# The Ways of the Sages and the Way of the World

The Minor Tractates of the Babylonian Talmud:
Derekh 'Eretz Rabbah
Derekh 'Eretz Zuta
Pereq ha-Shalom

Translated on the basis of the manuscripts
and provided with a commentary
by

Marcus van Loopik

J. C. B. Mohr (Paul Siebeck) Tübingen

*CIP-Titelaufnahme der Deutschen Bibliothek*

*Loopik, Marcus van:*
The ways of the sages and the way of the world : the minor
tractates of the Babylonian Talmud: Derekh 'Eretz Rabbah,
Derekh 'Eretz Zuta, Pereq ha-Shalom / transl. on the basis of
the ms. and provided with a commentary by Marcus van
Loopik. – Tübingen : Mohr, 1991
   (Texte und Studien zum antiken Judentum ; 26)
   ISBN 3-16-145644-0
   ISSN 0721-8753
NE: GT

© 1991 by J. C. B. Mohr (Paul Siebeck), P.O. Box 2040, D-7400 Tübingen.

The book was typeset and printed by Gulde-Druck in Tübingen on acid free stock paper from
Papierfabrik Buhl in Ettlingen and bound by Heinrich Koch in Tübingen.

Printed in Germany.

# Preface

The texts in this book contain the translation and commentary of the Derekh 'Eretz tractates. The book may contribute to a better understanding of early rabbinical literature. The interpretation of these tractates leads us to a deeper insight into the relation between law and morality and between the law and the spirit of the law. It shows us the customs, rules, and the way of life of the Torah scholars and of Early Chasidim. It also shows us the spiritual and social background of the New Testament and of the rabbinical period of the first centuries and later.

Some years ago Rabbi Y. Aschkenasy from Hilversum asked me to accept the heavy task of making a new critical edition of the Derekh 'Eretz tractates. I decided to carry the plan into execution, because I knew the need of a new critical translation and commentary of these texts and because of the great importance of these texts for the history of the Jewish religion and its ethical insights. The existing translations are lacking for critical notes and do not supply much parallels and commentary. During the research I could make use of the manuscript-copies, which were collected by Rabbi Y Aschkenasy.

I express thanks to Drs. T. de Bruin and Drs. D. van Uden, who did much work by collating a great part of the Mss. I also express my thanks to the "Makhon Kitbei Jad" in Jerusalem for the supply of photographs and microfilms of Mss. and I am very grateful to Mrs. K. Deen, who translated the text and the commentary from Dutch into English. The translation was subsidized by the B. Folkertsma-foundation for Talmudic Studies in Hilversum. Three years of the research were subsidized by the Dutch Organisation for Scientific Research (N.W.O.). I hope that this study may be of value to all who desire to study rabbinic literature and to learn from the words of the sages.

Great is the Torah for it gives to those that practise it life in This world and in the World to Come, as it is said: "For they are life to those that find them and health to all their flesh" (Prov. IV,22). M'Abot VI,7.

Marcus van Loopik

# Contents

## Translation and commentary

## Bibliography

Contents

# Index

# List of abbreviations

| | |
|---|---|
| 'Ab. Zar. | 'Abodah Zarah |
| 'Ar. | 'Arakhin |
| A.R.N. | 'Abot de-Rabbi Natan |
| A.S.T.I. | Annual of the Swedish Theological Institute |
| Ag. Ber. | Aggadat Be-Reshit |
| Ag. Sam. | Aggadat Samuel |
| Am. | Amos |
| Ant. | Antiquitates |
| – B.B. | Baba Batra |
| – B.M. | Baba Metzi'a |
| – B.Q. | Baba Qama |
| Bam. Rab. | Ba-Midbar Rabbah |
| Bar. | Baruch (Barukh) |
| Beg. | Beginning |
| – Bekh. | Bekhorot |
| Bel. | Bellum Judaicum (The Jewish War) |
| Ber. Rab. | Be-Reshit Rabbah |
| – Ber. | Berakhot |
| – Bik. | Bikkurim |
| C.E. | Christian Era |
| ca. | circa |
| Cant. | Canticles |
| cat. | catalogue |
| cf. | confer (conferatur) |
| chap. | chapter |
| char. | character |
| Chron. | Chronicles |
| curs. | cursorius (in italics) |
| D.E.R. | Derekh 'Eretz Rabbah |
| D.E.Z. | Derekh 'Eretz Zuta |
| Dan. | Daniel |
| De Virt. | De Virtutibus |
| De Spec. Leg. | De Specialibus Legibus |
| Deb. Rab. | Debarim Rabbah |
| – Dem. | Demai |
| Dt. | Deuterononium |
| E.J. | Encyclopedia Judaica |
| 'Eb. ha-'Ez. | 'Eben ha-'Ezer |
| ed. | edition; editor; edidit |

| | |
|---|---|
| – 'Ed. | 'Eduiot |
| 'Eikh. Rab. | 'Eikhah Rabbati |
| En. | Enoch |
| - 'Er. | 'Erubin |
| Est. | Esther |
| Ex. | Exodus |
| Ez. | Ezekiel |
| fol. | folio (foliant) |
| Gad. | Gadol |
| Gal. | Galatians |
| Gen. | Genesis |
| Germ. | German |
| Gerush. | Gerushin |
| Gez. | Gezeilah |
| – Git. | Gittin |
| h. | halakhah |
| H.T.R. | Harvard Theological Review |
| – Hag. | Hagigah |
| Heb. | Hebrew |
| Hebr. | Hebrew; Hebrews |
| Hil. | Hilkhot |
| – Hor. | Horaiot |
| Hos. | Hosea |
| Hosh. Mishp. | Hoshen Mishpat |
| HUCA | Hebrew Union College Annual |
| – Hul. | Hullin |
| Is. | Isaiah |
| Isr. | Israelitish |
| 'Issur. Bi'ah | 'Issurei Bi'ah |
| J.B.L. | Journal of Biblical Literature |
| J.Q.R. | Jewish Quarterly Review |
| J.Th.S. | Jewish Theological Seminary |
| Jac. | Jacobus (James) |
| Jad | Jad ha-Hazaqah = Mishneh Torah |
| Jalq. | Jalqut (Shim'oni) |
| Jalq. ha-Makh. | Jalqut ha-Makhiri |
| Jalq. Re'ub. | Jalqut Re'ubeni |
| J.E. | Jewish Encyclopedia |
| – Jeb. | Jebamot |
| Jer. | Jeremiah |
| Jor. De'ah | Joreh De'ah |
| Josh. | Joshua |
| Jub. | Jubilees |
| Jub. Vol. | Jubilee Volume |
| Judg. | Judges |
| Kal. | Kallah |
| – Kel | Kelim |

| | |
|---|---|
| – Ker. | Keritot |
| – Ket | Ketubot |
| Lag. | Lagarde |
| l.c. | loco citato |
| Lev. | Leviticus |
| M- | Mishnah |
| M. G. W. J. | Monatschrift für Geschichte und Wissenschaft des Judentums |
| – Ma'as. | Ma'aserot |
| – Ma'as. Shen. | Ma'aser Sheni |
| Macc. | Maccabees |
| – Mak. | Makkot |
| – Makhsh. | Makhshirin |
| Mal. | Malachi |
| Mas. Soph. | Massekhet Sopherim |
| Mas. | Massekhet |
| Mas. Kal. | Massekhet Kallah |
| Mas. Kal. Rab. | Massekhet Kallah Rabbati |
| Mas. Sem. | Massekhet Semahot |
| Mat. | Matthew |
| – Meg. | Megillah |
| Mekh. | Mekhilta |
| Mekh. de-R. Jishm. | Mekhilta de Rabbi Jishma'el |
| Mekh. de-R. Shim. bar Johai | Mekhilta de Rabbi Shim'on bar Jochai |
| – Men. | Menahot |
| Mi. | Micah |
| Midr. Leq. Tob | Midrash Leqah Tob |
| Midr. Ag. | Midrash Aggadah |
| Midr. | Midrash |
| Midr. Tan. | Midrash Tanna'im |
| Midr. Teh. | Midrash Tehillim |
| Midr. ha-Gad. | Midrash ha-Gadol |
| – Miqw. | Miqwa'ot |
| Mishl. | Mishlei |
| – M. Q. | Mo'ed Qatan |
| Ms(s). | manuscript(s) |
| N. S. | New Series |
| Nah. | Nahum |
| – Naz. | Nazir |
| – Ned. | Nedarim |
| Neh. | Nehemiah |
| – Nid. | Niddah |
| Num. | Numeri (Numbers) |
| op. cit. (o.c.) | opero citato |
| Opp. | Oppenheimer |
| 'Or. Haj. | 'Orah Hajjim |
| O. S. | Old Series |

| | |
|---|---|
| par. | parashah; paragraph |
| per. | pereq |
| – Pes. | Pesahim |
| Pes. Zut. | Pesiqta Zutarta |
| Pes. Rab. | Pesiqta Rabbati |
| Petiht. | Petihta |
| P. R. E. | Pirqei de-Rabbi 'Eli'ezer |
| Prov. | Proverbia (Proverbs) |
| Ps. de-R. K. | Pesiqta de-Rab Kahana |
| Ps. | Psalms |
| – Qid. | Qiddushin |
| Qoh. Rab. | Qohelet Rabbah |
| Qoh. | Qohelet |
| R. | Rabbi; Rab |
| r. | remez |
| – R. ha-Sh. | Rosh ha-Shanah |
| R. E. J. | Revue des Etudes Juives |
| Rab. | Rabbah; Rabbati |
| Rabad | Rabbi 'Abraham ben David |
| Rabb. | Rabbinic |
| Radbaz | Rabbi David ben Solomon ibn Abi Zimra |
| Rambam | Rabbenu Mosheh ben Maimon |
| Ramban | Rabbi Mosheh ben Nahman |
| Ran | Rabbenu Nissim (Gerondi) |
| Rashba | Rabbi Shelolmo ben 'Abraham 'Adret |
| repr. | reprint |
| Riph | Rabbi Jitzhaq Alphasi |
| Ritba | Rabbi Jom Tob ben 'Abraham 'Asulai |
| Rosh | Rabbenu 'Asher |
| S. E. R. | Seder 'Eliahu Rabbah |
| S. E. Z. | Seder 'Eliahu Zuta |
| Sam. | Samuel |
| – Sanh. | Sanhedrin |
| Sed. 'Ol. | Seder 'Olam |
| Seph. | Sepher |
| – Shab. | Shabbat |
| – Sheb. | Shebu'ot |
| – Shebi. | Shebi'it |
| Shem. | Shemot |
| Shem. Rab. | Shemot Rabbah |
| – Sheq. | Sheqalim |
| Shir ha-Shir. Rab. | Shir ha-Shirim Rabbah |
| Shul. 'Ar. | Shulhan 'Arukh |
| sim. | siman (§) |
| Soph. Sal. | Sophia Salomonis |
| – Sot. | Sotah |
| Span. | Spanish |

| | |
|---|---|
| squa. | square |
| – Suk. | Sukkot |
| Syr. | Syrian |
| – Ta'an. | Ta'anit (Ta'aniot) |
| – Tam. | Tamid |
| Tan. | Tanna'im |
| Tanh. (Jash.) | Tanhuma (Jashan) |
| Targ. Pseudo Jon. | Targum Pseudo Jonatan |
| Targ. | Targum |
| Tb- | Talmud Babli |
| Teh. | Tehillim |
| – Tem. | Temurah |
| – Ter. | Terumot |
| Test. Iss. | Testament of Issahar |
| Tj- | Talmud Jerushalmi |
| Tos-; Tos. | Tosephta |
| vs. | verse |
| Waj. Rab. | Wa-Jiqra Rabbah |
| Za. | Zachariah |
| – Zeb. | Zebahim |
| Zut. | Zutarta |

# Introduction

## The Minor Tractates Derekh 'Eretz Rabbah, Derekh 'Eretz Zuta, Pereq Ha-Shalom

### 1. The Minor Tractates

Derekh 'Eretz Rabbah, *Derekh 'Eretz Zuta* and *Pereq ha-Shalom* are part of the so called 'Minor Tractates' of the Babylonian Talmud. *Derekh 'Eretz Rabbah* and *Derekh 'Eretz Zuta* contain mainly standards of decent behaviour and rules of etiquette customary to the circles of Tannaitic as Amoraic Torah scholars and students. *Pereq ha-Shalom* contains a collection of mainly Tannaitic and Amoraic statements concerning peace, ending with a statement about seven qualities of the sage and seven qualities of an uneducated an uncivilised person, extracted from M'Abot V,7.

The names *Derekh 'Eretz Rabbah* and *Derekh 'Eretz Zuta* are not original, as appears from the arrangement of the manuscripts of these Minor Tractates, which are part of the Babylonian Talmud. Yet, these tractates are mentioned under the names of *Derekh 'Eretz Rabbah* and *Derekh 'Eretz Zuta* (and *Pereq ha-Shalom*) in very early publications of the Talmud, together with the so called Minor Tractates: *M'Abot*, *'Abot de Rabbi Natan* [a], *Massekhet Sopherim*; *Massekhet Semahot*; *Massekhet Kallah*; *Massekhet Kallah Rabbati*; *Massekhet Derekh 'Eretz Rabbah*; *Massekhet Derekh 'Eretz Zuta*; *Pereq ha-Shalom*; *Massekhet Gerim*; *Massekhet Kutim*; *Massekhet 'Abadim*; *Massekhet Sepher Torah*; *Massekhet Tephillin*; *Massekhet Tzitzit* and *Massekhet Mezuzah*. In most Talmud editions the Minor Tractates are fit into Seder Neziqin, after Massekhet 'Edujot. However, in the Edition Vilna (1843) the tractates have been added after Massekhet Baba Qamma. *Derekh 'Eretz* is included in Ms. Munich, a manuscript of the Babylonian Talmud from the fourteenth century.[1]

There is a division of opinion about the number of tractates that belong to the Minor Tractates of the Babylonian Talmud. For instance, Me'iri (*Beit*

---

[1] See Ms. München (1342), Kön. Hofbibliothek, (M. Steinschneider), no. 95, fol. 565b-567a. See facsimile edition of H. Strack, Leyden 1952. This Manuscript has D.E.Z. I–IX and D.E.R. III–IX, placed after M'Abot! D.E.R. I is rendered under the denominator of *'Arajot Pereq 'Aleph* in the Mishnah-codex Kaufmann A 50, at the end of Seder Nashim; see the facsimile edition of G. Beer, Jerusalem 1968, p. 525.

*ha-Behirah*) and Ramban (comments on Neziqin a.l.) made an enumera-
tion of the Minor Tractates without mentioning *Derekh 'Eretz, Massekhet
Semahot, M'Abot* and *'Abot de Rabbi Natan*.[2] In the first edition of the
Babylonian Talmud (Venice 1532) *Massekhet Semahot, Massekhet Kallah*
and *Massekhet Sopherim* were added, but not the tractates of *Derekh 'Eretz*
and *'Abot de Rabbi Natan*, which were not included until the third edition of
Venice (1550).[3] Probably, the parts of *Derekh 'Eretz*, which originally were
autonomous units, have been integrated in the Babylonian Talmud, in
some versions of it, in post-Gaonitic days.


### 2. *The concept 'derekh 'eretz'*[4]

In the tractates of *Derekh 'Eretz Rabbah* and *Derekh 'Eretz Zuta*, a compilation of a number of more or less aggadian statements and stories has been
formed under the denominator of the concept 'derekh 'eretz'. For a better
understanding of what connects these statements and stories , which have,
for the major part, been linked together associatively, a further explanation
of the concept 'derekh 'eretz' is needed.

Literally, 'derekh 'eretz' means 'the way of the earth' or 'the way of the
world', and the concept refers, in a broad sense, to human behaviour and
human observations in general.[5] The term 'derekh 'eretz' is one of the most

---

[2] See *Derech Erez Sutta*, ed. A. J. Tawrogi, Königsberg 1858, introduction, p. I.

[3] For a short survey, see introduction to *Pseudo Eliahu Zuta*, ed. M. Friedmann,
Jerusalem 1969, pp. 1−2. In, for instance, the third Venician edition of the Babylonian
Talmud (1550), tractates of *Derekh 'Eretz* were admitted. See also the survey of the
rendering of the *Derekh 'Eretz* tractates by M. Higger, *Massekhtot Ze'irot*, repr.
Jerusalem 1970, p. 175. See also M. Steinschneider, *Catalogus Librorum Hebraearum*,
Berolini 1852, copy Hildesheim 1964, no. 1405, no. 1410, no. 1636, no. 1637. C. Wolff,
*Bibliotheca Hebraea*, vol. II, Bologna 1967, p. 1283, n. 139. See note 1, in Ms. Münich of
the Babylonian Talmud the tractates of *Derekh 'Eretz* can be found and D. E. R. I can be
found in the Mishnah Ms. Kaufmann A 50.

[4] See in connection with the different notions of the concept 'derekh 'eretz', for
instance, S. Krauss, in: *R. E. J.*, XXXVII (1898), p. 37 ff. M. Higger, *Massekhtot Ze'irot*,
Jerusalem 1970, introduction, p. 1 ff. M. Kadushin, *Worship and Ethics*, A Study in
Rabbinical Judaism, Northwestern University Press 1964, chap. III. M. Kadushin,
*Organic Thinking*, New York 1938; repr. New York s. a., pp. 117−130 a. o.

[5] Alternative terms are: 'orah hajjim', 'minhag (ha)-'olam', 'derekh ha-'olam', 'darkhan shel benei 'adam', 'noheg she-be-'olam', 'minhag derekh 'eretz', 'nimus 'olam',
'millei de-'alma', 'millei de-derekh 'eretz'. Cf. for instance the introduction to *Pseudo
Eliahu Zuta*, ed. M. Friedmann, p. 5; TbPes.122a; TbBer. 7b; TbShab. 33b and Mas.
Kal. Rab., ed. N. N. Coronel, 11a and 11b.

differentiated terms in the rabbinical tradition. The term is found only a few times in the tractates of *Derekh 'Eretz*, namely in the sense of a rule of decent conduct[6], a rule about proper table manners[7], and a form of refinement which may be expected of pious Torah scholars.[8]

Based on the use of the expression 'derekh kol ha-'aretz' in the Tenakh and the use of the term 'derekh 'eretz' and related expressions within the rabbinical traditions, one can distinguish roughly between the following meanings. In the Tenakh the concept points to sexuality as a form of universal behaviour[9] and to natural death of human beings.[10] It is likely that, in that period, the concept has pointed to all human customs concerning sexuality and death.[11] In the rabbinical tradition the concept of 'derekh 'eretz' points to: 1) natural processes and observations concerning fixed rules of nature's ways in general; 2) natural processes and events and man's reactions to them, which have to do with his physical existence, like, for instance, a disease with a natural course, or a natural death, or the moving of one's bowels; 3) rules concerning matters that influence health favourably or unfavourably and that are, in one way or another, related to proper care of one's body and the ways the body should function. For instance, in *Derekh 'Eretz* one finds rules concerning the visiting of the privy or the bathhouse, rules for proper dressing and undressing, nourishment, bloodletting and such; 4) sexual behaviour as a form of general human behaviour; 5) practical, normative and ethically coloured rules about sexuality and intramarital relationships; 6) work as a form of general behaviour; 7) practical and, sometimes strongly, ethically coloured rules for civilised behaviour in social contracts and especially in the conduction of trade; 8) human reactions and motives to act; 9) practical rules of life and advice; 10) standards of decent behaviour, for instance, concerning the relationships between the young and the old, Torah scholar and student, parents and children, students among themselves, husband and wife etc.; 11) table manners; 12) normative rules with a moral tenor (often to be combined with the uses of the concept mentioned above); rules that belong to this category are often derived from the Torah; 13) proper religious customs; 14) advises

---

[6] Cf. D. E. Z. III,1 and D. E. R. V,1-b.

[7] See D. E. R. VI, 7-b.

[8] See D. E. R. V,3. See also the opening of D. E. Z. I: 'The ways of the sages are ... '

[9] See Gen. 19:31 and cf. Gen. 31:35 referring to menstruation, which is natural to mankind.

[10] See II Kings 2:2.

[11] See introduction to *Pseudo Eliahu Zuta*, ed. M. Friedmann, p. 2−3.

and, in certain circles compulsory, aggravations of general standards, a way
to express special piety.

The concept 'derekh 'eretz' has a descriptive as well as a prescriptive
notion. In the descriptive sense the concept points to experiences and
observations that are universally human, concerning both man himself and
his relation with surrounding nature and its laws. Where 'derekh 'eretz'
refers to these laws of nature the concept sometimes has a pseudo-scientific
character and a prophesying notion which is here and there incorporated
into practical advice. In relation to man himself the concept points to acts
which are characteristic to man, and to reactions which are universally
human. The concept has a prescriptive notion where is points to standards
of decent conduct, practical rules of life and rules of conduct stated by a
sense of morality. One specific way of using the concept of 'derekh 'eretz' is
using it to refer to the atmosphere of the ethical. In the early rabbinical
traditions one will seek in vain for a definition of ethics or a systematic
approach of ethical questions, since there was no distinction between
ethical and other religious obligations. There was, however, a strong sensitivity for matters with ethical implications. It is this sensitivity for the field
of ethical matters which is denoted with the concept 'derekh 'eretz'.[12]

The relation between the descriptive and the prescriptive use of the
concept 'derekh 'eretz' had been phrased by M. Kadushin, as follows: 'It
denotes at once universal human traits and those human traits that are
"proper", good. Such a double use of the term reveals in a single phrase the
assumptions which together constitute the rabbinic "definition" of the
ethical: Good actions, motives and outlooks have there ground in human
nature; good actions, therefore, can and should be universal human
traits.'[13] Within the rabbinical tradition the concept 'derekh 'eretz' is mentioned in relation with good actions and rules of life which were not first
revealed to Israel on Mount Sinai, but had been known to earlier generations of all mankind, because they relate to common sense and to universal
rules of civilisation which are indispensable conditions for the proper
functioning of a human society.[14] The term 'derekh 'eretz' refers to social
and civil conduct resting in universal human insights.

---

[12] In connection with this, see M. Kadushin, *Worship and Ethics*, chap. III ("The
Sphere of Ethics and Morality") and introduction.

[13] See M. Kadushin, *Organic Thinking*, p. 122.

[14] Cf. the explanation of Abrabanel in his commentary on M'Abot III,17. See also the
commentary of Almosnino on M'Abot l.c. Compare Rambam, *Shemoneh Peraqim* V,
a. o.

In the rabbinical tradition the rules under the denominator 'derekh 'eretz' can be derived from the Torah, which is understandable on the basis of the fact that the Torah gives, apart from the rules that apply only to Israel, a number of universal rules of decent and civil conduct. This is the origin of the rabbinical expression: 'The Torah teaches us "derekh 'eretz"'.[15] In a number of cases, however, the term 'derekh 'eretz' points to rules of conduct borne on religious motives, which can, in fact, only apply to Israel, such as the advice to light the lights of Sabbath as early as possible on Friday evening in order to add to the holiness by extending the duration of the Sabbath as much as possible.[16] Sometimes 'derekh 'eretz' is counted among the commandments that are compulsory for Israel, as can be understood from the statement: 'It is the undeveloped who possess 'derekh 'eretz' (civilisation and good manners) and the rest of the commandments' (but no knowledge of the explanation of the Scripture in the oral tradition).[17]

By studying the rules compiled in the tractates of *Derekh 'Eretz* under the denominator of the concept 'derekh 'eretz', one acquires insight in the way in which, in certain circles, the concept was realised in practice; one learns its relation with rules of conduct which applied to said circles. Much of what can be found in *Derekh 'Eretz* concerning rules of conduct is the reflection of a lifestyle which was customary in the groups of pious Torah scholars and their students. These rules could be denoted with the term 'derekh hasidut', 'the way of the pious'. The sages imposed on themselves severe aggravations of norms and adhered to extra rules, apart from the rules which applied to everyone, to remain far from transgression or even the suspicion of transgression and to avoid putting any fellowman to a disadvantage or to advance oneself. In this way the rules of *Derekh 'Eretz* form a sharpening as well as a broadening of the existing norms and *halakhah*.[18]

From the tractates of *Derekh 'Eretz* one acquires a special understanding of the sharp notion of the rabbis concerning the ethical, and insight in the way the sages and the early Hasidim lived. Characteristics of the practical piety which hasidic sages who lived in accordance with the rules of *Derekh 'Eretz* tried to connect with intensive study of the Torah are: emphasis on a

[15] Cf., for instance Siphrei, Be-Ha'alotekha, pisqa 102; Ber. Rab. XX,12; Ber. Rab. XXXI,10; Waj. Rab. XXVI,7; TbSot. 44a; TbHul. 84a and many other sources.

[16] See Mekh. de-R. Jishm., Be-Shallah, ed. M. Friedmann, 25b. TosSot. IV,1 and TbShab. 23b.

[17] See S. E. R., ed. M. Friedmann, p. 69.

[18] *Halakhah* is literally 'the path', i. e. 'the path man must take' as denomination of accepted standards which are lawful within the community.

positive social attitude through acts of charity and giving help to the poor;
combining the appeal to love God with the appeal to love and honour one's
neighbour; combining piety with humbleness and tolerance; emphasizing
trying to avoid transgression (expressed in the appeal to 'jir'at het' (fear of
transgression, fear of God); accepting aggravations of common rules to
keep oneself and others far from transgression and to practise cleanness of
thought and intentions; striving toward an asymmetrical position of oneself
and one's fellowman by estimating the honour and the interests of the other
higher than one's own; sobriety; emphasis on the act next to study; maintaining reserve in the contact with woman, for fear of being seduced into
transgression; fulfilling one's religious and social duties for the sake of
Heaven and not for one's own; a strong consciousness of the presence of the
Shekhinah[19]; exemplary love and reverence for the Torah and the handling
of holy texts; and especially characteristic for those who live according to
the rules of *Derekh 'Eretz* great caution in the contact with sectarians and
illiterates who think lightly of the instructions of the Torah and who may
have a bad influence.

### 3. Backgrounds

As said, the rules of life one finds in the tractates of *Derekh 'Eretz* have
functioned notably in circles of Torah scholars.[20] The Major part of these
rules originated from these circles and have not been popularised and
started to function in wider circles until later. Compared to *Derekh 'Eretz
Zuta*, *Derekh 'Eretz Rabbah* contains more stories; however, the opinion
that the stories in *Derekh 'Eretz Rabbah* were intended to popularise the
rules stated in *Derekh 'Eretz Zuta* and to introduce them into wider circles,
is not correct, since *Derekh 'Eretz Rabbah* contains a lot of material that
cannot be found in *Derekh 'Eretz Zuta* and the statements in *Derekh 'Eretz
Rabbah* also were primarily directed at the circle of Torah scholars.[21] The
names *Derekh 'Eretz Rabbah* (the Major Derekh 'Eretz) and *Derekh 'Eretz
Zuta* (the Minor Derekh 'Eretz) are not, as the names may indicate, a larger
and smaller reflection of the same discussion, but refer to two independent
collections of statements. In *Derekh 'Eretz Zuta* as well as in *Derekh 'Eretz*

---

[19] The immanent presence of God in the world.
[20] See also M.B. Lerner, in: *The Literature of the Sages*, I, (Compendia Rerum
Iudaicarum ad Novum Testamentum), ed. S. Safrai, Assen / Maastricht 1987, p. 397 ff.
[21] See S. Krauss, in: *R. E.J*, XXXVII (1898), p. 213; S. Krauss regarded D. E. R. as a
popular version of the rules in D.E.Z.. See, on the other hand, the opinion of
M.B. Lerner, op. cit. in note 20, p. 380.

*Rabbah* one often finds references to the 'talmid hakham', the sage and Torah scholar.[22]

The piety, the 'hasidut' in the tractates of *Derekh 'Eretz* does not belong to the piety of the simple and illiterate pious men, but to the piety of the Torah scholars who try to combine study with practical piety. It is remarkable that in a number of places in *Derekh 'Eretz* there are warnings against contact with the "am ha-'aretz', the compatriot who is more interested in worldly matters than in holy matters, notably against sharing a meal with one of them, because of the danger of eating something which is prohibited and not prepared according to the refined prescriptions of the oral tradition.[23] It is even more remarkable to find in *Derekh 'Eretz* the direct context of the warning not to share a meal with a (priest who is also an) "am ha-'aretz'[24] for fear of eating prohibited food, and the warning of being reserved in taking the vow and oath, and in the contact with women. This combination was typical for the milieu of the so-called 'associated' or 'haburim'. The term 'haburim' refers to groups of 'united' who were characterised by their strict observance of all religious prescriptions (notably those concerning cleanness) and who tried to keep as much distance as possible between them and those who did not live strictly by the rules.[25]

In a number of places in *Derekh 'Eretz* customs are mentioned, which are in paralleltexts ascribed to certain pious and specially refined circles in Jerusalem.[26] In A. R. N. [b] XXVI (26b) a statement is referred to from the so-called *Megillat Hasidim* (The Role of the Pious), which is also mentioned in D. E. Z. II,23.[27]

---

[22] For confirmation of this allegation one can refer to a number of places: D.E.Z. I (beginning); D.E.Z. II (ending); D.E.Z. IV (beginning); D.E.Z. VI (beginning); D.E.Z. VII (beginning); D.E.Z. VIII,12. See also D.E.R. V,4 and D.E.R. VI,3-d. Further cf. S.E.R. VI, ed. M.Friedmann, p. 33: "Any sage in whom there is no knowledge, an animal is better than he." And see M. Friedmann, op. cit., introduction to *Pseudo Eliahu Zuta*, p. 6, where he explains the word 'knowledge' in the statement mentioned above as 'knowledge of "derekh 'eretz"'. Cf. Waj. Rab. I,6 and A.R.N. [a] (64a) a.o.

[23] See D.E.Z. I,15 and D.E.Z. IV,1 · Compare the well-known statement of Hillel from M'Abot, as rendered in D.E.Z. III,15: 'And an ""am ha-'aretz" cannot be a pious man (other version: "parush" = segregated = Farisean) . . .'

[24] See D.E.Z. I,15 and D.E.R. I,35.

[25] Cf. TosDem., II,2.

[26] See D.E.Z. V,3 and cf. TbGit. 87b (Mishnah); TbSanh. 23a; Mekh. de-R. Jishm., Mishpatim, par. 20, ed. M. Friedmann, 98b.; 'Eikh. Rab. IV,4. See also D.E.R. VIII, 2 and cf. TosBer. IV,9; TjDem. IV [24a]; Tj'Ab. Zar. [39c]; TbB.B 93b..

[27] For further details cf. S. Safrai, ('Teachings of Pietists in Mishnaic Literature'), in:

## 4. The oldest literary information

In general, the tractates of *Derekh 'Eretz* contain gnomic statements, i.e.
sharply formulated statements of wisdom, and practical rules. One can
determine a great resemblance in style with the *Book of Proverbs, Sepher
ben Sira, Sophia Salomonis* and *Pseudo-Phocylides*.[28] One must not forget,
however, that the rules of *Derekh 'Eretz* are much less universal statements
of wisdom and much more concrete rules of conduct, tied to very specific
human situations, and much like the ones found in the halakhah.[29]

Characteristic for the style of *Derekh 'Eretz* is the, very often anonymous, oral tradition of statements which are, in other parts of the tradition,
clearly ascribed to certain persons.[30]

A lot of material in *Derekh 'Eretz* is derived from traditions from the
Talmud and Midrash, but in a large number of cases original traditions have
been preserved in *Derekh 'Eretz*, for which no direct parallels can be found
in the tradition. It is proved from parallels that early *Derekh 'Eretz* literature has existed which dates back to the Tannaitic period.[31] This was
referred to by the Amoraim[32] in their discussions concerning the *Mishnah*.
For instance, in a discussion in the Babylonian Talmud[33]it appears that, as
early as the times of Rabbi Jehudah ben 'Ilai (Tanna of the fourth generation), a collection of rules by the name of *Hilkhot Derekh 'Eretz* must have
been known which (see context) apparently was regarded as a secondary
collection of traditions, apart from the rest of the oral traditions. It is not
correct to suggest that the name *Hilkhot Derekh 'Eretz* in itself is a reference to a collection which is cognate to *Pirqei ben 'Azzai*.[34] For the manuscripts refer to *Derekh 'Eretz Zuta* (I—IX) as being *Hilkhot Derekh 'Eretz*
(see below). In his comment on the said Talmud text, Rashi refers to,

---

*J.J.S* (1965), pp. 15—33. And see S. Safrai,('Mishnat Hasidim be-Siphrut ha-Tanna'im'), in: *'Ein Joseph. Qobetz le-Zikhro shel Y. Amorai*, Tel Aviv 1973, p. 136 ff.

[28] See S. Krauss, in: *R. E.J*, XXXVII (1898), p. 58 ff.

[29] Indeed the first chapter of D. E. R. consists mainly of halakhic formulations concerning sexual relationships, most of which have been recorded in later halakhic works.

[30] On the other hand, the tractates of D. E. contain credited statements which had
been handed down anonymously in other parts of the tradition. This points possibly to
the old age of the texts and their independence.

[31] This is from the first two centuries of the Christian era and it precedes the finishing
of the editing of the *Mishnah* by Rabbi Jehudah ha-Nasi, about 210 C. E.

[32] The generation between the finishing of the Mishnah (about 210 C. E.) and the
finishing of the Babylonian Talmud (about 500 C. E.).

[33] See TbBer. 22a.

[34] I.e. D. E. R. III—IX. See B. Lerner, in: *The Literature of the Sages*, I, p. 387.

among others, *Darkhan shel Talmidei Hakhamin*.[35] In TjShab. VI,2 under
the header of 'derekh 'eretz', a custom is mentioned – known as a Tannaitic
tradition in the time of Rabbi Johanan and Rab Shaman bar 'Abba – which
matches a rule of conduct from *Derekh 'Eretz Rabbah* (beginning). In *'Abot
de Rabbi Natan*[36] referring to *Megillat Hasidim*, a statement is made which
is also handed down in *Derekh 'Eretz Zuta* (II). This might indicate that
*Derekh 'Eretz Zuta* I–III, as a literary unit is a Tannaitic collection from the
circles of early Hasidim, which was already referred to in *'Abot de Rabbi
Natan*. Therefore the assumption that *Derekh 'Eretz Zuta* I–III (IV)
roughly dates back to Tannaitic times, is justified.[37] This does not alter the
fact that, presumably, the final editing did not take place until Gaonitic
times.[38] Countless Tannaitic traditions that are quoted in the Talmud and
the Midrash, can also be found in the tractates of *Derekh 'Eretz*, sometimes
even in a more original form. In *Massekhet Kallah Rabbati* a kind of
'gemara'[39] is given with traditions from *Derekh 'Eretz Zuta* (I–III) and
*Derekh 'Eretz Rabbah* (III–XI), and with some traditions which can be
found in other places of *Derekh 'Eretz*. M. Friedmann has the opinion that a
large part of the content of *Massekhet Kallah Rabbati* was formed in the
school of Raba (third century) whose name is often mentioned in *Massekhet
Kallah Rabbati*.[40] This implies, at least, that the major part of the traditions
from *Derekh 'Eretz Zuta* I–III and *Derekh 'Eretz Rabbah* III–XI and a
number of statements from other parts of the tractates of *Derekh 'Eretz*
must have been known quite some time before the Babylonian Talmud was
finished in 500 C. E. Another opinion says that Raba in *Massekhet Kallah
Rabbati* refers to Raba, the Gaon of Pumbeditha (seventh century).[41] Most
likely *Massekhet Kallah Rabbati* is a product of Gaonitic times. From
Gaonitic times the traditions from *Derekh 'Eretz* were handed down by

---

[35] D. E. Z. I,1 ff.

[36] A. R. N. [b], XXVI (p. 52).

[37] See L. Ginzberg, in: *J. E.*, IV, col. 530 and see M. Higger, *Massekhtot Derekh
'Eretz*, New York 1935, introduction p. 19; and D. Sperber, *Massekhet Derekh 'Eretz
Zuta*, Jerusalem 1982, p. 179. Cf. also P. Rubanov, in: *Horeb*, VII (1943), p. 214.

[38] See M. B. Lerner, in: *The Literature of the Sages*, I, ed. S. Safrai, pp. 382–383.

[39] I.e. a kind of explanation which can be compared to the discussions of the Babylonian Amoraim about the Mishnah in the Babylonian Talmud, called 'gemara'.

[40] See among others M. Friedmann's opinion in his edition of S. E., introduction to
*Pseudo Eliahu Zuta*, p. 15.

[41] See M. Higger, *Massekhet Kallah*, New York 1936, introduction, p. 113. See also
A. Aptowitzer's opinion, 'Le Traité de "Kallah"', in: *R. E. J.*, LVII, 1909, p. 248. A. Ap-
towitzer connected the name Raba with the eighth century student of Rab Jehudai Gaon.
See also B. Lerner, in: *The Literature of the Sages*, I, ed. S. Safrai, p. 396.

different names, connected with the originally separate units *Derekh 'Eretz* is compiled of.[42]

There is a special relation between the tractates of *Derekh 'Eretz Zuta* and the sixth chapter of *Pirqei 'Abot* , called the *Pereq Qinjan Torah* (The chapter of the acquiring of the Torah).[43] On Sabbath-afternoons, as early as Gaonitic times, other traditions were studied under the name of *Pereq Qinjan Torah* (or *Pereq Rabbi Me'ir* or *Baraita de 'Abot*), of which a part has been preserved in a number of Mahzorim[44], next to the statements which, according the rendering in *Pirqei 'Abot* in the *Mishnah*, make up the sixth chapter of *Pirqei 'Abot*. In a number of cases these traditions include parts of the first chapters of *Derekh 'Eretz Zuta*.

Rab Shalom Gaon already mentioned the Babylonian custom of studying the sixth chapter of *Pirqei 'Abot* on Sabbath afternoons.[45] In the version of the Siddur by Rab 'Amram Gaon[46] (died about 875), parts of the first chapters of *Derekh 'Eretz Zuta* are found in the rite of Sabbath afternoons, obviously to be studied after midday's prayers. This custom is confirmed by a remark in the Siddur of Rab Sa'adjah Gaon (882−942), in which studying of the sixth chapter of *Pirqei 'Abot* and *Jir'at Het* (denoting the first four chapters of *Derekh 'Eretz Zuta* in old scripts) is prescribed.[47] Based on all this, it is quite understandable that parts of the tractates of *Derekh 'Eretz* were handed down into a large number of Mahzorim, since it was the custom to study parts of *Derekh 'Eretz* on Sabbath afternoon. Also, other than liturgical sources confirm that in Gaonitic times parts of *Derekh 'Eretz* were known.[48]

---

[42] For a detailed listing of these early sources see, among others M. Higger, *Massekhtot Derekh 'Eretz*, introduction, chap. IV. See also D. Sperber, *Massekhet Derekh 'Eretz Zuta*, p. 167 ff.

[43] See M. Higger, 'Pereq Qinjan Torah', in: *Horeb* II (2) (1935); en M. Higger, 'Massekhet 'Abot u-Pereq Qinjan Torah', in: *Horeb*, IV (1937); See M. Hacohen, in: *Sinai Jub. Vol*, 1985, ed. J. L. Maimon, p. 419 ff. See also D. Sperber, *Massekhet Derekh 'Eretz Zuta*, pp. 147−145. S. Sharbit, 'Minhag ha-Qeri'ah shel 'Abot ba-Shabbat . . .', in: *Bar Ilan*, XIII (1976), p. 169 ff.

[44] Special books of prayers with ritual, often poetic, additions for the holy days.

[45] See Siddur Rashi, sim. 516, ed. S. Buber / I. Freimann, p. 529.

[46] See ed. N. N. Coronel, Warsaw 1865 (repr. Jerusalem 1965), Seder Minha le-Shabbat, pp. 30−31; the edition Warsaw is based on Ms. British Library, Or. 1057 (Marg. 206), a manuscript with additions that are nor original; the parts cannot be found in other versions. In this matter, see *Seder Rab 'Amram Gaon*, ed. G. Goldschmidt, Jerusalem 1972, in notes on p. 80. See also remarks of D. Sperber, *Massekhet Derekh 'Eretz Zuta*, p. 172.

[47] See ed. I. Davidson a. o., pp. 122−123.

[48] Rab Sherira Gaon, for instance, the father of Haj Gaon, mentioned *Hilkhot Derekh*

## 5. Some remarks concerning the manuscripts

As was mentioned above, the arrangement of the tractates of *Derekh 'Eretz* as can be found in the editions of the babylonian Talmud, is not original. The manuscripts give arrangements entirely different from the one of *Derekh 'Eretz Rabbah*, *Derekh 'Eretz Zuta* and *Pereq ha-Shalom*. In this matter the manuscripts of *Derekh 'Eretz* can be arranged in four groups.[49]

I Manuscripts by the name of *Jir'at Het* (Fear of Transgression) as a separate denotation of *Derekh 'Eretz Zuta* I–IV and IX.; and by the name of *Derekh 'Eretz Ze'irah* (*Qetannah*) (the Minor Derekh 'Eretz) as a denotation of *Derekh 'Eretz Zuta* V-VIII. This arrangement is undoubtedly the oldest as appears from the mention of these parts of *Derekh 'Eretz* by Gaonitic sources.[50]

II Manuscripts by the name of *Massekhet Derekh 'Eretz* or *Hilkhot Derekh 'Eretz*, as denotation of *Derekh 'Eretz Zuta* I–IX and by the name of *Pirqei ben 'Azzai* as denotation of *Derekh 'Eretz Rabbah* III–IX. As for *Derekh 'Eretz Rabbah* this is the most original arrangement.[51]

III Manuscripts by the name of *Derekh 'Eretz* or *Derekh 'Eretz Zuta* as denotation of *Derekh 'Eretz Zuta* I–IX, and by the name of *Massekhet Derekh 'Eretz* or *Hilkhot Derekh 'Eretz* as denotation of *Derekh 'Eretz*

---

*'Eretz* as one of the *baraitot keti'ot* (minor independent Tannaitic traditions); see *'Iggeret Rab Sherira Gaon*, ed. M. B. Lewin (1922), p. 47; and see *Teshubot ha-Geonim*, ed. A. E. Harkavy, sim. 380. Another example could be the testimony of the Karaite Qirqisani (first half of the tenth century) who mentioned *Jir'at Het* as one of his sources (the name of D. E. Z. I–IV). See also W. Bacher, in *J. Q. R.*, VII (1895), pp. 697–698. See I. Abrahams, in: *J. Q. R.*, X (1898), p. 660; and see I. Abrahams, in: *M. Steinschneider Festschrift*, repr. Hildesheim 1975, p. 72, referring to *Kitab al Anwar*, ed. A. E. Harkaby. See also A. Büchler, *Types of Jewish Palestinian Piety*, London 1922, p. 33, note 1. See *Perush Rab Haj Gaon*, on Seder Tohorot, ed. Berlin 1921, p. 37ff. See S. A. Poznanski, in *M. G. W. J.*, LXI (1917), p. 229ff. See *Halakhot Gedolot*, ed. I. Hildesheimer, Berlin 1888 (Ms. Roma, about 1000), containing D. E. R. II, D. E. Z. I–IV, D. E. Z. V-VIII and D. E. Z. IX; and many other sources. See S. Safrai, 'Teachings of Pietists in Mishnaic Literature', in: *J. J. S.* (1965), p. 27.

[49] See for the arrangement following in the text: M. Higger, *Massekhtot Ze'irot*, pp. 7–8; see M. Higger, *Massekhtot Derekh 'Eretz*, introduction, p. 15ff. See also D. Sperber, *Massekhet Derekh 'Eretz Zuta*, appendix 7, p. 178.

[50] As with Rab 'Amram Gaon, Rab Sa'adjah Gaon, in *Halakhot Gedolot*, with the Karaite Qirqisani and others. For details see the literature mentioned under note 48. This arrangement can also be found in a number of genizah fragments.

[51] A manuscript with a similar arrangement was, for instance, known to Rashi, to the author of *Mahzor Vitry*, to the Tosaphists, to Rabbi 'El'azar ben Jehudah of Worms and to the author of *Seph. ha-Roqeah* and others.

*Rabbah* III–XI (sometimes supplemented with the first chapters of *Derekh 'Eretz Rabbah*).[52]

IV Manuscripts by the name of *Derekh 'Eretz Rabbah* (or *Massekhet Derekh 'Eretz* or *Middat Derekh 'Eretz*) denoting *Derekh 'Eretz Rabbah* I–XI, and by the name of *Massekhet Derekh 'Eretz Zuta* denoting *Derekh 'Eretz Zuta* IX–XI (V-VIII or I–XI).

M. Higger (see note 43) marked group I as the Gaonitic arrangement. This arrangement is in fact the oldest. Group II was marked by him as the French version and Group III as Sefardic version (Spanish), which also must include the fourth group.[53] Opposing an arrangement of the manuscripts on different critical apparatuses based on the groups mentioned above, as in the edition of M. Higger, it must be said that some manuscripts correspondent more, in many places, with manuscripts from other groups than with manuscripts from their own group. More confusing still is that M. Higger has placed the less reliable rendering of the *Derekh 'Eretz* tradition in the *Musar* literature within the apparatus of the manuscripts. Based on the arrangement of certain manuscripts no conclusion can be made regarding their disposition and quality. Choosing a certain version must be done case by case, also taking into consideration criteria concerning the content of the text.

As basic text for the translation of *Derekh 'Eretz Zuta* in this book Ms. Oxford Bodleian (cat. A. Neubauer, no. 896) was chosen, a manuscript written in Lybia in 1203, according to the catalogue A. Neubauer – A. E. Cowly. As basic text for the translation of *Derekh 'Eretz Rabbah* Ms. New York, Jewish Th. Sem (cat. E. N. Adler, no. 2237) was chosen. This manuscript was written in the Provence in 1271 (see cat. E. N. Adler, Cambridge 1921, p. 81). For the translation of the text of *Derekh 'Eretz Zuta* X and *Pereq ha-Shalom* we used the same manuscript cat. E. N. Adler, no. 2237.

---

[52] Strikingly, in some manuscripts with this arrangement the second chapter of D. E. R. is combined with the third chapter of D. E. R. Cf. for instance Ms. Oxford Bodleian (cat. A. Neubauer no. 2239) and Ms. Oxford Bodleian (cat. A. Neubauer no. 2257) and Ms. New York, Jewish Th. Sem. (cat. E. N. Adler no. 1909) and Ms. New York, Jewish Th. Sem. (cat. E. N. Adler no. 2237) and Ms. Epstein, *Mi-Qadmoniot ha-Jehudim*, II 1887; and in *Mahzor Vitry*, ed. S. Hurvitz, repr. Jerusalem 1963, p. 721 ff. and Talmud Babli, third ed., Venice.

[53] See M. B. Lerner, in: *The Literature of the Sages*, I, ed. S. Safrai, p. 381 note 89, referring to M. Higger. D. Sperber, *Massekhet Derekh 'Eretz Zuta*, p. 178, denotes this group as being Italian, without motivation.

The basic text for the translation of *Derekh 'Eretz Zuta* I−IX is a manuscript with the oldest arrangement and with a reliable and complete rendering of the text. Its versions, as a rule, correspondent with genizah fragments and they can be defended on the basis of criteria regarding content. Indeed, the manuscript of *Derekh 'Eretz Rabbah* and *Derekh 'Eretz Zuta* X−XI does contain a younger arrangement of the text (group IV), but still it dates back to the thirteenth century and it renders the text completely and in reliable way (in its commentary *Derekh 'Eretz Zuta* XI is corrected here and there on the basis of other manuscripts). The fragmentary character of many other manuscripts made these unsuitable for serving as a basic text.

## 6. Structure

*Derekh 'Eretz Rabbah* I is also called *Pereq 'Arajot* (The chapter of the prohibited sexual relationships) on the basis of its designation in the *Mishnah Ms. Kaufmann A 50*. The content of this chapter consists mainly of Tannaitic halakhic statements.[54] This fact is, however, mitigated by the fact that this chapter also clearly contains post-Talmudic material.[55] In *Ms. Kaufmann* this chapter is mentioned at the end of Seder Nashim. In *Halakhot Gedolot* (ed. A. Hildesheimer; repr. Jerusalem) *Derekh 'Eretz Rabbah* I is mentioned separately under the denominator of *Hilkhot 'Arajot*. In *Pes. Zut.* ,'Aharei Mot, at Lev. 18,23 (ed. S. Buber) *Massekhet 'Arajot* is referred to as being a part of the Mishnah.[56]

Apparently the content of *Derekh 'Eretz Rabbah* I was regarded as part of the Mishnah, under the name of *Massekhet 'Arajot*. There has been a division of opinions about the relation of *Derekh 'Eretz Rabbah* I with *Massekhet Kallah*. It is often expressed that *Derekh 'Eretz Rabbah* I originally was a part of *Massekhet Kallah*.[57] However, it is more acceptable that *Massekhet Kallah* was part of the *Derekh 'Eretz* traditions in general, since sexual relationships also belong to the notions of the concept 'derekh

---

[54] See M. Higger, *Massekhtot Ze'irot*, pp. 21−22, 31.

[55] Cf. M.B. Lerner, in: *The Literature of the Sages*, I, ed. S. Safrai, p. 385, referring to M. Higger. See also our commentary on this chapter.

[56] Cf. M.B. Lerner, in: *The Literature of the Sages*, I, ed. S. Safrai, p. 383, referring to *Halakhot Gedolot*, ed. S.A. Traub., 81b.

[57] See among others, the opinion of the Gaon of Wilna on D.E.R. I, and cf.. S. Krauss, in: *R.E.J*, XXXVI (1898), p. 32 ff. and J. Reiffman, 'Kunteres ruah hadashah', in: *Beit Talmud*, IV (1885), p. 84 a. o.

'eretz'. In their present forms *Derekh 'Eretz Rabbah* I and *Massekhet Kallah* are to be regarded as clearly separate literary units.[58] *Derekh 'Eretz Rabbah* contains very old Tannaitic traditions, but also some of later date. From the arrangement of those manuscripts which have *Derekh 'Eretz Rabbah* III—IX but not *Derekh 'Eretz Rabbah* I, it becomes clear that this chapter was only added much later to the tractates of *Derekh 'Eretz* which are known to us. At the ending of *Derekh 'Eretz Rabbah* I there is mention of the grandson of Rabbi Jehoshua ben Levi, a much later tradent than those mentioned in other parts of *Derekh 'Eretz*. On many counts the content of this chapter depends on discussions in the Babylonian Talmud, which means that the editorial closing of the material in this chapter took place after the closing of the Babylonian Talmud.

Originally, the second chapter of *Derekh 'Eretz Rabbah* (*Pereq ha-Minim*) was like *Derekh 'Eretz Rabbah* I a separate unit and was added to *Derekh 'Eretz Rabbah* III—IX only later. Indeed, there are manuscripts which mention *Derekh 'Eretz Rabbah* III—IX by the name of *Pirqei ben 'Azzai* but leave out *Derekh 'Eretz Rabbah* II. In *Massekhet Kallah Rabbati* there are comments on the statements of *Derekh 'Eretz Rabbah* III—IX, but there is a notable absence of the traditions of *Derekh 'Eretz Rabbah* I and II. *Derekh 'Eretz Rabbah* II has a structure entirely its own, and a very methodical composition. The first part of the chapter consists of a summing up of twelve rows of unvirtuous persons, each row followed by quotations from Scripture. Following these, twelve rows of virtuous persons are mentioned, also followed by quotations from Scripture. The rest of the chapter has an entirely different form and content. The ending, an explanation of Dt. 32:1, is a mystical text of which the style is similar to the style of mystical works from the Gaonitic era.[59] The language at the beginning of this chapter as regards the virtuous and unvirtuous persons is in many places very archaic by nature.

Based on the beginning of the summing up of the unvirtuous persons, this chapter is usually called *Pereq ha-Minim* (the Chapter of the Sectarians). In Ms. E. N. Adler, no. 1745, however, this chapter is called *Pereq ha-Ma'asim* (the Chapter of the Acts).

*Derekh 'Eretz Rabbah* III—IX, called *Pirqei ben 'Azzai* in manuscripts with the oldest arrangement, also originally constituted a separate literary unit, closed with an admonition. However, one can argue that, originally,

---

[58] See introduction to *Pseudo Eliahu Zuta*, ed. M. Friedmann, p. 13; and cf. M. Goldberg, *Derech Erez Rabba*, Breslau 1888, introduction, p. VI.

[59] For details see commentary.

*Derekh 'Eretz Rabbah* III was not attached to *Derekh 'Eretz Rabbah* IV-IX. It was connected to *Derekh 'Eretz Rabbah* IV-IX only later on and has given them the name *Pirqei ben 'Azzai*. In other places in the tradition, a lot of material from the said chapters is quoted as baraita. Save one possible exception, none of the tradents mentioned in this unity is of later date than Rabbi, which makes the supposition of M. Goldberg, that most part of *Derekh 'Eretz Rabbah* IV-IX had found its fixed form by the end of the third century, a plausible one.[60]

In TbPes. 86b (see the comments of Rashi on this tradition), as early as 200, it is referred back to traditions of norms of decent conduct accepted by the sages, which are mentioned in *Derekh 'Eretz Rabbah* VI and VIII. Cf. the mention of 'good manners' according to a tradition in *Derekh 'Eretz Rabbah* VI in the second generation of Amoraim in a tradition in TbBeitza 25b.

It is part of the universally accepted views that *Derekh 'Eretz Rabbah* III strongly bears on traditions from *'Abot de-Rabbi Natan* XIX.[61] The content of *Derekh 'Eretz Rabbah* III mainly consists of statements of wisdom, whereas the contents of *Derekh 'Eretz Rabbah* IV-IX for the greater part consists of rules of etiquette. The majority of statements from *Derekh 'Eretz Rabbah* (I)III−IX as well as the statements from *Derekh 'Eretz Zuta* I−IV date back to as early the Tanaitic era. From all sorts of overlaps in the text it appears that this literary unity of *Derekh 'Eretz Zuta* III−IX must have been built up from originally much smaller units which are very difficult to reconstruct.

*Derekh 'Eretz Rabbah* IV as well as *Derekh 'Eretz Rabbah* V start off with the words 'le-'olam' (always). S. Krauss spoke of *Pirqei le-'Olam* basing himself on the fact that the opening words are the same and the contents of the two chapters are coherent to a high degree.[62] Both chapters describe norms of decency for Torah scholars concerning their social behaviour and support them with examples. The words 'Therefore Rabbi Jehoshua ben Levi says...' at the ending of *Derekh 'Eretz Rabbah* V may be regarded as a closing to *Derekh 'Eretz Rabbah* IV-V.[63]

---

[60] See M. Goldberg, *Derech Erez Rabba*, introduction, p. V.

[61] Cf., for instance, M. Goldberg, *Derech Erez Rabba*, introduction, p. V. M. Higger, *Massekhtot Ze'irot*, introduction, p. 13 and 23. M.B. Lerner, in: *The Literature of the Sages*, I, ed. S. Safrai, p. 386, note 136, proposes that reading 'R. Natan' in Ms. A. Epstein is a possible reference to A.R.N.

[62] See S. Krauss, in: *R.E.J.*, XXXVI (1898), p. 32.

[63] See S. Krauss, in: *R.E.J.*, XXXVI (1898), p. 35.

*Derekh 'Eretz Rabbah* VI and *Derekh 'Eretz Rabbah* VII are also related as regards content. Chapter VI contains quite some stories and rules about table manners, which the opening of chapter VII links up to. Next, rules are given on how someone is to behave in the privy. S. Krauss denotes these two chapters as *Pereq ha-Nikhnas* based on the opening words of *Derekh 'Eretz Rabbah* VI.[64]

*Derekh 'Eretz Rabbah* VIII and IX are called *Pereq ha-Nikhnas II* by S. Krauss, based on the opening words of chapter VIII. Like *Derekh 'Eretz Rabbah* VI and VII, in the manuscripts these chapters are distinguished clearly as separate units. Chapter VIII deals with table manners and soon reverts to rules of conduct that have a strong ethical nature, implicating one must not create false expectations with one's neighbour and that one must not disadvantage one's neighbour in any way. Chapter IX contains rules concerning table manners, supplemented with narrative material for illustration. In a number of manuscripts the ending of *Pirqei ben 'Azzai* is explicitly indicated at the closing of *Derekh 'Eretz Rabbah* IX.

*Derekh 'Eretz Rabbah* X and *Derekh 'Eretz Rabbah* XI are called *Pirqei ha-Nikhnas III*, by S. Krauss (see note 62). However, the two chapters are entirely different and they must have been handed down separately from the chapters I−IX (see all the manuscripts that have *Derekh 'Eretz Rabbah* I−IX but not *Derekh 'Eretz Rabbah* X and XI. Chapter X is devoted to conduct in the bathhouse and in this matter a number of old traditions have been changed as regards their meaning. *Derekh 'Eretz Rabbah* XI contains rules that contribute to one's wellbeing and health, and is supplemented with a number of statements of wisdom at the ending, after which it is closed with some blessings.


In a number of manuscripts *Derekh 'Eretz Zuta* I−IV and *Derekh 'Eretz Zuta* IX are called *Massekhet Jir'at Het* (Fear of Transgression). This title, *Jir'at Het* can already be found in the Siddur of Sa'adjah Gaon (see above) and with the Karaite *Al Qirqisani* (see under note 48). This part of *Derekh 'Eretz* consists mainly of short statements and contains no narrative material. It breathes the atmosphere of *Pirqei 'Abot* and *'Abot de Rabbi Natan*, statements in the New Testament and in *Didache*. Here in particular, one finds the characteristics of the admonitions from the circles of the Hasidim, such as the emphasis on humility, forgiving, tolerance, charity, ascesis, joy

---

[64]  See S. Krauss, in: *R. E. J.*, XXXVI (1898), p. 32.

in fulfilling the commandments, voluntary aggravations in order to remain far from transgression, and such. The reference mentioned above of *Megillat Hasidim* in *'Abot de Rabbi Natan* [b] XXVI notably relates to a statement in *Derekh 'Eretz Zuta* II. Elsewhere in the Rabbinic tradition a number of statements are referred to as being of Tannaitic origin.[65]

*Jir'at Het* belongs, as we see it, to the oldest parts of the *Derekh 'Eretz* literature (see above). The closing part of chapter I, in which rows of persons are mentioned who have remained undamaged after death, or who have entered paradise alive, was not added until much later (presumably not sooner than the tenth century).[66] The mention of Rabbi Jehoshua ben Levi at the end of the last row is based on Talmudic tradition and in itself it proves that the addition must have been made later.

Almost all statements in *Derekh 'Eretz Zuta* I—IV are anonymous, in *Derekh 'Eretz Zuta* IV only Tannaitic spokesman are mentioned. It is remarkable that *Derekh 'Eretz Zuta* IV is not incorporated in *Massekhet Kallah Rabbati*, contrary to the chapters I—III. It is not unlikely that chapter IV was added to I—III in a later stage and that the closing admonition of chapter IV served as a conclusion of I—IV in total. Chapter IX, considered to be a part of *Jir'at Het* in a number of manuscripts, is an originally independent chapter that was added later (this explains why a number of manuscripts mention chapter IX only after *Derekh 'Eretz Zuta* V-VIII and not directly after chapter IV).[67] Chapter IX is also greater in size than the other chapters.[68] At the end of *Derekh 'Eretz Zuta* IX, one finds a closing formula of the same kind as the closing formula of *Derekh 'Eretz Zuta* IV. This closing formula can be found in the manuscripts which consider *Derekh 'Eretz Zuta* I—IV and IX a unity as well as those which don't place chapter IX after chapter IV. This is why it is not unlikely that this closing formula originally functioned as a closing of chapter IX as an independent unit. It must be clear that there is a considerable time interval between the origin of the independent units and their final editing as a

---

[65] See the commentary and cf. M. B. Lerner, in: *The Literature of the Sages*, ed. S. Safrai, p. 382, note 99.

[66] See the commentary and cf. the opinion of A. J. Tawrogi, *Derech Erez Sutta*, Königsberg 1885, introduction, p. II. On the other hand, see the opinion of S. Krauss, in: *R. E. J.*, XXXVII (1898), p. 45.

[67] See also D. Sperber, *Massekhet Derekh 'Eretz Zuta*, p. 180, referring to L. Ginzberg.

[68] Cf. in particular S. Krauss, in: *R. E. J.*, XXXVI (1898), pp. 31—32, pp. 44—45. According to A. J. Tawrogi, *Derech Erez Sutta*, introduction, p. III, *Derekh 'Eretz Zuta* IV served as an example for the realisation of *Derekh 'Eretz* IX.

unity. Derekh 'Eretz Zuta V-VIII is also an originally independent unit, called *Massekhet Derekh 'Eretz Ze'ira* (the Minor Derekh 'Eretz). In the Talmud editions as from *ed. Frankfurt* (1720–1723) (they are not mentioned in *ed. Frankfurt* 1699) these capita are said to be borrowed from the *Mahzor Vitry*. The chapters contain many anonymous rules for the right conduct of Torah scholars and their students, which are found in practically all other rabbinical sources. It was added to *Jir'at Het* much later and it is probably written by a single author (it is much more a unity than *Jir'at Het*) in the post-Talmudic era.[69] M. B. Lerner points to a number of polemic statements at the end of chapter VIII, which indicate, according to the author, that *Massekhet Derekh 'Eretz Ze'ira* must have played a part in an anti-Karaite polemic.[70]

*Derekh 'Eretz Zuta* X, *Pereq Rabbi Shim'on*, this is also an originally independent chapter with a clear-cut closing formula. It was named after the man who made the statement mentioned first in the text. Its beginning is based on Talmudic messianic traditions. Certain anti-Karaite tendencies are not foreign to its content.[71] In manuscripts with the oldest arrangement it is not mentioned.

*Derekh 'Eretz Zuta* XI. In a number of manuscripts this chapter is mentioned at the end of *Derekh 'Eretz Zuta*, but clearly distinguished from it (only after the specification of the end of *Derekh 'Eretz Zuta* this chapter is mentioned separately). The designation of this chapter as *Derekh 'Eretz Zuta XI* is in fact not correct and serves only purposes of convenience. *Pereq ha-Shalom* is a completely independent unit of a strongly stylized collection of statements about peace, borrowed from the Talmud and the Midrash. Based on the manuscripts it is evident that Pereq ha-Shalom was added to the rest of *Derekh 'Eretz* only much later.[72]

[69] See A. J. Tawrogi, *Derech Erez Sutta*, introduction, p. IIff. See D. Sperber, *Massekhet Derekh 'Eretz Zuta*, p. 179.

[70] See M. B. Lerner, *The Literature of the Sages*, I, ed. S. Safrai, p. 383.

[71] Cf. M. Higger, *Massekhtot Derekh 'Eretz*, p. 248.

[72] See also D. Sperber, *Massekhet Derekh 'Eretz Zuta*, p. 181.

# List of Manuscripts

New York, Jewish Theological Seminary , cat. E. N. Adler, p. 81, no. 2237. Miscellany, partly described by A. Neubauer, *R. E. J.*, X, 100. Written by Jacob Machir called 'Camprat Dawjan de Vives', ca. 1271, censored 1575. Cf. the description by M. Higger, *Massekhtot Derekh 'Eretz,* introduction, pp. 44−45. D. E. R. I−IX; D. E. Z. I−IV, IX, X, V-VIII.

Oxford, Bodleian, cat. A. Neubauer, I, p. 190, no. 896. Fol. 1−224. Minhagim (Siddur) in Arabic, of Rabbi Shelomo ben Natan, containing 30 chapters, of which the last is headed: '... *Massekhet 'Abot we-Qinjan Torah we-Jir'at Het we-Derekh 'Eretz*', preceded by the preface. The latest authority quoted by the author is Rabbi Jitzhaq. Over some words in *'Abot* is written the Arabic translation in Magrebi char. The manuscript is written in 1203 in Qa' la Barqa (cyrenaica) in Lybië. D. E. Z. I−IV, IX, V-VIII.

Oxford, Bodleian, cat. A. Neubauer, I, p. 785, no. 2257 · Talmudical treatises: *Hilkhot Sopherim*, *Massekhet Semahot*, *Massekhet Kallah*, fol.111b: *Massekhet Derekh 'Eretz Rabbah*, fol. 118: *Massekhet Derekh 'Eretz Zuta*, and fol. 121b: *Pereq ha-Shalom*. The treatises-mentioned are written in Ital. Rabb. char.
End date 1582. Cf. the description by M. Higger, *Massekhtot Derekh 'Eretz*, introduction, p. 41. D. E. R. I−XI; D. E. Z. I−IV, IX−X, *Pereq ha-Shalom*.

Oxford, Bodleian, cat. A. Neubauer, I, p. 815, no. 2339. Midrashim and Agadic treatises. Fol. 9: *Derekh 'Eretz Zuta*, the end of IV, IX and X. Fol. 11b: *Pereq ha-Shalom*. Fol. 54b: *Middat Derekh 'Eretz*, identical with *Massekhet Derekh 'Eretz Rabbah* (II and III in the editions make in the Ms. one chapter). Fol. 67: *Derekh 'Eretz Zuta*, I−IV, continuation of fol. 9ff. Syr. Rabb. char. Cf. the description by M. Higger, *Massekhtot Derekh 'Eretz,* introduction, p. 40. D. E. R. I−XI; D. E. Z. I−IV, IX−X, *Pereq ha-Shalom*.

Oxford, Bodleian, cat. A. Neubauer, I, p. 784, no. 2255. Fol. 58. *S' Derekh 'Eretz*, beg. with chap. I−III; V (= VII and VIII in editions); end with beg. of VII (= X in editions). Germ. Rabb. char. (many pages are obliterated and injured). Cf. the description by M. Higger, *Massekhtot Derekh 'Eretz*, introduction, pp. 27−28. D. E. R. III-VIII, IX.

Oxford, Bodleian, cat. A. Neubauer, I, p. 306, no. 1100. Opp. no. 59. Siddur acc. to Rabbi Simha of Vitry (Mahzor Vitry acc. to modern title page; see Luzzato, *Qeren Hemed*, III, p. 200ff.). Part IV *Hosha'not*. Fol. 243: beg. with introduction *Darkhan shel Talmidei Hakhamim* and seven chapters. At the end: *Seliqa Darkhan shel Talmidei Hakhamim*. Next comes *Pereq ben 'Azzai* and five chapters: *Le-'olam tehe*, *Lo jippater*, *Ha-nikhnas le-beit-*,*Shenajim she-haju*, and *Lo 'adam*. Germ. Rabb. char. (the oldest hand aproaches to the square char.), most of the liturgies with vowel points. Cf. the description by M. Higger, *Massekhtot Derekh 'Eretz*, introduction, p. 33. D. E. Z. I−IX; D. E. R. III−IX, X (begin) XI (begin).

Oxford, Bodleian, cat. A.Neubauer, I, pp. 301–302, no. 1098. Miscellaneous. Fol. 105: *Massekhet Derekh 'Eretz*, six chapters (the printed *Massekhet Derekh 'Eretz Zuta*. Chap. I ends '*Ajn tobah* . . . , beg. of the third chapter of the editions. II = III of the editions. III = IV; IV = V, ends 'midda'at ha-beriot'; V = VI; VI = VII, VIII and IX of the editions). Fol. 108b: . . . *u-Peraqim de ben 'Azzai* . . . : six chapters (the printed *Massekhet Derekh 'Eretz Rabbah*. I = III of the editions; II ends 'Hareni niphtar' (= IV); III = V; IV = VI; V (end wanting) = VII; VI (begin wanting) = VIII, with additional par., many varriations from the editions.
The copy was made by *'A "zaq* (fol. 81). On fol. 69b birth of Shemarjah, twelfth of Nissan 5330 = 1570. Old Germ. curs. char. The margins of the last five leaves are mended with fragments of an old French poem (char. of the end of the 13th or beginning of the 14th century. Cf. the description by M. Higger, *Massekhtot Derekh 'Eretz,* introduction, pp. 25–26. D. E. Z. I–IX; D. E. R. III–IX.

Oxford, Bodleian, cat. A. Neunauer, I, p. 19, no. 120. Fol. 193: sentences in Hebrew and Arabic. Fol. 194: . . . . *Shemu'el ha-Qatan 'omer* . . . Ibid. *Qinjan Torah* (chap. VI of M'Abot). Fol. 199: sentences (*Jir'at Het*). Fol. 205: *Nathil Derekh 'Eretz*. At the end of the Ms.: prayer in Arabic. Written by Jishma'el ben Joseph ha-Sopher ben Shemu'el ha-Melammed. Span. Rabb. char. Two hands.
Cf. I.Abrahams in: *J. Q. R.* X (O.S.), 660–661. M. *Steinschneider Festschrift*, pp. 72–75. W. Bacher, *J. Q. R.* (O.S.) VII, 679–698. Cf. the description by M. Higger, *Massekhtot Derekh 'Eretz,* introduction 19. *Jir'at Het* (D.E.Z. I–IV,IX) and *Derekh 'Eretz Ze'ira* (D.E.Z. V-VIII). The text agrees closely with the text in *Halakhot Gedolot*, ed. A. Hildesheimer.

Oxford, Bodleian, cat. A. Neubauer, I, p. 83, no. 38 Fol. 133b: *Jir'at Het*. Fol. 143b: *Derekh Eretz*. Owner: Jehudah ben Jitzhaq ben Jehudah. Syr. Rabb. char. See for further information what is said about Ms. Oxford, Bodleian, cat. A. Neubauer, no. 120. D.E.Z. I–IV, IX, V-VIII.

Oxford, Bodleian, cat. A.Neubauer, I, p. 194, no. 904. Fol. 215b *Hilkhot Derekh 'Eretz* (cf. cat. A. Neubauer, no. 120). Only four chapters. Owner: Rabbi Jitzhaq (at beginning injured and pale). Written by Joseph ben Shemu'el "ha-Qatan" (?); (another part of the Ms. was finished 5241 = 1481). Span. Rabb, char.
D. E. Z. I–IV (IV: partly).

Oxford, Bodleian, cat. A. Neubauer, I, p. 853, no. 2422. Fol. 57: *Mas' Gerim, Seder Tanna'im we-'Amora'im*. Ms. additions to *Mas' Derekh 'Eretz* and *Taqqanot* of Rabbenu Gershom and Rabbenu Tam. Germ. curs. char. D.E.Z. V-IX

London, Montefiore Libr., H. Hirschfeld, *Descriptive Catalogue of Hebreww Mss of the Montefiore Library*, London 1904, no. 64. *J. Q. R.* (O.S.) XIV, p. 173. *Kisse Kabod*. The tractates *Kallah, Sopherim, Derekh 'Eretz*, with the commentary of Judah Abbas. In the last named tractate chapters III and IV are written as one chapter. It is also incomplete, and contains only about a third of chap. VI. After fol. I lacuna. With regard to the author, see M. Steinschneider in: *J. Q. R.* (1899), p. 333. Span. Rabb. char. D. E. R. I-VI (VI: partly).

London, Jews College, A. Neubauer, *Catalogue of the Hebrew Mss. in the Jews College*, London, p. 11, no. 28[19]. Fol. 146b-150: *Massekhet Derekh 'Eretz (Zuta)*. Fol. 150ff. *Massekhet Kallah*. Germ. Rabb. char. D. E. Z. I–IX.

London, Montefiore Libr., H. Hirschfeld, *Descriptive Catalogue of the Hebrew Mss. of the Montefiore Library*, London 1904, no. 431[21]. Fol. 76: *Darkhan shel Talmidei Hakhamim* · No.'s 15−22 Ital Rabb. char. Various hands. End 15th century? D. E. Z. I−IX (IX: partly).

Cambridge UB, S. M. Schiller Szinessy, *Catalogue II* (never published), p. 96, no. 40[20]. D. E. Z. V-IX.

Cambridge UB, TS SN 329/482. D. E. Z. VII and VIII.

Mishnah codex Kaufmann A 50. See the facsimile edition of G. Beer, Jerusalem 1968, p. 525. *'Arajot Pereq A'*. D. E. R. I. Cf. M. Higger, *Massekhtot Derekh 'Eretz*, p. 15.

New York, Jewish Theological Seminary, cat. E. N. Adler, no. 4465a. See the description by M. Higger, *Massekhtot Derekh 'Eretz*, introduction, p. 29, no. 6. D. E. Z. I−IX (*We-zeh Hilkhot Derekh 'Eretz . . .*) and D. E. R. III−IX (*Pirqei ben 'Azzai*).

New York, Jewish Theological Seminary, cat. E. N. Adler, no. 7246. D. E. Z. I−IX.

New York, Jewish Theological Seminary, cat. E. N. Adler, p. 72, no. 428. Mishlei with Jewish Persian translation. *Mas' Derekh Eretz* ditto. Cf. M. Higger, *Massekhtot Derekh 'Eretz*, introduction 16. D. E. Z. V-VIII.

New York, Jewish Theological seminary, cat. E. N. Adler, p. 19, no. 2542. Begin: *Nathil be-Derekh 'Eretz Qetannah*. D. E. Z. V, VI (begin).

New York, Jewish Theological Seminary, cat. E. N. Adler, p. 19, no. 1909. *'Abot de Rabbi Natan, Massekhet Derekh 'Eretz* (Rabbah and Zuta), *Massekhet Kallah* and *M'Abot* with commentary. D. E. R. I−XI; D. E. Z. I−IV, IX, X; *Pereq ha-Shalom*.

Milaan, Ambr., C. Bernheimer, *Codices Hebraici Bibliothecae Ambrosianae*, Milaan 1933, no 14[6]. I. Textus interior: Pentateuchus vocabilus, accentibus . . . II. Textus maginalus: inc. fol. 226 ff.: *Massekhet Derekh 'Eretz Rabbah. Ha-meqaddesh 'ishah hare zeh 'oser 'alaw sheba 'arajot . . .* Sacer textus charactere italico huente, marginalis rabbinico exeratus (saec. XV).

München, Kön. Hofbibl., cat. M. Steinschneider, *Die Hebr. Handschriften der Kön. Hof- und Staatsbibliothek in München*, no. 95. Fol. 565b-567a: *Derekh 'Eretz*. Written in 1342. Cf. H. Strack's facsimile edition, Leiden 1912. Fol. 565b second col.: *'Ahel Mas' Pereq 'Eretz . . .* = D. E. Z. I. Fol. 566b, first col.: Seliq Mas' *Derekh 'Eretz . . .* = D. E. Z. IX, end. Fol. 566b, first col. *Hai lekha Pirqei ben 'Azzai* = D. E. R. III. Fol. 567a, second col.: *Shalemu Pirqei ben 'Azzai* = D. E. R. IX, end. Cf. the description by M. Higger, *Massekhtot Derekh 'Eretz*, introduction, pp. 28−29. D. E. Z. I−IX, D. E. R. III−IX.

München, Kön. Hofbibl., cat. M. Steinschneider, o.c., no. 232[10]. Fol. 85: *'Injan Derekh 'Eretz*, from *Derekh 'Eretz Zuta*. Chap. V-VIII, I−IV (fol. 86b,5); IX (fol. 88b,2) with var.; then, sayings with numbers: *Sheba debarim tzawah ha-qadosh rabbeinu 'et beno . . .* Many notes, which are partly removed. Sabb. ben Mosheh, physician from ?? . . . , acquired the Cod. as inheritance with the brothers Hillel and Sal. . . . (or . . .) 1380 (or 1420?). Ital Rabb. char. (ca. 1400).

München, Kön. Hofbibl., cat. M. Steinschneider, o.c., no. 264[5]. Miscellaneous. Fol. 96: *Hilkhot Derekh 'Eretz*. Span. curs. f. 192 ff., a. 1363. D. E. Z. I, II, (partly).

Moscow, cat. A. Katsh, *Ginzei Russya*, no. 249. D. E. Z. I–IV, IX.

Vatican, cat. S. E. Assemani, p. 290, no. 303. Anonymous. Fol. 225a-229: *Hilkhot Derekh 'Eretz*. Begin: *Darkhan shel Talmidei Hakhamim* .... Rabbinicis litteris exaratus, olim Palatinus. 16th century? (Is codex partim decimoquarto, partim decimosexto Christi seculo videtur exeratus).

Oxford, Bodleian, cat. A. Neubauer – A. E. Cowley, no. 2643. Ms. Heb. d.46. Cowl. 39. 14b (fol. 85). Fragment of *Massekhet Derekh 'Eretz* , beg. *Mishnah middah she-notelin 'aleha sahar*, followed by the chap. *Rabbi 'Eli'ezer ha-Kappar*, incomplete. Syr. Rabb. char. D. E. Z. IV, IX.

Oxford, Bodleian, cat. A. Neubauer – A. E. Cowley, no. 2661. Ms. Heb. c.17. Cowley 56. Fol. 6b: *Derekh Eretz Zuta*, ends *U-tepajjes 'otam*. Syr. squa. char. See the description by M. Higger, *Massekhtot Derekh 'Eretz*, introduction, p. 19. D. E. Z. I.

Oxford, Bodleian, cat. A. Neubauer – A. E. Cowley, no. 2261. Ms. Heb. c.17. Cowley 56. Fol. 10: *Derekh 'Eretz Zuta*, II *we-'eino she-lekha* to III *'al menat – le-shallem we-'im* · No sections for *'Abot* or *Derekh 'Eretz*. Large Syr. char. D. E. Z. II–III.

Oxford, Bodleian, cat. A. Neubauer – A. E. Cowley, no. 2669. Ms. Heb. d.47. Cowley 67. Fol. 14: *'Abot* VI,9 (*kol ha-niqra*), ending with *Seleq Pirqa. Seleq 'Abot we-Qinjan Torah*; followed by *Derekh 'Eretz Zuta* (headed *Jir'at Het*).
Syr. squa. char. D. E. Z. I (partly).

Oxford, Bodleian, cat. A. Neubauer – A. E. Cowley, no. 2669. Ms. Heb. d.47. Cowley 67. Fol. 15: D. E. Z. I, beg. *'Al jehi Pirqekha*, to II *'eini jodea*. Fol. 16: D. E. Z. IX, beg. "om' mahaloqet", ending with *Seleq Jir'at Het*, followed by the common prayer *Jotzer 'Or*, with variations. Syr. squa. char. D. E. Z. I–II, IX.

Oxford, Bodleian, cat. A. Neubauer – A. E. Cowley, no. 2833. Ms. Heb. b.10. Cowley 267. Fol. 84 D. E. Z. IX (*she-lo jahseru* to the end of the chapter, with the colophon *Seleq Derekh 'Eretz Rabbah*, followed by the chapters V-VIII, headed *Derekh ('Eretz Zuta)*. Syr. Rab. char. D. E. Z. IX, V-VIII.

Oxford, Bodleian, cat. A. Neubauer – A. E. Cowley, no. 2833. Ms. Heb. b.10. Cowley 266. Fol. 66. D. E. R., par. 8 (*lo jishlah 'adam*) to the end of the section, followed by par. 10, headed *Pereq H(et)'*, to *'arumim ruban*. Fol. 66b is blank. Syr. Rabb. char. See the description by M. Higger, *Massekhtot Derekh 'Eretz*, introduction, p. 45. D. E. R. VIII, X.

New York, Jewish Theological Seminary, cat. E. N. Adler, p. 19, no. 229. The like of *Derekh 'Eretz Zuta*. Parts of D. E. Z. VI-VIII.

New York, Jewish Theological Seminary, cat. E. N. Adler, no. 409. *Massekhet 'Abot, Pereq Qinjan Torah, Jir'at Het. Jir'at Het* beginning: *Talm' Hakkam*, end: *Be-Mosheh mah katub* .... Cf. the description by M. Higger, *Massekhtot Derekh 'Eretz*, introduction p. 20. D. E.. Z. I (partly).

New York, Jewish Theological Seminary, cat. E. N. Adler, no. 1111. Fragments of D. E. Z. VIII. Cf. the description by M. Higger, *Massekhtot Derekh 'Eretz*, introduction, p. 22.

New York, Jewish Theological Seminary, cat. E.N. Adler, no. 1177. Fragment of D.E.Z. I(end)-II(begin). Cf. the description by M. Higger, *Masekhtot Derekh 'Eretz*, introduction, p. 22.

New York, Jewish Theological Seminary, cat. E.N. Adler, p. 19, no. 1329. Parts of D.E.Z. I -III. See the description by M. Higger, *Massekhtot Derek 'Eretz*, introduction, p. 20.

New York, Jewish Theological Seminary, cat. E.N. Adler, p. 19, no. 1745. Parts of D.E.R. II.

New York, Jewish Theological Seminary, cat. E.N. Adler, p. 19, no. 2101. The like of *Derekh 'Eretz Ze'ira*. Scribe: Jitzhaq ben Mosheh ben Shemu'el ha-Sephardi, ca. 1135. Fragments of D.E.Z. II (from *'Im haphetz 'atta le-hitrahheq* [II]), D.E.Z. III, D.E.Z. IV (from: *she-lo shimmashta ke-jozte bo* , D.E.Z. V (numbered as chap. I) VI (numbered as chap. II), VII (numbered as chap. IV and VIII (numbered as chap. IV). Cf. the description by M. Higger, *Massekhtot Derekh 'Eretz*, introduction, p. 17.

New York, Jewish Theological Seminary, cat. E.N. Adler, no. 2149. Fragments of D.E.Z. I−III. See the description by M. Higger, *Massekhtot Derekh 'Eretz*, introduction, p. 22.

New York, Jewish Theological Seminary, cat. E.N. Adler, no. 2157. Fragments from the beginning of D.E.Z. VII.

New york, Jewish Theological Seminary, cat. E.N. Adler, no. 2840. Parts of D.E.Z. VIII. See also the description by M. Higger, *Massekhtot Derekh 'Eretz*, introduction, pp. 22−23.

New York, Jewish Theological Seminary, cat. E.N. Adler, no. 3051. Fragments of D.E.Z. VII from *Shomea u-mosiph* (VII). See the description by M. Higger, *Massekhtot Derek 'Eretz*, introduction pp. 23−24.

Cambridge, Westm. Coll., no. 97−98. Fragments of D.E.Z. I.

London, OR 5558A (PS 103707). Parts of D.E.Z. I ('Jir'at Het'). From *Darkhei Talmidei Hakhamim* to *Harheq me-ha-ki'ur u-min ha-domeh*.

Cambridge UB, TS III, 32. Last word of D.E.Z. VI. Begin of D.E.Z. VII (numbered as chap. III), end: *she jehe tzanua be-ma'asaw*. (VII,12).

Cambridge UB, TS III 142. End of D.E.Z. I, from *'Am ha-'aretz shema tehallel qodshei shamajim* (I) to end of D.E.Z.I, D.E.Z. II from begin to *we-da she-bein ha-jom le-mahar*.

Leningrad, cat. A. Katsh, *Ginzei Russya*, no. 4. *Jir'at Het* = D.E.Z. I, parts of D.E.Z. II, IV, IX. *Derekh 'Eretz*: D.E.Z. V, VI, parts of D.E.Z. VII and VIII. See the description by M.Higger, *Massekhtot Derekh 'Eretz*, introduction p. 24.

Leningrad, cat. A. Katsh, *Ginzei Russya*, no. 6. *Jir'at Het* = D.E.Z. I−IV, part of D.E.Z. IX. See the description by M. Higger, *Massekhtot Derekh 'Eretz*, introduction, pp. 24−25.

Cambridge UB, TS 12.729. Cf. S. Schechter, *J. Q. R.*, XIV (1902); pp. 509–510. Square char. with a turn to cursive, but of earlier date than fragm. XL (= 14th century)... The second leaf reproduces a few passages from the minor tractate D. E. Z. Text reproduces on p. 475–476.

Cambridge, UB TS, III 33. Part of D. E. Z. VII. From begin to *Talmid hakham tzarikh she-jehe tzanua be-ma'asaw*.

Cambridge, Trinity College Library, cat. H. Loewe, pp. 64–65, no. 74. Leafs of liturgy. In the margin, top, bottem and sides portions of *Massekhet Kallah* and *Derekh 'Eretz*. Date: 14th century. Text and notes in the margin in Franco-German hand.

Ms. A. Epstein. For Ms. Epstein in *Mi-Qadmoniot ha-Jehudim* (1887) see bibliogaphy. Cf. M. Higger, *Massekhtot Derekh 'Eretz*, introduction pp. 45–46.

Leningrad, cat. G. Katsch, *Ginzei Russya*, no. 215 (Geniza). D. E. Z. I–III.

London, BM, br. 1389. Cf. G. Margolianth, *Cat. of the Hebr. and Samaritan Mss.*, London 1915, IV, p. 153. Moral and ethical excerpts from Talmud and Midrash, devided into 11 sedarim. Imperfect. Possibly compiled by a rabbi of Augevin, England. Date 14th century. See A. Marmorstein, *J. Q. R.* N. S., XIX, p. 17f.

New York, Jewish Theological Seminary, cat. E. N. Adler, p. 141, no. 2345. Hebrew-Persian miscellany. Containing *Derekh 'Eretz*.

Oxford, Bodleian, cat. A. Neubauer, no. 563. Fol. 141b, parts of D. E. Z. I. In the middle: *Hilkhot Derekh 'Eretz*. End of the page: chap. II, begin. Fol. 124a-b: rest of chap. II. and begin of D. E. Z. III (numbered as chap. I). Fol.134a: D. E. Z. III to the end, begin of D. E. Z. IV (numbered as chap. II). Fol. 134b-144a: rest of D. E. Z. IV and begin of D. E. Z. V (numbered as chap. III). Fol. 144b: rest of D. E. Z. V, D. E. Z. VI and begin of D. E. Z. VII (numbered as chap. IV). Fol. 145a: rest of chap. VII, begin of D. E. Z. VIII (numbered as chap. V) Fol. 145b: rest of D. E. Z. VIII to "sopho le-hitnasse bahem she-n'" (VIII,8). Begin of D. E. R. VI. Fol.146a-146b: rest of D. E. Z. VI to *We-lo johez 'adam perusa*.

Paris, Consistoire Israelite, no. 94 (82). Lost in the Second World War. Cf. M. Schwabe, "Les Mss. du Consistoire de Paris", in: *R. E. J.*, LXII, (1911).

Paris, Consistoire Israelite, no. 102. Lost in the Second World War. Cf. M. Schwabe, "Les Mss. du Consistoire de Paris", in: *R. E. J.*, LXIV, (1912).

Paris, Bibl. Nationale, H. Zotenberg, *Catalogue des Mss. Hebreux et Samaritains a la Bibliotheque Imperiale*, p. 115, no. 716. Fol. 273–274: *Derekh 'Eretz Zuta*. Date: 14th century.

Paris, Bibl. Nationale, Hebreu, no. 1391. *Massekhet Derekh Eretz Zuta*. A lot of sentences in D. E. Z. I–II are missing. Fol. 1a: D. E. Z. I), part of D. E. Z. II (begin). Fol. 1b: end of D. E. Z. I, D. E. Z. II, (part). Fol. 2a: rest of D. E. Z. II, begin of D. E. Z. III. Fol. 2b: rest of D. E. Z. III. Begin D. E. Z. IV. Fol. 3a: end of D. E. Z. IV. Begin of D. E. Z. V., begin of D. E. Z. VI. Fol. 3b: end of D. E. Z. VI, D. E. Z. VII. Fol. 4a: D. E. Z. VIII, begin of D. E. Z. IX. Fol. 4b-5a: rest of D. E. Z. IX, begin of D. E. Z. X. Fol. 5b: rest of D. E. Z. X and addition of a hasidic text. Fol. 6a -7b: *Pereq ha-Shalom* XI (short version). (The text of *Pereq ha-Shalom* does not concur with the Basic Ms., but with the other manuscripts). Writing, cf. the char. of Ms. New York, cat. E.N. Adler, no. 2237.

Strassburg (Strasbourg), University Library, no. 172/3. Provided with vowels. Fol. 2b: D.E.Z. II, 13 – D.E.Z. II,21 (from "tebaqqesh 'elbonekha" to "hewe ratz"). Fol. 3a: D.E.Z. I,34 – D.E.Z. I,41 (from "le-Dawid 'abdi" [Ps. 89,4] to "we-Serah bat 'Asher we-jesh 'om' "). Genizah.

Vatican, cat. S.E. Assemani (*Codices Hebr. et Samar.*, Rome 1756, p. 33), no. 44.: *Massekhet Derekh 'Eretz'* Tractatus de Viae Terrae... This text, however, is not of D.E.

Wien, Cat. A.Z. Schwarz, *Die Hebr. Mss. in Osterreich,* (Bibl. Isr. Kultusgemeinde Wien), Leipzig 1931, pp. 17–18. no. 32. Lost in the Second World-War. A) *Massekhet Derekh 'Eretz*. Begin fol.1: *Ben 'Azzai 'omer kol ha- noten* ...end: fol. 7:... *bi-mehera be-jameinu... Seleq dabar 'eretz.* D.E.R. I–XI. A.Z. Schwartz l.c.: "Varianten aus dieser Ms. bei A. Epstein *Miqqadmoniot ha-Jehudim,* p. 113ff. M. Goldberg in der Edition (Breslau 1888) gibt pag. XV, Anm. nur an, diese abgedrückten Varr. benützt zu haben, bringt aber unter H 1 auch eine Reihe von anderen, die zum Teil nicht in dieser Ms. stehen." B) *Derekh 'Eretz Zuta.* Begin fol. 7: *Darkhan shel Hakhamim.* End fol. 10:... *we-khen jehi ratzon... Seleq* (end D.E.Z. IX). Variants of this Ms. have been used by A.J. Tawrogi (ed. of D.E.Z.). Date: 14th century. Germ. Rabb. char.

The description of some other Mss. of less interest is found in M.Higger, *Massekhtot Derekh 'Eretz*, introduction, p. 18ff.

# Translation and Commentary

# Pereq 'Arajot

## *Derekh Eretz Rabbah, chapter I*

**[Let Me begin Derekh 'Eretz.]**

**1. One who betroths a woman, makes (thereby) seven relations prohibited to himself. They are: her mother, her mother's mother, her father's mother, her daughter, her daughter's daughter, her son's daughter, and her sister while she is (herself) alive.**

**And all these who are prohibited to him, the interdict is not (even) lifted, except in the case of his wife's sister, who is prohibited only during her (i. e. his wife's) lifetime.**

Relevant scripture quotations: Lev. 18:17−18.

By sanctification is meant the official act of betrothal. Through betrothal, a man joins a woman to himself. The act takes place through the transfer of money or a document given to the woman ; or through sexual intercourse (see MQid., beginning). In TbQid. 2b the term 'sanctification', i. e. the betrothal, is explained as an act in which the woman is dedicated to the man. She becomes 'heqdesh', i. e. something which has been dedicated, thereby the man is forbidding her for all other men. Another consequence of this 'sanctification' is that the man makes a number of relatives of his future spouse forbidden for himself, while in turn a number of the man's relatives become forbidden for the woman, also after divorce or death of the partner. (In this connection cf. TbJeb. 40b; 95a; Rambam, *Jad*, Hil. Jebamot, I, 13.)

In TbJeb. 40b are mentioned the same relatives of a 'jebamah' (wife of a brother who has died childless; see Dt. 25:5−6) who has been released by 'halitzah'. The 'jabam' may no longer marry any of those women since for him the 'jebamah' is considered in this respect as a woman divorced from him (cf. TbSot. 43b). These then are the relations of the wife or betrothed whom the man may not marry (also after divorce), and whom − with the exception of the sister of the betrothed or wife − he may not marry even after the death of his wife. Thus, what holds for the 'jabam' with respect to the relations of the 'jebamah', also holds implicitly for the man with respect to his wife's relations. (See further: Shul. Ar., Eb. ha-Ez. 162,3; Me'iri, *Beit ha-Behirah*, on TbJeb. 40b; see *Mahzor Vitry*, ed. S. Hurwitz, p. 724; Pes. Zut., ed. S. Buber, 51a; see *Halakhot Gedolot*, ed. I. Hildesheimer, repr. Jerusalem 1980, II, p. 30; Rambam, *Jad*, Hil. 'Issur. Bi'ah, II,7.10. *Tur*, Eb. ha-Ez., 66. Texts concerning

forbidden relationships in general: TjJeb. II,4 [3a]; TbJeb. 20aff.; TbSanh.
75a; *She'iltot*, 'Aharei Mot 96e and 161ff; Rambam, *Jad*, Hil 'Issur. Bi'ah,
I,1−6, and other sources; see also M. Higger, *Massekhtot Ze'irot*, pp. 92 and
143.)

In connection with the reading *ha-'ishah* (the woman) instead of *'ishah* (a
woman) see the *Tosaphists* on TbQid. 2a. *Ha-'ishah* is clarified by them as the
woman discussed in the Torah (see Dt.22:13 or Dt. 24:1). *Except in the case of
his wife's sister . . .* , see Dt. 25.

## 2.  **And never does he disqualify his wife (from sexual intercourse with him) because of (intercourse with) her mother, her daughter or her sister.**

By entering a relationship of betrothal (or marriage) a sexual relationship with
seven listed relations of the woman becomes forbidden for the man. If sexual
contact occurs nonetheless with one of the listed relations, the woman does not
become forbidden for the husband. There are different reasons for this. 1)
Sexual intercourse with a forbidden relation (as listed) can never constitute a
valid bond which could render impossible a continuing relationship with the
man's wife (see e.g. *Shul. Ar.*, Eb. ha-Ez. 15:1 and 44:6. 2) Another com-
plementary argument may be taken from Num. 15:3. Only intercourse between
a woman and another man makes the woman forbidden for her husband; this
then does not apply to intercourse between the woman's husband and one of
her close relations (such as her sister). (Cf. TbJeb. 95a en TjJeb. X,8 [11a]). 3)
In TbJeb. 95a, we find the following a fortiori reasoning: if she (the wife) may
still return to her husband after involuntary intercourse with another man
(considering that through the betrothal her husband makes all other men
forbidden to her), he may even more so return to her having involuntary
intercourse (by mistake) with the sister of his wife (of whom only a small
number of relations are forbidden for her husband). See also Siphrei, Naso,
pisqa 7, ed. H. S. Horovitz, p. 11;

See TbJeb. 95a: It would be logical to assume that a man should have to be
divorced from his wife after intercourse with a close relationship of hers by
analogy of the obligation to divorce after the commission of adultery by his
wife.

Here the question is justified as to why only three of the seven listed
forbidden relations are explicitly mentioned in this statement. The answer is
that all seven relations are meant, but precisely these three are mentioned here
because the close relationship of these three to the wife can especially wrongly
provoke the thought that a relationship between them and the husband should
be reason for divorce. See Rambam, *Jad*, Hil. 'Issur. Bi'ah, II,10; *Riph* on
TbJeb. 22a and *Rosh* on TbJeb. 22a.

In this statement in *D. E.* there is a discussion about not disqualifying the
married woman. A clear exception is made in the tradition with respect to the

betrothed woman (see TbJeb. 95a and cf. TjJeb. X,8 [11a]). See TbJeb. 94b, which contains a statement by Rabbi 'Aqiba that the wife's sister, whom the man has married by mistake, must be divorced, with the result that the man may no longer return to his own wife (for she has become the sister of a divorced woman). This statement is remarkable in the light of the Mishnah (see TbJeb. 94a), according to which a husband in such a case may return to his wife. It is evident from the rest of the gemara that Rabbi 'Aqiba discusses the betrothed woman, whereas the Mishnah discusses the married woman. In the gemara there is mention of a man who mistakenly thinks his wife is dead and marries her sister, after which the wife returns alive. If a man had sexual relations with the sister of his betrothed, there is the chance that the betrothal is invalid because of the possibility that a certain condition on which the validity of the betrothal depends has not been fulfilled. In that case then, the man's relationship with the sister may well be lawful, forbidding further relations with his betrothed. In order to eliminate all misunderstanding and to prevent others from suspecting an illegal return by the man to his betrothed, the sages determined that, in the event of a betrothal in such a situation the man ought to be divorced from his betrothed as well as her sister. If the man is married to his wife, there can then be no discussion of conditions.

The relation initiated with the sister simply is not legal in any way and the man can return to his lawful wife, even if the relationship with the sister was intentional. See Rambam. *Jad*, Hil. Gerush., X,8, concerning the matter of the difference between married and betrothed. See also *Halakhot Gedolot*, ed. I. Hildesheimer, II, p. 30, and other sources.

**3a. When she (i.e. a betrothed or a married woman) has had intercourse (with another man), if under force she is permitted to him (i.e. she may continue to live with her husband), but (if she has had intercourse) willingly she is prohibited to him.**

Relevant Scripture passages: Lev. 18:16,20; Num. 5:13; Dt. 22:23−27.

If a betrothed or married woman has intercourse with another man out of her free will, then she may not return to her husband. In this case, a betrothed woman may not marry her betrothed and the husband of a married woman must divorce his adulterous wife. See TjSot. IV,4; TbSot. 27b; TbJeb. 51b and 56b and 100b. See *Tur*, Eb. ha-Ez. 6; *Shul. Ar.*, Eb. ha-Ez. 11 and 187,17; cf. Lewin B.M. Lewin, *Ginzei Qedem*, II, p. 27 and other sources. Cf. also Rambam, *Jad*, Hil. 'Ishut, XXIV,19; Rambam adds to the case of forced intercourse, on the basis of mentioned Talmud passages, the case of a woman who mistakenly had intercourse with another man. Cf. MJeb. X,1; TjJeb. X,7 [10c] and TosJeb. XI,5; TbJeb. 87b ff.

**3b. But if she is the wife (or betrothed) of a priest, whether (she had intercourse with another man) under force, or willingly, she is prohibited to him (i. e. she may not continue to live with her husband).**

Relevant Scripture passages: Lev. 21:7; Dt. 24:4.

The background of the rule that the wife of a priest may not return to her husband after rape or voluntary intercourse with another man, possibly accounts for Lev. 21:7. Although the term 'halalah' (Lev. 21:7) has a very specific technical meaning in the rabbinic tradition, in the first instance it literally means 'the one who has been pierced', which might be interpreted as a woman who has been profaned by sexual relations outside the bond of marriage. This can be the result of rape or intercourse engaged voluntary. According to the tradition, the betrothed or wife of a priest who has been raped or voluntary had sexual relations with another man may not return to her husband because of 'be'ilat zenut' (a relationship in the realm of harlotry). As a result of such intercourse, a woman enters into the sphere of 'zenut', even though such intercourse may have been involuntary. A priest may not be married to a woman who may be called 'zonah' (harlot). Cf. Rambam *Jad*, Hil. 'Issur. Bi'ah, XVIII,6.

While a non-priest may take his wife back after she has been raped, this is forbidden for the priest. In the gemara we encounter the following reasoning: If it is explicitly stated in the Torah that the wife of a non-priest may not return to him only when she commits voluntary adultery, one must then conclude that the wife of a priest may not return to her husband even after forced adultery. See TbJeb. 56b and 100b; TbKet. 51b. Cf. also the version of D. E. R. by the Gaon of Vilna, who has inserted a piece borrowed from the gemara after the statement discussed here (see TbKet. 51b).

**4. When a divorced woman is betrothed (with another man) and has had intercourse (with her new betrothed) whether under force or willingly, she is prohibited to return (i. e. she may not return to her former husband) · For Rabbi Jishma'el said: '"Her former husband who has sent her away (may not take her again to be his wife after that she is defiled)" (Dt. 24:4).' And whence is her defilement? This, however, is what the sages say: 'When she (i. e. is married woman) has had intercourse under force, she is permitted to him (i. e. she may return to her husband) but when (she had intercourse with another man) willingly, she is prohibited to return to him (i. e. she may not continue to live with her husband). But the wife of a priest, whether she had intercourse under force or willingly, is prohibited to (return) to him.'**

**[An other more consistent reading according to other Mss.: If a divorced woman is betrothed (to another man) and has had intercourse, whether**

**under force whether willingly, she may return. If (however) a divorced woman is married (to another man) and has had intercourse, whether under force or willingly (add: she may not return). These are the words of Rabbi Jishma'el, for Rabbi Jishma'el said: 'it is forbidden, because it is written: "Her former husband who has sent her away may not take her again to be his wife, after that she is defiled."' And whence is her defilement? The sages say: 'As long as she is not married with another man she may return to him (i. e. to her first husband), after that she is married to another man she may not return to him.']**

Relevant Scripture passage: Dt. 24:4.

A woman who is betrothed or married and whose husband has himself divorced from her may not return to her husband if she has entered into a relationship with another man and has had intercourse with this man. In the printed version of *D. E. R.* (see also the manuscripts), we find the addition that this is the opinion of Rabbi Jishma'el, and then follows a tradition of Rabbi Jishma'el, in which he quotes Dt. 24:4. Following that is an explanation of the quotation mentioned. According to this explanation, a married woman is defiled if she has voluntary had intercourse with another man. If she has been forced to have intercourse with another man, then she is not considered defiled, and she may return to her husband. Cf. the opinion of Rabbi Jishma'el in TbKet. 51b with reference to Num. 5:12; cf. also TbJeb. 56b. This statement is in clear contradiction to the preceding one, which deals with a divorced woman and in which no distinction is made between voluntary and forced sexual intercourse on the part of the woman. See the reading of the Gaon of Vilna (cf. TbKet. 51b) who attributes the part concerning the divorced woman not to Rabbi Jishma'el (see Mss. of *D. E.*) but to Rabbi José ben Kippar in the name of Rabbi 'El'azar ben Shamua. This reading is not, however, corroborated by the manuscripts. It is, however, possible to read the last line like the Gaon : *But this* (i. e. not the married woman but the divorced woman who has been betrothed to a new man and has had intercourse with that man) *whether she had intercourse under force whether willingly is prohibited* (to return) *to him* (i. e. her first husband).

One finds an interesting reading in the *Halakhot Gedolot*, l.c. *The sages say that, as long as she is not genuinely married to another man, she may return to him* (her first husband)*; if however she is married to another man, then she may not return.* This reading is in place of what in our reading in *D. E.* follows the words *And whence is her defilement?* This in fact constitutes the opinion of Rabbi 'El'azar ben 'Azarjah (cf. Siphrei, Ki Tetze, pisqa 270 and Midr. Tan., ed. D. Z. Hoffmann, p. 115; TbJeb. 11b and TjJeb. X,7 [10c], and other sources).

According to this opinion, the words *after she has been defiled* in Dt. 24:4 are explained as applying to the time after she is married to another man, for then sexual relationship may be assumed. If she was only betrothed to the second man, according to this explanation, it is assumed that she has not yet been defiled (a sexual relationship in this case probably not assumed). The sages (in these sources) also do not permit the divorced woman to return to her first husband after having only been betrothed to another man.

With reference to Dt. 24:1−4, one can distinguish two kinds of explanations which emphasize *'and if she goes and becomes another man's wife'* (vs. 2) and explanations which emphasize *'after she has been defiled'* (vs. 4). In the latter case the main question concerns whether she has actually had intercourse with another man, and in the former case it concerns whether or not she has entered into a valid relationship with another man. A connection between the two explanations is possible in the sense that sexual intercourse is assumed in the marriage relationship but not in the betrothal relationship. The position that a divorced woman may not return, even after betrothal, can also rest on the opinion that the betrothal of a divorced woman does not at all exclude sexual intercourse. See however Rambam, *Jad*,Hil. Gerush., XI, 12, where the author explicitly separates in this case the betrothal of a divorced from sexual relations.

From the fact that the woman may not return to her first husband, even after forced intercourse with her betrothed, it is evident that the position in *Derekh 'Eretz* that the betrothal is reason within itself to prohibit her return concurs with the standpoint of the sages in the Talmud (see also TbQid. 5a).

**5. Rabbi José ben Kippar explained [in the name of Rabbi 'El'azar ben Shamua]: 'None of the women who are prohibited to him on account of incest do inquire a 'get' from him, when he had intercourse with (any of) them, except his wife's sister, his brother's wife and a married woman, because there may come a time when their prohibition will be lifted up.'**

A relationship by the man with one of the forbidden relatives, who in technical terms must be considered as "arajot' and with whom he may have no intercourse on pain of death or 'karet', is illegal and simply a form of fornication. In this case, then, there can be no question of the realization of a legal relationship in the sense of a betrothal or marriage. After intercourse with such a forbidden relation, an act of divorce is not required to allow the woman to be able to marry another man. For certain of these forbidden relationships, however, there are situations which make up an exception to this rule: the sister of his wife after his wife has died; the wife of his brother, who has died childless, in the situation requiring a marriage with the 'levir' (see Dt. 25:5−6); the wife of another man, permitted him after divorce or the death of her husband.

In TbJeb. 94b we find the following explanations of Rab. If a man is betrothed, he can in certain situations wrongly assume that his future wife has died, and mistakenly marry her sister. If his wife indeed turns out to be alive, one could think that his betrothal was not legal because certain conditions were not fulfilled. In that case the relationship with the sister was indeed legal, and he must give his wife as well as her sister a document of divorce. If the man in this situation was married, there can be no discussion of conditions. His wife may return to him and he does not have to be divorced from her sister. A similar situation may arise if a man wrongly assumes that his betrothed brother has died end enters into a marriage with his brother's wife. When a man's woman enters into a relationship with a man who incorrectly assumes that the woman is divorced or that her husband has died (and when the woman may marry again on the strength of the testimony of **one** witness and a decision of the 'beit din'), then the woman must have herself divorced from both men. See also Rambam, *Jad*, Hil. Gerush., X,5,8,9,10. See TbJeb. 88b and 94a.

**6. And the following explanation was given by Nehunja ben Haqanah [better reading: Hanina ben 'Uri] in the name of Rabbi Natan: Anyone who belongs to the category of those who may not enter (by marriage into the assembly of the Lord; cf. Dt. 23:3—9) (when such a person has never-theless married a Jewess) the child is disqualified (to belong to Israel) and he disqualifies (the Jewish mother from marrying a priest) by having intercourse (with her). And they are: an Ammonite, a Moabite, an Egyptian [ an Edomite], a slave, a bastard, a 'natin', a Samaritan and a 'halal' (i. e. is a disqualified priest).**

Relevant Scripture passage: Dt. 23:3—9.

A child born from a relationship between an Israelite and any of the persons named in this passage is disqualified from belonging to the community of israel and from marrying into that community, and is certain disqualified from the priesthood. In *D. E.* there is the addition of the category of the 'halal' (the profaned) and the slave. It appears here that it is primarily aimed at disqualification on the matter of the priesthood. Adults and boys from the age of nine years and one day who fall under one of the listed categories disqualify the daughter of a priest from marrying a priest and from eating from the 'terumah' of her father, and they disqualify a Levite or an Israelite from marrying priest by having intercourse with them. A child from such a relationship is likewise disqualified. See TosNid. VI,1; TjJeb. VII,5 [8b]; TbJeb. 68a and 76b and 77b; see TbQid. 67a and 74b; TbNaz. 23b and TbHor. 10b: Rambam, *Jad*, Hil. 'Issur. Bi'ah, XII,17ff.; *Tur*, Eb. ha-Ez. 4, and other sources.

With regard to a *slave*, one notices that in many respects he was indeed considered a Jew if he was circumcised, but no more. Where marriage relationships were concerned, he counted as a Jew only after his emancipation. See S. Safrai, in: *The Jewish People in the first Century*, ed. S. Safrai a. o., II, p. 752: 'Despite the fact that slaves were for many purposes considered as Jews, in marital matters they were considered to be gentiles until they had been granted their freedom. Therefore, members of those families within which servants or maids had been assimilated but not freed, were considered to be impure lineage and thus disqualified from marriage, particularly within priestly families.' Cf. also TosQid. V,2; Siphra, 'Emor, VIII and TbKet. 14b. A. Büchler, 'Familienreinheit und Familienmakel in Jerusalem vor dem Jahre 70', in: *Festschrift Adolph Schwartz zum 70 Geburtstag*, ed. S. Krauss, Berlin 1917, pp. 133–162 (English translation in A. Büchler, *Studies in Jewish History*, Oxford 1956, pp. 64–98. See also *Shul. Ar.*, Eb. ha-Ez. 44,8.

A *mamzer* (*bastard*) is defined in the tradition as a child born of a relationship which is punishable by 'karet' or death. See e.g. TbQid. 74b and MJeb IV,3.

In connection with a *natin*, see I Chron. 9:2; Ezr. 2:43 and 8:20; Neh. 3:26. They are considered as descendants of the Gibeonites, whom Joshua made servants of the Temple (Jos. 9:27; in connection with their position see further in MQid. I,4ff. Cf. TbJeb. 78b and see *Encyclopedia Miqra'it*, sub 'netinim'.

A *halal* (*disqualified priest*), one who has been profaned, is a child born of a relationship between a priest and a woman forbidden to him; par example a divorced woman, an adulterous woman (i.e. a harlot, there are different opinions about this term), a profaned (disqualified) woman (i.e. a woman who has had a relationship with a member of one of the categories listed in Dt. 23:3–9 and listed here in *D. E.*), a proselyte woman (according to one opinion a woman who became proselyte after the age of three years), a freed bond maid, and a woman who has been subjected to lascivious intercourse. See MJeb. VI,5; TbJeb. 60b/61a and TbQid. 78a. Also the child of a male proselyte was considered to be a 'halal'. A 'halal' is also a child born of a marriage between a high priest and a woman who was not a virgin at the time of marriage, such as a widow, a divorced woman or a woman who has been raped (cf. Lev. 21:7,14).

**7. The daughter of a 'halal' is fit (to marry a priest) although he (i.e. her father) belongs to those who may not enter (into the community of Israel). [better reading: intercourse (i.e. marriage) with a 'halal' is (nevertheless) legal, although he belongs to those who may not enter (the community of Israel).**

The remark here requires further clarification. This rule states that the daughter of a 'halal' is suitable for marriage with a priest, although the 'halal' himself belongs to that category of men who may not have relations with the daughter of a priest, a Levite or an Israelitish woman without disqualifying them for priests. In MQid. VI,6 (cf. TbQid. 77a), it is stated to the contrary that the daughter of a 'halal' is always excluded from marrying a priest. The commentator from *Nahalat Ja'aqob*, Jacob Naumburg, points out in his commentary on D. E. R. I, that the opinion of Rabbi Dostai ben Jehudah is given here, asserting that the sons of Israel are a purification for disqualified women, and that the daughters of Israel are a purification for the disqualified sons of priests. This means that a marriage between someone who is disqualified and someone who is not removes the disqualification for the children born of that marriage. See TbQid. 64a and 74b and 77a. According to this position a daughter born of the marriage between a profaned son of a priest and an Israelish woman who has not been disqualified, is qualified, just as is a son born of such a relationship. This explanation is not very probable in relation to the text of *D. E. R.*. See the reading in Ms. Kaufmann; cf. the reading in *Halakhot Gedolot*, ed. I. Hildesheimer, II, p. 31. A marriage with a 'halal' is a breach of a commandment, but it is still legal (as opposed to a marriage with a non-Jew, which is not at all valid). Noticing this fact the last reading has 'bi'at halal' instead of 'bat halal': *A relationship with a 'halal' is legal, although he himself belongs to them who may not enter* (the community of Israel). We prefer the reading such as in *Halakhot Gedolot*, and read *bi'at halal* and consider this tradition as a remark added in clarification of the special position of the 'halal' among the listed categories, considering that a marriage (sexual relationship) with a 'halal' is legal (although a marriage with someone falling into one of the categories listed in Dt. 23:3−9 is not). See also TbJeb. 37a. Some manuscripts mention the statement in the name of Rabbi Hanina ben 'Uri speaking in the name of Rabbi Natan.

**8. If a man has had intercourse with any of the women who are prohibited to him on account of incest, he is still permitted to (marry) her (near) relations.**

**One who has had intercourse with a married woman is permitted (to marry) her daughter.**

See the other sequence in Ms. Kaufmann [a 50] and cf. *Halakhot Gedolot*, ed. I. Hildesheimer, p. 31 (see there the critical apparatus) with the following opening: 'Rabbi José ben Kippar presented this midrash in the presence of the sages in the name of Rabbi 'El'azar ben Shamua ...' Midr. ha-Gad. about Lev. 20:14, ed. A. Steinsalz, 1976, p. 567 reads: 'Rabbi Hananjah bar 'Idi presented this midrash in the presence of the sages in the name of Rabbi Natan.' See TbJeb. 97a and cf. TjJeb. IX,8 [10c]; TbJeb. 94a and 94b (MJeb. X,3).

A number of relationships which are prohibited in the Torah are illegal and do not at all formalize a legal relationship by which some relations of the partner (in this case the woman) are forbidden for the other. These include relationships which are punishable by death or 'karet' or relationships with non-Jewish (non Israelitish) woman. See in this connection *Shul. Ar.*, Eb. ha-Ez. 15.

As example there is mentioned here in *D. E.*, the married woman with whom no one but her husband, on pain of death, may have intercourse. Cf. Lev. 18:16,20; Num. 5:13; Dt. 22:23−27. If another man has intercourse with her anyway (unintentionally) he may then marry one of her relatives afterwards, even if it is her daughter. If a man receives incorrect news that his wife is dead and meanwhile marries her sister, after which his wife turns out to be alive, he may return to his wife and the relatives of her sister will still be permitted to him. He can for example marry the daughter of the sister after divorce or death of his wife. Cf. Rambam, *Jad*, Hil. Gerush., X; *Shul. Ar.*, Eb. ha-Ez. 15,27; and other sources.

**9. This is the question which putted Rabbi José ben Taddai, a man of Tiberias, to Rabban Gamli'el: 'If I, being permitted to (have intercourse with) my wife, am prohibited to (marry) her daughter, should it not be a logical reasoning that I am (the more so) forbidden (to marry) the daughter of a married woman, with whom I may not have intercourse?' He said to him: 'Go and provide me (with a wife) for the High-priest concerning whom it is written: "A virgin of his own people shall he take to wife" (Lev. 21:14). Then I will provide you (with wives) for the whole of Israel.' Another interpretation (in refutation of the reasoning of Rabbi José ben Taddai): We do not use a logical reasoning (a fortiori) to abrogate a law of the Torah. Rabban Gamli'el then excommunicated him.**

Rabbi José ben Taddai of Tiberias, puts a question to Rabban Gamli'el which can only be intended ironically. See R. Halperin,'*Atlas 'Etz Hajjim*, IV, Tel-Aviv 1980, p. 226: Rabbi José ben Taddai a Tanna of the fourth generation at the time of Rabban Gamli'el the second.

The reasoning behind the question of Rabbi José is as follows: If I may not have a relationship with the daughter of someone (i.e. my legal spouse) with whom I may have a legal relationship and with whom I may have intercourse, how much more forbidden must it be for me to enter into a relationship with the daughter of someone with whom I may not have a legal relationship and with whom I may not have intercourse, i.e. the daughter of a married woman. Thus, to this reasoning, it would seem that a man may only marry the daughter of a widow or a divorced woman.

Rabban Gamli'el demonstrates the senselessness of this reasoning through his attempt to show that, according to this assertion, the high priest of Israel would not be able to marry at all, although the Torah commands him to do so! In any case the high priest absolutely may not marry a widow or divorced woman, and accordingly to the same a fortiori reasoning, he should also certainly not be allowed to marry the daughter of such women. According to this reasoning, daughters of married women also do not come into consideration, meaning that the high priest must leave unfulfilled the instruction in the Torah that he marry a virgin from among his people. Making a rule that would prohibit a high priest from marrying would mean a negation of the authority of the Torah!! The other side of Rabban Gamli'el's refutation is that not all nubile women are daughters of deceased or divorced mothers. If one enforced the stated rule, there would remain too few nubile women, and many men in Israel would not be able to fulfil the commandment given to them in the Torah to beget offspring. Therefore Rabban Gamli'el states ironically: if you accomplish the impossible by giving a woman to the high priest, then I too shall accomplish the impossible and provide all of Israel with marriageable women.

One may make no logical deduction on the basis of a hermeneutic principle with the aim of weakening the Torah. This explains why the student of Rabban Gamli'el is expelled according to an addition in most of the manuscripts. It is a very serious matter to want to destroy the Torah with halakhic reasoning! See also the commentary in *Nahalat Ja'aqob* on this passage.

In connection to the name Taddai, see (among others) J. Klausner, *Jesus von Nazareth*, Seine Zeit, sein Leben, seine Lehre, erw. Auflage Jerusalem 1952, p. 388. See Midr. ha-Gad. on Lev. 20:14, ed. A. Steinsalz, p. 576, where it reads 'Rabbi Joseph ben Haddai' and 'and he said to him one is not using halakhic conclusions in order to weaken even one word of the Torah'. See also Jalq., 'Emor, r. 731, where it reads 'Rabbi José' and 'Rabbi Shim'on ben Gamli'el'. The concluding remark about the excommunication is missing there as in Jalq. Re'ub., 'Emor, p. 74 (where it reads 'Rabbi José ben Hazzai'); see further M. Higger, *Massekhtot Derekh 'Eretz*, pp. 267–268. See especially *Halakhot Gedolot*, ed. I. Hildesheimer, *Hil 'Arajot*, p. 31.

**10. If a man has had intercourse with any of the women who are prohibited to him on account of incest, he (thereby) does not disqualify them (by intercourse) concerning (her rights in relation to the) priesthood.**

In this passage it is explicitly stated that a woman who had an incestuous relation with a man (a relation punishable by 'karet' or death) is not disqualified to marry a priest. In the light of other traditions, this passage is very remarkable! A child born of such an incestuous relationship is considered a 'mamzer'. Cf. TbQid. 74b and MJeb. IV,3. Another rule in the tradition states that if a child is disqualified through a relationship of the mother, the mother herself will be disqualified by a fortiori reasoning. The mother has committed a transgression and the child has committed no transgression! See TjJeb. VII,5 [8a]; TbJeb. 56b and 69a; TbQid. 77a; Rashi on TbJeb. 15b and TbNid. 69b.

Another well-represented position in the tradition is that a woman who has an extra-marital sexual relationship (and then by a fortiori reasoning in the instance of a relationship sharply forbidden in the Torah) must be regarded as a 'zonah' (harlot) whom a priest may not marry See Lev. 21 and cf. MJeb. VI,2: TjJeb. VI,5 [7c] and VII,5 [8b]; TbJeb. 59b and 61b and 76a; TbSanh. 51a and TbTem. 30a and other sources. Cf. Rambam, *Jad*, Hil. 'Issur.Bi'ah, XVIII,1. A general rule formulated in the Mishnah is, that a woman who has had an incestuous relationship (or even just a relationship forbidden in the Torah) is forbidden for members of the priesthood (see MJeb. VI,2 and cf. Rashi and Tosaphists on TbJeb. 61a.

In order to avoid these difficulties, the Gaon of Vilna suggested in his notes on *D. E. R.*, that the word **not** be omitted from the text, so that the woman would indeed be disqualified, according to the same statement. Unfortunately, this plausible assumption is not confirmed in the manuscripts, although it is confirmed in the reading of *Halakhot Gedolot*, ed. I. Hildesheimer, l.c. For potential solution of listed difficulties concerning the text, M. Higger (*Massekhtot Derekh 'Eretz*, pp. 267−268) points to TbJeb. 61b, which contains the opinion of Rabbi 'Aqiba that 'zonah' in Lev. 21 is an unmarried public woman, in contradiction to the more common opinion that this word refers to a woman who has had a relationship that is forbidden in the Torah. According to the authority here in *D. E.*, the consequence of Rabbi 'Aqiba's opinion should be that a woman who is not 'muphqeret' (a public harlot) should – in the strictest sense – be allowed to marry a priest. Such an explanation of Rabbi 'Aqiba's words, however, is improbable. Another possibility assumed by M. Higger would be that there is a difference between Babylonian traditions and traditions from 'Eretz Jisra'el. According to the tradition of 'Eretz Jisra'el, the woman should indeed be disqualified after an incestuous relationship, but not so according to a Babylonian tradition. In connection with the tradition of 'Eretz Jisra'el M. Higger cites the *Riph* and *Rosh* on TbJeb. 22a; TjJeb. II,8 [4a] and VII [8b]; he also cites B. M. Lewin, *Ginzei Qedem*, II, p. 28; *Me'iri* on TbJeb. 69a and 69b.

In MJeb. VI,2 and the gemara in TbJeb. 53b and 61b, however,there is no evidence of contradiction to the general opinion that a woman who has had an incestuous relationship is no longer suitable to marry a priest. A priest may not marry a woman who is like a 'zonah'. According to the Rabbis, by a 'zonah' is meant: a proselyte, a freed bondwoman (a non-Jewish female slave that is set free), or a woman who has had a relationship which falls under the category 'be'ilat zenut' (par example a Jewish woman freed from captivity by gentiles). There are different views about the explanation of the term 'be'ilat zenut'. According to one opinion, there is mention of harlotry if a negative command in the Torah has been broken through the sexual relationship or if it hinders the fulfilment of a positive command (see MJeb. VI,5; TbJeb. 61b and Rashi on TbJeb. 53b and TbQid. 77a; see TbGit. 81a and TbSanh. 51b and TbSanh. 76b; Jalq., Pinhas, r. 774; Rambam, *Jad*, Hil. 'Issur. Bi'ah, XVIII,1; *Tur*, Eb. ha-Ez., 33; and other sources.).

According to another opinion, every extra-marital relationship is already to be considered meretricious and a form of harlotry (cf. TbJeb. 59b and 61b and 76a; TbSanh. 51a and TbTem. 29b and 30a; TjJeb. VI,5 [7c] and TjJeb. VII,5 [8b])". Others define harlotry as a relationship which is incestuous in nature and punishable by 'karet' or the death penalty (see e.g. *Hassagot Rabad* on Rambam, *Jad*, Hil. 'Issur. Bi'ah, l.c. and Tosaphot Jom Tob on MJeb. VI,5;

see also the Tosaphot on TbJeb. 61a and cf. *Tur*, Eb. ha-Ez. 6 and 26 and *Bajt Hadash* and *Beit Joseph* on that passage).

The general opinion, however, shared by all is that a woman who had an incestuous relationship is disqualified in all instances for members of the priesthood. See also especially *Riph* on TbJeb. 21b and *Rosh* on TbJeb. 21a. Discussion concerns only women who have to do with lesser transgressions. The only solution here is to accept the reading suggested by the Gaon and given in *Halakhot Gedolot*, in which the negation particle **lo** (*not*) is missing, and to assume that the woman is indeed to be disqualified in this case. See finally the construction of L. Ginzberg mentioned by M. Higger (*Massekhtot Derekh 'Eretz*, p. 269): 'not only that the child is a 'mamzer', but such a person disqualifies them as far as (relationship with) members of the priesthood are concerned.'

**11. (If a man has had intercourse with) a menstruant, although he deserves for this intercourse (the penalty of) 'karet', the child is qualified [to stand and ] to bring sacrifices upon the altar.**

If an existing relationship is lawful and no transgression has been committed in initiating the relationship, neither the mother nor the child is disqualified in connection with the priesthood. How strongly sexual intercourse with a menstruating also is condemned neither the mother nor the child is disqualified by it. In connection with this see Lev. 21:14−15, for in the Torah is says; 'he shall not marry' and 'he shall nor profane'. 'Marry' refers to betrothal or marriage, and 'profane' refers to the transgression committed in entering into the relationship. If there is no mention of a legal betrothal or marriage in the case of sexual intercourse with a menstruating woman, then the child from that relationship is qualified, and accordingly the mother is not disqualified. See Siphra, 'Emor. per. II,5 and compare TbJeb. 49b and 60a and TbQid. 68a; Rambam, *Jad*, Hil. 'Issur. Bi'ah, XVIII, 1 and 5; *Shul. Ar.*, Eb. ha-Ez. 44,7. An Israelite woman or Levite woman that is the daughter of a woman who has had intercourse during menstruation may marry a priest. The son of a priest, who has had intercourse with a menstruating woman, may bring offerings to the altar.

**12. A woman who has had intercourse with that which is not a human being, although she deserves for this (the penalty of) 'karet', she is not disqualified from (her rights concerning) priesthood.**

A Woman who has had intercourse with 'someone who' is not a man, i. e. an animal, is not disqualified to marry a priest. If she herself is the daughter of a priest, she may still eat from the 'terumah' of her father. This still applies even though she may put to death if the sexual act was intentional. See Lev. 20:16 and cf. TbJeb. 59b. Even if she has been warned previously and there are witnesses to the incident, she is still not disqualified. She definitely is not regarded as a 'zonah' as result of the intercourse with an animal. There is no question of 'be'ilat zenut' (an act of harlotry) because only when she has had intercourse with a human being can there be discussion of 'be'ilah' (intercourse). According to one opinion, she should even still be able to marry a high priest (provided she was a virgin beforehand) , because she is not considered to have had intercourse. See TjKet. I,3 [25b]; TbJeb. 59b; Rambam, *Jad*, Hil. 'Issur. Bi'ah, XVIII,1.

**13.  Rabbi José said: 'It once happened to a girl [at Haitali] that, while the girl was clearing the house, an ape came and had intercourse with her from the rear. The case came before the sages, they did not disqualify her from (her rights concerning) priesthood.'**

Also a name of the locus of the incident was added in the parallel in TbJeb. 59b and in manuscripts. Cf. TosNid. I,9. See the transcription by Jastrow, *Dictionary*, under the title Hitlu and Hitlut. See S. Klein, *Beiträge zur Geographie und Geschichte Galileas*, Leipzig 1909, p. 47. See also M. Ginsberg, in: *The Minor Tractates of the Talmud*, ed. A. Cohen, II, London 1965, p. 533, note 47: Haitali, Babylonian form of Aitalu, the modern Aiterun and N. W. of Qadesh. See the Mss. on D. E. R. I. See R. Rabbinovicz, *Seph. Diqduqei Sopherim*, repr. New York 1960, on TbJeb. 59a; see notes in *Halakhot Gedolot*, ed. I. Hildesheimer, p. 32 and see the variants listed there. According to the reading in TbJeb. l.c. Rab Dimi is the authority and a dog living in the wild had sexual intercourse with a girl. After this incident Rabbi still considered the girl suitable for marrying a priest,while Rab Samuel remarked that she was even suitable for marrying a high priest. Cf. also TbTem. 30b; Rambam, *Jad*, Hil. 'Issur. Bi'ah, XVIII, 1−5. The reading in the babylonian Talmud contains more details and is probably more authentic.

**14.  The following are forbidden relations in the second degree (i. e. by rabbinic decision): his father's mother, his mother's mother [the wife of his mother's father] the wife of his father's father [some Mss add: the wife of his mother's father, the wife of his son's son, the wife of his daughter's son and the wife of his father's maternal brother] and the wife of his mother's paternal brother. Bar Kappara adds: the mother of his father's father and the mother of his mother's father.**

See Lev. 18 in which are listed relationships forbidden with among others the following: the mother, the father's wife, the father's sister, the mother's sister, the wife of the father's brother, the son's wife, the son's daughter, and the daughter's daughter. All of these relationships explicitly forbidden in the Torah are considered as "arajot", forbidden relationships of the first degree. 'Shenijot', forbidden relations of the second degree, are forbidden on the grounds of oral tradition and are based on the decisions of the sages. They are not explicitly mentioned in the Torah, but are derived from the above mentioned "arajot'. See TbJeb. 21a; TjJeb. II,4 [3c]; enumerations in Rambam, *Jad*, Hil. 'Issur. Bi'ah, I,6; *Shul. Ar.* Eb. ha-Ez. 15,2.4.6.7.8.9; *Semag*, Lowin 110; cf. also *Me'iri* on TbJeb. 21a.

According to the opinion of Raba, a hint is given in the Torah itself on relationships in the second degree. In Lev. 18:29 it states "For whoever do any of these abominations, the persons that do them shall be cut off from among their people." "These abominations" refers to the major transgressions, from which one may conclude that there are also less serious transgressions. According to Raba, these are the forbidden relationships of the second degree; see TbJeb. 21a. In the *She'iltot* ('Aharei Mot 97) and in TjJeb. II,4 [3c] we find the same statement and there the authority is Rab Huna; cf. Midr. ha-Gad. on Lev. 18,30.

The 'shenijot' are relationships forbidden by the sages. Upon transgression, a betrothal or marriage is still legal and a child born from such a relationship is not a 'mamzer'. It is certainly urged that such a relationship be broken up and that the woman be given a document of divorce. The woman receives in that case no 'ketubah'. See TosJeb. II,4; Pes. Zut., 'Aharei Mot, ed. S. Buber, 52a; B. M. Lewin, *'Otzar ha-Ge'onim*, Teshubot on TbJeb. 21a, p. 25; and *Ginzei Qedem*, II, pp. 27–28; *Riph* on TbJeb. 21a; Rashi on TbJeb. 21a; *Shul. Ar.*, Eb. ha-Ez. 15,1.

*Bar Kappara adds...* See the remarks by *Me'iri* on TbJeb. 21a. The two relationships added by Bar Kappara are not found in all traditions and according to Me'iri they are not found in Sephardic sources! The addition of Bar Kappara is missing in the Talmud Babli, though Rambam does name the mentioned categories.

**15. The wife of one's father's brother is prohibited to him, but his daughter (i. e. a man's cousin) is permitted to him. His father's brother is permitted to his wife (i. e. the nephew's wife) and to his daughter.**

The wife of the father's brother is forbidden for a man, according to the Torah. See Lev. 18:14. A distinction is made between the wife of the brother of the father from the same father, and the wife of the brother of the father from the same mother, but different fathers. The first relationship is mentioned in Lev. 19:14 and is therefore a forbidden relationship in the first degree. The second is a relationship derived by the sages and is therefore a forbidden relationship in the second degree. See TbJeb. 21b; Rambam, *Jad*, Hil. 'Ishut, I,6; *Shul. Ar.*, Eb ha-Ez. 15,17; cf. *Halakhot Gedolot*, ed. I. Hildesheimer, (Hil. 'Arajot), p. 32.

A marriage between a man and his niece (the daughter of his father's brother) is permitted, but a marriage with his aunt (the wife of his father's brother) is forbidden. An uncle (the father's brother) may marry the wife and daughter of his nephew (the son of his brother).

**16. The wife of his mother's brother is prohibited (to a man) but his daughter (i. e. a man's cousin) is permitted to him.**

**His mother's brother is permitted to his (i. e. the nephew's) wife and to his daughter.**

As a relationship with the wife of the father's brother (from the same father) is explicitly forbidden in the Torah, the rabbis by analogy have made forbidden a relationship with the wife of the mother's brother. This last prohibition was thus derived by the rabbis from a prohibition in the Torah, and a derived prohibition involves merely a forbidden relationship of the second degree. The daughter of the mother's brother is, however, permitted for a man. The mother's brother may marry the wife and daughter of his nephew (i. e. the son of his sister).

**17. The wife of one's father-in-law (when she is not his wife's mother) or the wife of his son-in-law (when she is not his own daughter) are permitted to him; but the sages say: 'The wife of his father-in-law is prohibited to him for the sake of false appearance, but her daughter (i. e. the daughter of the wife of his father-in-law, when she is not his wife's sister) is permitted to him.'**

The wife of one's father-in-law is permitted. In this case it is of course meant that the wife of his father-in-law is not the mother of his own wife, for she is forbidden for him according to a prohibition in the Torah, see Lev. 18:17. Concerning the wife of his son-in-law it is of course meant that she is not his own daughter, for a man's daughter is forbidden for him, according to the Torah, see Lev. 18:17. According to the sages in *D. E. R.* and according to a tradition in the Talmud Jerushalmi the wife of a man's father-in-law is forbidden to him, see TjJeb. II [3d] and Pes. Zut., 'Aharei Mot, ed. S. Buber, 52a, and Rabbenu Tam, *Seph. ha-Jashar*, sim. 101 (ed. Rosenthal, 1898, p. 210), and *Tur, Eb. ha-Ez.* 15, and *Meʾiri* on TbJeb. 21a. This is to avoid false appearance, lest people wrongly assume that she is also the mother of his wife. The Babylonian tradition in TbJeb. 21a and 21b, however, does permit a man relationship with the wife of his father-in-law. Cf. TosJeb. III,1; *Sheʾiltot*, 'Aharei Mot, 97; and B. M. Lewin, *'Otzar ha-Geʾonim*, Teshubot on TbJeb. 21a, p. 25.

In *Halakhot Gedolot*, ed. I. Hildesheimer, (Hil. ʿArajot), p. 32, one finds both readings and there is directed to a tradition as in TjJeb. l.c. that the sages forbid these relationships (here with the wife of the father-in-law as well with the wife of the son-in-law) because of false suspicion. Cf. also *Seph. ha-Jashar*, l.c. and other sources.

From the commentary on TbJeb 21a, it becomes clear that the argument avoiding false suspicion proved valid in respect to the wife of the father-in-law, because this woman in general was not so well known in the man's circles and could easily be mistaken for the mother of his wife. In reference to TbJeb.21a see e.g. *Mordekhai*; *Rosh; Hiddushei Ramban*; *Hiddushei Rashba*; *Hiddushei Ritba*.

Should such a marriage take place, it need not to be dissolved. Cf. *Tzemah Tzedeq* 40; see however Rabbenu Tam with the contradictory opinion in *Seph. ha-Jashar*, ed. Rosenthal, p. 210. The commentaries in reference to TbJeb. 21a do point to the tradition from the Talmud Jerushalmi but remain explicitly in keeping with the Babylonian tradition. Cf. e.g. *Riph*, *Mordekhai*, *Me'iri*, *Rosh*, and *Qorban Netan'el* on TbJeb. 21a; Rambam, *Jad*, Hil. 'Ishut, I,6; *Hiddushei Ramban*; *Hiddushei Ritba*; *She'iltot we-Teshubot Radbaz*, and other sources. on TbJeb. 21a. See also *Shul. Ar.*, Eb. ha-Ez. 15,24. Additionally see B. M. Lewin, *'Otzar ha-Ge'onim*, Teshubot on TbPes., p. 16 (39), note 8, and on TbJeb, p. 25 (57), note 17.

From the fact that a relationship with the wife of the son-in-law is mentioned neither by Rambam or in the *Shul. Ar*, it would appear that this relationship was permitted in accordance with the Babylonian tradition. The wife of the son-in-law is also not mentioned in TjJeb. l.c., see B. M. Lewin, *'Otzar ha-Ge'onim*, TbJeb., p. 25 [57], note 18. The wife of the son-in-law is mentioned, however, by a number of Rishonim (see *Mordekhai; Me'iri*; Rabbenu Tam (*Seph. ha-Jashar*); *Hiddushei Rashba; Hiddushei Ritba*; and other sources.

A man is permitted to the daughter of the wife of his father-in-law. This applies after the death of his own wife, because the daughter concerned is the sister of his wife. Cf. the gemara in TbJeb. 21a and cf. *She'iltot*, 'Aharei Mot, 97; *Me'iri* on TbJeb. 21a.

## 18. The daughter of one's stepson is prohibited to him, but the stepson's wife is permitted to him. His stepson is permitted to his (i. e. the stepfather's) wife and to his daughter.

The daughter of a man's stepson is forbidden to him on the basis of of the Torah. Cf. Lev. 18:17: "You shall not uncover the nakedness of a woman and her daughter, and you shall not marry *the daughter of her son* and the daughter of her daughter." The forbidden relationship of the first degree is mentioned in this context as an introduction to what here immediately follows. A man is permitted the wife of his stepson and a stepson may marry the wife of his stepfather (this means, of course, that the wife of his stepfather is not his own mother).

A man may also marry the daughter of his stepfather, provided that she has a different mother and thus is not his half-sister. See TosJeb. III,1 and see TjJeb. II [3d]; TbJeb. 21a-b; cf. *She'iltot*, 'Aharei Mot, 97. See B.M. Lewin, *'Otzar ha-Ge'onim*, Teshubot on TbJeb. 21a and on TbPes. 16a; *Halakhot Gedolot*, ed. I. Hildesheimer, II, p. 32.; *Tur*, Eb. ha-Ez. 15; *Shul. Ar.* 15,21. In Pes. Zut., 'Aharei Mot, ed. S. Buber, 52a, however, we find another tradition. According to this tradition the wife of a man's stepson is forbidden to him to avoid false suspicion ('mar'it 'ajn'). Additionally, according to this version based on the opinion of the sages a stepson may have no relationship with the daughter of his stepfather if she has grown up with him and his brothers. This is again to avoid false appearances as one could incorrectly think that the stepsister is his real sister. See also *Hiddushei Ramban* on TbJeb. 21a, according to which the Talmud Jerushalmi as well as *Halakhot Gedolot*, would forbid a man the wife of his stepson to avoid false appearances. The version of H*alahkot Gedolot* known to us, however, report differently.

### 19. A man may marry the wife of his brother's son and the wife of his sister's son.

This is the same relationship as mentioned in D.E.R. I,15, according to which tradition the brother of the father may marry the wife of the nephew. A man is also permitted to marry the wife of his sister's son. This is the same relationship as mentioned in D.E.R. I,16, according to which the mother's brother may marry the wife of the nephew.

### 20. When a man wants to remarry his divorced wife after her marriage (with a second husband who died or divorced her) she is prohibited to the (first) husband and she must be released by 'halitzah' (from the levir, when her first husband has died childless), but (in that case) her associate (i.e. the second wife of the first husband) is permitted to the levir.

A man who takes back his former wife may not have intercourse with her after she has been married to another man who has since died or also given her a document of divorce. This means, that he may not take her back and that she must be freed from the obligation to the levir through the ritual of 'halitzah' if her first husband has died childless. If her former husband who wishes to take her back may not have intercourse with her, then neither may his brother in the case of levirate marriage. No one may be the levir for a woman who was forbidden for his brother who died without issue. N.B. in the text the use of the words *after she has been married to another man*, and see the commentary on D.E.R. I,4. It is obvious that the opinion (of Rabbi 'El'azar ben 'Azarjah) is assumed, that she may not return after a marriage only (but may possibly return after a betrothal). The reading here in *D.E.* concurs with the version in TbJeb.

12a; according to the tradition in TjJeb. II [10a] a woman in this situation, however, should be permitted to the levir. See also Ms. Kaufmann A 50 on D. E. R. See Mss. and *Riph* on TbJeb. 12a. The *Riph* names a tradition in the name of the Talmud Jerushalmi that does concur with the Babylonian tradition and with D. E. Cf. finally Rambam. *Jad*, Hil. Jibbum, VI,13. The rival woman of the woman in question may enter into levirate marriage, for her relationship with the deceased brother was still legal.

## 21. And when a man has had sexual intercourse with the sister of his sister-in-law who is released from him by 'halitzah', he may not live with her as husband and (if he dies childless) she must be released by 'halitzah' from the levir.

Just as the sister of the wife remains forbidden for a man as long as his wife is still living – even after being divorced from his wife – the sister of the sister -in-law, who has been freed of her obligations to the man by the ritual of 'halitzah', remains by analogy forbidden for the man as long as the sister-in-law by whom 'halitzah' has been performed is still alive. Cf. TbJeb. 44a and the Mishnah in TbJeb. 44b.

The manuscripts and parallels give different readings. According to the reading in TjJeb. IX,2 [10a] no man may marry the sister of the woman who has been freed of her obligations to him through 'halitzah'. If he does so anyway and dies childless, then she may enter into a levirate marriage. This is in accordance with a rule formulated in the context (ibid. h. 5) that if a woman is forbidden for her husband on the basis of a rule formulated by the sages (and not explicitly on the basis of the Torah) and if she is not forbidden for the levir, she may enter into marriage relationship with this levir if her husband has died childless. Cf. likewise the Mishnah in TbJeb. 84a. This tradition in the Talmud Jerushalmi is in contradiction with the reading in the basic manuscript of D. E. See (however) Ms. Kaufmann A 50, with a reading that partially concurs with the Jerushalmi tradition. Likewise in contradiction to the reading in *Halakhot Gedolot*, ed. I. Hildesheimer, (Hil. 'arajot), p. 33.

See the Manuscript variants, especially Ms. Kaufmann A 50, that gives in agreement with the tradition in TjJeb. and *Halakhot Gedolot* the addition that the rival wife of the sister-in-law in question may enter into a levirate marriage. According to the tradition in D. E. the sister of a woman who has been released by 'halitzah' stays forbidden for the levir. The reading in D. E. is problematic in the light of the general rule that a woman who is 'shenijah' (forbidden in the second degree) in relation to her husband but is not forbidden in relation to her levir, is forbidden for her husband but not for her levir (after the death of her husband). See TjJeb. l.c. and cf. TbJeb. l.c.; cf. Rambam, *Jad*, Hil. Jibbum, VI,13; Rambam mentions as exception the case mentioned in which a woman who is divorced marries another man and then returns to her first husband after the death of her second husband or after divorce. See *Tur*, Eb. ha-Ez. 174.

## 22.  The wife of a physically fit man who has a brother, who is crushed in his private parts, is permitted to the husband, but she is prohibited to (marry) the levir (when her husband dies childless).

By *crushed in his private parts ('petzua dakkah')* is meant a person whose testicles are crushed in an accident. Cf. e.g. TbJeb. 75b and Rambam, *Jad*, Hil. 'Issur Bi'ah, XVI,1 and 9. A relationship with the person mentioned falls under these relationships forbidden in the Torah, and sexual intercourse and marriage with such a person constitute a breach of a negative command. If a healthy brother of a man whose genitals has been crushed dies childless his wife may not enter into a levirate marriage with his brother(the 'petzua dakkah'), for such a marriage is permitted only when there is the intention to beget offspring for the brother who has died without issue. In this case, the levir belong to the category placed outside of the community of Israel. See Dt. 23:2 and TjJeb. IX [10a]; TosJeb. IX,2; TbJeb. 79b; Rambam, *Jad*, Hil. Jibbum, VI,4. Although a marriage between a 'jebamah' and a 'petzua dakkah' is prohibited, 'halitzah' has to be performed nonetheless, for marriage concluded despite the prohibition would still be valid. Cf. e.g. MJeb. II,3−4, and other sources.

## 23.  The associate of a wife suspected of adultery is permitted to (live with) the husband, but she is prohibited to (marry) the levir (when her husband dies childless).

The rival wife of a 'sotah' (a woman suspected of adultery) still has an undamaged relationship with her husband, as she has committed no transgression. She is thus still permitted for her husband. If her husband dies childless, however, as the rival wife of a 'sotah' she may not enter into a levirate marriage. Cf. TbJeb. 11a. The reason for this is given in TbJeb. 11a by Rab. On the basis of Num. 5:13 uncleanness is attributed to the 'sotah'. This means that her case is comparable to a case of incest and on this account the rival wife may not conclude a levirate marriage. See further discussion in which a distinction is made between a biblically forbidden 'sotah' and a 'sotah' forbidden on the basis of the words of the sages (i.e. a woman who married a second husband under honest misapprehension). In the last case the rival wife may of course enter into a levirate marriage. See Rambam, *Jad*, Hil. Jibbum, VI,19, where the author elaborates conclusions on the basis of discussions conducted in the Babylonian Talmud. The rival wife of a wanton 'sotah' (against whom there are witnesses) may not enter into a levirate marriage. But the rival wife of a 'sotah' whose guilt by her own intentions has not yet been established by the time of her husband's death, may conclude a levirate marriage. See *Maggid Mishneh* on Rambam,

*Jad*, l.c. and see references of *Rabad* in connection with TbJeb. 11a; cf. also *Shul. Ar.*, Eb. ha-Ez. 173,11.

To judge from discussions mentioned, this part of D. E. would be concerned only with a 'sotah' who commits adultery intentionally and in the presence of witnesses, after which her husband dies childless.

**24. And when a man has had intercourse with the sister of his brother's divorced wife [or with the sister of his brother's halitzah] she may live with him, but (when he dies childless) she is prohibited to the levir (i. e. to the brother who once married her sister).**

If a man has himself divorced from a woman, her relations remain forbidden to him, including her sister as long as his divorced wife remains alive. His brother, however, may marry the sister of his former wife. Should the brother who is married to the sister of the divorced wife die (childless) then the brother for whom she is still the sister of his former wife who is still alive, may not conclude a levirate marriage with her. Cf MJeb. in TbJeb. 40a. Relatives of the 'halutzah' are permitted for the remaining brothers who are exempt through the 'holetz'. There are additions in the Mss. which mention the sister of the 'halutzah' along with the sister of the divorced wife.

**25. [When a woman married to one who is crushed in his private parts and who has a brother who is physically fit, she is permitted to the levir, but she is prohibited to the (physically unfit) husband. A woman who is suspected of adultery is prohibited to the one as well as to the other (i. e. to the husband and to the levir); so a women released by 'halitzah' is prohibited to the one (who released her) as well as to the other (.i. e. to his brother, the levir)]. When a woman is married with a man who is crushed in his private parts and who has a brother who is (likewise) crushed in his private parts, she is prohibited to the one as well as to the other (i. e. to the husband as well as to the levir).**

Compare the commentary in reference to D. E. R. I,22.

**26. A female proselyte, a freed captive woman, a freed female slave, a widow of mixed family, a woman suspected of adultery (as long as her innocence is not proved), a woman released by halitzah, a divorced woman and a 'halalah' (i. e. the female issue from a priest's illegitimate relation) are disqualified from marrying a priest. When they are married to an Israelite, their daughters are fit regarding priesthood (i. e. to marry a priest).**

A priest may not marry a 'zonah' (harlot]. See Lev. 21:14. Considering that even a forced relationship with a worshipper of idols makes a woman 'zonah' (cf. e.g. Rambam. *Jad*, Hil. 'Issur. Bi'ah, XVIII,3 and cf. MJeb. VI), it is understood that a female proselyte (who became according to one tradition a proselyte after the age of three years), a freed captive woman, a freed female slave and other women who may have had intercourse with idolaters are considered as 'zonah' and forbidden for a priest.

A woman who is the widow of a man from mixed family may also not marry a priest. Although she herself may not be from a family which is disqualified with respect to the priesthood, she has been married to a man from a family which is doubtful in the sense of causing disqualification to women who marry one of their members. As a result of this relationship, the woman is possibly disqualified. Cf. TosQid. V,2; M'Ed. VIII,3; TbQid. 75a and other sources. A dubious family is one in which there are 'netinim', 'mamzerim', slaves, disqualified priests etc. Cf. MQid. VI,4; TbQid. 69b and TbKet. 14a-b. From the traditions it is evident that there have been different opinions with respect to the widow of a man from a mixed (dubious) family. See e.g. M'Ed. l.c.; TbKet. 13a-b. Rabban Gamli'el is of the opinion that such a widow is disqualified, even if one would accept witnesses for her qualification. From TbQid. 75a it would seem that this general rule was accepted. Rabban Gamli'el is speaking expressly on the basis of a decree by Rabban Johanan ben Zakkai that it is not acceptable for a court to make a statement in such a case about qualification or disqualification.

A 'sotah' (a woman suspected of adultery) may not have the chance to marry a priest if her husband dies and her innocence has not been proven or if she has not drunk from the bitter water.

A 'gerushah' (*a divorced woman*) is forbidden to a priest on basis of the Torah (see Lev. 21:7). From this the the Rabbis made conclusions for the case of a 'halutzah' ( *a woman released by 'halitzah*).

A *halahah* (a disqualified woman) is forbidden to a priest on basis of the Torah (Lev. 21:14). When, however, a disqualified women marries an Israelite, the daughters from such a relationship may marry a priest. This opinion one finds in MQid. VI (cf. TbQid. 77a). This tradition is not in accordance with the opinion of Dostai ben Jehudah in D. E. R. h.l. Dostai ben Jehudah thinks that a daughter from a marriage of a 'halal' (disqualified priest) with a qualified Israelitish woman may also marry a priest. According to the general opinion in the Mishnah, however, a child born from a 'halal' is disqualified in all cases.

**27. One who has had sexual intercourse with a (non-Jewish) maidservant is liable to the penalty for violating fourteen negative commandments and to the penalty of 'karet' (i. e. of being cut off)by the hand of Heaven: (He is guilty) because of (transgressing :) 'You shall not sow your vineyard with two kinds of seed' (Dt. 22:9), because of (transgressing) 'You shall not plough with an ox (and ass together)' (Dt. 22:10), because of (transgres-**

sing) 'You shall not wear a mingled stuff' (Dt. 22:11), because of (transgressing) 'You shall not murder' (Ex.20:13 and Dt. 5:17), because of (transgressing) 'You shall not commit adultery' (ibid), because of (transgressing) 'You shall not steal' (ibid.), [because of (transgressing) 'You shall not bear false witnesses' (ibid.)], because of (transgressing) 'You shall not covet' (Ex. 20:14 and Dt. 5:18), because of (transgressing the prohibition of having intercourse with) one's father's wife, because of (transgressing the prohibition of having intercourse with) one's brother's wife, because of (transgressing the prohibition of having intercourse with) a menstruant, because of (transgressing the prohibition of having intercourse with) a (non-Jewish) maidservant, because of (transgressing the prohibition of having intercourse with) a heathen woman, and because of (transgressing the prohibition of having intercourse with) a harlot.

One who had a relationship with a non-Jewish maidservant has violated fourteen negative commandments. Spoken is of a non-Jewish female slave, who is not emancipated and who is not a proselyte in all respects. Though maidservants normally were baptized in the 'miqwah', concerning marriage they were reckoned as non-Jewish women. See S. Safrai, as mentioned in D. E. R. I,6. Cf. TbJeb. 23a.

The prohibition to marry a non-Jewish woman in the Torah concerns in the first place the Canaanitic nations (see Dt. 7:1—2). In Neh. 10:31 the prohibitions concern non-Jewish women in general. Cf. the reasoning of Rabbi Shim'on in TbQid. 68b: "'For he shall turn away thy son' (Dt. 7:4), which includes all who may turn away.' Here every person who serves idols is implicated. Cf. also Rabbi Shim'on in TbSanh. 21a in relation to Dt. 17:17 and see *Mishneh Keseph* at Rambam, *Jad*, Hil. 'Issur. Bi'ah, XII,1.

In connection with 'you shall not sow' (Dt. 22:9) and in connection with 'you shall not plough ox and donkey together' (Dt. 22:10) and 'you shall not wear a garment of two kinds' (Dt. 22:11) it is to say, that these laws forbid mixtures and are connected with the verdict of mixed marriages.

The quotations 'you shall not kill' and 'you shall not commit adultery and 'you shall not steal' and 'you shall not covet' do not really fit into this saying about a relationship with a non-Jewish maidservant. These quotations originally belonged to a saying about adultery, as in Siphrei Zuta, Shelah, pisqa 39 (ed. H. S. Horovitz, p. 289). The tradition here in D. E. R, is a mixture of a tradition transmitted by Rab Dimi in Tb'Ab. Zar. 36b and TbSanh. 82a and a tradition like the tradition in Siphrei Zuta l.c.

*The wife of the brother* and *the wife of the father*. Possibly here in D. E. is suggested, that a non-Jewish woman will have a history, in which she was not always living in accordance with the prohibitions of incest. A relationship with her may be a relationship with a woman who has and/or has had an incestuous relationship. Cf. the reconstructions of the Gaon of Vilna, who leaves out all passages, which do not fit into the context of the relationship with the non-Jewish maidservant. The basis manuscript has to be complemented with the words 'you shall not bear false witnesses' (Dt. 5:20 and Ex. 20:16) with help of the other manuscripts.

A transgressions brings in its train other transgressions and lies in order to conceal it.

**28.  If an Israelite has profaned himself and his seed with a heathen woman, he shall have no 'awakening' (i. e. no children who will give instruction) among the sages and no 'responding' (i. e. no children who will respond) among the students. If he is a priest, he shall have no son to offer an offering to the Lord of hosts.**

A child born from a relationship of a Jew with a non-Jewish mother is not considered as a Jew and he is disqualified in relation to the priesthood. Cf. e.g. TbQid. 77a; cf. MQid. III,12 and also Rambam, *Jad*, Hil. 'Issur. Bi'ah,, XV, 3−4.

The background of this saying is found in a tradition ascribed to Rab and in relation to Mal. 2:11−12: 'The Lord will cut off the man that does this, the master and the scholar, out of the tabernacle of Jacob, and him that offers an offering unto the Lord of Hosts.' The words are explained as: if he is a scholar, he shall have no awakening (i. e. teaching) among the sages and none responding among the disciples; if a priest, he shall have no son to offer an offering unto the Lord of Hosts.

The saying contains halakhic as well as aggadic notions.

**29.  One who marries a woman befitting him, Elijah kisses him and the Holy One blessed be He loves him. But one who marries a woman not befitting him, Elijah binds him and the Holy One blessed be He lashes him [other reading: the Holy One blessed be He hates him and Elijah lashes him].**

This saying corresponds with a well known tradition from the Babylonian Talmud in the name of Rab Hamnuna (TbQid. 70a). In the tradition mentioned priests, Levites, and Israelites, are warned not to marry a woman who is not befitting to them (i. e. a woman, that will have disqualified offspring; see also the commentary on D. E. R. I,6). The transgression of the prohibition to marry a disqualified woman eventually means a threat to the integrity of the priesthood. In later traditions the expression 'she-'einah hogenet ' (*not befitting him*) is explained in a more extensive meaning, i. e. a wife that is married on the ground of unjust motives (see *She'iltot*, Wa-Era, sim. 41.). Par example one who marries a wife because of money, because of voluptuousness, because the high social position of her family etc. Such an explanation of the expression may be assumed to be present in the gemara of TbQid. 70a. See especially the commentary on D. E. Z. X,10.

**30. Woe to the one who disqualifies his seed and who blemishes his family and who marries a woman not befitting him.**

*Pogem mishpehato* (*who blemishes* **his family**). A great importance was attached to the good name of the family. Circles of the priestly caste toke care that no marriages were contracted with persons of families to which belonged persons, who might be disqualified. In case of doubt one kept distance of these families as a whole. Cf. TbJeb. 64b; TbKet. 28b; Ber. Rab. C,7 and Bam. Rab. XXIII,1.

**31. Everyone who (continually) declares (others to be) disqualified, is (himself) disqualified and he never speaks in praise of (anybody in) the world.**

See commentary in relation to D. E. Z. VIII,14.

**32a. 'Abba Hilpa would say: 'Do not be careless in making vows lest you be led to violate oaths.**
**32b. And be not the guest of an unlearned priest lest he cause you to eat from what is consecrated to Heaven.**
**32c. And do not converse much with women, because when one converses much with women it is only about unchastity.'**

32a. See the commentary on D. E. Z. I,16. Most of the parallels (so TbNed. 20a: baraita) are without a deliverer!! D. E. R. I is not in all respects dependent on other sources and it certainly contains very old traditions! Only according to A. R. N. [a], XXVI (41b) and A. R. N. [b], XXXIII (36b) the saying is transmitted by Rabbi 'Aqiba. Here in D. E. R. the author is 'Aba Hilpa (Tanna). See the remarks by A. Büchler, *Types of Jewish Palestinian Piety*, repr. London 1922, p. 66, note 2 in reference to K. Kohler: 'who sees in the title Abba a characteristic of the Essene . . .'

This saying (see also 32b and 32c) connects the contents of this chapter about forbidden relations with the rest of Derekh 'Eretz. The theme is to make a fence around the Torah and to keep distance from transgression.

See the discussion in the commentary on D. E. Z. l.c.

32b. On the basis of the arguments in the commentary on D. E. Z. l.c. we choose here for the reading *kohen 'am ha-'aretz* (*unlearned priest*) in stead of *'am ha-'aretz* (unlearned person).

32c. The sayings in 32a, 32b and 32c form (as sayings of Abba Hilpa) a unity in accordance with the tradition in TbNed. 20a and parallels. Also this saying about conversation with women belongs to the statement of Rabbi 'Aqiba in A.R.N. as mentioned above. In circles of pious men the association with women was restricted to the minimum. Any kind of association with women – and not in the least 'sihah' (lighthearted conversation about idle matters) and 'sehoq' (flirting) – may lead to serious transgressions.

See also D.E.Z. III,12!

**33. Rabbi ['Aha the son of Rabbi ('Aha of the school of Rabbi)] Joshia would say: 'Everyone who gazes at women will ultimately come to transgression.'**

On the basis of other manuscripts and parallels the basis manuscript must be corrected and it must be read: Rabbi 'Aha(i) bar Joshia. See TbNed. 20a. Rabbi Aha(i) bar Joshia was a Tanna of the fifth generation. See in connection with him R. Halperin, *'Atlas 'Etz Hajjim*, IV, pp. 137–138, sub 'Aha(i) bar Joshia.

The reading in TbNed. l.c. is Rabbi 'Aha be-Rabbi (be-Ribbi) Joshia. See H. Freedman, translation of Massekhet Nedarim, in: *The Babylonian Talmud*, ed. I. Epstein, III, p. 57, note 2: 'Berabbi or Beribbi is a contraction of Be Rab, belonging to the school of an eminent teacher.' In that case we have to translate: Rabbi 'Aha of the school of Rabbi Joshia!

**34a.  And the sages say: 'Everyone who looks upon the heel of a woman, it is decreed over him (by Heaven), that he will beget children with physical blemishes.**
**34b.  And everyone who has no shamefacedness will easily sin, for it is said: "The display of their countenance bears witness against them" (Is. 3:9); and everyone who has shamefacedness will not easily sin, for it is said: "And that fear of Him may be before your face, that you sin not" (Ex. 20:17).'**

34a. It is remarkable that in TbNed. l.c. the saying of D.E.R. I,34a is also ascribed to Rabbi 'Aha of the school of Rabbi Joshia. See TbNed. 20a and the interpretation of the saying of Rabbi 'Aha of the school of Rabbi Joshia by Rab Joseph: 'Rabbi Joseph said: "This (i.e. the heel of a woman) applies even to one's own wife when she is niddah."' In the context of this explanation in TbNed. 20a the sayings here in D.E.R. come into the domain of voluntary strengthening of general rules as was ordinary in circles of the ancient pious men. The central theme in all these sayings on the end of D.E.R. I is the concept 'sejag la-Torah' – the making of a fence around the Torah, in order to keep oneself from transgression as far as possible ('le-harhiq me-'abeirah').

34b.  See for commentary on this saying D.E.Z. VIII, 10.

**35. Rabbi Jehoshua [other reading: Rabbi Maisha the grandson of Rabbi Jehoshua ben Levi] said: 'Everyone who sees a naked body and does not feed his eyes on it, will merit to receive the Countenance of the Divine Presence, for it is said: "And shuts his eyes from looking upon evil" (Is. 33:15). And what is written after that? "He shall dwell on high" (Is. 33:16), and it says "Your eyes shall see the King in his beauty" (Is. 33:17).'**

The basis manuscript has to be corrected with the help of the other manuscripts. A better reading is: *Rabbi Maisha (Mesha) the grandson of Rabbi Jehoshua ben Levi.* 'Receiving the countenance of the Shekhinah' is the reward for the intimate relationship with God in doing the religious commandments. It is spoken of the presence of the Shekhinah especially in relation to studying as a religious duty. Cf. eg. M'Abot III,5; TbTam. 32b; Tj'Er. V,1, and other sources. Lightheartedness results in the departure of the Shekhinah. Cf. TbShab. 30b: 'This teaches you that the Divine Presence rests upon man neither through gloom, nor through sloth, nor through frivolity, nor through levity, nor through talk, nor through idle chatter, save through a matter of joy in connection with a precept...' The religious experience of Gods presence is only guaranteed by a correct lifestyle and obedience to the 'mitzwot'.

# Pereq Ha-Minim

## *Derekh 'Eretz Rabbah, chapter II*

**1. Concerning the heretics, the apostates, the informers, the wicked, the hypocrites (annunciators), and the Epicureans, Scripture says: 'But a hypocrite cannot come before His countenance' (Hiob 13:16).**

The common feature of the groupings listed here is that they pose a threat to Judaism from within. Although the rabbinic tradition is not preeminently dogmatic, there are in fact a number of premises upon which the Jewish way of life is based, in accordance with the precepts of the oral and written tradition. Here we find reaction against groupings which deny these premises or otherwise threaten the physical survival of the community from within, especially against groupings which abandon the monolatristic concept of God; completely or partially deny the authority of the tradition; abandon the belief in the World to Come and the concept of resurrection, reward and punishment connected with that belief; and wilfully displace themselves from the community and threaten the community.

In MSanh. X,1 (cf. TbSanh. 90b), the only comment about the groupings mentioned is that they will have no share in the World to Come. In TosSanh. XIII,4 and in Tb.R. ha-Sh. 17a, eternal punishment in the Gehinnom is dealt out to similar groupings. That indicates a reaction against real threat that these groupings posed for Judaism, particularly in the second century C. E. The heart of the tradition mentioned probably predates the fall of the Temple and was directed against Sadducees and Hellenized Jews. See L. H. Schiffman, 'At the crossroads: Tannaitic Perspective on the Jewish-Christian Schism', in: *Jewish and Christian Self-definition*, ed. E. P. Sanders a. o., II, London 1981, p. 143; J. Guttmann, 'Ueber zwei Dogmengeschichtlichen Mischnastellen', in: *M. G. W. J*, XLII (1898), p. 289 ff.

See here in D. E. the reading of the Gaon of Vilna which, in accordance with D. E. R. II,7, quotes Ps. 9:18 instead of Hiob 13:16, and reads 'mehallelei shem shamajim' (the people who profane the Name of Heaven) instead of 'u-mehannephim'.

*Minim (heretics)*. This term refers to groupings which were perceived as a threat not so much because of deviating behaviour as because of deviating doctrines and concepts. The 'Birkat ha-Minim', the 'blessing' against the heretics in the Eighteen benedictions, shows that the concept 'minim' already clearly referred to certain groupings in the first century. Cf. TbBer. 28b and

TjTa'an. II [65c]. In TjSanh. X,6 [29c] (Amoraic source), there is a discussion about twenty four groupings of 'minim'. The term 'minim' refers not only to Jewish-Christian groupings (e.g. TosHul. II, 24 [22]; TbShab. 116a; TbGit. 45b) but also refers to Jewish groupings (cf. e.g. TosBer. IX,5; TosB.M. II,33; TjSanh. X,6 [29c]) and to Jewish, non jewish, and Jewish-Christian Gnostics (cf. e.g. MMeg. IV,10; TbMeg. 15a; MBer. IX,7; TbSanh. 37a). In any case the reference concerned mostly those groupings which, despite their deviating doctrines, had to be considered as Jewish or wished to belong to Judaism, especially Jewish-Christian and / or Jewish-Gnostic groupings.

In the printed editions of D.E., one does find as result of censorship the reading 'tzaddoqim' instead of 'minim'.

In connection with the term 'minim' see (among others): A. Marmorstein, in: *Huca*, X (1935), p. 223ff. and see G.F. Moore, *Judaism*, III, Cambridge 1930, p. 68ff. (repr. New York 1971, I, p. 243ff., I, pp. 365−366, II, p. 250 and p. 356); A. Büchler, *Studies in Jewish History*, pp. 245−247; and see *E.J.*, XII, col. 1ff.

In connection with 'Birkat ha-Minim' cf. TbBer. 28b and TbMeg. 17b; TosBer. III,25 and TjBer. II,4 [5a] and TjBer. IV,3 [8a]; J. Mann (Genizah-fragments), in: *HUCA*, II (1925), p. 306 and S. Schechter (Genizah-fragments), in: *J.Q.R.*, X (1898; repr. 1966), p. 657 and p. 659. In genizah-fragments (of 'Birkat ha-Minim') 'minim' are mentioned along with 'notzrim'. See I. Elbogen, *Die jüdische Gottesdienst in seiner geschichtlichen Entwicklung*, Hildesheim 1967, pp. 36−40; cf. I. Elbogen, *Ha-Tephillah be-Jisra'el*, Jerusalem 1972 pp. 27−29, p. 31 and p. 40.; R.T. Herford, *Christianity in Talmud and Midrash*, New York 1966, pp. 125−135; J. Heinemann, *Ha-Tephillah bi-Tequphat ha-Tanna'im we-ha-'Amora'im*, Jerusalem 1966, p. 142; S. Lieberman, *Tosephta Ki-Pheshutah*, I, New York 1956, p. 53ff.; E. Bickermann, in: *H.T.R.*, LV (1962, p. 171, note 35; R. Kimelman, in: *Jewish and Christian Self-definition*, ed. E.P. Sanders a.o., II, p. 226 and L.H. Schiffman, in: o.c., p. 150ff.

*Meshummad* (*apostate*). This literally means 'one who has been destroyed'. It actually refers to someone who ignores the commandments of the Torah and Jewish law. In Tannaitic sources, the term applies to someone who wilfully commits transgressions. See L.H. Schiffman, in: *Jewish and Christian Self-definition*, ed. E.P. Sanders a.o., II, p. 145. In TbHor. 11a (TosHor. I,5), we find a halakhic definition of 'meshummad' as one who violates certain dietary restrictions. According to another opinion it even refers to someone who wears a garment of wool and linen (see Siphra on Lev. 1:2, where the 'meshummad' is described as one who does not accept the covenant; cf. TbHul. 5a, where the 'meshummad' is equated with someone who pours idolatrous libations and one who violates the Sabbath in public. It is also stated here that the 'meshummad' is excluded from those who may send voluntary offerings to Jerusalem, from which it is evident that they were Jews. No repentance is expected from them, however in contrast with the 'resha'im'. Cf. also Tb'Ab. Zar. 26a-26b and TbGit. 45b, where they are mentioned separately from the 'Gojim'. A 'meshummad' is therefore to be considered as a Jew who wilfully breaks the commandments which determine the manifestation of his Jewish identity, thereby consciously distancing himself from that identity.

*Mesorot (informers, denunciators)*. This term primarily refers to people who denounced Jews or fellow Jews), who practised rituals forbidden during the Hadrianic persecutions, and possibly to people who denounced Jews for other reasons in other periods as well, such as by giving information on tax evaders to the occupying authorities. Cf. the opinion of Rashi on TbR. ha-Sh.17a, who considers the informer's offence to cause financial loss to fellow Jews (cf. also TbB. Q. 5a), and see Rambam, *Jad*, Hil. Hobel u-Mazziq, VII,1 ff.; and see J. Schechter, *'Otzar ha-Talmud*, Tel-Aviv 1963, sub 'masoor', 'moser' etc.

In TbB. Q. 119a, there is a discussion about the right to confiscate the possessions of an informer, and in another tradition, an attempt on the life of an informer is not deemed as punishable if it enhances the security of the community (see Tb'Ab. Zar. 26b and cf. TbSanh. 57a and TosB. M. II, end). This tradition is comprehensible only in the situation in which informers posed a real threat for the community; see also H. Freedman, translation of TbSanh. in *The Babylonian Talmud*, ed. I. Epstein, London 1935, p. 389, note 2.

*Resha'im (transgressors, wicked)*. On the basis of the coherence between traditions in which the term 'resha'im' is used, this category can be identified with the 'poshe'ei Jisra'el', the rebellions of Israel. Cf. Ps. 37:38 and Hos. 14:10, where 'poshe'im' and 'resha'im' are mentioned jointly. In the parallels in TosSanh. XIII,4 and TbR. ha-Sh. 17a, it states that the 'poshe'ei Jisra'el' ('resha'im') will remain in the Gehinnom for twelve months, as opposed to other groupings mentioned here in D. E. R. which will have absolutely no part in the World to Come. In the period of the Hashmoneans, the 'poshe'ei ba-Torah' (transgressors against the Torah) were a well known group. Cf. I. Macc. 14:14 and II Macc. 6:21.

In Waj. Rab. II,9, it is stated that the offerings of the 'rish'ei Jisra'el' are accepted, and hope is expressed that the 'rish'ei Jisra'el' will be brought back under the wings of the Shekhinah. In connection with this group, there is no mention of a wilful break with Judaism. See Tb'Er. 19a (cf. TbHag. 27a) which contains a statement by Resh Laqish that Gehinnom will have no hold over the people in this category and that they are full of 'mitzwot'. Cf. further TbKer. 5b and *Tosaphists* on TbGit. 19a; S. E. R. III, ed. M. Friedmann, p. 15 and L. Ginzberg, *Geonica*, II (1909. repr. New York 1968), p. 370. In *HUCA*, X (1935) A. Marmorstein demonstrates on the basis of the texts that the members of the group referred to by those terms were not antinomistic, that they did not deny the authority of the Torah and believed in resurrection, and that they were members of the local synagogues and communities. A. Marmorstein notes as a distinguishing feature of this group that its members did not recognize the authority of the prophets and hagiographers as part of Scripture (see Tanh. J., 'Eqeb, § 1; Tanh., ed. S. Buber, 10a.).

Although they were circumcised and belonged to the community, they were accused of assimilation and they were supposed to have kept Israel from keeping the Torah and performing the 'mitzwot'. Cf. Midr. Shir ha-Shir., ed. L. Grünhut 10a and Sed. 'Ol., ed. A. Marx, III, p. 9. In S.E.R. III, ed. M. Friedmann. pp. 14−15, on the one hand it is stated that the 'resha'im' and the 'poshe'ei Jisra'el' neglect the study of the Torah, but on the other hand they are defended with the argument that they say their prayers, go to the synagogue and perform 'mitzwot'. In Midr. Teh. 1 (ed. S. Buber, 6b) however, it is claimed that they serve other Gods. On the basis of the passages mentioned here and by A. Marmorstein l.c. the impression arises that the term 'resha'im' refers not so much to one specific group, but rather to Jews in general, who on the one hand assimilate into their non-Jewish surroundings, and on the other hand remain faithful to Judaism in many respects. See, however, S. Krauss, in: J. Q. R., V (1893; repr. 1966), p. 133: a 'rasha' was supposed to have denoted a certain sect; in connection with that S. Krauss refers to TosBer. III,25 and other sources. In our opinion 'resha'im' were perceived to be a less acute threat then the other groupings mentioned.

*Hanaphim* (*annunciators, hypocrites*). In connection with this term see W. Bacher, in: *M. G. W. J.*, XX (1871), p. 208 ff. The Targum on Hiob translates the term 'hanaph' with 'delator' (informer). See the Targum on Hiob 13:16; 15:34; 17:8; 20:5; 27:8; 34:30; and see Midr. Teh. 52 (ed. S. Buber, 86b). See further TbJoma 81b and Qoh. Rab. IV,1 and Jalq., Ez., r. 341. The term 'hanaph' also has the meaning of 'flatterer', 'pretender'. On the basis of the relationship with the context of TbSot. 42b (a statement of Rabbi Jeremiah bar 'Abba) and Midr. Teh. 101,3, we opt here the meaning of 'flatterer' in the sense of collaborating and currying favour with the occupying authorities and enemies of Israel.

*Appiqorosin* (*Epicureans*). The term is derived from the name Epicurus, founder of a Greek school of philosophy (342/1−270 B.C.E.) whose point of departure was the denial of providence and the relationship between gods and men. See S. Krauss, *Griechische und Lateinische Lehnwörter im Talmud, Midrash und Targum*, II, repr. 1964, p. 136 ff. The explanation from the Amoraic period based on Semitic derivation are of no matter here (see TbSanh. 99b-100a and TjSanh. X,1 [27d] and cf. L. H. Schiffman, in: *Jewish and Christian Self-definition*, ed. E. P. Sanders a. o., II, p. 141 ff. and notes on p. 348.

In connection with the denial of providence as a distinguishing feature of the 'appiqorosin', see also Josephus, Ant. X, and cf. S. Lieberman, *Greek in Jewish Palestine*, repr. New York 1963, p. 30 and *E. J.*, I, p. 665 and cf. the definition of Rambam, *Jad*, Hil. Teshubah, III,8. An Epicurean is one who denies the involvement of God in the affairs of men and the world and thus the authority of revelation, divine judgement, the World to Come and the like. L. H. Schiffman, l.c., points out the correspondences described by Josephus between the ideas of the Epicureans and of the Sadducees, and he points out that traditions such as in MSanh. l.c. were especially targeted at Sadducees and Hellenized Jews. It is certain that the aversion to the groupings mentioned here in D.E.R. has very old roots and has to do with the problems appearing from the Seleucidic period onwards. See L.H. Fischmann, o.c. , p. 348, note 159.

**2. Concerning the fear-inspiring, the impudent, the proud, the haughty, the malicious, the violent, Scripture says: 'For the arms of the wicked shall be broken, but the Lord upholds the righteous' (Ps. 37:17).**

*'Eimtanim (fear-inspiring* persons)*. Cf. Targ. Onk. and Targ. Ps. Jon. on Dt. 2:10, where "eimtan' is used as translation of 'ha-'eimim'. The word *gaphtan* (*impudent*) arose from 'geiftan' and from 'geiwtan' and 'ga'awatan' (proud). See M. Jastrow, Dictionary, I, New York 1950, p. 236, col. b, sub 'geiwtan', with the meaning of 'haughty, 'proud'. The word *zahtan* (*proud*) may have derived from 'zeihtan' and was formed with the help of the stem 'zahah' or 'zuah' (to be proud, overbearing). Cf. in this connection Targ. on Ps. 44:19 'u-zehuhit libna' (made haughty our heart), ed. Lag. (cf. Mss. 'zehuhin') 'zehu-hin'. Cf. also TbHul. 7a 'mazhihin' (mazhihin). cf. TbSot. 47b 'zehuhei leb' ('zehuhei leb' or 'zehihei leb') and cf. TosSot. XIV,9 (ed. S. Lieberman, *Seder Nashim*, p. 238, and cf. S. Lieberman, *Tosephta Ki-Pheshutah*, VIII, p. 755, l. 52−53. See the remark by S. Krauss, in. *R.E.J.* XXXVI (1898), p. 33. He interprets the absence of the difficult term 'zahtanim' in A.R.N. [b], XXXV (43a) and the replacement of the term in S.E.R. XV (traditional. ed.; see to the contrary ed. M. Friedmann XVI, p. 71) with 'nahnatin' as proof of the genuine character of the text in D.E.!! (n.b., there are however readings of S.E.R. in which the term 'we-zahtanin' is used, see e.g. ed. M. Friedmann l.c.).

**3. Concerning those who devise evil, who invent (evil) plans [other reading: who obscure their utterances], who spurn with their lips and who make smooth their tongue, Scripture says: 'Let their way be dark and slippery, the angel of the Lord pursuing them' (Ps. 35:6).**

*Horeshei ra* (people *who devise evil*). The term refers to people who prepare evil schemes and wicked plans. In connection with the term see Prov. 3:29 and 14:22. Cf. also Hiob 4:8 and the 'hiph'il'-form in I Sam. 23:9 and compare with that Ps.3:29 and 6:14 and 14:22. Cf. especially Seph. Ben Sira 7:12 (ed. M.Z. Segal, p. 43) and 27:22 (ed. M. Z. Segal, p. 168). Of concern here are very old terms which can indicate the great age of traditions in this chapter of D.E.

*Mehashebei debarim* (people *who invent evil plans*).

In the Tenakh 'mehashebei-' (who think of) is connected with 'ra' (evil) or 'awen' and the like. Cf. Ez. 11:2; Mi. 2:1; Ps. 10:2; Ps. 21:12; Ps. 35:20; Ps. 36:5).

One reading in the manuscripts of D. E. is 'mahshikhei debarim' (those *who obscure their utterances*). Cf. Hiob 38:2 'mahshikh 'eitzah'. Ms. Jewish Theological Seminary, cat. E. N. Adler, no. 1745 reads 'mehappekhei derakhim' (overturners of ways). On the basis of that reading, the reading 'mehappekhei debarim' (those who twist their words) is more plausible, especially because this reading is to be found in the parallels A. R. N. [b], XXV (43a) and S. E. R., XVI (ed. M. Friedmann, p. 77). Given this information, an original reading 'u-mehappekhei debarim' (those who twist their words) is not impossible. Cf. also wordings in TbPes. 113a. But the reading 'u-mahshikhei debarim' (those who obscure their utterances) also deserves consideration. These solutions fit into the entire sequence in which different forms of misuse of human speech are dealt with.

*U-maphtirei shepha* (people *who spurn with their lips*). Those who make gestures of contempt with their lips, who spurn with their lips, who draw their mouths out of contempt. Cf. especially the passage in Ps. 22:8 [7]: 'All who see me mock at me, they make mouths at me, they wag their heads' and cf. passages in Pes.Rab., XXXVIII, ed. M. Friedmann, 163a. In connection with the opening of the mouth to make contemptuous gestures, see passages in Ps. 35:21 and Hiob 16:10 and see S. Krauss, *Talmudische Archeologie,* III, repr. Hildesheim 1966, IX, p. 12. Cf. in parallels (S. E. R. l.c.) mention of the different readings 'Ma'amiqei shepha' (those who make their language deep, those who speak unfathomably) and the reading (A. R. N. l.c.) 'mamtiqei shepha' (those who use sweet [flattering] language).

*U-mahliqei lashon* (people *who make smooth their tongue*). The basis manuscript required a minor correction. The expression seems to have been borrowed from biblical use of language. Cf. Ps. 5:10; Prov. 2:14, 7:5, 28:23 and 29:5. See A. R. N. l.c. with the reading 'ba'alei lashon ha-ra' (those who speak gossip).

**4. They who smite in secret and who openly revile, who disgrace the public and who create dissension are destined to become like Korah and his assembly, concerning whom Scripture says: 'And the earth closed upon them' (Num. 16:33).**

On the basis of the passage of Scripture cited, it can be stated that the transgressions of Korah and his assembly may serve as a guide to the explanation of the transgressions mentioned here. *Makkin ba-sater* (*who slay in secret*) must also then not be taken in the sense of physical aggression, but rather as a verbal act, one of slander. Cf. in this connection the passage in Dt. 27:24: ''arur makkeh re'ehu ba-sater' ('cursed be he who strikes his neighbour in secret') with Ps. 101:5: 'melashni ba-seter re'ehu' ('he who slanders his neighbour in secret'). In reference to Dt. 27:24, see (among) others Rashi, who explains that passage in

the sense of slander. In A. R. N. [b], XXXV (43b), we find the interpretative
reading: 'men'atzim ba-sater' (who blaspheme, who insult in secrecy).

*Meharrephim be-galuj (who openly revile)*. Those who speak scornfully
about their fellow men in public. See, however, the explanation in the parallel
in S. E. R., XV (ed. M. Friedmann, XVI, p. 77) in which the passage is rendered
interpretatively as 'those who curse God in public'. In connection with the
event of Korah and his company in the background, we choose the reading in
D. E.: those who speak scornfully about their fellow men.

*U-Mazzilei rabbim (who disgrace the public)*. The basis manuscript reads 'u-
mazzilei 'et ha-rabbim', which is grammatically inconsistent. The stem 'nazal' is
possibly an allusion to the fact that Korah brought many others down with him
into the earth when his entire assembly was swallowed up (see Num. 16). The
reading 'melawwim be-ribbit' (who lend on interest) in Ms. cat. E. N. Adler,
no. 1745 is clearly corrupt and does not fit within this context. See TbSanh. 109b
(cf. Jalq., Korah, r.752) and the interpretation of Num. 16:33 that Korah and
his assembly will have no part in the World to Come.

5. **Concerning those who store up fruit, who unsettle the market, who
make the ephah small [and the 'sheqel' great] and who lend on interest,
Scripture says: 'The Lord has sworn by the pride of Jacob: If I ever forget
any of their works' (Am. 8:7).**

This passage is rendered in TbB. B. as a baraita! *Those who store up fruit*, i. e.
for purposes of speculation, in expectation of a period of scarcity. In Ms. cat.
E. N. Adler, no. 1745 and in TbB. B. 90b we read 'otzerei' (from ''atzar' = to
gather) in stead of 'otzerei', from ''atzar' = to withhold, to held fast).

*Maphqi'ei she'arim (who unsettle the market)*. I.e., those who unsettle the
market by driving up prices in time of threatening or actual scarcity, or even
withholding products and driving up prices in order to create a false impression
of scarcity. In connection with the term 'maphkia she'arim', cf. also MTa'an.
II,9 (see the explanations in ed. Ch. Albeck, *Seder Mo'ed*, Tel-Aviv 1973,
p. 37.; and see Rashi in reference to TbMeg. 17b.

*Maqtinei 'eiphah (who make the ephah small)*. This term was clearly borrowed from Am. 8:5, as was the addition *and the 'sheqel' great*, which is found in
the manuscripts and in the parallels. The ephah was a volume measure of
roughly 40 litres; If the volume was made smaller, the buyer received too little
for his money. The 'sheqel' was the weight with which the buyer's money was
weighed in the time when there were still no minted coins of good quality and
one could make a coin inconspicuously smaller by shaving off a bit of the
precious metal from the edge. If the 'sheqel' – the control weight – was too big,
then the buyer had to pay relatively too much money. It is difficult to determine
if a later addition is under discussion here. See the deviating reading in
A. R. N. [b], XXXV (43b), which, in our opinion, must be considered as a

secondary interpretative reading. See there the reading: 'those who reduce the measures', and the explanatory addition 'in order to thereby make a profit in the land of Israel'. See S. E. R., ed. M. Friedmann, introduction, pp, 49–50.

**6. The following do not leave (their possessions) to their children and if they leave (them) they will not do successfully [other reading: They will not leave (them) to their grandchildren]: the dice gambler, one who lends on interest, the raiser of small cattle, one who transacts with money derived from (the produce of) the sabbatical year and with money that has to come from overseas countries, and a priest and Levite who borrow (in advance) on their portions (i. e. their shares in the 'terumah' or tithes).**

*The dice gambler.* The player with the dice. This refers to a dice game in which money was won or lost. *Qubja* (dice) is derived from Greek 'kubeia'. Cf. here MSanh. III,3: 'These are disqualified from acting as judge or witness where a financial matter is concerned): the dice gambler, one who lends money on interest, one who flies pigeons, one who transacts with money derived from the produce of the Sabbatical year.' Cf. TbSanh. 42b; TosSanh. V,2; TjSanh. III,5 [21a], which contains the addition of (among others) breeders of small cattle. Cf. Tb'Er. 82a; TbR. ha-Sh. 22a; M'Ed. II,7 and cf. Rambam, *Jad*, Hil. 'Edut, X,4 and *Shul. Ar.*, Hosh. Mishp., 34,16(29–32). Persons in the categories mentioned are excluded because of their professions from having any say in financial-judicial matters, considering that they showed no respect in their dealings from the proprietary rights of others, or speculated without making a constructive contribution to the community for their profit. See also L. Cohn, in: *M. G. W. J.*, XX (1871), p. 494. In the Tos. l.c., there is the additional reason that the subject here concerns habits which are difficult to break, the consequences of which cannot be amended in the short run.

*The raiser of small cattle.* There was a great aversion to those who kept small cattle, since keeping small cattle was apt to cause destruction to another's territory; it was also considered to be a form of robbery and an offense to raise small cattle within the boundaries of Israel as it rendered the land unsuitable for cultivation (see in this connection MB. Q. VII,7; TosB. Q. VIII,10 and 11; TbB. Q. 79b.

*Money from overseas countries.* Those who will get money from overseas regions will not bequeath anything to their children, but for a reason different from that of the individuals in the previous mentioned categories we encountered in the listing of those excluded from acting as judge or witness in decisions concerning financial matters. There was a great danger that the money being carried over long distances could be lost as the result of a storm or robbery. Cf. here also D. E. Z. X.

*A priest and a Levite who borrow...* I.e. a priest and a Levite who claim in advance to the 'terumah' and tithes, respectively, of a certain person. Every priest and Levite eventually has equal rights to these but may not assert special rights to a previously determined share. Note the much clearer formulation in other manuscripts: 'and should they bequeath (to their children), they will not bequeath to their grandchildren. Cf. also the reading of the Gaon of Vilna on D.E.

**7.  Concerning the heretics, the apostates and those who profane the Name of Heaven, Scripture says: '[The wicked] shall return to the nether-world, all the nations that forget God' (Ps. 9:18). And it says: 'That which is crooked cannot be made straight' (Qoh. 1,15).**

This passage shows strong resemblance with the passage at the beginning of this chapter. The Gaon of Vilna has used the verse cited here from Ps. 8:18 with the passage at the beginning of this chapter, and has mentioned on this place a different passage with other references (Hiob 13:16 and Ps. 101:7) under the influence of TbSot. 42a. The manuscripts, however, do not support such a change. See also the censored reading of 'tzaddoqim' instead of 'minim'.

**8.  Concerning those who coo like doves, who make vehement motions with their hands when talking and who stamp with their feet and who walk on their tip-toe, Scripture says: 'Let not the foot of pride overtake me, let not the hand of the wicked drive me away' (Ps. 36:12).**

*Those who coo like doves.* Only Ms. cat. E.N. Adler, no. 1745 has the clear reading of 'ke-jonim' (like doves). We find this wording in Is. 38:14 and 59:11, where it is used in expressions of anguish. Here in D.E., the expression most likely alludes to the mannerism of proud men. 'Menimin' comes from 'num' (to speak); cf. further the reading in Jalq. ha-Makh. on Ps. 36:12 ('ha-menahamin') and cf. this with the Targ. on Nah. 2:8 ('menahamin ke-qol jonim') as a translation of 'menahagot ke-qol jonim'; cf. the manuscript reading in D.E. 'we-ha-menahamin' of 'naham' = to be agitated, to make a noise. Cf. TbBer. 3a: 'menahamenet ke-jonah', cooing (in mourning) like a dove.

*Ha-meniphim (who make vehement motions).* Along with *who coo* it is an expression for an animated manner of talking with pride and exaggerated gesticulations as a display of self-importance.. Cf., e.g. TbJeb. 63a, where the term concerned denotes the swaying movement of the standing corn as an image of proud attitude. The expression 'heniph jad' (gesturing with the hand) is an expression haughtiness as well as of an aggressive threat. See e.g., Seph. Ben Sira 12:18 (ed. M.Z. Segal, p. 75, and see p. 81) and Seph. Ben Sira (ed. M.Z. Segal, p. 225) and cf. Is. 10:32, 11:15, 19:16, and Za. 2:13. It is possible, then, that people who gesticulate in an agitated and threatening manner while speaking are referred to here in D.E. See also the readings in the manuscripts of 'ha-mepappin' from 'paphah', derived from 'pèh' with the meaning 'to mouth', 'to talk in a proud manner'. See also the reading of 'ha-megappephin' from 'gaphaph' (to join, to press, to close) and the special meaning 'to fold hands in idleness' (cf. M. Higger, *Massekhtot Derekh 'Eretz*, p. 104: 'who wring their hands'; cf. also the Targ. on Qoh. 4:5: 'the fool fold his hands and eats his own flesh'. This reading has possibly evolved from another reading 'u-menaph-nephin'. See also *Ma'alot ha-Middot*, ed. Eshkol, Ma'alat Derekh 'Eretz, p. 298.

*Who stamp with their feet.* This is possibly an expression for a self-assured, somewhat aggressive manner of walking or otherwise for an agitated gesture of contempt. Cf. here, S. Krauss, *Talmudische Archäologie*, III, (chap.) IX, p. 12.

*Who walk on tiptoe.* Walking on tiptoe can be explained as an expression of pride and as representation of the fact that someone wants to appear greater than he actually is. In manuscript one finds the addition 'and who wink with their eyes'. In connection with this addition, cf. Is. 3:16 and the explanation thereof in TbShab. 62b: 'They filled their eyes with paint and winked'. See the context in Is. and in Tbsanh. l.c. and cf. TbJoma 9b; Waj. Rab. XVI,1 (ed. M. Margulies, p. 341 ); Jalq., Is., r. 397 and other sources. It is possible, however, that the addition here can be explained as a supplement to the corrupt text of D. E. R. II,8 'and those who are wise in their own eyes' (in Ms. cat. E. N. Adler, no. 1745, the two passages have been merged together).

**9. Concerning the haughty of spirit and those who slander, who talk obscenely and who are wise in their own eyes, Scripture says: 'For behold the day** *of the Lord* [read: that comes]. It burns as a furnace' (Mal. 3:19) (4:1).

In our basic text there is an erroneous quotation which, with the help of the other manuscripts, must be corrected to read 'ha-jom ha-ba' ('that comes').

*Medabberim nebalah* (*who talk obscenely*). Who talk with an overtone of foolishness. See 'nabal', Compare the use of the term in Is. 9:16 and Is. 32:6. In the parallels 'medabberim kazab' (who speak deceptive language) appears as an interpretative rendition of the more archaic expression 'medabberim neba-lah'.

**10. Concerning some one who marries off his daughter to an old man, who marries off his son who is a minor to a (mature) woman, who returns a lost article to a heathen and who does a favour to one who will not acknowledge it, Scripture says: 'The Lord will not be willing to pardon him' (Dt. 29:19).**

The statement here in D. E. R. is based on a tradition as ascribed to Rab in TbSanh. 76b. The point of departure in that context is based on Lev. 19:29: 'Do not profane your daughter to cause her to be whore.' According to Rabbi 'Eli'ezer that refers to someone who marries off his daughter (who is still

young) to an old man who will not be able to fulfil the sexual desires of the
vivacious young woman, with the possible result that she will commit adultery
with other men. Following that is a statement ascribed to Rab. Also, if an adult
woman is married off to a minor (a boy who is not yet thirteen years and one day
old or who does not even have two pubic hairs (cf. MNid. V,9), there is the
danger of the woman committing adultery because the boy will not be able to
fulfil her desires. According to general opinion, however, a valid marriage
cannot be performed if the male is a minor. Cf. e.g. MJeb. X,8−9; TbJeb. 62b,
91b, 96b, 112b; TbQid. 14a, 44b and 50b. The reason for that is that such an act
would be tantamount to prostitution. Cf. also *Shul. Ar.*, Eb. ha-Ez. I,3 and 43,1
and see Rambam, *Jad*, Hil. 'Issur. Bi'ah, XXI,25.

In the tradition perhaps one might find traces of the supposition that such a
marriage would be possible just before the thirteenth year. See the gemara in
TbSanh. 76b and Rashi and *Tosaphists* in that text, and see *Bajt Hadash* on Eb.
ha-Ez. and *Turei Zahab*, on Eb. ha-Ez. 3. The halakhah, however, forbids such
a marriage. See *Shul. Ar.* l.c. and see *'Otzar Poseqim*, Eb. ha-Ez. I,14.

*Who turns a lost article.* See the explanation of Rashi on Rab's statement in
TbSanh. 76b, that the return of lost goods applies only with respect to fellow
Israelites. The return of lost goods to heathens only increases the possessions of
those who have robbed Israel. In TbB. Q. 113b, we find in the name of Rabbi
Shim'on the statement that it is permissible to keep the lost article of a heathen
and that it need not be returned. Cf. also TbB. M. 24b, where the argument
appears that heathens themselves do not return lost objects. In the gemara of
TbB. Q. 113b, there is a discussion of the possibilities of justifying this rule on
the basis of the Torah. See Dt. 22:1−3 where there is a discussion about the lost
goods of 'your brother'. i. e., of an Israelite and not of a heathen.

Yet another reason is added here in D. E.: *and doing good to one who will not
acknowledge it.* Returning stolen goods to the heathens by Israel will bring
about no change in the understanding between heathens and Israelites, but will
only mean a strengthening of the position of the enemies of Israel. Cf. analogous reasons in Rambam. *Jad*, Hil. Gez. we-'Abeidah, XI,2−3 and *Shul. Ar.*,
Hosh, Mishp., 266,1. In contrast to our statement in D. E., seems the tradition
in TosB. M. II,27 to deal with the stray cattle of heathens until the point that
one has returned it to the responsibility of the owner. That tradition, however,
concerns cattle, and in that tradition both the duty to prevent stray cattle from
causing harm to others and the preservation of good understanding with the
non-Jewish community play a role. Cf. also TosB. M. II,33. See also the
opinion of the pious Pinhas ben Ja'ir in TbB. Q. that restitution is always
mandatory in case not returning something to a heathen would mean the
desecration of God's name.

**11. Concerning tax collectors, confiscators, exchangers of money and pu-
blicans (i. e. farmers general of taxes), Scripture says: '[your riches] and**

**your merchandise [your wares of exchange], your marines, your traders [other reading: your sailors], your chalkers [and the exchangers of your wares and all your men of war that are in you with all the company which is in the midst of you] shall fall into the heart of the seas, in the day of your ruin.' (Ez. 27:27).**

*Gabba'im* (*Tax collectors*). Mobile tax collectors, who entered houses with their money bag, as opposed to the 'moshekhim' who possessed a box. See MB. Q. X,1−2 and TbB. Q. 113a. The 'moshekhim' were the so called 'publicani', the farmers general of taxes, and the 'gabba'in' were their agents who collected the taxes. Both the 'publicani' and their agents, the 'gabba'in' were classified along robbers and disqualified as witnesses (see MSanh. III,3 and TbSanh. 25b and TosSanh. V,5), and their money was not accepted for 'tzedaqah'. See MB. Q. X,1−2 and TbB. Q. 113b. They were not accepted in the circles of the 'habberim', the holy law-abiding men. Cf. TosDem. III,4.

*Haramim* (*confiscators*). The Romans imposed the so-called 'arnonia', a very arbitrary seizure of natural goods (such as grain, bread, wine, oil, meat, clothing and the like; cf. A. R. N. [a], XXI) and even of livestock and people, whom they forced into labour (the so-called 'angaria'; cf. among others MB. M. VI,3). Confiscation was also used as punishment for tax evasion. Cf. e. g. TbPes. 112b and TjKet. VII,3.

The quotation from Ez. is given incorrectly in the basis manuscript.

**12.   Concerning some one who deceives his partner (in business), who does not return a lost article to its owners, who lends money to his fellow with the intention to take away from him his house or his field (when he cannot pay back the money) who lives with his wife in an obscene manner and who makes false accusations of wanton behaviour against her in order to divorce her, Scripture says: 'I the Lord search the heart. I try the reins' (Jer. 17:10).**

All the things mentioned here have in common that they are committed in secret and cannot be controlled by human judgement. The matters mentioned here are finally left to the judgement of heaven. Cf. also A. Büchler, *Studies in Sin and Atonement*, London 1928, p. 401, note 4, in reference to Philo, *De Spec. Leg.* I, 235 and *De Virt.* XI). In connection with the citation from Jer. 17:10, it should be noted that in that passage, the words 'I the Lord' are especially important and are explained in the tradition as a warning added to certain 'mitzwot' that God will hold man responsible for commandments which have to do with inner attitudes or the keeping of which is difficult to supervise outwardly. Cf. e. g. A. R. N. [a] XVI (32b) in connection with Lev. 19:18; cf. also Rashi concerning Lev. 19:14, and other sources.

Compare Ms. cat. E. N. Adler, no. 1745 with the reading 'ha-shoqer 'al . . . lib'alo' ('to become his owner', instead of ' . . . li-be'alaw' = 'to its owners') and cf. the reading in *Seph. ha-Roqeah*, Hil. Teshubah, § 29, which is obviously explainable by the absence of the words 'who does not return a lost article to its owners'. 'Lib'alo' seems to be a corruption of 'li-be'alaw' ('to its owners').

*False accusations*. In connection with "alilat debarim', see Dt. 22:13–14,17. It is a technical term referring to the accusation by the husband that his wife was not a virgin at the time of their marriage and that she had extramarital relations in her father's house prior to the marriage.

**13. Concerning those who are insulted and do not insult, who hear [themselves reviled and do not answer, who are performing (the commandments)] from love, and who rejoice about their sufferings, Scripture says: 'But they that love Him be as the sun when he goes forth in his might' (Judg. 5:31).**

See the commentary on the term "alub' (forbearing) with reference to D. E. Z. I,1 and II,11. The basis manuscript is defective and must be supplemented with help of the manuscripts and the parallel in TbShab. 88b and other sources. See the remark of S. Krauss in *R. E. J.*, XXXVI (1898), p. 33, note 6, that the form 'ne'elabin' is considered to be more original than the form "alubin', as in S. E. R.; cf. *Seph. Diqduqei Sopherim*, on TbShab. 88b.

**14. Concerning those who are contemptible in their own eyes [and those who are despised in their own eyes], who subdue their inclination and who are making humble their spirit Scripture says: 'Thus says the Lord, the Redeemer of Israel, his Holy One, [to him who is despised of men, to him who is abhorred of nations, to a servant of rulers. Kings shall see and arise, princes and they shall prostate themselves]' (Is. 49:7).**

In the manuscripts and variants, see the addition 'we-hanibbazin be'eineihem' (who are despised in their own eyes) and compare with that the statement in Ps. 15:4 'nibzeh be-'einaw nim'as'. On the basis of this quotation from Psalms, M. Friedmann (S. E. R. XVI, p. 78) gives preference to the other sequence in S. E. R.

This statement, just as the previous one, fits into Hasidic milieu. In the quotation given (Is. 49:7), there is the concept of elevation as reward for suffering and humilation. See the entire quotation as given in the manuscripts.

**15. Concerning trustworthy men, those who keep hidden a secret, who return things entrusted to their care, and who return a lost article to its owner, Scripture says: 'Mine eyes are upon the faithful of the land, that they may dwell with me' (Ps. 101:6).**

The basis of this statement is formed by Prov. 11:13: 'He who goes about as talebearer reveals secrets, but he who is trustworthy in spirit keeps a thing hidden.' In actuality, the categories mentioned after 'ba'alei 'emunah' (trustworthy men) comprise a more detailed rendition of this term. The restitution of a deposit is mandatory on the basis of the Torah (cf. Lev. 5:21ff. and 6:1–5), just as is the command to restore things that have been found (see l.c. and cf. Dt. 22:1–3–. The command to reveal no secrets plays an important role in the administration of justice. If a judge reveals even 22 years later how a fellow judge voted, then he may still be punished for that, according to a tradition handed down by Rabbi 'Ammi. See TbSanh. 32a and TbB. Q. 99b and Siphra, Qedoshim, XIX (ed. M. Weiss, 88a) and other sources.

**16. Concerning someone who loves his wife like himself and who honours her more than his (own) body, and who leads his children on the right path and who marries off a wife to his son, just before puberty when he is still young and before he is coming into the power of sin, Scripture says: 'And you shall know that you tent is in peace. When you shall visit your habitation you shall miss nothing. You shall know that your seed is plenty and your offspring like the weed of the earth' (Hiob. 5:24–25).**

From TbJeb. 62b (cf. TbSanh. 76b), it is clear that the statement mentioned here in D. E. R. is a baraita. Honouring one's spouse more than oneself. Where honouring one's father and mother is concerned the term 'kabed' (to honour) means actual care. Here in in D. E. the term can be explained, analogous to that interpretation. A man must care for his wife, more than he can actually afford to, and he must care for her more than he can possibly care for himself. Cf. e.g. TbHul. 84b; MKet. V,9; TbB.M. 59a and Jalq., Ps., r. 871. Another known rule is: she rises with him but she does not go down with him; i. e. the husband is obligated to provide for his wife in accordance with the living standard to which she is accustomed, even if this is higher than his own. See TjKet. V [30a] and TbKet. 48a and 61a. A connection is made between this rule and the statement here in D. E. in *Teshubot Maharam* (TbB. B. 80a), mentioned in Ch. Z. Taubes *'Otzar ha-Ge'onim le-Massekhet Sanhedrin*, Jerusalem 1966, p. 338, on TbSanh. 76b.

Furthermore respect for the woman is especially associated with sexuality. In a statement by Rabbi 'Eli'ezer and Rabbi Jehudah, the words 'ha-'oseh hephtzei 'ishto' (see the reading in S.E.R., ed. M. Friedmann, XVI, p. 78) are connected in Mas. Kal. (ed. Vilna/Romm, 51a) and Mas. Kal. Rab., II (ed. Vilna/Romm, 52b) with an expression of respect for the woman during sexual advances by the man. See S. E. R., ed. M. Friedmann, XVI, p. 78, note 37, where the author assumes that the original reading was 'ha-'oseh hephtzei 'ishto' ('who fulfils the wishes of his wife') and says that the reading 'he who loves his wife more than himself and honours her more than he honours himself' is a more detailed explanation of the original words. This opinion, however, is not free of doubt.

*Who marries off a wife to his son.* The passage 'who marries off a wife to his son, who is still a minor (or more freely: if he is still young), if he is not far from reaching adulthood' forms a potentially serious halakhic problem. See Lev. 20:10. Scripture specifies no age at which a son must be married. From the rabbinic tradition emerges the general opinion that a marriage with an under-age boy (see also the commentary on D.E.R. II,1) is not legally valid and is therefore not permitted. Cf. among others MJeb. X,9−9; TbJeb. 62b, 91b, 96b, 112 b; TbQid. 19a, 50b and cf. traditions in Ch.Z. Taubes, o.c., on TbSanh. 76b and see B.M. Lewin, *'Otzar ha-Ge'onim*, on TbJeb. 96b, pp. 191−194; *Shul. Ar.*, Eb. ha-Ez., 43,1; *'Otzar Poseqim*, Eb. ha-Ez. I,14; Rambam, *Jad*, Hil. 'Issur. Bi'ah, XXI,25 and other sources.

On the other hand one finds in the tradition the assumption that a marriage between an adult woman and an under-age boy is allowed (see *Tosaphists* on TbSanh. 76b in reference to TbKet. 90a and the Mishnah contained in that text, where it is remarked that the 'ketubah' of a woman married with an under-age man is considered to be valid; cf. the gemara in TbSanh. 76b and *Bait Hadash* on Eb. ha-Ez. 1 and *Turei Zahab* on Eb. ha-Ez 1,3; *Beit Shemu'el* on Eb. ha-Ez. 1,3 and see B.M. Lewin, *'Otzar ha-Ge'onim*, on TbJeb. 96b, § 459; and see *Tarbitz* I, p. 91; A. Ehrman, *Massekhet Qiddushin*, 1967, pp. 219 and 202. Along with TbJeb. 90a the gemara in TbSanh. 76b (TbJeb. 62b) would especially lead to the assumption that a marriage with a male of minor age is possible. From the reaction in the gemara, however, it can appear that 'samukh le-pirqan' must not be interpreted as 'just before puberty' but as 'just after reaching their age' (thirteen for a boy), as it is to be found back in commentaries. In TbQid. 19a, Resh Laqish does present the question of whether or not an under-age male may enter into marriage, and in Mekh. de-R. Jishm., Mishpatim, par. 3 (ed. M. Friedmann, 78b) there is explicit mention of marrying off 'banim qetanim' (sons who are still under age [or young]). In TbQid. 19a, we find in the name of Rabbi Jannai a halakhic decision handed down stating that a marriage relationship with an under-age male is not possible, and the question is whether the term 'qetannim' in the Mekh. l.c. is to be considered as a strictly technical term or just a term for a young age right after the thirteenth year.

The omission in a number of manuscripts of D.E. of the term 'qatan' (which probably belongs to the original reading) is probably connected with the problem mentioned and possibly represents an attempt to avoid a contradiction with the accepted halakhah. It is the question, however, of whether 'qatan' here in D.E. must be viewed as a strictly technical term or as a term which only indicates the young age of a boy right after he has reached the age of thirteen. In practice, the average age for a boy to marry was about eighteen years (cf. e.g. M'Abot V,21 and cf. TbQid. 29b). The economic situation did not allow a very early marriage for a son. Cf. e.g. MB.B. VI,4 and TbSot. 44a; see also L. Finkelstein, *'Aqiba, Scholar, Saint and Martyr*, Philadelphia 1936, p. 22: 'Among the poor a man usually passed his thirtieth year before he could think of taking a wife.' See TbQid. 29b and the reason of marrying off boys (when they were young) that they would not follow the wrong path and would not be kept from studying the Torah. Cf. also Rambam, *Jad*, Hil. Talm. Torah, I,5 and *Shul. Ar.*, Jor. De'ah, 246,2.

See the remark of M. Friedmann in connection with S. E. R., according to whom the reading 'and he who marries a woman to his son who is "qatan" before he commits transgression' is original. The words 'samukh le-pirqo' are thought to have been added later.

**17. Concerning some one who loves his neighbours, who displays attachment to his relatives, who marries the daughter of his sister and who lends a 'perutah' to a poor man in the time of his need, Scripture says: 'Then you shall call and the Lord shall answer' (Is. 58:9).**

The basis of this statement is found in Is. 58:7 ff.: 'Is it not to share bread with the hungry, and bring the homeless poor into your house, when you see the naked, to cover him, and not to hide yourself from your own flesh? ... Then you shall call, and the Lord will answer...' This passage also occurs as a baraita in a previous mentioned context of Talmud Babli (see TbSanh. 76b and TbJeb. 62b). The words 'and not to hide yourself from your own flesh' refer here to two things: 1) friendly association with others in the neighbourhood (*he who loves his neighbours*) and 2) entering into marriage with a relative, e.g.: the daughter of a sister (*who marries the daughter of his sister*). In the rules concerning forbidden marriage relationships, it is striking that there is no mention in the Torah of a forbidden marriage with the daughter of a sister. From this the rabbis have concluded that such a marriage is permissible, even desirable. Also, the marriage between Caleb and Miriam is put forth as a proof of the desirability of such a marriage. Cf. TbB. B. 110a and see also Ch.Z. Taubes, *'Otzar ha-Ge'onim*, p. 438, on TbSanh. 76b.

Especially in the early literature of the Second Temple Period, one finds emphasis on endogamous marriage with relatives. See S. Safrai, in: *The Jewish People in the First Century*, ed. S. Safrai a.o., II, Assen / Amsterdam 1976, p. 754. In the rabbinic period, there was no explicit emphasis placed on endogamy, but a marriage with the daughter of a sister was considered highly commendable. Along with TbJeb. 62b and TbSanh. 76b, cf. also TosQid. I,4 and MNed. VIII,7 and IX,10. This is all in contradiction to the Damascus Sect (*Damascus-scroll*, V), Samaritans, Christians, and Karaites. See S. Krauss in: *Studies in Jewish Literature in Honour of K. Kohler*, Berlin 1913, pp. 165–175, and see C. Rabin, *Qumran Studies* (Scripta Judaica 2), Oxford 1957 pp. 91–92.

The reason for the custom of marrying the daughter of a sister is that the natural love for relatives, added to the love between a man and a woman, provides a guarantee for a strong marriage. See *Maggid Mishneh* on Rambam, *Jad*, Hil. 'Issur. Bi'ah, II, 14. Another reason, which has already been encountered in TbB. B. 110a, is the observation that there was a special relationship between an uncle and a niece on the basis of popular perception that many children bear a resemblance to the brother of the mother. Cf. also Ch. Z. Taubes l.c. In *Seph. Hasidim* (ed. R. Margaliot, Jerusalem 1957 = version Bologna) § 485, p. 331, there is additional mention of the superstition that on the basis of that relationship, the children of the sister will have the same good and moral characteristics as their mother's brother. Rashi in his commentary on TbJeb. 62a explains that the stimulus applies only with respect to the daughter of the sister, because she is just as dear to the brother as his sister. The love between brothers is less in general, so the rule does not apply with respect to the daughter of a brother. Through Rab Sherira Gaon we know of the explanation that a marriage with the daughter of a brother is undesirable because it is irreconcilable with the duty regarding marriage with a levir, as the brother would die without sons. This is a remarkable argument, considering that the rabbis have interpreted 'ben' in Dt. 25:5 to mean 'child' and not only 'son'. See MJeb. II,5 and TbJeb. 22b and other sources. In the case of a daughter, then, the marriage with a levir is not possible. See on the whole question in *Seph. Hasidim*, ed. R. Margaliot, notes to a statement of Rabbi Jehudah ha-Hasid, p. 16, § 21, note 32; see also *Tosaphists* on TbJeb. 99a). According to some Rishonim, however, marriage with the daughter of a brother also deserves preference (cf. *Tosaphists* on TbJeb. 62b and *Maggid Mishneh* on Rambam, *Jad*, Hil.'Issur. Bi'ah, II, end. In the Testament of Rabbi Jehudah ha-Hasid, *Seph. Hasidim* l.c.) we already find the opinion that a marriage with the daughter of one's brother or sister is not to be permitted because of danger of genetic degeneration (see the sources mentioned).

18. **Concerning some one who acknowledges (the righteousness of his sentence) in sincerity and concerning those who repent in uprightness and who receive those who repent and who teach them not to return immediately to their (former) transgressions, Scripture declares: 'Then shall your light break forth as the morning' (Is. 58:8).**

See the different manuscript readings, such as the reading 'ha-megajjerim' or 'ha-mitgajjerim' (see *Reshit Hokhmah*) with the meaning ' those who proselyte wholeheartedly'. See also the reading 'ha-menahagin' ('those who lead the community with righteousness'). According to the content of the reading 'ha-matzdiq 'et ha-din' ('he who wholeheartedly accepts the judgement passed on him') would be very appropriate here. The words ''et ha-din' after an expression like 'ha-matzdiq' are sometimes absent. The term 'ha-matzdiq' may therefore be read as 'ha-matzdiq 'et ha-din'. Those who accept the judgement and repent wholeheartedly comprise an appropriate unit. Cf. also M. Ginsberg, in: *The Minor Tractates of the Talmud*, ed. A. Cohen, II, p. 450. The reading in manuscripts 'ha-mitwaddin' (who confess) point in the same direction!

A condition for a sincere and unreserved repentance is sincere and unreserved acceptance of punishment imposed or of the negative consequences of a deed as punishment. The second step in the process of repentance is turning away from the transgression in order to prevent it from being repeated. Cf. also M'Abot I,8 after the transgressor has accepted the judgement passe upon him and punishment in sincere repentance, he is then at once to be treated as an innocent.

19. **Concerning those who judge in righteousness, who reprove in truth, who perform (their duties in) cleanness and who are pure of heart, Scripture declares: 'Surely God is good to Israel, to the pure of heart' (Ps. 73:1).**

*Danin be-Tzedeq*. This may refer to the thoroughness of judicial investigation previous to reaching a judgment. Another notion to be expected in the realm of literature concerning 'derekh 'eretz' concerns the necessity to combine justice with compassion and justice with love in the trial process as much as possible. In this connection see Dt. 1:16 and II Sam. 8:15 and the discussion concerning those passages in TbSanh. 6b and parallels. See also TbSanh. 7b (ed. A. Steinsalz, "ijjunim' on p. 33).

*We-'osei tehorah* (*who perform cleanness*). See the interpretation of M. Higger, *Massekhtot Derekh 'Eretz*, p. 107: 'Who prepare food on accordance with Levitical precautions.' Cf. statements in TosDem. III,1; TbBer. 19a; TbGit. 62a and other sources. See also in the translation of M. Ginsberg, in: *The Minor Tractates of the Talmud*, ed. A. Cohen, p. 540: 'Who perform (their daily tasks) in a state of (ritual) cleanliness.' In this context of D. E., however, one expects more metaphorical meaning. In the Tenakh the stem 'tahar' ('tahor') already bears a moral meaning. See e.g. Num. 5:28; Prov. 15:26, 20:9, 30:12; Ps. 51:9.12. For the expression 'bar lebab' (*pure of heart*) see Ps. 24:4; Ps. 73:1 and cf. Waj. Rab. XVII,1.

20. **Concerning those who sigh, who grieve, who look forward to salvation, who mourn for Jerusalem, Scripture declares: 'To appoint unto them that mourn in Zion to give them a garland for ashes' (Is. 61:3).**

Since the destruction of the Temple in the year 70 C. E. (and possibly since the destruction of the First Temple in Babel; cf. Is. 61:3), there have constantly been small groups which regularly fasted and mourned over the destruction of the Temple. Cf. TosSot. XV,11 and TosB. B. II,17 and TbB. Q. 59a and

TbB. B. 60b; Pes. Rab. XXXIV; Midr. Teh. 137 (ed. S. Buber, §6, 262b); Jalq., Is., r. 504 and Jalq., Ps, r. 885.

This statement evokes a special association with the expressions as well as the content of the statement about those who mourned for Zion (cf. Is. 61:3) in Pes. Rab., XXXIV (Jalq, Is., l.c.), where special emphasis is also placed upon daily praying in anticipation of salvation. Cf. also S. E. R., XIX, ed. M. Friedmann, pp. 110 and 112 in connection with the term 'metzaphim li-jeshu'ah' ('who look forward to salvation').

No relationship, however, can be clearly demonstrated with those who mourned for Zion from the Pesiqta. Similar groups have existed since the fall of the Temple. In light of this, a dating of the period of those who mourned for Zion from the Pesiqta is certainly of no decisive importance for the dating of the passage here in D. E. Cf. A. Goldberg, *Frankfurter Judaistische Studien*, *Erlösung durch Leiden*, Frankfurt am Main 1978, p. 131 ff., in connection with various hypotheses concerning such dating.

### 21. Concerning those who are merciful, who feed the hungry and who give drink to the thirsty, who clothe the naked and who distribute alms, Scripture declares: 'Say to the righteous that it shall be right with him' (Is. 3:10).

In relation to this passage, see the Scripture passage quoted here in the context of TbQid. 40a: 'Say the righteous, when he is good...' (Is. 3:10). The righteous one who is good is one who is good to Heaven and who is good to man. The second part of the quotation, implied in the quotation here in D. E., is important: 'that they shall eat the fruit of their doings.' The lending of various kinds of support summed up here to one's neighbour will immediately yield fruits to the righteous. This positive social attitude and the immediate positive response to this comprise an immediate reward. Cf. also the tradition about actions, the fruits of which one already enjoys in this world, in MPe'ah I,1; TosPe'ah I,1; TbShab. 127a; cf. Siphrei Dt., pisqa 324; A. R. N. [a], XL (60b) and other sources.

### 22. Concerning the meek [other reading: the poor], the bashful, the humble of spirit, those who are yielding to subscription into public service and those who have faith (in the divine promises), Scripture says: 'And you shall decree a thing and it shall be established unto you. A light shall shine upon your ways' (Hiob 22:28).

See other manuscripts here in D. E. with the reading "onijjim' (the poor) instead of "anawim' (the meek). The reading of *the meek* in the basis manuscript appears at first glance to concur more with the concepts mentioned in the passage. See, however, the combination in Is. 66:2: 'Poor and humble of spirit'. It is difficult to be absolutely certain about the best reading, all the more so in specific early Tannaitic milieu in which the notions of 'onijjim' (the poor) and 'anawim' (the meek) were felt to be very closely related. The wording in this passage is most likely very old! See, in connection with that, D. Flusser, in: *Israel Exploration Journal*, X (1960), p. 1 ff. It would be obvious to assume that "anawim' was mistakenly written in stead of "onijjim', considering that 'jod' and 'waw' are easily interchanged in manuscripts.

*Nohim la-tishhoret* (*yielding to subscription*). See also D.E.Z. II, 15 (cf. M'Abot III,12 and other sources), we have chosen for the explanation of this term as follows: the forms of forced labour imposed by Roman authorities, i.e., the conscription of young men. See also other possible explanations in the commentary with reference to the expression in D.E.Z. l.c.

*Ba'alei habtahah* (*who have faith*). In connection with this expression cf. Mekh. de-R. Jishm., Jitro, par. 2 (ed. M. Friedmann, 60a) in reference to Ex. 18:21: 'Ba'alei 'abtahah' are 'men of truth'; 'haters of profit' refers to those who are reverse to taking money in trial. / The expression 'ba'alei habtahah' refers primarily to people who place trust in divine promises (see *Dictionary*, ed. M. Jastrow, sub 'habtahah') and therefore do not aim for earthy gain, and who manage to bear losses, relying on the divine promises of the World to Come. Cf. also in a statement by Rabbi 'El'azar ha-Mode'i in the direct continuation in the Mekh. l.c.: 'Brave men' ("anshei hail' = men of strength or as explained also in the Mekh. l.c. rich men) that is 'ba'alei 'abtahah'./ Cf. also the use of the term 'habtahah' in Ber. Rab. LXXVI,2: 'The righteous do not rely on (promises for) This World' Cf. especially D.E.Z. II, 10 and the commentary there.

An explanation of the expression 'ba'alei (h)abtahah' in the sense of trust in divine promise can be linked here in D.E. with the appeal for patience with occupying authorities, for humility, and for tolerance of poverty. The expression 'ba'alei habtahah' was obviously already known in the time of Rabbi 'El'azar ha-Mode'i, a student of Rabbi Johanan ben Zakkai. The passage in D.E. possibly sheds more light on this expression as a reference to people who refrain from publicly resisting the occupying authorities. Rabbi Johanan ben Zakkai and some of his followers are known for their aversion to confronting the Roman authorities. The truly brave men and heroes are they who manage to bear their fate and trust on divine promises.

**23. Concerning those who take pains for the Torah, who learn Torah for its own sake, who take every opportunity to perform the commandments and who watch anxiously at the doors of the temples (i.e. at the doors of the houses of study and prayer) Scripture says: 'Happy is the man that hearkens to me, watching daily at my gates, waiting for the posts of my doors' (Prov. 8:34).**

*Heikhalot* (*temples*) refers to houses of prayer. Only in Jalq. ha-Makh. do we find a parallel. There we find in addition to the passage a deviating quotation which actually belongs to the passage immediately following.

24. **Concerning those who pursue righteousness, who seek peace for their people, who share in the sufferings of the community and who stand by them in the hour of their distress, Scripture says: 'The Lord is good, a stronghold in the day of trouble. And He knows them that take refuge in Him' (Nah. 1:7).**

25. **On account of four things an eclipse of the sun takes place: on account of a president of the Court who died and was not mourned according to the halakhah, on account of a betrothed maiden who cried out aloud (for help) in the city (when someone tried to rape her) and when there came none to rescue her, on account of a man who lies with a man, on account of two brothers whose blood was shed at the same time.**

This passage concurs with a baraita mentioned in TbSuk. 29a. In a number of manuscripts, there is the addition of a related baraita which we find in TosSuk. II,5. Human transgressions diminish the light streaming from heavenly bodies. The traditions according to which the sun and the moon do not want to shed their lights because of human transgressions are known. Cf. Waj. Rab. XXXI,9; Midr. Teh. 19,11 and TbNed. 39b; Num. Rab. XVIII,16,20; Jalq., Jo., r. 538 and Jalq., Ps. r. 673, and other sources.

26. **On account of four things the money of householders is confiscated by the government: on account of (keeping) documents (of indebtedness) that are payed (in the hope of claiming payment again), on account of those who lend money on interest, on account of those who withhold the payment of a hired labourer, on account of some one who has the power to protest (against wrongdoing) and who does not protest and on account of those who mark out (sums of money) for charity in public, but do not give it (actually).**

This passage is based on a baraita in TosSuk. II,5. As was the case with the immediately preceding passage, the text of D. E. is most closely related to the reading in TbSuk. 29a.

*On account of documents that are payed*, i. e. on account of those who keep in their possession bills of indebtedness which have already been settled, in the hope of claiming payment once again. Cf. Rashi on TbSuk. l.c.

*Who lend money on interest.* It is forbidden for a Jew to lend money to another Jew on interest (cf. Ex. 22:24; Lev. 25:35−37 and Dt. 23:20−21; Ez. 18:11−13.

*The power to protest.* See especially Rashi in connection with TbSuk. l.c. Only the 'householders', i. e. the well-to-do and owners of real property, had the opportunity, because of their wealth, to protest against transgressions within the community (especially in order to protect the weak against injustice). Attention was paid especially to them. Cf. here e.g., the tradition in TbShab. 55b, where nearly the same statement is used in connection with Pinhas, who had not warned Hophni and thus was also found guilty: 'because it was possible to Pinhas to protest to Hophni, but he did not'. Because of their position of power, householders had the ability to put others in society in disadvantage as well as to support the community, especially through act of charity. If they abused their position, it was considered appropriate to punish them by confiscating their positions (according to the rule 'middah ke-neged middah').

The practical background of this passage is undoubtedly the fact that the behaviours mentioned gave others the impression that someone had merely increase his possessions and spent nothing. In addition to the fact that someone who did not devote himself to the good of the community consequently became unpopular. It was conceivable that someone who was was guilty of that could attract attention from the treasury and be accused of tax evasion, in which case all his possessions were confiscated (cf. e.g., TbPes. 112b).

**27. On account of four things the properties [of householders] fall to the state treasury: on account of those who delay the payment of a hired labourer, on account of those who take the yoke from their neck and place it on the back of their fellowmen and (the sin) haughtiness of spirit is counterbalancing them all (i.e. this sin is as heavy as all the things mentioned together).**

This passage is found in TbSuk. 29b but is not found in the context of TosSuk. l.c.

*Tamjon (treasury)*, i.e. the Roman treasury (Greek: tameion).

*Kobesei sakhir (who delay the payment)*. Rashi on TbSuk. l.c. explains this term to refer to those who postpone payment of their hired servants, as oppose to "osheqei sakhir', explained as referring to those who deny the duty to pay (their hired servants). See also *Maharasha* on TbSuk. l.c., who explains "osheqei sakhir' to mean those who reduce payment under the pretence of unclear arrangements. This distinction is somewhat artificial, though, as both terms carry the meanings mentioned (cf. Lev. 19:13 and Dt. 24:14).

*Poreqei 'ol (who remove the yoke)*. This expression refers to people who individually shirked the duty to pay taxes, thereby additionally burdening the rest of the community since it was required in the various tax districts that a certain amount of money in taxes be collected. Tax evasion was very common in 'Eretz Jisra'el (see e.g., TosSot. V,7; MNed. III,4; TbB.B. 127b and TbB.Q. 113a). If someone was discovered to the guilty of tax evasion, his possession were confiscated (cf. also TosMa'as. Shen. III,8).

*Gassut ha-ruah (Haughtiness of spirit)*. An arrogant attitude is seen as counterbalancing all transgressions mentioned in this passage. In connection with the nature of that wording, cf. MPe'ah I,1 and TosPe'ah I,1–2 and parallels. An arrogant attitude, refusal to help the poor, and the placement of one's burdens upon other people could draw the attention of others (and thus treasury) to one's wealth. In connection with that cf. TjNed. IX,3 [41c].

The passage is understandable in light of the fear of fiscal agents and malicious informers from the ranks of the Jewish community. This situation was typical in the early centuries of the era of 'Eretz Jisra'el. Cf. especially the commentary on D. E. R. I,1, sub 'mesorot'.

**28a.  Rabbi Jehudah ben Dostai [better reading: Rabbi Dostai ben Rabbi Jehudah] said: 'Always contend with the wicked and do not envy those who work unrighteousness, for it is said: "They that forsake the Law praise the wicked' (Prov. 28:4).'**

In the basis manuscript, Rabbi Jehudah ben Dostai is named as the author. In other manuscripts, we find mentioned: Rabbi Dostai ben Rabbi Jehudah. [In TbMak. 7a, a Tanna with the name of Jehudah ben Dostai is mentioned as speaking in the name of Shim'on ben Shetah, cf., however, R. Rabbinovicz, *Seph. Diqduqei Sopherim*, on TbMak. l.c.; in the manuscripts, we find a better reading: 'Rabbi Dostai ben Jehudah' in name of Rabbi Shim'on; see also A. B. Hyman, *Toledot Tanna'im we-'Amora'im*, I, repr. Jerusalem 1964, p. 325 and see the parallel in TosSanh. III,11 with the reading Dostai ben Jehudah. Cf. in TbB. Q. 83b a statement in the name of 'Rabbi Dostai ben Jehudah' and the reading in manuscripts of 'Rabbi Jehudah ben Dostai'.]

The better reading in D. E. is also undoubtedly 'Rabbi Dostai ben Jehudah', a Tanna from the fifth generation and a pupil of Rabbi Shim'on. In the parallel of our statement here in D. E. R., Rabbi Dostai ben Rabbi Mattun is mentioned as the author (see TbBer. 7b). The use of 'tanja' must clearly refer to a Tannaitic tradition (cf. also TbMeg. 6b and see W. Bacher, *Die Aggadah der Tannaiten, II*, repr. Berlin 1965, p. 391; he prefers the reading Rabbi Dostai ben Jehudah as in D. E.!). The reading 'Rabbi Dostai ben Jannai' in a manuscript of D. E. must be the result of an incorrect interpretation of an abbreviation.

The reading in D. E. *always contend with the wicked* is much sharper than in TbBer. l.c.: 'it is permitted to contend with the wicked'.

**28b.  And should a man whisper to you: '(But is it not written:) "Do not contend with evildoers, neither envy those that work unrighteousness" (Ps. 37:1).' Turn off your hand (i. e. do not contend longer) and say to him: "'contend not with evildoers"' (means:) in performing evil deeds, "neither envy them" (means:) to act like the workers of unrighteousness.'**

Haphekh jadekha (*turn off your hand*). Cf. I Kings 22:34 and II Kings 9:23 as reference to turning the reins and withdrawing oneself from battle. It is possible to render the expression here in D. E. with: 'turn away from him with the words...'

29. **Above (in Heaven) there is no sitting, no eating, no drinking [no sleeping] no procreation, no enmity, no hatred, no envy, no rivalry, no obduracy, no weariness and no hindrance.**

In TbBer. 17a, Rab is mentioned as passing on the related tradition. From parallels, it appears that 'lema'alah' (*above*) means 'the world of the angels'. In the parallel TbBer. 17a (and other parallels) it is remarkable that "olam ha-ba' (the World to Come) is represented in exactly the same way (the term "olam ha-ba' can also refer to the life after death, to the world of spirits). There is only stated additionally that, in the World to Come, the righteous will be provided with honour and they will sit together, enjoying the glory of the Shekhinah. In the listing, then 'there is no sitting' is left out.

In the most direct parallels of this passage, one does not find the version of D. E. but rather the version concerning the World to Come as in TbBer. 17a (cf. A. R. N. [a] I, (3a); Mas. Kal. Rab., ed. N. N. Coronel, 4a; S. E. Z. XIX, ed. M. Friedmann, p. 26; and Jalq., Ber., r. 111. Only Jalq. Re'ub., Naso (end) has the same version as in D. E. concerning the world above. Cf. e.g. Ber. Rab. LXV,2 and TjBer. I,1 [2c] in relation to 'there is no sitting' and the world of angels (see also D. Halperin, *The faces of the Chariot*, Tübingen 1988, pp. 149–150) and see the following passage here in D. E. Probably this passage in D. E. R. II,28 belongs to a mystical milieu and forms a mystification of old traditions about the World to Come.

In D. E. R. the tradition known from TbBer. 17a was probably used. There are, incidentally, very old traditions concerning the differences between the world of humans and the world of angels with some concurring elements. Cf. especially P. Schäfer, *Rivalität zwischen Engelen und Menschen*, Berlin /New York 1975, especially p. 51 ff. In connection with the preference of the reading in agreement with TbBer. 17a over the reading in D. E., see M. Higger, *Massekhtot Ze'irot*, p. 23. There M. Higger calls the reading in D. E. defective. In reference to the version concerning the World to Come there is the problem that there is discussion in yet other traditions of a meal in the World to Come for the righteous (cf. e.g., TbKet. 111b and TbB. B. 75a) and even of procreation (see TbShab. 30b). The term "olam ha-ba', however, sometimes refers to the Messianic Age. In the gemara of Massekhet Kallah Rab. l.c., the solution is sought in a difference between the World of Souls and the situation after the resurrection after the Messianic Age. In other traditions there is mention of angels and righteous people who feed from the glory radiating from the Shekhinah.

30. 'Give ear you heaven and I will speak' (Dt. 32:1), This is (in accordance
with) what David the king of Israel has said: 'He made darkness His hiding
place, places surrounding Him (His shelter)' (Ps. 18:12). In reference to
Whom did David speak this verse? He only spoke it with reference to the
Holy One blessed be He and he praised Him that He is Ruler in His high
place [in His world], that He is unique, that He is One, and that His Name is
One and that He dwells in three hundred and ninety heavens, that His
Name and attributes are inscribed upon each one of the heavens and that in
each one of them are ministering angels, Ophanim, Seraphim, Cherubim,
celestial spheres and the Throne of Glory. You must not wonder at this
thing, for behold a king of flesh and blood has many habitations, one for
warm weather and another for cold weather, and you must take a view of it,
how much more (this holds true of) the king of Worlds to whom all things
belong.

As long as Israel performs the will of the All Present, He dwells in
'Arabot, the seventh heaven, and He does not remove from them in any
way, for it is said: 'From between the two Cherubim, and He spoke unto
him' (Num. 7:89). But in the our of wrath He ascends and stays in the
upper-Heavens and all people cry and weep, but their voice is not heard and
they decree fast-days and roll themselves in dust, cover themselves with
sackcloth and shed tears.

The words of Dt. 32:1 are the introductory words of the final portion of this
pereq. With respect to the section following these words see S. Krauss, in:
*R. E. J.*, XXXVI (1898). S. Krauss remarks that the style indicates correspondences with mystical words from the period of the Ge'onim. Direct parallels are
to be found in later sources, not before the tenth century. Dt. 32:1 is connected
to Ps. 18:12 (II Sam. 22:12) and a mystical massage contained within that
passage. In the passage Ps. 18:12, the basis manuscript mentions one word
more than in other manuscripts. The Masoretic punctation in Ps. 18:12 places
the cesura as follows 'jashet hoshekh sitro...' ('He made darkness His hiding
place'), cf. however, II Sam. l.c. where another cesura is used, because the
word 'sitro' is missing there. No meaning must be attached to the more exten-
ded quotation in the basis manuscript, because (as in II Sam.) the word 'sitro'
has probably also been omitted.

*Three hundred ninety firmaments.* This number is based on gematria. In
Hebrew the number value of the word 'shamajim' (Heaven) is 390.

*As long as...* Here is recorded also the tradition of seven heavens, which is
mentioned in TbHag. 12b and attributed to Resh Laqish. In A. R. N. [a]
XXXVII (55b), Rabbi Me'ir is mentioned as the authority of this passage. Cf.
also S. A. Wertheimer, *Battei Midreshot*, II (*Pereq Ra'ajot Jehizqe'el*). Accor-

ding to W. Bacher, *Die Agada der Tannaiten*, II, p. 65, note 3, the reading
'Rabbi Me'ir' is preferable, certainly in combination with a statement by Rabbi
Jehudah, such as in TbHag. 12b. The reading 'Rabbi 'Eli'ezer', such as in Deb.
Rab. II,32 and in Midr. Teh. 114 (ed. S. Buber, § 2, 236a) and the reading
'Rabbi Jirmejahu ben 'Eli'ezer' in Jalq., 'Eqeb, r. 855 are, according to W. Ba-
cher, based on wrongly interpreted abbreviation which really refers to Rabbi
Me'ir.

According to the opinion of G. Scholem, the idea of the existence of seven
heavens had evolved very early from the idea of three heavens. The various
concepts of 'heaven' in the Scriptures probably support that. In IV Ezra
VII,89−90, there is already development of the idea of seven heavens in the
description of the seven stadia, through which the soul passes in the afterlife.
See G. Scholem, *Major Trends*, repr. London 1954, p. 54, in reference to
*Ascensio Isaiah*. The basis of the tradition in D. E. is thus very old.

The notion that God retires to higher realms because of human transgressions is undoubtedly connected to older rabbinic traditions, according to which
the Shekhinah retired up from earth to the seventh heaven because of human
transgressions since the generation of Adam onwards. Cf. e.g. Ber. Rab.
XIX,7; Midr. Shir ha-Shir. Rab. V (beginning); Bam. Rab. XIII,2; Tanh.
Jash., Pequdei, § 6; Tanh. Jash., Naso, § 16; Pes. Rab., V, ed. M. Friedmann,
18b.

In this later mystical tradition here in D. E., Gods lowest station – if Israel
commits no transgressions – is in the seventh heaven (clearly a more mystical
representation). It is remarkable, however, that Gods presence between the
wings of the Cherubim on the cover of the Holy Ark is mentioned along with the
argumentation. This is, as we may assume, the consequence of the original
representation in the midrash in which the Shekhinah retires from earth to the
seventh heaven. In early sources as Waj. Rab. XXIX, 11 and others it is said
that the seventh heaven is God's most esteemed residence.

# Pirqei Ben 'Azzai

## *Derekh 'Eretz Rabbah, chapter III*

**1a. Ben 'Azzai said: Whoever lays the following four things to heart and set them before his eyes will never commit a sin again: Whence he came, whither he goes and who will be his judge [and what will become of him in the future].**

**1b. Whence he came? From a place of darkness and gloom. Whither he goes? To a place of darkness [and gloom]. (Another tradition:) whence he came? From a place of uncleanness. And whither he goes? To cause others to be unclean. (Another tradition:) whence he came? From fetid moisture and from a place where the eye cannot see. And whither he goes? To the netherworld and a place of destruction [other reading: to be judged] in Gehinnom and to be burnt by fire. Who will be his judge? This will not be of flesh and blood but the Lord of all works blessed be He [before Whose face there exists no injustice, no forgetfulness, no partiality and no taking of bribes]. And what will become (of him) in the future? Dust, worms and maggots, for it is said: 'How much less man, that is worm, and (the son of man that is) maggot.' (Hiob. 25:6).**

'Aqabja ben Mehalal'el (an early Tanna from the period preceding the fall of the Second Temple) must be considered as the authority for this statement, which is based on the tradition in M'Abot III,1. In the original version three things are listed. In the versions in A. R. N. [a], XIX (35a) and A. R. N. [b], XXXII, (35a/b), four things are listed, whereby the words *and what will become of him in the future* appear in addition to *and whither he goes*.

The beginning of the basic text in D. E. (1a) is inconsequent in that it mentions that there are four things but lists only three. With the aid of the other manuscripts, we must add the words *and what will become of him in the future*. See M. Higger, *Massekhtot Ze'irot*, pp. 13 and 34. All of chapter III in D. E. R. is supposed to have been borrowed from the traditions in A. R. N. [a].

In D. E. R., there could have been an error concerning the authority (according to the opening words of D. E. R. III: Ben 'Azzai), because the chapter is not beginning with a statement of Ben 'Azzai but with the statement of 'Aqabja ben Mahalal'el, which was connected with the death of Rabbi 'Eli'ezer (see the further context here in D. E. R.). From A. R. N. [a] XXV, it is clear that statements of Ben 'Azzai were mentioned in an original connection with the story of the death of Rabbi 'Eli'ezer, thus giving rise to the error. Cf. also M. Gaster, *Seph. ha Ma'asiot*, New York 1968, § 126, pp. 86–87, and introduction, p. 34.

The parallels based on D. E. have taken over the four sections, and they mention Ben 'Azzai as the authority. According to one tradition, going back to Rabbi Levi, 'Aqabja ben Mehalal'el's statement is based on an interpretation of Qoh. 12:1: 'Remember your Maker in the days of your youth.' Here the word 'Bore'akha' (your Maker) is interpreted as 'Be'erekha' (your Source, your Origin) and as 'Borekha' (your Tomb) and as 'Bore'akha' (your Maker and your Judge). See TjSot. II,2 [18a] and parallels.

Concerning the elaboration of the saying of 'Aqabja ben Mehalal'el, the different parallels provide various options. *Whence he came* is explained differently in D. E. R. and in the versions of A. R. N. In D. E. as *from a place of darkness*. In A. R. N. [a], XIX (35a) with an addition: 'Rabbi Shim'on says: "He comes from a place of darkness and he returns to a place of darkness. He comes from a stinking drop, from a place where the eye cannot see."' In A. R. N. [b], XXII (35a-b) we find these additions: 'Rabbi Shim'on ben 'El'azar says: "⟨from where he comes⟩ means from a place of fire and he returns to a place of fire, ⟨from where he comes⟩ means from a place beyond and he returns to a place beyond, ⟨from where he comes⟩ means from a place where no creature's eye can see, ⟨from where he comes⟩ means from a place of uncleanness and he returns (to such a place) and makes others unclean."' In these versions we see a further application of the statement in polemic against gnostics, who seek the essence of man in the soul, which was born of pure light and returns to pure light. The body is considered to be inferior and to be the work of the demiurge. We find that the version in M'Abot is already in some way to be interpreted as an antignostic reaction. No distinction is made between body and soul, and the entire person is made responsible for his deeds. We consider the version in M'Abot, which is less clearly polemic than the versions in A. R. N., to be original. The additions in A. R. N. [b] l.c., ascribed to Rabbi Shim'on ben 'El'azar, comprise a clear remembrance of Gnostic concepts against which the polemic is directed. See S. Lieberman, *Tosephta Ki-Pheshutah*, V, pp. 1292–1293. According to S. Lieberman the original reading is according to which a man goes to a place of maggots and worms. This answer, which originally accompanied *and whither he goes* is placed in D. E. R. and in A. R. N. after the additional words *and what will become of him in the future*.

The quotation of Hiob 25:6 in the basis manuscript of D. E. R. is incomplete and must be corrected. See eventually the manuscript in A. Epstein, *Beiträge zur jüdische Altertumskunde*, I, 1887, p. 113 ff.; see also A. R. N. [a], XIX (35a), notes of ed. S. Schechter, where Rabbi Natan is mentioned as the authority in stead of Ben 'Azzai.

**2. Rabbi Shimʿon said: (A man is full of) worms during his life and (full of) maggots when he is dead. Worms during his life, these are vermin. Maggots when he is dead, this is what swarms when he is dead.**

The statement ascribed here in D.E. to Rabbi Shimʿon is ascribed in A.R.N. [a], XIX (35b) and in Mas. Kal. Rab. (ed. N.N. Coronel, 11b) to Rabbi ʾEliʿezer ben Jaʿaqob. In fact, the name Shimʿon must be associated with the statement following (D.E.R. III,3), which in A.R.N. [a] l.c. is ascribed to Rabbi Shimʿon ben ʾElʿazar! See M. Higger, *Massekhtot Zeʿirot*, p. 34, where he states that he prefers the reading of ʾEliʿezer ben Jaʿaqob in A.R.N. l.c. over the reading of Rabbi Shimʿon in D.E.R.

The statement represents an explanation of Hiob 25:6 (cf. also Is. 14:11 and cf. Midr. Qoh. Rab. V,3). One finds a related statement in *Seph. Ben Sira* 10:9,11 (ed. M.Z. Segal, p. 61). *Seph. Ben Sira* 10:9: ʿhe whose body is full of maggots while he is still aliveʾ. See the explanation of M.Z. Segal on p. 62: he whose entrails rot even during his life. See *Seph. Ben Sira* 10:11: ʿWhen a man dies, he inherits worms and maggots, lice and creeping things.ʾ See especially the parallel in *Reshit Hokhmah* (Derekh ʾEretz, shaʿar II, beginning). Along with the inter-pretation of the words ʿshe-marhish be-motoʾ (ʿand what swarms when he is deadʾ) M. Ginsberg (in his translation of D.E.R. in: *The Minor Tractates*, ed. A. Cohen, p. 534) also suggests the possibility of interpreting the words as the fact that ʿhe feels the bite of the maggots even when he is dead.ʾ He refers to TbShab. 13b: ʿWorms are as painful to the dead as a needle in the flesh of the living.ʾ

**3. Rabbi ʾElʿazar [ben Jacob] said: ʿMan is comely and praise-worthy but brings forth (from his body) a hideous matter. To what can this be compared? To a large salon in the middle of which an outlet pipe of a tannery was fixed [whoever passes says: "How comely this salon would be if not an outlet of a tannery was fixed in the middle of it"]. So a man is comely and praiseworthy but he brings forth a hideous matter (and yet he is haughty)! If he would bring forth from his bowels foliatum or balsam or any other kind of aromatic spice, how much more would he pride himself over the (other) creatures.ʾ**

The better reading is ʿRabbi ʾEliʿezer ben Jaʿaqobʾ, as in a lot of manuscripts. In the wording of A.R.N. l.c., and in Mas. Kal. Rab. l.c. the order of the authorities of this saying and the preceding one is inverted (see also D.E.R. III,2). Here in D.E. Rabbi ʾElʿazar ben Jaʿaqobʾ is named as the authority. The reading in A.R.N. (cf. Mas. kal. Rab.) citing Shimʿon ben ʾEliʿezer as authority deserves preference. The reading in A.R.N. and Mas. Kal. Rab. is also preferable to the reading in D.E. in other respects. On the basis of these parallels, it is better to correct and read: ʿSo is man: if now (ʿwe ʿatta ʾimʾ) when he emits an un(be)coming thing (from his bowels) he prides himself (read: 'mitga'eh' instead of 'na'eh u-meshubah'), should he emit from his bowels foliatum, balsam or any other kind of aromatic spice, how much more would he pride himself over other creatures!'

The reading in D. E. is clearly secondary with respect to the reading in A. R. N. See also M. Higger, *Massekhtot Ze'irot*, p. 34. See the reading in A. R. N., ed. S. Schechter, hosaphah b of version [a], 79b, more related to the reading in D. E. R. h.l. Other manuscripts in D. E. read 'man is decorous and praiseworthy but emits an unbecoming thing *out of his mouth.*' This is an application of the statement as an admonition not to say indecent things. In the original statement, however, there was an unambiguous reference to the human intestinal tract and the habit of eliminating bodily waste (see especially the reading in Mas. Kal.Rab. which confirms this opinion). We therefore also prefer the reading in the basis manuscript without the addition of 'mippiw' ('out of his mouth'). In the mentioned quotation of *Seph. Ben Sira* 10:9ff., it is probable that an allusion was already made to the rotting process in the human intestines. 'Teraqlin' (*salon*) is the Greek 'triklinion'; 'pelaiton' is the Greek 'pholiaton' (*foliatum*), a pleasant smelling oil or salve made from leaves, especially from the leaves of the nard plant. See S. Krauss, *Lehnwörter*, II. ''Apharsamon' (*balsam*) is the Greek 'apobalsamon', sap from the balsam tree.

**4. When Rabbi 'El'azar ben 'Azarjah was about to die his disciples visited him and they sat down before him and said: 'Our master, teach us only one thing more.' He said to them: '[My children] what shall I teach you? Go and be careful for the honour of your fellow and when you stand up to pray, know before Whom you are standing and praying, for on that account you will enter into the life of the World to Come.'**

As in the other statements preceding in this chapter, it is apparent in D. E. that the bearer of the tradition has been incorrectly recorded. It is not Rabbi 'El'azar ben 'Azarjah but Rabbi 'Eli'ezer (ben Hyrkanos) who is really meant here. See the parallels and see W. Bacher, *Die Agada der Tannaiten*, I, p. 103ff.

The direct relationship established between respect for one's neighbour and respect for God (the latter in the specific form of 'kawwanah' during prayer) is remarkable. The emphasis on 'kawwa-nah' during prayer is typical for the Hasidic milieu. In this connection cf. TbBer. 32b. The emphasis on fear and/or love for God in direct connection with love and respect for mankind is distinctly characteristic of early sources. Cf. e.g., Jub. 36:4−8 and *Seph. Ben Sira* 27:30−28:7; Mark. 12:28−34; Luke 10:25−28 and see *Seph. Pitron Torah* (ed. E. E. Urbach, 1978, p. 79ff.); cf. Test. Dan 5:3 and Test. Iss. 5:2 and 7:6; A. R. N. [b] XXVI, and other sources. See especially D. Flusser, in: *H. T. R.*, LXI (1968), pp. 107−127.

The reading of the parallel in TbBer. 28b is more extensive. There one finds, in the middle of Rabbi ʾEliʿezer's answer, the following teaching: 'Keep your children from meditation (philosophical meditation?) and set them between the knees of scholars.'

The meaning of the words 'dabar ʾehad bi-lebad' (*only one thing*) is clarified by the reading in TbBer. 28b, where the disciples ask him to instruct them in the 'way of life', i.e., the manner in which to gain entrance into the World to Come. The reading in D.E.R. was not derived from the reading in the Babylonian Talmud, but is dependent on the tradition in A.R.N. [a] l.c. See also M. Higger, *Massekhtot Zeʿirot*, p. 34.

**5. Five things we have learnt from Rabbi ʾElʿazar [better reading: Rabbi ʾEliʿezer] when he was about to die, and we rejoiced over them more than we rejoiced (over them) during his life. They are: a ball, a shoe form, an amulet, tephillin and a round cushion are susceptible of uncleanness and one may immerse them (for purification) just as they are. Go and be careful (regarding those ordinances) for they are important ordinances [established ordinances], which were told to Moses on (Mount) Sinai.**
**[End of chapter]**

The Tradition in D.E.R. is derived from the tradition in A.R.N. [a], XIX (35b). The correct reading is 'Rabbi ʾEliʿezer (ben Hyrkanos), as in A.R.N.. With respect to Rabbi ʾEliʿezer's last words, the tradition in A.R.N. was transmitted by Rabbi ʾElʿazar ben ʿAzarjah. This may have led to the error in D.E.R. (see manuscripts) of considering the halakhot taught here as the final words of Rabbi ʾElʿazar ben ʿAzarjah. M. Higger (*Massekhtot Zeʿirot*, pp. 23−24) also feels the correct reading is the one that considers the statement to be the final words of Rabbi ʾEliʿezer (ben Hyrkanos). Cf. also Rashi and *Tosaphists* in reference to TbSanh. 68a; see A.R.N. [a], XXV. It is remarkable, however, that in TosKel. II,6 a portion of the halakhot belonging to Rabbi ʾEliʿezer's final words is attributed to Rabbi ʾElʿazar ben ʿAzarjah! Cf. also the clearly incorrect version in A.R.N. (ed. S. Schechter, hosaphah b, version [a], 79b) with: 'Rabbi ʾElʿazar ben ʿAzarjah spoke: Rabbi ʾElʿazar ben ʿAzarjah taught this five things.' The rendition there is not entirely correct, moreover it is (in reality) Rabbi ʾElʿazar who is passing the words of Rabbi ʾEliʿezer.

See also the version about the instruction by Rabbi ʾEliʿezer from his deathbed in A.R.N. [a], XXV (40b-41a), according to which tradition the lucidity and dignity with which Rabbi ʾEliʿezer answers halakhic questions just before his death provide proof for Rabbi ʾElʿazar ben ʿAzarjah that Rabbi ʾEliʿezer, although excommunicated, will have part in the World to Come. Cf, also J. Goldin, *The Fathers according to Rabbi Nathan*, p. 199 and Rashi and *Tosaphists* in reference to TbSanh. 68a.

A 'kaddur' is a *ball* , usually made of leather and filled with hair, wool or rags. An "immum'is a *shoe form* made of leather and filled with hair, wool or rags. In TbSanh. 68b there is discussion about a new, unworn shoe which is still on the 'immum' (last). Cf. MKel. XXVI,4. A 'Qamea' is an *amulet*, frequently in the form of a leather pouch containing magical herbs, written texts etc. A 'keset 'agulah'is a *round cushion*, often made of leather, used as pillow for the head while reclining during a meal.

Let us make a few observations about the halakhot taught by Rabbi 'Eli'ezer. All the objects mentioned have in common that they are made of leather and contain a hollow which can be filled. Considering that these objects do contain a hollow, but only a hollow in which to fill them up and which is normally not opened, there is a difference of opinion. Rabbi 'Eli'ezer claims that the (contents of) the objects mentioned can still become unclean, while the Sages claim that the objects cannot become unclean because they are usually closed. N. B. a leather utensil can only become unclean if it has a receptacle, i.e., a hollow in which something can be placed. Everyone agrees, however, that the things mentioned can become unclean if the leather cover is ripped open. The issue of discussion is whether the leather casing and its content are to be considered one thing in this case and that the object can be cleaned by immersion or weather the leather casing must be considered as a separate barrier between the object to be cleaned and the water, requiring that the water casing be removed in the cleaning process before immersing the contents. According to Rabbi 'Eli'ezer, the contents and casing comprise one and the same thing, and the object may be immersed in its entirely for cleaning. According to the Sages, however, the casing (which acts as barrier) must be removed first. See also *Nahalat Ja'aqob* on D. E. h.l. and see J. Goldin, o.c., p. 196, note 9 and see commentaries in connection with TbSanh. 68b.

*And we rejoiced over the more...* I.e., they rejoiced because his teaching, which had been rejected in his lifetime when he was excommunicated, was accepted when he lied on his deathbed.

*Halakhot gedolot (important ordinances)*. See TbSheb. 45a and TbB.M. 112b, where the term is explained as 'halakhot qebu'ot' (fixed laws), i.e., laws based on very old traditions. In the passage in A. R. N. [a], XXV (40b), we find the reading 'halakhot gedolot', while according to the reading in A. R. N. [a] XIX (35b) the words 'halakhot qebu'ot' are used.

## Derekh 'Eretz Rabbah, chapter IV

**1.  You should always be pleasant on entering and pleasant on leaving and you should spend little time to worldly affairs (business) and occupy yourself with the Torah.**

A definite correspondence with the wording in A. R. N. [a], XLI (65b−66a) is to be established here. As in comparison with contextual connections and wording in Mas. Kal. Rab. (ed. N. N. Coronel, 13a) we may suppose the following original connection (see also notes in S. Schechter's edition of A. R. N., l.c.). First, there is a statement: *Spend less time on worldly affairs (business) and occupy yourself with (the study of) the Torah*, along with the accompanying example of Rabbi Shim'on bar Jochai (mentioned in A. R. N. [a], l.c.). Secondly, there is the statement 'and submissive to the people of your house (only in Mas. Kal. Rab., l.c.), along with the story of Rabbi Shim'on ben 'El'azar as example (in D. E. R. and in A. R. N. [a] the statement is not mentioned but the story is). Thirdly, there is also the statement *You should always be pleasant on entering and pleasant on leaving (a house)*, along with the story of Rabbi Tarphon as example (mentioned in A. R. N. [a], XLI (67a), but in the wrong place). If we accept this hypothesis, the stories serve as examples for the statements (originally) preceding them.

*You should always be pleasing on leaving and entering* must then be explained with reference to the example of Rabbi Tarphon mentioned in A. R. N., and it must be explained as a duty to honour a bride by inviting her over, looking after her, and escorting her away. Without this specific example, one might wonder whether the statement refers to the duty to led an old, learned, or important person precede oneself out of respect upon entering and leaving a house, or one might wonder if the statement applies to the manner of greeting upon meeting and leaving a host etc. Accepting the hypothesis given also means that the original connection in both D. E. R. and Mas. Kal. Rab. and even in A. R. N. has not been preserved.

**2a.  It happened to Rabbi Shim'on ben 'El'azar, when he came from Migdal Gader ['Eder] from the house of his master and when he was leisurely riding on his ass along the seashore, that he changed upon a certain man who was extremely ugly. He said to him: 'How ugly are your works.' [another reading: 'How ugly are the sons of Abraham our father.' Or: 'Are all people of your city ugly like you?'] He replied to him: 'What can I do**

(about it), go and speak to the Craftsman Who made me.' Immediately he
(i. e. Rabbi Shim'on ben 'El'azar) dismounted from the ass, prostrated
himself before him and said to him: 'I humble myself before you, forgive
me.' He replied to him: 'I will not forgive you until you go to the Craftsman
Who made me and say to Him: 'How ugly are your works.' He followed him
[about] half a mile and more. When the people of his town heard [about his
arrival] they went out to meet him and spoke to him: 'Peace be with you
Rabbi.' He said to them: 'Who are you calling Rabbi?' They replied to him:
'Him who walks behind you.' He said to them: 'If it is him (you are calling
Rabbi) may there not be many like him in Israel!' They replied to him: 'God
forfend! What has he done to you?' And he said: 'This and so he has done to
me.' They said to him: 'Nevertheless, forgive him.' He said to them:
'Behold, I forgive him, but only on the condition that he will not act in the
same manner again.'

The following story of Rabbi Shim'on ben 'El'azar could be a more detailed
elaboration of the statement 'and be submissive to the people of your house',
which has been preserved only in the version in Mas. Kal. Rab. (ed.
N. N. Coronel, 13a). The same story, as an example of an attitude of tolerance,
is attributed in TbTa'an. 20a-b to Rabbi 'El'azar ben Rabbi Shim'on. See,
however, R. Rabbinovicz, *Diqduqei Sopherim*, a.l., I, p. 122 and other parallels to D. E. R. from which the correct reading appears to be 'Rabbi Shim'on
ben 'El'azar'. He was a contemporary of Rabbi Jehudah ha-Nasi and he was
problably the son of 'El'azar of Bartota. See Encyclopedia Iudaica XIV, col.
1554.

The location of the place 'migdal g"d"r' ('migdal '"d"r') is problematic. A
place with the name 'migdal 'Eder' is mentioned in Gen. 35:21−22 and has
been located to the area of Jerusalem. See B. Z. Segal, *Ha-Geographia ba-
Mishnah*, Jerusalem 1979, pp. 121−122. See also *E. J.*, XIV, p. 105. To the
contrary see W. Bacher, *Palestina*, p. 280 and see W. Bacher, *Die Agada der
Tannaiten*, II, p. 424, who identifies the place with Magdala on the Lake of
Tiberias, in explanation of the words "al shephat ha-jam' (*along the seashore*).
It is better to read 'Migdal Gadar' and to identify the place with Gadar(a) by the
Lake of Tiberias. See J. Goldin, *The fathers according to Rabbi Nathan*, p. 219,
note 9 and see B. Z. Segal, o.c., p. 57. Different places with that name have
existed. In this connection A. Neubauer, *La Géographie du Talmud*, repr.
Hildesheim 1967, pp. 243−244, mentions a place called 'Migdal Gador', where
there was a small river next to an important school. That would serve as an
excellent explanation of the reading "al shephat ha-nahar' ('along the river',
see TbTa'an. 20a-b and the manuscripts of D. E. R.) instead of the reading "al
shephat ha-jam' ('along the seashore').

In any case one might think of a place by the Lake of Tiberias. According to the basic manuscript the reading 'Migdal Gadar' deserves preference above 'Migdal 'Eder'. That reading remains problematic. The words 'kamah mekhu'arin ma'aseikha' (*how ugly are your works*), can perhaps be translated as 'how ugly are your deeds' (cf. M. Higger, *Massekhtot Derekh 'Eretz*, p. 61) and could be interpreted as evidence that Rabbi Shim'on ben 'El'azar incorrectly assumes a correspondence between the man's appearance and his deeds. The addition of the word 'reiqah' ('empty headed person') in manuscripts and parallels is evidence of the negative disposition of Rabbi Shim'on ben 'El'azar toward the ugly man. It is possible, however, to translate the term as 'in what ugly fashion you were made'. Cf. the opinion of M. Higger, *Massekhtot Ze'irot*, p. 24, who assumes that the author in D. E. has made use here of the tradition in TbTa'an. 20a-b.

**2b. And that same day Rabbi Shim'on sat (in the house of study) and expounded: A man should always be pliant like the reed and not hard (unyielding) like the cedar.**

**When the four winds of the world get up, the reed is bending with them hither and thither. When the winds die down it remains standing on its place. What is the ultimate fate of the reed? It will be found worthy to make a pen from it to write a Torah-scroll with it. But the cedar is not like that. When the North-west wind gets up [other reading: when all the winds of the world blow upon it, they cannot move it from its place but when the southern wind blows upon it] it uproots it and overturns it on its face. And the result is that it is standing on its roots (i. e. that it will be fully uprooted). [What is the ultimate fate of this cedar?] There will come demolishers [better reading: woodcutters] and carpenters and they will cut him and they will ceil their houses with it and what is left they will throw in the fire. Therefore the sages say: 'Be pliant like the reed and not hard (unyielding) like the cedar.'**

In TbTa'an. 20a-b and TbSanh. 105b-106a, the comparison of the cedar tree and the reed is mentioned in the framework of a statement by Rabbi Jonatan in connection with the curse of 'Ahijah the Shilonite and the blessing of Bileam the wicked. The tradition in D. E. has probably been derived from the tradition in the Talmud. In D. E. R., the comparison between the cedar and the reed has been put into the mouth of Rabbi Shim'on ben 'El'azar in connection with the preceding story about Rabbi Shim'on ben 'El'azar. N. B., in Mas. Kal. Rab. (ed. N. N. Coronel, 13a), the comparison appears anonymously after the story about Rabbi Shim'on ben 'El'azar. In the basis manuscript of D. E. R. and related parallels, the comparison of the cedar and the tree is widened with various elements. The Gaon of Vilna reconstructed the text in an interesting way: 'When the east, north, or west (as is normal) wind blows, the tree is partially uprooted at most, but if thouthern wind blows, then the tree is completely uprooted. Confirmation of the image yields the perception that a tree develops roots which help it to withstand normal winds such as the wind from the east in the winter, the wind from the west in the summer, and the wind from the north, which blows regularly. The tree may then be partially uprooted. Should (on a rare occasion) the wind blow from the south, against which the tree's roots structure has not grown to protect the tree, then the tree will be blown about. See in this connection the explanations of A. Steinsalz to TbSanh. 106a (ed. A. Steinsalz, II, p. 462). And in connection with the strength of the wind from the south, see Rashi in reference to TbB. B. 25b and TbGit. 31b). In light of the above mentioned explanation we give preference to a reading such as the one in TbTa'an. 20a-b. Cf. also the reading in A. R. N. [a], XLI (66a). The readings in the basis manuscript of D. E. R. and in Mas. Kal. Rab. are corrupt.

*Nimtza 'erez zeh she-'omed 'al shoreshaw* (*and the result is that it is standing on its roots*) is problematic at first glance and appears to be so from the different variants. In Ms. Oxford Bodleian, cat. A. Neubauer, no. 1100 perhaps provides a solution: 'This cedar is (finally) found thrown on its roots ('mushlah' in stead of 'she'omed'). Cf. also the reading in *Pirqei Rabbenu ha-Qadosh* in: ed. L. Grünhut, III, p. 88: 'muttal 'al shoreshaw' ('lifted up on its roots'). The words 'she 'omed 'al shoreshaw' so clearly mean that the tree's roots are no longer under ground, so that the tree may be considered as dead. See the commentary in reference to D. E. Z. VIII (beginning) in connection with the possible political implications of the original background of this comparison between the cedar and the reed.

*Soterin* (literally *demolishers*, wreckers). Another reading is 'kotetin' from 'katat' (to hammer, to pulverise). Another reading is 'sotetin' from 'satat' (to cut stone, to polish). Another reading 'koretin' (*woodcutters*). We choose here in D. E. the reading 'sotetin' (cf. also A. R. N. [a], l.c., and Mas. Kal. Rab., l.c.) with the meaning of 'woodworkers', *woodcutters*.

*Mekattetin*, which might be translated as *carpenters*. Cf. the reading and translation of M. Goldberg, *Derech Erez Rabba*, Breslau 1888, p. 6 with 'Zimmerleute' for the reading 'mesattetin'.

In connection with the choice of the reading 'sotetin' (*woodcutters*) the reading 'u-mesattetin 'oto' (*and they will cut it*, 'and they will work it') is not improbable. See the manuscripts in D. E. R. and see also the reading in A. R. N. [a] and in Mas. kal. Rab. l.c.

*And they will ceil (cover)*, can best be retained. See especially the extra addition in the reading in *Pirqei Rabbenu ha-Qadosh*: 'houses and a toilet' or 'houses and a toilet and a bathhouse' See ed.L. Grünhut, *Seph. ha-Liqqutim*, III, XI,3, p. 88 (cf. Ed. M. Higger, in: *Horeb* (1942) a. o.).

3a.  **How does a man honour his teacher? When both of them are on the
way he lets him (i. e. his teacher) walk on his right and does not let him walk
on his left.**

A norm of etiquette is given here. In TbJoma 37a, a related statement is
ascribed to Rab Jehudah. On the basis of TbHul. 91a and Rashi in connection
with Tb'Er. 54a, it appears that this statement concerns a baraita. Cf. Is. 63:12;
Ps. 109:31 and Ps. 110:,1,5; God walks on the right of man. It is an honour to
walk on someone's right side. The most religious duties are fulfilled with the
right hand, and the right hand is the symbol of power and protection. Cf. in
Tb'Er. 54a the story of the teaching of Moses and Aaron, who still sits on the
left of Moses when alone with him, because his teacher comes to sit to the right
of him (see on that passage the commentary by Rashi).

3b.  **When there are three (men walking together) [and with them is a sage]
the Rab [better reading: the sage] (goes) in the middle, the more important
(of the other two) on his right, and the less important on his left.**

This norm is also implied in the representation of the story about the teaching of
Moses in Tb'Er. 54b, from which it is apparent that the origin of the norms may
be sought in the milieu of the 'talmidei hakhamim'. After the sons of Aaron also
come in and heard their lesson from Moses, Aaron, who first sat to the left of
Moses, still sits to his left, while Eleazar sits to the right of Moses and Ithamar to
the left of him. Rabbi Jehudah criticized this representation of events and
remarked that Aaron always sat on the right of Moses when his sons were
present. Subsequently it is stated in the gemara that the opinion of Rabbi
Jehudah concurs with a baraita that the Rab walks in the middle with the more
important pupil to his right and the less important to his left. The statement
here in D. E. R. concurs with the baraita recorded in Tb'Er. 54b (cf. especially
also TbJoma 37a).

M. Higger, *Massekhtot Ze'irot*, points out that the original version would
have been 'we he-hakham be-'èmtza' ('and the *sage* in the middle), a reading
from 'Eretz Jisra'el as opposed to the Babylonian reading, in which 'hakham'
was replaced by 'rab' (teacher). According to this assumption, then, the basis
manuscript of D. E. R. has a Babylonian version. See especially the manuscripts of D. E. R. which read:' If there are three of them and a *sage* is among
them, then the sage walks in the middle...' This is supposed to have been the
original version of 'Eretz Jisra'el. Cf. also TjBer. V,4 [9c].

In connection with MJoma in TbJoma 37a ('the deputy high priest at his [the
high priest's] right and the head of the family at his left') a tradition corresponding to the statement in D. E. R. h. l. is recorded as a baraita. Following a
statement by Rab Jehudah: 'One who walks at his master's right is a boor'.
Remarkably Rab Jehudah's statement is explained in the discussion to mean

that in all situations, a student must walk to the left of his teacher, even when the teacher is accompanied by two students. This raises the problem that the tradition of Rab Jehudah does not concur with other traditions, according to which the more important student walks to the teacher's right and the less important one to the teacher's left, should they be together as three. This contradiction in the discussion about the tradition of Rab Jehudah is solved by assuming that it is implied in other traditions that the students actually walk somewhat behind their teacher and not alongside him. The tradition in D. E. R. offers a better solution here and shows that a distinction must be made between the situation in which a teacher is accompanied by only one student (as assumed in the tradition of Rab Jehudah) and the situation in which a teacher is with more than one student!

D.E.R. gives here a solution, which was not known in the in the context of this Babylonian Amoraic discussions!!!

3c. **And so we find in connection with the three angels who came to Abraham. They were: Gabriel, Michael and Raphael. Gabriel to overthrow Sodom [and Gomorrah], Raphael to heal Abraham and Michael to bring good tidings and to bless Sarah. Michael, now, was in he middle [,Gabriel on his right and Raphael on his left].**

The basis of this image given here of the three angels who visit Abraham must in all possibility be sought in old Targum traditions on the book of Genesis. It is explained that the three men in Gen. 18:2 (see Targ. Pseudo Jon.) are three angels, each with a separate task. One angel is to announce that a child will be born to Sarah, another is to save Lot and his family, and another is to bring destruction to Sodom and Gomorrah. In relation to that, a number of singular forms are explained further on. The words 'I will surely return to you this time next year' in Gen. 18:10 are explained to be the words of the angel who announces that a child will be born to Sarah. From Gen. 19:1 and 5, it appears that two angels are on their way to Sodom and Gomorrah. One of the angels clearly already had accomplished his task). One of the remaining angels is charged with the task of saving Lot and his family (cf. Gen. 19:21−22) and the other angel must destroy Sodom and Gomorrah (see Gen. 19:25; cf. especially the tradition as preserved in Tanh., Wa-Jera, ed. S. Buber, § 20; and Tanh. Jash., idem, § 8). Not until a later stage are these three angels identified as Michael (the messenger to Sarah), Gabriel (the angel of judgement, as the agent of the destruction of Sodom and Gomorrah), and Raphael as the rescuer of Lot and his family (cf. Ber. Rab. L,2).

It is possibly a later development that Raphael is attributed with the role of the healer of Abraham (no support for this quoted from scripture), while Michael and Gabriel retain the functions originally ascribed to them. Cf. TbB. M. 86a; Midr. ha-Gad. on Gen. 18:2, ed. M. Margulies, p. 291, and other sources. Actually according to those last traditions, the rescue of Lot and his family is not mentioned at all. This problem is mentioned in the gemara of TbB. M. l.c. (cf. Midr. ha-Gad. l.c.), and there is concluded that Michael must have two tasks and accompanies Gabriel in order to rescue Lot. See also the solutions suggested in Mas. Kal. Rab. (ed. N. N. Coronel, 13a).

The tradition that holds that the angels accomplish one task each probably belongs to the original form of the tradition (cf. targ. l.c.; Tanh. l.c.; Midr. ha-Gad. l.c. Later Raphael was attributed with the role of healer of Abraham, through which the tradition of Lot became a problem for which different solutions have been offered. In D. E. a remark about the rescue of Lot and his family has been completely omitted. The heart of the baraita here in D. E. R. we find in balanced form in TbJoma 37a without elaboration of the various tasks of the angels. Michael walks in the middle. According to a tradition ascribed to Rabbi Hijja (cf. Ber. Rab. XLVIII,10 (ed. J. Theodor / Ch. Albeck, p. 485); cf. Midr. ha-Gad. on Gen. 18:3 and cf. Midr. Leq. Tob ,ibid., and other sources), Michael is the angel whom Abraham addresses with the words 'My Lord, if I have found favour in your sight' (Gen. 18:3). Michael is addressed as the greatest of the three angels.

According to the tradition here in D. E. R., based on a tradition like the baraita in TbJoma 37a, Michael (as the most important) also, then, walks in the middle. Cf. also Dan. 10:21 and Dan. 12:1, where he is mentioned the prince of Israel. Gabriel, the angel of judgement, is second in order and thus, according to this tradition, he walks to the right of Michael. Raphael, third in order, walks to the left of Michael.

**4a.** **When Abraham our father saw the ministering angels the Divine Presence appeared and stood above him. He said to them: 'My Lords wait for me until I have taken leave of the Divine Presence, Who is greater than you', for it is said: 'and he said: "My Lords if now I have found favour in your eyes, pass not away, I pray you, from your servant" (Gen. 18:3). '**

D. E. R. IV,4 from the words *When Abraham our father saw* up to the words *they have only just arrived* is only loosely connected to the context and thus comprise an interruption. We possibly may regard this as a later insertion into the original context. M. Goldberg, *Derech Erez Rabba*, p. 7, note 9, expresses the same opinion. On the other hand must be admitted that there are strong contextual relations with the preceding and following passages in D. E.

The manuscripts show different readings. The basis manuscript cites Gen. 18:3, whereas other manuscripts cite Gen. 17:22. The reading in the basis manuscript is undoubtedly preferable. The word ''Adonai', however, is rendered incorrectly in the basis manuscript as 'J''J', the name for God. According to the explanation of Gen. 18:3, the word ''Adonai' must refer to the angels, and the verse is read as: 'My lords, if I have found favour in your eyes

...' in the sense of 'My lords, wait for me, until I have taken leave from the Shekhinah'. According to previously mentioned explanation of Rabbi Hijja, "Adonai' refers especially to Michael, the greatest of the three angels. Cf. Ber. Rab. XLVIII,10; Jalq., Wa-Jera, r. 82.; idem, 'Eqeb, r. 856; and cf. TbSheb. 35b: 'All the names mentioned in Scripture in connection to Abraham are sacred, except this which is secular, it is said: 'And my lord, if now I have found favour in your sight.' Cf. TjR. ha-Sh. I,2 [56d]; TjMeg. I,4 [71d]; Mas. Seph. Torah, in: *Massekhtot Qetannot*, ed. M. Higger, p. 32; Midr. Ag., ed. S. Buber, p. 40 (on Gen. 18:3); Midr. Leq. Tob on Gen 18:3 and Jalq. Re'ub. on Gen 18:3 [90a]; and Rashi on Gen. 18:3, and other sources.

The question concerning whether "Adonai' is addressed to God or the angels is a subject of discussion in an early Tannaitic tradition. See TbSheb. 35b and parallels. See also Ber. Rab. XLVIII, 10 (ed. J. Theodor / Ch. Albeck, pp. 486–487 and *Tosaphists* on TbShab. 127a, sub 'di-khetib', also ed. A. Steinsalz, p. 561; and see Rashi in reference to TbSheb. 35b. In a conflicting tradition, "Adonai' in Gen. 18:3 is, however, interpreted as referring to God. According to this explanation, Abraham requests God to wait until he has finished speaking with the angels, which serves to prove the rule that it is more important to receive guests than the Shekhinah! See the statement of Rab in TbShab. 127a; cf. TbSheb. 35b; Midr. Teh. 18,29; Midr. Ag. on Gen. 18:3 (ed. S. Buber, p. 40); Midr. ha-Gad. on Gen. 18:3 and see also *She'iltot*, Wa-Jera 11; and see further M. Kasher, *Torah Shelemah* (Hebr. ed.), p. 744, § 50.

The quotation (see manuscripts D. E. R.) from Gen. 17:22 'When he had finished talking with him, God went up from Abraham' is explained in the midrash as if Abraham first ended his talk with God before God left him. In reference to that passage, we find in Ber. Rab. XLVII,6 (cf. Jalq., Lekh le-Kha, r. 82, and D. E. R. V, beginning) the statement that an important person must ask consent of an unimportant person before leaving him, and the other way round. The argumentation, however, is incomplete, and Gen. 17:22 can also serve as proof of the custom that an unimportant person (like in D. E. R. h.l.) asks consent of an important person in order to leave of him. In Tanh. Jash., Wa-Jera, § 8 Gen. 18:33 is cited as proof that an important person (God) asks consent of an unimportant person (Abraham) to leave. See especially *Perush Maharzav* on Gen.l.c. Cf. also A.R.N. [a], XXXVII (56a) and A.R.N. [b], XL (56a). The strong relationship of the statement here in D. E. R. with the traditions mentioned clarifies the alternative reading of the manuscripts which cite Gen. 17:22.


**4b. And when Abraham had taken leave of the Divine Presence he stood and bowed before them and invited them to take place beneath the tree, for it is said: 'Let now a little water be fetched (and wash your feet)' (Gen. 18:4) and after that (it is said:) 'And I will take a morsel of bread' (Gen. 18:5).**

**But (when the angels came to Lot) what did he say to them? 'Stay the night and wash your feet' (Gen. 19:2).**

**Others say: 'He spoke wise words to them, thinking by himself: If they (i. e. the people of Sodom) will see them with their hands and feet washed, then they will kill me, my wife and my children. But when they see the dust (still) on their feet, then they will say (to themselves): they have only just arrived.'**

Abraham first takes leave of the Shekhinah before turning to his guests to offer them hospitality. The Midrash subsequently deals with the difference between Abraham and Lot. While it is said that Abraham had first water brought so that they may wash their feet (Gen. 18:4), after which he invites them to rest and eat (Gen. 18:4−5), Lot suggests first to his guests that they spend the night, and then wash their feet and go on their way (cf. Gen. 19:2). The reading which we find in the basis manuscript would suggest that Abraham is more hospitable than Lot, who does not first offer his guests something to eat. It is most improbable, however, that this interpretation concurs with the original intention of the tradition. It is not at all relevant to the following *Others say ...* , which leads into another subject (namely, the order of washing and staying overnight). The expression *others say* indicates that the problem of washing before or after sleeping overnight must have played a role in the directly preceding passage, but with another (unmentioned) explanation! According to Gen. 19:3 Lot very willingly gave a feast for his guests. This leads us to conclude that after the words *others say* the text goes immediately into further elaboration of the problem of the order in washing and staying overnight. See also M. Goldberg, *Derech Erez Rabba*, p. 8, note 3, where he states his assumption that the words *and after that (it is said): 'And I will take a morsel of bread'*, must be considered as a later insertion and must be deleted because they interrupt the cohesiveness of the text. M. Goldberg's assumption, unfortunately, is not confirmed by the manuscripts of D. E. R.

On the basis of the tradition in Ber. Rab. L,4 (ed. J. Theodor / Ch. Albeck, II, p. 520), however, we find A. Goldberg's assumption to be correct. The midrash deals with the contrast between the words of Abraham (who invites first his guests to wash heir feet before resting, see Gen. 18:4) and the words of Lot (who first invites his guests to rest and spend the night over before washing their feet). In the first clause of the tradition of D. E. R., the theme of Abraham's aversion to idolatry, which could explain the difference between the words of Abraham, is missing (see Ber. Rab. l.c.). The background of that explanation is a tradition which is ascribed to to Rabbi Jannai the son of Rabbi Jishma'el, in which it is assumed that Abraham suspected his guests of being Arabs, who worshipped the dust of their feet (see TbB. M. 86b and parallels; cf. also the statement of Rabbi Levi in Ber. Rab. XLVIII,9 and parallels). Out of fear of idolatry, Abraham has his guests wash their feet immediately. Lot was less scrupulous.

A second theme is subsequently brought up in Ber. Rab. L,4 with the introductory words 'we-jesh 'omerim' (in D. E. R. h.l. : ''aherim 'omerim'), *others say*. It is assumed that Lot intentionally let the dust remain on his guest's feet so that the residents of Sodom would have the impression that Lot's guests had just arrived and he had not yet offered them hospitality. If the residents of Sodom suspected Lot of offering hospitality to his guests, then Lot and his family would have to fear for their lives. In Sodom, the offering of hospitality was severely punished. Cf. e.g., TbSanh. 109a-b and Ber. Rab. XLIX,6 among other sources.

An interesting variation on Ber. Rab. L,4 brings up yet another reason for Abraham's behaviour. Abraham has his guests wash their hands before eating, in compliance with the halakhic rule and duty of 'netilat jadajim' (washing the hands before a meal). Lot, however, did not concern himself with that duty. See Ber. Rab. l.c., ed. J. Theodor / Ch. Albeck, II, p. 520; and M. Kasher, *Torah Shelemah*, on Gen. 18:4 (Hebr. ed., p. 746, § 60).

### 5. He who walks behind his master may not leave him before first obtaining his permission.

The continuity of the chapter that was interrupted with the presentation of exegetical elaborations after 'When saw Abraham' is here continued. Two different traditions are merged together here. According to the tradition in TbJoma 37a already mentioned, it was a good habit, for a student to walk somewhat behind his teacher, and in any event he should never walk before him. This tradition is connected here in D. E. to another tradition which holds that one may not take leave of one's teacher without first asking his consent. See the reconstruction of S. Krauss, in: *R. E. J.*, XXXVI (1898), p. 208 based on TbJoma l.c.: He who walks behind his teacher is arrogant, and it is never permitted to leave him from behind without first requesting his consent. Neither the manuscripts nor the parallels support this reconstruction.

For further information on exegetic backgrounds concerning the custom of asking consent of someone before taking leave of him, see (in reference to Gen. 17:22) Ber. Rab. XLVII,6 and cf. Jalq., Lekh le-Kha, r. 82 and in reference to Gen. 18:33 see A. R. N. [a], XXXV 956a] and A. R. N. [b], XL (56a) and cf. Tanh. Jash., Wa-Jera, § 8 and see especially Maharzav on Ber. Rab. XLVII,6 and *Mattanot Kehunah* on that text, and see D. E. R., V (beginning). Cf. the reading in Mas. Kal. Rab. (ed. N. N. Coronel, 13b and ed. M. Higger, p. 319).

### 6. [When two persons enter a house, the Rab enters first and then the student follows.]

**When they are both sages, equal in learning, the master of the house enters first and then the guest.**

**And when they are leaving, the guest goes out first and after him the master of the house.**

In the reading of *Menorat ha-Ma'or* (Al Nakawa) (ed. H. G. Enelow, IV, p. 409), yet another statement is added at the beginning: 'End the Rab enters the house first, and then the student follows...' This addition is not found in other parallels and manuscripts of D.E.. But the addition does make the succeeding statements flow better! On the basis of the story of Honi the circle maker in TbTa'an. 23b, one expects at first glance an additional theme. The host enters first and exits last so that his wife is not left alone in the house with his guest(s). In the circles of pious 'talmidei hakhamim', it was the custom to avoid false appearances and false rumours whenever possible. That appears not to be the only theme, however, considering that the statement already suggests that if the man of the house is the student, the Rab enters first and exits last. The theme mentioned can be defended nonetheless. The statement about the Rab will be in reference to a house of study! The custom of Honi the circle maker also did not apply to the Rab but to the guests whose character he did not know well, thus prompting his custom.

7. **One who leaves his master, whether he be greater than his master, or his master be greater than he, he should say: 'Behold, I am leaving.'**

The term 'gadol' (great) can refer to importance, i.e. one's social position or, in this context, the extent of one's knowledge of the Torah, as well as to age. A reason is given in TbJoma 53a as to why one should not leave one's teacher suddenly or unannounced. It is improper to turn one's back to a teacher.; instead, one must look back in order to show that one does not desire to take leave of him. It is even said of Rabbi 'El'azar and of Raba that they took leave of their colleague-teacher by walking backwards with their faces toward their teacher. That is all stated in the context of a discussion about the manner in which one was obliged to leave the Temple. No discussion is necessary concerning the fact that in the circles of the 'talmidei hakhamim' those customs are connected with the consciousness of the Divine Presence, the Shekhinah, which is especially connected to the presence of the teacher. Cf. TbBer. 64a; Mekh, de-R. Jishm., Amalek, par. 1 (ed. H. S. Horovitz, p. 196); Jalq., Shem., r. 270 and r. 393; Shir ha-Shir. Rab. II,5; Midr. Teh. 25,6; Tanh., Ki-Tissa, § 27; Ber. Rab., ed. J. Theodor / Ch. Albeck, p. 684; and other sources.

Thus, it is more than a matter of politeness to take leave of a student, colleague or teacher in a special way. The examples of the leave-taking between Abraham and God cited in the sources fit into that context, also! See then also the commentary and parallels in connection with D.E.R. IV,4. Ber. Rab. XLVII,6 is the source for our statement. Cf. Jalq., Lekh le-Kha, § 82.

## Derekh 'Eretz Rabbah, chapter V

**1. One should not leave, neither his master nor his fellow, unless he leaves when he has obtained (previously) his permission.**

One may not leave one's teacher without telling him and without first asking his consent. The overlapping of this statement with the statements in chap. IV (end) shows that Pirqei ben 'Azzai (D.E.R. III–IX) does not constitute a complete editorial unity, but has been assembled from various fragments. Cf. in this connection the custom (also mentioned in TbBer. 31a and parallels) of not leaving a colleague sage learned in the Torah without saying to him some words about halakhah.

**2. All men can learn good manners from the All Present, Who said to Abraham: 'Do you have any further need of Me? He replied to Him: "Lord of the World, no (lit. yes)."'**

This statement should be considered as a paraphrased rendition of an exegetic tradition such as in A. R. N., XXXV (56a) and A. R. N. [b], XL 56a). Cf. Tanh. Jash., Wa-Jera, § 8 and cf. *Maharzav* on Ber. Rab. XLVII,6. Gen. 18:33 serves as the starting point for this statement: 'And the Lord went His way, when He had finished speaking to Abraham, and Abraham returned to his place' This is explained as meaning that Abraham did not return to his place before God Himself told him that He was leaving and so, as it were, asked him for consent. One may assume that the tradition here in D.E.R. is a later rendering of an older exegetic tradition. See also M. Goldberg, *Derech Erez Rabba*, p. 9, where the words 'Who said to Abraham: "Have you any further need of Me?" He replied to Him: "Lord of the World, no"', are regarded as a gloss which replaced the quotation: 'And the Lord went His way, when He had finished speaking to Abraham.' Cf. the manuscripts and cf. the attempt by the Gaon of Vilna, here in D.E.R. h.l., to insert Gen. 18:33 and thus adapt it more to the sources mentioned.

Abraham's answer to God is missing in the basis manuscript of D.E.R. Most other manuscripts read 'hen' (*yes*). One may assume that there is an euphemism here and that, in actuality 'lo' (*no*) is meant.

**3. A man should never enter the house of his fellow suddenly. And all men can learn good manners from the All-Present, Who stood at the entrance of the Garden (of Eden) and called to Adam (to announce His Presence), for**

**it is said: 'And God called unto the man and said unto him: Where are You?' (Gen. 3:9).**

The desirability of knocking before entering into some place and of announcing one's arrival beforehand goes back to a very old tradition. In TbNid. 16b, reference is made to Ben Sira in connection with the custom of not entering into a house suddenly and unannounced. The statement as such does not appear literally in *Seph. Ben Sira* (cf. S. Schechter, in: *J. Q. R.*, III (1881), p. 693), but there does appear a variant. See *Seph. Ben Sira* 21:22−23, ed. M. Z. Segal: 21:24, p. 127 and notes on p. 129): 'The foot of a fool (sets out) quickly for a house ... one who is unwise peers from the gate at a house.' Cf. also *Pirqei Rabbenu ha-Qadosh*, ed. S. Schönblum, p. 14 and p. VIII; N. Brüll, *Jahrbücher für jüdische Geschichte und Literatur*, VII, p. 48.

In MTam. I,2 we also find an old tradition containing this rule of etiquette. It is assumed here that the person presiding over the lottery of the priests knocks at the door of the place where the priests are spending the night, even if the door is not closed. In TbPes. 112a and other sources, the admonition not to enter a house suddenly, is attributed to Rabbi ʿAqiba, and in TbNid. 16b (cf. Waj. Rab. XXI,8 and other sources), this admonition is passed by Rabbi Shimʿon bar Johai. On the basis of Ex. 24:16, and old tradition presents God as an example because He calls to Moses first before approaching him further. See Mekh. de-R. Jishm., Jitro, Ba-Hodesh, par. 2, ed. H. S. Horovitz, p. 207, and other sources.

The form of the tradition (for which Gen. 3:8−9 serves as basis) here in D. E. R. is found only in later sources. Cf. *Midr. ʾAleph Beit de-Rabbi ʿAqiba*, in: A. Jellinek , *Beit ha-Midrash*, III, p. 61; Jalq., Ber., r. 27 and cf. Mas. Kal. Rab. (ed. N. N. Coronel, 16b).

**4. There is a story about four elders who were on their way to attend to a private counsel (with the highest Roman authorities) and they had a certain companion there, a philosopher. They were: Rabban Gamliʾel, Rabbi Jehoshua, Rabbi ʾElʿazar ben ʿAzarjah, and Rabbi ʿAqiba. Rabbi Jehoshua said to Rabban Gamliʾel: 'Would you want us to pay a visit to our companion, the philosopher?' He replied to him: 'No'. In the morning he said again to him: 'Do you want us to pay a visit to our companion, the philosopher?' He replied to him: 'Yes'. He (Rabbi Jehoshua) went and knocked on the door. The philosopher debated in his mind and said (by himself): 'This can only be the good manners of a sage.' (When he heard knocking) a second time, he got up and washed his face and feet. (When he heard knocking) a third time, he arose and opened the door. And he saw the sages of Israel, some coming from here [and some coming from there] (i. e. all together and one on the side of the other). They were: Rabban**

**Gamli'el [in the middle] and Rabbi 'El'azar and Rabbi Jehoshua on his right and Rabbi 'Aqiba on his left. The philosopher debated in his mind and said (by himself): How shall I greet the sages of Israel. If I say 'Peace upon you Rabban Gamli'el', It would happen to me that I degrade the sages of Israel; and if I say 'Peace upon you all sages of Israel', I would degrade Rabban Gamli'el. As soon as he reached them he said to them: 'Peace upon you, all sages of Israel, headed by Rabban Gamli'el.'**

The story which follows here offers an illustration which popularizes the above-mentioned admonition not to enter a house suddenly. It also illustrates the custom (mentioned in D. E. R. IV (end) that teacher and students walked or set with each other according to their rank. In this story are mentioned four elders which (in accordance with the use of the language of that time) refers to four men learned in the Torah. Cf. e.g., the use of the term 'zeqenim' (*elders*) in TbQid. 32b.

'Malkut penimit' is a *private counsel* with the highest Roman authorities. In a number of traditions, it is mentioned that the four sages, Rabban Gamli'el (the second), Rabbi Jehoshua (ben Hananjah), Rabbi 'El'azar ben 'Azarjah, and Rabbi 'Aqiba, undertook together a journey to Rome. Cf. M'Er. IV,1−2; Siphrei, 'Eqeb, pisqa 43 (ed. L. Finkelstein, pp. 94−95), idem, pisqa 318 (p. 316); 'Eikh. Rab. V,18; TbMak. 24a-b; Shem. Rab. XXX,9. See L .Ginzberg, *Genizah Studies in Memory of Solomon Schechter*, I, New York 1928, p. 219; *Mishnat Rabbi 'Eli'ezer*, ed. H. G. Enelow (repr. 1970), p. 103 and cf. also TosJoma II,12 and MMa'as. Shen. V,9; Siphra, 'Emor, per. XVI,2; TbSuk. 41b; TosSuk. II,11, and other sources. D. Herr, in: *Sripta Hierosolymata*, XII, Jerusalem 1971, p. 138, notes.

The philosopher, whom Rabbi Jehoshua wishes to visit (according to this story in D. E.) is according to a number of scholars Flavius Josephus, and the visit must have taken place at the end of the first century. See J. Deerenbourg, *Essai sur l'histoire et la geographie de la Palestine d'apres les Talmuds et les autres sources rabbiniques*, Paris 1887, p. 334; E. Renan, *Les Evangiles et la Seconde Generation Chretienne*, Paris 1881, p. 307; W. Bacher, in: *R. E. J.*, XXII (1891), p. 143; H. J. Zimmels, in: *R. E. J.*, XXIII (1892), p. 318; S. Krauss, in: *R. E. J.*, XXXVI (1898), p. 209; H. Graetz, in: *M. G. W. J.*, XXVI (1877), p. 355; N. Brüll, *Jahrbücher*, IV, p. 401 ff.; H. Vogelstein and P. Rieger, *Geschichte der Juden in Rom*, I, America 1940, p. 33, note 3; see especially W. Bacher, *Die Agada der Tannaiten*, I, p. 79 ff.; M. Goldberg, *Derech Erez Rabba*, p. 10, note a; G. Allon. *Toledot ha-Jehudim be-'Eretz Jisra'el bi-Tequphat ha-Mishnah we-ha-Talmud*, ed. S. Safrai, repr. 1975, pp. 148 and 354; L. Finkelstein, *'Aqiba Scholar Saint and Martyr*, p. 151.

The four sages are supposed to have visited Rome in connection with the intended execution of Flavius Clemens (a relative of Vespasianus), who was accused of atheism by Emperor Dominitianus in connection with his conversion to Judaism. See Flavius Josephus, Ant. IV, 435 and cf. *Dio Cassius* (67,14:1−2). The incident described must have occurred around 95 C.E.

L. Finkelstein (l.c.)explains that Rabban Gamli'el's initial refusal to handle Rabbi Jehoshua's first request and his approval of his second request according to the tradition here in D.E. are evidence of the fact that the well known conflict between the two men was still noticeable but was already less intense. See TbBer. 27b-28a in reference to this conflict.

As Nasi, Rabban Gamli'el walks in the middle, while Rabbi 'El'azar ben 'Azarjah (as co-Nasi, according to the Babylonian Talmud, ibid.; or as 'Ab Beit Din, according to TjBer. IV,1) and Rabbi Jehoshua ben Hananjah (the teacher of Rabbi 'Aqiba) as second in rank, walks to the right of Rabban Gamli'el, and Rabbi 'Aqiba, as lowest in rank, walks to the left of Rabban Gamli'el (that appears to be an original element, considering that later traditions certainly tend to emphasize the role of Rabbi 'Aqiba!).

From the fact that the philosopher assumes that a Sage is knocking at his door because somebody knocks at the door gently before entering, one may assume that the story is a special illustration of that rule of etiquette. It is thus better not to read 'we'amad' (so the basis manuscript) but to read 'we-taphah' ('and he knocked') in agreement with the manuscripts here in D.E.R. Finally, the order in which one greets a group of people plays a role. One gets the impression that the entire story was formulated especially as an example of a number of norms of etiquette.

## 5. **We learn this (rule of good manners) not from Rabban Gamli'el, but from the Divine Presence, for it is said: 'I saw the Lord sitting on his throne, and all the hosts of Heaven standing by Him on His right and on His left' (I Kings 22:19).**

The statement made here gives the impression of being an interpolation and interrupts the continuity with the text following. See also the Gaon of Vilna, who dates the entire statement back to D.E.R, IV (story of Abraham and the angels), where it is placed (in IV,4b) after the words *only just arrived* and changed to :'And not only from the angels do we learn this, but also from the Shekhinah.' See also the opinion of M. Goldberg, *Derech Erez Rabba*, p. 11, note 5. According to M. Goldberg, the tradition here in D.E.R. V, was clearly added in by someone who was not familiar with the content of related passages in D.E.R. IV.

See also the order in Ms. Kal. Rab. (ed, N.N. Coronel, 13a-b and 16b). Because of the logical sequence between the two stories of Rabban Gamli'el in Rome and the story of Rabbi Jehoshua (see the following passages in D.E.R. V) we prefer the order found in D.E. Cf. the opinion of S. Krauss, in: *R.E.J.*, XXXVI (1898), p. 209.

**6. Always let all people regarded by you as robbers, but pay the same honour to them as to Rabban Gamli'el.**

It happened that Rabbi Jehoshua invited a man and gave him food and drink and also took him up to the roof (to sleep) and then took away the ladder from under him. What did that man do? He arose in the middle of the night, took the belongings (of Rabbi Jehoshua) and wrapped them up in his garment. And when he tried to descend, he feel down and broke his neck. In the morning Rabbi Jehoshua found him and said: 'Worthless man, do so people of your kind (always) act?' He replied to him: 'Master, I did not know that you had removed the ladder from under me.' He spoke to him: 'Worthless man, do not you know that (already) since yesterday we are on guard against you?'

Hence Rabbi Jehoshua [ben Levi] said: 'Always let all people be regarded in your eyes as robbers, but pay the same honour to them as to Rabban Gamli'el.'

The beginning of this passage is a logical transition between the story of Rabban Gamli'el in Rome and the subsequent story of Rabbi Jehoshua and the thief. This story culminates in the repeated maxim *Always let all people be regarded in your eyes as robbers . . .*, which is attributed in the basis manuscript to Rabbi Jehoshua and in a number of other manuscripts to Rabbi Jehoshua ben Levi. W. Bacher, *'Amora'ei 'Eretz Jisra'el* (Hebr.) I, 1925, p. 133, note 4) assumes that the statement and event mentioned concern Rabbi Jehoshua ben Levi, in which case Rabban Gamli'el (in D. E. R. V,6) is Rabban Gamli'el the third, the son of Rabbi Jehudah ha-Nasi! This would thus mean, that this statement was wrongly associated, in the context of D. E. R., with Rabban Gamli'el the second from the time directly after the fall of the Temple. See further M. Ginsberg, in: *The Minor Tractates of the Talmud*, ed. A. Cohen II, notes to transl. of Mas. Kal. Rab., p. 509, note 3, where the translator assumes that Rabban Gamli'el in this statement (D. E. R. V,6) is Rabban Gamli'el the first. There are, however, no compelling reasons for completely excluding the possibility that 'Rabban Gamli'el' refers to Rabban Gamli'el the second (who despite the conflicts with his colleagues, was respected for his contributions to the halakhah) even if Rabbi Jehoshua ben Levi (who lived much later) is responsible for the transmission of the statement here. This is not improbable, for it is unlikely that Rabbi Jehoshua ben Hananjah would pay such homage to Rabban Gamli'el the second, considering that Rabban Gamli'el had humiliated him. See TbBer. 27b-28a.

## Derekh 'Eretz Rabbah, chapter VI

**1a. One who enters a house, whatever the master of the house tells him (to do) he must do.**

A guest must do whatever the host instructs him to do. This statement is attributed in TbPes. 86b to Rab Huna, who must have drown on traditions which already existed concerning 'derekh 'eretz'. Cf. also the opinion of M. Higger, *Massekhtot Ze'irot*, p. 24. In TbPes. 86b, the statement appears with the curious addition of 'hutz mi-tzé' (except...?). This addition, however, does not appear in all readings of the Talmud. See R. Rabbinivicz, *Seph. Diqduqei Sopherim*, on TbPes. l.c., III, p. 262. And see *Me'iri* on TbPes. l.c., who suggests omitting the inappropriate words. In this connection, see TbPes., ed. A. Steinsalz, *'Ijjunim*, where different explanations of the addition are given. 1) As guest, one is obliged to do everything except something for which it is necessary to leave the house. The host has authority only in his own house. 2) A guest is not required to leave the house immediately, should he be instructed to do so. This would be humiliating. 3) 'Mi-tzé' is also used in reference to excrement. A guest is not required to execute an order which involves contact with filth. 4) 'Tzé' is also explained to be an abbreviation for 'tzad 'issur' (something forbidden). A guest is not required to carry out an order which involves a transgression or a matter which is connected with transgression. This explanation corresponds to an addition in D.E.R. in Ms. Oxford, Bodleian, cat. A. Neubauer (I, p. 306), no. 1100: 'When it concerns something which is permitted', i.e., only then a guest is required to carry out an instruction from the host. The words which have been added in this manuscript should be considered as a later addition, in agreement with the addition in TbPes. l.c. See M. Goldberg, *Derech Erez Rabba*, p. 12ff. 5) 'Tzé' is also interpreted as an abbreviation for 'Tzadoqi' and 'Appiqoros'. Should a host fall under one of these cursed categories, a guest may not even be obedient. 6) 'Tzé' is also interpreted as an abbreviation of 'tzorekhei 'ishah' (the needs of the wife [of the host]). A guest is not required to be obedient in connection with the needs of the housewife, for he must keep his distance from her.

**1b. This happened to Rabbi Shim'on ben Antipatros, who was (often) visited by guests. He urged them to eat and to drink and they had vowed [by the Torah that they would neither eat nor drink] but they made themselves liars (and broke their vow). And on the moment of their departure he would flagellate them. These happenings came to the notice of Rabban**

**Johanan ben Zakkai and the sages and they were angered by this matter. They said: 'Who will go and inform us about it?' Rabbi Jehoshua said to them: 'I will go and see what he is doing.' They said: 'Go in peace my master and teacher' [better reading: He went and found him sitting at the entrance of his house and he said to him: 'Peace be upon you, my master and teacher.'] He (i. e. Shim'on ben Antipatros) said to him: 'Are you needing something?' He said: '(I need) a lodging.' He said to him: 'Stay in peace.' They sat down and occupied themselves with the study of the Torah until evening. In the morning he (i. e. Rabbi Jehoshua) said to him: 'I go to the bathhouse.' He said to him: 'as you wish.' But Rabbi Jehoshua was afraid that he would beat him at his thighs. After he came out (of the bathhouse and returned) they ate and drank. He said: '[who] will accompany me (on my way back)?' He said: 'I will.' And Rabbi Jehoshua was debating in his mind and said (unto himself): 'What have I to report to the sages who sent me?' Rabbi Jehoshua turned around. He said to him: 'Why did you turn around?' He replied: 'I have something to ask you. Why did you flagellate the people who were your guests and why did you not flagellate me?' He said to him: 'You are a great sage and you have good manners; but the people who were my guests, I pressed them to eat and to drink and they had vowed by the Torah (not to eat and drink) and they made themselves liars. And so I heard from the mouth of the sages, that whoever vows by the Torah and makes himself a liar (by violating his vow) has to be given forty lashes.' He said to him: 'And this you are (really) doing?' He replied: 'Indeed.' He (i. e. Rabbi Jehosua) said to him: 'I order you to give them two times forty (lashes), [forty lashes] of you and forty (lashes) of the sages who sent me.' Rabbi Jehoshua went and reported to the sages what he had seen regarding (the behaviour) of Shim'on ben Antipatros.**

The story that follows here serves as an illustration of the previous statement about obeying the master of the house. Shim'on ben Antipatros, i. e. Shim'on the son of Antipatros. The manuscripts read: '*Rabbi* Shim'on ben Antipatros'. It is unclear, however, if he can be considered as one of the rabbanim. See R. Halperin. *'Atlas 'Etz Hajjim*, IV, p. 30 and cf. A. B. Hyman, *Toledot Tanna'im we-'Amora'im*, III, p. 1161. The name 'Antipatros' may have been derived from a place name. See S. Krauss, *Lehnwörter*, II, p. 70; and S. Krauss, in: *R. E. J.*, XXXVI (1898), p. 209; and M. Higger, *Massekhtot Derekh 'Eretz*, p. 194 and notes; and other sources.

The story about Shim'on ben Antipatros, as given in D. E. R., raises a number of questions. In this connection, see especially commentaries on *Tur*, Or. Haj., 170. 1) How could the guest be forced to eat and drink and then promise not to do so and break the promise immediately? 2) If one understands the command to eat and drink as a proleptic way of speaking and assumes that this command is prefaced by the promise not to eat and drink, there still remains the question why the guests break their promise immediately and without dispute. 3) In the situation mentioned in point 1, the question concerns how to explain 'we-gazar' (he urged, referring to a coercive command) if one does not assume that the guests do not at all want to eat and to drink? How is this to be explained? One solution would be to assume that the guests had promised Shim'on ben Antipatros (or anyone else) beforehand not to eat and drink in the house of the host. Without altering the text, this explanation may be given with some difficulty.

It is clear from the story that the aversion of Shim'on ben Antipatros to making vows is very central to the story. It is possible that he invited guests whom he suspected of taking such vows in order to force them into breaking their vows and to be able to punish them. Considering that they did not dare to oppose their host, they broke their vow and thus deserved corporal punishment. This also explains why it is not stated in the text that Rabbi Jehoshua made a vow. He still feared, however, the punishment because he did not know the reason for the punishment of the others! In any case, Rabbi Jehoshua would have refused to break his vow without some dispute if he was forced to make a vow and to break that vow immediately. As a sage he simply did not make such frivolous vows, and Shim'on ben Antipatros realised that. This point of view is also confirmed in the reading in Midr. ha-Gad. (see Midr. ha-Gad. on Num. 30:3). In Midr. ha-Gad. making and breaking of vows is central to the context (unlike in D. E. R., where obeying one's host is of main concern). Also, in the reading of Midr. ha-Gad. one does not find a command to eat and drink preceding a remark about guests making a vow! The story in Midr. ha-Gad. probably takes place in the original setting, unlike the story here in D. E. See also the opinion of M. Higger, *Massekhtot Ze'irot*, p. 42. In D. E. R., the connection between the story with the context was fabricated. The construction in the reading in Midr. ha-Gad. is more balanced. Based on Midr. ha-Gad. it is more logical to assume that Rabbi Jehoshua upon taking his final leave feared that he would still be hit.

*'Ameru lekh le-shalom Rabbi u-mori (they said: 'Go in peace, My master and teacher')*, as the words are the singular, it is improbable that these words were spoken by colleagues of Rabbi Jehoshua (to Rabbi Jehoshua) for they would have addressed him with the plural 'Rabbenu u-morenu'! It is read then: 'They said to him: "Go in peace." He went and found him (i. e. Shim'on ben Antipatros) sitting in the gate of his house, and he said to him: "Peace be with you, my Rabbi and teacher."' According to some manuscripts Rabbi Jehoshua spoke the above-mentioned words 'Rabbi u-mori' to Shim'on ben Antipatros. This makes the transition to the following words more clear.

In connection with the words 'lekh le-shalom', which are spoken upon taking leave, see TbBer. 64a and R. Rabbinovicz, *Seph. Diqduqei Sopherim*, on

TbBer. l.c. In connection with the greeting 'Rabbi u-mori', see TbPes. 51a and cf. S. Krauss, *Talmudische Archäologie*, III, chap. IX, p. 16. If one greeted someone with the words 'Peace be with you, Rabbi', one was answered with 'Peace be with you, my Rabbi and my Teacher.

The reading in the basis manuscript must be corrected to 'mi malweni' (*who will accompany me*; 'who will see me out?') in stead of 'malweni'.

The commandment not to break an oath or a vow is a so called 'negative command' in the Torah. Cf. Lev. 5:4; Num. 30:3 and Dt. 23:21). All open and conscious violations of a negative commandment which cannot be righted by fulfilling a positive commandment can be punished by flogging. In this connection see especially TbTem. 3a-b and cf. MMak. II,4, and other sources. Cf. also Rambam, *Jad*, Hil. Sanh., XVIII,1. One possible reading is (according to the manuscripts): 'I order you to punish them with forty lashes for me and (another) forty lashes for you and (another) forty lashes for the scholars.' The reading in the basis manuscript is defective here. A second possible reading is: 'I order you to punish them with forty lashes and (another) forty lashes; that is forty lashes for you and another forty lashes for the scholars.'

2a. **A man should never be hot tempered during his meal (when something happens against his will).**
2b. **It happened that Hillel the Old had a certain dinner party, when a poor man came and stood at his door and said: 'Today I am to marry a woman and I have no provisions (for the wedding-feast).' His (i.e. Hillel's) wife took the entire meal and gave it to him. And after that she kneaded other dough and cooked another stew, came in and placed it before them. He (i.e. Hillel) said to her: 'My daughter, why you did not bring it to us (sooner)?' She told him all that happened. He said to her: 'My daughter I, too, did not judge you in the scale of guilt but in the scale of merit, because everything you have done you have done for the Name of Heaven.'**

In Talmudic literature we can only find related sayings about the behaviour of pious men, like the remark by Rab 'Adda bar 'Ahabah ('Amora of the sixth generation): 'The disciples of Rab 'Adda bar 'Ahabah asked him: "To what do you attribute longevity?" – He replied: "I have never displayed any impatience in my house and I have never walked in front of any greater man than myself, nor have I ever meditated (over the words of the Torah) in dirty alleys, . . .' See in connection with the patience of Hillel TbShab. and parallels. Parallels of this saying in D. E. R. are only found in later literature; e.g., Mas. Kal. Rab., ed. N. N. Coronel, 16b.

3a. **One should leave a portion (lit. a border) of the food in the stewpot and one should not leave a portion of the food in the dish.**

**3b.  It happened to Rabbi Jehoshua that he was the guest of a widow. She served him food cooked in a stewpot, he ate and did not leave a portion of it. A second time ( being her guest) she served him up food cooked in the stewpot and he ate and did not leave a portion of it. The third time she spoiled his meal with salt and as soon as he tasted it he withdrew his hand from it and ate his bread dry. She said to him: 'Why did you withdraw your hand and did not eat (of it)?' He said to her: 'I have already eaten earlier in the day.' She replied to him: 'If you have (already) eaten you should be modest in eating bread in the same way as you are modest in eating pounded beans.' [Another reading: She said to him: 'Why you ate much bread but only little pounded beans, did not the sages say that one should leave a portion of the food in the stewpot, but one should not leave a portion of the food in the dish?']**

This tradition is closely related to the traditions mentioned in Tb'Er. 53b. According to the opinion of S. Krauss, in: *R. E. J.*, XXXVI (1889), p. 210 and W. Bacher, *Die Agada der Tannaiten*, I, p. 181, the reading here in D. E. R. has been derived from the reading in Tb'Er. 53b. It would be better to say, that Tb'Er. 53b in some respects contains a better and more original reading. The differences, however, may show that we find in D. E. an independent reading. In Tb'Er. 53b the entire construction is more balanced. In the reading in D. E. R., emphasis is placed on the norm of leaving a portion of food (pe'ah) over only in the stewpot, but not on the dish. Therefore, the original introductory sentence 'Hence Rabbi Jehoshua said: "No one has ever had the better of me ..."' (see D. E. R. VI,3b.) was placed at the end.

Originally this introductory sentence might have come first, with the story (told in the first person) following it. See so Tb'Er. l.c.

With the help of Tb'Er. 53b and parallels, one can reconstruct the answer of the woman as follows: *She said to him: 'If you have already eaten, you should be moderate in eating both bread and pounded beans (i. e., not only in eating pounded beans). Is it possible that you did not leave a pe'ah over the former meals (and are now doing so as compensation)? But did not the sages say: "One is not to leave a pe'ah in the stewpot, but one is to leave pe'ah in the dish."'* In other words, the host must put out all the food in the stewpot into the dish for the guest, and the guest must leave something in the dish for the host and not eat all the food served to him as that could be taken as a sign of gluttony. The woman clearly resents Rabbi Jehoshua for always eating everything that is served to him and not leaving anything over in the dish. See also the reading in 'Eikh. Rab. I,19 and *Menorat ha-Ma'or* (of Jitzhaq 'Aboab), § 317, and other sources. See the *Tosaphists* on Tb'Er.53b: only someone who eats everything from the dish is considered to be a glutton. Cf. also Tb'Er. l.c., ed. A. Steinsalz, *'Ijjunim*, p. 233.

One can see what remains in the dish, but one cannot see what remains in the stewpot. One therefore does leave a pe'ah in the dish, but not in the stewpot. See further *Shul. Ar.*, Or. Haj., 170,3. Cf. also the rule in D. E. R. IX,1 and in D. E. Z. V,1: One may not wipe a dish completely clean with a breadcrust. Cf. the translation by M. Higger, *Massekhtot Derekh 'Eretz*, p. 367: 'When a guest is offered pastry, he should always leave some, but he should not do so when he is offered a boiled dish.' This is another interpretation of the reading in conformity with the reading in Tb'Er. 53b.

In the manuscripts of D. E. R., however, we find another reading: *She said to him: 'You eat much bread, but only a little of the pounded beans?! Did not the sages say: "One is to leave pe'ah over from (the food in) the stewpot, but one is not to leave pe'ah over from (the food in) the dish."'* We also find this reading in Tb'Er., Ms. Munich (see R. Rabbinovicz, *Seph. Diqduqei Sopherim*, p. 206, where he plausibly explains this reading to mean that it is inappropriate and lacking in taste for one to leave over food for the host in the dish from which one has eaten. Cf, also the reading in Midr. ha-Gad. on Gen. 24:19, ed. M. Margulies, p. 389, and cf. the reading in: M. Gaster, *Seph. Ma'asiot*, p. 155. This is the most convincing reading in the context of the discussion between Rabbi Jehoshua and the woman, considering that in her answer she takes away from him his excuse of leaving so much behind in the dish as compensation for the other times, when he left little or nothing in the dish. Thus the reading in Ms. Munich on Tb'Er. 53b, also deserves preference. The custom mentioned that one did not completely wipe a dish clean with a piece of bread does not at all imply that one had to leave some food on the dish for the host! See the remarks of M. Goldberg, *Derech Erez Rabba*, p. 16 and see S. Krauss, *Talmudische Archäologie*, III, chap. IX, p. 269, note 419.

3c. **Hence Rabbi Jehoshua said: 'No one has ever got the best of me except this woman, a little boy and a little girl.' It happened to Rabbi Jehoshua, that he was walking across a field and chanced upon a little girl. She said to him: 'Why are you walking in a field?' He replied to her: 'I am walking on a (trodden) path.' She said to him: 'If that is a path, then no others than robbers like you have trodden it down.'**

**And another time it happened to Rabbi Jehoshua, that he was on his way and met a little boy, who was sitting at a crossroad. He said to him: 'My son, by which road can I come to the city, by this or by that way?' He replied to him: 'See the two roads before you, this one is long and short, and that one is short and long.' He walked along the short and long road. When he reached the wall of the city he chanced upon gardens and parks surrounding it. (He turned back) and saw the same little boy sitting on his place. He said to him: 'Did I not ask you (by which road I come into the city) and did you**

**not say to me, that I could come into the city by this road, being short and long?' He replied to him: '[Master] are you not a great sage, and this is your wisdom?' Rabbi Jehoshua went and kissed him upon his head and said: 'Happy are you, O Israel, for all of you are sages, great and small.'**

*Hence Rabbi Jehoshua said...*

As in Tb'Er.53b, a formulation in the first person also deserves preference in this segment of the stories about Rabbi Jehoshua. The structure in the version in Tb'Er.53b is preferred.

From the wording in TbB.Q. 81b (cf. TbTa'an. 6b), it is evident that the custom of not using already trodden paths on another man's territory was viewed as an expression of special piousness. As in the case of the widow, it is clear that the girl expected a sage to behave in a special way. The fear of causing harm to one's fellow man is a feature of 'hasidut'!

*And another time it happened to Rabbi Jehoshua ...*

Again, as in Tb'Er. 53b, a version in the first person is to be preferred. Rabbi Jehoshua is misled. The road he should have chosen in the first place was long and short. On first sight it was long where distance was concerned, but on closer inspection it was short because it led directly to the city and was without obstacles. The road which he wrongly chose was short and long. Where distance was concerned it appeared to be short, but in the end it was long because it was not possible to go directly to the city via that route.

Here, then, we have the unmistakable moralizing teaching that one should not choose the way which appears to be easiest, but should choose the way which he is certain it will lead him to his destination.

See the manuscripts with the addition 'we-qarpiphim'. ('qarpiph' is an enclosed space outside a settlement). See the more complete answer of the boy in Tb'Er.53b: "Turning back I said to him, 'My son, did you not tell me that this road was short?' He replied: 'And did I not also tell you: but long?'".

**4. How does one dance before a bride? Beth Shammai says: 'The bride (is praised) as she is.' And Beth Hillel says: '(With he words:) beautiful and graceful bride.' (The sages of) Bet Shammai said to (the sages of) Beth Hillel: 'According to your words, even if she were lame or blind one should say to her: "beautiful and graceful bride!?" But the Torah says: "Keep you far from a false matter".' (The sages of) Beth Hillel replied to (the sages of) Beth Shammai: 'Imagine that someone has made a bad purchase in the market, should one praise it in his eyes or deprecate it in his eyes? Of course one should praise it! Therefore the sages have said: "The disposition of a man should always be one of compassion with his fellowmen."'**

How should people sing about the bride while she is dancing?

Should they sing the same words of praise, even if they are exaggerated in the case of a certain bride, or should they sing about her actual qualities? There was a difference of opinion concerning this question between the school of Hillel and the school of Shammai, doing justice to the truth took precedence over expressing compassion with an ugly bride. In the school of Hillel, however, compassion with the bride took precedence over the truth, and every bride, whether beautiful or ugly, was to be eagerly praised in song.

It is well-known that a number of decisions made by the school of Shammai were utterly positive toward and protective of women. Their decision here signalized the danger that which is meant to be reverence of the bride can degenerate into a meaningless compliment. In TbKet.16b-17a we find this discussion between the two schools recorded as a baraita.

M. Higger (*Massekhtot Ze'irot*, p. 25) suggests that it is possible that intro-ductory wording has been omitted from D. E. R. h.l., and that the following remark preceded the discussion between the two schools: 'One should always be in solidarity with his fellowman.' This maxim (*The disposition of a man should always be* . . . , attributed to the sages) is attributed to the school of Hillel in both the Ms. versions in TbKet. l.c. (See R. Rabbinovicz, *Seph. Diqduqei Sopherim* a.l.) and in Mas. Kal. Rab. (ed. N.N. Coronel, 17a and cf. ed. M. Higger, p. 323 ff.) · The wording in TbKet. l.c appears to be original. (See also M. Higger, *Massekhtot Ze'irot*, l.c.) .

In the gemara in Mas. Kal. Rab. l.c., it is argued in favour of the school of Hillel that the praises sung for a bride may be sung for her character and not just for her physical appearance.

## 5.  A man should not break of 'Who brings forth' (i. e. the piece of bread on which the benediction 'Who brings forth' is pronounced at the beginning of the meal) from a place where the bread is soft but from a place where the bread is hard (i. e. well baked to a crust).

The word 'ha-mittah' in the basic manuscript bears no meaning. See the manuscripts, which give 'ha-Motzi' as the name for the piece of bread which is broken off when the blessing 'Blessed are You King of the world Who brings the bread out of the earth' is said. (Cf. in that connection TbBer. 35a) Compare the manuscript reading 'ha-perusah', which refers to the same piece of bread. (For additional background of this statement, see the commentary on D. E. Z., VI, 4).

## 6.  And one should not take in his hand (a piece of bread) [as big as] an egg, and if he does so, he surely is an insatiable eater and glutton.

A baraita which mentions customs of the sages may be involved here. From the wording, we may assume that the size of the piece of bread which is broken off when the blessing is uttered at the beginning of the meal is under discussion here. According to one opinion, the size of the piece of bread must not be smaller than an olive. (Cf., e.g., TjBer. VI,1 and cf. TbBer. 46a: The host, not the guest, breaks the bread because the host will not hesitate to break off a piece of good size.)

On the other hand, the piece broken off must not be too big so as not to create an impression of gluttony. Only on Sabbath is an exception made to this rule. In honour of the day, then, one may break off a large piece of bread, but only if he has not done so on other days. If he takes a great piece of bread on the Sabbath as well as on other days, to do so would be a sigh of gluttony. See TbShab. 117b and cf. TbBer. 39b, and other sources. Concerning breaking of bread in general cf. also D. E. Z., VI,4). One should not take in his hand a piece of bread larger than that which will fit decently into the mouth. Breaking off a piece of bread with one's teeth from a big piece in the hand was considered very indecent in the circles of the sages.

The reading 'we-lo johetz beitza' ('he should not take an egg') here in the basic manuscript of D. E. R. must be amended to 'we-lo johetz perusah ke-beitza' ('a piece as big as an egg').

Cf. also M. Goldberg, *Derech Erez Rabba*, p. 19, with the suggested reading 'we-lo jokhal 'adam' etc., in agreement with *Tur*, Or. Haj. 167; cf. also the manuscripts of D. E. R. h.l.

**7a.  And one should not drink his cup in one draught and if he drinks (it in one draught) he surely is a soaker and an insatiable person.**
**7b.  And how many pauses should he make when drinking? Two (pauses) is a sign of good manners, three (pauses) that he belongs to the arrogant.**

This statement is quoted in TbPes. 86b as a baraita and has obviously been drawn from Derekh 'Eretz traditions known at the time. Different rules concerning 'derekh 'eretz' are mentioned in the wording in connection with Rab Huna, the sun of Rab Natan. In the same wording, see also the tradition here in Derekh 'Eretz mentioned in the framework of a story about the visit of Rabbi Jishma'el ben Rabbi José ben Lakonia (a Tanna of the fifth generation; see TbB. M. 88a) .

*And how many pauses . . .* , to empty a goblet in three draughts is arrogant and exaggerated, and to empty it in one draught gives an impression of gluttony, to empty it in two draughts is considered to be decent. (See especially also the commentary in reference to D. E. R., VIII, beginning.)

**8.  And a man should start to eat garlic or onions [from the top but] only from (where) the leaves (sprout). And if eats (first from the top), he surely is an insatiable person.**

In connection with this statement, see the commentary and parallels in reference to D. E. Z., VI,5.

## 9. And one should not drink two cups before reciting Grace after the meal, because it makes him appear a soaker and an insatiable person.

There appears to be no direct parallel for this statement, and the statement does not appear in Mas. Kal. Rab.

Different interpretations are possible. The statement possibly means that one should not drink two goblets of wine prior to saying the 'Birkat ha-Mazon' after a meal, as that would then mean that grace would be said over a third goblet of wine. After drinking two goblets of wine, one would not be able to concentrate to say grace with proper attention after the meal. Cf. e.g., the interpretation of Rosh of the statement of Rab Nahman bar Jitzhaq in TbBer. 51b: '... What is the second cup of punishment? Rab Nahman bar Jitzhaq said: "a second cup"' (i.e. when saying grace after the meal). Cf. also *Nahalat Ja'aqob* on D. E. R. h.l. and cf. TbPes. 110b. If the explanation of Rosh in TbBer. 51b is correct, we find there a parallel in the tradition. See, however, the explanation of Rashi in TbBer. l.c., where the term 'second cup' is explained in line with the wording immediately following concerning the fear of drinking a even number of goblets of wine, because even numbers were supposed to bring misfortune. Cf. TbPes. 110b concerning fear of demons. Rashi explains the text immediately following the statement of Rab Nahman bar Jitzhaq in TbBer. 51b (in connection with the number of goblets) to be merely an example of what can lead to a slackening of attention (through fear and superstition) when saying grace.

If the explanation of Rab Nahman bar Jitzhaq is interpreted in the sense of Rashi, then a parallel with the text here in Derekh 'Eretz is not at issue, considering that a completely different theme (gluttony) is under discussion in Derekh 'Eretz. See also the opinion of M. Goldberg, *Derech Erez Rabba*, p. 20.

Another possible interpretation – the one which is most probable – is that one is not to drink two goblets of wine during 'Birkat ha-Mazon' itself. To drink more goblets of whine while saying grace after the meal would probably give the impression that the wine was not being drunk for the grace, but purely out of desire to drink. One must say the grace after the meal over the goblet with proper attention and with the right intentions. Cf. M. Goldberg l.c. and *Nahalat Ja'aqob* on D. E. R. h.l., and other commentaries.

1. **When two (persons) sit at one table, the greater one (elder or more important one) puts forth his hand first and then the smaller (younger). And if he (i. e. the younger) puts forth his hand (first), then he is a glutton.**

In the Babylonian Talmud, the Jerusalem Talmud, and the Tosephta, we find the same tradition formulated in different ways. The one who breaks the bread for the blessing and who says the blessing may put out his hand first to take bread, or he may be the first to dip and taste his bread (which was often used as a spoon. cf. TbBer. 47a; TbGit. 59b; TjBer. VI,1 [10a]; TosBer. V,7.) That custom does not differ essentially with the custom described here in D. E. according to which the right to sample the food first is reserved for the oldest or most venerable person who broke the bread and said the blessing. (Cf. the wording in TbBer. 46a-47a). An exception was made in the situation involving a host and guests. It was usually the host who broke the bread, though he could, out of respect, let his teacher or another venerable person among his guests break the bread. There is no real contradiction between the version in D. E. R. and the parallels mentioned, considering that in the circles of the sages it must have been customary to let the oldest guest and the guest most respected for his knowledge of the Torah say the blessing while breaking the bread so that he would have been the first allowed to sample the bread. Cf. also the tradition in TbBer. 47a ascribed to Rab.

Under discussion here are rules of etiquette which could be applied flexibly.

2. **It happened that Rabbi 'Aqiba prepared a meal for his pupils and that he served two dishes for them, one half done and the other (well) cooked. First he served to them the half done. The clever among them took hold of the stalk with one hand and tried to tear a piece off with the other hand, but it did not come off. He withdrew his hand from it and ate his bread dry.**

**But the stupid among them took hold of the stalk with one hand and did bite a piece off with his teeth [another reading: took it with both hands and tore it apart]. Rabbi 'Aqiba spoke to him: 'Not so, My son, but place your heel on it in the dish!' After that he did serve for them a (well) cooked dish. They ate and drank and were satisfied. After that he said: to them: 'My sons, I only did all this to you to test you whether you have good manners or not.'**

The story about Rabbi 'Aqiba and his students which follows illustrates the admonition not to behave as a glutton. This story is known only from the Derekh 'Eretz tradition. 'Aqiba has two dishes served. One of the dishes is still raw ('haj') or half done ('na'', cf. the use of this word in, e.g., TbPes. 41a), and the second dish is well cooked. 'Aqiba first has the raw dish served.

The behaviour of the ignorant pupil, who bites off the stalk with his teeth and leaves the rest on the dish, is objectionable for the others present, and moreover it is unhygienic. (The Rabbis of the Talmudic period already recognized the possibility that diseases could be spread through saliva. Cf. among others, S. Krauss, *Talmudische Archäologie* , chap. IV, p. 251.

The behaviour of the ignorant pupil spurred Rabbi 'Aqiba to make his ironic remark. In a statement attributed to Rabbi Shim'on ben Gamli'el, the Medes were praised for the fact that they did not bite off their food with their teeth but cut it, and that they did not kiss someone on the mouth but on the back of the hand. Since we assume that the Medes did not kiss someone on the mouth but on the back of the hand for hygienic reasons, we assume that they also did not bite off their food for hygienic reasons. Cf. Ber. Rab. LXXIV,2 and other sources. Cf. especially TbBer. 8b and Midr. ha-Gad. on Gen. 31,2 (ed. M. Margulies, p. 547), where Rabbi 'Aqiba is mentioned as the authority!

### 3.  A man should not eat before the fourth hour (of the day) and he should not wash himself in the bathhouse before the fourth hour.

It is not good for one to eat before the fourth hour. One calculated the day from 'netz ha-hammah', the point at which the first rays of the sun became visible. The day was divided into hours (considered to be dependent on the time of the year and the lengthening and shortening of daylight). On the average, the sun in Israel rises about 6:00 a.m. our time. The fourth hour correspondents roughly to 10:00 a.m. our time. See E. Z. Melamed, *Pirqei Minhag we-Halakhah*, Jerusalem 1970, p. 30.

Further information about the custom of the morning meal in the Tannaitic period is contained in a baraita in TbShab. 10a and in TbPes. 12b. Gladiators eat in the first hour (about 7:00 a.m.), robbers eat in the second hour (about 8:00 a.m.), owners of inherited wealth eat in the third hour (about 9:00 a.m.), ordinary people eat in the fourth hour (about 10:00 a.m.), and day labourers in the field eat in the fifth hour (about 11:00 a.m.). Finally, sages, who pray and study before eating, eat in the sixth hour (about noon). See further discussion concerning that in the gemara in TbShab. 10a. In reference to another version of the baraita, see also R. Rabbinovicz, *Seph. Diqduqei Sopherim*, and M. Higger, *'Otzar ha-Baraitot*, VI, p. 402. Such a tradition is undoubtedly the background to the admonition not to eat before the fourth hour, for less-respected people such as robbers and gladiators – certainly no sages – eat before the fourth hour.

According to one explanation in Tosaphot on TbPes. 107b, there are definite indications that the fourth hour did not refer to the fourth hour of the day, but that one was to understand the fourth hour to be the fourth hour after arising. In TbPes. 107b., it is said that King Agrippa ate in the ninth hour and that kings arise in the third hour of the day. (Cf. MBer. I,2 and TbBer. 8b-9a.) In other words, king Agrippa ate in the sixth hour after arising, which concurred with the habits of the sages, as we saw in the baraita mentioned. (Cf. *Tosaphists* in reference to TbPes. 107b; the explanation of the *Tosaphists*, however, seems rather contrived.)

Beside the duty first to pray and study before eating, one finds another reason for not eating very early in TbBer. 44b. One was especially not to eat vegetables before the fourth hour as it would be unpleasant for others who observed the custom of not eating before the fourth hour. In talking with someone who had already eaten, they would have to inhale his breath (which bore the smell of food) while they themselves had not yet eaten.

Health reasons for the eating regulations are also suggested, in the gemara of Mas. Kal. Rab. (ed. N.N. Coronel, 18a and in ed. M. Higger, pp. 335−336). One was certainly not to eat a heavy meal to early. In our opinion, the most important reason for the eating regulations was the custom of the sages first to pray and study in the mornings. Cf. the tradition of Rabbi Hanina, who reproved early bathers and told them they should first devote attention to studying (TjBer. III,4 [6c], and cf. the instructions concerning that in TbBer. 22a. It is understandable that the first meal was eaten so late in the day in light of the fact that, in the Tannaitic period, one usually ate only two meals a day. See S. Krauss, *Talmudische Archäologie*, III, chap.IX, p. 26ff.

## 4. Hot water in large quantities is harmful to the body, in a small quantity it is beneficial to the body. Wine in a large quantity is harmful to the body, in a small quantity it is beneficial.

'Hamin' without any additions, means 'warm water' (Latin: calidae). Cf. S. Krauss, *Talmudische Archäologie*, I, chap.IV, p. 210 and p. 667, note 13. In all probability, bath water and bathing in water are under discussion here, but it is certainly not impossible that drinking warm water is also meant. Cf. also the drinking of wine in the text following the statement. While bathing in hot water, one also drank some of the hot water (sometimes with herbs; see S. Krauss, o.c., ibid., pp. 210−228; cf. TbShab. 41a; TbShab. 119a; TbB.B. 146a. It was especially considered very healthy to take hot baths. Cf. TbGit. 68a, MNed. XI,1 and TbNed. 80a, Tb'Er. 55b, TbHul. 24b, Waj. Rab. XIV,3 and other sources. Like other things, done in an excessive way bathing too often in hot water was considered harmful to one's health.

In an aphorism involving numbers in TbGit. 70a and A.R.N. [a] XXXVII, (55a), and other sources, seven things are mentioned which are good in small amounts and harmful in excessive amounts, including the two things mentioned here: warm water and wine. This statement most certainly is rooted in the Tannaitic period. In other traditions, it is emphasized that one must rinse oneself off with cold water after taking a hot bath. It is also stated that one must especially not rinse one self off with warm water as this would weaken the bather's constitution, apart from the fact that it would mean wasting warm water, which was expensive. Cf. D. E. R., X (end), and the parallels mentioned there and cf.especially TbShab. 40a; TjShab. III, 4 [6a] and TbTa'an. 23a. Cf. also S. Krauss, *Talmudische Archäologie*, I, chap. IV, p. 228 ff. and notes, p. 682. In reference to health and wine cf., e.g., TbBer. 35b; TbB. B. 12b; TbB. B. 88b; Tb'Ab. Zar. 40b.

**5.  Three things are of equal importance: wisdom, fear and meekness.**

See our remarks in the commentary in reference to D. E. Z., V,5. One can consider the statement here in D. E. R. as a reaction to a discussion about the importance of the order of (especially) 'jir'ah' (fear) and 'anawah' (meekness). The discussion was prompted by an old statement attributed to Rabbi Pinhas ben Ja'ir about the degrees of sacredness in which he placed 'jir'ah' above 'anawah' (according to TjShab. I,3, on the basis of Prov. 22:4).

It appears, that the statement of Rabbi Pinhas ben Ja'ir contains some exegetical difficulties resulting in different versions. Considering that, on the basis of Prov. 22:4, one may conclude that "anawah" must be considered more important than 'jir'ah' ('The heel of meekness ["anawah"] fear of the Lord ["jir'ah"]', i.e., 'fear of the Lord' is not more than the heel of 'meekness'). There are also other versions of the statement of Pinhas ben Ja'ir in which the order of the two concepts is reversed and according to which 'fear of the Lord' ('jir'ah') is only a preliminary step toward the higher 'meekness' ("anawah"). See all parallels and the commentary referring to D. E. Z. l.c. Also, see, especially the statement of Rabbi Jehoshua ben Levi in Tb'Ab. Zar. 20b. Rabbi Jehoshua ben Levi considers "anawah' to be most important; cf. Tb'Ab. Zar. 16b. In connection with the entire issue, see especially the commentary of the *Tosaphists* in reference to Tb'Ab. Zar. 20b and various versions of the statement of Rabbi Pinhas ben Ja'ir in which it is stated – on the basis of the statement here in D. E. R. – that one of the three characteristics (wisdom fear and meekness) has not any value without the other two.

**6a.  One who is entering a privy should not turn his face to the east and his back to the west (or his face to the west and his back to the east) but (he should turn) to the sides (i. e. to the north and the south). And he should not uncover himself until he sits and he should not wipe himself until he sits and he should not wipe with the right hand but with the left.**

**6b.  It happened to Rabbi 'Aqiba that he followed Rabbi Jehoshua to watch**

**his behaviour [other Mss. add: He saw that he entered the privy just
(turning his face and back) to the sides (i. e. south and north) and that he did
not uncover himself until he was seated and that he did not wipe (himself)
with the right hand but with the left] and ( after watching these things) he
asked: 'Why one does not wipe with the right hand?' Rabbi 'Eli'ezer said:
'Because one eats with it.' Rabban Gamli'el said: 'Because one points with
it the accents (i. e. the cantillations) of the Torah.'**

The custom described here is mentioned in the sources of the story about Rabbi
'Aqiba which follows in the text. The custom goes back to the time before the
destruction of the Temple. Cf. TjBer. IX,8 [14b-c]; TbBer. 61a and 62a;
A. R. N. [a], LX (64b), and other sources. In the tradition just mentioned and in
parallels, a number of acts are mentioned which were not allowed to be carried
out near the Temple or the Temple Mount (see MBer. IX,5) because these acts
were perceived to be insulting for the Holy Presence there. According to the
gemara, these acts included urinating or defecating with the genitals or rectum
exposed in the direction of the Temple Mount and the Temple. According to
TbBer. 61b and Tj. l.c., there were different opinions. According to Rabbi
Jehudah, the rule not to consult nature east or west (i. e., with the rectum or the
genitals in the direction of the Temple) applied only when the Second Temple
was still standing.

   The origin of the custom, then, clearly must be sought in the Second Temple
Period. According to Rabbi José in the Jerusalem Talmud, the rule applied
only from 'Ha-Tzophim' (Mount Scopus) and the inner side of it (i. e., the side
closer to Jerusalem than Mount Scopus, the side facing the city) and not the
other side of Mount Scopus, from which the Temple was no longer visible.
According to the version of Rabbi José's opinion in the Babylonian Talmud,
the rule applied only when Jerusalem and the Temple were in sight (thus in an
open place and not surrounded by walls which would obstruct the view of
Jerusalem and the Temple) and at the moment that the Shekhinah was still
remaining on the Temple Mount. Cf. also the opinions of Rabbi Johanan and
Rab according to the version in TbBer. l.c.) According to Rabbi 'Aqiba, the
rule applied in all places (except in accordance with the condition set forth in
the version in TjBer., l.c. – those surrounded by walls). Therefore, the rule also
applied outside of Israel (and it also applied after the fall of the Temple.) From
the context of the story of Rabbi 'Aqiba which follows in the text, it is clear that
he still considered the rule to apply in his time also. From the gemara it is clear
that the opinion of Rabbi 'Aqiba deserves preference. For regions in Galilee
and parts of Judea, which were neither west nor east of Jerusalem, majority
opinion held that another rule applied, namely, that the genitals or rectum
should face east or west (and thus with the sides toward Jerusalem), and not
north or south (i. e., in the direction of Jerusalem; cf. also Siphrei, Ki-Tetze,
pisqa 257, ed. L. Finkelstein p. 281, a statement of Rabbi Jishma'el).

The reading in the basis manuscript of D. E. R. must be corrected with the aid of the manuscripts and the parallel in TjBer. l.c. to read: '. . . panaw le-mizrah we-'ahoraw le-ma'arab' (i. e., not with his face to the east nor his posterior to the west, or vice-versa). The explanation in the commentaries (see commentaries in connection with with *Shul. Ar.*, Or. Haj. 3,5 and with Siphrei, Ki-Tetze, pisqa 257, ed. M. Friedmann 120b) in connection with the opinion that the forbiddance especially concerns baring one's posterior to the west because of the presence of the Shekhinah in the west, deviates from the mentioned traditions of 'Eretz Israel. The notion of the Shekhinah in the west is according to L. Finkelstein (Siphrei l.c.) of Babylonian origin.(See TbB. B. 25a, and especially the explanation of L. Finkelstein on Siphrei l.c., p. 281, note 11, in which he shows that the tradition in Siphrei deals with a prohibition (which also held in Galilee) that one was not to turn to the south or the north. According to our opinion the text in Siphrei l.c. pertains to a southern tradition and to the forbiddance to direct one's posterior to the north and his face to the south. However, the opinion that the presence of the Shekhinah in the west is only a Babylonian tradition is dubious. See in this connection M. Goldberg, *Untersuchungen über die Vorstellung der Shekhina in der Frühen Rabbinischen Literatur*, pp. 365–371!

*He did not uncover himself until he sat down.* Cf. TbTam. 27b, where it appears that the admonition not to undress oneself while standing applied especially on open land and was meant to prevent one from being seen naked by others. Cf. Rabbenu Gershom and others in that source. The words . . . *and he did not wipe himself until he was seated* are difficult to understand. These words are missing in other manuscripts of D. E. R., possibly because they were not well understood.

In the tradition in TjBer. l.c., with which the tradition in D. E. shows strong agreement, we find the wording 'he did not sit own until he rubbed.' The word 'shiphsheph' (rubbing) can be explained as 'he did not sit before rubbing (the rectum).' Cf. Jastrow, *Dictionary*, sub 'shaphaph'. An explanation like that makes no sense, better seems the reading in the basis manuscript of D. E. of 'he did not wipe himself until he sat down'.

We mention here the word order in the Talmud Jerushalmi, but with the following explanation: 'he did not sit down until he dug a hole' (in accordance with the translation of TjBer. l.c., ed. M. Schwab : *The Talmud of Jerusalem*, I, New York 1969, p. 170, in reference to Dt. 23:14). It is prorbably appropriate here to think of the habit of scraping away earth with the feet before defecating in order to be able to cover up the excrement as soon as possible after defecation. One finds a conformation of this explanation in the Torah, see Dt. 23:14 (13): 'You will have a spade with your tools, and when you are sitting outside you will dig a hole with it and cover your excrements.' This text of the Torah is mentioned in the context of Siphrei l.c.!!

The reading in the basis manuscript in D. E. R. VII,6b is much too short, and

gives the impression of being a shortened version of a much lengthier source.
The other manuscripts have supplemented the tradition here to conform with
the description of events in the sources.

The words 'we-sha'al' (*and he asked*) in the basis manuscript must be deleted.
The text which follows those words has nothing to do with a question put to
Rabbi Jehoshua by Rabbi 'Aqiba.

The matter here concerns a separate baraita from a Tannaitic discussion. See
TbBer.62a (the baraita is missing in Ms. Munich). The reading in D.E.R.,
however, deviates from the reading in TbBer. l.c. According to the reading in
TbBer. l.c., Rabbi Jehoshua says: 'because one writes with it' (i.e. with the
right hand), whereas according to D. E. h.l., he says: 'because he drinks with it'.
According to TbBer. l.c. it is Rabbi 'Aqiba who says: 'because one points with it
to the accent of the Torah (scroll)', and not Rabban Gamli'el, as according to
the version in D. E. R. h.l. (See also the version in A. R. N.[a], XL (64b), where
the reason of eating and drinking is ascribed to Rabbi Jehoshua, and the reason
of pointing to the accents in the Torah is ascribed to Rabbi 'Eli'ezer. It is
difficult to reconstruct the correct reading.)

See Rashi in reference to TbBer.62a with the explanation that accents
(cantillations) indicate up- and downward motion with the hand in accordance
with musical accents in the Scripture, as such a motion was customary during
the reading of the Torah in Israel.

7. **A man should not rejoice among people who weep and he should not
weep among people who rejoice; he should not stay awake among people
who sleep and he should not sleep among people who are awake; he should
not be standing among people who are sitting ad he should not sit among
people who are standing.**

**A general rule regarding this matter: A man should not do differ his
disposition from the disposition of his fellow and of other men.**

For remarks, see commentary in reference to D.E.Z. V,6.

## Derekh 'Eretz Rabbah, Chapter VIII

**1a.** **One who visits a home should not say to them (i. e. to the host or the servants) 'Serve me up, that I may eat', until they say it (i. e. until he is invited to eat).**

**1b.** **When they mix for him a cup (of wine) he must drink with interruptions. And how many pauses he should make? (If his wine is mixed ) with warm water three times, and with cold water four times.**

**1c.** **About which matters is spoken (here)? About a cup (served) in Galilee but as far as a cup (is served ) in Judah one may make a pause in his drinking as often as one desires.**

A guest must wait until he is offered something; he may not ask for food or drink himself. In the period of the Tanna'im and Amora'im, wine was much stronger than it is at present, and it had to be mixed with water. Cold wine was normally composed of one part wine to two parts water, and warm wine was composed of one part wine to three parts water. Wine was more intoxicating when drunk warm than when drunk cold. See S. Krauss, *Talmudische Archäologie*, II, chap. VI, p. 241 and p. 616, note 724; and cf. especially TjMa'as. Shen. III,8 [50d].

In the circles of the sages, it was considered extremely indecent to empty a goblet of wine in one draught. See D. E. R., VI, 7 and parallels. At the same time one was advised not to empty the goblet in too many draughts and not to take too many pauses while drinking, as that could be taken a sign of false modesty and considered exaggerated. See the baraita in TbPes. 86b and cf. D. E. R. l.c. According to that baraita, taking two pauses (i. e., three draughts) was a sign of haughtiness. There is a clear difference between the baraita and the text here. When drinking warm wine, one has to take three pauses (i. e., drink the wine in four draughts), and when drinking cold wine, one has to take four pauses (i. e., drink the wine in five draughts). It is possible that one was supposed to drink cold wine in more draughts than warm wine because cold wine was usually poured out in greater quantities than warm wine, since it was not as intoxicating as warm wine. An exception was made in instances when smaller goblets, such as those in Judea, were used. In such instances, one was allowed to drink the goblet empty in fewer draughts, possibly even in one draught. See also S. Krauss, *Talmudische Archäologie*, III, p. 59; cf. TbPes. 86b.

See, however, the remarkable translation by M. Higger, *Massekhtot Derekh 'Eretz*, p. 74; 'not more than three times in cases of warm liquid, and not more than four times in the case of cold liquid'. See the commentary in *Nahalat Ja'aqob* on D.E. h.l., where it is incorrectly assumed that the goblets used in Judea were larger, so that one in Judea could drink a goblet empty in as many draughts as one liked.

**2. A man should not say to his fellow: 'Come and eat (in return for) what you gave me to eat.' Because that is a kind of usury. In Jerusalem they used to give in return (for the meal) gifts to their children.**

Eating meals together was important to the sages, and among them there was the custom of inviting each other for meals and of reciprocating invitations. The meaning of the statement here in D.E.R. can be understood only in light of traditions which the wording is closely related to the wording in D.E.R. h.l.

See D.E.R., VIII,5; Mekh. de-R. Jishm., Mishpatim, par. 13, ed. M. Friedmann, 89b; TosB.Q. VII,8 (cf. idem VI,14); Tj'Ab. Zar. I,3 [39c]; TjDem. IV [24a]; TbHul. 94a. One finds there the following statement, either anonymous or attributed to Rabbi Me'ir: 'One must not urge his neighbour to be his guest, knowing that he will not accept (eat).' This is used in the wording of the traditions mentioned as an example of 'genibat da'at' (the stealing of thoughts, i.e., the creation of false ideas and deception). In giving someone such invitation, one misleads that person and quite wrongly places demands on that person's sense of gratitude. With the aid of the parallels mentioned, one can supplement the statement in D.E. as follows: 'One may not say to a companion: "Come and eat with me just as you gave me a meal", knowing that his companion cannot accept the invitation, for that would be like usury.' In giving such an invitation, one makes the impression of wanting to do something in return for a companion without in fact being ready to do so – and thus escapes his obligation to that person. He earns another's appreciation free, without effort, just as one earns interest.

It is quite possible, however, that this element was given a different meaning in D.E. than in the sources. The statement *A man should not say: 'Come and eat ...'* means that when one is inviting someone to be his guest for a meal, one should be careful not to give the guest the impression that he is being invited in return for a meal he gave the host. Unselfishness and true hospitality are lost in situations in which something is done in return for something done. A stronger motive behind the statement may be to prevent a host from inviting someone to a meal expressly in return for a meal, with the hope that the guest will be afraid of creating the impression of wanting to be paid in kind for his earlier hospitality to the host and therefore will eat less. That would amount to profit for the host.

The continuation of the text with the words *In Jerusalem they used to give in return for the meal ('mappala') gifts ("aspatatja') to their children* offers great difficulties for interpretation. The concept of "aspatatja' (here translated as *gifts*; see basis manuscript) is difficult to place. On the basis of related parallels,

S. Krauss (*Griechische und Lateinische Lehnöwrter im Talmud, Midrash und Targum*, I, p. 11) suggests the reading of "askepasra' (Greek: 'skepastra' = cover, curtain); along with that, he reads "aphla' in stead of 'mappalah', which is derived from 'epulae' (meals). The complete meaning, then, is as follows: during meals in Jerusalem, the curtain before the entrance way was raised as a sign that no more guests were to come in. There is indeed a tradition found in 'Eikh. Rab. IV,4, TosBer. IV,9 and TbB. B. 93b in which that custom is confirmed. The manuscripts in D. E. R., however, do not confirm that convincingly. 'Mappala' is also interpreted here in D. E. as 'mappula' ('mappah' ; 'mitpahat' = bandage, wrap), terms which appear in the parallels mentioned. See ' Eikh.Rab. l.c.; TosBer, l.c. and TbB. B. l.c. 'Mappula' is a partition, a curtain. Cf. S. Krauss, *Talmudische Archäologie*, III, p. 43, note 309. In combination with the word order in D. E. that interpretation is not free of problems. One could invert the words and with the help of the manuscripts read: 'hophkhin mappula le-'akhsania she-la-hem' (they turned the 'mappula' for their guests [in order to show that no more guests could be received]).

One finds an interesting tradition in the parallels which are closely related in terms of content with D. E. R. These parallels appear in TjDem. l.c. and contain the following:

(U-be-Jerushalajim hajah hophekh philkijah ['ikhlijah] di-jemina le-shim'olah [de-shim'ola li-jemina]): *In Jerusalem, people were accustomed to turning the 'philkijah'* (other versions: 'ikhlijah', or: 'philbijah' or 'piwla' cf. also 'Ahabat Tzion ed. B. Ratner on TosDem., IV, p. 109) *from right to left [or: from left to right]*. See the interpretation of J. Levy, *Neuhebräisches und Chaldäisches Wörterbuch*, sub "ikhlijah'. One was was supposed to have turned the right side of the curtain toward the left if the eating hall was full and no guests could be received.

A more likely explanation is that in TjDem. and Tj'Ab. Zar. There is a discussion about a 'fibula' (a kind of clasp for clothing). See the reading in 'Eikh. Rab. and see especially *Mattanot Kehuna* on 'Eikh. Rab. l.c. In certain circles in Jerusalem, one was supposed to move the 'fibula' from right to left as a sign that the wearer had already been invited to have a meal with someone; this would then make it impossible for one to give an insincere invitation to someone. Cf. also in 'Eikh. Rab. l.c. the custom in certain circles in Jerusalem of rolling up the left sleeve as a sign that one had been invited to a meal. See especially Jastrow, *Dictionary*, sub 'piwla'; cf. S. Lieberman, *Tosephta Ki-Pheshutah*, I, 1956, p. 63; J. N. Epstein, *Tarbitz*, V (3), p. 27. In terms of content, such an explanation would fit extremely well here in D. E., but it would not do justice to the text as such. See, however, the attempt in *Mattanot Kehuna* l.c. to connect the reading "aphsatatja' with the reading 'philbijah'.

See also the reconstruction suggested by the Gaon of Vilna; *In Jerusalem, however, they used to exchange invitations with another ('hophekhin 'et ha-'akhsanja she-la-hem zeh la-zeh')*.

This reading, however, also does not do complete justice to the readings in the manuscripts of D. E.. Cf. the reading in *Tur*. Or.Haj., 170 (*Beit Joseph*) and the reading in Ms. Epstein (in *Qadmoniot ha-Jehudim*), and see also *Nahalat Ja'aqob* on D. E. R. h.l. with the reading : "akhsanja le-nesu'im': *In Jerusalem, one was invited to a wedding in exchange for an ordinary meal.*' This version, though, also does not do justice to the readings of the manuscripts available.

The reading which does the most justice to the versions in the manuscripts of D. E. R. is *U-be-Jerushalajim haju hophekhin 'aphsanja le-taphla she-la-hem* ,interpreted as: *And in Jerusalem(when one was invited to dine), one would in return give gifts to their children (of the hosts).* See the translation of M. Higger, *Massekhtot Derekh 'Eretz*, 1935, p. 74 and see ibid., p. 224, note 8. He interprets "aphsanja' (Greek 'opsonion') as 'doron' (gift), with reference to TbSanh.18b and TjSanh.II(20c) and Shir ha-Shir. Rab. I,12. The Greek word 'opsonion', however, is very freely interpreted here. The word normally means: provisions, allowance, wages. In this case though, it applies to the reading in the manuscripts of D. E. The giving of gifts to the members of the host's household fits into the section dealing with inviting someone in return for previous invitations, and possibly it was intended to avoid the impression that the guest was seeking some advantage. The guest thus could enjoy the hospitality of his host in an unselfish manner. It is even possible that the statement about the giving of gifts in D. E. h.l. can be explained in light of a more extensive original tradition in which was discussed the bad custom of offering a gift to someone with the knowledge that he would not want to accept it, as can been seen in the related context in TjDem. l.c. and Tj 'Ab. Zar. l.c. The tradition and context here in D. E. R. is based on statements attributed to Rabbi Me'ir in TbHul.94a and TosB. B. VI,14. M. Higger, *Massekhtot Ze'irot*, 1970, p. 24, notes that the version in TbHul. is (in context) more complete than the version in D. E. R. Here in D. E. R., however, there are extra elements present which have to do with sources from 'Eretz Israel!!

3.  **A man should not send to his fellow a jug of wine while its mouth is filled with oil (i. e. with a layer of oil floating on the wine), because this may lead to death. It happened that a certain man arranged a feast for his son and when he saw that a company of people had arrived and had taken place for a meal, he came in to serve wine [other reading: to bring oil]. When he saw that it was filled with oil [other reading: wine] he strangled himself (of shame) and died. Therefore the sages said: 'A man should not send to his fellow a jug of wine and put (a layer of) oil at its mouth, because this may lead to death.'**

A man should not sand to his fellow a jug of wine when the mouth of it is full of oil, i. e., when oil is floating on top of the wine. One is not to mislead another by sending him a jug of oil which actually consists of only an upper layer of oil floating on top of wine or (according to one parallel) water. Cf. a reading in TosB. B. VI,14. See *Hasdei David* (ed. B. A. Ratner) on TosB. B. l.c. and cf. Mas. Kal. Rab., ed. M. Higger, IX, p. 334. In the parallels a connection is established between this statement and the other statements here in D. E. R. and other statements related to D. E. R. See TosB. B. VI,14; TbHul.94a, the statement here is mentioned next to the statements of Rabbi Me'ir as a separate baraita.

There was the danger that one could invite guests, assuming that he had an entire jug of oil with which to light candles or prepare food, and then do something to himself out of shame upon suddenly realising that he would not be able to entertain his guests because he in fact had only water or wine and not the oil necessary for preparing the meal. Cf. *Hasdei David* on TosB. B.VI,14 and cf. *Rashi* and *Maharasha* in connection with TbHul. 94a and *Nahalat Ja'aqob* in connection with D. E. R. h.l. Cf. the reading of the Gaon of Vilna, and see other sources.

The reading in the basis manuscript raises problems and must be corrected. According to the reading in the basis manuscript, the host would want to pour out wine for his guests, but to his horror he would assume from the layer of oil in the jug that he only had a jug of oil. This reading, however, does not clarify why a jug of water in stead of wine is discussed in, e.g. Mas. Kal. Rab. l.c. and Tos.B. B. l.c. It is apparent from the beginning of the section (*while its mouth is filled with oil*) that the person who sent the jug fully intended to create the impression that the entire jug was filled with oil. This intention is found in all the parallels; cf. especially the reading in Mas. Kal. Rab., ed. M. Higger, IX, p. 334. It can be assumed here that the matter concerns oil, which was more expensive than wine. We therefor give a preference here (in accordance with the commentaries mentioned and with M. Higger, *Massekhtot Derekh 'Eretz*, p. 225 and others) to the reading which is in agreement with the tradition in TbHul.94a: 'He went in to bring oil, saw that it was full of wine and hanged himself.' This reading contradicts the reading of the basis manuscript in D. E. R. h.l.

The concept of 'genibat da'at' (intentional deception) is also of central concern here. The giver of the jug (it is not impossible that a gift is involved in this situation) wanted to give the impression that he was sending a jug of expensive oil when in fact he was sending a jug of wine (or even water), which is cheaper. Such deception – which at first glance appears innocent (as the sender was not expecting any illegal gain) – can lead to very serious consequences. It is also a form of false generosity!

**4.  A man should not say to his fellow: 'Take oil' of an (in reality) empty jar (knowing that his fellow for some reason will not do so), because he would display false generosity to him.**

No one may say to a companion: 'take oil' (oil used as salve) from an empty jar, knowing beforehand that he will not accept the offer anyway. See the explanation in Mas. Kal. Rab., ed. M. Higger, IX, p. 335. That would be 'to steal thoughts' or, to use the words in D. E. 'doing a favour (and gaining gratitude) for nothing', i. e., showing false generosity. The companion would be grateful for an empty offer. According to the readings in TbHul. 94a and TosB. B. VI,14, those words are from a statement made by Rabbi Me'ir. (In this connection, see W. Bacher, *Die Agada der Tannaiten*, II., p. 16. In other sources the statement is mentioned but attributed to no one; see parallels apparatus.

Compare other closely related examples given in the parallels (TbHul. 94a and TosB. B. l.c. in the name of Rabbi Me'ir; without attribution in Mekh. de-R. Jishm. l.c., TosB. Q. VII,8; TjDem. l.c. and in Tj'Ab. Zar.l.c. In the parallels there appears the term 'genibat da'at'. These examples include the following: 'He should not open casks of wine (for a guest) which are to be resold to the shopkeeper, unless he informs the guest of that.' I.e., one should not open a cask of wine for the guest and let him think that he is so important that a cask of wine is especially opened for him, letting him think that the wine left over after the meal will shortly go sour, and not telling him that which has not been used will go back to the shopkeeper (according to prior arrangements). That also constitutes false generosity.

One should also not offer a gift to someone knowing that he will not be able to or will not want to accept it. This also constitutes false generosity. Cf. D. E. R. VIII,5. The expression used for these situations in the parallels is 'miphne she-to'eno ta'anat hinnam' (because he unjustly lays claim). This means that one exacted gratitude from someone without having done something to deserve it. Another expression used (also found in D. E. R. VIII) is 'genibat da'at' See also the expression 'mehanehu tobat hinnam' (doing a favour without effort). Especially in connection with the statement here in D. E. R. that one was not to offer someone oil while knowing that the jar is empty, it is suggested in the gemara in TbHul.94a that an exception be made when such behaviour is intended to accord the guest special honour.

## 5. A man should not urge his fellow to dine (with him), knowing that he will not dine. And he should not offer him many gifts, knowing that he will not accept (them).

These statements (compare commentary D. E. R. VII,2 and 4 and 5) are handed down in the name of Rabbi Me'ir in TosB. B. VI,14 and in TbHul.94a; and they are recorded without attribution in other parallels. To urge someone to come to dine or to offer him gifts with the knowledge that he will not be able to accept is a form of false generosity. See further commentary in reference to D. E. R. VIII,2.

6. **A man should not offer new wine to drink, pretending that it is old (wine), because this is a kind of robbery.**

One should not serve new wine and pretend that it is old wine, for that is a form of robbery. We do not find this statement in the parallels mentioned! A number of manuscripts in D. E. R. h.l. read: 'A man should not serve old wine and pass it off as new wine.' The remark that the behaviour described is a form of robbery possible places the statement somewhat outside of the context of the text which precedes it, in which there was no mention of robbery but of false generosity. It is possible to give a sensible explanation of the alternative reading in the manuscripts, according to which one should not serve old wine and pretend that it is new wine. This probably refers to the situation in which a wine seller wanted to sell new wine to his customer and let him have a taste of old wine, whereby the buyer was misled and thought he was buying new wine of exceptional quality. This was a form of deception and in fact of robbery, in the sense that the wine seller intentionally put his customer at a disadvantage.

According to the reading in the basis manuscript, however, the situation is the other way round, and it is stated that one should not serve a guest new wine and pretend that it is old wine. This reading would bear upon the situation in which, e.g., an innkeeper would give a guest new wine and pass it off as old wine, and thereby cheat the customer. This would therefore also be a form of robbery in the sense that the innkeeper intentionally put the customer at a financial disadvantage.

7. **When one is offering drink to assdrivers [ better reading: when he is pouring out wine (slowly to leave the sediment) for assdrivers] he should not say to them: 'remove this (wine or sediment) and put it to the other (wine)', for this is a kind of robbery.**

This statement can be interpreted correctly only with the aid of the parallel in TosB. M. III,27 (cf. TjB. M. III [9c] and TbB. M. 60a [see MB. M. IV,11] and cf. R. Rabbinovicz. *Diqduqei Sopherim* on TbB. M. l.c., Ms. Hamburg): 'One does not mix the sediment of wine (that one is not selling at a given moment) with the wine (that one is selling at a given moment ; and without the customer telling that). But one has to give him the sediment from the wine (i. e. one is allowed to add to the wine the sediment from the wine that a customer is buying). How it is in practise? This means that if one is pouring out ('shopheh'; the Mss. in D. E. R. h.l. have the readings 'shopheh' and 'shophekh'!!) wine (i. e. pouring it slowly into the jugs) for ass drivers then one is allowed to add to the customer's wine the sediment from that wine, but not from any other wine. As it is said: "When one is adding to the customers wine, to day's sediment must be added to to day's wine, and tomorrow's (yesterday's) sediment must be added to tomorrow's (yesterday's) wine."' Cf. especially Rashi in reference to TbB. M.6

In Ms. Oxford, Bodleian, cat. A. Neubauer (I, p. 306) no. 1100 and in Ms. Munich (cat. M. Steinschneider) no. 95 the word 'shopheh' (pouring wine slowly into a jug) is used and in Ms. New York, J.Th.S. (cat. E.N. Adler) no. 4465a the word 'shophekh' is used! These readings deserve preference over the reading 'mashkeh' in the basis manuscript. 'Shaphah' means to pour out slowly so as to leave the sediment behind, especially when selling wine. The reading 'shopheh' establishes a direct relationship to the source in Tos. l.c. In agreement with that source, the explanation of that statement here in D. E. is as follows: *If one pours out wine and gives it to the ass drivers, one should not say to them; 'remove the sediment from this wine and mix it into that wine (i. e. other wine than that which the sediment came from).'*

N.B. cf. the analogous expressions in D.E.R. h.l. and in Tos. l.c. Upon delivering or reselling the wine, the ass drivers would not inform the recipient that the wine was mixed with sediment from other wine, which – apart from the fact that the seller would gain an unjust profit in reference to the volume of the wine – in many cases would have a bad effect on the quality of the wine.(Cf. TbB. M.60a, concerning the duty to inform the customer if the wine has been mixed). The recipient would thus be deceived. Cf. also, e.g., the forbiddance in MB. M. IV.11 to sell wine mixed with water to vendors even if they knew about the mixture, for they would buy and sell it and simply cheat other people! Cf. TjB. M. III [9c] and other sources.

This statement in D. E. R. has also been interpreted wrongly by commentators. Cf.,e.g., the reading 'silqu mi-zeh u-tenu la-zeh' in stead of 'silqu 'et zeh u-tenu la-zeh' suggested by the Gaon of Vilna, and cf. the translation of M. Ginsberg in *The Minor Tractates of the Talmud*, ed. A. Cohen, II, p. 55: 'Take away this man's cup and pass it to someone else.' The suggestion is that he has already had his drink when in fact he has not. Cf, also the interpretation of M. Higger, *Massekhtot Ze'irot*, p. 75: 'He must not say to his servants: "Remove the good wine and give them the bad wine instead."' In this situation, one may assume that the assdrivers have been drinking at an inn and have already drunk so much that they would not notice that the good wine had been replaced by bad wine (on the suggestion of the innkeeper) and that they would believe that they had been drinking only good wine. If the innkeeper charges them for the price of good wine, then that is a form of robbery. We find, however, that the original version and meaning must be sought in reference to TosB. M. III,27, and to TbB. M.60a [see Ms. Hamburg], in agreement with the previously mentioned commentary, according to which it is a form of robbery if a seller lets assdrivers mix sediment with wine to which it does not belong. In light of that commentary the reading in the basis manuscript is vindicated. N. B.: the statement following (i.e. D. E. R. VIII,8) is related to the same context in MB.M. IV,11 and provides further evidence that a source of the statement here in D. E. R. must be sought in this and related sources.

8. **When one is passing sellers of produce in the market place, one should not say to them: 'How much (do you ask) for this article?', when he has no intention of buying it. Because he encourages the mind of the seller (that he will sell it). [Other reading: He enlarges the mistake of the seller (i. e. his false hope to sell it)].**

This statement is analogous to a statement in MB. M. IV,10 which is connected with Lev. 25:17: 'You shall not wrong one another, but you shall fear your God; for I am the Lord your God.' This passage is explained as referring to wronging people with words (as opposed to the passage in Lev.19:14 which is explained as referring to material fraud and oppression). MB. M. IV,10: 'Like as the law against defrauding applies to buying and selling, so does it apply to spoken words. A man may not say: "How much is this thing?", if he does not wish to buy it.' Cf.TbB. M.85b andTbPes. 112b; Pes. Rab., pisqa 42.

A rather analogous statement appears in TbB. M. 85b in the name of Rabbi Jehudah: 'One may not feign interest in a purchase when he has no money, since this is known to the heart only, and of everything known only to the heart it is written "And you shall fear your God" (Lev.25:17).' Here, it does not concern a matter which falls under the jurisdiction of and is punishable under halakhah. No one else can determine whether someone's interest in the goods for sale is genuine or feigned; it is a matter of the heart, and therefore it is said that Heaven can determine the genuineness of the interest. Concerning matters which involved internal intentions which cannot be ascertained by the outside world, Scripture adds the words 'and you shall fear your God.' The term 'masur li-lebab' (left to the heart only) refers to matters of the heart, for which there are no hard and fast halakhic rules but which must be determined by the individual's sense of ethics.

The expression 'she-mashbiah da'ato' (satisfying or encouraging his mind) refers to a seller who is wrongly satisfied with the thought of selling something. Cf. the other version 'she-mashbiah ta'uto', i.e. enlarging the mistake of the seller (in selling his article). See also the reading 'she-mashbiah 'eino shel mokher', i.e., for thereby he ('enlarges the eye' and) induces the seller to overcharge other buyers. Cf. M. Higger, *Massekhtot Derekh 'Eretz*, p. 75.

**1a. A man should not break bread over a dish but a man may wipe the dish with a peace of bread [another reading: ... and a man should not wipe the dish with a piece of bread].**

A man should not break bread over the dish, so that no crumbs fall into the dish. Others might find crumbs in a dish unappetizing and not wish to eat further. Cf. the explanation in *Nahalat Ja'aqob* on D. E. R., h.l., and cf. *Magen 'Abraham* in *Shul.Ar.*, Or. Haj. 170. The reading in the basis manuscript "abal meqanneah 'adam qe'arah' (may wipe...) contradicts the readings in Ms. Oxford Bodleian (cat. A. Neubauer I, p. 306) no. 1100 , and in Mas. Kal. Rab. (ed. M. Higger, IX, p. 333, and ed. N. N. Coronel, 18a) and D. E. Z., V,1, where the text reads 'we-lo jeqanneah et ha-qe'arah' (may not wipe...). We give preference to the version in agreement with the reading in D. E. Z., l.c., according to which it is not permitted to wipe a plate completely clean with a piece of bread. That is indecent, and one would thereby give the host the impression that he had not got enough to eat or, worse still, that he was simply a glutton. On the other hand, it is also indecent for one to leave a large portion of food which has been served to him untouched on his plate. See our explanation in connection with D. E. R., VI,3a-b.

**1b. And a man should not leave crumbs [other reading: gather crumbs and leave them] on the table, because he hurts (with this) the feelings of his fellowman.**

One should not gather the crumbs and leave them on the table, for in doing so, he hurts the feelings of his fellow man. It is possible that the appetites of the other guests at the table will be ruined upon the sight of the crumbs gathered together. Concern not only with the rights but with the feelings of one's fellow man is characteristic of the way of Derekh 'Eretz.

**2. A man should not bite from a piece of bread and return it into the dish. And similarly should not bite (something) from a piece of bread and give it (i. e. the rest) to his fellow, because not all tastes are the same.**

One may not bite off a piece of bread and leave the rest on the dish. Cf. also the parallels with the reading 'and leaving it on the table.' See D. E. Z., VI,6 and other places.

D. E. R. gives a reading that is analogous to the version of the statement that appears in TosBer. V,8 (ed. S. Lieberman, p. 26).

In the Tosephta, the reading is: 'One may not bite off a piece of bread and leave it (the rest of it) on the dish ('li-qe'arah') *because that is dangerous to life.*' Apart from the risk that the sight of such a piece of bread may cause someone not to eat further and thus to harm himself, we may also assume here that there is the danger of spreading disease.

In D. E. R. h.l. (see the text following ), we find the reason that the indecent behaviour mentioned may ruin another person's appetite, which is sufficient reason for disapproving of such behaviour. It is also objectionable for a person at the table to offer someone a piece of bread from which a piece has been bitten off. This embarrasses another person, which may cause him to accept the bread reluctantly.

**3a. A man should not drink from a cup and give it to his fellow, and this is because of danger to life.**

**3b. It happened that Rabbi 'Aqiba was the guest of a certain man, and that he (i. e. that man) offered him a cup (of wine) from which he had (previously) tasted. Rabbi 'Aqiba said to him: 'Take and drink it (yourself).' [Again he offered him cup (of wine) from which he had (previously) tasted. Rabbi 'Aqiba said to him again: 'Take and drink it (yourself)']. Ben 'Azzai said to him: "Aqiba, how long will you give to drink cups (of wine) from which (previously) has been tasted?'**

**3c. Another time it happened that Rabbi 'Aqiba was the guest of a certain man and that he (i. e. that man) took a piece of bread and did rest the dish on it – -Rabbi 'Aqiba snatched it and ate it. He said to him: 'Have you not another piece of bread to eat than the pieces of bread on which I do rest the dish?' He said: 'It seemed to me that you would be scalded with tepid water, but now (I notice) that you are not even scalded with boiling water.'**

3a. *A man should not drink...*

One should not drink from a cup and pass it on to a fellow man because of danger to life. In TbTam. 27b, we find a more detailed description of the recommended practise of not offering to somebody else a cup from which one has drunk. That text deals with a rule of behaviour passed on by Rab Huna to his son Rabbah.

The edge of a cup from which someone has already drunk must first be cleaned before the cup is passed on to someone to drink from.

If the cup contains wine, the edge of the cup must be wiped before the cup is passed on to someone else. If the cup contains water, then it is sufficient to pour out a bit from the side from which someone has drunk (to do that with a cup of wine would mean wasting the wine.)

The expression *because of danger to life* used here in D.E.R. acquires a special meaning in the tradition in TbTam. l.c. In that text is mentioned an example of someone with a weak constitution who did not want to accept a cup offered to him from which someone else had already drunk. He pretended not to be thirsty when in actuality he was thirsty but did not drink from the cup because someone else had already drunk from it, and he died as a result of his thirst. The expression : *danger to life* is also explained to apply in the situation in which the health of someone at the table who may not dare to refuse a cup (from which someone else had already drunk) offered to him may be threatened by the very aversion with which he nonetheless does drink from the cup. See *Be'er Heitab* in *Shul. Ar.*, Or. Haj. 170 and see *Nahalat Ja'aqob* on D.E.R., h.l.; cf. *Magen 'Abraham* in *Shul. Ar.* l.c., where the argument concerning the danger of transmitting disease is also mentioned.

### 3b. *It happened that Rabbi'Aqiba...*

This illustrative story about Rabbi ʿAqiba is not found in early sources. The version of the story in the basis manuscript of D.E. is incomplete. After the words 'Rabbi ʿAqiba said to him: "take and drink it"', it is better to add, with the help of manuscripts, the words: 'Again (the host) handed a goblet (of wine) from which he (previously) tasted. And (again) said Rabbi ʿAqiba to him: "take and drink it."' In light of that, Ben ʿAzzai's exclamation ("Aqiba how long will you give to drink goblets [of wine] from which [previously] had been tasted?') is understandable. In most of the manuscripts of D.E. these words of Ben ʿAzzai are not directed at ʿAqiba but at the host who offers to Rabbi ʿAqiba goblets from which he has already drunk. Cf. also the corrections in the edition of the text of the Gaon of Vilna.

### 3c. *Another time it happened that Rabbi ʿAqiba ...*

This story about Rabbi ʿAqiba illustrates the rule derived from a baraita that one is not to support a dish of food on a piece of bread because one should treat food with respect. See D.E.R., IX, 5 and the commentary in that passage. By taking the piece of bread away from under the dish, Rabbi ʿAqiba subtly tried to show his objection to the habit of supporting the dish with bread. The statement *It seemed to me that you would be scalded with tepid water, but now (I see to my embarrassment) you are not even scalded with boiling water* is a proverbial statement which appears in other places in the tradition. Cf., e.g., TjBer. II,8 [5b], where the statement is used in the situation in which people are not sensitive to symbolic treatment or even when repeated and show no comprehension until they are reprimanded explicitly. See the manuscripts in D.E. with the deviating reading: 'But now (I see to my embarrassment) you are only scalded with boiling water.'

4. **And a man should not drink his cup and place it on the table, but he should hold it in his hand until the attendant comes and he shall give it to him.**

This warning is based on the fear that by putting the cup back on the table, wine will be spilled on the table or on the cloth covering the table. The fear of spilling wine was certainly justified considering the form of drinking cups in the first centuries. In reference to that, see S. Safrai, 'Home and Family' in *The Jewish People in the First Century*, II, ed. Safrai a. o. II, pp. 742–743: 'The usual cup of this period bore little resemblance to that of today; it had a wide mouth, but the base was so narrow that it could not be set on the table when filled. It was served directly into the diner's hand, and when he was finished with it, he placed it in a special metal stand, called the "cup container", or laid it on the table.' In reference to 'cup containers', cf. TbPes. 55b and MKel. XVI,2. That explanation about the form of cups may also explain why the rule about putting a cup back on the table does not appear in later traditions. Another form for drinking cups perhaps made the rule superfluous.

5. **Rabbi said five things (concerning bread): One should not place row meat on bread and not on a cup [another reading: and not a cup on bread] and not a dish on bread, and one should not throw bread around and do rest a dish on bread, and one should not sit on food because one should handle articles of food respectfully.**

The tradition mentioned here goes back to an anonymous baraita in TbBer.50b. According to the version in D. E. R., Rabbi is supposed to have been the author of the baraita. The central point that unifies the elements listed in this baraita is the duty to treat food – especially bread – with respect. The version in TbBer. l.c. is shorter and more comprehensible · Only four things are mentioned in that text, as opposed to five in D. E. R. On the basis of the version in TbBer. we can reconstruct the text in D. E. R. as follows: 1) we may not place raw meat on bread, 2) we may not pass a cup (full of wine) *over* bread nor a dish *over* bread, 3) we may not throw bread, 4) we may not rest a dish *on* bread, and 5) we may not sit on articles of food, because we must handle food with respect. For the most part the manuscripts of D. E. R. confirm this reconstruction.

Under the second point, D. E. R. h.l. actually says *and not a cup on bread* (in stead of passing over bread), to which is added another element which does not appear in this form in TbBer. l.c.: *and not a dish on bread.* It appears that five different things are mentioned here in D. E. when, in fact, six are listed. As a result, the fourth point *and we may not rest a dish on bread* is missing in other manuscripts of D. E. and in the version in Mas. Kal. Rab. (ed. M. Higger, IX, p. 334), although it may have belonged to the original version (cf. TbBer. l.c.).

Obviously this element was found to be superfluous upon the reading of the
second point of *and not a dish on bread*.

It is a bad practise to put raw meat on bread. It is possible that blood from the
meat will remain behind on the bread, rendering it unsuitable for consumption.
One may also not pass a full cup of wine over bread so that no wine will be
spilled on the bread and make it unpalatable. One may also not throw pieces of
bread. Pieces of bread were thrown sometimes in jest. Cf. TjDem. VII,1 [26a],
Ber.Rab. LXV,15 and cf. S. Krauss, *Talmudische Archäologie*, III, chap.IX,
pp. 51–52. From the discussion in TbBer. l.c., it appears that the rule (which
prevailed among the sages) of not throwing pieces of bread was accepted in the
time of Rab 'Ashi and Mar Zutra, while the throwing of other items of food was
either under discussion or accepted.

The conclusion, therefore, is that it was permitted to throw food other than
bread, provided that it was not made unpalatable or unsuitable for consumption.

One did use a piece of bread to stabilize a dish of food, as tables were often
imperfect in those days and were not easily placed level on the floors of that
time. Bread consequently acquired a less appetizing appearance. See in that
connection also the remark by Samuel (recorded in TbBer. 50b): 'A man may
use bread for any purpose he likes.' In the context from that statement,
however, it means that one was allowed to wipe his hands with a piece of bread
after the meal, even though this contradicted the forbiddance to waste food.
From a discussion with Rab Sheshet in TbShab. 50b, it appears that the opinion
of Samuel rests on the assumption that bread was not easily made unsuitable for
consumption and still could be eaten after such use. (Cf. *Shul. Ar.*, Or. Haj. 171
and see TbShab. 50b, ed. A. Steinsalz and id. TbShab. 143a. Cf. MShab. XXI,3
and cf. TbBer. 52b and the *Tosaphists* in that text and the opinion of Rashi, and
cf. *Shul. Ar.*, Or.Haj. 180,4 and other sources.

### 6.  One who is invited to a meal should not take his portion and give it to the attendant lest something untoward happen to the meal, but he should take it and keep it in front of him and after that give it to him.

*Lest something untoward should happen at the meal.*

These words are understandable only in light of a parallel in TbHul. 107b,
which is more complete than the version in D. E. R. h.l. TbHul. 107b (cf. idem
105b) contains the following baraita: 'Our rabbis taught: "A man should not
give any bread to the attendant, while the cup (of wine) is in his hand (i. e., in
the hand of the attendant) or in his host's hand, lest something untoward
happen at the meal."' The host might be annoyed at such behaviour and might
choke while drinking, or he might look with anger at the attendant, who might
become frightened and spill the wine and thus cause an unfortunate accident.
See commentaries in reference to TbHul.107b. He could spill the wine on the

bread and thereby ruin the meal. The tradition is understandable in light of the practise of putting bread in the mouth of the attendant in jest (see TbHul. l.c.) or of the practise among guests of offering out of kindness some of the meal to the attendant. The host's dismay at guests giving away food to the attendant is understandable, considering his fear that there won't be enough food left for the guests. Cf. S. Krauss, *Talmudische Archäologie*, III, chap.IX, p. 48.

In connection with the parallel in TbHul. l.c., the words can also be explained as follows: 'But he should take it and keep it in front of him and give it to him (the attendant) afterwards.' The guest is to wait to give something to the attendant until the host has set his cup down and/or given the guest permission to give something to the attendant, or he is to wait until after the meal. In *Magen 'Abraham* and in *Lebushin* (of Mordehai Jaffe) on *Shul. Ar.*, Or. Haj. 170.18, the words *lest something untoward happen to the meal* are explained as follows: so that nothing unfortunate will happen to the rest of the meal, with the result that the portion of food given away turns out to be necessary for the guests. Cf. also *Nahalat Ja'aqob* on D. E. R. h.l. We however, give preference to the explanation given above which concurs with the tradition in TbHul. l.c., according to which there is the fear that an accident will happen with wine. This also connects with the statement from D. E. mentioned earlier concerning the admonition not to waste food.

7a.  **Guests who are invited by a host may not leave unless they have got permission of the master of the house. [Another reading: should not give anything from what is set in front of them to the host's son or to his servant unless they have got permission of the master of the house.]**

Visitors may not go out unless they first receive permission from the master of the house. The basis manuscript shows here a remarkable deviation from the other manuscripts in D. E. and from the source of the statement, a baraita in TbHul.91a. In light of the direct result (see D. E. R. IX,7b.) the reading which concurs with TbHul.94a undoubtedly deserves preference. In TbHul. l.c., the reading is: 'Guests are not allowed to give anything from what is (set) before them, not to the son and not to the daughter of the host...' There exists the possibility that the master of the house only wants to provide a small meal for his guests or that he has only a small amount of food in the house. If the guests give away from the food given to them to the children or the servants of the master of the house, there may be nothing left over for the guests. This would shame the master of the house extremely. In TosBeitza. IV,10, it appears that it was customary in some places to give food to the guests upon leaving. Cf. MHul. VIII,2; Tj'Ab. Zar. III,1 [42c]; Siphra (ed. Weiss, 78c) and cf. S. Krauss, *Talmudische Archäologie*, III, chap. IX, p. 263, note 338. Guests were also supposed to give nothing of these gifts to the son or daughter of the host, in order not to give the impression of not appreciating what was provided for them. In reference to Tos. l.c., see S. Lieberman, *Tosephta Ki-Pheshuta*, V, pp. 1013–1014.

**7b.** **It happened to a certain man that he invited guests in a year of scarcity and there were three (guests). And he had (only) three eggs and set these (eggs) before them. When the son of the house came in and stood in front of them, one (of them) took his portion and gave it to him, and so the second and the third. When his father came in and discovered that he had taken one (egg) in his mouth and two in his hands he remained standing and lifted him up to full height and dashed him to the ground so that he died. And also his mother, as soon as she saw her son dead, she placed herself on the roof and fell down [from the roof] and died. And also the father, as soon as he saw this happen placed himself on the roof, fell down and died.It turned out that three persons were killed for such (a trivial) thing!**

This story is mentioned in the source TbHul. 94a in direct connection with the remark: 'Guests (who are visiting a host) are not allowed to give anything from what is before them...'

The final sentence in the version in D. E. is ascribed in themanuscripts (with the exception of our basis manuscript) as well as in the version in TbHul.94a to Rabbi ʾEliʿezer ben Jaʿaqob. The version in D. E. R. is based on the tradition in TbHul.94a. See also M. Higger, *Massekhtot Zeʿirot*, 1970, Mabo p. 26.

# Pereq ha-nikhnas

## Derekh 'Eretz Rabbah, Chapter X

**1a. One who enters a bath-house should say: 'May it be Your will, O Lord, My God, that You cause me to enter in peace and that You cause me to depart in peace and that You cause me to return in peace, and that You save me from this (fire and heat) and from what is like it in the future.'**

This prayer, uttered upon entering and leaving a bathhouse, can be understood in light of the real dangers to which a visitor to a bath house was exposed. A fire was lit under the floor of the hotroom ('caldarium') of a bathhouse in order to heat kettles filled with water. Between the floor (which rested on pillars) and the place where the fire was stoked, there were spaces through which intensely hot air could rise to warm the floor. If the floor and surrounding walls collapsed, the visitors could fall into the fire or into the boiling water in the kettles, which were heated next to the caldarium. Cf, e.g., the story of the miraculous rescue of Rabbi 'Abbahu after the floor of a bathhouse collapsed. Cf. TbKet. 62a and TjBeitza I,6 [60c]. See also TbPes. 122aff., where Rabbi José warns that one should not enter a new bathhouse because of the danger that the new floor will collapse. Cf. TjM. Q. I,2 [80b]. According to a tradition in TjBer. IV,4 [8b] and other sources, Rabbi Mana made his last will upon entering a bathhouse which had a heated bath. See the version of the prayer in TjBer. IX,6 [14b]: 'May it be ... that You rescue me from being burned upon the fire', and cf. the version in D. E. R. h.l. and in Tos. l.c.: 'May it be ... that You make me enter in peace.'" See also the prayer of Rab 'Aha upon leaving the bathhouse; 'I thank You ... that You have saved me from the fire.' (See TbBer. 60a).

Cf. also the version of the prayer said upon leaving the bathhouse in Mas. Kal. Rab. (ed. M. Higger, chap. IX, p. 337): 'I thank You ... that You have saved me from death by drowning and by fire.' In connection with the dangers in bathhouses, see S. Krauss, *Talmudische Archäologie*, I, chap.IV, p. 676, note 109 and p. 220; and see S. Krauss, in: *R. E. J.*, XXXVI, (1898), p. 213.

Another real danger for visitors to a bathhouse was that of taking a bad fall on the smooth marble floor. Cf. TbHul. 145b.

Parallels of this statement in D. E. are found in the Tosephta as well as in both the Babylonian and Jerusalem Talmuds.

The reading in D. E. R. shows the most correspondences to the reading in TosBer. VII,17 (ed. S. Lieberman, I, p. 38; ed. M. S. Zuckermandel, p. 16). The version in the Tosephta (cf. the version in TjBer. IX,6 [14b]) also ends with the words: 'and save me from this and from similar things in the future.' It is acceptable to assume that the original version ended in agreement with the Tosephta and the Jerusalem Talmud) with the above-mentioned prayer for being spared of harm in the future, and not with the notion (found in the Babylonian Talmud, TbBer. 60a) of accidents and death as atonement of transgressions, for a prayer usually end positively. See S. Lieberman, *Tosephta Ki-Pheshutah*, I, p. 119, l. 80. The notion of accident and death as atonement, which appears in the middle of the prayer (and not at the end, as in TbBer. 60a) in the Tosephta and the Jerusalem Talmud, has clearly been omitted from the version in D. E. The concluding words *and that You save me from this and from what is like it in the future* actually refer to that notion. (In the Babylonian Talmud, the words 'and save me from this...' appear before the notion mentioned, such order is clearly incorrect. See, however, M. Higger in: *Massekhtot Ze'irot*, p. 26, where he expresses the opinion that the tradition here in D. E. R. has been borrowed from the Babylonian Talmud (TbBer. 60a.).

1b.  **And how should one act before one enters? One takes off his shoes and removes his turban and his cloak and looses his girdle and one takes off his shirt and after that one looses his underwear.**

In the circles of the sages one tried to adhere to a certain order when undressing and dressing in the bathhouse. In D. E. Z., one finds a parallel which mentions other names for articles of clothing and another order in which they are removed when one is in a bathhouse. See D. E. Z., VIII, end. According to D. E. R. h.l., one removes one's clothes in the following order: shoes, hat, 'talith', girdle, shirt, and undergarment. In connection with 'pirsaqi' see in Ms Oxford Bodleian (cat. A. Neubauer, I, p. 815) no. 2339 the variant derived from ''aphqarsuto', which can be retraced to ''aphqarsin' and ''aphiqarsin' = Greek 'epikarsion', undergarment; see S. Krauss, *Griechische und Lateinische Lehnwörter im Talmud, Midrasch und Targum*, I, sub ''aphqarsut', and see M. Jastrow, *Dictionary*, II, p. 107; see also other sources.

The sequence in which first the shoes are removed and the girdle is removed before the shirt appears plausible, unlike the reading in Mas. Kal. Rab. (ed. M. Higger, chap. IX, p. 336; ed. N. N. Coronel,18a), which gives the sequence of shirt, girdle, hat, and undergarment. In practise, after the coat is removed (cf. D. E. Z. l.c.), one will have first removed shoes (for hygienic reasons), then hat, and then the girdle so that one's shirt and undergarment can be removed. Thus, underclothes were probably removed last. That which was removed last was put back on first.

1c.  **When some one has washed himself and come out of the bath and when one has brought him a towel, he should dry his head (first) and after that all his limbs. When one has brought him the oil, he should oil his head (first)**

**and after that the rest of his body [and after that he puts on his underwear] and he gets into his shirt and he girds himself with his girdle and he covers himself with his cloak.**

Along with a certain order for undressing and dressing the pious sages also had a specific order in which they dried off and oiled the different parts of their bodies. After bathing, one dried oneself off, applied oil to the skin, and put one's clothes back on. This tradition is missing in the parallel context of Mas.Kal. Rab. The statement as such appears only in D. E. In TbShab. 61a we find a related tradition concerning the order in which one was to apply oil to the skin. And from the related context in TjShab. VI,2 [8a], it is explicitly clear that the parallel in TbShab. 61a was derived from the 'derekh 'eretz' traditions already known in the period of the Talmud! See in this connection the commentary by M. Higger in relation to TjShab. l.c. in *'Otzar ha-Baraitot*, VI, p. 358; and see M. Higger, *Massekhtot Ze'irot*, pp. 26−27 and 32; see further commentary to D. E. R., X, 1d. The reading of this statement and the statement directly following is more complete in D. E. R. than in the Babylonian Talmud l.c. and the Jerusalem Talmud l.c.!! According to M. Higger the words 'because it is the king of all the limbs' (following on the words '... he should anoint his head first') in TbShab.61a were added later. See M. Higger, *Massekhtot Ze'irot*, pp. 26−27. From the sequence mentioned here in D. E. R. in which one put one's clothes back on, it is obvious that it was customary for one to dress in the reverse order in which one had undressed.

**1d.  And (after that) he puts on his shoes, [he puts on] the right (shoe) first and then the left, and when he takes off his shoes [he takes off] the left (shoe) first [and then the right]. It is the same in connection with the tephillin, (he puts on) that of the hand first [and then of the head], and when he removes (them) [he removes] that of the head first and then that of the hand. If he has a servant or a son (to help him) they may put it on for him.**

According to D. E., when putting on shoes, the rule was to put on first the right shoe and then the left shoe; when removing shoes, it was proper to remove the left shoe first because the left shoe is put on last. The same rule applied for 'tephillin': the 'tephillin' for the head, which were put on last, were removed first. The tradition mentioned here belongs to very old rules of 'derekh 'eretz' which had already been adopted in the Babylonian and Jerusalem Talmuds. This tradition is mentioned in TbShab. 61a and in TjShab. VI,2 [8a] in connection with an incident between Rabbi Shim'eon ben 'Abba and Rabbi Johanan (so Jerushalmi), or between Rab Shaman bar 'Abba and Rabbi Johanan (Babli). The issue here concerns the same people. Rab Shaman bar 'Abba, an

Amora of the second generation who went from Babel to Israel, is the same
person as Rabbi Shim'on ben 'Abba, pupil of Rabbi Johanan. Compare TbKet.
23a with TjKet II,6, and see R. Halperin, '*Atlas 'Etz Hajjim*, IV, p. 305.

Rabbi Shim'on ben 'Abba (as he was called in Israel) assisted Rabbi Johanan
in putting on his sandals. He first put the right sandal on Rabbi Johanan, and
then the left sandal. According to the version of TjShab. l.c., Rabbi Shim'on
ben 'Abba acted in that case in accordance with '*d*erekh *'eretz'*. Rabbi Johanan,
however, adhered to another tradition and wanted the left sandal to be put on
first. According to TjShab. l.c., the opinion of Rabbi Johanan concurred with
the *Rishonim*, and in his surprise over what Rabbi Shim'on ben Abba did, he
called him 'Babylonian'. Obviously, the custom practised by Rabbi Shim'on
ben 'Abba (which is in accordance with the rule in D. E. R.) is connected to a
Babylonian rule of behaviour. Therefore, the rule in D. E. R. h.l. involves a
Babylonian tradition! This Babylonian rule of behaviour which Rabbi Shm'on
ben 'Abba practises is supported in a baraita recorded in TbShab. l.c. in the
name of the rabbis in general. The content of that baraita must date back to old
'derekh 'eretz' traditions. See the parallels and see the commentary of M. Higger, '*Otzar ha-Baraitot*, IV, p. 385 and M. Higger, *Massekhtot Ze'irot*,
pp. 26−27. From the rest of the context in TbShab.61a, it appears that the
Babylonian Amora'im of the fourth and fifth generations accepted both of the
above mentioned practises and that they valued neither one above the other but
sought a compromise between the two.

2a.  **Who has entered a bathhouse should not exercise (in order to perspire)
[and he should not scrape himself] and he should not rub (with oil) [another
reading: and he should not let his limbs be broken] on the marble (floor).**
2b.  **It happened (however) to Rabban Gamli'el, who was weak, that one
smoothed out oil for him on the marble, but he did not accept it.**

One who visits a bathhouse should not 'become fatigued'. The Hebrew term for
that phrase 'hit'ammel', also appears in MShab. XXII,6. Cf. TbShab. 147b and
TosShab. XVI(XVII),22 (ed. M.S. Zuckermandel, p. 136). See Rabbenu
Hanan'el on TbShab. l.c. and see *Nahalat Ja'aqob* on D. E. R. h.l. and see
commentaries in reference to MShab. l.c. and see especially S. Lieberman,
*Greek in Jewish Palestine*, pp. 73−79. See also S. Krauss, *Talmudische
Archäologie*, I, chap. IV., pp. 230−231. The matter here concerns the practise
of applying oil to oneself and then exerting oneself afterward with vigorous arm
and leg movements in order to induce perspiration. Through perspiration,
impurities are driven out of the body through the pores in the skin and are then
separated away along with the oil from the skin with a scraper (see the term 'le-
hitgarger'). Such strenuous bodily exertion was forbidden especially on the
Sabbath. If the interpretation here in D. E. R. is correct, such athletic activities

carried out in public were absolutely disapproved of in circles of the sages, on regular days as well on the Sabbath. One possible reason for the disapproval of the sages is that such athletic activities reminded them of the emphasis placed in Greek culture on the development of the body, a concept which they detested. It is also possible, however, that the chance that other guests at the bathhouse could be hindered or even harmed as the result of other guests engaging in strenuous exercise also was a reason for the disapproval of the sages. See, however, the explanation of Rashi in reference to TbShab. 147b and Rambam, *Jad*, Hil. Shab., XXI,28 and M. Jastrow, *Dictionary*, II, p. 1098, and other sources in which 'hit'ammel' is explained as referring to a vigorous form of massage. The use of the verb in the sense of physical exercise (see especially TosShab. l.c.), however, is quite clear in the sources mentioned. A further indication of the relationship between D. E. R. h.l. and the context in MShab. l.c. is the addition of the phrase 'we-'eino mitgarger' (*and should not not scrape himself*) in the other manuscripts. There was criticism of scraping away in public bodily impurities released through perspiration as well as of the strenuous activity carried out to encourage perspiration.

Cf. also S. Krauss, in: *R. E. J.*, XXXVI, (1898), p. 212.

The expression 'we-'eino mishtammesh' is interpreted in various ways in the commentaries. Considering the connection with the tradition in MShab. XXII,6, one would be tempted to read 'we-'eino memashmesh' (*and he does not rub himself [with oil] on the marble [i. e., on the large common floor of the bathhouse]*). The forbiddance to rub oneself with oil possibly stemmed from the danger that oil could be spilled on the floor and that other guests at the bathhouse could slip on the floor. This explanation, however, does not fit in the direct context, according to which an exception is made for people who are physically weak. Because of this, we give extra consideration to the alternative reading in other manuscripts. The other manuscripts in D. E. give the reading 'we-'eino mishtabber' (*and he may not let himself be broken*) on the marble floor. Cf. also the reading in Mas. Kal. Rab., ed. M. Higger, chap. IX, p. 338 and ed. N. N. Coronel, 18b.

The expression 'to let your limbs be broken' is explained as a technical term for a very vigorous form of massage, and it is possibly intended as a denigrating term referring to the practise of working oil in the body by rolling the body over a marble slab, which has been smeared with oil. Cf., e.g., TosDem. I,9; TosTer. X,10; TosShab. III,7; TosShab. XVI,4; TosShebi. VI,9; TjShab. VIII, 8 (38b) and see other sources. See notes in M. Higger, *Massekhtot Derekh 'Eretz*, p. 300. Cf. especially S. Krauss, *Talmudische Archäologie*,I, chap. IV, p. 230: 'Neben der Methode des Einreibens war es auch üblich, Öl auf eine Marmorplatte oder auf eine lederne Unterlage zu giessen, um sich darauf herum zu wälzen ("mit'aggel") und so das Öl auf sich wirken zu lassen. Von dieser Methode, die zwar für Kranke ihre Bequemlichkeit hatte, bei Gesunde jedoch nicht gern gesehen wurde, sagte man wegwerfend "mishtabber", "sich zerbrechen", nämlich auf den harten Fliesen.' Cf. also S. Krauss, in: *R. E. J.*, XXXV,(1898), p. 212.

This explanation can be associated with the following text in D. E. according to which an exception was made for Rabban Gamli'el. See J. Kanovitz, *Me'arekhot Tanna'im*, 1976, p. 275; the Rabban Gamli'el here is supposed to be Rabban Gamli'el the second, the Nasi of Jabneh). Because he was physically weak at the time, it was permitted for him to be rubbed with oil, in a reclining position. The wording here may be interpreted as follows: 'It once happened that they poured smooth oil ("halephu") on the marble for Rabban Gamli'el, who was weak.' Cf. the interpretation of M. Higger, *Massekhtot Derekh 'Eretz*, p. 113: 'He was offered oil while on the marble floor.' The term 'halephu' is interpreted differently here. See the reading in *Mahzor Vitry* (ed. S. Hurwitz, p. 733): 'hippilu lo', one threw for him oil on the Marble floor. Cf. S. Krauss, in: *R. E. J.*,XXXVI, (1898), p. 212: 'On fit couler pour lui de l'huile sur le marble, mais il ne voulut pas en profiter.'

A completely different reading is suggested by M. Ginsberg, *The Minor Tractates of the Talmud*, ed. A. Cohen, II, p. 561: 'It once happened that they begged Rabban Gamli'el, who was weak, to urinate on the marble floor.' M. Ginsberg suggests that 'mashtin', (to urinate) should be read in place of 'shemen' (oil). See also *Nahalat Ja'aqob* on D. E. R. h.l. in reference to *Seph. 'Agguda* with the reading 'we-'eino mashtin'.

**3. Rabbi Shim'on [ben Gamli'el] said: 'One who lets his limbs be broken on the marble (floor) is the companion of an ass and who eats on the market place is the companion of a dog', and some say that he is also unfit to testify (in case of a lawsuit).**

'Rabban Shim'on ben Gamli'el says: "One who has been massaged (literally, who has had his limbs broken) is the companion of an ass.' See the reading in Mas. Kal. Rab., ed. M. Higger. chap. IX, p. 338, with the reading: 'Rabban Gamli'el...' We assume that the manuscripts of D. E. R., h.l. refer to Rabbi Shim'on ben Gamli'el the second. There appears to be a contradiction, though, especially with the TosTer. X,10. Cf. also TosShebi. VI,9, which indicates that Rabbi Shim'on ben Gamli'el permits the massaging of oneself with oil on a marble slab, even in the case of a priest who uses the oil of the Terumah. As the person here is also Rabban Shim'on ben Gamli'el the second, an explanation must be sought for the contradiction between the two traditions. In D. E. 'shish' refers to the marble floor of the bathhouse.

Massage performed in public in the manner described above was criticized, but it was performed on marble slabs especially meant for that purpose which were probably concealed in separate, screened-off places. Under those conditions, then, massage was obviously permitted, judging from the traditions in the Tosephta mentioned above. Only an animal rolls itself over the floor in public.

A sage does not do that, or at least does not do that in view of public. Eating in public also likens a person to an animal. An observation concerning such behaviour appears in a baraita in TbQid. 40b. It is also stated there that someone who eats in public (i. e., at the market) is unfit to act as a witness in a trial. Lack of self respect makes one unfit to give testimony because it was assumed that such a person would not be likely to feel ashamed of giving false testimony. The tradition in D. E. was probably the source of the tradition in TbQid.40b. Cf. also TjMa'as. III,5 [50c]. Cf. M. Higger, *Massekhtot Ze'irot*, 1970, p. 27.

### 4. **A man may cite rules related to the privy in the privy and (rules) related to the bathhouse in the bathhouse.**

One may talk about matters concerning the privy in the privy, and one may discuss matters concerning the bathhouse in the bathhouse. In Tj'Ab. Zar. III,4 [42d] and in TjShab. III,1 [6a], that opinion is attributed to Rabbi Jehoshua ben Levi in a discussion about how Rabban Gamli'el the second would have answered someone who asked him why he (Rabban Gamli'el) was bathing in a bathhouse dedicated to Aphrodite. Concerning the question see M'Ab. Zar. III,4 and cf. Tb'Ab. Zar.44b and TbShab. 40b. He is supposed to have answered, in accordance with the Mishnah: 'We may not answer (questions relating to Torah) in a bath.' The discussion in the gemara concerns how he could have even answered that question in the bathhouse, considering that Rabban Gamli'el would have adhered to the rule (passed on by Rabbi Johanan) that: 'It is permitted to ponder (over matters of Torah) in any place except a bath and a privy.' According to this strict rule, one is not even allowed to meditate on religious matters in a bathhouse or in a toilet; it is improper to do so because one is unclothed in such places. An attempt was already made to solve this problem in a Tannaitic tradition by assuming that the Mishnah was incorrect and that, according to the original version, Rabban Gamli'el did not speak until he had left the bathhouse. See Tb'Ab. Zar. l.c.

In connection with the matter, Tj. l.c. quotes to the contrary the opinion of Rabbi Jehoshua ben Levi. This opinion is easier to understand in consideration of the background of the opinion in the example of Rabbi Me'ir and his pupil Rabbi Shim'on ben 'El'azar, cited in Tj. l.c. (cf. TbShab. 40b). While in a bathhouse, the pupil supposedly asked Rabbi Me'ir a halakhic question concerning whether it was permissible to perform certain actions in the bathhouse, Rabbi Me'ir supposedly answered him, 'It is forbidden.' Their discussion concerned actions forbidden on the Sabbath. From Rabbi Me'ir's opinion it appears that it was permitted to discuss a halakhic matter in a bathhouse if the intention was to prevent possible transgression.

In Tj. l.c., it is additionally stated, in the name of Judan, the father of Rabbi Matanja, that it was allowable to ask halakhic questions about bathing, but that

it was not the practise to answer such questions in the bathhouse. In Tj'Ab. Zar.
l.c., one also finds the opinion, attributed to Rabbi Samuel bar 'Abdimi
('Abdumi), that it was indeed permissible to ask halakhic questions about
bathing while in the bathhouse, but that the humidity in the bathhouse was bad
for the teeth – meaning that it would thus be better to wait till one was out of the
bathhouse before even speaking.

From TbQid. 33a, it appears that the admonition (see the above mentioned
opinion ascribed to Rabbi Johanan) not to meditate upon religious matters in
unclean places or places where people are not clothed was intended to prevent
from unintentionally talking about such matters. Only someone who, by force
of habit, meditated on religious matters unintentionally was to be excused. Cf.
also TbBer. 24b; TbMeg. 28a and TbZeb. 102b.

**5. One should not ask and reply (i. e. discuss religious matters) in any place
where the majority of the people present are undressed, and (even) not in a
place where the majority is dressed (and only a minority is undressed).
Whether the majority of the people present are dressed and (only) a
minority is undressed, or the majority is undressed and the minority dressed, all are (regarded as) undressed.**

One does not ask questions and give answers in any place where the majority of
those present are undressed. This same applies in places where the majority of
people present are dressed. If anyone present is undressed, then everyone
present is considered to be undressed. According to this opinion, therefore, it is
forbidden to ask questions and give answers concerning the Torah and oral
tradition in any place where naked people are present, even if most of the
people present are dressed. This opinion concurs with the reading in the
manuscripts in D. E. R., h.l. The basis manuscript, however, requires a slight
correction. This reading and interpretation in D. E. concurs with the interpretation of M. Higger, *Massekhtot Ze'irot*, p. 113. The above mentioned explanation is basically in agreement with the parallels in TbShab. 10a and other
sources, in which it is stated that it is forbidden to study the Scriptures, to pray
etc., in a place where undressed people are present. Cf. the same tradition in
TosBer. II,20 and in TjBer. II,3 [4c]. The explanation also concurs with the
preceding statement in, in which the question of discussing halakhah in a place
where people are likely to undress. See, however, the explanation of M. Ginsberg, in *The Minor Tractates of the Babylonian Talmud*, ed. A. Cohen, II,
p. 561; like the Gaon of Vilna, he suggests that 'to ask questions and give
answers' means to greet someone and return the greeting. Cf. TbShab. 10a and
Waj.Rab. IX,9, and other sources, where 'Shalom' is mentioned as one of
God''s names. The word 'shalom' is generally uttered in a greeting and thus
should not be spoken in a place where the majority of people present are not
dressed. This interpretation, however, requires adaption to the parallels in the

Babylonian and Jerusalem Talmuds and the Tosephta. According to TbShab. 10a (TosBer. l.c. and TjBer.l.c.), it is allowed to greet people in a place where some people are dressed and others are not. Here in D.E.R. one should replace 'we-lo' with 'ella' and read: 'One does not greet someone or return a greeting in any place where the majority of people present are undressed, *but* (in stead of : and even not) one does do so in a place where the majority of people are dressed.' This reading, however, is not confirmed by the manuscripts. It is additionally stated in TjBer. l.c. that it is not permitted to greet people in places where the majority of people are *usually* unclothed, regardless of the actual situation at a given moment. Cf. S. Lieberman, *Tosephta Ki-Pheshuta*, I, p. 26. By implication, then, it is allowed, according to that tradition, to greet people in places where usually only a minority of people are undressed. In line with the above mentioned interpretation of M. Ginsberg and the Gaon of Vilna, also the subsequent text of the statement in D.E.R. must be revised in order to stay in keeping with the parallels. See the suggestion of the Gaon of Vilna in agreement with the reading in *Mahzor Vitry* (ed. S. Hurwitz, p. 733) to revise the text. According to that revision the reading is then as follows: 'One is not to give or return a greeting in any place where the majority of people are undressed, *but* one is to do so in a place where the majority of those present are dressed. If the majority are dressed and the minority are not, *then it is as if everyone is dressed*. If (however) the majority are undressed and (only) a minority are dressed, then it is as if everyone is undressed.' Cf. notes in *Mahzor Vitry* l.c., ed. S.Hurwitz. The text in *Mahzor Vitry* does contain the reading 'we-lo' (and not) in stead of ''ella' (but). There remains a question, however, as to what extent the reading in *Mahzor Vitry* actually support the reconstruction suggested by the Gaon of Vilna. We prefer the first explanation given, according to which the phrase 'to ask questions and to give answers' refers to the discussion of Torah and halakhic issues in the bathhouse. This explanation does complete justice to the manuscript versions of D.E. (with the exception of the version in *Mahzor Vitry*, which partially suggests another interpretation. The remarks about the proportion of clothed people to unclothed people present in a given place, especially in the bathhouse, can be understood in light of the division of bathhouses at that time. Bathhouses were divided into at least three rooms. The actual bathing room, where the bath was located and where everyone was undressed, was called the 'caldarium' ('beit penimi'). Located closer to the entrance of the bathhouse was another room, called the 'apodyterion' (probably the place known in Hebrew as 'beit ha-hitzon') where people changed their clothes and where both dressed and undressed people were present. A third room, called the 'palaestra' by the Romans, was meant for clothed people only. There was also often mention of a fourth room, called the 'tepidarium' by the Romans ('makom ha-zei'ah' in Hebrew), which was intended for perspiration. Cf. the parallels mentioned previously and cf. S. Krauss, *Talmudische Archäologie*, I, chap. IV, p. 218.

6. **A man should not put a question (about Torah) to his fellow in the bathhouse on account of danger and if someone (nevertheless) puts a question to him, he must say to him: 'It is a bath-house!' And some say that he may answer him and that it does not matter.**

One may not ask a acquaintance a question in a bathhouse because of danger, and if one asked a question, he should reply: 'This is a bathhouse!' Other Manuscripts of D. E. R. and the version in Mas. Kal. Rab. (ed. M. Higger, chap. IX, p. 338) add in the word 'shalom' after 'jish'al' and thus give the following reading: 'One is not to greet an acquaintance in the bathhouse ...' It is not clear to what extent it is forbidden or allowed, with no distinction made between a clothed or unclothed majority of people present as in the previously mentioned sources, to greet. It is also not clear what danger is involved in the act of greeting someone in a bathhouse.

We prefer the reading from the basis manuscript without the addition of the word 'shalom', and we believe that the statement here, just like the preceding one, concerns the asking of questions about Torah (i. e., halakhic questions) in the bathhouse. One can regard this a direct supplement to the formulation of the problem from D. E. R. X,4 and to the opinion that one may ask halakhic questions in a bathhouse which deal with bathing itself. From Tj'Ab.Zar. II,4, it appears that there was an opinion according to which it was absolutely advised not to discuss halakhic issues in a bathhouse and that one was surely not obligated to reply when asked questions about halakhic questions. (Judan, the father of Rabbi Matanja, said: 'One may ask halakhic questions (in the bathhouse) concerning bathing, but it is not the custom to answer such questions.') According to the version here in D. E., when faced with such questions, one is supposed to answer: 'This is a bathhouse.', i. e., it is inappropriate to give an answer while in the bathhouse. Compare this with the answer of Rabban Gamli'el to a person who asked a question in the bathhouse, according to the tradition in M'Ab. Zar. III,4: 'One does not answer in a bathhouse.' Cf. Tb'Ab. Zar. 44b; TbShab. 40b; Tj'Ab.Zar. III,4 (42d) and TjShab. III,1 [6a].

*Because of danger* – this possibly refers to the opinion of Rabbi Samuel bar 'Abdimi ('Abdumi), recorded in Tj'Ab. Zar. l.c., according to which it is better to wait until after leaving the bathhouse before asking halakhic questions, because the humidity in the bathhouse can harm the teeth. According to this opinion, then, it is better not to speak at all in a bathhouse. The term 'miphnei ha-sakkanah' (because of danger) generally refers to matters and situations which pose threat to health.

*Others say ...* This contrary opinion, according to which it is permitted to discuss halakhic questions relevant to bathing in the bathhouse, concurs with the opinion of Rabbi Jehoshua ben Levi. See Tj'Ab. Zar.l.c. and TjShab. l.c. See also D. E. R. X,4 regarding the attitude of Rabbi Me'ir, who replied to his pupil in the bathhouse. Cf. Tj'Ab.Zar. l.c., TjShab. l.c., and TbShab. 40b. Cf.

TbShab. ibid. concerning a story about Rabbi, who gave a halakhic instruction in the bathhouse.

There clearly have been various opinions about the issue of speaking about halakhic matters in the bathhouse. The tradition here in D.E. is undoubtedly secondary and comprises traditions recorded in the parallels mentioned.

### 7. A man should not stretch out his legs in a bath-tub, while he is laying in it in his full length, because this is a disgrace to him.

''Ambati' = Greek 'Ambatè' (bathtub). One may not dangle the feet in a bathtub, i.e., one may not stretch out the legs while lying stretched out in the bathtub, for it is improper to do so in a public bathing facility. Considering the correspondences to the statement immediately following in D.E., the background to this statement must be sought in TosMiqw. V,14ff. The original tradition, recorded in the Tosephta, however, was quite different: 'He who jumps into the *Miqweh* is contemptible...' According to the commentaries (cf., e.g., *Hasdei David* by Pardo a.l. [ ed. Livorno, 1776, repr. 1971, p. 39]), one sometimes did jump into the miqweh from the edge out of excessive religious strictness. One jumped into the water in order to be surrounded completely by water for an instant. To step into the water by using the steps descending into the pool would cause an undesired separation between the body and the water. It was considered contemptible and asocial to jump into the miqweh, because water could be splashed out of the miqweh (important if it was a small miqweh) meaning that less than the prescribed amount of water would be left in the bath for the next person. Some Miqweh's contained only the amount of water prescribed for ritual purification. Cf. TosMiqw. I,17 and cf. TbQid. 66b. In *Seph. ha-'Eshkol*. Hil. Miqw., sim. 60 (repr. of ed. Halberstadt, Tel Aviv, 1962, p. 148), there is also reference to the danger that the water can be splashed out of the miqweh before the person jumping is even himself immersed, with the result that he also would not be bathing in the prescribed amount of water. According to another explanation (found in, e.g., *Keseph Mishneh* on Rambam, *Jad*, Hil. Miqw., I), one easily gives the impression by jumping into the miqweh that his primary purpose is to play and indulge in frivolity rather than to be ritually cleansed. Cf. also the subsequent text in Tos. l.c. The prohibition not to go into the miqweh two times in a row is explained in a similar manner. One immersion is sufficient for ritual cleansing. Someone who immerses himself more than once is considered to have intentions other than to be purified.

The rule just mentioned, which in the Tosephta bears upon behaviour in the Miqweh, underwent a change of meaning in D.E. and came to be applied to the situation in the bathhouse. The development of the change is clear from Mas. Kal. Rab., which contains the following version: 'And one may not rest his feet at the edge of the bath and jump into the bath from the edge.' Mas. Kal. Rab.

reads 'we-jehe qophetz' (jump) in place of 'we-jehe robetz'! See ed. M. Higger., chap. IX, p. 339 and ed. N. N. Coronel, 18b.

The version in D. E. R. should be regarded as a further deviation from the source in Tos l.c. The term 'robetz' must have evolved from 'qophetz'.

See S. Krauss, *Talmudische Archäologie*, I, p. 677, note 123, with the following explanation, which differs completely from the text in D. E. R., h.l.: 'Nicht soll man die Füsse in die Badewanne hängen lassen, auch soll niemand sich darin hinkauern...' In that passage S. Krauss repeats 'we-'al' (and not) before 'we-jehe robetz'. He considers both terms to refer to the intention to urinate in the bath. (His interpretation, however, is not plausible.) We prefer the reconstruction that concurs with the reading in Mas. Kal. Rab. l.c. The question remains, however, as to whether the version in D. E. R. h.l. was an intentional deviation from that reading. The reason for forbidding jumping into the bath from the edge in a bathhouse must be sought in connection with the danger and the inconvenience such behaviour caused to other bathers as well as in the intention to prevent wastage of water.

**8.  And a man should not say to his fellow 'press your hands on me' (i. e. immerse me completely) in the bath-house. [And who says so will not depart from there undamaged; Rabbi Jehudah spoke: 'About which situation is spoken here? When there is little water, but when there is plenty of water, then a person who acts this way is praiseworthy.']**

The reason behind the admonition not to let himself be pressed under water by the hand of his fellow, must also be sought in TosMiqw. V,14ff. There it is stated that it is contemptible to have oneself immersed in the water by the hand of another bather. The reason for this is probably connected with the excessive stringency in religious ritual's intended to ensure that one was completely immersed in the water for the ritual cleansing. In a small miqweh there was the complaint that the volume of the immersed body and that of the hand of someone else immersing the body was to great and that so much water was lost, that it was possible that less than the forty 'se'ah' required was left in the miqweh. See, e.g. *Hasdei David*, l.c. on Tos. l.c.

That rule originally applied in a private miqweh, is applied here in D. E. R. to the situation in a public bathing facility. One finds a direct indication of the origin of this statement in D. E. in an addition made in a number of manuscripts of D. E. In the manuscripts appear the following words, ascribed to Rabbi Jehudah: 'Rabbi Jehudah said: "What is the issue here? The situation that there is too little water. If there is much water, then the person doing this is to be praised."' Then sufficient water has been left in the bath. It is not probable, however, that the problem of water wastage was the motive here in D. E. behind encouraging such moderate behaviour in a bathhouse, which contained reasonable large baths. The above mentioned addition does not appear in the basis manuscript. One must therefore assume that the original reason has been altered in D. E. R. In this connection cf. *Keseph Mishneh* on Rambam, *Jad*, Hil. Miqw., I,19, where such behaviour (it is: having himself immersed by the hand of another bather) is condemned as frivolous behaviour and opposition to a non-functional conception of bathing as merely a source of recreation is expressed. Such an explanation applies very well in the context of D. E. R. h.l. The sages opposed the influence of the Greco-Roman bathing culture in which ritual purification and cleansing in general were of secondary importance. From the additions in the manuscripts of D. E. R., it appears that the practise of pressing someone under the water with the hand was considered dangerous. Cf. The statement of Rabbi Jehudah in TosMiqw. V,14: 'Rabbi Jehudah said: "Hold him down with your hand until he expires."' Cf. also S. Krauss, *Talmudische Archäologie*, I, chap. IV, p. 677, note 123. S. Krauss applies the addition made in the manuscripts of D. E. according to which Rabbi Jehudah made an exception for instances in which there was much water: 'In vielem Wasser jedoch lässt man sich wohl nur der grösseren Sauberkeit wegen u.z. ganz leicht niederdrücken.'

One also finds, however entirely different explanations for the practise mentioned here in D. E. Cf., e.g., M. Ginsberg in *The Minor Tractates of the Babylonian Talmud*, ed. A. Cohen, p. 562: 'A man should not say to his fellow in a bath-house: "Rub me in well with your hand" and he who says so will not depart from there unscathed. Rabbi Jehudah said: "'This only applies when there is little water (when the rubbing may arouse unclean thoughts), but when there is plenty of water it is all right."' Cf. also S. Lieberman, *Greek in Jewish Palestine*, p. 92 ff. Cf. also the explanation of M. Higger, *Massekhtot Derekh 'Eretz*, p. 14, where he explains the words 'deros jadkha 'alai' (lay your hand on me) to mean: 'Attack me with your hands to wrestle with me.' These last explanations, however, completely ignore the source in TosMiqw. l.c.

### 9. [One who reads (the Shema) twice] and one who immerses himself twice, such a person is contemptible.

He who immerses himself twice is contemptible. As for the two preceding statements, the basis for this statement is found in TosMiqw. V,14. It is meant here that one may not waste water in the miqweh during ritual purification out of excessive strictness. One immersion is sufficient during ritual purification. Water is already lost because a certain amount remains on the body. For other bathers, then, there may not be the required forty 'se'ah' of water in the bath. So much water remains on the body, that it is even more senseless to immerse oneself twice for ritual purification in a very small miqweh containing just forty 'se'ah'. There was already too little water left over after the first immersion. Cf. MMiqw. VII,6. Moreover, immersing oneself twice, one gives the impression of having other purposes than just undergoing ritual cleansing, for one immersion is enough for one to be purified. Cf. *Seph. ha-'Eshkol* (repr. of ed. Halberstadt, Tel-Aviv, 1962, sim.60, p. 148) and cf. *Keseph Mishneh* on Rambam, *Jad*, Hil. Miqw.,I,9. This explanation concurs with the version in the basis manuscript.

In the reading in Mas. Kal. Rab. (ed. M. Higger, IX, p. 339) and in the manuscripts. of D. E. R., one finds the following addition: 'He who reads twice and who immerses himself twice is contemptible.' The word 'reads' refers to the recitation of the Shema. Cf. TbBer. 33b and MBer. V,3. It is forbidden to say any word or sentence of the Shema twice at once, for that may give the impression that one recognizes two Gods. The recognition of two Gods is dualism. In TbBer. l.c., a further distinction is made between someone who repeats words from the Shema (this is contemptible) and someone who repeats sentences from the Shema. Someone who repeats sentences must be silenced.

See the suggestion in *Nahalat Ja'aqob* on D. E. R. h.l. to read: 'he who washes himself twice' in place of 'he who reads twice.' This supposition is not confirmed in the manuscripts.

We believe that the remark about reading the Shema twice must be regarded as a later addition, and that the incorrect suggestion that it was forbidden out of fear of dualism to bath twice, was based on that addition. Cf. *Hasdei David* on Tos Miqw. l.c., where dualism is also mentioned in connection with bathing.

In our opinion, the original reason for forbidding bathing twice at once was the intention to discourage an exaggerated ritual of purification and to discourage bathers from wasting water. See also the context which directly follows here in D. E. R. in connection with doing harm to the community. Cf. TbKer. 8a-b and the opinion of Rabbi 'Aqiba that someone who is obligated to undergo a ritual bath five times requires only one immersion to become clean.

There are indications in the tradition that there existed the custom of immersing oneself more than once, because one immersion was considered insufficient in certain cases. Cf. TjSheb. II,1 and cf. *Seph. ha-Zohar*, Wa-Jera, 102b and *Seph. Hasidim*, ed. M. Margaliot, 1957, § 394, p. 285 and notes;

## 10.  Who covers himself in his cloak and stays in the room where they sweat, such a person is robbing the community.

Bathing facilities contained small rooms in which people were to sweat; these rooms corresponded to what the Roman called the 'tepidarium'. After using such a room, it was considered a good practise to leave it as soon as possible in order to make room for someone else. It was considered asocial of someone to use the room after getting dressed. The clothing absorbed the warm humidity. Cf. also the commentary in *Nahalat Ja'aqob* h.l. A person who does so is called a 'robber of the community', for his behaviour amounted to an abuse of facilities meant for the whole community.

**11. Who washes himself with cold water and sluices himself with lukewarm water, such a person is robbing the community. What should he do (to indemnify the public)? He should go and dig wells, ditches and caves and he should repair roads, paved high ways and he will be forgiven.**

He who rinses himself off with warm water after bathing in cold water is considered to be a robber of the community. One must use warm water sparingly. One usually bathed in warm water, then went into the 'tepidarium' to sweat and then rinsed off with cold water (as for a refreshing shower after bathing). Cf.,e.g. TbShab. 40a and other sources. In connection with the halakhah concerning the Sabbath, one does find opinions that it is permitted to rinse oneself off with warm water. See especially the meaning of Rabbi Shim'on in TbShab. 39b, who permits it; cf. TosShab. III,4 and TjShab. III [6a], According to Rabbi Jehudah it is only permitted to rinse off with cold water, and according to Rabbi Me'ir, it is not permitted to rinse off at all. The essential issue is to what extent the fear that one uses water on Sabbath that has been warmed up on Sabbath, is justified. It is suggested in the gemara that an opinion such as Rabbi Shim'on's only applies when water heated by a natural source (as in Tiberias) is used. The statement here in D.E. concerns the possibly wasting of water and, in contrast to the opinion of Rabbi Shim'on as explained above, concerns the situation in which warm water is scarce and in which there is no access to water heated by a natural source. The use of too much warm water constitutes an abuse of community supplies, as it is possible that too little warm water would be left over for others.

Also compare TbShab. 41b. One strengthens his body by rinsing off with cold water after taking a warm bath, but one who rinses off with warm water after taking a warm bath weakens his body and looks like iron which has not been hardened with cold water after being forged. Note the direct correspondence between the wording in TbShab. 41b and the wording of the parallel in Mas. Kal. Rab., ed. M. Higger. chap. IX, p. 340: 'He who washes himself with warm water and does not rinse himself off with cold water ..'

**What should he do? ...**

What should someone do who has harmed the community? This statement goes back to a baraita which deals with the problem of people who have robbed the community and wish to repent. Cf. TosB.M. VIII,26; TbBeitza. 29a. From the context in TosB.M. VIII,26 and in TbB.Q. 94b and other sources, it appears that those who have done harm to others and want to abandon their harmful practises must either restore items they have stolen to the owners in their original condition or compensate the owners in some other way. Sometimes it was impossible to compensate those who have been wronged because they are not aware that they have been wronged. The entire community may have been wronged, for example, by tax collectors and keepers of livestock. In such instances the repentant individual must finance projects for the community so that those he has wronged profit from those projects. In the parallel in TbB. Q. 94b, Rab Hisda is supplied with specific information concerning projects intended for the good of the community, such as wells, ditches, and caves (for the provision of water to the general public, which includes those persons who have been wronged; cf. also TbBeitza. l.c.). Projects also include the repair of paved roads, as mentioned in D. E. R. h.l. The reading in the basis manuscript (*and theatres*) is not correct. Theatres were considered heathen, and the hostile opposition to them was so great that people even refused to help in constructing them (cf. Tb'Ab. Zar. 16a). It is better to interpret 'teratiot' as a form of ''asteratiot' = 'strata' (paved ways). Support for this interpretation can be found in TbM. Q. 5a, which, like D. E. R., mentions the repair of 'wells, ditches and caves' and of roads ('u-metiqin et ha-derakhim') and of 'cleaning the roads of thorns, mending the broadways and paved highways (... "'astrata'ot")'. The term 'teratiot' here in D. E. refers thus to 'paved highways'. Cf. the translation of M. Ginsberg, in: *The Minor Tractates of the Babylonian Talmud*, ed. A. Cohen, II, p. 562: '... or repairing highways and streets and then he will be forgiven.' See also the reading in Ms. Oxford Bodleian (cat. A. Neubauer I, p. 815) no. 2339, which still mentions 'samekh' in: 'we-teratsiot'!

The concept of reconciliation and forgiveness, by what can be placed under the rabbinic concept of 'gemilut hasadim' (the rendering of charity and services to others and to the community) is very old and already appears in Seph. Ben Sira (ed. M. Z. Segal, 3:28, p. 19; cf. idem notes, p. 20 : 'Just as water can extinguish a raging flame, so can charity ("tzedaqa") extinguish transgressions.' Cf. Dan. 4:24 and A. R. N. [a], IV (11a).

# Pereq Ha-Jotzee

## Derekh 'Eretz Rabbah, chapter XI

**1a.** **One who sets out on the way alone before cock-crow, his blood is upon his head.**
**1b.** **Rabbi Josijah said: 'He should not set out on his way before the cock crows at least twice. And what kind of cock? They spoke about the average type (i. e. the type, which crows not too early and not too late), for it is said: "Who has put wisdom in the Ibis and who has given insight to the cock" (Hiob 38:36).'**

**One who sets out on the way alone...**

This is a warning warning not to begin on a journey alone before the cock has crowed; Rabbi Josijah's additional remark that one should wait until the cock has crowed at least twice before starting on a journey alone, and the remark that the cock should be one that crows neither to early nor too late, all appear in TbJoma 21a as well as in D.E.R. The beginning of the statement 'If one starts on a journey before the cock has crowed, his blood is on his head', is recorded in TbJoma 21a in the name of Rabbi Sh(e)ila (a Tanna of the third generation). The addition of the reference of Hiob 38:36 here in D.E. does not appear in TbJoma. 21a. M. Higger (*Massekhtot Ze'irot*, p. 27) assumes that the reading in TbJoma was derived from the tradition in D.E. and that it was abridged! Rabbi Sh(e)ila is not mentioned in D.E. as the person passing on the tradition. The addition of Hiob 38:36 in D.E. should be considered secondary as its content has little bearing on that preceding.

The cock crowed before "ammud ha-shahar', the time in which the light of morning first becomes visible. Cf.TbPes. 2b. From the parallels, it appears that the fear of demons was the reason for the warning. To be in the dark alone was considered especially dangerous. Cf, e.g., TbPes. 112b and Rashi on TbMeg. 3a and TbJoma 21a; TjShab. II [5b] and other sources. According to a statement by Rabbi José ben Rabbi Jehudah in TbPes. 112b, it was considered especially dangerous to be out on certain nights. The cock's crow was an announcement of daybreak and therefore was supposed to cause the demons to flee. Cf., Ber. Rab. XXXVI,1; cf. TbHul. 91a, where Rabbi Jitzhaq remarks, in connection with Gen. 32:25, that a sage may not be out on the road at night because the being with which Jacob fought retained its power at night but lost it when daylight appeared. One could, however, suggest another reason in the context of the rules of behaviour in D. E., which was especially intended for those in the circles of the sages. See D. E. Z., IV, 1 (cf. TbBer. 43b and other sources), where a sage is warned not to go out into the dark (alone) so that he can not be suspected of perverse or illicit deeds. See also Rashi in reference to TbTa'an. 10b and a well-known statement by Rab, with a third reason, namely, that one may travel only after daybreak and before nightfall. Rashi indicates that a sage may not expose himself to unnecessary dangers. If he goes out alone into the dark, he could be assaulted by thieves or he could fall into a pit with no one around to help him. (Cf. Waj. Rab. XXVI,7)

*Rabbi Josijah said...* According to Rabbi Josijah, one must wait until the cock crows twice before beginning a journey alone. The cock might give his first crow very early, at the end of the first nightwatch after midnight (cf. MJoma. I,8), i. e., at 4.00 or 5.00 in the morning. In our opinion, the quotation from Hiob. 38:36 was added in later as a reference. The concept 'sekwi' from the quotation is explained in a few baraitot as the common word for a cock. According to TbR. ha-Sh. 26a the term was supposed to be the word for a cock used in Ken Nishraja (Kennesrin, south of Aleppo). According to TjBer. IX [13c] [cf.TbBer. 60b] a cock was supposed to have been called 'sekwi' in Rome (Idumea is probably meant, see M. Schwab, *The Talmud Jerusalem*, p. 157, note 9).

In later commentaries 'sekwi' is derived from the stem 'sakha' (= to see) and 'sekhija' (waiter, seer). As watchman, the cock is the first to see the light of day. Cf., e.g., M. Jastrow, *Dictionary*, II, p. 1571. In connection with 'sekwi' in the meaning of cock, see further L. Köhler/ W. Baumgartner, *Lexicon*, Leiden 1958, p. 921; see further commentaries on the berakhah in the mourning prayer: 'Blessed are You, O Lord our God Who has given to the cock ("sekwi") intelligence to distinguish between day and night.'

## 2. A man who returns from a journey and (immediately) visits a bath-house, undergoes a bloodletting, gets intoxicated and has marital inter-course on the floor, his blood is upon his head.

A variant of this statement appears in TbGit. 70a in the form of a number proverb. According to M. Higger, the reading here in D. E. R. is earlier, given the wording 'damo be-rosho' (his blood is on his own head) in place of 'dies immediately'. On this point, however, D. E. is very stylized. An entire series of statements is mentioned in which those words appear again and again.

*And he who copulates on the floor.* These words, which appear in here in D. E. R., may represent the merging of two phrases that appear separately in TbGit. 70a as 'he who sleeps on the floor' and 'he who copulates'. (Cf. the reading of the Gaon of Vilna.)

From the commentary of Rabbi Johanan on the above mentioned number statements in TbGit. l.c., it appears that just just doing the different tiresome and enervating activities mentioned one after the other was judged to be a threat to health, even to life. A number of baraitot point especially to the dangerous combination of bleeding himself and having sexual intercourse without resting and eating in between. In connection with resting after blood-letting, see the remarks of Rab and Samuel in TbShab. 129b and other sources.

### 3. One who kills a louse on his bed and who stands naked in the light of a candle or in the moonlight, his blood is upon his head.

There is not a direct parallel for the combination of acts mentioned here. The forbiddance to kill a louse on bed is possibly based on the opinion that it is unhygienic to do so. In combination, however, with the following forbiddance to stand naked in front of a candle, one could also understand the forbiddance to be directed against superstition. This bears a striking connection to a related statement preserved in Midr. Ma'aseh Torah (see, A. Jellinek, *Beit ha-Mid-rash*, II, p. 96): 'He who does (these) four things, his blood is on his head. He who sits in the *shadow of a corpse*. He who stands naked in front of a candle...' (It should be stated, however, that another version of the same Midrash, has a different reading of the statement: 'He who does (these) four things... He who extinguishes the candle with his mouth. He who sits in *the shadow of a candle*. He who stand naked...'. Cf. *Pirqei Rabbenu ha-Qadosh* in *Seph. ha-Liqqutim*, ed. L. Grünhut, III, pp. 69—70. Night was associated in antiquity with demons and death. It was possible considered dangerous to sleep near a corpse (however small) for death brings death.

Along with the warning not to stand naked in candlelight, one also finds the warning not to copulate or urinate by candlelight. Cf. TbNid.16b-17a and other sources. From the context it appears that such actions were condemned as indiscreet. (See TbNid. 16b, where it is concluded on the basis of Hiob. 3:3 that it is not proper to copulate during the day. The original reason for these statements in D.E., however, must probably be sought in a form of superstition. Note, e.g., TbPes. 112b: 'You may not travel alone at night and you may not stand naked in front of a candle, for it is taught: "He who stands naked in the light of a candle will become epileptic (i.e., he will be overtaken by a demon), and he who copulates in candlelight will have epileptic children."' It appears that the fear of demons prompted these warnings. Cf. also MShab. II,5: 'If a man puts out a lamp (on the Sabbath) from fear of gentiles or robbers or of an evil spirit...' Commentators usually interpret 'evil spirit' psychologically, in the sense of hypochondria and anxiety. In this case, extinguishing the candle would calm someone down. Cf. Rambam, Bertinora, Kahati and others. See A. Marmorstein in *Tzion* (1887), p. 22 and in *Mitteilungen zur Jüdischen Volkskunde*, XXX (1927), p. 31. See also A. Marmorstein in: *M. G. W.J.*, LXXII, (1928) p. 391 and S. Krauss in: *M. G. W.J.*, LXXII, (1928), pp. 477—478. The term 'evil spirit' also refers, however, to a demon. Cf., e.g.,

Tos'Ab. Zar. I,16: 'One may not travel with a caravan... not even out of fear of
gentiles, robbers, or an evil spirit (demon)...' Cf. M'Er. IV,1 and other
sources. In MShab. l.c., 'evil spirit' probably also refers to a demon. Cf., e.g.,
*Rabbenu Nissim* on TbShab. 29b and *Riph* a.l., in Talmud Babli ed. Vilna/
Romm, 13a: '... because of an evil spirit which appears before him, and so that
he becomes calm when he can't see him.' See especially A. Marmorstein in
*M. G. W. J.*, LXXII (1928), p. 391 and cf. J. Bergmann in *M. G. W. J.*, LXXI,
(1927), pp. 162–165; cf. also other sources. It was possible felt that the scanty
light that burns on the evening of Sabbath draws the attention of demons to an
ill or anxious person who, despite or even because of the light, cannot see well
in the darkness but feels that he can de seen by demons. The shadows caused by
the flickering light make the person uneasy, and he can be put at ease only when
the light is extinguished. It is thus understandable that it was considered
dangerous to stand naked in front of a candle because that could attract the
perverse attention of demons (despite the general notion that light of a torch for
example, drove demons away; cf. e.g., TbBer. 43b). There were also many
superstitious fears associated with moonlight and shadows in the moonlight.
Cf., e.g., TbGit. 70a and TbPes. 111a. See also G. Dalman, *Arbeit und Sitte in
Palestina*, I, repr. 1964, p. 13.

4. **One who drinks liquids, that have been uncovered overnight and that
are mixed with water, his blood is upon his head, because of the danger.**

The forbiddance to drink liquids diluted with water which have stood uncovered for a night also arose from superstition. See TbNid. 17a a warning attributed
to Rabbi Shim'on bar Johai that one should not drink liquids which have been
diluted with water and which have stood uncovered overnight. It is added in the
gemara of TbNid. l.c. that the warning applies only to liquids contained in a
vessel made of metal or alum crystals. The background to the statement in the
gemara is contained in TbPes. 112a in a warning against drinking water from
rivers and pools for fear of the night demon Shabriri, who was supposed to
cause blindness. Following the warning in TbPes. 112a, there appears the
incantation 'Shabriri, Beriri, Riri, Jiri, Ri, I am thirsty for water in a white
glass.' The incantation was supposed to protect one from Shabriri, who was
supposed to be rendered powerless by the gradual abbreviation of his name.
This incantation is comparable to the one recorded in Tb'Ab. Zar.12b: '... Shabriri... which prevail in white vessels.' It appears from these statements that
clear, shining vessels were supposed to be especially attractive to the demon
Shabriri. This notion was probably influenced by the interpretation of his name
as the *shaph'el* form of the stem 'barar' (to shine brightly) and thus as a
euphemism for a causer of blindness. Cf. the expression 'sagi nehor' (literally
'rich of light' and euphemism of blind) 'sanwer', the *saph'el* form of 'nur' (to
shine). Cf. especially the Targum Onkelos on Gen. 19:11, where 'be-sanwerim'

is translated in Arameic as 'shabrirja'. The name 'shabriri' is also interpreted as
a combination of 'shober ra'aja' (breaker of the eyesight, or something similar
in meaning. See *Arukh ha-Shalem*, ed. A. Kohut, sub 'Shabriri'. The name
'Shabriri' was supposed to be a corruption of 'shabkhiri', a Persian word for
night blindness.

According to the opinion of M. Higger, *Massekhtot Ze'irot*, p. 27, the version
in D. E. is the original version and 'because of danger' was added later on the
basis of TbNid. l.c.

### 5. One who drinks from brooks, rivers and pools with his mouth or (by drawing the water) by one hand, his blood is upon his head [because of leeches].

See the suggestion of S. Krauss, *Taludische Archäologie*, III, chap. IX, p. 242,
note 27, to read 'u-me-ha-berikhot' in stead of 'u-me-ha-midbarot' (deserts; we
translated *pools*) from 'berikhah' (lake). This warning appears in Tb'Ab. Zar.
12b in which it is also warned that one should not drink water from rivers and
other bodies of water with his mouth or from his hand. This manner of drinking
does not permit one first to inspect the water for the presence of organisms. The
possibility of swallowing a leech was especially feared (see the gemara in
Tb'Ab. Zar. 12b). Note the addition of 'ha-nima shira' in some manuscripts of
D. E. R. h.l. See the explanation in *Nahalat Ja'aqob* as 'a worm that lives in
water' and see the reading given by the Gaon of Vilna. The words 'ha-nima
shira' literally mean 'string of silk', and serve as a description of the glittering
form of the leech in water. Cf. also TbShab. 90a: 'The worm... the worm of
silk... are all dangerous (for one who eats them).' See M. Higger, *Massekhtot
Ze'irot*, p. 27 in connection with the opinion that the addition in the manuscripts
of D. E. R. represents an adaption by later writers in the D. E. tradition to the
gemara in Tb'Ab. Zar. 12b.

### 6. One who undergoes a bloodletting and fasts (immediately), his blood is upon his head.

To fast after letting blood was considered health threatening. See especially the
statement of Rab and Samuel in the context of TbShab. 129a: 'Rab and Samuel
both say: "If one makes light of the meal after bleeding his food will be made
light of by Heaven, for they say: He has no compassion for his own life, shall I
have compassion unto him?"' Further in the text: 'Rab and Samuel both say:
"He who is bled must (first) partake of something and then go out. For if he
does not eat anything, if... he meets a homicide he will die..."' Rab advises
that, in any case, one should eat meat after being bled (life for life), and Samuel
advises that one should drink wine for the replacement of the blood. According
to Rab, one should even sell his sandals and the beams of his house if necessary,

in order to obtain food after having been bled. It was considered especially dangerous for one to engage in activities which taxed the body and not to rest directly after having been bled. Cf. D. E. R., XI,2. See also especially the further context in TbShab. 129a; cf. also TbNid. 17a and TbKet. 77b.

### 7. **They who write Scrolls, Tephillin and Mezuzot, they and their traders (i. e. who sell their products for them) and the traders of their traders (i. e. traders to whom their traders sell) will never see a sign of blessing.**

Cf. the versions of this statement in baraitot in TosBik. II,15 and TbPes. 50b · Those who copy holy writings from scrolls, tephillin and Mezuzot, and the intermediaries who arrange the ultimate sale of the copies will never see a sign of blessing. Their activities are not blessed, and the intermediaries will not enjoy the reward of their labour. Cf. especially the statement in D. E. Z. X,8: 'Four perutot are without a sign of blessing. They are the wages of scribes, the wages of interpreters...' Cf.TbPes.50b. The writing out of holy texts is the fulfilment of a 'mitzwah' and must be done for the sake of Heaven, not for the sake of financial gain. It is improper to accept payment for copying holy texts. See TbPes. 50b: 'But if they engage for its own sake, they do see (a sign of blessing).' In a number of traditions it is unacceptable to sell, for example, a copy of a Sepher Torah, even if one has more copies of it, and even if the proceeds are used to procure another Sepher Torah or to buy food. See the opinion of Rabban Shim'on ben Gamli'el in TbMeg. 27a: 'Even if a man has no food and he sells a Sepher Torah... he will never see a sign of blessing', i. e., he will come to no good with that money. The ideal behind the objections was that every man should make his own copy of the Torah. This ideal was based on Dt. 31:19: 'Now therefore write this song ...'; cf. TbSanh. 21b and TbMen. 30a. In practise, however, only the command to have a Sepher Torah in one's possessions was followed; to make actually a copy oneself remained an ideal.

Another reason that the above activities were not sanctioned was that there was the risk that one could make errors while copying texts or sell texts with small unknown mistakes. The consequences of such mistakes, however, are not negligible. See the explanations in the gemara of Mas. Kal. Rab. (ed. M. Higger, chap. X, p. 341). The survival of the world is considered to be dependent on the perfection of the Torah. Cf., e.g., Tb'Er. 13a; Waj. Rab. IXX,2; Shir ha-Shir. Rab. XV,11; Tanh., Ber-Reshit, § 1; TjSot. II,4 [8a] and other sources. In one tradition (A. R. N.[a]. XXXVI (54b) concerning occupations (such as medicine) in which even the smallest mistake could have very far-reaching consequences, it is even stated that professional scribes of holy texts were among those who have no part in the World to Come. Cf. TbQid. 82a and TbB. B. 21a.

## 8. Traders of unclean fish and unclean fat will never see a sign of blessing.

Traders of unclean fish and of unclean fat will never see a sign of blessing. This statement is missing in TbPes. 50b. The selling of unclean fish refers to the mixing of the inwards of clean fish with those of unclean fish, which yield a mixed product, the cleanness and origin of which can no longer be ascertained. Such a product is then sold as clean fish. Cf. TbB. M. 61b. Also the fat of clean animals was mixed with the fat of unclean animals and sold as clean fat. It was thus forbidden for a jew to sell and use products of a non-jew in which fats has been worked. Cf., e.g., TjTer. VIII.

## 9. One who deals in reeds and vessels will not see a sign of blessing.

According to the explanation of this baraita in TbPes. 50b, dealers in reeds and vessels will never see a sign of blessing because they are exposed to the evil eye. The large volume of these products might give others the impression that business dealing in such products are doing extremely well, which could give rise to jealousy. See M. Higger, *Massekhtot Ze'irot*, p. 27, where he claims that the baraitot in D.E. predate their parallels in TbPes. 50b!! The explanatory addition which appears in TbPes. 50b does not appear in D. E. R.

## 10a. Rabbi 'Aqiba: 'One who works on the end of the day preceding Sabbath-days and on the end of the day preceding festival-days from the ninth hour and afterwards will never see a sign of blessing.'
## 10b. 'And who works on the Ninth of Ab will not see a sign of blessing.'

He who works on the evening eve of the Sabbath or on the eve of holidays (from the ninth hour onward) will not see a sign of blessing. He will not enjoy the rewards of activities he carries out that time. This statement appears in an anonymous baraita in TbPes. 50b as a more detailed explanation of MPes. IV,1 ff.: 'He who does work on the eve of the Sabbath and on the eve of festivals from 'minhah' onward will never see a sign of blessing.' See also in the gemara: 'An industrious man who suffers loss – (that is) he who works the hole day and works on the eve of the Sabbath.' It is possible that the version here in D. E. R with Rabbi 'Aqiba as authority is older. See also M.Higger l.c.!

While one was not to do work on the eve of Pesah from midday onward, one was not to work on the Sabbath and holidays from 'minhah' onward. In this case, 'minhah' refers to the 'little minhah', from 9.30 hour of the day onward (from about 3.30 p.m.); cf. TbBer. 26b and '*Ijjunim*, in ed. A. Steinsalz a.l.; cf. also TosBer. III,1; cf. G. Dalman, *Arbeit und Sitte,* I, pp. 617–618.

*And who works on...* Unlike the previous statement concerning work on the eve of the Sabbath and holidays this statement is also in the tradition ascribed to Rabbi 'Aqiba, cf. TbTa'an. 30b. See also *Halakhot Gedolot*, ed. E. Hildesheimer, Hil. Tisha be-'Ab, p. 391 and cf. *Riph* on TbTa'an. 30b, where Rabban Gamli'el is mentioned as authority for this statement.

In an anonymous tradition in MPes. IV,5 it is stated that one may do work in a place where work is customary done on the Ninth of Ab, but one may not do work in a place where it is not the custom to work on the Ninth of Ab. It is also stated that scholars may do no work anywhere and that if they have the choice, they will choose to follow the strictest rule. The scholars apply the stricter rules to themselves. By not working, they can concentrate better on fasting and did not risk of not being able to complete the fast as a result of bodily exertion. Some manuscripts of D. E. R. h.l. omit this statement.

### 11. Rabbi 'Aqiba said: 'Scholars should abstain from work on the Ninth of Ab, and everyone should consider himself a scholar.'

Sages and scholars may not do work on the Ninth of Ab. Where not doing work on this day is concerned everyone should act as a scholar and sage. This entire statement is ascribed here in D. E. to Rabbi 'Aqiba. According to MPes. IV,5 (Tb. 54b), however, the tradition is as follows: 'And the sages do not work anywhere (on the Ninth of Ab). Rabban Shim'on ben Gamli'el said: "(In this matter) a man must always consider himself as a sage."' Cf.TbBer. 17b and TbTa'an. 30b. The reading according to a baraita in TbTa'an. 30b is: 'It is also taught: "Rabban Shim'on ben Gamli'el said: One must always consider himself as a sage so that he may feel the fast more strongly."' The tendency to apply to everyone the stringent rule that applied to sages was typical for the circles of the D. E. traditions. In connection with the statement ascribed to Rabban Shim'on ben Gamli'el in MPes. l.c., see F. Böhl, *Gebotserschwerung und Rechtsverzicht als etisch-religiöse Normen in der rabbinischen Literatur (Frankfurter Judaistische Studien)*, Band I, Frankfurt am Main 1971, pp. 21 ff.

### 12. One has told: At one time Rabbi 'Aqiba and (other) scholars were sitting under an olive tree at a table, because of the danger (i. e. the heat of the sun) and he said: 'They who cut down trees and who raise small cattle and traders in a marketstand will never see a sign of blessing.'

They who cut down trees, they who rise small cattle, and they who trade on the pathway will never see a sign of blessing.

This baraita appears anonymously in TbPes. 50b, where yet a fourth category is mentioned: '... and those who cast their eyes on the better portion (when sharing with another person).' The baraita, attributed to Rabbi 'Aqiba here in D. E., is introduced here in D. E. by a historical remark about Rabbi 'Aqiba. This clearly indicates that this reading in D. E. is older than the reading in TbPes. l.c.! The reading in D. E. R., in which only three categories are mentioned, correspondents remarkably to the version in the baraita in TosBik. II,16.

(see ed. S. Lieberman, I, p. 293; see especially the commentary in Mas. Kal. Rab., ed. M. Higger, chap. IX, p. 343.) The practise of sitting under an olive tree to avoid the danger of sunburn might have been the direct impetus behind Rabbi 'Aqiba's remark about wrongness of cutting down a fruit tree! In Ber. Rab. LXII,7 (cf. TjBer. II [5c]), it is mentioned that Rabbi 'Aqiba (among others) specifically chose a certain fig tree under which he gathered usually with his pupils to give them lessons. To cut down a fruit tree is a transgression of a prohibition in the Torah. According to Dt.20:19ff. one may not even cut down a fruit tree in order to facilitate an end to battle while besieging an enemy in a city. One may definitely not destroy any fruit tree without a compelling reason to do so. In the tradition, an exception is made only – in time of war – in the case of wild trees which bear no edible fruit and for fruit trees which no longer produce fruit. An exception was also made in the case of trees which threatened the health of healthy fruit trees; cf., e.g., TbB.Q. 91b and Siphrei (on Dt.), pisqa 204; and Rambam, *Jad*, Hil. Melakhim, VI,8 and cf.S. Krauss, *Talmudische Archäologie*, chap. VI, p. 207.

Just like those who cut down fruit trees, owners of livestock (sheep and especially goats) were considered among those who destroy the land (Israel). Owners of livestock were not only considered robbers because they let their animals graze on someone else's land, but they were also considered responsible for rendering the land unsuitable for further cultivation. In this connection, cf. commentary and parallels in connection with D. E. R., II,6, where owners of livestock are ranked among those who will leave no money for their progeny. See the gemara in Mas. Kal. Rab. l.c., where it is suggested that the 'slaughterers of livestock' be read in place of 'owners of livestock'. There are no sound reasons, however, for amending the baraita accordingly.

*'Taggarei simta', traders in a market stand.* Cf., however, J. Levy, *Wörterbuch über die Talmudim und Midraschim*, sub 'simta', derived from 'semita' (narrow path, narrow road) and opposed to 'pelatja' (broad road). 'Taggarei simta' thus refers to merchants who sell their wares while on the road. Cf. also S. Krauss, *Griechische und Lateinische Lehnwörter im Talmud, Midrasch und Targum*, sub 'simta'.

In TosBik. II,16 (ed. S. Lieberman, I, p. 293), one finds also the reading 'shemittah'. See H. Freedman in the translation of TbPes. 50b, *The Babylonian Talmud*, ed. Epstein, *Pesahim*, p. 245: 'Trading with the produce of the Sabbatical year is forbidden.' See also MSanh. II,3 and S. Lieberman, *Tosephta Ki-Pheshutah*, II, p. 85. 'Taggarei simta' is better explained, however, as 'traders in marketstands', in accordance with M. Higger, *Massekhtot Derekh 'Eretz*, p. 116. Cf. M. Jastrow, *Dictionary*, II, p. 981, sub 'simta'. He derives the meaning of 'marketstand' from (among others) Siphra, Be-Har, VII beginning of par. VI (ed. Weiss, 109c) in connection with the sale of slaves: 'we-lo ja'amidennu be-simta we-ja'amidem 'al 'eben ha-leqah', 'and he shall not place him [the slave] in a "simta" and he shall not place him on a (so called) "sellingstone"', this is based on Lev. 25:42. Cf. Jalq., Be-Har, r. 667 with the reading 'we-lo ja'aseh simta we-ja'amidem 'al 'eben ha-leqah' and see other parallels. The meaning of 'marketstand' in the above-mentioned places is contested. Cf. J.Perles in: *M. G. W. J.*,, XXIV, (1873), p. 371, where an entirely different explanation is given. 'Simta' is read also as 'timsa' from the Greek 'timesis' = public appraisal and bidding in public. In TjShab. I [2d] (cf. TbShab. 7a), there is spoken of 'simta she-bein ha-'ammudim' (simta between the pillars). In TbKet. 84b 'simta' is contrasted to 'reshut ha-rabbim' (a public place visited by many people). These references indicate that 'simta' refers to a place set off by pillars near a market place or square. These pillars were obviously used by the merchants for setting up temporary marketstands. This explanation also clarifies the reading 'ja'amidennu be-simta' (siphra l.c.) as well as the readings 'ja'aseh simta' (make a simta) and '"taggarei simta' (merchants in marketstands) here in D. E. R. See further S. Lieberman, *Tosephta Ki-Pheshutah*, l.c., and see Rashi and *Me'iri* in reference to TbPes. 50b and cf. Rashi, commentary on Lev. 25:42 and Rambam, *Jad*, Lo Ta'aseh 258 and *Massekhet 'Abadim*, ed. M. Higger, 1930, p. 57. See especially the explanation of Rashi on TbPes. 50b. Merchants in marketstands had a strident and ostentatious way of selling their wares, and consequently they attracted the evil eye of others, i. e., they provoked the jealousy or irritation of passers-by whose negative disposition towards the merchants would somehow have an effect on them. See also *Nahalat Ja'aqob* on D. E. R. h.l. The commentaries give the same explanation concerning people who destroy fruit trees or keep livestock. They, too, attracted the evil eye of others, which ultimately meant that their activities would not bring success. Cf. the addition in TbPes. 50b: ' . . . and they who cast their eyes at the better portion.' To do so also made one unpopular among others. See the explanation in the gemara l.c.: 'What is the reason? Because people gaze at them.'

**13. One who sells his (Torah-)Scroll, though he does need it (i.e. the money for his living) [another reading: though he does not need it (i. e. the Sepher Torah, because he possesses another Scroll)] and one who sells his daughter (as a handmaid) though he has nothing to eat, will never see a sign of blessing.**

Anyone who sells his (Torah) scroll although he does need the money from the sale will never see a sign of blessing. This statement was apparently derived from the gemara TbMeg. 27a, which contains a related statement ascribed to Rabbi Shim'on ben Gamli'el: "Come and hear: A man should not sell a Sepher Torah even though he does not need it (i. e.: even though he has another Sepher Torah)." Rabban Shim'on ben Gamli'el went further and said: "Even if a man has no food and he sells a Sepher Torah or his daughter, he will never see a blessing."' See also M. Higger, *Massekhtot Ze'irot*, p. 27.

The manuscripts of D. E. R. read: "aphilu she-'ein tzarikh lo' (although he does not need it; i.e. that Sepher Torah). The same reading also appears in TbMeg. 27a and in the commentary of *Rabbenu Hanan'el, Rabbenu Nissim, Riph* and *Rashi*. In the basis manuscript of D. E. R., however, we find the reading "aphilu she-tzarikh lo' (even though he does need it; i.e., the money of the sale). This reading also appears in another version of the baraita in TbMeg. 27a in the *She'iltot*, Noah, sim.5. (Cf. the remarks of S. Lieberman, *Tosephta Ki-Pheshutah*, II, pp. 853–854, in reference to TosBik. II,15.

In the same context of TbMeg. 27a there appears Rabban Shim'on ben Gamli'el's statement that a Torah scroll may not even be sold in order to acquire a newer one. According to Rabbi Me'ir, it is permitted to sell the Torah scroll only if the money from the sale is to be used to finance the study of the Torah or to help marry off a daughter, provided that there is no other way of obtaining money. Cf. TbB. B. 151a and *Tosaphists* on TbB. B. 8b.

*Anyone who sells his daughter*. On the basis of Ex.21:7 it was in principle permitted for a Hebrew man to sell his daughter under the age of twelve into bondage to another Hebrew. See, e.g., MKet. III,8 and cf. TbKet. 40a-b. This was, however, permitted only in circumstances of great need. Cf. Tos'Ar. V,7 and cf. Rambam, *Jad*, Hil. 'Abadim, IV,1–2. From the text here in D. E., it appears that Rabbi Shim'on ben Gamli'el disapproves categorically the sale of Hebrew girls to other Hebrews to work as servants. In the post-Biblical period, the sale of Hebrew girls into slavery was probably only a theoretical possibility, the sale of Hebrew slaves was probably rarely realized. In that connection, cf. M. Stern in *The Jewish People in the first Century*, ed. S. Safrai a.o., II, p. 629: 'In principle the institution of Jewish slavery was never abolished... On the other hand, it is quite evident that Jewish slaves were not common. Actually in the last century of the Second Temple Period, we have no concrete example of a Jewish slave. One can possibly speak of a gradual withering away of the institution of Jewish slavery and its almost-disappearance.' Note further the literature mentioned by M. Stern and cf. especially G. Allon, *History of the Jews in Palestine in the Period of the Mishna and the Talmud*, II, pp. 228–229. In reference to the aversion to selling Hebrews into slavery, cf. TbGit. 65a; TbQid. 69a and Tb'Ar. 29a.

**14. Rabbi Jitzhaq says: 'Slanderers, such persons belong to the shedders of blood, because it is said: "You shall not go up and down as a talebearer among your people, neither shall you stand idle by the blood of your fellow" (Lev. 19:16).'**

There is no known parallel outside of D. E. to this statement. "Okhelei qurtzin' ('qartzin') is: slanderers informers. The current expression, however, is "okhelei qurtzin' (literally: 'eaters of pieces', i.e., those who eat flesh torn from someone's body), which refers to slanderers and informers. Cf. L. Köhler/

W. Baumgartner, *Lexicon*, 1958, p. 1121. M. Higger (*Massekhtot Derekh 'Eretz,* p. 312 also reads "okelei qurtzin', although the expression does not appear in the manuscripts of D.E. The term "'okhelei qurtzin' ('qartzin') appears in Dan. 3:8 and Dan. 6:25. Cf. Targ .Onkelos on Lev. 19:16, where 'lo telekh rakhil' is translated as 'lo teikhol qurtzin'. Cf. also Targ. Pseudo Jon. on Lev. 19:16: 'lo meikhol qurtzin...'. Cf. the use of the term in TbBer. 58a "akhal beh qurtzin bi-malka' and A.R.N. [a] XVI: "okhilo qurtza 'etzel shilton'; cf. also TbGit. 56a. The term actually means to speak slanderously of someone before the authorities (the Romans). See further Targ. Prov. 11:13; Targ. Prov.20:19 and other sources. See M. Jastrow, *Dictionary*, II, pp. 1343, 1344, 1425.

In the statement of Rabbi Jitzhaq, a slanderer and informer is equated to someone who spills blood. The background of this statement is the text coherence in Lev.19:16ff.: 'You will not go around among your people as a slanderer, and you shall not stand forth against the life (lit. stand near the blood) of your neighbour, I am the Lord.' Rabbi Jitzhaq explains the connection of his statement with Lev. 19:16 as follows: Someone who is responsible for the conviction and execution (carried out by a third party) because he informed on and slandered that person is regarded as if he killed that person himself. It is also stated elsewhere in the Tenakh that one should not kill. The words 'you shall not stand forth against the life of your neighbour' imply then that it is also considered murder when one intentionally passes on information on someone which leads to his death at the hands of a third party (the Roman authorities). Cf. Rambam, *Jad*, Hil. De'ot, VII,1 and see *Keseph Mishneh* on that passage. See *Alsheikh* in reference to Lev. l.c. and *Qitzur Shul. Ar.,* 'Issur Rekhilut, § 30!; and other sources.

This statement probably must be interpreted in light of the appearance of informers and traitors who informed the Roman authorities.

### 15. Rabbi 'Eli'ezer says: 'One who hates his fellow, such a person belongs to the shedders of blood, for it is said: "And if a man should hate his fellow and lie in wait for him, and smite him mortally that he die" (Dt. 19:11).'

An anonymous more extensive parallel to this explanation (ascribed to Rabbi 'Eli'ezer) on Dt.19:11 is found in Siphrei. Dt., pisqa 168 (cf. Pes. Zut. on Dt. 19:11 [ed. S. Buber, 32a]). It was characteristic of the circles of the D.E. traditions that the very consideration and intention of harmful deeds were judged in terms of the most extreme consequences possible. Cf. also the atmosphere in Mat. 5:22 and Did.3:1ff., in which anger and murder are directly linked with each other.

**16.  Ben 'Azzai says: 'One who hates his wife is a shedder of blood, for it is said: "And lay wanton charges against her" (Dt. 22:14). In the end he hires [(false) witnesses] and hastily has her brought to the place of stoning.'**

Ben 'Azzai judges hating one's wife in terms of the worst consequences. Hating one's wife can lead to one's falsely accusing his wife, by hiring false witnesses if need be. With reference to Dt.22:14 ff., under discussion here is the situation in which a man who does not love his wife (see Dt. 22:13) falsely accuses her of having had sexual relations with another man during her engagement (when she was still under the authority of her father) and accuses her of not being a virgin at the time of marriage. A woman was executed by stoning for such behaviour (see Dt. 22:21).

*In the end he hires witnesses* (see the addition in the manuscripts) *and hastily has her brought to the place of stoning.* See the explanation of Rashi on the nearly identical wording in TbKet. 45a 'They bring them (the false witnesses against the woman) early to the place of execution, so that they cannot escape their doom and that they get it over as soon as possible.'

There is no directly related variant to this statement outside of D. E. Cf. the related anonymous tradition in Siphrei Dt., pisqa 235 (ed. L. Finkelstein , p. 267) in reference to Dt.22:13: 'If a man marries a woman and develops an aversion against her (lit. hates her)...' With reference to this verse and its further context (the same as here in the statement of Rabbi Jitzhaq), it is implied in a listing of transgressions that minor transgressions lead to increasingly serious ones. The man's aversion to his wife eventually leads to the shedding of blood. Given the context of the passage quoted from Scripture 'the shedding of blood' also refers to falsely accusing one's wife of not being a virgin at the time of marriage. Cf. also the statement of Rabbi Me'ir in TosSot. V,11, ascribed to Rabbi 'Aqiba in A. R. N. [a], XXVI (42a), that someone who takes an incompatible woman as his wife (not for the sake of heaven and not out of affection) will develop an aversion to her and ultimately wish for her death. Cf. S. Lieberman, *Tosephta Ki-Pheshutah*, VIII, p. 6662; cf. also the commentary to D. E. R. I, 29.

**17.  Rabbi José says: 'One who fixes (calculates) the end (i. e. the time of redemption and the coming of the messiah) and who hates scholars and their students [and a false prophet] and similarly one who speaks slander, has no share in the World to Come.'**

Like the preceding statement by Rabbi Jitzhaq, this statement, ascribed to Rabbi José, does not appear as such in the sources. According to S. Krauss, in *R. E. J.*, XXXVI (1898), p. 218, Rabbi José is Rabbi José ha-Gelili. Given the context of the statement, however, it is more likely that W. Bacher (in *M. G. W. J.*, XLII (1898), p. 505 ff. is correct in suggesting that 'Rabbi José' refers to Rabbi José ben Halaphta (of the generation after the Bar Kochba period). Cf. also W. Bacher, *Die Agada der Tannaiten*, II, p. 159, note 7. According to W. Bacher, the statement here in D. E. involves a specific group of people who tried to predict the moment that the messiah would come, hated scholars and engaged in slanderous behaviour, probably to the extent of acting as traitors and informers. These groups are supposed to have been Jewish-Christian sects. The addition in some manuscripts of the words 'and a false prophet' may well confirm that assumption. The statement is directed at a group of heretics who had strong eschatological expectations, appealed to prophecy and who were hostile to scholars. The words 'he will have no part in the World to Come' were a set expression used to resist sectarian tendencies in Judaism, especially in the second century of the common Era. Cf. J. Guttmann in: *M. G. W. J.*, XLII (1898), p. 289 ff. in connection with MSanh. X,1. See also I. H. Schiffman in: *Christian and Jewish Self-Definition*, ed. E. P. Sanders, II, p. 139 ff.

Statements directed against concrete expectations for the future are especially understandable as a reaction to the Bar Kochba uprising and its consequences. See S. Klausner, *Die Messianischen Vorstellungen des Jüdischen Volkes im Zeitalter der Tannaiten,* Krakau 1903, p. 27 ff. and see A. Silver in: *Messianism in the Talmud Era*, ed. L. Landman, New York 1979, p. 425 ff. See also "Vorzeiten und Berechnung der Tag des Messias" in Commentary on Mat., ed. H. L. Strack / P. Billerbeck, IV, 1928 , p. 977 ff.

*Those who hate the sages and their disciples*. According to the tradition, these people do study the Torah, but not in houses of study and together with other people. They avoid coming together with the sages and thus miss the practical and instructive daily contact with them. They do not study to put their knowledge to practical use or to adapt it to the norms of the community. See the use of the expression 'haters of the sages' in TbBer. 63b, TbTa'an. 7a, TbMak. 10a and TbJoma 72b.

The term 'lashon ha-ra'' is also used to refer to the deeds of informers who represent someone in a bad light before the authorities. This interpretation especially clarifies the strong reaction against such people in which it is stated that they will be denied a share in the World to Come. In connection with 'lashon ha-ra'', cf. Ber. Rab. XCVIII,19 (Tb'Ar. 15b) and Deb. Rab. V,7, and other sources.

**18. Rabbi Me'ir says: 'Whoever has a synagogue in his town and does not visit it, deserves death. How much more then (when one does not visit) a house of study in which are (learned) many thousands and myriads of precepts of which is spoken in the Torah!'**

**[Rabbi Me'ir says: 'Whoever has a scholar in his neighbourhood and does not serve him deserves death, for it is said: "Because he has despised the**

**Word of the Lord" (Num. 15:31) and it is said: "So says the Lord: What unrighteousness have your fathers found in Me, that they are gone far from Me" (Jer. 2:5).']**

According to Rabbi Me'ir, anyone who has a synagogue in his city and does not visit it deserves to die. Resh Laqish claims that a person who does not visit the synagogue must be called 'shaken ha-ra'' (a godless resident). According to a statement by Rab Huna in TjBer. V [8d] (and parallels) one who does not go to the synagogue is even denied a part in the World to Come. Most of the manuscripts of D. E. R., however, read *house of study* instead of *synagogue*". Considering that the tradition goes back to Rabbi Me'ir, the alternative reading 'house of study' would not be inappropriate. See, however, the text following the statement: 'How much more so this is true for the house of study ..') From this text it appears that the reading 'synagogue' of the basis manuscript must be retained. A similar statement by Rabbi Me'ir is recorded in A.R.N. [a], XXXVI (55a): 'Anyone who lives in a city that has a house of study and does not go there will have no share in the World to Come.' In Siphrei Num., pisqa 112 (ed. H.S. Horovitz, p. 121), Rabbi Me'ir explains Num. 15:31 ('Because he has despised the word of the Lord, and has broken his commandment, that soul should be utterly cut off...') to mean that that soul will have no part in the World to Come. The tradition states: 'Rabbi Me'ir used to say: "He who studies the Torah but does not teach it is alluded to in ⟨He has despised the word of the Lord⟩."' A version that partially corresponds to that statement was added into some manuscripts of D. E. R.: 'Rabbi Me'ir said: "Anyone who has a sage at his side (in his vicinity) and does not serve him deserves to die, for it is said: ⟨Because he has despised the word of the Lord...⟩"' Cf. also, *Menorat ha-Ma'or*, of Al-Nakawa, ed. H.G. Enelow, p. 410 and *Reshit Hokhmah*, Per. Derekh 'Eretz, sha'ar I and cf. the extensive version in *Ma'alot ha-Middot*, ed. Eshkol, repr. Jerusalem 1978, p. 218, used by M.Higger in *Massekhet Derekh 'Eretz*, p. 314. Rabbi Me'ir is addressing here people who do not visit the house of study, who do not want to share their knowledge with others and who avoid the instructive daily contact with sages. Where that is concerned, the context of D. E. R., XI,18 bears directly upon that in the preceding text concerning those who despised scholars and their disciples. The addition in the manuscripts which mention Num.15:31 establish a connection between the context of TbSanh. 99a and Siphrei Num., pisqa 112 and the struggle against heretical groups. The positions on halakhah and the oral tradition as a whole are central to the context under discussion and are directed against groups that question the absolute authority of the oral tradition or against groups that teach halakhot that deviate from the generally accepted halakhah.

How much more so this is true for the house of study ... It is rather common in the tradition to value the house of study more highly than the synagogue. This has to do with the special emphasis placed on the importance of studying the

Torah as a guide for behaviour and on the importance of the oral tradition. Consider, for example, the fact that it was deemed especially commendable to go from the synagogue to the house of study (see TbBer. 64a and parallels), and the fact that it was permitted to convert a synagogue into a house of study (see TbMeg. 27a and other sources).

**19. Who makes his way in public with his shoes unlaced (to be conspicuous), such a person belongs to the haughty of spirit. And for what reason can it be said of haughtiness of spirit, that it is like worship of idols? For it is said: 'And you shall not bring an abomination in your house' (Dt. 7:26), and in another verse it is said: 'Everyone that is proud in heart is an abomination (to the Lord)' (Prov. 16:5). As (the word) 'abomination' (has to be explained) there (i.e. in Dt. 7:26), so (it must be explained as reference to worship of idols) here (i.e. in Prov. 16:5).**

*One who makes his way in public...* Anyone who unlaces his sandals and then goes to the market is considered haughty. Note the additions in the manuscripts: 'He who walks with his "santar" (a kind of cloak) hanging sideways (over his shoulder) and his cap turned backwards or has his legs crossed or holds the straps of his phylacteries in his hand and puts them back while walking on the market belongs to the haughty of spirit.' (This is missing in Mas. Kal. Rab., ed. Coronel, 9a.) In Mas. Kal. Rab. l.c. , there appears the explanation according to which the behaviour is described as an attempt to be eccentric. A parallel to the statement is not found outside of the D. E. tradition, with the exception of Mas. Kal. Rab. l.c.

*And for what reason it can be said of the haughty...*

Haughtiness of spirit is like worship of idols. This section must be distinguished from the one preceding it. It is based on a baraita ascribed to Rabbi Shim'on bar Johai. See TbSot 4b. The statement is based on a 'gezerah shawah' (analogous reasoning). The analogy rests on the fact that the same term 'to'ebah' is used in two different contexts. Considering that the term 'to'ebah' is associated in Dt. 7:24 with idols and the worship of idols, the same must be true of the use in Prov. 16:5, which also deals with pride. Thus, a relationship is established between pride and idolatry. The reading in TbSot. 4b is presumably older.

**20. He who is about to sleep on his bed should say: '(Blessed are You, O Lord our God, King of the World) Who causes the bands of sleep to fall on the eyes of man.'**

**And he who awakes from his sleep should say: 'My God, the soul which You have given me is pure.'**

**He who is turning on his side from his sleep should say: 'Blessed Who opens the eyes of the blind.'**

The source of these berakhot is to be found in TbBer. 60b. The tradition in TbBer. is more complete and contains deviant wording. The wording 'heblei sheinah 'al 'einei 'adam' (*bands of sleep on the eyes of man*) deviates from that in TbBer. 60b, which reads 'heblei sheinah 'al 'einaj' (bands of sleep on my eyes), but concurs with that in Ms. Munich on TbBer. l.c. See R. Rabbinovicz, *Seph. Diqduqei Sopherim*, I, p. 173 and cf. B.M. Lewin, *'Otzar ha-Ge'onim*, on TbBer. l.c.: *Perush Rabbenu Hanan'el*, p. 67. See also B.M. Lewin, *Ginzei Qedem*, I, pp. 35−36; cf. *Seph. ha-Roqeah*, sim. 345; and see other witnesses mentioned by B.M. Lewin. To the contrary, cf. *Seder Rab 'Amram Gaon*, ed. 1865 (repr.1965) pp. 1 and 19 and see id. ed. D. Goldschmidt, Jerusalem 1972, pp. 2 and 54; and see , *Siddur Rab Sa'adjah Gaon*, ed. I.Davidson / S. Assaf a.o., Jerusalem 1963. p. 87. See further differences in the wording between D.E. and TbBer. l.c.

*My God the soul that You gave me was pure* ... It is plausible that this blessing is a reaction to the sectarian concept of original sin. Cf. J.Scheftelowitz in *M.G.W.J.*, LXX, (1926), pp. 272−273 and see I. Jacobson, *Netib Binah*, I, 1978, pp. 162−163. In connection with the concept of the purity of the soul and the duty for man to keep the soul pure, cf. TbShab. 152b; TbB.M. 107a; TjBer. II,3 [4d]; and other sources. Cf, also Soph. Sal. 8:19−20 (cf. id. 4:15; Waj. Rab. XIV,2). See R.H. Charles, *The Apocrypha and Pseudepigrapha of the Old Testament*, II, 1913 (1976) in connection with II En. 30:16, p. 450, notes. The concept of the purity of the soul at birth has parallels in Platonic thinking. The concept of the body as a source of evil (which was bound to the notion of a pure soul and which was current in Greek thought) is not so found in either the rabbinic tradition or in Soph. Sal.

*He who is turning on his side from his sleep* in D.E. correspondents to TbBer. 60b 'He who opens his eyes'. See the version of the Gaon of Vilna of D.E.R. h.l., in which the reading 'blessed are You who looses them that are bound' is suggested in connection with 'He who is turning...' According to TbBer. l.c., this is to be said after he is stretching himself and sits up.

The wording from D.E.R. XI,20 onward should be regarded a secondary addition made to chap. XI intended as a good conclusion of a literary unit. Cf., e.g. Ms. Oxford Bodleian (cat. A.Neubauer, I, 306) no. 1100, which does not contain the text from D.E.R. XI,20 onward. In connection with these berakhot see also I. Elbogen, *Der jüdische Gottesdienst in seiner Geschichtlichen Entwicklung*, p. 89ff. Although these berakhot were incorporated in Siddurim, there was definitely no general obligation to say them. See also the commentary D.E.R. XI,21 Cf. also *Seder Rab 'Amram Gaon*, ed. D. Goldschmidt, p. 2.

**21.  He who enters a privy should say: 'Be honoured, you honoured ones, servants of Heaven, give honour to our God [remain standing on your places and be on your guard], help me [watch over me], wait for me until I enter and come out, for this is the way of men.' He who leaves a privy should say: 'Blessed is He Who formed man in wisdom.'**

One said a berakhah upon entering and leaving the 'beit ha-kisse' These berakhot were connected with the fear of demons. The 'beit ha-kisse' was obviously regarded as a place where one was especially vulnerable to attacks by demons. One often relieved oneself in an isolated place, and the danger of being attacked by demons was considered to be especially great at night, especially since one relieves himself not in company of others, but on one's own. Cf. the context of TbBer. 62b and see S. Krauss, *Taludische Archäologie*, I, p. 47ff. The blessing was uttered in request of the help and protection of benevolent forces (angels), and it was uttered to dispel one's fear. To utter such a berakhah was considered to be the practise of the pious and thus was not considered to be a common obligation. In this connection, cf. *Shul. Ar.*, Or. Haj. 33.1 and *Turei Zahab* and *Beit Joseph* in reference to *Abudarham* and *Hiddushei Ribash* and other sources. See also I. Elbogen, *Der Jüdische Gottesdienst in seiner Geschichtlichen Entwicklung*, p. 89ff. With reference to 'asher jatzar' (*Who formed man in wisdom*), cf. I. Jacobson, *Netib Binah*, I, p. 156 and cf. other sources.

The version of the berakhah spoken upon entering the 'beit ha-kisse' recorded in D.E.R. h.l., correspondents for the most part to the wording given in TbBer. l.c. as a correction of an earlier mentioned version passed by 'Abajje. See the further additions in the manuscripts of D.E. The version in D.E. is shorter than the version in TbBer. l.c. (see supplements in manuscripts of D.E. in line with the Babylonian Talmud). See TjBer. IX, h.4 (14a), from which it appears that there definitely was no fast wording for these berakhot in the Tannaitic period. From other parallels it is also evident that there were great differences in wording in much later traditions. Cf., e.g., *Siddur Rab Sa'adja Gaon*, ed. I. Davidson / S. Assaf a.o., p. 87; cf. the version in the commentary of *Rabbenu Hanan'el* in B.M. Lewin, *'Otzar ha-Geonim*, on TbBer. 60b, I, p. 67; cf. *Seph. ha-Roqeah*, Hil. Berakhot, sim. 344, ed. Jerusalem, 1967, p. 236. The wording here in D.E.R. is based on the above-mentioned wording of 'Abajje and thus must be considered to be an addition from no earlier than the end of the fourth century C.E. See M. Goldberg, *Derech Erez Rabba*, p. V.

**22.  When he washes his face he should say: 'Blessed is He Who removes the bands of sleep from my eyes and slumber from my eyelids.'**

**23.  When one has put on his clothes and goes out into the street, one should say: "May it be Your will. O Lord, My God, that you make me enter [better**

reading: that You support me] and lead me in peace and uphold me in peace and let me obtain grace, favour and mercy in Your eyes and in the eyes of all who behold me and cause me to return to my house in peace [and deliver me from the hand of the enemy and from everyone who lurks for me by the way] and deliver me from the influence of an evil tongue and let me not be accustomed to any transgression, iniquity or failure and let me not stumble in matters of halakhah [or in any matter whatsoever and deliver me from all kinds of things that cause damage and all kinds of affliction that break forth and come upon the world, that they do not injure me by day or by night, Amen]. May it be Your will [other reading: The will of the Holy One blessed be He] that He causes me [us] to behold the rejoicing of Israel in Jerusalem [other reading: Of Jerusalem and her comfort, Amen.]

[End of Massekhet Derekh 'Eretz, it contains nine chapters]

The wording of the berakhah in D. E. R. XI,23 deviates greatly from that in the traditions in TbBer. 60a-b. The wording of the blessing said upon washing one's face (D. E. R. XI,22) also appears in TbBer. 60b. and concurs more or less with the wording in D. E. R. The prayer spoken by one who has got dressed and is leaving the house recorded in D. E. is an amalgamation of two separate prayers in TbBer. 60a-b. The text in D. E. represents a selective combination of diverse elements made on the basis of the Talmud tradition. Cf. M. Higger, *Massekhtot Ze'irot*, p. 28. What is recorded here as a prayer spoken upon leaving the house is recorded in TbBer. 60a and other sources as an expression of thanks made upon leaving a village or city: 'When he is outside, he says: "I give thanks to You, O Lord, my God, that you have brought me out of this city in peace, so may You guide me in peace and support me in peace and make me proceed in peace and deliver me from the hands of all enemies and who lie in wait by the way."' It is notable that a related prayer, spoken upon leaving the house, as well as the village, appears in *Seder Rab 'Amram Gaon*.

The rest of the formulations in D. E. R. partially concur with the words uttered – according to TbBer. 60b – upon washing one's face (rather than with those spoken upon leaving the house, as here in D. E. R.). See also *Siddur Rab Sa'adja Gaon*. Cf. also in TbBer. 60b the words spoken before one goes to sleep.

# Jir'at Het

## *Derekh 'Eretz Zuta, chapter I*

**1. The ways of scholars (sages) are to be: meek, humble of spirit, diligent and filled (with knowledge), forbearing and beloved by all, humble to the members of his household, in fear of transgression and judging a man according to his deeds.**

A number of later sources (especially Mahzorim) begin this chapter with: 'Rabbi Me'ir said...' See especially Me'iri's introduction to M.'Abot, *Beit ha-Behirah*. See also Ha-Kohen in *Sinai*, Jub. Vol., ed. J. L. Maimon, Jerusalem 1985, p. 418 ff., which discusses the problem of different versions of M'Abot, especially in Yemenite manuscripts in which sections of the beginning of D. E. Z. are combined with *Pereq Qinjan Torah*, (i. e., the sixth chap. of M'Abot, also known as *Pereq Rabbi Me'ir* (cf. Mas. Kal. Rab. VIII and S. E. Z. XVII, which contain material of *Pereq Rabbi Me'ir*) on account of the opening words of the chapter) to form the seventh chap. of M'Abot. See also M. Higger in: *Horeb*, IV, (1937), p. 110 ff. Because of the close relationship between the beginning of D. E. Z. and the sixth chapter of M'Abot – *Pereq Qinjan Torah* –, Rabbi Me'ir is cited in a number of Mahzorim as the spokesman in the opening words of D. E. Z. In Mas. Kal. Rab. (ed. M. Higger, chap. III, p. 212), the opening of Derekh 'Eretz Zuta is ascribed to Rabbi Jehudah. It is possible that the reading in Mas. Kal. Rab. is the original reading and that the reading 'Rabbi Me'ir' came about because of the close relationship between the opening lines of D. E. Z. and *Pereq Qinjan Torah*. See S. Sharbit, in: *Bar Ilan*, XVII (1976), p. 184, mentioned by D. Sperber, *Massekhet Derekh 'Eretz Zuta*, p. 77, notes.

This statement lists qualities and behaviour among that were characteristic of scholars. It was assumed that one had to possess those qualities in order to study the Torah successfully.

Those qualities define more closely the ideals regarding study in the spiritual world of the rabbis.

*'Anawah (meekness)*. The rabbis especially considered it necessary for one to be meek in order to acquire insight into and knowledge of the Torah. Moses, the great teacher and the recipient of the revelation, was considered an especial example of meekness in some traditions that were based on Num. 12:3: 'Now the man Moses was very meek, more than all men that were on the face of the earth.' See Mekh. de-R. Jishm. (ed. J. Z. Lauterbach, pp. 273–274): '"But Moses drew near unto thick darkness" (Ex. 20:21). What brought him this

distinction? His meekness...' This old midrash is based on *Seph. Ben Sira* 45:4–5 (ed. R.H. Charles, *The Apocrypha and Pseudepigrapha*, I, p.458): 'For his faithfulness and meekness, He chose him out of all flesh...' Cf. ed. M.Z. Segal, p.307 and cf. also ed. M.Z. Segal, p.7.: 'For fear of the Lord is wisdom and instruction, and faith and meekness are well pleasing unto him.'

The tradition concerning the relationship between "anawah' and wisdom and between "anawah' and the privilege of acquiring wisdom and receiving revelations, is very old. See also the references in the above-mentioned Mekhilta text to Is. 57:15; Is. 61:1; and Ps. 51:9. In those references a connection is established between "anawah' and the presence of the Shekhinah. In connection with "anawah', see D. Flusser, in: *The Israel Exploration Journal*, X, no. I (1960), pp. 1–13. In further reference to Moses and "anawah', see, e.g., Siphrei Num., pisqa 110 (ed. H.S. Horovitz, p.99); A.R.N. [a], IX (21a) and A.R.N. [a], XXXIII (38a); Mas. Kal. Rab., ed. M. Higger., chap. III, p.215; and other sources. See also L. Ginzberg, *The Legends of the Jews*, repr. Philadelphia 1968, II: pp.305, 323 and 339; III: pp. 59, 118, 126, 141, 168, 209, 242, 256, 336 and 413; V: p. 416; VI: pp. 61, 91, 97, and 140.

The terms "anawah' and "anaw' were especially connected with 'hasidut'; in that connection meekness was mentioned as a prerequisite for receiving the 'Ruah Qadosh' (Holy Spirit). Cf. A. Büchler, *Types of Jewish Palestinian Piety*, p. 8; see TjSot. 24b; TossSot. XIII,3; TbSot. 48b; and cf. Shir ha-Shir. Rab. VIII,9.3; cf. also TbNed. 38a; TbShab. 30b, and other sources.

"Anawah' is listed as one of the 48 prerequisites for the study of Torah. Cf.M'Abot VI,5; S.E.Z., XVII (ed. M. Friedmann, p. 18); S.E.R., XIV (ed. M.Friedmann, p.63ff.); Mas. Kal. Rab. VIII (in Babylonian Talmud, ed. Vilna /Romm, p.45a). Cf., e.g. Siphrei, 'Eqeb, pisqa 45; TbTa'an. 7a; Tanh., Ki-Tabo, § 3; Shir ha-Shir. Rab. I,2. Cf. S.E.R. VI (ed. M. Friedmann, p. 31): 'A man shall keep himself close to the way of meekness and after that he shall ask insight from the Omnipresent.' Cf. S.E.Z. III (ed. M. Friedmann, p. 177), where it is stated that one must be meek in order to receive the Torah. Those traditions which state that only people who are modest and humble retain knowledge of the Torah also bear relation to the statement here in D.E.Z. Cf., e.g., D.E.Z. VIII, 1. and Tb'Er. 54a, Tb'Er. 55a, TbSot. 21b and other sources. Some of the characteristics listed here in D.E. as being necessary for sages were also considered necessary for individuals functioning as judges in the courts of justice ('beit din'). Cf. TossSanh. VII,1; TjSanh. I,4 [7c] and TbSanh. 88b and TosHag. II,9 and Deb. Rab. I,10 and Midr. ha-Gad. on Dt. 1:15 and Rambam, *Jad*, Hil. Sanhedrin, II,7.

*'Shephal ruah' humble of spirit).* See notes concerning meekness.

*Zerizut (diligence* [in learning and fulfilling his duty and in doing positive things]). The concept of 'zerizut' implies a positive attitude in the fulfilment of duties and the intention to do so as quickly and thoroughly as possible. Cf. the opposition of 'zariz' (industrious) to 'shaphal' (indolent) in TosJeb. IV,8.

'Zerizut' expresses the eagerness to do things as quickly as possible. Cf. Targ. Pseudo Jon. on Lev. 24:12: '...quick ("zariz") in making decisions in legal matters concerning finances and slow in concluding legal matters of life and death.' Cf. especially TbPes. 4a: 'The zealous ("zerizim") do their religious duty as quickly as possible.' Cf. TbPes. 89a; TbJoma 28b; TbNaz. 23b; TbHor. 11a; TbMen. 43b; Mas. Sopherim. XVIII,5. In Mas. Sopherim XVIII,5 (in Babylonian Talmud ed. Vilna /Romm, 42b): 'And they bring them (their children) to the houses of prayer in order *to make them active in fulfilling the mitzwot.*' In that connection, cf. especially TosBekh. VI,10: 'If his son is industrious (i. e., diligent and learns quickly ["zariz"]) and if he retains what he has learned...' (cf. TbQid. 29a). See alsoespecially the explanation in *Mesillat Jesharim* of M.Ch. Luzzato, chap. VI, that 'zerizut' particularly refers to attitudes toward positive duties and the eagerness and devotion in fulfilling such duties. In the framework of the statement of Pinhas ben Ja'ir upon which *Mesillat Jesharim* is based, one can also place the concept of 'zerizut' in the context of 'hasidut'.

*Memulla (filled* with knowledge and a desire to learn). One finds that the terms 'zariz' and 'memulla' appear together in TbQid. 29b. (In the parallel to this tradition in TosBekh. VI,10, the word 'memulla' does not appear. In the commentaries on TbQid. l.c., the reading 'memulla' is generally explained to mean 'filled with a desire to learn Torah.' In another reading of the tradition in TbQid. l.c., however, the word 'memulla*h*' (salted) appears. *Riph* however reads 'memulla'.

'Memulla' can also be explained to mean: filled with knowledge of the Torah and the precepts. Cf., e.g., M'Abot IV,20: 'Rabbi said: "Look not at the jar but on what is in it, there may be a new jar that is *full* of old wine ."'' Wine here is an allegory for knowledge of the Torah. Cf. also, *Seph. Ben Sira*, 2:16 (cf. ed. M. Z. Segal, p. 8): '... will be *full of* (knowledge) *of the Law.*' Cf. especially the expression in TbSanh. 70b: 'jehe li ben zariz u-memulla ba-Torah' (that I may have a son who is diligent and filled with [knowledge of] the Torah). See also H. J. D. Azulai in *Kikkar L 'Adon* on D. E. Z. h.l. with the reading 'zariz be-mitzwot u-memulla be-mizwot'.

'Memulla' is also explained to mean: full of good intentions and qualities. See the reading 'memulla kol tob' in *Menorat ha-Ma'or* of Al-Nakawa, ed. H. G. Enelow, IV, p. 400 and in *Reshit Hokhmah*, Sha'ar I (ed. Amsterdam, p. 306). Cf. also the explanation on D. E. Z. h.l., in *Nahalat Ja'aqob*; see also D. Sperber, *Massekhet Derekh 'Eretz Zuta*, p. 13: 'u-memulla middot tobot' (and full of good qualities).

An entirely different interpretation of 'memulla' appears in the gemara of this statement in Mas. Kal. Rab., ed. M. Higger, chap. III, p. 212. It is read in that source to mean 'taking the place of one's forefathers and continuing the tradition.' Cf. TbHor.11b: '... memalle maqom 'abotaw' (... filling the place of his fathers).

Along with the reading 'memulla' (filled), one also finds in the baraita quoted in TbQid. 29b the reading 'memulla*h*' (salted). Cf. also the reading 'zariz u-mutzlah' (industrious and successful [in the study of the Torah]) in *'Ein Ja'aqob* on TbQid. l.c. (113b). One also finds the reading 'zariz u-mutzlah' in a number of manuscripts of D. E. Z. h.l. See also the interpretation of 'memulla*h*' in Mas. Kal. Rab. l.c. as "arib" (spiced, well mixed, well seasoned) in the sense that one is pleasing to all people as opposed to unpleasing in the way of unsalted or unspiced food. Some manuscripts in D. E. Z. h.l. have the reading 'u-me'urab' (well mixed). Cf. also Targ. Onkelos on Ex. 30:35, where 'memulla*h*' is translated as 'me'urab'. In this connection, cf. also the statement in TbKet. 17a (and other sources): ' At all times man's disposition shout be sweet in associa-tion with other men : 'me-'urab 'im ha-beriot'). Cf. also D. E. R. VI, end.

In association with the concept 'zariz' and with TbQid. 29b, 'memulla*h*' could very well be interpreted as 'salted' in the sense of 'sharp-witted, pithy'. See also in A. J. Tawrogi, *Derech Erez Sutta*, Königsberg 1858, p. 5; in the explanation of A. J.Tawrogi 'memulla*h*' is compared with the Latin expression 'salem habere' (to be sharp-witted). Cf. also the opinion of S. Krauss, in: *R. E. J.*, XXXVII (1898), p. 51. See the explanation of *Nahalat Ja'aqob* on D. E. Z. h.l. of 'memulla*h*' as flavoured (mixed) with all *middot*, i. e. with pleasing qualities.

*'Alub (forbearing,* tolerant and forgiving). Moses was considered to be a model of someone who was "alub' as well as "anaw'. Cf. A. R. N. [a], XXXV (38a): 'Who is the most tolerant? He who is as tolerant ("'alub") as Moses, for it is said (Num 12:3): "Now the man Moses was very meek ('anaw)..."' It is evident from this example that the conceptual relationship between "alub' and "anaw' was strong. The concepts "alub' and "anaw' belong to the sphere of 'hasidut'. Cf. Büchler, *Types of Jewish Palestinian Piety*, p. 14ff.

The quality of "alub' also included patience and disregard of imputations and derision. See especially TbShab. 88b. Cf. in the parallels apparatus the parallel mentioned. Cf. also S. E. Z., IV in the commentary *Jeshu'ot Ja'aqob* (repr. Jerusalem 1978, p. 178): "Alub' refers to one who remains silent when someone puts him to shame or damages his honour. In a statement, ascribed to Rabbi Alexandari, an explicit connection is made between maintaining silence in face of denigration and derision, and 'hasidut'. See Midr. Teh. 86,1; 'He who hears himself cursed and keep silent though he has the means to stop it . . . So David heard himself cursed, and kept silent. Therefore he calls himself "hasid" as God is called "Hasid" . . . ' Cf. Midr. Teh. 16,11; Jalq. Ps., r. 834. See A. Büchler, o.c., p. 15.

*. . . beloved by all . . .* The high esteem of others, just like meekness, was one of the 48 characteristics one should have in order to study the Torah success-fully. Cf. M'Abot VI,5: "ahub', which is explained in most commentaries to mean: beloved among the people. Cf. S. E. Z., ed. M. Friedmann, XVII and XVIII and Mas. Kal. Rab. VIII (in Babylonian Talmud); cf. also S. E. R. XIV (ed. M. Friedmann, p. 63ff.) From S. E. R. l.c., it is clear that the concepts

mentioned were included in the guidelines established for correct behaviour in the house of study. In S.E.R. l.c., it is stated 'beloved Above and desired [among men] below'. According to one tradition in M'Abot VI,1 (cf. S.E.Z. XVII, ed. M. Friedmann, pp. 15−16 and Mas. Kal. Rab. VIII), someone who occupies himself with studying the Torah was considered a beloved friend of God ('rea 'ahub').

The omission of 'among everyone' after 'beloved' in some manuscripts of D.E.Z. makes possible the interpretation 'beloved by God'. Most manuscripts, however, support the reading 'beloved among (all) people'. In any case, there is no conceptual contradiction between the readings 'beloved by God' and 'beloved among people'. The duty to make oneself beloved among people is stressed even more strongly in A.R.N. [a], XXXIII (38a): 'Who is a hero? . . . And there are those who say: "He who wins the love of one who hates him (an enemy)."' With respect to the time of the pious sages, the words 'among everyone' from the basis manuscript must be interpreted broadly and include those who are not friends. Cf. also the concept "alub' (tolerant and forgiving) in the lines immediately preceding here in D.E.Z. See, however, the manuscripts with the reading "ahub le-kol jode'aw' (beloved by all who are acquainted with him) and cf. also D.E.Z., II,14:'Beloved among all and even more so among the members of his household.' It is also stated that a judge must be beloved among people. Cf. TosSanh. VII,1; TjSanh. I,4 [7c]; TbSanh. 88b; TosHag. II,9; TbTa'an. 16b and Midr. ha-Gad. on Dt. 1:15 and cf. Rambam, *Jad*, Hil. Sanhedrin., II,7.

*Humble in spirit to the members of his household.* To behave with a lack of modesty toward the people with whom one lives, creates an atmosphere which may lead one to commit serious transgressions in relationship with others. Avoidance of any situation which could lead to such transgression was an example of *'hasidut'* that was characteristic of the sages. Emphasis was placed on this 'middot' (qualities) because of the risk of committing transgressions.

*Jare het (fearing transgression).* To fear transgression was also one of the 48 qualities one had to possess before engaging in the study of the Torah, according to M'Abot VI,5 ('be-jir'ah'). Cf. S.E.Z., ed. M. Friedmann, XVII, p. 18 and Mas. Kal. Rab. VIII. Note especially the statement of Hillel in M'Abot II,5: 'An uncivilized person is one who does not fear God (i.e., does not fear committing transgressions), and an ignoramus is not a *hasid* . . .' See especially the commentary of Rashi and Rambam in reference to Hillel's statement in M'Abot. The listing in M'Abot V,6 (and parallels) of characteristics that a sage was required to possess is related to the listing of qualities here in D.E.Z.

'Jir'at het' (the fear of [committing] transgression) represents the motivation to avoid evil which is the first step in the development of the sage and his intuitive ability to avoid evil through exercising his knowledge and refinement. To attain the level of a 'hasid', it is additionally necessary to have thorough knowledge of the Torah. 'Jir'at het' is typical of the world of 'hasidut'. It does not represent a halakhic rule but is one of the characteristics among the others mentioned in the beginning of D. E. Z. that one is required to possess in order to gain knowledge of the Torah and to be able to live in accordance with the commandments. 'Jir'at het' is not only the first such quality mentioned as being necessary for gaining knowledge of the Torah, but is also a quality to be refined by the sage in order to sharpen continually his ability to define transgression. With reference to this aspect of 'jir'at het', cf. A. Büchler, *Types of Jewish Palestinian Piety*, p. 29: 'The sin-fearing quality would then refer to the deliberate avoidance of an action that constituted an offence only for the very sensitive donor, but was for the average and observant Jew not approaching a sin.' The 'hasid' is not content with minimum standards of conduct but resolves to go far beyond the letter of the law. It is clear that the explanation in the broad sense of 'jir'at het', along with "alub', "ahub' etc., concurs with the definition of 'jir'at het' given above by A. Büchler.

*Judging a man according to their deeds.* With reference to the definition of 'doresh' (here translated as: judging), see among others A. J. Tawrogi, *Derech Erez Sutta*, p. 1, where 'doresh' is explained to mean: judging.

And similarly M. Ginsberg in *The Minor Tractates of the Talmud*, ed. A. Cohen, II, p. 567. See also other sources. Note, however, the interpretation of M. Higger, *Massekhtot Derekh 'Eretz*, p. 33: 'He inquires after everyone's welfare in terms of his vocation.'

## 2. And he says: 'Whatsoever exists in this world, I have no desire for it, because this world does not belong to me.' He sits, wrapping himself in his cloak at the feet of the sages and no man sees any evil in him.

*Whatever exists in this world...* The sages placed grate emphasis on the World to Come, and also stressed the importance of this world. But the world is according to them not an end in itself but rather place of preparation for the World to Come. Cf. especially M'Abot IV,16. In connection with M'Abot l.c., see E. E. Urbach in *Sepher Jobel le-Jitzhaq Baer*, ed. S. W. Baron a. o., Jerusalem 1961, p. 48 ff. One does not find in rabbinical sources the opposition between the material (body) and the spiritual, furnished as a reason for renouncing This World, as suggested by Philo and in I En. 48:6−7 and I En. 108:7−9. According to the rabbis, the value of This World rested in its connection with the World to Come. In connection with the problem of dualism, see D. Flusser in: *Tarbitz*, XXVIII (1958), p. 158 ff. It was not assumed that This World is to be only enjoyed and that this enjoyment is an end in itself. Cf. TjNed. I,1; TbNed. 9b; TosNaz. IV,7; Bam. Rab. X,7 and cf. Bam. Rab. XII,10. In the very early tradition (allegedly from the period of Shim'on the Just) mentioned in the sources previously cited, the desire to become a Nazirite was defended by the motivation to avoid committing sins through self-indulgence: 'Wretch! Why do you vaunt yourself in a world that is not yours, with one (i. e., yourself) who is destined to become worms and dust?' (TbNed. l.c.). Cf. the statement by Rabbi 'Aqiba in M'Abot III,13.

As a result of suffering and persecution, strong emphasis was placed on the value of *'jissurin'* (suffering) and on the importance of reward in the World to Come as compensation for the suffering endured in This World, especially as a result of situations after the fall of the Temple and in the Bar Kochba period. Because of the expectation of reward in the World to Come, it was feared that the enjoyment of This World will prevent one from being rewarded in the World to Come. Those who enjoy This World have actually already received their reward. In this connection, cf. TbSanh. 101a and TbQid. 40b. See especially Tb'Ar. 16b and E. E. Urbach in *Sepher Jobel le-Jitzhaq Baer*, p. 61. In this source of D. E., however, the reason for expecting one's reward in the World to Come is linked to the idealization of poverty and extreme austerity in certain circles. This reason appears in older traditions. Cf. the tradition in TbTa'an. 24b, concerning Rabbi Hanina ben Dosa, who chose to remain poor in order not to endanger his share in the World to Come by becoming wealthy in This World. Cf. also the tradition concerning Ben He He in TbHag. 9b (cf. S. E. Z., ed. M. Friedmann, pp. 176 and 181. See especially D. Flusser, in: *Israel Exploration Journal*, X (1960), pp. 1–13, concerning sources in Qumran and the New Testament.

The enjoyment of This World is subject to certain limitations and is not to be the primary goal underlying one's behaviour. The proprietary rights of This World rest with God, which has consequences for one's behaviour in This World. Cf. TosBer. IV,1 and parallels. One can not enjoy This World without first saying a 'berakhah' confirming God's deeds.

In further connection with asceticism in the Second Temple period, see J. A. Montgomery, in: *J. B. L.*, (1932), pp. 184–213; and Y. Baer, *Jisra'el ba-'Ammim*, Jerusalem 1955, p. 22ff. See also E. E. Urbach, o.c., p. 48ff. in reference to ways of fasting as a form of atonement after the omission of the sacrificial rites after the fall of the Temple, and in connection with the still common motive the fear of being forced by the 'jetzer ha-ra'' to commit sin, as a reason far fasting. See also P. Hacohen Peli in: *E. J.*, III, col. 678.

### 3a.  **He sits, wrapping himself in his cloak at the feet of the sages and no man sees any evil in him.**
### 3b.  **He questions according to the subject matter and answers according to the halakhah.**

3a. Compare the commentaries in M'Abot. I,4: 'José ben Jo'ezer said: "Let your house be a gathering place for the sages, cover yourself with the dust of their feet (i. e. sit amidst the dust of their feet)..."' Rashi explains sitting at the feet of the sages as a metaphor for serving the sages (cf. also Bertinoro). Sitting at the feet of the sages, however, must be interpreted not only as a call to modesty, it must also be interpreted literally. Compare the commentaries (of M'Abot) of *Rabbenu Jonah Gerondi* and *Rabbenu Jitzhaq of Toledo* and others. In this connection see M. Aberbach in: *HUCA*, XXXVII (1966), p. 111 ff. See also S. Safrai in: *The Jewish People in the First Century*, ed.S. Safrai a.o., II, p. 737. M. Aberbach, o.c., p. 112 explains: 'For junior pupils, as well as school children, seating on the bare dusty floor was generally the rule. There they would sit, probably in crosslegged position, holding their scrolls, when studying Bible, between their knees.' Cf. A.R.N. [a], VIII (19a). Cf. also, e.g., Act. 2,3; TbBer. 23b; TbShab. 30b; TbSanh. 6b; and TbHul. 6a; A.R.N. [a] VI; TbM. Q. 16b and TjM. Q., III [83a]. In the Tannaitic and Amoraic periods it was not unusual for sages themselves to sit on the floor (see all references mentioned in M. Aberbach, o.c., p. 114 ff.

The great majority of the manuscripts (including the Genizah-fragments) of D.E. read: 'He sits (and studies) soiling ('metanneph' in place of 'mit'atteph') his cloak at the feet of the sages. This reading bears a stronger connection to the tradition in M'Abot I,4. M. Aberbach, o.c. p. 118, explains the reading 'u-metanneph' (soiling his cloak) as a reference to the fact that the cloak became dirty because it was spread out on the dusty floor. It was especially important to spread the cloak out on the floor in the winter for protection against the cold, which rose up through the stone floor. Sitting on a cold stone floor could be harmful to one's health. Cf. TjBeitza I,6 [60c]. On the basis of the explanation advanced by M. Aberbach the term 'u-mit'atteph' (wrapped in his cloak) could also be explained to mean that the cloak was spread over the legs and knees for protection from the cold. We choose the reading 'u-me'atteph kassuto' from the basis manuscript of D.E.Z.

Among the sages, however, wrapping oneself up in one's cloak had another purpose. "Atiphah' (to wrap oneself up) was customary in various religious activities: The 'tallit' was spread around the entire body and especially over the head. Cf., e.g., TbM. Q. 24a: 'Wrapping not done in the manner of the Ishmaelites (=Arabs) is not proper wrapping.' See S. Krauss, in: *H.U.C.A.*, XIX (1945−46), p. 135 ff. Cf. I. Elbogen, *Der jüdische Gottesdienst in seiner geschichtlichen Entwicklung*, p. 500. Wrapping oneself was part of every significant act of sacredness and solemnity, but it was customary only among scrupulous and prominent scholars. They wrapped themselves, for example, for attending the administration of justice by judges (cf. TbShab. 10a) for attending the official dissolution of vows (cf. e.g. Tb'Er.64b; TbNed. 77b; TosPes. I,28 and Tj'Ab. Zar. I [40a]), for visiting the sick (cf. TbShab. 43b and TbNed. 40a), for praying (cf. TbShab. 10a), for welcoming the Sabbath (cf. TbShab. 119a, and for learning mystical traditions (cf. MHag. II,1; TosHag. II,1, ed. S. Lieberman, p. 3 and TjHag. II,4 and TbHag. 14b; see further TbR. ha-Sh. 17b, TbTa'an. 20a and other sources. The common feature of the activities mentioned here is that they are sanctified by the presence of the Shekhinah. See also S. Krauss, o.c., p. 147 and see M. Ydit in: *E.J.*, VIII, col. 2 ff. The Shekhinah was assumed to be present especially during prayer and study. (See the commentary to D. E. R. I, end.)

The given explanation of the basis manuscript in D. E. Z. applies here, because disciples revered rabbis and masters so much that they considered them to be a guarantee of the presence of the Shekhinah. See especially S. Krauss, o.c., pp. 146–147. Cf. Mekh. de-R. Jishm., Jitro Amaleq, par. 1 (ed. H. S. Horovitz p. 196; ed. M. Friedmann, 59a): 'Everyone who welcomes the face of the sages welcomes, as it were, the face of the Shekhinah.' Cf. also Tj'Er. V,1; TbBer. 64a; Shir ha-Shir. Rab. II,5; Midr. Teh. 25,6; Tanh. Ki-Tissa, ed. S. Buber § 15, 58a; Ber. Rab. LXIII, ed. J. Theodor / Ch. Albeck, p. 684; cf. also the forbiddance to walk past a scholar with one's head uncovered. See especially Mas. Kal. Rab. (in Babylonian Talmud ed. Vilna/Romm, 52a) and the commentary by S. Krauss, o.c., pp. 144–145. One sat at the feet of the sages because it was forbidden to raise oneself above the Shekhinah. In connection with the forbiddance to raise oneself above the Shekhinah, cf. Ber. Rab. XLVIII,7 (ed. J. Theodor / Ch. Albeck, p. 482); Midr. ha-Gad. on Gen. 18:1 (ed. M. Margulies, p. 290); Ag. Ber. XIX; Deb. Rab. XI,2; Tanh. Wa-Jera, § 2 (ed. S. Buber § 4); Midr. Teh. 18,29 and cf. Jalq, Ps., r. 831 and cf. TbBer. 6a.

It is striking that 'wrapping oneself' is mentioned in parallels in combination with sitting on the floor. Cf. on the basis of MHag. II,1 TosHag. l.c.; TjHag. l.c. and TbHag. l.c.; TbNed. 77b; TosPes. I,28 and other sources. Cf. especially the history of Hillel in TbShab. 31a, according to which he wrapped himself and sat down on the floor in order to answer questions. See A. Büchler, *Types of Jewish Palestinian Piety*, p. 11, where the author clearly states that Hillel's act of wrapping himself in his garment had a special religious significance. For another version of this example of Hillel see A. R. N. [b], XXIX (30b).

On the basis of the information given above, the act of wrapping oneself in one's cloak and of sitting on the floor at the feet of the sages can be attributed to a special sensitivity to the presence of the Shekhinah, of Whom the sage present was considered to be a representative. Such sensitivity was particularly strong among the 'hasidim' (cf., e.g., the practise among the 'hasidim' of keeping the head covered at all times and of not moving about with completely erect posture, out of reverence for the constant presence of the Shekhinah. Cf. the statement of Rabbi Jehoshua ben Levi in TbQid. 31a; cf. also the later tradition of Rab concerning the ten characteristics of 'hasidut'. (See *'Otzar ha-Ge'onim*, ed. B. M. Lewin, Shabbat, p. 110; cf. *Seph. Juhasin,* 200; see *Seph. ha-'Orah* of Rashi, ed. S. Buber, p. 1; see *Seph. ha-Pardes* of Rashi in: *M. G. W. J.*, LII (1908), p. 716; see also S. Krauss, o.c., p. 148.

*And no man sees any evil in him...* The sage must fear a bad reputation, for a bad reputation would mean desecration of God's name ('hillul ha-Shem'). The sage in particular must have an irreproachably reputation because he ultimately sets the standard by which people regard the Torah (cf., e.g. TbJoma 86b). He must avoid matters that may lead others to suspect him of committing a sin, even if such suspicion is unjustified. He must avoid all matters that include even the slightest chance of involving a sin. With this in mind, then, the reading of 'debar ki'ur' (an unbecoming thing) in some parallels of D. E. Z. is remarkable. The expression of 'ki'ur' refers even to things which in the strictest sense are not forbidden, but which may be perceived by a refined individual to lead possibly to sin. See also the commentary in D. E. Z. I,13!

See *Mahzor Vitry*, ed. J. Hurwitz, p. 721 and cf. *Menorat ha-Ma'or* of Al-Nakawa, ed. H. G. Enelow, IV, p. 400 and *Reshit Hokhmah*, D. E., sha'ar I. On the other hand the term 'ki'ur' may specifically refer to sexual transgression. Cf. J. Maier, *Jesus von Nazareth in der Talmudischen Uberlieferung*, Darmstadt 1978, p. 158. This would confirm the reading 'dabar "erwah' (a matter of forbidden sexual relations) in a number of manuscripts of D. E. Z. We prefer the interpretation from the basis manuscript of D. E. Z. given above for a sage had to refrain from becoming concerned in something that involved even the slightest hint of transgression.

3b. *He questions according to the subject matter . . .* In the learning process of the sage, the asking of questions and the giving of answers while studying with others was of greatest importance. During study, the student had to behave modestly and correctly, especially toward the teacher. Cf., e.g., TbShab. 3b: 'Said Rabbi Hijja to Rab: "Son of illustrious ancestors. Have I not told you that when Rabbi is engaged in one tractate, you must not question him about another, lest he not be conversant with it. For if Rabbi were not a great man, you would have put him to shame, for he might have answered you incorrectly . . ."' It was esteemed improper to ask questions about topics not under discussion, for one could publicly embarrass the teacher by doing so. A pupil had to show respect to the teacher in his manner of asking questions as well as his manner of giving answers. Cf. also Tossanh. VII,10 and Tanh., Ha'alotekha, § 11 (ed. S. Buber, § 20, 28a); cf. also TosMeg. IV,24 (ed. M. Lieberman, Mo'ed, p. 360); and see other sources. See the explanation in *Mahzor Vitry* on the basis of M'Abot. VI,6 (ed. S. Hurwitz, p. 542): 'He must ask questions dealing with the halakhah under discussion at that moment. And if he is asked a question he must respond with an adequate answer.' It is necessary to ask relevant questions and to give answers according to the current tradition in order to increase one's knowledge. Cf. especially M'Abot. VI,6, cf. S. E. Z., ed. M. Friedmann , XVII, p. 19 and Mas. Kal. Rab. VIII and cf. D. E. Z. III, 16; M'Abot II,5 and other sources.

Asking questions and giving answers in the house of study served not only to increase a pupil's knowledge but also to improve attention and concentration. It was esteemed an indispensable part of the learning process which helped the student to attain independence in understanding and applying the tradition. (See S. E. R. XIV, ed. M. Friedmann, p. 64). One was to ask questions only with the intention of contributing to the discussion or of increasing knowledge, not with the intention of displaying one's knowledge. This was also a reason why one was to concentrate only on matters under discussion. Cf. A. R. N. [a], XL (63b).

### 4. Be like a leather bottle [not ] split open, which is not opened to let in the wind; and like a deep (garden) bed which retains its water; and (be) like a coated vessel (which is coated with pitch), which preserves its wine and like a sponge which absorbs everything.

'Nud baqua' is a leather bottle which has burst or split open. Cf., e.g., TbHul. 14b in relation to the stem 'baqa' (to tear, to split), cf. TjQid. I,4 [60a] and Tj'Ab. Zar. V,10 [45a]. 'Nud' refers not only to a bottle filled with wine but also to one filled with air. Cf. the use of 'nud' in Mekh. de-R. Jishm., Be-Shallah, on Ex. 15:8 (ed. M. Friedmann, 40a), which mentions a hermetically sealed leather bottle which takes nothing in and lets nothing out. Cf. Jalq., Be-Shallah, r.248 and Jalq. Hiob, r.927. In the Targ. on Sam. 19:13 the term refers to a goatskin filled with air. The basis manuscript here in D. E. Z. reads: 'Be like a leather bottle split open ("baqua"), that is not open (i. e., that has no opening).' This reading is problematic because it contradicts itself. A bottle that has been torn or split open is by definition not hermetically sealed. On the basis of the manuscripts here in D. E., however, we can arrive at various possible solutions to this problem: 1) a reading without 'baqua': 'Be like a leather bottle that is not opened (i. e., that has no opening)...' The term 'baqua' also does not appear in A. R. N. [a], XLI (p. 67): 'Be like a leather bottle that has no opening.' This reading is also chosen by A. J. Tawrogi, *Derech Erez Sutta*, p. 2; in M. Higger, *Massekhtot Derekh 'Erez*, p. 35; in D. Sperber, *Massekhet Derekh 'Eretz Zuta*, p. 13, and in other editions. It also appears in D. E. Z. I, h.l. in some manuscripts. The word 'baqua' is not missing, however, in the same manuscripts in the context of D. E. Z.II,14! Remarkably 'baqua' appears in the Genizah fragments of D. E.. It is therefore plausible that the word 'baqua' did appear in the original version of D. E., but with a negation particle preceding it: 'Be like a leather bottle *not* split open, to let the wind in.' See D. E. Z. II,14. in Ms. Oxford Bodleian (cat. A. Neubauer) no. 1100. This reading was later combined with the explicative reading in A. R. N. l.c.: 'Be like a leather bottle that has no opening .' The combined version is thus: 'Be like a leather bottle *not* split open so that it has no opening to let the wind in.' As a result of a misreading , the negative element for 'baqua' fell away and 'a bottle split open' was read in place of 'a bottle *not* split open'. In accordance with this reconstruction we could accept the reading of Ms. Oxford Bodleian (cat. A. Neubauer) no. 1100 in D. E. Z. II,14: '... a leather bottle *not* split open...'

2) Some manuscripts in D. E. Z. (in chap. I, h.l., and in chap. II l.c.) read: 'Be like a leather bottle split open to let the wind in.' The parallel in A. R. N., however, does not confirm this reading. Moreover, the word 'baqua' probably

has a negative meaning in this context. The word 'ruah' certainly has a negative meaning in light of its immediate context: 'Be not like a wide opening letting the wind in.' It is improbable that 'ruah', here with the meaning of 'wind' refers to the knowledge of Torah that the student is supposed to acquire and retain.

In light of the words which immediately follow ('be like a deep bed at a low level...'), it is clear that the image of the leather bottle applies to one who does not lose any of the valuable knowledge he has gained of the Torah and acquire in its place useless knowledge (air). Cf. the reading that appears in some manuscripts here in D. E. Z.: 'Be not like a leather bottle... that is not swollen up (does not drip; she-'ein nitphah) to let the wind in.' It is remarkable that this corrupt reading appears in a few Genizah fragments.

See also especially S. E. R. XIV (ed. M. Friedmann, p. 62): 'What is he (man) like? He is like a leather bottle filled with water. The water is poured out and flows away. In a short while there is nothing left in the bottle. But he who occupies himself with the words of the Torah – what is he like? He is like the deepest bed...' Note the context of this reading, which is closely related to that in D. E. Z.!!

*...and like a deep bed (i. e. on a low level)* ... A sage must be like a deep flowerbed that not only does not let the water (the words of the Torah) escape, but also draws water to it. Cf. also the explanation of M. Ginsberg in his translation of D. E. Z. in *The Minor Tractates of the Talmud*, ed. A. Cohen, II, p. 65: 'Such a bed yields good produce, so must a scholar study continuously and raise good students.' Cf. also the closely related context in Tb'Er. 54a in a statement ascribed to Rabbi 'Eli'ezer: 'Why it is written "His cheeks are like balsam beds"? (Cant. 5:13). If one makes himself like a bed through which everyone walks and like balsam with which everyone perfumes himself his learning will be preserved.' Subservience and humility are necessary for acquiring and retaining knowledge of the Torah. Cf. the comparison in D. E. Z. VIII,1, where knowledge of the Torah is compared with water that flows only downward (i. e., to a humble person). See the parallels and commentary in that text.

*... like a vessel which is coated with pitch* ... In connection with the use of closed, pitch-coated bottles and jugs for keeping wine, see S. Krauss, *Talmudische Archäologie*, II, chap. IV., p. 236ff. The stopper of an earthenware jug containing wine was coated with pitch to prevent leaking or evaporating.

The expression 'qanqanah zephutah' was attributed to Rabban Johanan ben Zakkai as characterization of the astonishing memory of his pupil Rabbi 'Eli'ezer ben Hyrcanos, who forgot nothing. See M'Abot II,8; cf. A. R. N. [a], XIV (29b) and cf. A. R. N. [b], XXIX (29b). Cf. also the statement by Rabbi Jehudah ben Teima in A. R. N. [a], XLI (67a).

*... and like a sponge which absorbs everything* ... A student who is eager to absorb much knowledge is compared with a sponge because a sponge has a great absorption capacity. The image of a sponge is also used in Siphrei, 'Eqeb,

pisqa 48 in a positive way in a statement by Rabbi Jehudah to characterise a student who is eager to learn. He soaks up knowledge without discrimination and insatiably, like a sponge. A sponge is the opposite of 'mokh', an absorbent wool-like substance with much smaller absorption capacity than a sponge. Unlike the student compared to a 'mokh', the pupil who is like a sponge absorbs all information, not only that which he himself considers necessary. See also A. R. N. [a], XLI (67a), where sages and especially students in general are compared (in the framework of the statement attributed to Rabbi Jehudah ben Teima) with a sponge and a bottle of wine sealed and shut with pitch, as opposed to the godless, who are compared to a funnel and a tube. See the further context in A. R. N. l.c., which bears a strong connection to D. E. Z. h.l.

In other parallels, the image of a sponge is not used in a positive manner. See, e.g., M'Abot V,15. A sage who is compared with a sponge is someone who indiscriminately absorbs knowledge and who produces that knowledge in a undifferentiated manner, without distinguishing between primary and secondary matters, like a sponge wrung of liquid. See commentaries and see especially A. R. N. [b], XLV (64a, A. R. N. [a], XL (64a). According to the parallels mentioned here, the ideal image for a sage is a fan which can take up everything (rough kernels as well as finely ground meal) but retains only fine meal (the essence). A student who is like a fan hears everything but retains only what is essential, unlike students who are like a funnel, which lets everything flow through it and which retains nothing, or like a strainer, which lets the wine pass through and retains only the sediment from the wine. These more differentiated parallels associated with M'Abot V,15, in which the sponge has a negative meaning, are probably a later development. In any case, there is no need to adapt the text here in D. E. Z., as A. J. Tawrogi does, to the tradition in M'Abot V,15 by reading: '... and not like a sponge...' See A. J. Tawrogi, *Derech Erez Sutta*, p. 2. Despite the grammatical possibility of A. J. Tawrogi's suggestion, the manuscripts of D. E. do not justify it. Apart from that, the parallels also give a positive image of a sponge, as is evident from the statement of Rabbi Jehudah ben Teima. One also finds in Mas. Kal. Rab. (ed. M. Higger, p. 228) a version like that in D. E. Z. h.l.

### 5. **Be not like a large door which lets in the wind; and be not like a small door, which disgraces the worthy; but be like the lower threshold, on which everyone treats; and like a low peg, on which everyone hangs (his things).**

This statement is interpreted in the commentaries as a warning that one should be discriminating in making friends and tolerating people and that one should not associate carelessly with insignificant and shallow people. Cf. the interpretation of A. J. Tawrogi, *Derech Erez Sutta*, p. 2 notes and in M. Ginsberg in *The minor Tractates of the Talmud*, ed. A. Cohen, II, p. 567. This interpretation is secondary.

*A wide door* is better interpreted as an image of pride. A wide door lets in much undesired air. Cf. Prov. 17:19: '. . . he who makes his door high seeks destruction.' Note especially the reading of the tradition in A. R. N. [a], XXVI (42a), ascribed to Rabbi 'Eli'ezer ha-Kappar. In that version one finds mention of the supporting upper beam of a door that no one can reach with his hand. The image of this beam contrasts directly with that of the threshold, which lies very low and which remains intact even after the building has collapsed. Cf. the text in A. R. N. l.c. and cf. especially D. E. Z. III,17. A high entrance can collapse easily. Cf. prov. l.c.

. . . *and not like a small door (a low entrance) which disgraces the worthy* – this is explained in the commentaries as a warning not to make exceedingly humiliating demands of people in order to test them for the worthiness of one's friendship and tolerance. That is unnecessary. Cf., e.g., A. J. Tawrogi, l.c.; D. Sperber l.c.; J. Harburger, *Massekhet Derekh Erez Sutta*, Bayreuth 1839, p. 12 and cf. other commentaries. The given explanation, however, is secondary. The original meaning of the statement here must also be sought in connection with A. R. N. l.c., which contains a statement attributed to Rabbi 'Eli'ezer ha-Kappar that mentions a very high threshold instead of a narrow and small entrance. A high threshold has the same fault as a low gate or small entrance, i. e., 'it devours faces'. Another reading asserts that a high threshold 'disgraces the worthy'. See A. R. N. l.c. (42a, notes in ed. S. Schechter). In order to cross over a very high threshold, one is forced to move upward, and at the same time one is forced to bend over in order to avoid hitting his head on the upper beam of the door. The phrase 'which devours faces' has two meanings: It refers to the fact that the face of the person crossing over the threshold is temporarily hidden from the view of the host inside the house, and it refers literally to the possibility that the person entering the house can injure his head on the crossbeam of the door. See the explanation in D. Sperber, o.c., pp. 85—86; S. Krauss, *Talmudische Archäologie*, I, pp. 336—337 (notes) and G. Dalman, *Arbeit und Sitte in Palestina*, I, p. 67 ff. In connection with the literal interpretation of 'devours faces', see especially J. Goldin, *The fathers according to Rabbi Nathan*, p. 200, note 23: 'Perhaps we have here a reference to carved reliefs, as would seem to be suggested by . . .'

More preferable, however, is the explanation that 'devours faces' refers to the fact that the face of the person entering the house is hidden from the view of the host because he must bend over in order to enter. This is especially pertinent where 'jeqarim' (important and respectable guests) are concerned. See the version '. . . which disgraces the worthy . . .'.

In our opinion, it is unnecessary as well as incorrect to explain ''asqopah ha-'eljonah' (a high threshold) in the version in A. R. N. l.c. to mean 'crossbeam', despite the fact that ''asqopah' can sometimes mean 'crossbeam' like 'mash-qoph'. Cf. S. Krauss, o.c., pp. 37 and 330 (note 475). Cf. also, e.g., Targ. Pseud.Jon. on Ex. 12:7,22,23 and cf. D. Sperber o.c., p. 86.

In the version in A. R. N. l.c., the word 'mashkoph' refers to crossbeam (comparable to a large gate in the version in D. E. Z. h.l.), which means that ''asqopah ha-eljonah' in the same text must mean something else. Cf. also the version in D. E. Z. III l.c., where it is said that the high threshold (''asqopah ha-'eljonah') injures the feet. Such a statement can apply only to a high threshold. A low entrance must therefore be considered an image of pride like a high gate or a high threshold. The doors of houses were rather low in general. See, e.g., Siphrei, Balaq, pisqa 131, ed. H. S. Horovitz p. 172; Bam. Rab. XX,25 and Tanh., Balaq, § 21; cf. S. Krauss, *Talmudische archäologie*, I, pp. 36 ff., and 334 (notes). Thresholds, however, could be rather high. Cf., e.g. TosShab. I,6. Especially that part of the threshold that was under or outside the door, intended to keep dust and dampness outside. Sometimes there was yet another, smaller threshold in the form of a small step outside the door. Cf. D. Sperber o.c., p. 36; and S. Krauss, o.c., pp. 37—38 and 336 (notes), and especially note 484.

The connections between the above mentioned sources are as follows:1) A sage may not be proud in the ways represented by a high gate (see D. E. Z. I), by an unreachable high crossbeam (see A. R. N.), or by a very high threshold (see D. E. Z. III) that one can stumble over. 2) But it is also not sufficient for a sage just to display reasonable modesty, as represented by a small door of normal height (see D. E. Z., I), by a high threshold, which signifies disgrace of the worthy as they must bend over in order to cross over the threshold (another reading in A. R. N. mentions a small gate which devours faces), by a threshold of medium high (see D. E. Z., III; this probably refers to the part of the threshold outside the door that served as a step) upon which one would sit when one was having problems or by a threshold of medium high (as added in A. R. N.) against which one could collide his feet. 3) The greatest humility and servility imaginable are demanded of the sage. He has to be like the lowest threshold that people crossed upon entering a place. This part of the threshold lay inside the door beyond the higher parts of the threshold below or at the outside of the door. This lower part of the threshold was usually more or less level with the entrance level of the building. Anyone who crossed the outer threshold also had to step on the lower threshold. See S. Krauss, o.c., p. 38 and D.Sperber, o.c., p. 36. The low threshold was a symbol of a servile, humble attitude. Cf. especially S. E. R. XIV, ed. M. Friedmann, p. 63, where the image of the threshold tread upon by everyone is explained to mean the sage's readiness to be of service to others 'to be like a plank spanning a river across which everyone walks, and to be like a light for many people.' Cf. also the context in Tb'Er. 54a., only when one is like something upon which everyone treads will the learning process be effective and the knowledge gained in that process be lasting. Learning is valuable only when it leads to one's putting himself at the service of others. Note also the remark by Rab in Mas. Kal. Rab., ed. M. Higger, chap. III, p. 228, ed. N. N. Coronel. p. 76:'Raba said: "In the same way that the sill guides the door to close and open, so humility is a fence to wisdom.'"

Secondary explanations in the manuscripts and parallels of D. E. Z. h.l. include those in which the image of the gate is associated with quickness to anger or with openness to involvement in wickedness and idol talk. Cf. the gemara of the version in Mas. Kal. Rab. (ed. M. Higger, chap. III, p. 228; ed. N. N. Coronel, 7b: 'that he is not impatient'. See also S. Krauss, o.c., p. 336, note 484, where the wording in Mas. Kal. Rab. is interpreted as 'that he is not inhospitable.' The gemara in Mas. Kal. Rab. also explains that impatience leads to the alienation of others, and ultimately to isolation. Despite the different versions, the basic meaning is the same: A high gate serves no function, it only lets air in. A small gate is merely an obstruction. A high threshold and even a threshold of medium high do not withstand the ravages of time and are of little use. Only the lowest part of the threshold is preserved and is useful. Similarly, then, only the most humble attitude will result in lasting knowledge for the sage.

6. **When you have suffered a monetary loss, remember Job, who was smitten financially and physically. When you have been smitten physically, remember Datan and Abiram who descended alive into She'ol.**

See the commentary of J. Naumburg in *Nahalat Ja'aqob*. a.l. One must put financial loss and physical suffering in perspective. One should never concentrate only at his own fate. The statement refers not only to Hiob, who lost all of his wealth, but also to the grievous lot of Datan and Abiram who were buried alive (see Num. 16:32). According to the explanation in Mas. Kal. Rab. (ed. Higger, chap. III, p. 230) the example of Datan and Abiram was added for the following reason. Hiob had undergone financial loss and physical suffering, but Hiob was not a Jew, which meant that Jews might not fell that they had anything to learn from the example of Hiob. Datan and Abiram were Jews, however, and their example was added to that of Hiob's for the sake of relevancy.

7a. **Do not stumble because of your eyes, for only the eyes are a stumbling-block.**
7b. **Do not cause yourself to be ashamed by your teeth, lest you eat much more than is sufficient.**

7a. Sin begins with seeing. According to a remark (based on a statement in Num. 15:39) by Rabbi Levi, contained in TjBer. I,8 [3c], the eyes and the heart are the mediators of sin since they incite one to commit transgression. See also parallels in which Gen. 3:6 (among other passages) is mentioned: TbBer. 12b; Bam. Rab. X,2; Bam. Rab. XVII,6; Tanh., Shelah, § 15 (ed. S. Buber § 31); Jalq, Shelah, r.750; Rashi on Num. 15:39 and other parallels. This statement fits completely into the context of the literature of D.E., in which much stronger restrictions were placed (as a manifestation of 'hasidut') on what was permissible. The presence of wrong intentions is already the beginning of the commission of sin. Those who are pious have to remain within the bounds of righteousness. The ideas implied here fall under the concept of 'refraining from all that might lead to the commission of sin' ('le- harhiq me-ha-ki'ur') and the concept of 'an extra fence around the Torah' ('sejag la-Torah'). In the framework of the concept of 'sejag la-Torah') cf., e.g., A.R.N. [a], II (7a) and the example of Hiob, who made the halakhah for himself even more stringent and who did not even *look* at a virgin. Cf. the context in A.R.N. [a], II (7b) and in A.R.N. [b], II (4b) and idem (7b); cf. *Seph. Ben Sira* 9:5 and other parallels; cf. especially those parallels mentioned in connection with D.E.Z., III,12: 'Levity with women leads to lewdness.'

7b. *Do not cause yourself to be ashamed by your teeth...*

After the phrase 'by your teeth', a number of Manuscripts add in the explanatory phrase 'by your mouth'. This addition, however, was put in later. The translation given here, 'do not cause yourself to be ashamed...', is supposed by the reading in D.E.Z. II,22. See the explanation of D. Sperber, *Massekhet Derekh 'Eretz Zuta*, p. 15: 'Do not fear to tell your mouth that is is enough...'. See the parallels apparatus for deviating readings by Jacob Naumburg in *Nahalat Ja'aqob*, a.l. and by the Gaon of Vilna, neither of which is supported by the manuscripts of D.E.Z.

A sage is moderate, especially where eating and drinking are concerned. A figurative interpretation (among others) is offered in Mas. Kal. Rab., according to which the image of moderation in eating is used as a symbol for moderation of sexual desires. Reference is made in this interpretation to Prov. 30:20: 'She eats and wipes her mouth.' There is no reason, however, not to interpret the statement here in D.E.Z. as an admonition not to eat too much. The admonition to be moderate in the consumption of food and drink applied especially to the sages and their students, and appears in many forms in the literature of D.E. Cf., e.g., D.E.Z. VII,3; D.E.R. VI,6ff.; D.E.R. VIII,1; D.E.Z VI,5.

## 8. **Do not inquire with the heretics, lest you be drawn into Gehinnom.**

Do not ask for help or information from heretics. A number of manuscripts read: 'we-'al tidrosh le-minut [min ha-minut]' (do not apply to sectarism). Cf. the use of 'darash le-...' in Dt. 12:30; I Chron. 22:19; and Ezra 6:21. The basis manuscript here in D.E.Z. reads 'we-'al tidrosh 'im ha-minim' (do not study with heretics or do not enter in discussion with heretics). The nuances in the meaning given here are confirmed in the parallels. One was not allowed to enter in discussion with heretics, to accept help from them (even medical help), or to have any other direct contact with them. It is impossible to give a more precise definition of 'min' (heretic), given the many meanings of this term. See our commentary to D. E. R., chap. II,1! In any case, it is conceivable that the term pertains to Jews who adhered to Christian and/or Gnostic principles. One was not to seek out contact with these people, even if he needed their help. Cf., e.g., the story in which Rabbi Jishma'el preferred a relative to die rather than be saved by a heretic. See Tb'Ab.Zar. 17a; in connection with the assertion that the story concerned a disciple of Jesus and a Christian sectarian, see R. T. Herford, *Christianity in Talmud and Midrash*, p. 143; cf. J. Klausner, *Jesus of Nazareth*, (translated by H. Danby), repr. Jerusalem 1952, p. 37 ff.; and cf. J. Maier, *Jezus von Nazareth in der talmudischen Uberlieferung*, pp. 144–180. The verb 'mashakh' plays a role in the story about the relative of Rabbi Jishma'el, just as it does in the conclusion of the statement here in D. E. Z. Tb'Ab. Zar. l.c. reads: 'It is different with the teaching of heretics ('minim'), for it *draws*, and one may be *drawn after them*.' Inconnection with the verb 'mashakh', see *M. G. W. J.*, LXXVII (1933), pp. 401 ff. Cf. sources in TosHul. II,22; Tj'Ab. Zar. II,2 [40d-41a]; TjShab. XIV,4 [14d-15a]; Midr. Qoh. I,8 and idem VII,26; cf. also J. Guttmann, in: *M. G. W. J.*, XLII (1898), p. 301.

Discussions with heretics ('minim') are especially disadvised. The term 'minim' applies principally to those groups of heretics with Jewish roots who derived their arguments in an antagonistic manner from the rabbinic traditions and Scripture. Cf. the tradition of Rabbi Johanan in TbSanh. 38b (ascribed to Rabbi Simlai in TjBer. IX,1 and in Ber. Rab .VIII,9; cf. also Shem. Rab. XXIX,1 and Deb. Rab. II,13). In such discussions, one ran the risk of being overcome and of becoming convinced of wrong ideas.

From the parallels brought into context with the concept of 'a fence around the Torah', it is evident that the statement applies to a situation in which certain halakhic rules were made more stringent, with the intention of keeping one as far as possible away from transgression. The statement here in D.E. applies to radicalization distinctive of the *'hasidut'* which meant that one accepted further restrictions for himself in order to avoid transgression. A sage was required to avoid all contact with the world of 'minut', and certainly not to initiate such contact.

### 9. If others speak of you a great (serious) evil, let it be small in your eyes. And if you spoke a slight evil of others, let it be great in your eyes until you go and pacify him.

Higher demands are placed here on the sage and his students in comparison with other people. He must place the interests of others above his own interests, interpret things in favour of others to his own disadvantage, and he must judge his own mistakes more harshly than he judges those of others. The generosity toward others may also be considered characteristic of 'hasidut'. Cf., e.g., M'Abot V,10. The pious man always thinks to the advantage of others and to

the disadvantage of himself. In A. R. N. [a], XLI (67a), the statement here in
D. E. Z. is placed – in slightly different form – within the framework of statements made by Rabbi Jehudah ben Teima. These statements were made after
the year 70 C. E.; more precise dating is difficult; cf. M'Abot. V,20. The version
in A. R. N. l.c. is more extensive and contains the addition of a positively stated
idea: If one has done much good for someone else, he must not be impressed by
it. If someone has done him good on a small scale, he must be greatly impressed
by it. There are striking figurative as well as literal correspondences between a
number of statements (attributed to Rabbi Jehudah ben Teima) in A. R. N. l.c.,
and a number of statements here in D. E. Z. I. Compare with the context of
A. R. N. l.c.: D. E. Z. I,1 the notion of being "alub'; D. E. Z. I,4 (Be like a
leather bottle...); D. E. Z. I,4 (and like a vessel coated with pitch... and like a
sponge); D. E. Z. I,6 (the idea of being able to tolerate pain etc); D. E. Z. I,9
(the concept of being patient and forgiving); D. E. Z. I,10 (the concept of love
and respect for the Torah); cf. also D. E. Z.,II,1.

10a. **Let not your (behaviour during) adolescence be evil, for this is not
praise to the Torah; but let your (behaviour during your) adolescence be
seemly, for this this means praise to the sages.**
10b. **Love the Torah and honour the Torah [love your fellowmen and
respect them].**

10a. The term 'pereq tov' or 'pereq na'eh' (as opposed to 'pereq ra') is
mentioned in a number of parallels in connection with the conditions that
judges must fulfil. Judges must have a good reputation as adults and must have
had irreproachable reputations in their youth. Cf. TosHag. II,9 (ed. S. Lieberman, p. 384; TosSanh. VIII,1; TjSanh. I,4 [7c]; TbSanh. 88b; Deb. Rab. I,10;
Rambam, *Jad*, Hil. Sanhedrin, II,7; and Midr. ha-Gad. on Dt. 1:15. In the
parallels mentioned, the term 'pereq' refers to one's conduct in life. The term
can particularly refer to puberty and early adulthood. Cf. the usage of the term
'pereq' in TbPes. 43a; TbKet. 49b and other texts. In TbTa'an. 16a-16b, which
mentions conditions with which an intercessor and representative of the community must comply, the expression 'perek na'eh' is explained to refer to
unblemished conduct during youth. The explanation of the text here in D. E.
follows similar lines in Mas. Kal. Rab., ed. Higger, chap. III, p. 234; ed.
N. N. Coronel, 8a, as well in *Seph. Ma'alot ha-Middot*, D. E., ed. Eshkol,
p. 304. Both sources contain remarks about good reputation. In contradiction
to parallels of D. E. Z. and to the commentaries in general, S. Krauss (in
*R. E. J.*, XXXVII (1899), p. 52) interpreted 'pereq' as 'study' (in connection
with Just. Nov. 146,1). Cf. also the same explanation in E. Ben Jehudah, *Millon
ha-Lashon ha-'Ibrit*, X, p. 5238 and cf. S. Lieberman, *Tosephta Ki-Pheshutah*,
V, p. 129.

See also the explanation of S. Krauss l.c. in connection with D. E. Z. II,10. He reconstructs the text here in D. E. Z. I, as follows (see also manuscripts): 'Ne te contente pas d'avoir une belle conduite et un savoir mediocre, car se ne serait pas un honneur pot l'enseignement, mais excelle dans les deux car c'est là l'honneur de l'enseignement' (''al jehi piqqadonekha tob we-pirqekha ra', she-'ein shibhah shel Torah, 'ella jehi tob bi-shenajjim she-ken shibhah shel To-rah'). This reconstruction requires a number of changes in the text that are not supported in the manuscripts. See also the commentary to D. E. Z. II,10. The occurrence of the term 'piqqadon' in some manuscripts (in addition to the term 'pirqekha' or as a replacement of it) is explainable as follows: Do not let your credit (i. e. your good deeds and virtues) and your way of life ('pereq') be bad but good (pleasing), for only good conduct does justice to the Torah, the sages and the righteous.

10b. *Love the Torah...* In the explanation of this statement in Mas. Kal. Rab., the concept of love of the Torah is based on Dt. 6:5: '... and you shall love the Lord your God.' On the basis of a well known hermeneutic rule, the accusative particle in this quotation is interpreted as a reference to the idea that one should love the Torah as well as God. In the explanation the concept of love of the Torah is based on Prov. 3:9: 'Honour the Lord with your wealth.' The accusative particle is also interpreted as an indication that one should love the Torah as well as God. Note well the emphasis on 'love of the Torah', and see the additions in a number of manuscripts of D. E. Z. in which love for one's fellow man is given special mention: *Love the Torah and honour the Torah, love your fellowmen and respect them.* Such additions were characteristic of the setting in which the traditions of D. E. were transmitted.

**11a. Set aside your will in face of the will of your neighbour, for so did Rachel towards Lea and David towards Saul.**
**11b. Set aside your will and the will of your neighbour in face of the will of Heaven, for so we find in connection with Jacob, that he did not kiss Joseph.**

A sage has to set aside his own will for the sake of the will of his fellow man. This is again a statement urging one to put the interests of others before his own, a typical way of *'hasidut'*. Cf. especially the commentary to D. E. Z. I,9. The example of Rachel and Lea is based on the midrash on Gen. 29:25. Cf., e. g., the explanation of this verse in TbMeg. 13b: 'Rabbi 'El'azar said: 'What is the meaning of the verse "He withdraws not His eyes from the righteous" (Hiob 36:7)? In reward for the modesty displayed by Rachel... She replied (to Jacob): "I have a sister older than I am, and he (my father Laban) will not let me marry before her." So he (Jacob) gave her certain tokens (to identify Rachel). When night came, she (Rachel) said to herself: "Now my sister will be put to shame (i. e., she will be identified as Lea without the tokens)." So she (Rachel) handed her tokens over to her. So it is written: "And it came to pass in the morning, behold it was Lea" (Gen. 29:25). Are we to infer from this, that up to now she was not Lea? What it means is, that on account of the tokens which Rachel gave to Lea, he did not know it until then..."' Cf. also TbB. B. 123a; 'Eikh. Rab. Petiht. § 24; and cf. Midr. Ag. on Gen., ed. S. Buber, pp. 76–77; cf. also Ag. Esther II,20, ed. S. Buber, p. 24; Jalq. ha-Makh. Ps., on Ps. 18:27; Ber. Rab. LXX,19; and Tanh., Wa-Jetze § 11. See also further references in connection with Gen. 29:25 in M. Kasher, *Torah Shelemah*, on Gen. h.l., § 74 and pp. 1171–1172 (notes).

The example of David, who subordinates his wishes to those of Saul, is based on I Sam. 24:7: 'And he said unto his men: "The Lord forbid that I should do this thing unto my master, the Lord's anointed, to stretch forth mine hand against him..."' Cf. also I Sam 26:9: 'And David said to Abishai: "Destroy him not, for who can stretch forth his hand against the Lord's anointed and be guiltless?"' See the gemara of the version in Mas. Kal. Rab. III, (ed. M. Higger, p. 236).

11b. *Set aside your will and the will of your neighbour...*

The example given here of Jacob, who did not kiss his son, was derived from Gen. 46:29: 'And Joseph made ready his chariot and went up to meet Israel his father to Goshen; and he presented himself to him, and fell on his neck, and wept on his neck a good while.' It is remarkable that it is not stated in this verse that Jacob kissed his son after seeing him again for a long time. It is only said that Joseph embraced his father and wept. Why is the same not said of Jacob? Did he not embrace his son and weep? According to the gemara of this tradition in Mas. Kal. Rab. l.c., Jacob was afraid that Joseph's lips were 'unclean' after contact with foreign women in Egypt. See further the gemara in Mas. Kal.Rab. l.c., which partially incorporates the gemara from TbB. M. 83b and in which the imperishability of Jacob's body is discussed (cf. D. E. Z., I, end). The closing words '... and he wept on his neck a good while' in Gen. l.c., are explained to mean that Joseph begged his father to kiss him. Jacob, however, controlled himself and subordinated Joseph's plea and his own desire to kiss Joseph to God's will.

In Rashi's commentary, however, Gen. 46:29 is explained differently. According to this explanation,the earliest witness for which is from the Gaonitic period (see *She'iltot we-Teshubot ha-Ge'onim*, ed. J. Musafia, Lyck 1864, sim. 45 and Midr. Ag. on Gen. 46:29 [ed. S. Buber, p. 105]), Jacob did not kiss Joseph because he did not want to interrupt his recitation of the (morning) Shema. Cf. the tradition in TbJoma 19b: 'R. 'El'azar Hisma said: 'Concerning him who, reading the Shema, blinks with his eyes, gesticulates with his lips or points with his fingers, Scripture has said: "You have not called upon Me, O Jacob!" (Is. 43:22)', i.e. as it were you have not said Shema for Me. Cf. *Hiddushei Halakhot we-'Agadot* of Maharasha on TbJoma 19b, where a connection is established between the explanation of R. 'El'azar Hisma and the midrash (which is not explicitly mentioned) in which Jacob is presented as an example because he did not kiss or embrace Joseph, or even wink at him because he did not want to interrupt the recitation of the Shema. Cf. also 'Ijjunim on Tb Joma 19b, Talmud Babli, Massekhet Joma, ed. A. Steinsalz, p. 81, in reference to Rabbenu 'Eljaqim. See also Sepher Minhah Belulah, cited by M. Kasher in Torah Shelemah, on Gen. 46:29, p. 1869, § 177. Traces of older traditions are clearly preserved in the sources mentioned. The explanation that Jacob did not want to interrupt the Shema certainly fits in with the tradition here in D. E. Z., in which Jacob is held up as an example of someone who subordinated his own wishes (as well as those of his son) to the will of God.

## 12. Love the 'perhaps' and hate the 'so what'. Rabbi Hidqah said this in another way: 'Love the "perhaps" and hate the "what of it".'

The readings in the manuscripts reflect a number of corruptions. On basis of the reading 'ha-kamah' M. Ginsberg (in The Minor Tractates of the Talmud, ed. A. Cohen, II, p. 569) reads: 'hate the "how much"'. Cf. also J. Harburger, Massekhet Derekh Erez Sutta, p. 17. One explanation of this reading is: 'Be adverse to saying: 'So and so has too much (while I have far less)' , or 'So and so is respected (while I am not respected).' Cf. J. Harburger. l.c. and M. Ginsberg l.c. It is more accurate, however, to read 'hakhi mah' ('so what'), as in the basis manuscript, in accordance with 'mah be-kakh' ('what of it') in the alternative statement by Rabbi Hidqa. See also the remarkable but secondary explanation of A. J. Tawrogi, Derech Erez Sutta, p. 5: 'Stelle keine behauptungen über Grösse und Weise eines Gegenstandes auf, die du nicht erhärten vermagst.' This explanation is based on the commentary Midrash Shemu'el on Tb'Abot II,10. Cf. with the basis manuscript Seph. Hasidim, ed. R. Margaliot (Bologna version), § 98; cf. also Nahalat Ja'aqob on D. E. Z. h.l.: "Always say to yourself: "Perhaps I am committing a transgressionin speaking so or in doing so ...'", i. e. make it a cherished habit to consider all possible consequences of your deeds before hand so that you do not commit transgressions. But be adverse to saying: 'So what', i. e., what evil is involved in it? Be adverse minimalizing the possible negative consequences of a deed. When considering whether or not to do something, one should always take into account one's own weakness and vulnerability to sin.

In Mahzor Vitry (ed. S. Hurwitz, p. 500), the statement by Rabbi Hidka (love the 'perhaps' and hate the 'what of it') is mentioned in connection with M'Abot II,1: 'Be careful with a minor 'mitzwah' as with a major one ... Weigh the loss of a 'mitzwah' (i. e. the exertion or deprivation) against the reward (the positive result ), and weigh the advantage (the temporary pleasure) of a transgression against the loss (the ultimately negative result).' Thus do not say 'what of it' in the sense of 'what evil is involved in it', but consider the ultimate negative result (of committing a transgression).

In connection with Rabbi Hidqa (see the different reading of this name in the manuscripts: Hidqa, *H*idqa, Sidqa, *H*izqijah) see R. Halperin, *'Atlas 'Etz Hajjim*. He is supposed to have been a Tanna of the fourth generation and one of the students of Rabbi 'Aqiba. Cf. also A. B. Hyman, *Toledot Tanna'im we-'Amora'im*, I, p. 411. In connection with the expression 'mah be-kakh' see TbShab. 105b ('Amar Rabbi Jehudah...'); cf. TosShab. XVII,9 and S. Lieberman, *Tosephta Ki-Pheshutah*, III, p. 286; cf. TjQid. IV, 7 [66b]. Rashi, (Me'iri and others) explain on TbShab. l.c.: Accounts that do not concern you ('mah lekha') and accounts that were possible important in the past but are no, longer of practical use, for example, they have already been paid off ('mah be-kakh'). Cf. also *'Ijjunim* on TbShab. h.l., Talmud Babli, *Massekhet Shabbat*, ed. A. Steinsalz, a.l. In the context of D. E. Z. h.l. 'what of it' can be explained as: Hate saying 'of what importance is it', for the smallest transgression can lead to the most serious consequences. This fits completely into the context of the text following.

### 13. Keep aloof from everything hideous and from whatever seems hideous, lest others suspect you of transgression.

The statement applies to the world of the pious and the concept of 'hasidut', according to which one was supposed to impose extra restrictions on oneself not only to avoid an explicit transgression, but also to avoid that which could lead to sin.
'Ki'ur' (*hideous*) refers to something inappropriate, objectionable, perverse, or to something which involves unethical behaviour. 'Ki'ur' also frequently refers to sexual perversity. See references in commentary to D. E. Z. I,2.

In TosHul. II,24 the statement 'Keep aloof from everything hideous and from whatever seems hideous' is attributed to Rabbi 'Eli'ezer. In Midr. Tan., ed. D. Hoffmann, pp. 134 and 160, it is attributed to Rabbi Jishma'el. See related statements in I Thess. 5:22 and Did. 2:1 (ed. J. P. Audet, Paris 1958, p. 228). From the various parallels it is evident that the term 'ki'ur' (something hideous) has a wide range of meanings and can refer to anything that could lead to the commission of sin or that could even remotely involve the suspicion of transgression. The term applies to things that, strictly halakhically speaking involve no transgression, but that tend to sin or create the impression of being connected with sin. Things that could also just give others the impression that one is committing transgression were also considered hideous. Cf., e.g. Midr. Tan. on Dt. 24:17 (ed.D. Hoffmann, p. 160): One must not even accept a pledge as guarantee from a widow of comfortable means, in order to avoid all suspicion of transgression. Cf. also, e.g., Bam. Rab. X,8: Someone in the function of judge must refrain from drinking wine; such a person even refrains from drinking grape juice, which is not forbidden for him) in order to avoid the appearance that he is drinking wine. Cf. also e.g.,TbHul. 44b: One may not conclude an agreement of sale with someone for whom he acts as a witness, in order to avoid creating the false impression that there is a connection between the nature of his testimony and the conditions of sale, even if the agreement was worked out objectively or involves no conditions favourable to the witness. The concepts that incorporate the avoidance of creating false impressions are 'miphnei ha-hashad' and 'miphnei mar'it ha-'ajn'.

See especially G. Allon in *Tarbitz*, XI (1940), pp. 135−136, in reference to Did. 2:1: 'My child, flee from all that which is bad or which even appears bad ...' G. Allon makes clear that the original intention behind the Hebrew variant (D. E. Z. h.l.) was to warn people to refrain from becoming involved in things that could be suspected of involving sin, even if strictly speaking they involved no transgression at all. According to G. Allon, the original meaning was somewhat distorted further on in Did. and in the parallels A. R. N. [a], II (5a) by the addition of and connection with the idea that a minor transgression leads to a major one. Originally, the term 'ki'ur' referred not to a transgression, but only to something associated with sin. The original intention behind refraining from things that are not clearly transgression in themselves (and thus were not explicitly forbidden) but that are considered improper by those who are more sensitive to such things, is given in a statement by Rabbi 'Aqiba, found in A. R. N. [a],.XXVI (41b): : 'Do not involveyourself with heathens... do not involve yourself in something dubious (in something that you are not sure is good) so that you do not involve yourself (finally) in something that is clearly wrong.' Cf. also A. R. N. [b], XXXIII (36a) and note the context in the statement by Rabbi 'Aqiba that, like D. E., warns against association with the heathens and with a priest who is an ignoramus, and against frivolously making promises and oaths etc.

The rule of refraining from everything hideous is extremely typical of the setting of '*hasidut*', in which it was appropriate for one voluntarily to impose restrictions on oneself that were harsher than that imposed by halakhah. This fits within the framework of the concept 'sejag la-Torah' (an extra fence around the Torah). See the parallels quoted in A. R. N. in which this concept is of primary importance; cf. also the explanation to the version in Mas. Kal. Rab. III (ed. M. Higger, pp. 241−242).

Certain things that were not forbidden by law were nonetheless considered by the pious to be transgressions. The beginning of sin is signified by the loss of a positive motivation not to transgress against the essence of the Torah and halakhah. Such loss of motivation can result in interpreting a rule only literally, rather than in accordance with a strong inner drive to realize the true meaning behind a rule (which always goes beyond its literal meaning). See also D. Flusser, *Jahadut u-Meqorot ha-Notzrut*, Israel 1979, pp. 232−233. D. Flusser suggests that both traditions (the first being that a breach of a minor command leads to the breach of a major one, the second being that one must avoid all that which is hideous) developed in circles of the early *hasidim* to whose setting also belonged the Sermon on the Mount in the New Testament. Cf. the use of the concept of 'minor command' ('mitzwah qallah') in Mat. 5:19. According to D. Flusser, this concept refers to the extraordinary stringent halakhic restrictions mentioned by Jesus in his speech in the subsequent verses of Matthew. The connection between the statement that 'one should keep aloof from everything hideous' and the idea that a breach of a minor commandment leads to a breach of a major one is understood when one considers that the term 'mitzwah qallah [qetannah]',(a minor commandment), could also signify a special clarification and extra tightening of a current norm. In such circles of 'hasidim' the further restrictions based on the explanation of the essence of the 'mitzwot' were no longer clearly distinguished from the 'mitzwot' themselves; the further restrictions therefore comprise 'a minor command'. Whoever breaks through the fence surrounding a commandment irreversibly commits a break of that commandment according to this way of thinking. The fence is considered to be standard and binding. The 'hasidim' considered the restrictions, which were initially voluntary, accepted norms. The very entertaining of wrong ideas was considered to be a sin. To covet was according to them to steal and to hate was to commit murder. See the explanation of D. Flusser in this connection on Mat. 5:17: 'I have not come to abolish but to fulfil.' According to the opinion of Jesus the more severe and radical explanation in his speech did not contradict the accepted 'mitzwot', but it was the Torah itself, a legitimate explanation of the 'mitzwot'. It was not a supplement that went above the 'mitzwot', but a clarification of the essence of the 'mitzwot'. According to this explanation, then, the discrepancy (suggested by G. Allon l.c). between the original version (keep aloof from everything hideous) and the addition in some parallels of the idea that the transgression of a *minor command* leads to that of a greater one does not exist; rather the addition of expression about a minor command is a logical supplement to the original version. Concern with the impression that one's actions make upon others and with making certain that others not suspect one of dubious behaviour figures not only the principle of keeping aloof from everything hideous, but also the admonition that one should be equally circumspect in observing a *minor command* as in observing a major one. From examples it is evident that D. Flusser's interpretation of the term 'minor command' is correct. Cf., e.g., the context in M'Abot II,1, in the famous statement by Rabbi; 'Which is the right course that a man should choose for himself? That which he feels to be honourable to the actor (himself) and which brings honour from mankind. Be as heedful of a light precept as of a grave precept...' Cf. also Siphrei Dt., pisqa 79 (ed. L. Finkelstein, p. 145) on Dt. 12:28; (cf. also pisqa 97 on Dt. 13:19, id. p. 157): '"All these words that I command you" – so that a *minor command* is as dear to you as a *major command*. "Whenever you do what is good and right" – that which is good in

the eyes of heaven and right in the eyes of man. Those are the words of Rabbi
'Aqiba ... And Rabbi Jishma'el said: "that which is right in the eyes Heaven."'
Cf. the reading in the TosSheq. II,1; cf. also the reading in Midr.Tan., ed.
D. Hoffmann, pp. 61 and 126. See L. Finkelstein l.c., where it is suggested that
concepts as 'miphnei hashad' and the idea that the possibility of suspicion by
others should influence behaviour are according to the ideas of the school of
'Aqiba, but not according to the school of Rabbi Jishma'el. See, however, a
remark by Rabbi Jishma'el in MSheq. III,2: 'For a man must satisfy mankind
like he must satisfy God, for it is said (Num. 32:22): "And be guiltless towards
the Lord and towards Israel." And it says (Prov. 3:4) : "You shall find favour
and good understanding in the sight of God and man."' Cf. also Midr. Tan., ed.
D. Hoffmann, p. 110 and the statement: 'Keep aloof from everything hideous',
ascribed to Rabbi *Jishma'el*. Cf. Midr. ha-Gad. ,Be-Huqqotai, ed. Ch. Rabin,
p. 659.

### 14. **Do not slander your neighbour, because there is no remedy for all who slander.**

There is no remedy for the slanderer. For the explanation of the words 'there is
no remedy for him', note the explanation in Mas. Kal. Rab. III, ed. M. Higger
p. 242, in which the snake is referred to as an image of a slanderer on the basis of
Is. 65:25. It was believed that in the messianic period the blind and the lame and
all animals except the snake will be cured of their ailments and tendencies. The
snake, however, is condemned to eat dust forever. Cf. *Ma'alot ha-Middot*,
sha'ar D.E., ed. Eshkol, p. 304 and Ber. Rab. XX,5; Siphra be-Huqqotai, ed.
I. H. Weiss, 111a; Midr. ha-Gad., Be-Huqqotai, ed. I. A. Rabin, p. 659; Waj.
Rab. XXVI,2; Ag. Ber. LXXVIII; and Ag. Sam., par. 28 (end); Tanh. Wa-
Jiggash, § 8.; Jalq., Is., r. 369: Jalq., Ez., r. 383 (end).

In this case, 'there is no remedy for him' means that 'he' will have no share in
the World to Come. Cf. especially, P.R.E. LIII (beginning), where, on the
basis of Num. 12:1ff. (the story of Aaron and Miriam, who spoke like slanderers against Moses), the following meaning is suggested: 'Anyone who speaks
against someone else in secret will have no share in the World to Come.' Cf. the
wording in *Battei Midreshot*, ed. S. A. Wertheimer, 'Pereq ha-'aharon me-
Pirqei de Rabbi 'Eli'ezer', p. 238: '...has no share in the World to Come.' Cf.
especially the wording in P. R. E. LIV and in *Menorat ha-Ma'or* of *Jitzhaq
'Aboab*, sim. 52, in the name of P. R. E.: 'There is no remedy for anyone who
speaks against his fellow in secret.' This suggestion is based on the interpretation of Ps. 101:5: 'I will destroy him who slanders in secret.' The snake, which
bears an eternal curse, is presented as an image of that notion. This is related to
Dt. 27:24: 'Cursed be he who slays his neighbour in secret.' (The word 'slays'
here is explained to mean 'slanders'. Cf. also the statement in TbSot. 42a
attributed to R. Jirmejahu b. 'Abba: 'Four classes of people will not receive the

face of the Shekhinah . . . the class of slanderers, for it is written: "A wicked man may not stay with you." (Ps.5:5)' Cf. TbSanh. 103a; Jalq., Hiob, r. 906; and Jalq. Hos., r. 524. The version of this same statement in Midr. Teh. 101, 3 reads: '. . . the class of slanderers, for it is written: "I will destroy him who slanders his neighbour in secret." (Ps. 101:5)' The expression 'not receive the face of the Shekhinah' means that the slanderer will have no part in the World to Come. Cf. also A. Goldberg, *Untersuchungen über die Vorstellung von der Shekhinah in der frühen rabbinischen Literatur, Talmud und Midrasch*, p. 309. The quotation from Ps. 101:5 is cited in a statement by Rabbi Joseph ben Zimra (see Tb'Ar. 15b) as proof that God punishes slanderers with an incurable form of leprosy (in which case ''atzmit' is interpreted as 'li-tzemitut' [forever]).

The expression "ein lo rephu'ah' (*there is no remedy for him*) can also be interpreted to mean that there will be no opportunity for repentance or atonement. Cf. the statement of Rabbi 'Aha bar Hanina in Tb'Ar.15b: 'If he has slandered already, there is no remedy for him.' Cf. also the context of this statement. In connection with the relation between 'rephu'ah' (remedy) and acts of repentance and reconciliation, cf., e.g., *Seph. ha-Roqeah*, § 28: 'For him there is no remedy and no possibility to repent.' Cf. H. M. Horovitz, *Kebod Huppah*, Frankfurt am Main 1888, p. 52, § 142 (also *'Otzar Midrashim*, ed. J. D. Eisenstein, p. 162 ff.): 'In four instances, remedy is not possible even after repentance.' Cf. also the statement of Rabbi Hama bar Hanina in TbJoma 86b: 'Repentance is great for it *heals* the world . . .' (cf. Jalq., Jer., r. 269.)

In short, several reasons are possible for the assertion that there is no remedy for those who slander ('lashon ha-ra''). Sins such as slandering, which are usually committed a number of times and thus become bad habits, are difficult to rectify because the victims are no longer known. Cf. also Rambam, *Jad*, Hil. Teshubah, IV,3. The immediate result and later consequences of slandering cannot be controlled. It is with good reason that slander is compared in a number of statements with the most serious sins, such as shedding blood.

## 15. **You shall not eat bread with a priest who is an ignoramus, lest you will desecrate what is hallowed to Heaven.**

It is forbidden for a sage to eat with a priest who is an ignoramus. It is not clear to whom this admonition is directed. There are two possibilities. 1) It may be directed at a 'zar', i. e., an Israelite not descended of priests, for he might give him to eat from the Terumah (which is forbidden for a non-priest). Cf. Lev. 22:10. It was no imaginary danger that a priest who was ''am ha-'aretz' (an ignoramus) could unwittingly give someone food from the Terumah. 2) The admonition may also be directed at a priest, for it was no imaginary danger that a fellow priest who was an ''am ha-'aretz' could unwittingly give him to eat a defiled Terumah (which was forbidden even to a priest). Cf. the explanation of Ran on TbNed. 20a and cf. the reading in *'Ein Ja'aqob* on TbNed.20a: 'Do not make a practise of visiting a priest who is an "am ha-'aretz', for it will result in him giving you unclean Terumah to eat.' Of the various kinds of Terumot the following should be mentioned here. 1) The *Terumah Gedolah* (see MTer. IV,3), which every Israelite who worked the earth had to give to the priest (at least 1/60 [usually 1/50] of the harvest), cf. Num 18:12ff. and Dt.18:4,5. 2). The *Terumah taken from the tithe* meant for the Levites, who set aside yet another tenth from their tithes for the priests. Cf. Num. 18:25,32. The Terumah was meant only for those who were priests or who were members of the household of a priest. Cf. Lev. 22:10; Num. 18:32; MJeb. VII,1; MTer. V and other sources.

The statement under discussion here, along with an admonition not to make promises frivolously (note D. E. Z. I and TbNed. 20a), is attributed in a reading and tradition in A. R. N.[a], XXVI (41b) and A. R. N. [b], XXXIII (36b) to Rabbi 'Aqiba. It seems therefore to be plausible that the admonition here is directed at the lay person, the non-priest, as he might eat from the Terumah, which is categorically forbidden for him, for the admonition is placed – as in the parallels – in the framework of the concept 'sejag la-Torah' and situations that can lead a man to sin. Cf. also D. E. R. I,32b. The reading in Mas. Kal. Rab. III (ed. M. Higger, p 242; ed. N. N. Coronel, 9a) and a single manuscript here in D. E. Z. and in D. E. R. I,32b read: 'You shall not eat bread with an ignoramus ("'am ha-'aretz").' With respect to that, there is a reference in Mas. Kal. Rab. to TosDem. II,3: 'He that undertakes to be an associate . . . and he may not be the guest of an ignoramus ("'am ha-'aretz).' An associate (someone who wished to belong to the circle of people who scrupulously put the rabbinical precepts into practise) was not permitted to eat with an illiterate and less scrupulous person because of the danger of eating food from which the Terumah, tithes etc, had not been derived. The wording here in D. E., however, is: ' . . . so that you not desecrate what has been sanctified for Heaven', whereas in the parallels we find: ' . . . so that he does not make him eat from the Terumah' and ' . . . that you do not make inappropriate use of sacred property.' These readings may indicate a warning not to eat from the Terumah, which means that it is most probable that also the reading here in D. E., warning a non priest not to eat with a priest who is an ignoramus, is correct. A change in the text of "'am ha-'aretz' to 'priest 'am ha-'aretz' is extremely unlikely considering that it became increasingly less important after the fall of the Temple to set aside the Terumah for the priest. It is therefore plausible to assert that the reading 'With *a priest who is* "'am ha-Aretz"' here in D. E. Z. (see the majority of manuscripts, and cf. A. R. N. l.c. and TbNed. l.c.) is the original reading!

### 16. **You shall not be unbridled in vowing, lest you will make inappropriate use of oaths.**

This statement is missing in most of the manuscripts. According to parallels in A. R. N. [a], XXVI (41b) and A. R. N. [b], XXXIII (36b) (ascribed to Rabbi 'Aqiba) and in TbNed. 20a, this statement belongs to the one preceding it ('you shall not eat bread with a priest . . .') in D. E. Z. I,15. In the basis manuscript, one Genizah fragment and a few other manuscripts, however, the statement does appear. Through the influence of other parallels, this statement was probably added into the manuscripts very early on. The statement (see the parallels indicated) also fits within the concept of 'sejag la-Torah' (i. e., the imposition of further restrictions in order to avoid transgressions).

One should not make vows to liberally, for this can lead one to make an oath unintentional and thus break it. It is even considered a serious sin to break an oath inadvertently or to make a frivolous oath. In connection with vows, there is discussion here of a so-called 'shebu'at bittuj', which refers to the duty to carry out a deed or to refrain from it by an oath. In the Tenakh, a vow was acceptance of the duty to dedicate something to the Temple ('neder qodesh'), or of the duty to refrain from using a certain object or from doing something in connection with that object, or of carrying out a certain deed. It is evident from the Mishnah that in the rabbinical period a technical halakhic distinction was made between an oath and a vow. A vow means that one declares an object (or a person) forbidden for himself in connection with certain actions. One vowed sometimes not to make use of certain objects or good services offered to him as a punishment for not performing a certain action in the future. When one makes an oath, however, one commits himself to carrying out an action or to abstain from it by saying a formula typical for an oath (only when making an oath before a judge it was necessary to allude explicitly to one of the names of God.) An oath can also contain an assertion about the specific state of things. In common speech a difference is not always made between a vow and an oath; the transition from the one to the other is unclear. Cf., e.g., MNed. I,1 (TbNed. 22a); cf. also an explanation based on those sources in TbNed.80b: '. . . oaths too are included in vows . . .' Cf. also TosNed. V,3−5 ('we-nadar bi-shebu'ah'); and cf., e.g., MNed. I,4 and MB. Q. IX,10 which contains formulations in the form of both a promise and an oath.

Because of the fact that the difference between a (vow) promise and an oath is not always clear, the statement here in D. E. that one is not to deal with vows lightly, so that one does not violate an oath, is understandable. In this connection, see Mabo to Mishnah, *Nedarim*, ed. Ch. Albeck ( *Mo'ed*,), pp. 138−139. While the unintentional breaking of a vow is judged relatively mildly, the violation of an oath remains a serious matter. The prohibition against making an unnecessary oath ('shebu'at shaw'), for example, is part of the Ten Words. Cf. MSheb. III,9 and TbSheb. 29a. This explains in itself the general tendency

not to make an oath if there is no juridical necessity to do so. The reading in
A. R. N. [b], l.c., indicates likewise: '. . . so that you do not make an oath.' Cf.
also Mas. Kal. Rab. III, ed. M. Higger, p. 242: '. . . for promises lead to the
making of oaths.'

In a discussion in TbB.Q. 103b, it is said that it is impossible that Rabbi
Jehudah ben 'Ilai as well as Rabbi Jehudah ben Baba could have made a false
oath because both are known as 'pious men'! Cf. in Waj. Rab. XXXVII,1 (cf.
TbHul. 2a) Rabbi Jehudah's remark that it is better not to make a vow at all
than to fulfil a vow. According to a statement by Rabbi Jehudah in MDem. II,3
an associate may not carelessly make vows. In that statement Rabbi Jehudah
also warns that one should not associate with persons who are ignorami (who
belong to the "am ha-'aretz'). From this, then, it would seem that the warnings
here in D.E. (and in the mentioned parallels in A.R.N. ascribed to Rabbi
'Aqiba, and in TbNed. 20a) stem from norms particular to the 'Haberim', the
pious and law-abiding associates.

There is no question here of a categorical rejection of making vows and
certainly not of making oaths. The oath, which is made out of juridical necessity, is accepted and remains so. One is required by the Torah to take an oath
when serving as a witness in legal matters. Cf., e.g., Ex. 22:11; Num. 5:19,21;
Dt. 6:13; Dt. 10:20; cf. also Mekh. de-R. Jishm. on Ex. 22:10. See also TbSheb.
38b and other sources. One finds traces of an opinion, that one should avoid
involvement in situations that could lead to one's making a juridical oath (even
when acceptable in circumstances of necessity). Cf. Mekh. de-R. Jishm. on Ex.
22:10 (ed. M. Friedmann, 98b); TbSheb. 47b and TjSheb. VI,3 [37a]; TbGit.
35a; Waj. Rab. VI, ;Pes. Rab. XXII and other sources. The refusal to make
oaths, not necessitated by juridical circumstances, is also found in texts such as
Mat. 5:36ff. and Jac. 5:12. Cf., however, D. Flusser's opinion on the rejection
of oaths by the Essenes: D. Flusser, *Jahadut u-Meqorot ha-Notzrut*, p. 232, in
reference to Josephus *Bel.* II:135 and to the New Testament. Here he does not
distinguish between an oath made in court and one not made in court.

## 17. Keep aloof from grumbling, lest you grumble to others and lest you will add to transgression.

One should not carp and grumble, even if not directly to others, so that one
ultimately does not grumble to others and add to one's sins. Cf. also the
explanation in Mas. Kal. Rab. III, ed. M. Higger, p. 243. Through grumbling to
others and through the reaction of others, one will quickly commit worse sins,
such as hating, slandering, engaging in violence etc. This interpretation fits
within the context here in D.E.Z. in which the concept of 'sejag la-Torah' (the
imposition of further restrictions in order to avoid committing transgressions) is
of central importance. One should avoid situations tending toward sin that can
lead one to commit real transgressions. In D.E.Z. IX,1, the admonition not to

grumble is ascribed to Rabbi 'Eli'ezer ha-Kappar, a Tanna of the fifth genera-
tion. The reading there, which confirms the explanation given, is as follows:
'For if you grumble to others, you will be led to further sin.' To the contrary,
A. J. Tawrogi *(Derech Erez Sutta*, p. 6), incorrectly makes the following
interpretation: 'Tadle nicht zu viel, auf das du nicht das an anderen tadelts,
wobei du selbst beharrest.' This explanation is based on J. Harburger,
*Massekhet Derech Erez Sutta*, p. 17. Cf. also the reading of Rabbenu Jonah in
*Sha'arei Teshubah*, sha'ar 3, § 321: 'And the sages say: "do not grumble too
much, so that you are not led to sin."'

**18. There were seven Patriarchs with whom a covenant was made. And
they are: Abraham, Isaac, Jacob, Moses, Aaron, Pinhas and David. What
is written in connection with Abraham? 'In that day the Lord made a
covenant with Abraham, saying...' (Gen. 15:18). What is written in connection to Isaac? 'But My covenant will I establish with Isaac'(Gen. 17:21).
What is written in connection with Jacob? 'Then I will remember My
covenant with Jacob' (Lev. 26:42). What is written in connection with
Moses? 'For after the tenor of these words I have made a covenant with you
and with Israel' (Ex. 34:27). What is written in connection with Aaron? 'It is
an everlasting covenant of salt before the Lord (for you and your offspring)'
(Num. 18:19). What is written in connection with Pinhas? 'And it shall be
unto him and to his seed after him, the covenant of an everlasting priesthood' (Num. 25:13). What is written in connection with David? 'I have
made a covenant with my chosen, I have sworn unto David My servant' (Ps.
89:4).**

From here to the end of this chapter, there appear some numerical sayings, that
have no obvious connection with the directly preceding text, which contains a
series of statements made concerning the concept 'fence around the Torah'. In
some manuscripts the numerical sayings are missing. Those sayings were probably added at a early stage in the development of the text. See, however, the
opinion of S. Krauss in: *R. E.J.*, XXXVII (1899), p. 45 that the numerical
sayings belong to the original text version. The persons mentioned in the
sayings are all well-known within the tradition for possessing good characteristics. Abraham was known for his hospitality, Isaac for his self-sacrifice, Jacob
for his studiousness (note that 'tents' in Gen. 25:27 is interpreted as 'schools'),
Moses for his modesty, Pinhas for his zealousness for God, and David for his
willingness to repent and for his songs and praise, etc. Among other reasons
these men were esteemed for making a covenant owing to the possessing of the
above-mentioned attributes. Within the context of this chapter, then, this list
serves as an example of qualities for which a person who acquires that qualities
may be esteemed. In relation to all persons mentioned here one finds in the

Tenakh the use of the word 'berit' (covenant). In the explanation in Mas. Kal. Rab., III (see ed. M. Higger, pp. 243−244) the following is added in the form of a baraita: 'A covenant was also made with Israel... for it is said: "For after the tenor of these words I made a covenant with you and Israel."' (Ex. 34:27). This later addition was also absorbed in Ms. Oxford Bodleian (cat. A. Neubauer) no. 2339 in D. E. Z. h.l.

**19. Seven patriarchs have gone to rest in universal honour and the worm and maggots had no power over them. And they are: Abraham, Isaac, Jacob, [ Moses, Aaron and their father] Amram, [and] Benjamin and Isai the father of David [most Mss. omit Isai the father of David] and some say also David, because it is said: 'Therefore my heart is glad, and my glory rejoices, my flesh also dwells in safety' (Ps. 16:9).**

The basis manuscript mentions only six names, which indicates that the text requires correction. In addition to the names mentioned in the basis manuscript of D. E. Z. I, Mas. Kal. Rab. (ed. M. Higger, pp. 245−246) also mentions the name Kileab. It mentions: Abraham, Jacob, Amram the father of Moses, Benjamin the son of Jacob, Isai the father of David, and Kileab (the second son of David (see II Sam. 3:3). And in reference to another tradition David himself is mentioned. In a baraita in the parallel in TbB. B. 17a, however, other names are named: 'Our Rabbis taught: "There were seven over whom worms and maggots had no dominion: Abraham, Isaac and Jacob, Moses, Aaron and Miriam and Benjamin the son of Jacob... some say also David..."'

These names concur for the most part with those found in other readings in the manuscripts of D. E. Z. In any case, Moses and Aaron should be added in after Jacob in the basis manuscript, and Amram could be replaced by Miriam. In accordance with most of the manuscripts and the Genizah fragments, Isai must be omitted. The names Amram, Isai and Kileab (see the reading in Mas. Kal. Rab. l.c.) appear to have been introduced on the basis of another baraita: 'Our Rabbis taught: "Four died through the counsel of the serpent: Benjamin the son of Jacob, Amram the father of Moses, Isai the father of David and Kileab the son of David."' See TbB. B. 17a and cf. TbShab. 55b. Cf. also Jalq. II Sam., r. 151.

The central thought behind this statement is that Tzaddiqim should in fact not really die because death is the result of sin. Cf. TbShab. 55b: 'There is no death without sin.' The death of a righteous person is therefore problematic. Such a person does indeed die, but his body does not decay according to tradition. A closely related notion is that a number of Tzaddiqim died, as it were, unjustly and undeservedly. A 'tzaddiq' dies not as a result of committing sin, but as a result of Adam's sins and of the intrigues of the snake, all of which were beyond his responsibility. Cf., e.g., TbB. B. 17a: 'Our Rabbis taught: "Four died through the counsel of the serpent..."' Cf. also TbShab. 55b; cf. the

*Tosaphists* on TbShab. l.c.. Related to this are the traditions according to which a number of righteous men did not die in the hold of the Angel of Death but by a kiss from the Shekhinah. See TbB. B. l.c. and Rashi a.l. According to the tradition in TbB. B. l.c.: 'Our Rabbis taught: "Six there were over whom the Angel of Death had no dominion, namely: Abraham, Isaac and Jacob, Moses and Aaron and Miriam..." Rabbi 'El'azar said: "Miriam died also by a kiss..."' Cf. also Rabbi 'Aha bar Hanina's statement in TbShab. 55a that God instructed the angel Gabriel to place an ink mark on the forehead of the righteous ('tzaddiqim') so that the Angels of Destruction and the Decline would have no hold over them. Cf. Tb'Ab. Zar. 20a: the Angel of Death is hold responsible for the decay of the body after death. Cf. also Jalq., Ez., r. 350.

See here in D. E. Z. the manuscript readings that show 'shakhenu' instead of 'shakhebu'. This reading bears a stronger connection to the cited reference of Ps. 16:9: 'Therefore my heart is glad, and my soul rejoices, my body also dwells ('shakhan ') secure.' ('Kabod' [soul] is interpreted here as 'reputation', 'honour'). In the tradition the verb 'shakhab' is associated with a dignified and gentle death free of fear. Cf., e.g., Midr. Tan., ed. D. Hoffmann, p. 180: ' "To lie down" (shekhibah) means nothing other than a mind at peace, for it is said: "For then I should have lain down and been quiet; I should have slept; then I should have been at rest..."' (Hiob 3:13). Cf. also, e.g., Ber. Rab. LXII,2 and Midr. Leq. Tob., Wa-Jehi, ed. S. Buber, p. 114a. One can regard the reading 'shakhenu' as a later adaption to the passage Ps. 16:9 quoted in this statement. This passage, however, belongs only to the additional tradition concerning David. The manner in which this has been added could imply that it has been borrowed from the tradition in the Babylonian Talmud. In the Babylonian Talmud various arguments derived from Scripture are listed along with the different names. The reading of the baraita in the Babylonian Talmud appears to be more complete.

S. Krauss, in: *R. E. J.* ,XXXVII (1898), pp. 46–47, suggested that the original common binding factor which has given rise to this series of names must be sought in Scripture passages in which the verb 'shakhab' plays a role, e.g. Gen. 47:30: '... but let me lie with my fathers...' This applies to Jacob himself as to Isaac and Abraham. With respect to Moses one can refer to Dt. 31:16: '... Behold you are about to sleep with your fathers...' Since Aaron was mourned like Moses after his death, one can assume that also Aaron remained untouched after his death. (Cf. Num. 20:29 with Dt. 34:8) S. Krauss assumed that Miriam was originally listed in the series by analogy with Moses and Aaron, and that Benjamin's name was listed on the basis of a baraitathat has since been lost. With respect to David, however, it would have been more plausible in this case to cite II Sam. 7:12 because the verb 'shakhab' appears in that passage. It is also said that Solomon lay down by his forefathers (cf. I Kings 11:43), although Solomon is not mentioned in the series. Everything considered, we find S. Krauss's suggestion contrived. Neither the manuscripts nor the parallels confirm the suggestion at all. There is no special reason to doubt the originality of the Scripture references cited in TbB. B. l.c. (cf. TbShab. l.c.). The imperishability of Abraham's body is based there on Gen. 24:1 ('The Lord blessed Abraham *in all*'). With respect to the imperishability of Isaac's body Gen. 27:33 ('And I ate *of all*'). The imperishability of the bodies of Moses, Aaron and (by implication) Miriam, is based on Num. 33:38 and Dt. 34:5 ('... *by the mouth* of the Lord'). This passages belonged to the tradition that Moses, Aaron and Miriam died as a result of a kiss (by the mouth) of the Shekhinah. The imperishability of the body of Benjamin is convincingly based on Dt. 33:12: ... 'The beloved of the Lord, he shall dwell *in safety* ...' The version given in TbB. B. l.c. demonstrates that the list represents a compilation of original statement attributed to special individuals and that various arguments advanced in connection with those statements play a role in related traditions.

The meaning of the expression 'bi-khebod ha-'Olam', translated here as 'in universal honour' (i. e., without having lost respect in the eyes of the world), is best rendered in the variant of the statement in D. E. h.l. in *Seph. Hasidim*, ed. R. Margaliot (Bologna edition), § 1143, p. 569: 'Although these seven were buried and it would have been *no shame in the eyes of the world* had the worms gained dominion over them, the worms had no dominion over them...' Cf. also. e.g., Midr. Ps. 26, ed. S. Buber § 7: Jonah leaved This World as a fully righteous person ('tzaddiq gamur') and 'bi-khebodo', i. e., without damage to his good name and honour. Cf. also Jub. 4:23: 'And he (Enoch) was taken from amongst the children of man, and we conducted him into the Garden of Eden in majesty and honour...' ('le-gedolah u-le-kabod). See R. H. Charles, *The Apocrypha and Pseudepigrapha of the Old Testament*, II, p. 19.

The traditions based on Qoh. 7:1 further indicate that a good name and reputation exert a protective influence against death and decay and keep the body of the righteous person from decomposing. Among others, Moses, Aaron, Miriam and David are mentioned in the context of these statements. Cf. Qoh. Rab. VII,1 and Shem. Rab. LXVIII,1; Tanh., Wa-Jaqhel, § 1; Midr. Sam. XXXIII,2; Jalq., Qoh., r.973. Cf. also Kebod Huppah, ed. H. M. Horovitz, pp. 46—47. See also *'Otzar Midrashim*, ed. J. D. Eisenstein, I, p. 162ff.

20. **There were nine who entered the Garden of Eden alive. And they are: Enoch, Eliah, the Messiah, Eliezer the servant of Abraham, Hiram the king of Tyre, 'Ebed-Melekh the Cushite (= Ethiopian), Jabetz the grandson of Rabbi Jehudah ha-Nasi (read:the offspring of Jehudah), Bitjah the daughter of Pharaoh, and Serah the daughter of Asher. And some say: 'also Rabbi Jehoshua ben Levi'. [Another reading: Some say: 'Hiram the king of Tyre was expelled and in his place entered Rabbi Jehoshua ben Levi.' Or: Some say: 'Omit Hiram the king of Tyre and include Rabbi Jehoshua ben Levi in his place.']**

It is remarkable that no early parallels to this statement have been found. The statement already appears in the Genizah fragments of D. E. Z. Only in IV Ezra does one find a trace of existence of a tradition concerning a number of persons who did not die. See the remarks and references of R. H. Charles, *The Apocrypha and Pseudepigrapha of the Old Testament*, II , p. 576, note 26. He cites examples in which Enoch and Eliah, among others, are mentioned as not having died. Cf. Jub. 4:23; I En. 39:3 ff.; idem 70:1−3; II Hen. 36:2 in connection with Enoch. See also II En. 18:2, cited by M. Z. Segal, *Sepher Ben Sira ha-Shalem*, p. 340, l.20: And the angels hurried to Enoch and took him up to the highest heaven where the Lord received him and made him stand before Him for all time. In Josephus, *Ant.* I,3.4 and in Philo, *Questiones in Gen.* 86 (Cf. also Hebr. 11:5) it is also suggested that Enoch is immortal (although the LXX-text itself on Gen. 5:24 does not explicitly state that Enoch did not die. See I Hen. 99:52 in connection with Eliah.

The notion of the above mentioned individuals not dying especially plays a role in messianic expectations. In connection with Eliah, among others, cf. Mark. 9:2; Mat. 17:1 ff. and Luk. 9:28 ff.; IV Ezra 7:27,28; Deb. Rab. X,1; cf. also L. Ginzberg, *The Legends of the Jews*, V, pp. 96 and 164. Jeremiah, Barukh and Ezra are also mentioned in this connection. In connection with Ezra, cf. IV Ezra 14:9. In connection with Barukh cf. II Bar. 13:3 and 25:1 and cf. II Bar. 76:2. With respect to Jeremiah, see II Macc. 2:1 ff. and 15:13 and cf. Mat. 16:4. Cf. also L. Ginzberg, o.c., VI, pp. 400, 412, note 66. Also Jonah (who according to Midr. Teh. 26,7 also did not die) figures in messianic expectations. See L. Ginzberg, o.c., VI, p. 351, note 38. With regard to the notion of Eliah and Enoch not dying, cf. further the old traditions, mentioned in the commentary further on. See also A. J. Heschel, *Torah min ha-Shamajim*, II, London 1965, pp. 41−44 concerning Enoch and pp. 53−56 regarding Eliah.

K. Kohler in: *J. Q. R.*, V (1893), p. 417 (see also J. Scheftelowitz in: *M. G. W. J.*, LXV [1921], p. 112) contends that the statement here in D. E. Z. can be traced back to Essene tradition. This is a far-reaching conclusion which is certainly not applicable to all the persons referred to in D. E. Z. h.l. One can suggest, however, that the mention of Eliah and Enoch (who according to later rabbinical sources are considered to have died) dates back to very old traditions included in the writings read by the Essenes. None of the parallels of this statement as a hole, however, is very old! According to L. Ginzberg, o.c., V, pp. 85 and 96, note 67), it is difficult to date the entire series *before the tenth century*. The Genizah fragments here in D. E. possibly permit an earlier dating of the series.

The parallels give different readings with series of ten, eleven, thirteen or fourteen names. The reading with nine names here in D. E. Z and the reading with seven names in Mas. Kal. Rab. (ed. M. Higger, III, pp. 246−249; ed. N. N. Coronel, 9b) are probably the oldest. It is remarkable that the names Enoch, Eliah and the Messiah are not mentioned in the series in Mas. Kal. Rab.

The more extensive readings are later elaborations. The names of Jonadab ben Rekhab and of the bird Malchas were first added into *'Aleph Beit de Ben Sira* (see ed. in: *Ha-Tzopheh*, X, p. 269; and in *'Otzar Midrashim*, ed. J. D. Eisenstein, p. 50. In connection with the bird Malchas, see L. Ginzberg, o.c., V, pp. 95−96, note 67. See also I. Levi in *R. E. J.*, LXVIII (1914), p. 17. In *Pirqei Rabbenu ha-Qadosh* (ed. L.Grünhut in: *Seph. ha-Liqqutim*, III, p. 83) and in Jalq, Ez., r. 367 Metushalah and the sons of Korach are also mentioned in a list as being immortal. L. Ginzberg cites Christian influence with respect to the presence of Metushalah's name. See L. Ginzberg, o.c., vol. I, p. 142 and note 62; see also, V, p. 165.

Note in TbShab. 55b the rabbinical tradition (ascribed to Rabbi 'Ammi) that there is no death without sin. (Cf. Tb'Ar. 17a; Waj. Rab. XVII,1; Midr. Teh. 92,14 and Jalq., Ps., r. 840. The counterpart to this idea is that a person free of sin will not die. In connection with this thought, see Waj. Rab. XXVII,4 (ed. M. Margulies, pp. 628−629) and Qoh. Rab. III,14 and Bam. Rab. XIV; cf. also Pes. de-R. K., pisqa IX, ed. B. Mandelbaum, p. 152. Cf. also the idea that innocents do not die through faults of their own but as a result of the transgression of Adam. See. e.g., TbB. B. 17a; Siphrei, Ha'azinu, pisqa 339 (ed. L. Finkelstein, p. 388); Ber. Rab. XXI,1; 'Eikh. Rab. V,24; Tanh., Be-Reshit, ed. S. Buber § 17; Jalq, II Sam., r. 151.

There is, remarkably, no mention of the persons who supposedly entered Gan Eden alive in the extensive traditions and discussions concerning the death of the righteous in TbB. B. 17a, TbShab. 55b and Tb'Ar. 17a. This indicates that the statement here in D. E. concerns a later tradition. The various readings of that tradition were possibly spread in what L. Ginzberg calls 'popular circles' and dated back to very old sources. See L. Ginzberg, o.c., V, p. 163.

According to S. Krauss in: *R. E. J.*, XXXVII (1898), pp. 49−50 one could assume that this statement is directed against the exclusive claim of Christians regarding the continued existence of the body of Jesus of Nazareth. This is simply improbable, however, given for example that the immortality of Enoch was denied in the rabbinical tradition out of antagonism toward Christians concepts of immortality. Cf. among other sources, Ber. Rab. XXV,1 ff.; L. Ginzberg, *The Legends of the Jews*, V, p. 156; R. H. Charles, o.c., II, p. 488 (concerning II Bar. 13:3) and p. 514 (concerning II Bar. 59:5) and cf. Ber. Rab. XXV,1, ed. J. Theodor / Ch. Albeck, notes. See, A. J. Heschel, *Torah min ha-Shamajim*, II, p. 43. There is no doubt, moreover, that Jesus died.

In some parallels there appears the wording 'who did not taste death', either as a replacement of the wording 'entering Gan Eden alive', or as an addition. Cf. Jalq, Ez., r. 367; *Pirqei Rabbenu ha-Qadosh* in: L. Grünhut, *Seph. ha-Liqqutim*, III, p. 83;and *Midr. Ma'aseh Torah* in A. Jellinek, *Beit ha-Midrash*, II, p. 101 and cf. other sources. This wording has undoubtedly been borrowed from very old traditions. Cf. the usage of this wording in IV Ezra 6:26 and see Mark 9:1 and cf. Hebr. 2:9 (and Hebr. 11:15 with respect to Enoch ' tou mè

idein tanaton ') and Targ. Jer. on Dt. 32:1; cf. also Ber. Rab. XXI,5 and
TbJoma 87b and cf. other sources.

The wording in D. E. Z. h.l., concerning the entering of Gan Eden, however,
also has very old roots (cf., e.g. the tradition regarding the immortality of
Enoch in Jub. 4:23.

*Enoch* — Gen.5:24 underlies the idea of the immortality of Enoch, and can
serve as evidence of the death of Enoch as well as of his immortality. :'and he
was no more' may be a reference to the demise of Enoch. Cf. Ps. 39:14; Ps.
103:16; Prov. 12:7; Hiob 7:21; Hiob 8:22. The words 'and God took him away'
are associated, however, with the ascent of Eliah in Heaven (II Kings 2:3ff.). It
is generally understood that Eliah was immortal. This also explains discussions
in the rabbinical traditions as to whether Enoch did die (see below).

Some early sources more or less clearly suggest the immortality of Enoch. Cf.
Jub. 4:23; I Hen. 39:3ff.; I Hen. 70:1−3 and II Hen. 18:3 as cited by M. Z. Segal, *Sepher Ben Sira ha-Shalem*, p. 340, concerning 1.20; II Hen. 36:2; and
Philo, *Questiones in Gen.* 86 and Hebr. 11:5. Other early sources suggest on the
basis of the same quotation from Scripture that Enoch was very unique, but
they do not unequivocally assert his immortality. Cf., among others, Seph. Ben
Sira 44:16 (ed. M. Z. Segal 44:19, p. 307); Soph. Sal. 4:4−10 (Greek: 'metetetè'
as in Hebr. 11:5) Cf. Seph. Ben Sira 49:14 (ed. M. Z. Segal: 49:20, p. 337: 'we-
gam hu' nilqah panim', interpreted by M. Z. Segal on p. 340 as 'panim 'el
panim' (i.e. before the Shekhinah); cf. also. however, the explanation of
W. Bacher in: *J. Q. R.*, XII (1921), p. 281; W. Bacher reads 'me'al panim'
(away from the surface of the earth). Cf. the tradition in Josephus, *Ant.* I,3.4
(the Greek word 'anechoorèse', in that text Josephus also uses in connection
with Moses, see *Ant.* IV,48; Josephus does not deny the death of Moses). It
appears elsewhere that Josephus does not deny the death of Enoch. In *Ant.*
IX,2 (end) Josephus suggests the death of both Eliah and Enoch , saying: 'It is
written in the Sacred Books that they (Eliah and Enoch) disappeared, but so
that nobody knew that they died.' Cf. also L. Ginzberg. o.c.,V, p. 322.

The Targum Onkelos on Gen. 5:24 translates: 'lo-'amit jateh' ('God did not
let him die'). The expression 'we-'enennu' in Gen. 5:24 is rendered in some
manuscripts of the Targum as 'we-'itohi' ('and he was', i.e.: and he lived). The
Hebrew ''in' (aleph-jod-nun) can also be interpreted in Aramaic as affirmative
particle! See, however, Targum Onkelos, ed. A. Sperber, Leiden 1959, p. 8,
according to which the above-mentioned version of the Targum onkelos is not
original but is a later correction. The original reading is: 'we-'amit jateh' ('and
the Lord let him die'). There is reference in Ber. Rab. 25:1 to the idea of
immortality of Enoch, but it is represented as the idea of an Epicurean or a
heathen Matrona, and thus as an idea alien to Judaism that must be opposed.
Such opposition was probably based on the fear of deifying mortals. Cf. also
M. Kasher, *Torah Shelemah*, on Gen. 5:24, a.l., p. 358, note 60 and earlier cited

remarks, p. 139. That argumentation dates from the third century C.E.. In the
statement of Rabbi 'Abbahu quoted in this context, it is even suggested that
Enoch died before his time so that he would not commit serious sins as a result
of his unstable character. See also L. Ginzberg, *The Legends of the Jews*, V,
pp. 96 and 163−164. The tradition mentioned appears to have been inspired by
Soph. Sal. 4:10: 'And while living among sinners he was translated.' In the same
context of Ber. Rab. (XXV,1), a discussion between Rabbi 'Abbahu and
Epicureans is mentioned in which Rabbi 'Abbahu makes Enoch's death plausible. Rabbi 'Abbahu is also known for an anti-Christian polemic in which he
implicitly challenges the concept of the ascension of Jesus. (See TjTa'an. II,1
[65b] and cf. A.J. Heschel, *Torah min ha-Shamajim*, p. 43.) This indicates that
the denial of Enoch's immortality in the rabbinical tradition can probably be
explained as an anti-Christian polemic. Even in the time of 'Aqiba, there is
supposed to have been discussion concerning the reverence of Enoch. Cf. Midr.
Ag., ed. S. Buber., p. 15. Thus there is barely any trace left in the rabbinical
tradition of the legends concerning the immortality of Enoch that are well,
known from pseudo-epigraphic literatur. There are some traditions in which
Enoch is spoken of very positively, but his death is still not denied in those
traditions. Cf., e.g., Waj. Rab. XXIX,11 and Pes. de-R. K., XXIII (ed.
B. Mandelbaum, p. 344).

According to one tradition that has remained intact, however, Enoch (identified with Metraton) became an angel and was taken up into Heaven. These
and related traditions, however, do not say that Enoch was immortal. In Asc.
Is. 9:9 and later sources as Midr. ha-Gad. on Gen. 5:24 and *Seph. ha-Jashar* (in
A. Jellinek, *Beit ha-Midrash*, IV, pp. 129−130), Enoch's rise into Heaven in
connection with his becoming an angel is not distinguished from the rise of
others who did die! In Midr. ha-Gad., l.c., it is even said that all righteous
people (besides Enoch) were taken into Heaven after their deaths. See also
L. Ginzberg, o.c., V, p. 157 and cf. Rashi on TbB. B. 121b. Only in late mystical
tradition in Jalq. Re'ub. on Gen. 1 (52a) concerning Eliah's and Enoch's
becoming angels does it say that they did not die. There one finds a relationship
between becoming an angel and being immortal.

On account of the fact that Enoch's immortality is denied in the older
rabbinical traditions, L. Ginzberg suggests that the list of immortals such as
found here in D.E.Z. is a rather late tradition, dating from no earlier than the
tenth century of the C.E. (See L. Ginzberg. o.c., V, p. 96, note 67.) On the
basis of the material there is nevertheless reason to suggest that this tradition in
D.E. has very old roots. (See, e.g. K. Kohler in: *J. Q. R.*, V, [1893], p. 417)

*Eliah* — The tradition that Eliah was immortal is based on II Kings 2:1 and II
Kings 2:11, where it is said that God took him up to heaven in a storm. Cf. II
Kings 2:16,17, where it is written that his grave was sought in vain for three
days. In an earlier tradition such as I En. 99:52 (see *Seder 'Olam*, I [end]), there
is already allusion to Eliah's immortality. The many traditions about the bodily

manifestation of Eliah to later generations can also be understood on the basis
of explanations of II Chron. 21:12, according to which verse Eliah sent a letter
to King Joram. The midrash is based upon the opinion that in the verse
mentioned is referred to the period of the reign of King Joram himself. During
king Joram's reign, however, Eliah's place had already been taken by Elishah,
which means that the event described applies to the period after Eliah's ascent
into Heaven. In fact the event described in II Chron. 21:12 probably happened
in the period when Jehoshaphat, the father of Joram, was still alive and Joram
functioned only as regent in his father's place (and when Eliah had not yet
ascended into Heaven). In this connection, cf. *Seder 'Olam Rab.* XVII; cf. also
Rashi and Radaq with respect to II Chron. 21:12. See also *S. E. R.*, ed.
M. Friedmann, Mabo, pp. 18–19. Eliah was already considered a legendary
figure in the period of the Tenakh and associated with the coming of the
Messiah. Cf. Mal. 3:23ff. and *Seph. Ben Sira* 48:10; cf. also somewhat later
traditions such as Mat. 2:10ff.; Mat. 17:10ff.; Mark 9,11f.; and *Seder 'Olam
Rab.*, XVII and other sources. Cf. L. Ginzberg, o.c., IV, p. 217ff.

A number of old traditions, however, are absolutely unclear in regard to the
denial of Eliah's death. Cf., e.g., the LXX ('hoos eis ton ouranon') on II Kings
2:11 and the Targum, a.l. ('le-tzet shemaja') Cf. also *Seph. Ben Sira* 48:9, which
expressly reads 'ma'alah' and 'marom' but not 'shamajim'. Cf. the remarks of
L. Ginzberg, o.c., VI, p. 323, note 32 (end). Cf. also TosSot. 12,5. Josephus
suggests in *Ant.* IX,2 (end) the death of both Eliah and Enoch. The age of these
traditions shows that no reaction to Christian traditions is involved, unlike in
the later denial of the immortality of Enoch. See L. Ginzberg. o.c., VI, p. 323.
The same applies to the tradition preserved in the name of Rabbi José in which
Eliah's residence in Heaven is denied. See Mekh. de-R. Jishm., Jitro Ba-
Hodesh, par. 4 (ed. M. Friedmann, 65b) and cf. especially the gemara in
TbSuk. 5a. This tradition is actually not directed against the suggestion that
Eliah was immortal but it is directed against the notion of the bodily presence of
Eliah in a world-above conceived to be immaterial. From this arises the comparison with Moses, who is also not supposed to have been in Heaven during
the revelation of Mount Sinai. According to a Tannaitic solution concerning the
question of Eliah's presence in Heaven, Eliah was not taken into Heaven itself
but to a residence in the immediate vicinity of Heaven. (See TbSuk. 5a) This
may have influenced the old sources mentioned above in which Eliah's death is
not clearly denied. Cf. the contradictory opinion of M. Aberbach in: *E.J.*, VI,
col. 635, where the statement of Rabbi José is explained as an anti-Christian
polemic. Cf. also the note to TbSuk. 5a, *Babylonian Talmud*, ed. I. Epstein,
p. 15, note 3.

The problem of how Eliah could physically be taken into Heaven also figures
strongly in later, especially mystical traditions. Cf., among others, M. Zucker,
'*Al Targum Rasag al ha-Torah*, New York 1959, p. 106ff.; *Seph. ha-Zohar*, Wa-
Jaqhel, 191a; *Seph. Heikhalot* in A. Jellinek, *Beit ha-Midrash*, V, p. 176 and

*Tiqqunei Zohar* 70, 119b and Qimchi on II Kings 2:1. See also the many sources mentioned by A.J. Heschel, *Torah min ha-Shamajim*, II, p. 54ff.

It is difficult to establish the precise relationship between the traditions that describe that Eliah stayed in Heaven (or in the vicinity thereof) and those traditions that report that he stayed in Paradise. See L. Ginzberg, o.c., V. p. 323.

Although there is no question of a clear polemic against the immortality of Eliah as such, traditions have been preserved in which Eliah is treated less positively. Cf. among others Shir ha-Shir. Zuta VIII,6; cf. Shir ha-Shir. Rab. I,6; A.R.N. [b], XLVII (65a); Jalq, Kings, r. 217; P.R.E. XXIX (end); and S.E.Z. VIII (ed. M. Friedmann. 18b).

*And the messiah* — The words '. . . and the messiah . . .' are missing in Ms.Oxford Bodleian (cat A. Neubauer) no.2339 of D.E.Z. Ms. Oxford Bodleian (cat. A. Neubauer) no. 904 reads: '. . . and Moses . . .' (For traditions according to which Moses did not die, cf. Siphrei Dt., pisqa 387, ed. L. Finkelstein, p. 428. No early sources are found within rabbinical tradition that mention the Messiah's staying in Gan Eden and emphasize the fact that he did not die. The situation discussed here in D.E.Z. clearly takes place after the appearance of the messiah. Old traditions such as IV Ezra 14:9 that state that Ezra was taken into Heaven and stayed there with the messiah, involve the conception of a pre-existing messiah. Gan-Eden was also located in Heaven; cf., e.g., II En. 10. L. Ginzberg, o.c., V, p. 96, asserts that the situation described in IV Ezra took place after the appearance of the messiah. It is, however, evident in IV Ezra that the pre-existence of the messiah was assumed. Cf. IV Ezra 12:32 and 13:26. Cf. I En. 39:6ff.; 46:1ff.;48:2ff. 49:2ff.; 62:7 and 70:1ff. See finally the opinion of R.H. Charles, *The Apocrypha and Pseudepigrapha of the Old testament*, II, p. 621. R.H. Charles explains IV Ezra 14:9 as a reference to the pre-existing messiah. The messiah waits from the beginning of creation until his time has come. In IV Ezra 7:29−30 there is even mention of his death after that time. See M. Stone in: *Religion in Antiquity, Essays in Memory of E.R. Goudenough*, London 1968, pp. 215−232. Only in the later rabbinical sources of a mystical nature is the concept of the messiah staying in Gan Eden found, but that too concerns a pre-existing messiah who waits for his time to appear. This mystical idea was also described by Cabalistic writers as a part of the book of Enoch, see L. Ginzberg, o.c., I, p. 32. Cf. R. Patai, *The Messiah texts*, New York 1979, pp. 24−25. In I En. 71:14−17 there is mention of the identification of Enoch with the messiah. Those could be important in seeking a solution to the problem that it is clearly stated here in D.E.Z. that the messiah entered Gan Eden alive. There is probably a very old tradition suggested here in D.E.Z. which was transmitted in what one could call 'popular circles.' In connection with the idea of a time lapse between the first and second appearances of the messiah, cf. also, e.g., a statement by Rabbi Berekhjah in Ruth Rab. V,6 and cf. Bam. Rab. XI,2.

*Eliezer the servant of Abraham* — There are no early sources known according to which Eliezer the servant of Abraham did not die. In *'Aleph Beit de Ben Sira* (ed. in: Ha-*Tzopheh*, X, p. 267) it is said that Eliezer entered Gan Eden alive because of the great modesty he had learned from Abraham. According to Mas. Kal. Rab., III (ed. M. Higger, p. 75), Eliezer was taken into Gan Eden because of his prayer for Abraham. Cf. Gen. 24:12 and its context.

According to a tradition in P. R. E. XVI, Eliezer the servant of Abraham was unjustly suspected of having had sexual relations with Rebekka, and according to a tradition in Ag. Ber., Haj. Sarah, ed. S. Buber, p. 60 (noting as source Midr. 'Abkir), Eliezer was rewarded by being allowed to enter Gan Eden alive. Cf. Jalq., Haj. Sarah, r. 109. Cf. also other sources noted by L. Ginzberg, o.c., V, p. 263, note 301.

The parallel TbB. B. 58b mentioned in the commentaries is not really a parallel. In TbB. B. 58a one finds a curious report of a meeting between Rabbi Bana'a and Eliezer the servant of Abraham at the entrance of the grave of Abraham and Sarah while all of them are represented as living persons. Eliezer is clearly not regarded as one among immortals. This tradition can therefore not be used as support for the idea that Eliezer was immortal. It is impossible to trace this tradition concerning Eliezer the servant of Abraham, who (according to D. E. Z.) entered Gan Eden alive, back to an early time. See however K. Kohler in: *J. Q. R.*, V (1893), who refers to A. Geiger (*Zeitschrift der deutschen Morgenländischen Gesellschaft*, VI, p. 196ff.) and says that the tradition here is an old tradition from the Essenes.

*Hiram the king of Tyre* — The very negative image of Hiram in the rabbinical tradition makes the assertion that Hiram the king of Tyre entered Gan Eden alive problematic. Ez. 28:2 especially poses a problem, because it predicts the death of the king of Tyre, in the midrash identified as Hiram the king of Tyre, who lived at the time of the construction of the Temple. Hiram is strongly disapproved of in a number of traditions. Cf. TbB. B. 75a-b; TbHul. 89a; Mekh. de-R. Jishm., Shirah, par. 8 (ed. M. Friedmann, 48b); Mekh. De-R. Shim. bar Johai, p. 66, 91–92; Ber. Rab. XLVI,5 and XI,5; and Waj. Rab. XVIII,2; and other sources.

One possible solution of the problem would be to read 'Hiram from Tyre', thus not the king of Tyre, but the architect from Tyre and son of a widow from the tribe Naphtali (see I Kings 7:13ff. and cf. II Chron. 2:12–13 and II Chron. 4:11–16). In connection with genealogy see further Tb'Ar. 16a; Pes. Rab., pisqa 6: Josephus, *Ant.* VIII,3.4 and L. Ginzberg, o.c., VI, p. 295, note 61. Cf. also *Hiddushei Harshash* Ber. Rab. LXXXV,4. See L. Blau in *M. G. W. J.*, XLI (1879), p. 112. M. Ginsberg, translation of D. E. Z. in *The Minor Tractates of the Talmud*, ed. A. Cohen, II, p. 570, note 45; and L. Ginzberg, o.c., IV, pp. 155 and 259, note 62. See also Mas. Kal. Rab. (ed. N. N. Coronel, 9b), where it is suggested in the margin that the original reading was 'Mi-Ttzur', with a large 'mem'. The writers here have mistaken 'Mi-Ttzur' as abbreviation of

'Melekh Tzur' (King of Tyre). Cf. also the editions of D. E. Z. a.l., in editions of A. J. Tawrogi and D. Sperber; D. O. Straschun in: *Ha-Maggid*, IX (1865), p. 333, *Kaphtor u-Pherah*, ed. Z. H. Edelmann, Berlin 1851, 46a, mentioned in S. Krauss in: *R. E. J.*, XXXVII (1898), p. 48.

According to Mas. Kal. Rab, l.c., Hiram entered Gan Eden alive because he built the Temple. This refers to Hiram the architect. But it is also true that Hiram the king is credited in the tradition with building the Temple. In the manuscripts and parallels there is no support for the reading of 'Hiram from Tyre' instead of 'Hiram king of Tyre'. A special factor to be considered is that king Hiram has been attributed with an unusually long lifespan because various persons in the Tenakh (the same can be said of Serah bat Asher) have been identified as king Hiram. See Ber. Rab. LXXXV,4 and other sources, where Hira mentioned in Gen. 38:1 is identified as king Hiram the contemporary of David and with the king of Tyre mentioned in Ez. 28:2, where it is predicted how he will die at the hands of strangers (i.e Nebuchadnezar) as punishment for his excessive pride. Thus, according to generally accepted opinion, Hiram supposedly lived for more than 1200 years. It is certainly quite possible that the tradition about his extraordinary long life, together with Ez. 28:13, led to speculation about his acceptance into Gan Eden. In a later midrash *'Aleph Beit de Ben Sira*, Hiram the king of Tyre is named as one of those allowed to enter Gan Eden alive, in reward for his contribution to the building of the Temple. He supposedly stayed in Gan Eden for 1000 years but then had to leave because of his haughtiness, as derived from Ez. 28:2. The negative tradition of Ez., l.c., is enfeebled here by the notion that Hiram was driven out of Gan Eden after a period of time. In connection with this tradition must be understood the words: 'The king of Tyre removed (i. e.was driven away) and Rabbi Jehoshua ben Levi was allowed in his place.' (See the manuscripts of D.E.Z, h.l.) The word 'hutza" (was removed) does not refer to being removed from the list of immortals but to the removal of king Hiram from Gan Eden! King Hiram was then replaced by Rabbi Jehoshua ben Levi. See also D. Sperber, *Massekhtot Derekh 'Eretz Zuta*, p. 97. The interval between the passing of king Hiram (according to the midrash in the time of Nebuchadnezar (see Ber. Rab. LXXXV,4) and the passing of Rabbi Jehoshua ben Levi is possibly estimated at approximately 1000 years. Ez. 28:13 provides an important basis for this tradition: 'You have been in Eden, the Garden of God...' explained as a temporary staying in Gan Eden. We may assume that according to the Midrash, Hiram the king of Tyre is both rewarded for his help in building the Temple and punished for his extremely haughty attitude. The tradition here in D. E. Z., together with the remark that Rabbi Jehoshua ben Levi replaced Hiram the king of Tyre in Gan Eden probably comprises a later tradition in which (as in *'Aleph Beit de Ben Sira*) a negative and positive judgement over Hiram are synthesized.

*'Ebed-Melekh the Ethiopian* — 'Ebed-Melekh, who is named in Jer. 38:6, was one of the Eunuchs from the court of king Zedekia. He rescued Jeremiah from the pit into which Zedekia had him thrown. He is identified in the rabbinic tradition with Barukh, the servant and scribe of the prophet Jeremiah. (Cf. Jer. 32:12–16; 36:4–32; 43:1–7; and 45; The term 'Ethiopian' here is interpreted as a figurative reference to Barukh, who was distinguished like a black person among white people on account of his good deeds although there is no explicit discussion in rabbinical sources about the immortality of 'Ebed-Melekh we may reckon with a comparable tradition in a popular circuit of stories through the identification with Barukh. The tradition that Barukh did not die but was preserved for all time is very old and appears in II Bar. 13:3; 25:1 and 76:2. Cf. L. Ginzberg, o.c., VI, p. 411, note 66. According to the explanations in Mas. Kal. Rab., III (ed. M. Higger, p. 248) and in *'Aleph Beit de Ben Sira*, o.c., p. 267, 'Ebed-Melekh's entrance in Gan Eden alive was appropriate reward of saving a human live, i.e., for rescuing Jeremiah from the pit.

*Jabetz [ the grandson of Rabbi Jehudah ha-Nasi].* It is apparent from the context in the explanation in Mas. Kal. Rab., III, ed.M. Higger, p. 249, that Jabetz here refers to the biblical figure Jabetz and not to a descendant of Rabbi Jehudah ha-Nasi. Reference is made in I Chron. 4:10ff.: 'And Jabetz called on the God of Israel... and that Your hand might be with me and that You would work deliverance from evil... And God did as he asked.' 'Deliverance of evil' is explained as 'deliverance of death'. In a statement of Rabbi Jehudah ha-Nasi (TbTem. 16a and parallels), 'deliverance from evil' is interpreted as liberation from evil forces, sickness and pain.

The reading 'Jabetz the grandson of Rabbi Jehudah ha-Nasi' is corrupt. No grandson of Rabbi Jehudah ha-Nasi with the name Jabetz is known to have existed. Readings that name Jabetz as another person along with the son or grandson of Rabbi Jehudah ha-Nasi are also corrupt. Cf. the manuscripts on D. E. Z. h.l., that mentions the number nine, while in those manuscripts in fact ten people are listed. The name Rabbi Jehudah ha-Nasi, however, does not belong in the series of names. The assumption of D. Sperber, o.c., p. 98, that the original reading might have listed ten persons and that the names of Jabetz and the grandson of Rabbi Jehudah ha-Nasi were combined later in the list, is not convincing. Several individuals have attempted to make plausible the existence of a son of Rabbi Jehudah ha-Nasi with the name of Jabetz. See, e.g. I. H. Weiss, *Dor Dor we-Doreshaw*, vol.III, p. 57, note 2, based on TbKet.62b; cf. Krauss in *R. E. J.* XXXVII, 1899, pp. 48–49, where Jabetz is identified as the young deceased son of Rabbi, mentioned in TbSem. X. See also Tawrogi, o.c., p. 8; cf. the suggestion of Weiss, *Dor Dor we-Doreshaw*, II, repr. Jerusalem s. a., p. 57 to read 'Rabbi Jabetz'. The hypotheses here, however, are not convincing. Cf. also the manuscript-reading 'Jabetz the slave of Rabbi Jehudah ha-Nasi' in: *'Aleph Beit de Ben Sira*, ed. M. Steinschneider, p. 28.

In the Aggada (in Tannaitic tradition), Jabetz is identified as the judge

Othniel (the brother of Kaleb the Kenite; cf. Judg.1:16 and I Chron. 2:55. He is also identified as the brother of Simeon, mentioned in Judg. 1:17. There would therefore have been one person with both the name Othniel, Jabetz and the name Jehudah. See TbTem. 16a and the glosses of the Gaon of Vilna on that source. Cf. further Qoh. Rab. I,5; Shir ha-Shir. Rab. IV,7; Siphrei Dt., pisqa 352; TbSot. 11a; TbSanh. 106a; and Pes. de-R. Kah., ed. S. Buber, 22a.

The original reading in D. E. Z. might have been: 'Jabetz hu Jehudah' ('Jabetz – that is Jehudah' and thus not 'Jabetz the son [or grandson] of Rabbi Jehudah'). See J. Brill in *M. G. W. J.*, XLI (1897), p. 112. The error may have arisen over confusion resulting from a remark about Rabbi Jehudah ha-Nasi originally made in the margin of manuscripts of D. E., for it provides in TbTem. 16a an extensive explanation of the prayer of Jabetz in I Chron. 4:10 by Rabbi Jehudah ha-Nasi. Cf. also the explanations of L. Blau in: *M. G. W. J.*, XLI (1897), p. 112; S. Krauss, l.c..; L. Ginzberg, o.c., VI, p. 187; and M. Higger, *Massekhtot Ze'irot*, p. 131.

It is even more plausible to say that Jabetz is named in the original reading of this text in D. E. Z., on the basis of I Chron. 2:1−55, as a descendant of Jehudah: 'Jabetz the son of the sons of Jehudah'. This reading could than have been melded with the remark made in the margin about Rabbi Jehudah ha-Nasi, yielding the following reading: 'Jabetz the son of the son of *Rabbi Jehudah ha-Nasi*'.

Jabetz is esteemed in the tradition for the fact that he advised (wordplay on his name from the stem 'ja'atz') and instructed many of Israel in the Torah. See TbTem. 16a and parallels. See I Chron. 2:55: 'And the families of the Scribes which dwelt at Jabetz...', this is cited as a reference in the parallels; cf. especially Tanh., Tetzawweh, §9. According to an explanation by Rabbi 'Abbahu, Othniel revived through study the oral tradition, which had been forgotten to a large extent since the death of Moses. See idem TbTem. 16a, based on Jos. 15:17: 'And Othniel the son of Kenaz... took it.' (I.e., took Qirjath Sepher, literally: the city of the book and explained to mean that he won back the knowledge of the forgotten traditions, lost during the mourning period for Moses.) The entire context in Tem. 16a suggests that God rewarded Jabetz by hearing his prayer and spared him the influence of the evil force, sickness and pain. Wordplay makes here the identification of Othniel and Jabetz possible, Othniel being read as "Anahu El' (God has answered him). In S. E. R. VI (ed. M. Friedmann, p. 30) a cause-effect relationship is explicitly established between Jabetz effort with the Torah and Gods attention to his prayer, which resulted in Jabetz being spared of sickness and pain. It is striking that there is no mention of immortality as reward in these sources, which are not very late sources. In A. R. N. [a], XXXV, Jabetz is even called: A man good and righteous, a man of truth and pious. Only in the later source '*Aleph Beit de Ben Sira*, l.c., one does find a tradition comparable to that in D. E. Z. h.l. (cf. also Massekhet kallah Rab. l.c.). This, along with the factors mentioned, indicates that the listing of the entire series of immortals in D. E. Z. cannot be dated too early. In the reading concerning the immortals in *'Aleph Beit de Ben Sira*, o.c., it is striking that Jabetz is attributed with characteristics ascribed to the sages in the beginning of D. E. Z. I: 'He was meek, humble of spirit, filled with knowledge and a desire to learn, forgiving and beloved.'!! This implies a strong connection between the context of the first chapter of D. E. Z. as a whole and the series of immortals mentioned here as a part of it.

Cf. explanations in Ber. Rab., ed. J. Theodor / Ch. Albeck, pp. 96−97.

*Bitjah the daughter of the Pharaoh* − Cf. I Chron. 4:18. According to the version in Mas. Kal. Rab. III (ed. M. Higger, p. 246ff.), Bitjah was made immortal for the efforts in the liberation of Israel and for rescuing Moses. As just reward for saving human life, i.e., that of Moses and thus of an entire people, Bitjah was allowed to enter Gan Eden. Cf. the same reason for immortality of 'Ebed-Melekh the Ethiopian. A tradition concerning Bitjah's entrance alive into Gan Eden appears in Midr. Mishl. XXXI,9 (ed. S. Buber, p. 111, § 11) and later sources. No support for Bitjah's immortality is found in older sources, although she is portrayed in an usually positive light. According to some Amoraic traditions, Bitjah the daughter of the Pharaoh was proselyte. In TbMeg. 13a (cf. TbSanh. 19a) Rabbi Shim'on ben Pazzi gives an explanation on I Chron. 4:18: 'And his wife the Jewess bore Jered... And these are the sons of Bitjah the daughter of the Pharaoh, whom Mered took... ' The word 'Jewess' applies according to the explanation to Bitjah. In a further explanation, by Rabbi Johanan, Ex. 2:5 ('And the daughter of the Pharaoh went down to bathe in the river') is explained to mean that Bitjah purified herself of heathenism, i.e., that she underwent the ritual bath in converting to judaism. Cf. TbSot. 12b. In a related interpretation, Bitjah's husband Mered, is identified as Kaleb. The name Mered is supposed to apply to Kaleb's rebellion against the spies, and he is supposed to have taken suitable woman in taking the daughter of the Pharaoh, also a rebel, who fought against the heathenism of her father. Cf. also Waj. Rab. I,3, where a similar tradition is attributed to Rabbi Jehudah bar Shim'on, the son of Rabbi Shim'on ben Pazzi. Cf. also Deb. Rab. VII,5 on Dt. 28:6; P. R. E. XLVIII; and Jalq., Ex., r. 166.

In a statement by Rabbi Jehoshua of Sikhnin in the name of Rabbi Levi, Bitjah's name is interpreted as Bit J-H (Daughter of the Lord). Because she called Moses her son while he was not her son, God called her His daughter while she was not His daughter and while she belonged to a people other than the Israelites. Cf. Waj. Rab. I,3 and P. R. E. XLVIII. Early sources, however, never state that Bitjah the daughter of the Pharaoh did not die.

*Serah the daughter of Asher* — The name Serah appears a number of times in the Tenakh in connection with records of family generations. See Gen. 46:17; Num. 26:46; and I Chron. 7:30. Given that the sequence of traditions in the Tenakh are often interpreted chronologically in the midrash, the idea has risen that Serah was born while Joseph still lived (Gen. 46) and that she not only experienced the exodus from Egypt but also the entrance into the land Canaan (Num. 26) See, *Seder 'Olam Rab.* IX; cf. Ber. Rab. XLIV,9 (ed. J. Theodor / Ch. Albeck, p. 1182); and cf. also A. R. N.[b], XXXVIII (end). Because of her long life and her supernatural knowledge, Serah was able to tell where the chest containing Joseph's bones lay buried in the Nile, so that Moses could get the chest of bones and take it into the land of Canaan as promised. Cf. TosSot IV,7; TbSot. 13a; Mekh. de-R. Jishm., Be-Shallah, Petihta (ed. M. Friedmann, p. 24 a ff.) and see J. Horovitz, *Die Josepherzählung*, Frankfurt am Main 1921, p. 125 ff.; L. Ginzberg o.c.,II, pp. 116 and 181; idem, V, pp. 96, 165, and 356 (notes 295, 395 and 321). See also I. Heinemann, *Darkhei 'Aggada*, Jerusalem 1970, pp. 29−30 and 207, note 42, where he, in accordance with Grünbaum, derives 'Serah' from 'sara*h* ' (= to be left over) Cf. *Tosaphists* on TbSot.13a. In the midrash, a connection is established between the 'wise woman' in II Sam. 20:15 ff. and Serah the daughter of Asher. By means of a play of words, the words in II Sam. 20:15 ff. ('I am of them that are peaceable and faithful in Israel') are connected with the finding of Joseph's grave; in Ber. Rab. XCIV,9, they are explained to mean: 'I have perfected the people of Israel in Egypt, I have supplemented the trustworthy with the trustworthy, I have added the trustworthy Joseph to the trustworthy Moses.' See Maharzav a.l. In doing so she made possible the exodus from Egypt. See Mekh. de-R. Jishm. l.c.; Qoh. Rab. IX,9; Midr. Sam. XXXII; Jalq. Sam., r. 152. See also L. Ginzberg, o.c., II, p. 182.

In the version in Mas. Kal. Rab., l.c., II Sam. 20:15 is explained to mean that Serah the daughter of Asher perfected ('shalem') the number of those who entered Gan Eden alive. According to a tradition in P. R. E. XLVIII, Serah knew the secrets of deliverance and shared them with Abraham, Isaac , Jacob, and Joseph and his brothers. She learned the secret from her father Asher. This knowledge is also associated in the tradition with the deliverance to come. It is possible that the figure of Serah the daughter of Asher played a role in old eschatological traditions, such as those concerning Enoch and Eliah. Cf. here also L. Ginzberg, o.c., V, p. 96 and the sources referred to by L. Ginzberg in connection with Joseph's grave. Cf. also idem, V, p. 376, note 438.

In the tradition, however, she is possibly given immortality on completely different grounds. In the tradition, in which she is identified as the 'wise woman' from II Sam. 20:15, she is credited with saving the inhabitants of an entire city, something which not even Abraham was able to do. Cf. Shem. Rab. V,14 and Ber. Rab. XCIV,9 (ed. J. Theodor/ Ch. Albeck, a.l., notes) and cf. Ag. Ber. XXII and M. Kasher, *Torah Shelemah*, on Gen 46:17.

According to later sources, however, Serah gained immortality because she was the first to report Jacob that his son Joseph was still alive. See *'Aleph Beit de Ben Sira*, ed. in *Ha-Tzopheh*, vol. X, p. 269 and *Seph. ha-Jashar* on Gen. 45 (110a). Cf. Targum jer. on Gen. 46:17.

The so called Tomb of Serah bat Asher is still honoured to this day as a place of pilgrimage by the Persian Jewish community (see *E. J.*, vol. IX, col. 78.)

*Rabbi Jehoshua ben Levi* — The tradition that Rabbi Jehoshua ben Levi entered Gan Eden alive dates from the Talmudic period. SeeTbKet. 77b. His extraordinary piety and his self-offering solidarity with people who suffered from contagious afflictions of the skin are cited as reasons for his immortality. See the earlier commentary about Hiram the king of Tyre, who, according to an explanation on Ez. 28:2 ff. (where he is criticized for his haughtiness) and Ez. 28:13 (where allusion is made to his stay in Paradise), was sent away from Gan Eden after one thousand years and replaced by Rabbi Jehoshua ben Levi. This explanation is based on the reading of manuscripts in D. E. Z. ('And there are those who say: "Hiram king of Tyre was sent away and replaced by Jehoshua ben Levi."' The basis manuscript, however, reads: 'There are those who say: "Also Rabbi Jehoshua ben Levi."' This may be an earlier reading that was later replaced by a reading according to which Hiram was replaced in Gan Eden by Rabbi Jehoshua ben Levi, along with which is maintained the figure of nine immortals, as indicated at the beginning of this statement.

## Derekh 'Eretz Zuta, chapter II

**1. Let all your ways be for the name of Heaven. Love Heaven and fear Heaven.**
**2. Be frightened and rejoice about all the precepts.**

1. *Let all your ways be for the name of Heaven* ... Love for and fear of God should be the motivation behind all human actions. The concepts 'love' and 'fear' are very important here. In a number of manuscripts the concepts appear in reverse order. In both cases, however, the emphasis may be on 'love'. In one case 'love' is placed first in order to emphasize its importance, while in the other case 'fear' is placed first to indicate that it is a first stage in the religious development of human motivation, leading eventually to 'acting out of love.' 'Fear' applies to the fear out of committing sin and of being punished. 'Love' is the positive disposition to do good without expectation of gain. The greater esteem for acting out of love as opposed to acting out of fear has undergone historical development. See D. Flusser, 'A New Sensitivity in Judaism and the Christian Message'in: *H. T. R.*, LXI (1986), pp. 107−127. No clear distinction is made between fear and love in very old traditions such as Seph. Ben Sira and Jub. (cf. Jub. 36:4−8). Since the time of Hillel the Old, emphasis has been placed on love above fear. There were groups, however, which stressed acting out of fear. Cf. TjBer. IX [14b]. In connection with the relationship between love and fear, cf. A. Büchler, *Studies in Sin and Atonement*, London 1928, pp. 122−130 and the traditions mentioned there.
'Heaven' stands for 'God', see A. Marmorstein, *The Old Rabbinic Doctrine of God*, I, repr. Farnborough 1969, p. 105 ff. and E. E. Urbach, *Hazal*, Jerusalem 1978, pp. 56−63. Cf. further M'Abot II,1 and see in connection with the relation between acting for the name of Heaven and the voluntary halakhic restrictions of the sages: F. Böhl, *Gebotserschwerung und Rechtsverzicht als ethisch-religiöse Normen in der rabbinischen Literatur*, pp. 25−27 ff., p. 27: 'Wer um des Himmels Willen die Gebote tut is ein Frommer und Chasid.'

2. *Be frightened and rejoice* − Have fear and rejoice carrying out all commandments. In Mas. Kal. Rab. III (ed. M. Higger, p. 250), one finds the reading 'hadar we ..', 'Let your heart rejoice in beautifying every precept, i.e., in performing it in the most beautiful manner. Cf. Mekh. de-R. Jishm., Be-Shallah, par. 3 (ed. M. Friedmann, 37a). The reading that concurs with the basis manuscript of D. E. Z. is preferable because of the connection in the context. Cf. also the reading in A. R. N. [a], XLI (67a), where the following statement is attributed to Rabbi Jehudah ben Teima: 'Have love for Heaven

and fear Heaven. Have fear and rejoice in all commandments.' In D. E., l.c., the statement appears anonymously, accompanied by an introduction.

**3. Be like a leather bottle (not) split open, that is not opened to let in the wind, and (be) like a deep (garden) bed, which retains its water and like a coated vessel (which is coated with pitch), which preserves its wine.**

See the commentary in D. E. Z. I,4. D. E. Z. I—IV forms a unity but comprises a compilation of originally independent parts, which explains why some statements in these chapters appear twice. This statement in chap. II has been omitted in a number of manuscripts in order to harmonize the texts.

**4. Sit before the Elders and incline your ear and hear their words and listen carefully to the words of your fellows.**
**5. Do not be hasty to answer and give thought to answer with words according to the subjectmatter. Answer the first point first and answer the last point last.**
**6. And admit the truth, and do not speak before somebody who is greater in wisdom than you.**

4. See the commentary to D. E. Z. I,3.
5. *Do not be hasty to answer...* Cf. M'Abot V,7 and parallels. See D. E. Z., VII,1; and see D. E. Z. XI,25 and XI,27.

The habit of not answering hastily and of answering questions in the order in which they are asked is cited in M'Abot. l.c., as a feature typical of sages. Cf. also Qoh. 5:1 and Prov. 18:13 in this connection. For explanation, see especially the commentaries to M'Abot V,7 (Abrabanel; *Mahzor Vitry*, ed. S. Hurwitz, p. 542 and other commentaries). One should not seek to argue immediately, but answer only after considering the argument of the other person. One should try to understand another's arguments.

The basis of this statement is very old and is found in *Seph. Ben Sira* 11:7: 'Before you have examined blame not, investigate first and afterwards rebuke. Answer not a word before you hear and in the midst of a discourse speak not.' The statement here in D. E. Z. undoubtedly must be understood to apply to correct behaviour during discussions in the houses of study.

*And give thought to answer with words according to the subject matter...* Cf. M'Abot. V,7 and parallels. See D. E. Z. VII,1. See idem XI,25ff. Asking questions and adequately answering questions in connection with the topic under discussion is also noted as a characteristic typical of the sages. Cf. the commentary in connection with D. E. Z., I,3. In connection with the order in which questions must be answered, cf. the commentary to and parallels on D. E. Z. XI 25ff.; cf. D. E. Z. III,16 and D. E. Z. VII,1. Pupils of scholars must answer questions in the same order in which they have been asked. The answer must be to the point and deal with the subject of the question.

6. *And admit the truth...* Cf. M'Abot V,7 and parallels. See D. E. Z., VII,1 and idem D. E. Z. XI,25 ff. Acknowledging the truth is mentioned in M'Abot. l.c. as a typical characteristic of the sages. It is evident from the parallels that this rule belongs to those rules concerning behaviour in the house of study. Observation of these rules is esteemed essential for the gaining of knowledge. One is not to be ashamed to admit that he has not heard of a certain tradition before or that he has made an error in an argument. With regard to the various ways in which the rule is associated with Scripture in the parallels, see the commentary to D. E. Z. XI,34. Lev. 10:20 is especially important in this respect, with Moses put forth as an example.

**And do not speak before somebody who is greater ...** Cf. M'Abot V,7 and parallels. See D. E. Z., VII,1 and see D. E. Z., XI,25 ff. Not speaking before someone in one's presence greater than oneself was typical of the sages. For further explanations, see the commentary to D. E. Z., XI,30.

7. **If you desire to study, you should not say regarding what you have not heart of: 'I have heart'. And if one asks you a question regarding a matter and you are not well versed in it, you must not feel ashamed to say: 'I do not know', and if one is teaching you and you have not heart of it, you must not be ashamed to say: 'I have not heart of it, teach it to me'. And you should not look up to yourself by saying: 'I have not heart of it'.**

7. *If you desire to study ...* See M'Abot V,7 and parallels. See D. E. Z., VII,1. and D. E. Z. XI,25. Being honest and admitting that one has not heard of a certain tradition before is cited in M'Abot l.c. as a feature typical of the sages.

One is not to be ashamed of admitting that he is unfamiliar with a certain tradition and asking questions. Should others ask a question about such a tradition, one (even a teacher before students) should not be ashamed to say 'I have not heard of any tradition about that.' Cf. W. Bacher, *J. Q. R.*, XX (1908), p. 583, where he cites the example of Rabbi 'Eli'ezer's answer to a halakhic question put to him: 'I have not heard of that.' Cf. MNeg. IX,3; MNeg. XI,7; TbPes.38b; and TosJeb. III (end); cf. also TbJoma 66b and TbSuk. 27b. Note that Rabbi 'Eli'ezer's statement testifies to his good practise of not passing a tradition in the name of his teacher when he himself had not actually heard of the tradition.

The content of this statement in D. E. Z. is based in the milieu of the house of study and reflects a typical practise of the sages. The next line ('Do not yourself the favour of saying: ' I have not heart of that.') does not appear in most of the manuscripts of D. E. Z., and does not appear in M'Abot l.c. and parallels. In the commentaries, however, it is suggested that the addition should read: 'Do not yourself the favour of saying: "I have heard of that"', with the negation particle omitted. Cf., e.g., A. J. Tawrogi, *Derech Erez Sutta*, p. 10, with the reading: 'Und lass die Eigenliebe dich nicht verleiten zu sagen: "Ich habe es verstanden."' Cf. also J. Harburger, *Massekhet Derech Erez Sutta*, p. 21 and cf. the version of M. Ginsberg in *The Minor Tractates of the Talmud*, ed. A. Cohen, II, p. 571: 'And do not pretend to yourself: "I understood it."' It is possible, however, that the addition can be retained in the form transmitted by the basis manuscript of D. E. Z. This addition can then be viewed as a later mitigation of the preceding text. One should definitely admit one's ignorance but not use it, so to say, to one's own advantage. One might say: 'I have not heard of it' so as to avoid having the contribute to a difficult halakhic discussion, others must then answer in a difficult discussion. In such a case, one makes it too easy for himself, which also results in no progress in the learning process.

### 8. Perform deeds for the sake of performing (the deeds) themselves, and speak about them for their own sake, and make not a wreath with which to make yourself great and not a mattock with which to chop (other reading: with which to make a living).

This statement is ascribed in TbNed. 62a to Rabbi 'Eli'ezer the son of Rabbi Tzadoq (an elaboration on the statement attributed in M'Abot IV,5 to Rabbi Tzadoq). One finds both here in D. E. Z. and in TbNed. l.c. two readings: 'le-shem pe'ulatam' (for the sake of doing the deeds themselves) and 'le-shem po'alam' (for the sake of their Maker, i.e. for the sake of Heaven), both readings are possibly derived from 'le-shem Po'olam' (for the sake of doing it).

*Rosh* and *Ran* on TbNed. 62b read 'le-shem po'alam' to mean 'in the name of the Holy One, Who made them'. Cf. also the different readings in Siphrei, 'Eqeb, pisqa 48 (ed. L. Finkelstein, p. 114) and Jalq, 'Eqeb, r. 873 : 'le-shem p""lam' (ed. Saloniki: 'le-shem po'alam'). The basis manuscript here in D. E. reads 'le-shem pe'ulatan', do things for the sake of doing them. Cf, the statement of Ben 'Azzai in M'Abot IV,2: 'Because the one mitzwah brings with it another one, because the produce of a mitzwah is a mitzwah and the produce of a sin is a sin.'

Cf. D. E. Z. II,l in connection with the idea of doing the 'mitzwot' for the sake of Heaven.

*and speak of them for their own sake*... 'Them' possibly refers to words of Torah. In M'Abot IV,5 Rabbi Tzadoq's statement is as follows: 'Do not make a crown of them with which to adorn yourself or a spade with which to dig.' It is remarkable that the word 'them' is not clarified in that statement either. W. Bacher, *Die Agada der Tannaiten*, p. 48, note 3, suggests that the statement has been shortened and that it applies to the words of the Torah. See, however, Ch. Taylor, *Sayings of the Jewish Fathers*, repr. 1970, p. 68; Ch. Taylor interprets Rabbi Tzadoq's statement as forbiddance to make pupils a crown. See J. Harburger, *Derech Erez Sutta*, p. 21. J. Harburger claims that 'speak of *them* for their own sake' in D.E.Z. h.l. applies to good deeds. This is a plausible explanation that is confirmed by the readings in the manuscripts ('le-dabber bahem be-shemam' and 'le-dabber bahem be-shebah'). This interpretation also avoids the problem that the first part of the statement deals with good deeds and that after 'and speak about them' the subject is no longer 'good deeds' but 'words of Torah'.

One should speak of good deeds (and words of Torah) for their own sake, and not in order to adorn oneself. One should not do good deeds with a view to gaining respect and one should not study only to display one's knowledge and to gain attention. One should also not use good deeds (and study) as a spade with which to dig (into the ground) [another version: from which to eat]. In the commentary in Mas. Kal. Rab. IV (ed. Higger, p. 255), this is correctly associated with the forbiddance to earn one's living from the study of the Torah. A teacher is allowed to accept money only for his role in taking care of children but not for giving instruction. See notes to D.E.Z. IV,3.

A teacher is also not supposed to do good deeds with an eye to honour and personal gain. Love is supposed to be the motivating force behind studying as well as behaving. See especially I.B.H. Abram, *Joodse Traditie als Permanent Leren*, Waddinxveen 1980, pp. 223–228; see also sources mentioned there in connection with studying for the the sake of the Torah itself.

**9. Learn to take on you all the words of the Torah in affliction and do not resent an insult directed to you.**
**10. There is an propitious reckoning and a good paying, and there is assurance and there is truth.**

*Learn to take* ... A very similar statement is ascribed to Rabbi Jehudah ben Teima in the parallel in A.R.N. [a], XLI (67a). The statement there, however, reads: 'Learn to accept affliction and disregard an insult directed to you.' In that statement there is only mention of accepting pain and insult, not of studying the Torah. In TbShab. 88b, as in A.R.N. l.c., the same is also true. The statement of Rabbi Jehudah ben Teima here in D.E.Z. has probably undergone reinterpretation, resulting in the establishment of a special connection between tolerating suffering, and studying and practising the Torah.

Like the preceding statements in this chapter, this statement belongs to the milieu of Pereq Qinjan Torah (the sixth chapter of M'Abot) and is referred to for conditions necessary for successful study of the Torah. Special emphasis is placed on the connection between study and practise. In M'Abot VI,5 (and parallels) 'acceptance of suffering' is mentioned along with 'being tolerating and forgiving' ("alub") among the forty eight necessities for the study of the Torah.

In M'Abot VI,4 'a life of pain' is mentioned as a prerequisite for studying Torah and is defined as an ascetic way of life requiring little consumption of

food and drink, little sleep and few bodily pleasures. See parallels that use the expression 'to kill oneself for the sake of the words of the Torah.' Scripture quotations that support this include Num.19:14 and Hiob 28:13. Much eating and drinking causes drowsiness, and if one cannot study Torah day and night, the knowledge of the Torah will not be retained. Cf. among others, S. E. Z. XIV (ed. M. Friedmann, p. 64) and *Reshit Hokhmah*, Sha'ar Qedushah, VI-I. Cf. also the interpretation that differs from the above explanation in which this statement is read as: 'Learn to take on you words of the Torah *even* in time of affliction.' Cf., among others, M. Higger, *Massekhtot Derekh 'Eretz*, p. 37; and M. Ginsberg, translation in *The Minor Tractates of the Talmud*, ed. A. Cohen, II, p. 571. This interpretation, however, is not supported by the manuscripts.

*There is a propitious reckoning...* There is a beautiful reckoning and a good payment ('par'on tob') and there is assurance and there is truth. Be forgiving because you will be forgiven, and reparation will be made to you for past suffering, for your deeds will be considered and payment will be made for the suffering you have endured. From this arise security and truth. The words used here can be best explained in connection with the directly preceding statement

The basis manuscript, however, reads 'heshbon japheh u-pereq tob'. The term 'pereq tob' refers to an unblemished youth. See the notes to D. E. Z. I,10a. One must thus translate as follows: 'A well-ordered moral stock-taking ('heshbon japheh') and a virtuous adolescence ('pereq tob'); there is security and there is truth.' In D. E. Z. I,10a a virtuous youth is also mentioned in direct association with love for the Torah! See D. E. Z. II,11. In Mas. Kal. Rab. V (ed. M. Higger, p. 256), one finds the reading 'heshbon japheh u-pereq tob' explained as 'a good reputation and a virtuous adolescence'. The continuation of the manuscript-reading 'a man on whom one can depend and a man of truth' ['ish heshbon we-'ish 'emet'; in stead of 'we-jesh heshbon...'] also fits here. See also S. Krauss in: *R. E. J.*, XXXVII (1898), p. 52, where 'pereq' is given the peculiar meaning of 'study': 'On il a une belle conduite et un science profonde, il y a confiance et la verité.' Cf. also the commentary of S. Krauss in connection with D. E. Z., I,10a, mentioned in our commentary on that passage.

Because of the concurrence of the preceding context, however, one may assume that the reading 'pereq tob' (a virtuous adolescence) should actually be 'par'on tob' (a good payment, a good reward, or a good compensation). Most commentators and old editions reed 'a good payment'. Cf., e.g. *Derekh 'Eretz* , ed. Riva di Tarento; ed. J. D. Azulai (*Kikkar le-'Adon*), ed. A. J. Tawrogi and cf. ed. M. Higger and ed. D. Sperber. Cf. also *Menorat ha-Ma'or* of Al-Nakawa (ed. H. G. Enelow, IV, p. 402) and *Reshit Hokhmah*, Derekh 'Eretz, sha'ar I, and J. Naumburg in *Nahalat Ja'aqob* D. E. Z. a.l. The words 'a beautiful reckoning and a good paying' can in this case mean that one must be tolerant of other's insults because payment ('par'on') will be promptly made in compensation for the past. One can be certain ('habtahah') about that and rest assured that justice will finally be done to the truth ('"emet') of what has been suffered in silence. This explanation does justice to both the immediate context as well as the descriptive wording without verbs which are in the imperative mode! The notion of recompense for a forgiving disposition through Heaven is very old. Cf. *Seph. Ben Sira* 27:30 – 28,7; A.R.N. [b], XXVI (27a) and A.R.N. [a], XXVI (32b); Mat. 6:12; 6:14–15; 18:34–35; Luke 6:37–38; 9:4; and other sources. It is notable that such sources contain the affirmation that God will reward and forgive one who forgives his fellow man and the warning that God will withhold forgiveness from one who does not forgive to his fellow man. See also D. Flusser, in: *H. T. R.*, LXI (1986), pp. 107–127. A very closely related statement in Pereq Qinjan Torah (see M'Abot VI,4) appears to confirm the above-given explanation. Parallel to the context here in D. E. Z. II, that statement contains a call to study words of the Torah in a life of pain, privation and sobriety, and an admonition not to do so with the intention of gaining honour (cf. D. E. Z. II,8). This is then followed by an assurance of God's reward in the future: 'And your Employer is faithful to pay you reward of your work.' Cf. M'Abot II,16.

Other plausible explanations; In *Nahalat Ja'aqob* on D. E. Z. l.c. the reading 'a beautiful reckoning and a good payment' is connected with an explanation in *Reshit Hokhmah* (Derekh 'Eretz, Sha'ar I, and derived from *Menorat ha-Ma'or* of Al-Nakawa [see ed. H. G. Enelow, IV, p. 402]). The reading is interpreted as a description of correct behaviour for sages when conducting financial transactions. Such behaviour involves making calculations favourable for the other person ('a beautiful reckoning') and being willing to pay more than one has actually been charged ('a good payment').

## 11. Love the Torah and honour the Torah, love righteous deeds, love reproves, love rectitude [you should not run after honour and you should not be presumptuous in decisions].

In connection with the sequence of love for the Torah and fear of the Torah, see the remarks to D. E. Z. II,1 and D. E. Z. I,10b. The emphasis is unmistakable placed on love over fear here in D. E. Z. Note the addition in a large number of manuscripts: 'Love people and respect them.' This addition was probably derived from *Pereq Qinjan Torah*. See M'Abot VI,1: 'Rabbi Me'ir said: "Anyone who occupies himself with the Torah for the sake of the Torah itself... is called... a lover of God, a lover of people."' Cf. also M'Abot VI,6: 'A lover of God, a lover of people, a lover of righteous deeds, a lover of reproof and a lover of justice...' Cf. the context here in D. E. Z.

As with the other statements in this chapter of D. E. Z., there is a direct connection here with the forty eight characteristics and conditions necessary for the study of the Torah, mentioned in M'Abot. VI,5 and parallels. The explicit connection between love for God and love for people, as in the places mentioned in Pereq Qinjan Torah from which the addition in the manuscripts was derived, is especially typical of an specific Tannaitic milieu. See D. Flusser, l.c., in reference to Jub. 36:4−8,; Mark 12:28−34; Luke 10:25−28; and *Seph. Pitron Torah*, ed. E. E. Urbach, Jerusalem 1978, p. 79 ff.

... *love righteous deeds, love reproves* ... Note again the direct relationship with the listing of the forty eight conditions for the study of the Torah in M'Abot VI,6 and parallels. One again finds additions in the manuscripts that have been derived from M'Abot VI,6: 'love rectitude ... and do not pursue honour and do not be presumptuous in making decisions.' Cf. especially S. E. Z XVII (ed. M. Friedmann, pp. 18−19) and Mas. Kal. Rab. VIII. In connection with the addition 'we-lo tagis da'atkha be-hora'ah' ('and be not presumptuous in making decisions') in the manuscripts of D. E. Z., see a statement of Rabbi Jishma'el the son of Rabbi José in M'Abot.IV,7: 'He is presumptuous in making decisions (i. e. who makes legal decisions lightly) is a fool, godless, and is arrogant.' See also M'Abot VI,6; a sage may not be satisfied with a quickly-made decision. A good scholar and judge holds justice dear and takes no pleasure in indifferent or frivolous decisions, and condemns only with the greatest reluctance. Note the consequent text in M'Abot.VI,6.

On the basis of the parallels mentioned here in M'Abot etc. the reading 'tzedaqot' here in D. E. Z. is preferable to the reading 'tzaddiqim'. See manuscripts and cf. ed. Riva di Tarento and ed. A. J. Tawrogi.

## 12. And know the difference between to day and tomorrow, in connection to what is yours and to what is not yours [what is yours is (in reality) not yours], as for what is [not] yours, how you can regard it as yours?

We give the following reconstruction: 'And know the difference between today and tomorrow, in connection to what is yours and what is not yours; [what is yours is not yours,] and as for what is [not] yours, how you can regard it as yours.?' This reconstruction is based on the manuscripts. Paraphrased the reconstruction is as follows: Know that there may be a difference between today and tomorrow with regard to your possessions and those of another.; i. e. today you are rich and another poor, tomorrow someone else may be rich and you poor. What appears to be yours really is not yours at all; i. e., everything belongs to God, and it is His prerogative to distribute things among people differently tomorrow than today. If something that supposedly is yours is not really yours, why would you possess something that is not yours anyway? The basis manuscript concludes: 'As for what is yours, how you can regard it as yours?' One can explain this to mean: How can you regard anything at all as your possession? The intention is the same. One has no quarantined rights of possession. See also the manuscripts version with another (and probably secondary) concluding reading: 'What is yours is not yours. Of him who regards what is not his as his own, Scripture declares: "Woe to him that increases that which is not his" (Hab. 2:6).' The gathering of possession is very relative and is not essential for human existence. Cf. also D. E. Z. I,2. Compare with the reading in the basis manuscript the wording in a statement by Hillel in M'Abot I,14, which also ends with a rhetorical question. See A. Büchler, *Types of Jewish Palestinian Piety*, p. 38, note 3. A. Büchler refers to the statement in A. R. N. [b], XXVII (28a): 'Since which I possess is not mine, what for I require that which belongs to others.'

**13. Accustom yourself to end (your words) with goodness (or: accustom yourself to complete the good).**
**14. (Be) meek and beloved [by all] and humble of spirit [before all] and gentle of speech.**
   **[Be like a leather bottle not split open, that is not opened to let in the wind and (be) like the lower threshold on which every one treads.]**

13. *Accustom yourself to end with goodness* — an other interpretation of the same words 'accustom yourself to be perfect in goodness' and 'accustom yourself to complete (a) good (activity).'
   In an other way: Accustom yourself to end your activities with goodness and to complete a deal; end your words with good, i. e. with comforting expressions; accustom yourself to complete a good activity. Cf. also M. Ginsberg in: *The Minor Tractates of the Talmud*, ed. A. Cohen, II, p. 572.) The last interpretation means that one should not only begin a good deed but also complete it. A good deed is considered to the credit of the doer only if the doer completes that deed. Cf. Ber. Rab. LXXXV,3; TbSot. 13b and cf. other sources. The manuscript-reading 'gamur be-tobah' is not improbable in the sense of 'Strive to be perfect in doing good deeds.' Cf. the reading 'gomer be-tobah' in D. E. Z. ed. Riva di Tarento. Cf. D. E. Z. ed. A. J. Tawrogi, p. 13.
   14. *Meek and beloved...* See the commentary to D. E. Z. I,1. See the manuscripts with additions related to D. E. Z. I,4 and I,5.

**15. Be submissive to the superior and yielding to conscription (into public service; i. e. forced labour), of cheerful appearance and broad shouldered.**

See M'Abot III,12, where one finds the same wording ascribed to Rabbi Jishma'el. Cf. there the commentaries of, among others, Rashi, Rabbenu Jonah, Me'iri and Duran (Magen 'Abot). Cf. M'Abot, ed. Ch. Albeck. See especially the explanation of this statement from D. E. in Mas. Kal. Rab. IV (ed. M. Higger, p. 257), where the statement is interpreted as a compliant attitude toward the (Roman) authorities and the obligations imposed by them.
   'Qal le-Rosh' — obeying to the superior. In this instance, the word 'qal' can mean 'humble' as well as 'fast' and 'obliging'. Cf. also Rashi and Rambam in regard to M'Abot III,12.

*Nuach le-tishhoret* (*yielding to conscription*) — this similarly refers to a calm, unresisting attitude toward the 'tishhoret' ('angaria'), forced labour by the state. Cf. the explanation in Mas. Kal. Rab. l.c. Rashi on M'Abot III,12 associates the Term 'tishhoret' with 'shehwar', 'towncaptain' (cf. TbB.B. 47a) and explains it as 'the city treasurer', in reference to the Targum Onkelos on Num. 6:15, where the verb 'shahar' is used to refer to a fine ('to take away'). It is grammatically possible to derive 'tishhoret' from 'shehar': to declare a thing or a man free, to declare something as ownerless property, to confiscate, to press into public service. Cf. also Targum on I Sam. 12:3 and see M. Jastrow, *Dictionary*, II, p. 1551, sub 'shehar IV'. Note also the meaning of 'shehar' as to choose, to select, to inquire. One may understand the meaning of 'tishhoret' in the sense of conscription, the search for and the selection of workers. Along with the explanation in Mas. Kal. Rab. l.c., a tradition in S.E.R. I (ed. M. Friedmann, p. 5) confirms the interpretation of 'tishhoret' as forced labour. Cf. also TbBer.56a and Rashi, commentary on Gen. 15:18; Siphrei Deb., § 6; cf. Me'iri on M'Abot III,12; cf. Abrabanel in commentary on M'Abot l.c.

The derivation of 'tishhoret' from 'shahor' (black) provides a completely different meaning in the sense of 'those whose hair is still black', referring to youth. See commentaries to M'Abot III,12, such as those of Duran, Me'iri, Bertinoro and Abrabanel. Cf. Ch.Taylor, *Sayings of the Jewish fathers*, repr-.Jerusalem 1970, pp. 66−67; cf. the use of the term in, among others, 'Eikh. Rab. I,2 and 'Eikh. Rab. II,2; Cf. the expression 'tinnatzel mi-mal'akh ha-tishhoret' in D.E.Z. IX,7. One explanation here in D.E.Z.II is: Be obliging to the chief, i.e., the authority (cf. Rambam in reference to M'Abot l.c. ''al toqir naphshekha lo' (do not be haughty to him), and just be calm, i.e.self-assured and dignified, toward youth (cf., among others, Rashi, Rambam, Rabbenu Jonah, Bertinoro and Abrabanel on M'Abot III,12). Cf. also the explanation in *Nahalat Ja'aqob* on D.E.Z. h.l.: 'Be humble toward everyone, even toward a young person whose hair is still black.' See also the explanations in which 'tishhoret' is interpreted as age and adulthood. Cf. Rashi and Abrabanel on M'Abot III,12. And with this yields the following meaning: Be humble toward those in higher positions and toward older people.

The choice ultimately falls on the explanation that interprets the statement here in D.E. as call for a patient and tolerant attitude toward higher authorities and toward conscription into forced labour. This concurs with the explanation in Mas. Kal. Rab. l.c. It also connects with the text directly following in D.E.Z.: ... 'of cheerful appearance and broad shouldered', i.e., willing to bear burdens put upon one. See also the interpretation of the term 'ba'alei ''abtahah' (men of trust) in connection with the commentary on D.E.R. II,22!

*... of cheerful appearance ...* These words must be explained in direct association with a closely related statement by Rabbi Jishma'el in M'Abot 3,12: 'Be humble toward an authority... and receive everyone with joy.' Cf. also a

statement in M'Abot I,15, ascribed to Shammai: 'And receive everyone with a friendly and pleasant face.' Note further the use of the term 'To'ar tob' in the above-mentioned sentence in Shir ha-Shir. Rab. I,10 and other sources. See the manuscripts here in D. E. Z. with another reading: 'soher tob', a good business-man (also explained to mean someone who get along well with others). See also the reading 'shoher tob' (striving for the good, seeking good). The correspond-ence with M'Abot III,12 makes an explanation in the sense of 'cheerful appear-ance' more plausible.

... *and broad-shouldered* — This term does not appear in the closely related statement of Rabbi Jishma'el in M'Abot III,12 or in the parallel in Mas. Kal. Rab. IV (ed. M. Higger, p. 257). The term also does not appear in a number of manuscripts of D. E. Z. Ed. Riva di Tarento does not read 'we-rohab keteph' (and broad-shouldered) but 'we-rohab keseph' (and generous with money). Cf. also M. Higger in *Massekhtot Derekh 'Eretz*, p. 74. M. Higger reads 'we-rohab keseph' and gives the variant 'we-rewwah keseph' on the basis of Ms. New York, *J. T. S.* (cat. E. N. Adler) no. 1909 (we, however, read that as 'we-rewwah keteph') and the reading 'we-rewwah keseph' on the basis of Ms. Epstein (see M. Higger, o.c.,Introduction, p. 46). See A. J. Tawrogi, *Derech Erez Sutta*, Königsberg, p. 13, with the reading 'we-rewwah keseph' in refer-ence to a Ms. from the Codex Halberstam.

The reading 'and broad-shouldered' is to be preferred in connection with the interpretation already chosen for the context. The directive to be submissive to the superior and to yield to conscription into forced labour means that one should not seek confrontation with the authorities and that one should treat everyone in a friendly way and be ready to accept burdens without resistance.

**16. Keep aloof from that which leads to transgression, keep aloof from everything hideous and from what even seems hideous.**
**17. Shudder from committing a minor transgression, lest it leads you to commit a major transgression. Hurry to (perform) a minor precept, for this will lead you to (perform) a major precept**.

For further explanation, see the commentary to D. E. Z., I,13. The words 'harhek' and 'le-ki'ur' are missing in some manuscripts. The statement appears in nearly identical form in the closely related tradition in A. R. N. [a], II (5a), in connection with measures designed to prevent too-close contact with a men-struating woman or the wife of another man.

*Shudder from committing a minor transgression* ... Compare the commen-tary to D. E. Z. I,13. The wording concurs with the tradition in A. R. N. (a), l.c. There is also a strong agreement in the wording and thoughts in a statement by Ben 'Azzai in M'Abot IV,2 (and parallels): 'Ben 'Azzai said: "Run to do even a slight precept and flee from transgression; for a precept draws a precept in its train and a transgression draws a transgression in its train; for the recompense of a precept is a precept and the recompense of a transgression is a transgression."'

This reflects the psychological insight on the part of the rabbis that every transgression one commits weakens one's morale and that every good dead done strengthens one's moral. The lesser one's transgressions, the less likely one is to commit transgressions. A minor transgression precipitates a change in mentality that makes one liable to commit more major transgressions. Likewise, doing good deeds spurs one on to do more good deeds. With respect to the special meaning of the expression 'het ha-qal' (minor transgression) see the commentary to D. E. Z. I,13. Among the pious, the term 'minor transgression' and 'minor precept' ('mitzwah qallah') also referred to actions that were not generally forbidden but which were considered, among the more sensitive, to be related to sin or to lead one to commit sin. See especially D. Flusser, *Jahadut u-Meqorot ha-Notzrut*, pp. 232−233.

See the addition in the manuscripts: *'jehi habirekha mar'atkha'*, *'your neighbour may be your mirror [resemblance].'* In this connection, see the explanation in Mas. Kal. Rab. IV (ed. N. N. Coronel, 10b; ed. M. Higger, p. 264): 'When you speak about your fellow when he is not present, let his image always be before your eyes.' The same wording could also be interpreted here as 'your looking'. Cf. e. g., the use of 'mar'eh' in TbJoma 74b ('the pleasure of looking at one's wife'). Speak only about another person as if he is present. The preference here falls on the reading 'mar'ah', mirror. The interpretation thus is: 'Let your fellow be your mirror, for when you look at him you look at yourself.' Cf. Waj. Rab. XXXIV,14: 'Bar Kappara said: "Consider (see) his flesh as your flesh."' This interpretation connects the addition with what follows in the text: 'Let the honour of your neighbour be as dear to you as your own.' This means that one should treat his neighbour as he would himself, for he is like oneself, one's image. This direct connection with the context is also assumed in the version in Mas. Kal. Rab. IV, ed. M. Higger, p. 246. The explanation given here in D. E. Z. is directly connected to that given in the explanation of Lev. 19:18 ('love your neighbour as yourself'), according to which 'kamokha' (as yourself) modifies not 'love' but 'your neighbour'. Love your neighbour, as yourself, for he is like you, he is your image. See D. Flusser, in: *H. T.R.*, LXI (1968), pp. 107−127 (see especially p. 116); M. Buber in *A. S. T. I.*, IV (1965), pp. 13−17. H. Cohen, *Der Nächste*, Berlin 1935, p. 17, in reference to Naftali Herz Wessely and his translation: 'Liebe deinen Nächsten, er ist wie du.' Cf. also R. Rosenzweig, *Solidarität mit den Leidenden*, Berlin 1978, p. 136, note c. See also the commentary *Japheh To'ar* Ber. Rab. XXIV,7.

The concept of one's neighbour as one's equal and image is old. Cf., e.g., *Seph. Ben Sira* 27:30 − 28:7; cf. the statement of Hanina the observer of the priests, in A. R. N. [b], XXVI (27a) and cf. the statement of Bar Kappara in Waj. Rab. XXIV,14. Cf. especially A. R. N. [a], XVI (32b), where the words ''Ani ha-Shem' after the commandment about love in Lev. 19:18 are interpreted as: 'I have made him (just like you).' The concept of God's uniqueness and the concept of man as 'image of God' are the background of the notion of equality among people and the duty to respect and love them as oneself.

D. Sperber, *Massekhet Derekh 'Eretz*, p. 28, suggests yet another explanation: Let another be your image and mirror, i. e., let your image of yourself and your selfesteem depend on the reactions of others toward you. This explanation, however, bears a weaker connection to its immediate context.

**18. Let the honour of your neighbour be as dear to you as your own. And show respect to every human being.**

This statement, given anonymously here, is ascribed in M'Abot II,10 to Rabbi 'Eli'ezer. In one manuscript in D. E. Z. and in the reading of Mas. Kal. Rab., IV, ed. M. Higger, p. 264, one finds the statement: 'Let the money of your neighbour be as dear to you as your own.' This statement, too, was borrowed from M'Abot, where it is ascribed to Rabbi José. See also Lev. 19:18. The unusual form 'we-'ahabta *le*-re'akha' (literally: 'You will love *for* your neighbour') is interpreted to mean: You should wish *for* your neighbour what you would wish *for* yourself, and you should not wish *for* your neighbour what you would not wish *for* yourself. Cf. also TbShab. 31a; Ber. Rab. XXIV,7 and A. R. N. [b], XXVI (27a); cf. also the Targum Pseudo-Jon. on Lev. 19:18. See Ramban on Lev. 19:18. Both the honour and money of one's neighbour deserve to be loved as one's own honour and money. The essential thought here is that everyone is equal as an image of God. (See A. R. N. [a], XVI [32a]: 'Love your neighbour as yourself, for I the Lord have made him.' Cf. also a statement by Rabbi 'El'azar ben Shamua in M'Abot IV,12 in which respect for one's neighbour (student, college and teacher) is associated with respect for Heaven. Cf. also the following text here in D. E. Z.: 'And show respect to all men.' This can be interpreted as extension of the basic notion of the equality of all people because of their likeness to God as creation.

**19. Love the 'perhaps' and hate the 'so what'.**

See the entire different reading in Mas. Kal. Rab. l.c.: 'Love the one who reprimands you and hate the one who praises you.' It must be said that a reading such as the one in Mas. Kal. Rab. makes the associative connection with the subsequent text more understandable. A very large number of manuscripts in D. E. Z. have left out this statement (possible for editorial reasons, given that this same statement appears in D. E. Z. I,12; see the commentary there).

**20. Do not say: 'I will flatter this one that he will feed me', or 'I will flatter that one that he will give me to drink', or 'I will flatter this one that he may clothe me', or 'I will flatter that one that he may give me shelter'.**

A position of material independence, and especially the willing acceptance of such a position, deprives one of his spiritual independence, which means that one will not treat his benefactor objectively.

**21.  It is better to be ashamed of yourself than be put to shame by others.**
**22.  Let not your lips put you to shame and let not your mouth degrade you and let not your tongue cause you to be esteemed lightly and let not your teeth put you to shame and do not bow down to your words.**

21. *It is better to be ashamed of yourself* ... The theme in this statement as well as in its context is the willingness to be corrected by others. It is better to discover his own mistakes to improve his behaviour than to have to be corrected. This statement appears to have been borrowed from a proverb. A similar statement, ascribed to Rabbi 'Abba from Caesarea (or rather Rabbi 'Ada from Caesarea , an Amora of the third generation and pupil of Rabbi Johanan) is found in the context of TbTa'an 15b: 'One who is humiliated by himself is not like one who is humiliated by others.' TbTa'an. contains the suggestion to the Nasi and the 'Ab Beit Din that they should strew ash over their own head because it is better than letting someone else do so; cf. TjTa'an. II,1 [65a]. In the parallel in TosTa'an. (ed. S. Lieberman, p. 325) there appears a differently worded saying that calls people to repent: 'My sons, one should be shamed by his neighbour and not by his deeds. It is better that one should be shamed by his neighbour...' It is much better to admit one's mistakes and to let oneself be reproached than to make mistakes and deny and conceal them until they eventually come to light, only to make the shame yet greater. See S. Lieberman, *Tosephta ki-Pheshutah*, V, p. 1072.

See TbSanh. 42a: 'There is no comparison between declaring one's own disgrace and having another declare it.'

22. *Let not your lips put you to shame* ... A sage must speak in such a manner, that others respect him. The conclusion of the above-statement ... *do not bow down to your words*, can be interpreted in different manners. It is better for one to be careful with one's statements so that one need not retract statements and pardon himself. One should not make himself dependant on his words by making frivolous promises that one fulfils reluctantly or cannot fulfil at all, for this leads to shame. Words should not become idols to which one bows, i. e., one should not make them absolute and one should correct them as necessary. See *Nahalat Ja'aqob* on D. E. Z., h.l.

**23.  And if you desire to be attached to the love of a fellow man, concern yourself with his welfare.**

A most important parallel to this statement is A. R. N. [b], XXVI (26b), where the statement is introduced with: 'In the *scroll of the Hasidim*, it is said ...' (see, however, M'Abot, ed. L. Finkelstein, p. 112, 1.5, where is read 'harisim' in stead of 'hasidim'). From this it is apparent that there is a connection between statements from D. E. Z., I (part of 'Jir'at Het') and the milieu of the Hasidim. Moreover, it is also apparent that writings circulated among the Early Hasidim, the contents of which were related to the tractates of *Derekh 'Eretz*. In other words, the parallel A. R. N. [b] supports the assumption that old sections of D. E. Z., such as D. E. Z. Chapters I−II, belong to the milieu of the Hasidim!! See Siphrei, 'Eqeb, pisqa 48 (ed. L. Finkelstein, p. 112), where a tradition from the *Megillat Hasidim* is mentioned that possibly served as an explanation of Prov. 23:5, a verse that is also explained in D. E. Z. IV. Cf. also M. Higger, *Massekhtot Derekh 'Eretz*, introduction, p. 35, in connection with the tradition of the 'Early Hasidim'. See also S. Safrai, in: *J. J. S.*, XVI (1965), p. 15 ff. Typical of the milieu of the Hasidim was an unusually strong emphasis on respect for the person and goods of a fellow, based on the relationship of every person to God. Reference was already made in the preceding commentary to Lev. 19:18, where it is stated that it is expressive of love for one's neighbour to defend his rights and interests at least as strongly as one would his own. See Ramban in his commentary to Lev. 19:18: 'You shall love *for* him as yourself, that is to say, love *for* him the same goods as you love *for* yourself.' See the explanation in the gemara of Mas. Kal. Rab. IV, ed. M. Higger, p. 258: 'For it is written "Love your neighbour as yourself", through love for your neighbour, he is like you.' This means that if one wishes to be beloved by others, then he must first love others.

24. **And if you desire to keep aloof from failure, go, give thought, be aware and consider its end (i. e. the result of an act).**
25. **Let your soul cling to the precepts, sharp your knowledge and meditate at her gates (i. e. at the gates of wisdom).**

24. *And if you desire to keep aloof from failure* ... Various explanations are possible in connection with the last word 'sopho' (*its end*). The end (of failure) may refer to the ultimate consequences and negative effect of a transgression for the committer of a transgression in This World. It may also refer to the ultimate reward or punishment in the World to Come. Cf. the statement in *Seph. Ben Sira*: 'In all your doings remember the end, then you will never do corruptly.' In this case, however, "aharit' (the end) refers to death. Cf. *Seph. Ben Sira* 28:6 and *Seph. Ben Sira* 38:20 (ed. M. Z. Segal). This probably means that transgressions can result in early death. Cf. further M'Abot III,1 and D. E. R. III,1. Cf. also the statement of Rabbi Shim'on ben Natan'el in M'Abot II,9, according to whom the right way means anticipating the future, i. e., reflecting over the consequences of one's deeds beforehand. Rabbi Hidka is the authority in the parallel to this statement in D. E. Z. in Midr. ha-Gad. on Gen. 26:10 (ed. M. Margulies, p. 450). In D. E. Z. I,12 a closely related statement is

attributed to Rabbi Hidka: 'Love the "perhaps" ...', i.e., one should take into
account all possible effects of his deeds. Cf. also D.E.Z. II,19.

   25. *Let your soul cling to the precepts* ... One should cling to the precepts
like a man to his bride. Cf. TosJeb. VIII,7 and parallels. Cf. the reading in Mas.
Kal. Rab., ed. N.N. Coronel, 10a: 'attach yourself to the precepts, love your
soul, rejoice, sharpen your knowledge.' 'Shannen we-rannen' can be translated
as: sharpen your knowledge and rejoice [at her gates]. The verb 'ranan' means:
to meditate or to speak in a thoughtful manner as well as rejoice. Cf. the use of
this word in Ps. 51:16; Targ. Ps. 37:30; Targ. Ps. 1:2; Targ. Ps. 39:4; Targ. Prov.
15:28, and elsewhere. Cf. M. Jastrow, *Dictionary*, II, p. 1484: sub 'ran'. There
are deviating readings in the manuscripts in D.E.Z., such as 'shekhon we-
rannen' (dwell and meditate [rejoice]) and cf. G.J. Lipschütz, (*Regel Jeshara*)
a.l. 'shekhon we-reba'' (dwell and couch [at her gates] [i.e. the gates of the
academy]). It is possible that 'her gates' has only a figurative meaning. Cf. the
figurative meaning of waiting by the gates of wisdom in Prov. 8:34: 'Happy is
the man who listens to me, watching daily at my gates, waiting by my doors.' Cf.
also *Seph. Ben Sira* 14:20: 'Happy is the man, that meditates on wisdom... and
hearkens at her doors, who encamps round about her house...'
   A number of commentators, however, suggest that 'bi-pherateiha' (on its
aspects [details]) be read in stead of 'bi-phetaheiha' (at her gates). So they read:
'Sharpen your knowledge and meditate on its various aspects.' Cf. the Gaon of
Vilna on D.E.Z. a.l., in: ed. J.E. Landa; M. Higger, *Massekhtot Derekh
'Eretz*, p. 39; and M. Ginsberg in *The Minor Tractates of the Talmud*, ed.
A. Cohen, II, p. 573. The manuscripts, however, do not read 'bi-pherateiha'!

**26. If you have done much good, let it seem little in your eyes; and do not
say: 'I did good with my own (money)', but (say) 'From the good that one
did to me'. You (rather) should offer thanks that one cared for you and did
good to you! If a little good was done to you, let it seem much in your eyes
and do not say: 'Good was done to me because of my worthy acts', but say
'Good was done to me because of my unworthy acts'. For it is said: 'And He
repays them that hate Him to their face (i.e. immediately), to destroy them
(i.e. in the World to Come)' (Dt. 7:10).
If you did a little wrong, let it seem much in your eyes and say: ' Woe to me,
for I have sinned, woe to me that I have been made a stumbling-block (to
others).'
   But when much wrong is done to you, let it seem little in your eyes and
say: 'Only a little of my debts have I payed, I deserve (to be punished) much
more.'**

*If you have done much good...* One finds a strongly similar statement in A. R. N. [a], XLI (67a), ascribed to Rabbi Jehudah ben Teima. The version in A. R. N., l.c., is much shorter without Scripture quotations and deals exclusively with asymmetric relationship with one's fellow man. In D. E. Z. h.l. the Scripture quotations were added in and there is made a association with the relationship to God. It is possible that the far more extensive version in D. E. Z. with the addition of Scripture quotations is a further elaboration on the original shorter statement of Rabbi Jehudah ben Teima (whose statements appear anonymously scattered throughout the first chapters of D. E. Z.) in A. R. N. [a] l.c. This statement here in D. E. Z. is similarly worded in Midr. ha-Gad. on Gen. 26:10, but appears in connection with statements by Rabbi Hidka, with the addition of a digression over the quite different behaviour of 'Abimelekh.

A very similar statement, the source of which is unknown, also appears in Midr. ha-Gad. on Gen. 26:10, but in the name of Rabbi 'Eli'ezer. In that statement, the minimizing of one's many good deeds and the magnifying of one's bad deeds is cited as a characteristic of the righteous (ha-tzaddiqim) as opposed to the wicked (resha'im). The statement also concerns the asymmetric relationship with another in which his interests count more than one's own. Cf. The behaviour of the 'hasid' (the pious) is contrasted with the behaviour of the 'rasha'' (the wicked), cf. e.g. M'Abot V,10.11.13. The behaviour described here in D. E. Z. was typical of the milieu of the Hasidim, who placed heavier demands on themselves than on others. Here in D. E. Z. it is demanded that one put others higher than oneself. One must prize another's good deeds more than one's own. In addition to that there is the notion that one has no right to be treated well for what one has gained and that every shortcoming, however slight, must be considered reason for appropriate penance. If one is mistreated, one should bear in mind that it is not undeserved and that even worse treatment would be appropriate. It is never a profit if one does good deeds for others, for one can only give what one has received. Everything is owed to Heaven. Cf. D. E. Z. II,12 and D. E. Z., chap.I,2.

*And do not say: 'Good was done to me because of my worthy acts...'* The meaning of these words is based on an explanation of Dt. 7:10 that was current in the tradition that the wicked ('resha'im') are already rewarded in This World for the little good they have done and that only punishment awaits for them in the World to Come and nothing will impede their destruction. See the Targumim on Dt. 7:10; cf. the famous statement of Rabbi 'Aqiba in Mekh.de-R. Jishm., Jitro, par. 10 (ed. M. Friedmann, 72b); Siphrei, Wa-'Ethannan, pisqa 32 (ed. L. Finkelstein, p. 56; Midr. Tan. on Dt. 6:5; Tanh., Jitro, § 16 and other sources; Ber. Rab. XXXIII,1 (ed. J. Theodor / Ch.Albeck, p. 298); Waj. Rab. XXVII,1; A. R. N. [b], XLIV (62a); and parallels.

According to that tradition one must be happy with unpleasant things that have happened to him so that he can be sure of his reward in the World to Come. One must not rejoice about a life free of suffering considering that sins will then remain unrepented after his death. In the context of the tradition mentioned, there appears a statement in the name of Rabbi Me'ir, according to which the suffering that one undergoes is never equal to the sins he has committed. This notion concurs with the conclusion of the statement here in D. E. Z. Cf. Mekh. de-R. Jishm. l.c.; Siphrei, Wa-'Ethannan l.c., and parallels. It is thus plausible that the thought content of various other midrashim (in connection with Dt. 7:10) has been incorporated into the version of the statement in D. E. Z.

*Woo to me, for I have sinned...* An ostensibly minor sin by one person can lead to many more serious sins by others. One must judge a minor misdeed not only for the misdeed itself, but in the light of the most extreme possible consequences of that misdeed, which can have much more far-reaching effects than the initial transgression. In Mas. Kal. Rab. IV, ed. N.N. Coronel, 10b, one finds the reading: 'Woe to me that I have sinned, that a stumblingblock chanced upon me.'

## Derekh 'Eretz Zuta, chapter III

1. **Judge your words before they issue from your mouth and consider your deeds in accordance with 'derekh 'eretz' (good manners) and let a reward be given for every step you take.**

Judge your words... The reading 'judge your neighbour' instead of 'judge your words' in a number of manuscripts of D.E.Z. and Mas. Kal. Rab. (ed. N.N. Coronel, 11a) was most likely based on an error. The context indicates a general admonition that one should consider everything one is going to say and never say anything without having thought it out first. Cf. among other sources, D.E.Z. II,5, II,7, and II, 22; and D.E.Z. III,6. A well-thought-out and proper manner of speaking was highly esteemed among the sages. Cf. also M'Abot VI,6 and parallels and M'Abot I,5.

**...consider your deeds in accordance with 'derekh 'eretz'...**
One should consider one's deeds so that they comply with the often implicit norms of decency and humanity.

**...and let a reward be given to every step you take.**
One should make every step a fulfilment of a 'mitzwah' so that one becomes worthy in the eyes of Heaven with every step. The expression 'the reward of your steps' is current in the tradition and can refer, for example, to the profit gained for attending a synagogue (cf. TbSot. 22a) or the profit from doing a deed of charity. See Midr. Qoh. Rab. VII,2 [5].

2. **Acknowledge the justice of a (Divine) judgement over you and refrain from grumbling.**

The concept: 'tzidduq ha-din' implied here, is the acceptance of suffering and loss as a righteous judgement made in love. In MBer. IX,2 one finds an instruction to say the words 'dajjan 'emet hu' ('A righteous Judge is He'), a saying referring to God as a righteous Judge, upon receiving bad news. An attitude of meekness and an attitude of tolerance toward others is required of the sage here in D.E. An attitude of discontent, rebelliousness and vengefulness is considered objectionable. Cf., among others, D.E.Z. I,1 on 'alub' and I,9; and cf. D.E.Z. II,9; D.E.R. II,14; II,18. D.E.Z. III,2 deals primarily with the relationship between man and God. The concluding words of the statement, 'refrain from grumbling', also apply to that relationship. Those words mean that one should not complain about negative events, because all heavenly decisions are righteous. In D.E.Z.I,17 the words 'refrain from grumbling' apply to the relationship between people. See also the explanation in Mas. Kal. Rab. IV., ed. M. Higger, p. 243.

## 3. **Judge your neighbour turning the scale to the side of merit, and do not turn for him the scale to the side of guilt.**

See the commentary on M'Abot I,6, where a nearly identical statement is attributed to Rabbi Jehoshua ben Perahjah. The statement here is thus dated at least as far back as a century before Christ. Cf. also the story about Hillel the Elder in D. E. R. VI,2b

As in M'Abot, l.c., the statement here in D. E. Z. must be interpreted as every common inducement to give another person the benefit of the doubt and regard him innocent as long as no cogent proof of his guilt is produced. One should always try to think the best of another person. Nothing is worse than to misjudge someone. This general principle had a special application in the sentencing procedure, especially in situations in which a pronouncement of guilt would serve a punishment and in which a pronouncement of innocence would disadvantage no one. If the arguments for one's guilt are not stronger than the arguments for one's innocence, then he should be pronounced innocent. Upon passing a judgement that could involve punishment, one must be ready to pronounce someone innocent whenever possible, and pronounce someone guilty only when a judgement of guilt is absolutely unavoidable. Cf,. e.g., the rules pertaining the punitive judgments in MSanh. IV,1 and V,1 and in TbSanh. 40a. See also M'Abot VI,6 and parallels, where 'turning the scale to the side of merit' is mentioned as one of the 48 conditions that a 'talmid hakham' (a future sage and judge) must fulfil if his study is to be considered successful.

## 4. **Rejoice about your portion and enjoy the little you have, and do not hate him who rebukes you.**

Cf. the statement by Ben Zoma in M'Abot IV,1 (and parallels) '... Who is rich? Anyone who rejoices about his portion.' To rejoice about one's portion is cited in M'Abot VI,6 (and parallels) as one of the 48 characteristics necessary for successful study and required for a sage. The word 'portion' generally means one's lot in life, that which one must deal with in life. Cf. also the succeeding text in D. E. Z.: ... *and enjoy (we-na'eh) the little you have.* See the reading in the edition of D. Sperber, *Massekhet Derekh 'Eretz Zuta*, p. 31: 'u-ge'èh bi-me'utekha' (be proud on the little you have). This reading is not confirmed by the manuscripts. See the reading mentioned in A. J. Tawrogi, *Derech Erez Sutta*, pp. 17–18 with a different sequence ('Rejoice... and enjoy ..." is placed after the words of the next statement: 'be small in your own eyes' and cf. M. Higger, *Massekhtot Derekh 'Eretz*, p. 87. This sequence is not found in the manuscripts.

In Mas. Kal. Rab. IV (ed. M. Higger, p. 268) 'your portion' is explained to mean especially 'your wife'. This interpretation, however, limits the breadth of the text.

**Do not hate him who rebukes you**. Cf. the commentary to D. E. Z. II,11 and D. E. Z. IX,2, and see also the parallels mentioned there. See the deviating reading in Mas. Kal. Rab. l.c.: '... and hate the "what is in it"'.

### 5. **Be small in your own eyes. Let your share be blessed for ever, a benevolent eye and a humble spirit.**

Those words have been worked into the text in different ways in translations and commentaries. A. J. Tawrogi, l.c., establishes a connection with the preceding text and reads: '... then you will be blessed forever, and your eyes and your heart will be satisfied.' This version, however, does not justice to 'jehe' or 'jehi' (imperative tone). See, however, Ms. New York, *J. T. S.* (cat. E. N. Adler, p. 19) no. 1745, in which a reading appears to confirm similar interpretations. Cf. M. Ginsberg, in *The Minor Tractates of the Talmud*, ed. A. Cohen, II, p. 575: 'Your lot will always be blessed if you...' This reading is better but still does not fully do justice to the imperative forms. Cf. J. Harburger, *Massekhet Derech Erez Sutta*, p. 25. Equally unsatisfying is the reading of M. Higger in *Massekhtot Derekh 'Eretz* p. 40: 'Be small in your own eyes so that your share be blessed for evermore, regard people with a benevolent eye...' Like A. J. Tawrogi, M. Higger establishes a direct connection with the preceding text. The form 'jehe' ('jehi') makes this translation, however, implausible.

The translation 'let your share be blessed' does justice to the great majority of the manuscripts. The phrase 'a benevolent eye and a humble spirit' is to be understood as a further definition of 'share'. One should not strive for wealth but for a share consisting of a benevolent eye and a humble spirit. The phrase 'benevolent eye' (''ajn tobah') refers to the ability to give others generously and without jealousy. Cf. especially Prov. 22:9: 'He who has a benevolent eye, will be blessed.' Those who know to give and are humble will be forever blessed with a share in the World to Come.

'Nephesh hashubah' in the basis manuscript should be corrected on the basis of other manuscripts to read 'nephesh hashu**kh**ah' (humble spirit). See the parallel in TjBer.IV,2 [7d], where 'nephesh shephalah ruah nemukhah' (a humble soul and spirit) is mentioned as an example in connection with 'a benevolent eye'!! This parallel directly supports this correction. The same combination of characteristics is mentioned in TosSanh. VII,1 and TjSanh. I,9 [19c] as a feature of the sage! In both sources there is also mention of a 'heleq tob' in the sense of 'a good character'! See E. Ben Jehudah, *Millon Lashon ha-'Ibrit*, II, p. 1596, sub 'heleq'.

In M'Abot V,19 , someone who has a benevolent eye, a humble spirit and a humble soul is called a disciple of Abraham. In the passage concerning

Abraham's disciples, it is said that they will enjoy the fruit of their deeds in This World as well in the World to Come. This confirms our interpretation of D.E.Z., h.l. as: Let your share be blessed forever, i.e., in the World to Come, and strive to have a benevolent eye and a humble spirit, for those who know how to give will receive their share, and those who are humble will be raised.

**6. Accustom your tongue to say: 'I do not know', lest you will be led to tell a falsehood and be apprehended.**

Cf. the anonymous tradition in TbBer. 4a: 'Someone said: "'Accustom your tongue to say: I do not know, lest you be led to falsehood...'" This is the same tradition as in D.E. According to S. Krauss in: *R.E.J.*, XXXVI (1898), p. 42, the Talmud cites from 'derekh 'eretz' traditions in TbBer. 4a. Cf. also Rashi a.l. It is better for one, sage or student, not to speak about matters he is not sure of; it is becoming for a sage to admit if he does not know something. See further the remarks on D.E.Z. II, 7; D.E.Z. VII,1, and D.E.Z. XI (end).

**7a. If you are negligent in (the performance of) one precept, you will be in the end negligent in (the performance of) another. And likewise, if you make light of one precept you will in the end make light of another. And you will not be rewarded for your trouble.**

**7b. And likewise if you transgress the words of the Torah intentionally you will be made to transgress them intentionally and unintentionally.**

7a. The exact reading in the basis manuscript of the second part of the statement would be: ' .. and if you speak lightly of one precept, in the end you will make light of another.' The Hebrew is contrived, and the manuscripts have other readings. A number of manuscripts reads 'If you detach yourself from the performance of one precept by making light of it...' ("aqarta 'atzmekha le-haqel min ha-mitzwah'). This reading is somewhat more sensible but possibly is the result of a confusion with a corrupt earlier reading. We assume the reading to be corrupt. The original meaning might have been: 'we-khen ke-jotze bah 'im heqalta be-mitzwah 'ahat sophekha le-haqel be-'aheret.' Cf. the reading in *Nahalat Ja'aqob*: 'hakhi ke-jotze bah 'im heqalta be-mitzwah 'ahat...'. The variants may be understandable on the basis of an incorrectly interpreted abbreviation in this later addition to the text that readded: 'we-khen ke-jotze bah 'im heqalt" sophekha le-haqel be-'ah"'. Further variants have possibly resulted from this reading.

In the version of Mas. Kal. Rab.(ed. N.N. Coronel, 11a), the words 'ke-jotze bo' (see the manuscripts) are interpreted as a more precise definition of the preceding word 'mitzwah 'aheret' ('you will be in the end negligent in another similar precept'). The same is true of the interpretation of 'ke-jotze bo' of the next statement in D. E. Z. III,7a ('you will in the end make light of another similar precept'). Mas. Kal. Rab. l.c. reads: 'If you are negligent . . . in the end you will be negligent in another **similar** precept . . .' Accordingly, however, the word order in D. E. Z. III,7a (*and you will not be rewarded . . .*) must be altered. See below. The same reading and order apply to a number of manuscripts of D. E. Z. Cf. also J. Harburger, *Massekhet Derech Erez Sutta*, p. 25; M. Higger, *Massekhtot Derekh 'Eretz*, p. 40; M. Ginsberg in: *The Minor Tractates of the Talmud*, ed. A. Cohen, II, p. 575; and D. Sperber, *Massekhet Derekh 'Eretz Zuta*, pp. 32—33. The basis manuscript reads, however, 'we-khen ke-jotze bo' in D. E. Z. III,7a, and in D. E. Z. III,7b where the words serve as an introduction to the following statement. We find this letter view preferable, given the strong cohesion of content in the successive statements and the fact that they express the same thing. Cf. *Nahalat Ja'aqob* a.l.; cf. A. J. Tawrogi, *Derech Erez Sutta*, p. 18.

*. . . and you will not be rewarded for your trouble . . .* These words must be placed elsewhere and should be preceded by D. E. Z. III,7b: 'And likewise, if you transgress the words of the Torah intentionally . . .' One who no longer fulfils the commandments as precisely as possible or who always chooses for the interpretation involving the fewest restrictions and obligations possible and thus detracts from the essential meaning behind the commandments, places himself on a decline and will ultimately and unwittingly commit transgressions. He also undoes the profit yielded by his good deeds and efforts. Cf. the comparison of the scale in TosQid. I,13 ff. A. J. Tawrogi, o. c., suggests reading: 'sekher' (limit) instead of 'sakhar' and suggests the following translation: 'Dein Leiden (Vorwurf und Selbstklage) ist grenzenlos.' There is, however, no basis for such an interpretation.

The word 'tza'ar' (*trouble*) most likely refers to the effort of studying the Torah. Such effort is made in vain if one's behaviour becomes contrary to the precepts of the Torah. Cf. D. E. Z.II,9: 'Learn to take upon you all the words of the Torah in affliction ("tza'ar").'

*And likewise if you transgress the words . . .* One can extract different meanings from this statement. One transgression leads to another. Cf. a statement of Ben 'Azzai in M'Abot IV,2 and cf. D. E. Z. II,17 and D. E. Z. I,13. By committing a transgression, one becomes involved in situations in which he is forced to commit more transgressions in order to undo the consequences of the previous ones. Also, the commission of transgression weakens one's desire to do good and strengthens his desire to do evil, with the eventual result that he knowingly commits sins. In connection with the growing strength of the 'jetzer ha-ra'', see also the statement of Rabbi 'Assi in TbSuk. 52a and cf. Ber. Rab. XXII,6 (Rabbi 'Aqiba).

Another consideration in this vein of thought is that a person who is addicted to evil and who shows absolutely no desire to repent will not have offered the chance to repent by Heaven. One is forced to commit sin by the situation he has led himself into. Cf. TbJoma 39a and cf. a statement by Ben 'Azzai in Mekh. de-R. Jishm., Be-Shallah, ed. H. S. Horovitz / I. A. Rabin, p. 158; cf. also other sources. See L. Finkelstein, *Akiba: Scholar, Saint and Martyr*, p. 205; cf. also other sources.

## 8. **If you take money which is not yours, they will also take yours.**

The concept 'middah ke-neged middah' (measure for measure) figures in the background here. The sanction here applies to the transgression and thus constitutes appropriate punishment. Cf., e.g. the commentary of Rambam on Ex. 22:3 in reference to repayment double the worth of the stolen goods. Not only should the person robbed be compensated, but the thief must also make restitution to that person equal to the value of the loss he meant to cause the other person. He must thus admit his deed and suffer the loss he intended for the other person. See Rambam, *Jad*, Hil. Genibah I,4.

One should not rob another man of his possessions so that he himself will not be robbed. What one does not wish for oneself he must not do to others. See the statement very similar in the context of A. R. N. [b] XXXII (36a), attributed to Rabban Gamli'el. S. Krauss, in *R. E. J.*, XXXVI, (1889), p. 36, suggests that the statement in A. R. N. l.c. is secondary to the tradition here in D. E. Z. and is incorrectly ascribed in A. R. N. to Rabban Gamli'el! The statement in A. R. N. l.c. reads: 'If you do not wish that another take that which belongs to you, then you must not take that which belongs to another.' This makes one think of the negative wording of the command to love in Lev. 19:18 recorded in the name of Hillel. Cf. TbShab. 31a and cf. the later tradition passed on in the name of Rabbi 'Aqiba in A. R. N. [b] XXVI (27a).

The emphasis on identifying with one's neighbour in a loving manner also appears elsewhere in the first chapters of D. E. Z. Such identification leads one to wish good for his fellow because he wishes it for himself and to spare him unpleasant things because he wishes to be spared them himself. See D. E. Z. II,18 and II,23 and the accompanying commentary. Cf. further the commentary to D. E. Z. II,12.

## 9. **Be careful with sacred objects both when eating them and when giving them.**

Sacred things (namely the 'terumot' for the priests and the tithes for the Levites) must be ritually pure when eaten by priests and Levites. This is also true of the second tithe, which must be eaten by an Israelite in Jerusalem (when it is set free). The second tithe must also be ritually pure. Cf. Dt. 26:14ff.; cf. also J. D. Eisenstein, *'Otzar Dinim u-Minhagim*, repr. 1975, p. 245. Cf. also the admonition in D. E. Z. I,15 and D. E. R. I,32, that one should not be the guest of a priest who is an ignoramus so that he does not offer the 'terumah' to someone who may not eat from it, or so that he does not offer an unclean 'terumah' to someone who may eat from the 'terumah'. Great caution was especially exercised among the associates and the pious law-abiding.

One must also be careful in giving something that is sacred. The tithes and the 'large terumah' must be brought down on time and in the correct quantity. The Levites must be careful to carry down the small 'terumah' of their tithes to the priests. If an Israelite has promised to dedicate something to the Temple, he must carry that promise out. See the interpretation of M. Higger, *Massekhtot Derekh 'Eretz*, p. 40: 'Be careful... or giving away hallowed food.'

10. **Be forbearing and beloved when answering those whom you know.**

11. **Be forbearing and beloved by all men and most of all by the members of your household.**

10. **Be forbearing and beloved when answering...** In connection with the command to be submissive and worthy of being beloved (''alub we-'ahub'), see the commentary to D.E.Z. I,1. The characteristics mentioned here are especially associated with the manner in which a sage is to answer someone, he knows. Such a manner of answering most likely applied especially to the way in which a sage replied to students and fellow sages in the house of study. In answering a sage had to be patient, tolerant and amiable. Some manuscripts contain a longer reading: '... not only when answering those whom you know, but also when answering those whom you do not know.' This may be a later elaboration of the statement. **Answering**, then, may be interpreted to apply to the returning of a greeting. It was also good practise to return the greeting of someone one did not know. Compare the saying of 'Abajje: 'A man should always be subtle in fear of Heaven: "A soft answer turns away wrath" (Prov. 15:1), and one should always strive to be on best terms with his brethren and his relatives and with all men and even with the heathen in the street, in order that he may be beloved above and well-liked below and be acceptable to his fellow creatures.' – see TbBer. 17a.

11. **... forbearing and beloved to all men...** In some manuscripts the words 'forbearing and beloved' are missing. See the commentary to D.E.Z. I,1.

12. **The first stage of vowing is an opening to folly, the first stage of uncleanness is an opening to idolatry, [the first stage of) being lightheaded with women is an opening to unchastity.**

Three things are mentioned together in this statement: The making of vows, impurity in connection with the consumption of food), and contact with members of the opposite sex. This same combination appears in D.E.Z. I,13 and

I,15−16, concerning the avoidance of what is improper (in connection with women), not eating with an ignorant priest (in connection with the consumption of impure food), and restraint in making vows. It appears in D. E. R. I,32a-c (a statement by Rabbi Hilpa, concerning restraint in making vows, not eating with an ignorant priest, and restraint in contact with women. And it appears in TbNed. 20a as an anonymous baraita analogous to the content of the statement of Rabbi Hilpa in D. E. R. l.c., and to the content of a tradition in A. R. N. [a] I (3b), concerning not eating with unclean hands, not eating from a harvest from which the tithe has not been taken, and restraint in contact with members of the other sex.

It is clear from the texts mentioned and their context that the warnings in this statement in D. E. Z. comprise a closer definition of the concept 'sejag la-Torah' (a fence around the Torah) and that they apply especially to pious 'haberim', who were closed groups of especially law-abiding individuals who shielded themselves from committing transgressions by placing more restrictions upon themselves. See also A. Büchler, *Der Galiläische Am ha-Aretz des Zweiten Jahrhunderts*, p. 197. In connection with the words 'an opening to folly' see Qoh. 5:3: 'When you vow a vow to God, do not delay paying it, for there is no pleasure in fools . . .'

*The first stage of uncleanness is an opening to idolatry . . .* One manuscript (Ms. New York, *J. T. S.* [cat. E. N. Adler] no. 4465a) of D. E. Z. reads 'mam'eret' instead of 'tum'ah'. This alternative reading is accepted by D. Sperber, *Massekhet Derekh 'Eretz Zuta*, p. 33 and is interpreted as 'curse' ('me'erah'). See idem p. 11 and see the references there to Lev. 13:51−52 and Lev. 14:44.

From the above-mentioned traditions, which contain the same warnings, it is evident that 'tum'ah' (impurity) must be read here. The term probably refers to careless selection of a host, which carries, for example, the danger that one will eat impure food or food from which the tithe has not been taken. Cf. A. R. N. l.c.: 'tebalim'. Or the danger of eating hallowed food, which a non-priest may not eat. Cf. the commentary in reference to D. E. R. I, 32 in connection with *Ran* on TbNed. 20a. The remark here in D. E. Z. that impurity leads to idolatry is a possible allusion to the danger that one might consume food dedicated to idols by not paying attention to what one eats and with whom one eats. Cf., e.g., Tb'Ab. Zar. 29a-b and the forbiddance to drink the wine of heathens or even the wine of an Israelite that has been temporary in the storage of a heathen. The warning here in D. E. Z. most likely refers to the consumption of products the origin of which is not absolutely certain.

**The first stage of being lightheaded with women . . .** Compare, among others, Tb'Abot I,5 and Tb'Abot 3,13 with this statement. The background of this warning, as of the warning concerning vows and uncleanness, is the concept of 'a fence around the Torah' and of 'avoidance of the improper' (cf. D. E. Z. I,13). This warning applied to the pious who tried to avoid even approaching sin by applying extra restrictions to themselves. Frequent and frivolous conversation with a woman lead to unchaste behaviour. Those faithful to the laws not only avoided unnecessary conversation with women, they avoided even looking at women and, even more so, touching women. The very entertaining of unchaste thoughts about women was condemned. Cf. e.g., the precautions of Rabbi 'Eli'ezer to prevent himself from thinking about another woman. See TbNed. 20a and cf. TbB.M. 107b; Tanh., Naso, ed. S. Buber, § 13; and cf. the statement of Rabbi Johai bar Joshia in Mas. Kal. Rab. VIII (in Talmud Babli ed. Vilna/Romm, p. 51a): ...' Anyone who lets his thoughts centre on women will ultimately commit a transgression.' In connection to lightheadiness to women the terms 'sehoq' and 'sihah' appear along with the expression 'qallut rosh'.

13. **If you make yourself a surety (it should be) with the aim of paying (that surety). If you borrow (money), (it should be) with the aim of repaying. If you lend (money), (it should be) with the aim of not claiming it. Have in your mind to make a settlement.**

If one makes oneself a surety for another in order to help him meet financial obligations to another, one must pay off those obligations if the other cannot. If one borrows money, one must do so with the intention of paying it back as soon as possible.If one cannot repay a loan, one should not borrow. If one lends money, one must not expect repayment if the borrower cannot repay.

Most manuscripts, however, read: 'If you lend (money; it must be) with the object of claiming it.' We prefer, however, the reading of the basis manuscripts (and some genizah-fragments): '... with the object of **not** claiming it.' This reading concurs with the one in Mas. Kal. Rab. IV (ed. M. Higger, p. 271).

One should be strict with oneself in fulfilling financial obligations but less strict with others who owe money to oneself. This asymmetric situation advantageous to others and disadvantageous to oneself, is typical of the milieu of 'hasidut'. See also the commentary to D.E.Z. II,26. Cf. Ps. 37:21; cf. A. Büchler, *Types of Jewish Palestinian Piety*, p. 36ff.

*Have in your mind to make a settlement*... ('le-haphsiq 'et ha-heshbon'). This literally means to divide the bill, i.e., to void a part of the bill so that another no longer owes that part. Other interpretations include: Accustom yourself to reckon your accounts with a view to paying them up' (M. Higger); and 'Consider your plans and settle the bill completely' (cf. J. Harburger, o.c.). See also the reading in Mas. Kal. Rab., ed. N.N. Coronel, 11a-b: 'Hasten to consider and to settle your account.' Cf. A.J. Tawrogi, o.c. on D.E.Z. h.l.

14. **When one has acquired a good name, one has acquired it for himself; when one has acquired words of Torah, one has acquired the life of the World to Come.**

This statement is transmitted in M'Abot II in name of Hillel. Cf. A. R. N.[b], XXVI (27b), where stronger emphasis is placed on the importance of study than on the efforts for daily upkeep. A good name is not last upon death and do not pass on on inheritors, but it accompanies one in death. A good name is earned through studying the Torah; in this way one earns a share in the World to Come.

The commentaries assume a clear connection between the content of the statement of Hillel quoted here in D. E. Z. and the directly preceding text. One should stand by financial agreements and be compassionate toward others in financial agreements, for it is better to suffer financial loss than to lose one's good name. In acquiring a good name, one gains something that can never fall to anyone else. For the background to the statement of Hillel, see Prov. 9:12 and Prov. 20:1.

**15. A bashful man cannot learn and an irritable man cannot teach; and an unlearned man cannot be a 'parush' (i. e. a member of the circle of very observant Jews) nor can an emptyheaded man be sinfearing. And not everyone who engages in much business becomes wise**.

Like the preceding statement, this statement was made by Hillel. See M'Abot II,5; and cf. A. R. N. [a] XXVI (41b); and A. R. N. [b] XXXIII (36b). In the sources, the statement is also ascribed to Rabbi 'Aqiba (a later change). One who is sly and dares not ask questions or does not admit that he does not know something, will not learn. The asking and answering of questions in the house of study is an important part of the learning process. Cf. especially the commentary to D. E. Z. I,3 and II,5.

*And a irritable man cannot teach...* This is a continuation of Hillel's statement in M'Abot II,5. Along with a student's modesty and willingness to ask questions, patience on the part of the teacher is required in answering questions. He may not discourage students from asking questions by being irascible.

*And an ignorant man cannot be a 'parush'...* This is also part of a statement by Hillel from M'Abot II,5, but presented in a different order here in D. E. Z. In A. R. N. [a] l.c. and A. R. N. [b] l.c., this statement is ascribed to Rabbi 'Aqiba. A 'parush' is a strict observer of the Mosaic law and the rabbinical regulations, one who wants to be saintly and pure. The word 'hasid' is used instead of 'parush' in the parallel tradition in M'Abot II,5. The term 'parush' can help to explain the reading 'hasid'. The notion of 'parush' incorporates all forms of pious restraint such as from ritual impurity, idolatry, matters that hint at unchaste behaviour, the lighthearted making of vows etc. Cf. A. Büchler, *Types of Jewish Palestinian Piety*, p. 49 ff. and 63 ff.

The concept ''am ha-'aretz' refers to people who are civilized but possess no deep knowledge of the oral tradition of the Torah and the rabbinical regulations. Cf., e.g., the definitions in TbBer. 47b; TbBer. 50b; TbSot 22a; TbGit.

61a and other sources. The term ''am ha-'aretz' in those sources refers to someone who does not say prayers on time or correctly, who does not wear 'tephillin' or 'tzitzit', who does not put a 'mezuzah' on the door jamb, who does not know or observe the regulations of cleanness, who does not always set aside the 'terumah' and the tithes etc. See also A. Büchler, *Die Galiläische Am ha-Aretz des Zweiten Jahrhunderts*, passim.

Shallow study of the tradition, infrequent visits to the house of study and infrequent contact with the sages, along with to much emphasis on attentiveness to work and daily tasks and sustenance, make it impossible to become a strict observer of the law or to acquire 'hasidut'. Cf. especially TbBer. 47b.

There are, however traditions in which an ''am ha-aretz' is considered a 'hasid'. Cf., e.g. TbShab. 63a; cf. also the contradiction between the 'hasid' Haninah ben Dosa and the scholar Rabban Johanan ben Zakkai in TbBer. 43b or traditions in which a number of characteristics of a 'hasid' are attributed to an ''am ha-'aretz'. Cf., e.g., S. E. R. XV, ed. M. Friedmann p. 69: ' These are '"amei ha-'aretz" who have been instilled with the laws of "derekh 'eretz" and the other commandments and who refrain from committing transgressions and robbery and from doing all that is improper.' In connection with this wording see also D. E. Z. I,13 and D. E. Z II,16 and the commentary in that reference. See also S. E. R. XXIII, ed. M. Friedmann, p. 136 and S. E. R. XXVI, ed. M. Friedmann, p. 143. There is mention in other traditions of 'hasidim' who had no precise knowledge of the precepts of cleanness. Cf., e.g. A. R. N. [a] XXVII (28a) and parallels; cf. alsoS. Safrai in *J. J. S.*, XVI (1965), p. 25 ff. From such texts it would appear that among some 'hasidim' the emphasis was placed on 'good deeds' and interpersonal relations rather than on the study of the precepts of cleanness. It is especially evident from the last example from A. R. N. that scholars who scrupulously observed the law were suspicious of the knowledge of the Torah among **certain** 'hasidim'. It is not impossible that the reading 'parush' in the statement of Hillel represents a closer definition of 'hasid', because the term 'hasid' could also refer to people who were devout but not entirely strict in the observation of rabbinical regulations. A. R. N. [b] XXXIII (36b) contains a reading of the statement of Hillel with the more precise term 'parush' after 'hasid'! In other readings the term 'hasid' is replaced by 'parush'.

... *nor can an empty-headed man be sin-fearing*. In connection with the difference between a boor (an empty-headed man) and the ''am ha-'aretz' (an ignorant man), see, among others, Rambam and Rashi on M'Abot II,5. A boor is someone who is totally uncultured, while an ''am ha-'aretz' is basically civilized. In the D. E. tradition itself, the difference is defined in another way. In D. E. Z. X,11, for example, a boor is defined as someone who does read Scripture, but who does not know the oral tradition, i. e., who does not put the Torah in practise. An ''am ha-'aretz', however, is someone who does know something of the oral tradition, but who has no detailed knowledge of Scripture, which means that his actions are not based on a thorough explanation of the Scripture. An ''am ha-'aretz' may very well desire to act according to the oral teachings but cannot do so because he lacks knowledge of the Torah. Cf. also TbSot. 22a, where an ''am ha-'aretz' is defined by Rabbi 'El'azar as someone who has knowledge of both the Torah and the oral tradition, but not of the finer details of each one as they apply to daily life, because of too little contact with the sages. According to Rabbi Samuel bar Nahmani, such an individual is a boor. According to more widespread opinion, the description of an ''am ha-'aretz' of Rabbi 'El'azar is the correct one, and a boor is someone who does have knowledge of the Scripture but who has no knowledge of the oral tradition. See further TbBer. 47b. The conclusion, then, is that the ''am ha-'aretz' is someone who wishes to act according the rabbinical traditions and who has some knowledge of these traditions, but who does not set aside enough time to study and who is insufficiently motivated to study conscientiously. See the texts mentioned from S. E. R. XV, ed. M. Friedmann, p. 69; S. E. R. XXVII, ed. M. Friedmann, p. 136 and S. E. R. XXVI, ed. M. Friedmann, p. 143, where the ''am ha-'aretz' is discussed more or less favourably. A boor, on the other hand, has at most theoretical knowledge of the Torah, but no knowledge or motivation, necessary to put the Torah into practise anyway.

Hillel's statement, like the famous statement of Pinhas ben Ja'ir in connection with the list of virtues, assumes that 'hasidut' represents a higher degree of integrity than the fear of sin only. While the ''am ha-'aretz' can never attain the highest degree of perfection in his humane relations (cf. A. Büchler, o.c., p. 24ff.) the boor does not even possess the will or ability to avoid committing sin. See further A. Büchler, o.c., pp. 30 and 32−33.

Elsewhere in the tradition there is also evidence of the confidence of Hillel and his followers in the positive effect of the study of the Torah on human character, as well as of the opinion that a negative attitude is explainable as the result of lack of knowledge of the Torah. Cf., e.g., M'Abot I,12 and TbSanh. 31a concerning the attitude toward proselytes and cf. A. R. N. [a], III (7b) concerning the acceptance of students.

*And not everyone who engages much in business* ... Frequent occupation with business matters is usually the cause of neglect of the study of the Torah. Few great businessmen can be ranked among the sages. In connection with Hillel himself, see especially his statement in A. R. N. [b], XXVI (27b), in which he places the reward of the study of the Torah (the World to Come) above the material gains from business efforts. Cf. also the story in TbJoma 35b about Hillel's poverty, which did not prevent him from attending the lessons of the sages.

16. **Fifteen characteristics are mentioned in connection with a sage: (He is) decorous (pleasant) in his entering (and leaving), pious (modest) in his**

**sitting, inventive in fearing (transgression), alert in knowledge, wise in his ways, (his mind is) absorptive and retentive, (he is) attending frequently meetings (of the sages), answering many times (and fully), serving the sages frequently, (he is) asking according to the subject matter and answering in accordance with the halakhah, making additions to each chapter, going to the wise (to seek instruction from them) and he learns in order to teach and he learns in order to practise.**

Cf. also D. E. Z. VII,2 with other wording and cf. S. E.R · XIV (ed. M. Friedmann, p. 63), where a number of characteristics listed here are especially mentioned in connection with students and colleagues in the house of study. See also the correspondences with some of the 48 conditions necessary for successful study of the Torah listed in *Pereq Qinjan Torah* (M'Abot VI,5—6; cf. S. E. Z. XVII, ed. M. Friedmann, pp. 18—19 and Mas. Kal. Rab. VIII.

*Decorous (pleasant) in his entering (and leaving)* . . . Cf. D. E.R. IV,1. It is especially clear from the context in S. E. R. XIV (ed. M. Friedmann p. 63) that this statement applies to the entering and leaving of a house of study. Various interpretations are possible. The term 'na'eh' has, in connection with the compliance with certain precepts, the meaning of fulfilling a commandment with as much extra effort as possible and as decorously as possible. In this connection, cf. the statement of Rabbi Jishma'el based on Ex. 15:2 in Mekh. de-R Jishma'el, Be-Shallah, par. 3, ed. M. Friedmann, p. 37a.

It was considered a good practise to be the first to enter the house of study in the morning and the last one to leave it in the evening. In TbSuk. 28a, this practice is listed along with a number of other pious practices as characteristic of the devout way of life of Rabbi Johanan ben Zakkai. Cf. further Tb'Er. 21b; TbMeg. 15b and S. E. R. VIII.

It is also possible that reference is made here in Derekh 'Eretz Zuta to behaviour upon entering and leaving a house of study. It was considered highly improper to come late to lessons in the house of study, especially when one stepped over the heads of those already seated on the ground in order to sit close by the teacher. Cf., e.g., TbJeb. 105b; TbMeg. 27b; TbSot. 39a and TbSanh.7b. Cf. also other sources.

Upon leaving a house of study, as well as upon entering one, one was opposed to be patient and dignified. It was advisable for one to let those greater in years and knowledge precede when entering and for one to go first when leaving. The reverse was also possible, given the differences in local traditions concerning this custom. Cf. D. E. Z. VI,2a; and cf. D. E. R. IV, (end). Cf. M. Aberbach in: *HUCA*, XXXVII (1966), p. 107 ff.

*. . . pious ('hasid', modest) in his sitting. . .* 'Jeshibah' (sitting) is interpreted by A. J. Tawrogi (*Derech Erez Sutta*, a.l.) as 'academy' and by M. Higger (*Massekhtot Derekh 'Eretz*, a.l.*) as 'meetings of scholars'. In connection with the meaning of the term 'jeshibah' cf., among others, R. H. Charles, *The Apocry-*

*pha and Pseudepigrapha*, I, p. 517, note 29 in connection with *Seph. Ben Sira* 51,29. Cf. also *J. E.*, XII, p. 595 and *E. J.*, II, col. 199 ff.

The wording 'be-jeshibato' (*in his sitting*), however, applies to the act of sitting down and the manner in which one sits down in a house of study rather than to the house of study itself. It thus means that one should not rush to occupy a front seat. Cf. the commentaries. See the explanation in the parallel in S. E. R. XIV : 'Pious in his sitting in the house of study.'

The expression 'makkir 'et meqomo' (*knowing his place*) in M'Abot VI,6 (cf. S. E. Z., ed. M. Friedmann XVII, p. 18 and Mas. Kal. Rab., ed. N. N. Coronel, 14a) is also explained by M. Aberbach (in: *H. U. C. A.* XXXVII (1966), p. 119) to mean that one should be modest in seeking a place to sit in the house of study and not immediately take the best seat available. In M'Abot and the parallels mentioned 'jeshibah' (sitting in the house of study) is mentioned among the 48 conditions necessary for successful study of the Torah.

The word 'hasid' most likely means in this instance that the sage must take into account the sensitivities of others when taking a seat in the house of study.

*... inventive in fearing (transgression)...* The reading in D. E. Z. VII,1 reads "arum be-da'at' (deliberate in knowledge). The phrase means here in D. E. Z. III that one should be subtle in seeking new ways in which to fear God. Cf. the explanation of Rashi on TbBer. 17a, in which the same wording appears, and cf. the explanation in *Seph. ha-Roqeah*, Hil. Hasidut, ed. Jerusalem 1967, p. 17.

This term is particular to the milieu of the 'Hasidim', who take no pleasure in living only according to the generally accepted halakhah but seek a personal supplement to and realization of their sin fearing quality and accordingly impose more obligations and restrictions on themselves.

*... alert in knowledge...* ('piqqeah be-da'at'). Some of the manuscripts read: 'Wise in knowledge.'

*... wise in his ways...* Some of the manuscripts read: 'alert in his ways' and 'alert in his deeds'.

*... absorptive and retentive...* Read 'kones we-zakhran'. Cf. D. E. Z. VII,2. A good student absorbs and retains much knowledge. See also the different reedings in D. E. Z. VII,2. Cf. D. E. Z. I,4, where the absorption capacity and sharp memory of a good student are compared with a sponge and deep-lying flowerbed, respectively. See the commentary and parallels.

*... frequently attending meetings (of the sages)...* These words are missing in some manuscripts and parallels and in D. E. Z. VII,2. Cf. the reading 'sho'el ba-jeshibah' in *Menorat ha-Ma'or* of Al-Nakawa, ed. H. G. Enelow, IV, p. 492. Cf. *Reshit Hokhmah*, Huppat 'Elijahu, sha'ar 15. Cf. the reading 'ba-jeshibah' in: M'Abot VI,5 and parallels.

*... answering many times...* Cf. the commentary to D. E. Z. I,3; cf. also D. E. Z. II,5.

*... serving the sages frequently...* These words do not appear in a number of

manuscripts. To serve one's teacher is mentioned in M'Abot VI,5ff. Cf.
S.E.Z. XVII (ed. M.Friedmann, p. 18ff. and Mas. Kal. Rab. VIII (ed.
N.N. Coronel, 14a) as one of the 48 conditions necessary for successful study of
the Torah. It is essential to the learning process for one to serve his teacher. In
this way he has daily contact with the teacher. In a statement in TbBer. 7b, it is
said that it is even more important to serve the sages than to study. Before
Hillel's famous statement in M'Abot I,13 ('He who does not learn should be put
to death') one finds in TjNaz. VII,1 [56b] the alternative reading, ascribed to
Rabbi 'Aqiba: 'He who does not serve the sages should be put to death.' This
statement is associated there with a story in which Rabbi 'Aqiba wanted to fulfil
a 'mitzwah', but committed a sin out of lack of practical experience. See this
same story in D.E.Z. VIII,14a and the emphasis placed in that story on the
serving of the sages.

... *asking in accordance with the subject matter* ... See the commentary on
D.E.Z. I,3 and D.E.Z. XI, 31.

... *making additions to each chapter*... See the commentaries to M'Abot VI,6:
'Listens and makes additions.' Cf. D.E.Z. I,3 with commentary and parallels.
See especially in M'Abot I,13 a statement by Hillel about studying the Torah:
'He who does not make a contribution will come to an end' i.e., he who does
not add to his knowledge and to the tradition in an active learning process will
lose his knowledge. The aim in studying the Torah is that one will make his own
creative contribution to the learning process and that he will be able to provide
his own commentary to every chapter. He who is not personally involved in
studying and who makes no active contribution will ultimately lose his knowledge.

**17. Do not be like the highest threshold which injures the feet [and which
ultimately collapses] and not like the middle threshold, on which only the
troubled is sitting and which ultimately collapses. Be like the lower
threshold, on which most people tread and which remains on its place when
the whole building has fallen down in ruins.**

See the commentary to D.E.Z. I,5. It is not the haughty or somewhat modest
person but only the very humble person who serves people with his knowledge
who will endure, i.e. who will not lose his knowledge. Note the conclusion with
the preceding statement: 'Learn with the intention of teaching.' The cohesion is
especially clear in parallels as Tb'Er. 54a and S.E.R. XIV, ed. M. Friedmann
p. 63:... 'like a plank on which everyone treads, and like a tree in the shadow of
which everyone sits and a lamp that is the light for the eyes of many.' Cf. Mat.
5:14ff. To put one's knowledge into practise and pass it on to others is effective.
In this way, the knowledge one has gained acquires a meaning unprecedented
in greatness.

# Derekh Eretz Zuta, chapter IV

**1. Sages are pleasing (lend dignity) to a company, but the unlearned are not pleasing to a company.**

The term 'na'im' (pleasing, becoming) can be interpreted in different ways. It may mean according to our translation 'lending dignity to a company' as well as 'well-behaved among company.' On the basis of the parallels, the former interpretation is plausible. Ignorant persons are not welcome in the company of sages. The Hebrew concept 'haburah' (company) may specifically mean here a gathering of 'haberim': (associates), that is a group of sages who are associated with each other, who study together and who strive to live in strict accordance with the halakhah. See J. Heinemann in: *J.J.S.* XVI (1–4) (1962), p. 26; cf. TbBer. 47b.

The non-religion interest in worldly matters and the indifference to strict compliance with the law, characteristic of the "am ha-'aretz', could have negative influence on the 'haberim'. It was possible that "ammei ha-'aretz' wished to belong to groups that were faithful to the law, but they were not easily accepted. Cf. TosDem. II,2.

Eating meals together was an important part of the social life of the sages and 'haberim'. It provided the opportunity to discuss quietly matters of Torah and the tradition. Thus sages were also warned to avoid contact with "ammei ha-'aretz' and not to eat with them frequently because they were not interested in religious matters and only occupied themselves with gossip and idle talk. See further the parallels and the commentary to D.E.Z. VI,1. Cf. M'Abot III,3: 'Rabbi Shim'on said: "if three have eaten at one table and have not spoken there words of Torah, it is as if they have eaten sacrifices to the dead."'

**2. One who occupies himself with (the study of) Scripture (only) is of merit and is not of merit. (One who occupies himself with) 'mishnah' is of a merit for which he is rewarded. There is nothing more meritorious than (occupying himself with) 'talmud'. [Yet run always to the 'mishnah' more than to the 'talmud']**

To study Scripture is only partially meritorious. If one also occupies himself with the 'mishnah' (by gathering and learning halakhic rules), then he is not complete meritorious, but will be rewarded. He who occupies himself with 'talmud' (halakhic midrash), however, is the most meritorious of all. (In some parallels the saying is ascribed to Rabbi Shim'on bar Johai. See TjShab. XVI,1

[15c] and cf. TjHor. III, 7 [48c] and TjBer. I,5 [3b] and see Mas. Soph. XV [ed. M. Higger, pp. 277−278]). In compliance with some parallel texts, some manuscripts of D. E. Z. contain an addition that one should occupy himself more with 'mishnah' than with 'talmud'. In connection with the use of the terms 'mishnah' and 'talmud', see W. Bacher, *Die Exegetische Terminologie der jüdischen Traditionsliteratur*, repr. Darmstadt 1965, pp. 122−123 and 201. Cf. in Hebr. translation by A. S. Rabinovitz, *'Erkhei Midrash Tanna'im*, Tel-Aviv 1923, pp. 84 and 86. See Ch. Albeck, *Mabo la-Talmudim*, Tel-Aviv 1969, pp. 3−7.

In the Tannaitic period, the word 'talmud' generally meant midrash or oral tradition. In the statement of Rabbi Shim'on bar Johai, it is clear that 'talmud' means 'halakhic midrash', for halakhic midrash supposes both knowledge of Scripture and of halakhah and thus is more important than either of the two. In certain manuscripts in D. E. Z., in TbB. M. 33a and in Mas. Soph. XV, it is added: *Yet run always to the 'mishnah' more than to the 'talmud'*. See different wording in TjShab. XVI,1 [15c]. This remark could be explained entirely by the political circumstances in the time of Rabbi Shim'on, when all emphasis was placed on the gathering of halakhah to prevent knowledge of it being lost. Although the Talmud, the connection between Scripture and halakhah, should have been considered as more important, the gathering of halakhah had temporary priority. In a quieter political period, after most of the Tannaitic halakhic traditions had been collected, emphasis could again be placed on the 'talmud' (see below).

From parallels in TbB. M. 33a; TjHor. l.c. and Mas. Soph. l.c., it is clear, however, that the term of 'talmud' in the statement of rabbi Shim'on was interpreted differently in the period of the Amoraim to mean 'gemara' (the discussion of halakhic rules, especially those collected in the Mishnah; the derivation of the halakhot and the making of halakhic decisions). The word 'talmud' as used in the statement of Rabbi Shim'on could not yet have had this meaning. See W. Bacher, l.c. The interpretation of 'talmud' as 'gemara' lead to the perception of a tension in the statement from the time of Rabbi Shim'on (which was entirely or partially attributed to him) between the emphasis on 'mishnah' and 'talmud' (understood in the sense of 'gemara'), for which a historical explanation was sought (see below). See the parallel in TjHor. III,7 [48c], where it is taught in a related baraita: 'One who is ordering halakhot ('sodran') is preferable to the deductor (dialectician) of halakhot ('pilpelan').' This concurs with the opinion that 'mishnah' (the ordering) is prior to 'talmud' (deduction). See there the opinion of Samuel bar Nahman : '"mishnah" ranks above "talmud".' A statement by Rabbi Shim'on bar Johai is quoted in the same framework in confirmation of a previously cited tradition: '"mishnah" ranks above "miqra".'. Rabbi Shim'on bar Johai's statement quoted here correspondents with the first part of D. E. Z.: 'One who occupies himself with (the study of) Scripture (only)... it is a merit and it is not a merit.' It is stated additionally that the rabbis generally say that study of Scripture and 'mishnah' are of equal value. Cf. TjBer. I,5 [3b]. The rest of the words here in D. E. Z. referring to the relationship between 'mishnah' and 'talmud' are not attributed in TjHor. to Rabbi Shim'on bar Johai (as they are not in TjBer. I,5). In TjShab. l.c. the entire statement appears in the name of Rabbi Shim'on bar Johai. Cf. Mas. Soph. l.c. and cf. TbB. M. 33a, where the tradition appears anonymously.

According to the Amoraic interpretation of the statement of Rabbi Shim'on, 'mishnah' (the ordering of halakhot) is more important than the study of Scripture alone. The 'talmud' (the derivation of halakhot and discussions), however, is most important of all, for it makes possible the application of the precepts contained in the Torah. In various editions of TbB. M. 33a, the word 'gemara' is used instead of 'talmud'. Older traditions and the manuscripts, however read 'talmud'. See R. Rabbinovicz, *Seph. Diqduqei Sopherim* on TbB. M. h.l. R. Rabbinovicz suggests that the reading 'gemara' reflects a change made by a censor. Cf. also Mas. Soph. XV (ed. M. Higger, p. 277), where 'ha-Shesh' (the six orders) is read instead of 'talmud'. The addition and the extreme emphasis on the importance of 'mishnah' is historically under-standable. The collection of the halakhot was considered important in the time of Rabbi Shim'on, but was considered to be less important in the period of the Amoraim. Strong emphasis came to be placed on Talmud itself in the sense of gemara. Consequently, the emphasis on both 'talmud' and 'mishnah' in the statement of the time of Rabbi Shim'on bar Johai was viewed as a non-understandable paradox. An analysis of TjHor. l.c., indicates that there was a difference of opinion among the Amoraim regarding the degree of importance of 'mishnah' and 'talmud'.

Rabbi Samuel bar Nahman believed that 'mishnah' ranks above 'talmud', while Rabbi Johanan believed that 'talmud' is more important than 'mishnah'. These opinions bore on the ways in which the Amoraim attempted to explain the contradiction they perceived in the words ascribed to Rabbi Shim'on. On the one hand it is stated that it is most meritorious to study 'talmud', while on the other hand it is stated in addition to the words of Rabbi Shim'on: 'Always pursue "mishnah" more...' According to Rabbi Johanan (see TbB. M. l.c and cf.) the emphasis on 'talmud' and the opinion that it was most meritorious to study 'talmud', date back to the time of Rabbi, when the collected halakhah came under discussion. The remark that one should pursue 'mishnah' more than 'talmud' was according to the opinion of Rabbi Johanan added in the period after Rabbi. The emphasis on 'talmud' in the sense of 'gemara' was according to his opinion so strong that it was necessary to impress upon students the importance of the foundation of the 'gemara', namely 'mishnah', the teaching and passing on of Tannaitic halakhic traditions.

In Mas. Soph. XV (ed. M. Higger, p. 277 ff.; see the reconstruction of Ginz-berg in *Perushim we-Hiddushim bi-Jerushalmi*, I, New York 1941, p. 139; cf. the reading in TjHor. l.c.) one finds a completely different explanation (ascribed to José bar 'Abin) of the above-mentioned contradiction. The opinion that one should always pursue 'mishnah' more than 'talmud' could be explained on the basis of the period when the rabbis had not yet incorporated Tannaitic traditions into the Talmud. After most baraitot and tosaphot (i. e. nearly all Tannaitic halakhic traditions) had been incorporated into the Talmud, emphasis could be placed on the study of the Talmud as the greatest merit. See the reading in Mas. Soph. l.c.: 'But after Rabbi incorporated most 'mishnajot' (in the Mishnah) always pursue the Six Orders more than the Mishnah.' Cf. the reading in TjHor. l.c. (Ja'aqob Naumburg in *Nahalat Ja'aqob* on D. E. Z. h.l. renders the explanation of Rabbi José in accordance with the tradition in TbB. M.: 'But after... always pursue "mishnah" more than "talmud".') These are, however, retrospective explanations that are incorrectly based on the notion that the term 'talmud' in the statement of Rabbi Shim'on refers to the 'gemara'. It is quite possible to assume that the statement of Rabbi Shim'on was originally quite shorter and contained nothing about 'talmud' and the relationship between 'mishnah' and 'talmud'. Based on the reading of Rabbi Shim'on's statement in TjHor. l.c. and TjBer. l.c. this possibility cannot be excluded entirely.

3. **Make (teach) your Torah gratis, because the Holy One, His Name be blessed, gave her (i. e. the Torah) gratis; and exact no payment for her. But if you exact payment for (teaching) the words of the Torah, it will ultimately become evident that you are destroying the whole world.**

See the manuscripts from the parallels the starting point appears to be Dt. 4:5: 'Behold, I have taught you statutes and ordinances as the Lord commanded me...' This is explained to mean: As the Lord has Taught me these rules gratis I will also teach gratis. Moses is here the example of the teacher who like God teaches gratis. Cf. TbNed. 37a; TbBer. 29a; especially TjNed. IV,3 [38c]. Cf. further Midr. ha-Gad. on Dt. 4:5; Jalq., Wa-'Ethannan, r. 824; and Jalq, Prov., r. 960.

According to the gemara in TbNed. l.c., and the Mishnah in TbNed. 35a that one indeed may accept money for teaching Miqra, but not for teaching midrash, halakhot and 'aggadot. The reward for teaching Scripture actually comes from the care for children and not from teaching itself. In TjNed. l.c., it is said that one may accept reward for teaching Miqra and Targum, because only 'mishpatim' and 'huqqim' (interpreted as midrash and halakhot) and not Miqra and Targum are mentioned in Dt. 4:5. The version in D.E.Z. h.l. is clearly a parallel of the exegetical tradition based on Dt. 4:5. In D.E.Z., the Torah is discussed simply, with no distinction made between instruction in Miqra (and Targum) and instruction in the oral tradition. Cf., e.g., TbQid. 30a; the concept of 'Torah' may apply to the entire oral tradition. This lack of distinction can be explained by the fact that it is not the intention to present a halakhic rule in D.E.Z., but to present the intention of the above-mentioned midrash, according to which one may not accept payment for teaching Torah. In some parallels, the rule that one may not accept payment for teaching Torah is based on a comparison of the Torah with water. Knowledge of the Torah must be available free to everyone, just as water is free. Cf. Mekh. de-R. Jishm., Ba-Hodesh, par. 5 (ed. M. Friedmann, 67a) and parallels. The background principles of this statement in D. E. Z. are 'the study of Torah for the sake of Heaven' and 'the study of Torah (out of love) for the Torah itself'. Cf. D. E. Z. II,1 and D. E. R. XI,7. To accept payment for teaching the Torah is to threaten the existence of the world, cf., e.g., TbShab. 119a. To fail in teaching the Torah to e new generation brings close the end of society.

**4. Say not: 'I have no money', because all money belongs to you[better reading: to Him; or: to Me]. If you have been privileged to possess money, practise charity with it. As long as it is in your possession, acquire through it This World and inherit through it the World to Come. For it (the money) has wings and it will fly into the air (i. e. it will suddenly disappear), as it is said: ' When you set your eyes upon it, it is gone. It has made itself wings, like an eagle it flies to heaven' (Prov. 23:5).**

The reading of the basis manuscript 'because all money belongs to You' can best be corrected on the basis of other manuscripts to: '. . . to Me', or to: '. . . to Him'. This statement appears only in later parallels. The statement gives the impression of being a compilation of various older statements. See also the following statements beginning with 'Say not'. These highly stylized statements appear only in later sources, such as in 'Otiot de-R. 'Aqiba, Seph. Liqqutei ha-Pardes and Midr. ha-Gad.

In *Nahalat Ja'aqob* on D. E. Z. h.l. a connection is established between the content of D. E. Z. and the preceding statement. The argument that one has no money is no reason to ask for payment for teaching the Torah. All money belongs ultimately to God, and one who teaches Torah without being paid may trust that he will be provided for. This connection in content, however, is secondary. This statement is also recorded in the parallels independent of the statement preceding the one here in D. E. Z. The themes here in D. E. Z. are almsgiving and charity. Cf. D. E. Z. II, 12, where it is similarly stated that one cannot consider anything his personal possession and that God can make the rich poor and the poor rich at any moment. One has no right to complain if he has no money. Cf. D. E. Z. chap.I,6. The possession of money is only temporary, and if one has money, he should use it primarily for charitable purposes. The acquisition of wealth is only temporary and represents a test of one's readiness to help the poor. See Shem. Rab. XXXI,3 and parallels. One should take advantage of those times when he can give in order to acquire a share in the World to Come. The background idea here is that charity has a conciliatory effect. Cf. *Seph. Ben Sira* 3,30 (ed. M. Z. Segal, p. 19) and *Did*. IV.

In some parallels, a connection is made between almsgiving ('tzedaqah') and the rescue of the dead (and thus with a share in the World to Come), on the basis of Prov. 10:2: 'But almsgiving ('tzedaqah') saves one from death.' The word 'tzedaqah' (in the Tenakh: justice) is read here to mean almsgiving in the rabbinical sense. Cf., e.g., TbShab. 156b; TbB. M. 10a; Soher Tob on Prov. 10 (beginning); cf. also other sources. See S. E. Z. I, ed. M. Friedmann, p. 169; S. E. R. X, ed. M. Friedmann, p. 53; and cf. Shir ha-Shir. Zuta, ed. S. Buber, 8a; and *Seph. ha- Zohar* on Ex. p. 198.

Cf. M. Higger, *Massekhtot Ze'irot*, Mabo, pp. 10–11.

**5. Say not: 'That man is wise and I am not wise', because you have not served (the sages) as much as he did.**

**6. Say not: 'That man is rich and I am not rich', because not everyone is privileged to enjoy two tables.**

**7. Say not: 'That man is handsome and I am not handsome', because at the hour of your death you are both considered like carrion. And not only this but furthermore regarding carrion its (Jewish) owners may say to gentiles: 'Take the flesh for yourself and give us the hide.' But regarding you, no creature will care for (the dead bodies of both of) you.**

**8. Say not: 'That man is strong and I am not strong', because a strong man is only he who studies Torah, because there is said: 'Bless the Lord, His Angels, you mighty in strength that fulfil His word by listening to what His voice is speaking' (Ps. 103:20).**

5. *Say not: 'That man is wise...* Wisdom is not given, it is acquired only through study and through daily contact with sages and frequent visits to the house of study.

6. *Say not : 'That man is rich...* One should not envy another's wealth for no one is given two tables from which to eat. 'Two tables' can clearly be interpreted as a combination of knowledge and wealth (or knowledge and social prestige). A sage must not lament his poverty, for many material pursuits would only detain from studying. Poverty is a good sign, according to the tradition, for it shows that God has more interest in one's studying than in one's material matters. Cf. S. E. R. III (ed. M. Friedmann, p. 13) and Jalq., Sam, r. 165. Knowledge and social prestige occur rarely or never together. Cf. TbGit. 59a; TbSanh. 36a; *Menorat ha-Ma'or* of Al-Nakawa, ed. H. G. Enelow, III, p. 189; and M. Higger, *'Otzar ha-Baraitot*, X, p. 189, § 3.

'Two tables' can also be explained as This World and the World to Come. This explanation is based on the thought that the transgressors are already rewarded in This World (with prosperity) for their few good deeds, while the righteous in This World are already punished in This World for their sins (through for example oppression or poverty). See the remarks of S. Krauss in:

*R. E. J.*, XXXVI (1898), p. 43. S. Krauss suggests that Rabbi Johanan made use in TbBer.5b of the D. E. tradition about eating from two tables. There is no evidence, however, to support this suggestion.

7. *Say not: 'That man is handsome...* The only direct parallels to this statement are found in *'Otiot de-R. 'Aqiba* (see A. Jellinek, *Beit ha-Midrash*, III, p. 38 and cf. S. A. Wertheimer, *Batei Midrashot*, II, p. 381); In Midr. ha-Gad. on Lev. 12:1 (ed,. M. Margulies, p. 309); and in *Seph. Liqqutei ha-Pardes*, ed. M. Herschkovitz p. 88 (cf. A. Jellinek, *Beit ha-Midrash*, .I, p. 157). The statement is associated in those sources with Qoh. 3:19: 'The fate of men is the same as the fate of animals'. With respect to the relatively short lifespan of a person, everyone is alike. A body that was once beautiful remains behind as a useless, impure object. The cadaver of a pure animal, which may normally be eaten, may not be eaten by an Israelite if the animal has not been slaughtered according to the method prescribed. An animal may not be eaten, for example, if it has been torn, if it died through an accident or if it died a natural death. But the cadaver of such an animal, retains a certain value. Although the meat of such an animal may not be consumed by an Israelite, it may be sold to a heathen. Cf. Dt. 14:21. The hide of such an animal may be made into something by an Israelite. The dead body of a person, however, is of no practical value and would be of no interest to a heathen, i. e., even if it were sold, which of course would not be permitted. All people are alike in face of a speedy death. In the sources mentioned, one finds a much more extensive tradition concerning this, with the addition of the idea that it is a more serious defilement to touch a human cadaver than it is to touch a cadaver of an animal. Compare Num. 19:11 with Lev. 11:39. This same idea appears in S. E. Z. XXIV (ed. M. Friedmann, p. 42); cf. Tanh., 'Emor, ed. S. Buber, § 21, 49a; cf. Jalq. Qoh., r. 968. It is possible that the statement here in D. E. Z. was part of a more extensive midrash concerning Qoh. 3:19.

8. *Say not: 'That man is strong...* One should not envy the physical strength and masculinity of another, for true power and courage are spiritual power and courage, which are necessary for one to be able to put the Torah into practise and to control anger and evil intentions. Cf. in the parallels the use of Ps. 103:20 and cf. the version in *Halakhot Gedolot* (ed. E. Hildesheimer, p. 650), where Ps. 103:20 is added as a Scripture reference.

### 9. Let these words be in your heart: Know whence you came and whither you go and before whom you will have to give account and reckoning in the future.

These concluding words apply to the statements in D. E. Z. IV,4−8, all of which are introduced by the phrase 'say not'. This phrase is also cited in the sources quoted above (*Seph. Liqqutei ha-Pardes*, l.c.; cf. *Seder Jetzirat ha-Weled* in *Beit ha-Midrash* of A. Jellinek l.c. and in Midr. ha-Gad. on Lev. 12:1

l.c. Cf. also *Midr. 'Asseret ha-Dibrot* in A. Jellinek, *Beit ha-Midrash*, I, p. 157. The admonition actually dates back to a statement by 'Aqabjah ben Mehalal'el, of which only the beginning is given here in D. E. Z. See remarks to D. E. R. III,1.

**10. You may not cast your eyes on money which does not belong to you, because they (i. e. such eyes) even sink down (i. e. dim the light coming from) the gates of Heaven [other reading; because they cast you in the midst of darkness and gloom].**

The statements in D. E. Z. IV,9–22 like in D. E. Z. IV,4–9 appear in their entirely in *Seph. Liqqutei ha-Pardes* l.c. (cf. *Jetzirat ha-Weled* in A. Jellinek, *Beit ha-Midrash* l.c. and in *Midr.ha-Gad.* l.c.).

There are great differences in both the manuscripts and the parallels. One reading that is closely related to the basis manuscript of D. E. is found in S. E. Z. XVI (ed. M. Friedmann, p. 1; cf. Midrash Zuta on Qoh. 7:19). In the sources mentioned, this statement is said to come from the Mishnah! See S. E. Z.: '... for so teach the sages in the Mishnah...' See Midr. Zuta l.c.: 'De-tenan'. This method of citation is probably connected with the practise of studying the first chapters of D. E.Z, together with the sixth chapter of M'Abot and with the practise of transmitting them together in the tradition. This has resulted in parts of D. E. literature being regarded as a component of the sixth chapter of M'Abot. The statement here in D. E. Z. must be considered a counterpart to the statement in S. E. Z. IV,17.: 'Eyes that you do not cast on money that is not yours will give you light amidst thick darkness and gloom.' Eyes that are not jealous provide, as it were, light in darkness and allow one to see things stripped of darkness and removed from concealment. Jealous eyes, however, immerse one in darkness and deprive one of vision. In D. E. Z. IV,17 Is. 58:10 is cited as Scripture reference: '... Then shall your light rise in darkness and your gloom be as the noon-day.' The opposite image is depicted here in D. E. Z. IV,10. Jealous eyes will sink (read: 'me-shaqqe'ot') the light of the gates of Heaven (read 'she'arei raqia', as in the most of the manuscripts and add the word ''or' [light]). Cf. especially the commentary *Me'ir 'Einajjim* on S. E. Z. l.c.: Jealous eyes even extinguish the lights of the gates of Heaven. See also J. Harburger, *Massekhet Derech Erez Sutta*, p. 31: '... diese versenken die Pforten des Himmels.' and ibid. p. 30, note 6: '... dass gleichsam Sonne, Mond und Sterne nicht hervorkommen können um zu leuchten. Dem Neidischen scheint selbst die Sonne nicht freundlich.' See, however, the reading in S. E. Z. XVI, ed. Lewin Epstein and cf. the interpretation of A. J. Tawrogi, *Derech Erez Sutta*, p. 26: Do not cast your eyes on money that is not yours, for they will sink to earth, even if they are directed at the gates of Heaven.

A number of manuscripts of D. E. Z. and the parallels read: '... because they cast you in darkness ('she-hem ma'aphilot...'), in the midst of darkness and gloom.' See the commentary of M. Friedmann on S. E. Z. h.l. This is not an alternative reading but a more detailed explanation of a reading such as in the basis manuscript in D. E. Z. With reference to the phrase 'in the midst of night and gloom' cf. Prov. 7:9 and Prov. 20:20.

11. **Let not your ears hear idle words, because they are burnt first of the organs.**
12. **Let not your mouth speak calumny, for it is the first to be summoned for judgment.**
13. **Let there not be found with you any evil thing [or anything] which is robbed, because all your limbs will testify against you.**
14. **Let not your feet hurry you to (commit a) transgression, lest the Angel of Death is hurrying to get the start of you.**

11. *Let not your ear hear idle words* ... This statement is also cited as a tradition from the Mishnah in S. E. Z. XVI (ed. M. Friedmann, p. 2) and in Midr. Zuta on Qoh. 7:19. See the commentary to the previous statement. The statement appears in TbKet.5b as a baraita. See Rashi and others on Tb'Ab. Zar. 38a. The ear is the thinnest and softest part of the body and thus is the first to be scorched and burn if one is condemned to stay in Gehinnom. One notion behind this statement is that the part of the body where the process of transgression begins will also be condemned first. The instigator will be punished first. See the reading in *Seph. Liqqutei ha-Pardes* (ed. M. Herschkovitz, p. 88 and in *Seder Jetzirat ha-Weled* in A. Jellinek, *Beit ha-Midrash*, I, p. 157: '... for they let him hear first the judge of Gehinnom.' The words of the baraita in TbKet. 5a are also, however, interpreted figuratively. The Ear is the first to burn in the sense that the process of transgression begins with the ear. Listening to idle talk brings about idle thoughts and wishes, which leads to wrong behaviour.

12. *Let not your mouth speak calumny...* The tongue will be the first to account for its deeds. This also implies the judgement of Gehinnom. Cf. the reading in *Midr. 'Asseret ha-Dibrot* (in A. Jellinek, *Beit ha-Midrash*, I, p. 89): '... for all the parts of the body, the tongue is the first to burn and is the first to be condemned.' It is possible that an association with the procedures of execution by fire figures in this statement. The tongue was the first part of the body to burn when one was executed by burning. Cf. MSanh. VII (beginning) and cf. TbSanh. 52a ff.

13. *Let there not be found with you any evil thing (and any) stolen article...* Most manuscripts and parallels read: 'Let no stolen article be found in your hand.' This statement appears to be based on a tradition in TbTa'an. 11a. Cf. *Midr. 'Asseret ha-Dibrot*, in A. Jellinek, *Beit ha-Midrash*, I, p. 79. The notion that all parts of the body bear witness against one is based in TbTa'an. 11a on Is. 43,10: 'You are My witnesses, says the Lord ...'. After death, one must account

for all deeds to which the various parts of the body can attest, and those parts bear witness against one concerning deeds that have been done through them.

14. *Let not your feet hurry you to transgression...* One should not hasten to commit a transgression lest the Angel of Death inflict an early death before one has been able to repent. Let not the angel of death be as eager to take one's life as one was to commit transgressions!

15. **Fear not a court which is below (i. e. an earthy court), for the (earthy) witnesses against you are lovers of money. But fear the court which is above (i. e. the Heavenly court), because above there are witnesses against you [which do not love money] and moreover proclaim lawsuits against you from hour to hour.**

One must fear not earthy judgement but heavenly judgment, which is not corruptible. To clarify this statement, one can quote the words of Rabbi Johanan ben Zakkai spoken, according to the tradition, on his deathbed. See TbBer.28b and cf. A. R. N. [a], XXV. A person who has judged himself to be lacking must fear earthly judgment far less than heavenly judgment. An earthy court may be bribed by nice words and gifts and thus pass a favourable judgment, but the witnesses of the heavenly court cannot be influenced by nice words and gifts; rather, they are always ready to challenge one. See also the explicative reading in *Ma'alot ha-Middot* (ed. 'Eshkol, p. 309). Cf. also TbTa'an. 11a. Cf. TbHag. 16a and cf. *Midr. 'Asseret ha-Dibrot*, in A. Jellinek, *Beit ha-Midrash*, I, p. 79, where it is said that the two angels who accompany one throughout his whole life will testify about him.

In some parallels, one finds a revised reading: 'Fear the court below (the earthy court), even if they are found of money...', i.e., even if they can be influenced by bribe. Cf. *Menorat ha Ma'or* of Al-Nakawa, ed, H. G. Enelow, p. 43; cf. *Seph. ha-Musar* (of Rabbi Jehudah Kl"tz, ed. S.CH. Lieberman, Jerusalem 1967, p. 277) and *Reshit Hokhmah*, D. E., sha'ar III. See the reading in A. J. Tawrogi, *Derech Erez Sutta*, p. 27. This reading is not confirmed by the manuscripts in D. E. Z. and must be regarded as a secondary correction of the remark in the statement here in D. E. Z. that one need not fear the judgment of an earthy court because of its corruptibility. The meaning, however, is that one need not fear a wrong judgment, for the heavenly court will ultimately see the compensation. Sages must base their behaviour only on unshakeable fear of the heavenly court and not on influenceable human sanctions. The motivation to avoid evil must not depend on the extent to which one may expect human sanctions. Sages must not allow the lack of human sanctions or the possibility of avoiding such sanctions to influence their behaviour.

**16. If you have fulfilled My words joyfully, My (heavenly) family will go out to greet you. Even I Myself will go out to greet you and I will say to you: 'Your entering will be in peace.'**

This statement correspondents strongly with the context in TbKet. 104a and parallels. According to a statement by Rabbi Hijja bar Gamda made in the name of Rabbi José ben Sha'ul, a righteous individual will be welcomed after his death by other righteous people with the words: 'He shall enter into peace, they shall rest on their beds.' Cf.Is. 57:2. According to a statement in TbKet. l.c. by Rabbi 'El'azar (Rabbi 'El'azar ben Pedat; cf. W. Bacher *'Amora'ei 'Eretz Jisra'el*, II, p. 81), the righteous person who has died is met by three groups of angels. The first group says: 'Come in peace'. The second group says: 'He who walks in his uprightness' (Is. 57:2). The third group says: 'He shall enter into peace, they shall rest on their beds' (Is. 57:2). Cf. also the readings of this statement in BAM. Rab. XI,7 and in Midr. Teh. 30,3. The tradition most closely related to the one here in D. E. Z. is one passed on by Rabbi Jehudah bar Simon in the name of Rabbi Joshia. Cf. Midr. Teh. 30,3 in which it is said that God Himself, as it were, comes to meet the righteous who have died with the words: 'Your arrival is in peace.'

The statement here in D. E. Z. appears in similar form only in later sources, but giving the wording it quite possibly dates back to old traditions.

In connection with the term 'shahar' ('shiher') – the first official paying of respect to someone at dawn – see S. Krauss, *Talmudische Archäologie*, III, pp. 16 and 250, note 34; cf. also S. Krauss in *R. E. J.*, XXXVI (1898), p. 43. The image appears to have been derived from the practise of families in the Talmudic period of being the first in the morning to pay their respects to important people.

**17. If you have not turned your eyes to money, which does not belong to you, they will shine for you in the midst of darkness and gloom, because there is said: 'Then shall your light rise in darkness and your gloom be as the noon-day' (Is. 58:10).**

See the commentary on D. E. Z. IV,10.

**18. If you have not listened with your ears to idle words, they will cause you to hear (words to instruct you) [Mss.: words of peace in This World] for the life in the World to Come [other reading: for This World and for the World to Come], as it is said: 'And your ears shall hear a word behind you, saying, This is the way, walk in it ...'(Is. 30:21).]**

Ears with which one has not listened to idle words will let one hear (in) the life in the World to Come, according to the literal reading of the basis manuscript. A

number of manuscripts read: '... will let you hear peace in This World and in
the World to Come.' See the addition of Is.30:21 as Scripture reference in the
manuscripts. Cf. also the translation by M. Higger, *Massekhtot Derekh 'Eretz*,
pp. 44−45: 'If you have not suffered your ears to listen ... they will hear words
guiding you in This World and in the World to come.' We give preference to the
short reading of our basis manuscript.

**19.  If your mouth did not speak calumny, then on account of her all who
caused others to be slain will (themselves) be slain.**

The term 'ba'alei harugim' is difficult to interpret. It could apply to murderers,
but if it does, the term 'horegim' could also have been used. The term probably
applies not to murderers per se but to persons who have caused the death of
others through slanderous talk and betrayal. Those who refrain from slander
are rewarded in that slanderers are punished according to the most extreme
consequences of their behaviour. The term 'lashon ha-ra'' can also apply to
specific forms of betrayal; cf. TbKet. 49a; Deb. Rab. V,8 and other sources.
See also the interpretation in J. Harburger, *Massekhet Derech Erez Sutta*, p. 33:
'... Deines Mundes wegen werden ... alle die umkommen, *die damit töteten*.'

**20.  If your mouth has occupied itself with the words of theTorah, all who
live to the benefit of others (or: who are worthy of a blessing) will bless
themselves on behalf of it.**
**21.   If you withheld your hand from plunder, what can the workers of evil
do to you?**
**22.  If you did not close your hands from almsgiving, what can all owners of
silver and gold do to you?**
**23.  If your feet did not hurry you to an act of transgression, what can the
Angel of death do to you?**

20.  The basis manuscript reads 'ba'alei berukhim', which in this context is a
counterpart to the preceding 'ba'alei harugim'. This probably applies to persons who are a blessing to others, as opposed to 'ba'alei harugim' who cause the
death of others. Other readings, however, read 'ba'alei berakhah' (those who
utter a blessing). Cf. the explanation of M. Ginsberg in *The Minor Tractates of
the Talmud*, ed. A. Cohen, II, p. 580 that the term "ba'alei berukhim' means
those who are worthy of a blessing or who bless themselves with a blessing in
which they express the wish that they will be equally blessed as he who occupies
his mouth with the Torah. Cf. the reading in *Menorat ha-Ma'or* of Al-Nakawa,
ed, H. G. Enelow, p. 431, where Gen 12:3 is cited as Scripture reference, which
concludes with the words: '..And all generations of the earth will bless themselves with you ... '

Read in accordance with the manuscripts "aleikha' (on account *of you*) instead of "alaw' (on account *of it*).

### 24. **These words I discoursed before you, what you desire do it; but do not say: 'I was not warned'.**

See, among others, S. Krauss in: *R. E. J.* XXXVI (1898), pp. 31—32. S. Krauss regards these words as the official conclusion of D. E. Z. I—IV. While this may be so, it is also possible that these words are the original conclusion to the clear literary unit comprised by D. E. Z. IV,4—23. The numerous double texts in the first four chapters of D. E. Z. show that these chapters were compiled from loose fragments. See further the Introduction; it is not unlikely that chapter IV of D. E. Z. was added to chapters I—III in a later stage and that the closing admonition from then served as a conclusion of D. E. Z. I—IV!

# Derekh 'Eretz Ze'irah

## Derekh 'Eretz Zuta, chapter V

**1. He who is a sage, does not eat standing and does not drink standing and does not copulate standing and he does not wipe off the dish and he does not lick his fingers and he does not belch in front of his neighbour.**

This statement is composed of originally independent fragments. The listing of the first three things that a scholar must refrain from can be traced back to a tradition in TbGit. 70a: 'Three things weaken a person's body, and they are: eating while standing, drinking while standing, copulating while standing...'

The basis manuscript here in D. E. Z. reads 'we-lo-jashtin' (does not urinate). This is probably an incorrect interpretation of the abbreviation 'we-lo jsh"'('we-lo jeshammesh' = and does not copulate). In connection with 'we-lo-jashtin' cf. TbNid. 13a. The reading 'we-lo-jashen' is also an erroneous interpretation of the same abbreviation, but understandable on the basis of a tradition such as the one found in TbShab. 129b: 'For a master said: in five cases one is nearer to death than to life... who sleeps and rises (immediately)...' In accordance with the basis manuscript, one must read here in D. E. Z.: '... and does not copulate standing...' In the same context of TbGit. 70a, one finds a tradition in which the rabbis say that anyone who copulates standing becomes susceptible to muscle spasms. All the practices to be avoided listed here are mentioned among the practices that are injurious to one's health. Based partly on practical experience and partly on mild superstition, the warnings to avoid such practices must be understood as preventative measures against illness and bodily complaints. Cf. the commentary of M. Higger, *Massekhtot Ze'irot*, 1970, p. 139.

The continuation of the statement *And he does not wipe off the dish* .. belongs to another context of etiquette during the meals. Bread was used as a utensil with which to scoop food out of the communal dish. Cf. S. Krauss, *Talmudische Archäologie*, III, p. 51 ff. It was considered gluttonous to wipe a dish completely clean with a peace of bread and thereby give the host the impression that one's hunger was not satisfied. Cf. also the commentary to D. E. R. IX,1; and D. E. R. VI,3a-b.

... *and he does not lick his fingers* – bread was used as an utensil with which to scoop soft cooked food from the dish and thereby to prevent direct contact between the fingers and moist food. It was considered most improper and unhygienic to put one's fingers into one's mouth. This is comparable to the forbiddance to bite off a piece of bread and to put the rest back on the dish or to offer it to other guests, or to offer to other guests a goblet of wine from which one has already drunk. See D. E. R. IX,1. S. Krauss suggests that reference is made here in chap. V to the habit of lapping water like animals with the aid of their forelimbs. See S. Krauss, *Talmudische Archäologie*, III, p. 242, note 26. Cf. TbSanh. 68b; There is no special reason for S. Krauss's explanation in this case. Some manuscripts of D. E. Z. read 'with his lips' (which is difficult to clarify) instead of 'with his fingers'. It is thus possible that the original text read: 'One may not wipe the dish clean with a piece of bread, nor may he lick it.' Two versions have arose from it: '... and also not lick it clean with the fingers' and '... and also not lick it clean with the lips.' Cf. in manuscript Munich, Kön. Hofbibl. (cat. M. Steinschneider) no. 232(10) the reading '... and he will also not lick the dish clean with his lips.' This confirms the assumption made above.

... *and he does not belch in front of his neighbour.* The verb 'gasah' is interpreted as, among other things, 'to belch'. Cf. *'Arukh ha-Shalem*, ed. A. Kohut, II, (Vienna 1926), p. 326 and M. Jastrow, *Dictionary*, I, p. 260. See the reading 'we-lo-jitzhaq' (and he does not belch) in *Reshit Hokhmah*, pereq 'Anawah, sha'ar 7. The words 'in front of his neighbour' seem to affirm this interpretation. In TbNid. 63b, the term 'gasah' refers to a 'bloated feeling' as a sign of oncoming menstruation. In the same text, however, it is also interpreted as 'to belch'.

The term could mean 'to glut', 'to swallow large quantities.' Cf. the use of the term 'gasah' in Siphra, Be-Har, pereq IV,4 and Siphrei, Debarim, Pisqa 1 (ed. L. Finkelstein, p. 5) among other sources. This interpretation appears in A. J. Tawrogi, *Massekhet Derech Erez Sutta*, p. 29, notes.

In *Nahalat Ja'aqob*, a.l. J. Naumburg gives the following interpretation: The shifting back and forth of food from one side of the mouth to the other, in reference to an expression derived from the stem 'gus' (to stir) found in MMakhsh. V,11. For grammatical reasons, however, this interpretation is implausible.

## 2. (A further characteristic of the sage is) moderation in conversation, moderation in sleep, moderation in laughing, moderation in pleasure, moderation in 'yes, yes' and moderation in 'no, no'.

The things mentioned here that a sage must do in moderation were taken from a listing in *Pereq Qinjan Torah* (see M'Abot VI,5–6; and cf. S. E. Z. XVII, ed. M. Friedmann, p. 18 and cf. Mas. Kal. Rab. VIII, ed. N. N. Coronel, 13a).

The terms 'sihah' and 'sehoq' refer principally to speaking about non-religious matters and frivolous contact with women. Cf. S. Krauss, *Talmudische Archäologie*, III, p. 243, note 31; cf. also the commentary to D. E. Z. III,12.

... *moderation in 'yes, yes' and 'no, no'* ... The 'yes' of a sage must truly be yes and remain 'yes'. The same applies for 'no'. The sage must be trustworthy in his conduct so that others will trust him without him making superfluous affirmations, denials, or even oaths. Cf. especially Mat. 5:37 and ac. 5:12: 'Let your yes be yes and your no be no.' Cf. further S. E. R. XVIII (beginning) and Rambam, *Jad*, Hil. De'ot, V,13. Cf. the commentary to D. E. Z. III,12: 'The beginning of vowing...'

### 3. A man should always know with whom he is standing, with whom he is sitting, with whom he is eating, with whom he is drinking,with whom he is dining, with whom he is speaking and with whom he is affixing a signature to a document.

The practice of not standing, sitting, eating or drinking with just anyone or being the guest of just anyone or of signing an official document with just anyone is ascribed in old Tannaitic sources to the so-called 'pure-minded of Jerusalem.' In MGit. 9:8, it is said that the pure-minded of Jerusalem signed as witnesses the divorce act by writing: 'So and So, son of So and So' without adding 'witness'. They used as short a formula as possible. Cf. the *Tosaphists* on TbGit. 89a. The issue here concerns especially careful and scrupulous persons with refined manners. See the statement in name of Rab in TbSanh. 23a: Witnesses may not sign a deed unless they are aware who is to sign with them. The reason is the fear that the other witness may prove to be unfit. In that case both signatures are null, and the eligible signatory is thus put to shame (see the commentary of J. Schachter in *The Babylonian Talmud*, ed. I. Epstein, Seder Neziqin, III, p. 130, note 12. In connection to the term 'neqi'ei da'at Jerushala-jim' (the pure minded of Jerusalem) cf. J. Schachter in o.c., p. 131, in reference to Büchler's translation 'the cautious' and to Müller's translation 'the pious'. J. Schachter himself interprets the term to mean 'elegant circles'. Cf. also S. Krauss, *Talmudische Archäologie*, III, chap. IX, p. 55, with the translation 'the correct'. These more elegant circles were careful in selecting their guests and accepted an invitation to dine somewhere only if they knew with whom they would be eating, the intention being to avoid contact with godless people. Cf. also D. E. Z. IV,1. Possibly there is a connection with the 'men of Jerusalem' of whom it is said that they bound their Lulab with strands of gold; see MSuk. III,8; TosSuk. II,10; TbSuk. 37a (Ms. Ms. Munich: 'jeqirei Jerushalajim'!) and TbMen. 27a.

... *with whom he is sitting*... See the parallels. This actually means that one should know with whom he is sitting as a witness or judge at a trial. If a member of the elegant and pious circles did not know whether any other person present in the court had been disqualified as a witness, he did not take a seat in the proceedings, in order to avoid becoming involved in a dubious or fraudulent trial.

... *with whom he is dining, with whom he is speaking*... Law-abiding and scrupulous sages avoided contact with the "am ha-'aretz' in order to avoid becoming involved in gossip and confronting vulgar habits, which could lead to the discredit of their good name. Cf. also D. E. Z. IV,1 and the commentary there.

In the same context *with whom he is standing* has to be interpreted. Cf. the reading in Mekh. de-R. Jishm., Mishpatim, par. 20 (ed. M. Friedmann, 98b; ed. H. S. Horovitz / I. A. Rabin, p. 322): 'None of them went to a wedding before he knew who would be going with him.' Even being in the vicinity of unsuitable people was avoided by law-abiding and scrupulous sages. See Rashi on TbGit. l.c. It is noteworthy that the rules listed here are not introduced in D. E. Z. as pertaining to certain refined circles of people, but as general practices pertaining to no one in particular.

4. **By four things a sage (scholar) is recognizable: by his purse, by his cup, by his temper and by his attire. And some say: 'Also by his speech'.**

The statement appears as a baraita in the name of Rabbi 'Ilai in TbEr. 65b. Cf. in R. Rabbinovicz, *Seph. Diqduqei Sopherim*, a.l., the readings 'R. Pappa', 'R. 'Ilpa' and 'R. Shila'. Cf. R. Halperin, *'Atlas 'Etz Hajjim*, IV, p. 142. It is apparent here that the original statement was based on alliteration and that only three things were mentioned, beginning with the letter 'kaph': purse, cup and temper. One would have expected 'u-bekassuto' instead of 'u-be-'atiphato'. Cf. S. Krauss, *Talmudische Archäologie*, III, p. 241, note 13. S. Krauss suggests that the statement originally read: 'kiso, koso, we-kassuto'. The manuscripts, however, do not confirm this suggestion, and it is clear from Tb'Er.l.c. that 'u-be-'atiphato' (and by his attire) stems from another tradition. The reading in D. E. is less precise, considering that 'and by his attire' is simply added to the list of the alliterated elements and not introduced, as in Tb'Er. l.c., as a separate tradition. Cf. the opinion of S. Krauss in: *R. E. J.*, XXXVI (1898), p. 44. It is striking that in Tb'Er. it is less specifically stated: 'One recognizes *a man* by three things . . .' Cf. also the unspecified tradition in A. R. N. [b], XXXI (34b). S. Krauss. l.c., suggested that the fact that the statement in D. E. is applied to sages, explains the addition 'and by his attire'.

. . . *by his purse* . . . The scholar is recognizable by the way he uses money. Cf. the related tradition in A. R. N. [b] l.c. A Scholar or person is recognizable by the way in which he conducts financial transactions. If he deals only with his own advantage and in an unkind manner, then he is no scholar. Cf. also *Nahalat Ja'aqob* on D. E. Z., h.l. Cf. D. E. Z. III,13 and D. E. Z. II,23. Another possible explanation is that the scholar is recognizable by the extent of his generosity.

. . . *by his cup* . . . The scholar is recognizable by the account that he drinks (cf. A. R. N. l.c.) and by the way in which he drinks. See especially D. E. R. VIII,1b. The scholar does not drink great quantities at once and does not drink his goblet empty in one draft. He also does not drink from a goblet before offering it to someone else at the table. Cf. D. E. R. IX,3a-b. In short, the scholar can be recognized by his good table manners.

... *by his temper*... A scholar is tolerant and knows to control himself, even when he is insulted by others. Cf. also D. E. Z. I,1 at "alub'.

... *by his attire*... A scholar wears clean and simple clothing. Cf. the commentary to D. E. Z. VII,3: 'modest in his clothing.' Cf. *Seph. Ben Sira* 19:28−29 (ed. M. Z. Segal. p. 117): 'A man's attire proclaims his deeds (so the Syrian version; the Hebrew version reads: '(... and the laughter of his teeth) ... and the footsteps of a man tell about him.' Cf. in the parallels (A. R. N. l.c.; Seph. Ben Sira l.c.) the reference to a person's way of walking. See further the commentary to D. E. Z. VII,3.

... *by his speech*. On the basis of correspondences elsewhere in D. E., refraining from gossip must also be taken into consideration (cf., e.g., D. E. Z. I,14) as well as speaking with a soft voice (cf. D. E. Z. II,14) and speaking in a thoughtful and firm manner (cf. D. E. Z. II,5 and II,22, and D. E. Z. III,1 and III,6). A scholar speaks trustworthy and speaks only about relevant matters. Cf. D. E. Z. V,2: '... moderation in conversation', about idle matters. A scholar is very selective about those with whom he talks. Cf. D. E. Z. I,7, a sage avoids discussions with sectarians. Cf. also D. E. Z. V,3: A sage avoids the company of the ignorant "am ha-'aretz'. See also *Pirqei Rabbenu ha-Qadosh* in L. Grünhut, *Seph. ha-Liqqutim*, III, where Qoh. 1:17 is quoted in the explanation: 'Words of the sages heard in quiet are better than the shouting of him who rules among the stupid.'

## 5. **The adornment of the Torah is wisdom, the adornment of wisdom is fear, the adornment of fear is meekness, the adornment of meekness is (the performance of) the precepts, the adornment of the precepts is humility.**

See the various readings in the manuscripts of D. E. Z. Behind the adornment of the Torah there is a discussion about what is most important. If fear is the adornment of meekness, then meekness is the most important. If meekness is the adornment of fear, then fear is what is most important. See a statement ascribed to Rabbi Mana (or Mattana, according to the reading in Shir ha-Shir.Rab. I,9 and Jalq. ha-Makhiri on Prov. 22:4; or to Rabbi Jitzhaq son of Rabbi 'El'azar), see TjShab. I,3 and S. Lieberman, *Jerushalmi Ki-Pheshutah*, a.l., p. 35; cf. Midr. Prov. 15:32; Tanh., ed. S. Buber, Be-Ha'alotekha, § 16 and Jalq., Prov., r. 960 and Jalq., Ps., r. 870; cf. *Midr. ha-Gad.* on Dt. 23:15 and Midr. Tan., ed. D. Hoffmann, p. 148.

On the basis of Prov. 22:4 'fear of sin' is ascribed as the heel (of the sandal) of meekness ("anawah'). In this comparison meekness is considered more important than fear. It is also implicated that wisdom ('hokhmah') is more important than fear. Fear is the crown, the adornment, of wisdom. This correspondents with the reading in the basis manuscript of D. E. Z. : 'The adornment of wisdom

is fear.' As in the above-mentioned parallels one can support this statement
with Ps. 111:10: 'The beginning of wisdom is fear of the Lord.' The remark in
the above-mentioned parallels that fear is the heel of the sandal of meekness is a
possible contradiction to the basis manuscript of D. E. which states that meekness is the adornment of fear. Rather, it correspondents to those manuscripts
that read: 'The adornment of meekness is fear.'

A discussion about the importance of meekness and fear appears in the
traditions about a well-known statement by Pinhas ben Ja'ir about the scale of
virtues. The most prevalent version (see Tb'Ab. Zar. 20a and parallels) reads:
'... and meekness leads to fear...' In this statement, fear is considered to be
the higher goal to reach, to be attained through meekness. This seems to be the
original reading. Cf. Ms. Kaufmann on MSot. IX,14 and the reading given in
the margin of Ms. Parma on this passage from the Mishnah and cf. Ms. Leiden
of the Talmud Jerushalmi on TjShab. I,3 [3c]. Ms. Leiden l.c. reads: 'meekness
leads to fear, for it is written: "The heel of meekness, fear of the Lord."' (Prov.
22:4). From this it is apparent that the word "eqeb' (heel) in Prov. l.c. can also
be interpreted as '**goal**'.

According to this explanation, then, fear is to be attained by meekness. Cf.
also the corresponding genizah-fragments on Tj. l.c., in L. Ginzberg, *Seridei
Jerushalmi*, repr. Jerusalem 1969, p. 66. See, however, R, Rabbinovicz, *Seph.
Diqduqei Sopherim*, on Tb'Ab. Zar. 20a, p. 53, note 30 and the reference to,
among other sources, the *Riph* and *'Aggadot ha-Talmud* with a revised reading:
'Fear of sin leads to meekness.' See the reference in the *Tosaphot* on Tb'Ab.
Zar. 20a to TjSheq., with a corresponding reading (which, however, does not
appear in the readings of TjSheq. III [end] known to us). Only in the later
sources of the statement of Pinhas ben Ja'ir does this reading appear further.
Cf. *Seph. ha-Manhig*, ed. Rab Kook, p. 24.; Bahja on Dt. 23:10; and *Menorat
ha-Ma'or* of Jitzhaq 'Abohab, § 180. The revised reading is probably an attempt
to make the text correspondent with the explanation of Prov. 22:4, in agreement with the above-mentioned parallels, attributed to Rabbi Mana or Rabbi
Jitzhaq ben Rabbi 'El'azar. The statement of Rabbi Jehoshua ben Levi in the
context of the statement of Pinhas ben Ja'ir in Tb'Ab. Zar. 20a must be
similarly interpreted (cf. Tb'Ar. 16b): 'And meekness is the greatest of all.'
This is a corrective statement, added to the original version of the statement of
Rabbi Pinhas ben Ja'ir (according to which meekness leads to fear) and is meant
to oppose a contradiction to the current explanation of Prov. 22:4 at the time,
according to which meekness is more important than fear). Perhaps it is also to
be seen as an emphasis of the pious on meekness. The various readings in the
manuscripts of D. E. are therefore not coincidental, but bear a connection to
the problems mentioned. Cf. especially D. E. R. VII,5: 'Three things are equal
to each other: wisdom, fear and meekness.' This is clearly a reaction to the
discussion about the order of importance of meekness and fear and the relationship of wisdom to meekness and fear.

The wisdom of the sages is the adornment of the Torah. One honours the Torah by studying it. The adornment of wisdom is fear. Wisdom, which is expressed in the fear of committing transgressions is of greater value than wisdom that is not. The adornment of fear is meekness. One who is easily angered and is slów to forgive is much more likely to commit transgressions than a meek person. This reading from the basis manuscript concurs with the statement of Rabbi Pinhas ben Ja'ir that we consider to be original: ' ... meekness leads to fear of sin...' Meekness, however, is placed above fear, like in the statement of Rabbi Jehoshua ben Levi (see above) and in a statement ascribed to Rabbi 'Aqiba in A. R. N. [a], XXVI (41a-b).

The adornment of meekness is the precepts. One attains meekness through fulfilling the commandments. The adornment of the commandments is humility. One should not fulfil the commandments in order to attract attention; it is best to fulfil the commandments for the sake of Heaven.

**6. (A man) should not be awake among those who sleep, and he should not sleep among those who are awake; he should not weep among those who laugh and he should not laugh among those who weep; he should not sit down among those who are standing and he should not be standing among those who are sitting; he should not study Scripture among those who study the Oral Tradition and he should not study the Oral Tradition among those who are studying Scripture. As a general rule: no man should act differently from the usage of his fellowmen.**

Cf. D. E. R. VII,7. This summons to show solidarity with the situation and feelings of the community or a society in which one stays. The saying dates back to a statement, ascribed to Hillel, and transmitted in TosBer., II (end), in which one is cautioned not to deviate from others by being undressed or dressed while others are not, standing while others sit or sitting while others stand, or to laugh while others cry or cry when others laugh. The element of studying Oral Tradition and Scripture is added here in D. E. Z.! Cf. also a closely related statement by Hillel in M'Abot II,4: 'You may not separate yourself from the community.' See the accompanying explanation of Rashi and Me'iri, among others: be one with the community in time of need. Cf. also TbTa'an. 11a; cf. TbSem. chap. II; cf. also other sources.

A closely related tradition appears in a statement in S. E. Z. XVI (ed. Lewin Epstein, p. 60), ascribed to Samuel ha-Qatan, based on Prov. 24:17 (: 'You shall not rejoice over the fall of your enemies'): 'You shall not fear with those who do not fear, you shall not cry with those who do not cry...' Cf., however, a contradictory version in ed. M. Friedmann, pp. 12–13; and M. Friedmann's commentary there in which another explanation is provided. See S. Krauss, in: *R. E. J.*, XXXVI (1898), p. 45. According to S. Krauss, the statement in D. E. R. VII,7 (and thus by implication the statement here in D. E. Z. V) have

borrowed from the older Aramaic source in S. E. Z. l.c. The reading in D. E.
would thus be a younger Hebrew translation of the original Aramaic source.

D. E.R l.c. contains the addition of a concluding sentence: 'A man should
not deviate from the (mind and customs) of his companions and from other
men.' D. E. Z. h.l. reads: 'A general rule: A man should not deviate from the
customs of other men.' Cf. D. E. R. VI,4, which literally reads: ' A man's
thoughts must be mingled with the thoughts of (other) men', i. e. one should
always be emotionally involved with others and identify with them. Cf. TbKet.
17a and the explanation of S. Krauss, *Talmudische Archäologie*, III, p. 241,
note 6. Cf. also other sources. Cf. the statement of Rabbi Me'ir in Tanh., Wa-
Jera', § 11: 'A man must not deviate from the customs of the city (he comes to).'
See in the same strain of thought the aggadic example of Moses, who did not eat
on Mt. Sinai out of solidarity with the angels; and the aggadic examples of
angels who ate as if, out of solidarity with people. While the content of the
statement here in D. E. dates back to very old traditions, the form of the
statement was developed later.

## Derekh 'Eretz Zuta, chapter VI

**1. Four things are unbecoming for a sage (scholar): He should not be on the road after nightfall and he should not go out on the market (i. e. in public) scented; and he should not be the last to enter the synagogue and he should not frequent the meetings of ignorant persons.**

These for things do not comprise halakhic categories but involve special rules of behaviour that applied for scholars. More than ordinary conduct was expected of scholars. The statement here may have been basis of a more extensive, analogous baraita found in TbBer. 43b and parallels. The background of the rules of behaviour under discussion here is made clear in the gemara in TbBer. 43b. A scholar must avoid every form of false appearance, which could lead a scholar being unjustly suspected of something questionable, which in turn would defile God's name. A scholar may not go out alone into the dark so that he will not be suspected of untoward practises. Cf. the function of the concept 'desecration of God's name' ('hillul ha-Shem') in the context of TbJoma 86a. In TbPes. 2a, one finds avoidance of unnecessary danger as reason for not going alone in the dark. Cf. also D. E. R. XI,1 and the commentary in connection with reasons based on superstition for not going out alone into the dark. According to an opinion in TbBer. l.c., ascribed to Rabbi Johanan, a person was not to go out wearing perfume lest he be suspected of having homosexual contacts. Cf. also a statement of Beit Hillel, recorded in TosBer. VI,5 and TjBer. VIII,5 [12b].

A scholar was not to be last to enter a synagogue, lest others think that he came reluctantly and merely out of a sense of duty. TbBer. l.c. mentions 'house of study.' A scholar also must sit as little as possible with the "am ha-'aretz'. Cf. Ms. Oxford Bodleian (cat. A. Neubauer) no. 553: 'A sage must speak as little as possible with an "'am ha-'aretz".'

On the basis of the parallels, one may especially assume here that scholars were particularly supposed to avoid eating with the "am ha-'aretz'. By eating with an "am ha-'aretz' a scholar could be suspected of being careless in complying with the purity laws, pea, tithes, etc. A scholar must prevent others from suspecting that he behaves like the "am ha-'aretz' and that he has excessive interest in non-religious matters.

**2a. On entering the greater (the elder) precedes, on leaving the minor precedes. When ascending a staircase the greater precedes, when descending a staircase the minor precedes. Entering a meeting place (of scholars)**

**the greater precedes, on entering a prison the minor precedes. To pronounce a blessing the greater precedes.**

2b.  **And the passer-by greets one who is sitting.**

2a. *On entering the greater...* The word 'great' can refer to a person's age, social position, or knowledge of the Torah. In a parallel in Shem. Rab. IX,5, concerning the order of entrance, emphasis is placed on social status. Cf. also discussions in TjHor. III [48c]. In TbMeg. 28a, however, knowledge is stressed above social status. In TbBer. 46b, e.g., the importance of respect for a greater age is stressed. Cf. TbB. B. 120a; TjR. ha-Sh. II,6 [58b]; and TjSanh. I,2 [18c]; cf. also other sources. According to the tradition in TbB. B. 120a, the factor of age has precedence at a meal, and the extent of knowledge of the Torah has precedence in study groups.

In the context of D.E., one may interpret 'great' and 'small' to apply especially to knowledge of the Torah as well as to age. The practices mentioned here in D.E.Z. are also mentioned elsewhere in the tradition, as sign of respect for parents (Lev. 19:3) and older people in general (Dt. 1:15; Num. 11:15). See Rabbi's statement in TbBer. 61a. The great precede in all that is honourable and the small precede in all that is not honourable.

The order of entering into a house of prayer, of study etc., described in this statement does not concur with various parallels, which imply that important persons not only enter first but also leave first. Cf., e.g., TjHor. III [48c]; various readings of Siphrei on Dt. 1:15 (ed. L. Finkelstein, p. 25); and TosMeg. III,24 (cf. S. Lieberman, *Tosephta Ki-Pheshutah*, V, p. 24). One may assume that there were (local) habits that differed from each other. Most parallels contain a reading that states that is is an honour to leave a place first, which contradicts the tradition here in D.E.Z. See TbBer. 47a, where it is said that Rabin made an exception in entering through a gate that had no 'mezuzah' on it. Considering that it was nor honourable to pass through such a gate, he considered it proper for the 'smaller' to enter first. According to a baraita cited in the context of that opinion, the 'smaller' was the first to set foot on bridges and roads.

*When ascending a staircase...* Ascending and descending have also a symbolic meaning here.

*Entering a meeting place (Counsel Chamber) ...* The term 'beit ha-Wa'ad' translated here as 'Counsel Chamber', literally means 'the house of meeting'. This probably refers to a court of justice. Cf., e.g., the use of the term in MR. ha-Sh. IV,4 and see also D. Sperber, *Massekhet Derekh 'Eretz Zuta*, p. 26. 'Beit ha-wa'ad' can also mean, however, a house of study. Cf., e.g., M'Abot I,4.

In MSanh. IV,2 (cf. TosSanh. VI,2), one finds the tradition that, where legal decisions are concerned, one begins a discussion with the greatest and most learned persons in questions of finance, purity and impurity, and that only in matters of life and death ('dinei naphshot') does one begin with those who have the least knowledge, in order to prevent those people from being influenced by the testimony of those greater than themselves. In principal, then, it was the custom in the academy and in the court of law to let the most eminent scholar speak first. The statement in D.E., however, may also apply to the order in which people sat. Cf., e.g., TjKet. I,1 [25a] with respect to the practises in the court of law. In connection with the order of sitting, cf. further TbB.B. 120a and see *Shul. Ar.*, Jor. De'ah, 244,18 and see S. Krauss, *Talmudische Archäologie*, III, p. 45.

*To pronounce a blessing...* This may refer to the saying of the blessing at the beginning of the meal ('ha-Motzi') or to the saying of the blessing after the meal ('Birkat ha-Mazon'). The parallels especially confirm the latter possibility. See the context in TbBer. 46b and parallels. The person among a company of people who had the honour to wash his hand first, also had the honour of saying the 'Birkat ha-Mazon'. The honour of washing the hands first after the meal (or, when among many people of being the first of the last five to wash their hands) was reserved for the oldest (and the most venerable) person present, so that the honour of saying the 'Birkat ha-Mazon' after the meal generally fell to the oldest person present. The oldest person also had the honour of saying the blessing upon burning spices over a coal of fire at a feast.

The oldest person and the one with the greatest knowledge of the Torah was the first to be considered for saying a blessing. According to a tradition passed on in the name of Rabbi Johanan and Rabbi Shim'on concerning the saying of the blessing at the beginning of the meal, the host broke the bread and said the blessing and the guest said the 'Birkat ha-Mazon' after the meal. When no clear distinction was made between the duties of the host and guest, obviously the oldest person present broke the bread and said the blessing. According to a statement by Rabbi Johanan in TbMeg. 29a (see Rashi), it was condemned as a very serious transgression if a sage allowed an ignorant High Priest to utter the blessing, thereby putting himself in second place. Ignorance is never to be placed above the Torah. The custom of revering to the sages was not so much a sign of revering the sages as of revering the Torah.

### 3. **One should not seat himself in the presence of a greater (an elder) person.**

Nearly all the manuscripts read ('bi-phenei'). This renders the interpretation 'before the elders have taken their seat' less plausible. The term 'bi-phenei' must be translated as a definition of space, rather than as a reference to time. One may not lie next to a prominent person at a meal. This means then that one has to stay until one has received permission to take a seat (for example next to the seat of an important person) and so long as the prominent persons present have not taken their seats. Cf., e.g., TbBer. 46b and TjTa'an. IV,2 [68a] and TosBer. V,5 and TjKet. I,1 [28a] in a statement by Rabbi Alexandari.

According to the Jewish custom, the greatest person lies in the middle, the second greatest lies at the side near his head and the least eminent lies at the side near his feat. See TosBer. l.c. and TbBer. l.c.

According to an opinion of Rab Joseph, a pupil is not at all allowed to lie really next to his teacher at the celebration of the Seder, because he has, as it were, no free status and is subject to his teacher as he is subject to Heaven. Similarly, a woman is not to lie next to her husband in his house, considering that she is subject to his authority and not truly free. Cf. also *Shul. Ar.*, Or. Haj., 472,4. It is difficult to ascertain what may be assumed about situations other than the celebration of the Seder. It is clear from the context of TbPes. 108a that respect for those with greater knowledge was directly associated with respect for Heaven and for the Torah. See the statement of Rab Joseph in TbPes. 108a: 'The fear of your teacher is as the fear of Heaven.' Cf. also M'Abot IV,12; A.R.N. [a], XXVII; Tanh., Be-Shallah, § 26; and other sources.

In the strictest sense, the verb 'heiseb' refers to reclining, but it also refers to taking a place at a meal in general, even when there is no mention of the issue of actual reclining. It was unusual for most of the people, who lived simply, to have benches upon which to rest at a meal. See S. Krauss, *Talmudische Archäologie*, III, p. 44. Among those who lived simply, it was customary to lie at table only at a feast.

### 4. When one is about to break a peace of the loaf of bread (at the beginning of the meal) one should break a piece of the place that is well-baked.

The piece of bread that was broken off for the saying of the 'ha-Motzi' at the beginning of the meal is to be taken from the thoroughly baked side of the bread (i.e., the top and sides of the bread). Cf. Rashi on TbSanh. 102b the reading 'me-heikha de-qadim' (of the part that is baked first) instead of 'me-heikha de-qarim' (of the part that has formed a crust). Cf. in TbSanh., ed. Steinsalz, p. 488, reference to later halakhic discussions concerning this matter. In any case, the blessing is not to be spoken over a piece of bread taken from the soft inside of the bread. Cf. also D.E.R. VI,5 and the reading 'mi-maqom ha-qasheh' (of the hard part of the bread). The reasons behind this custom are not entirely clear. In M. Goldberg, *Derech Erez Rabba*, p. 19, it is suggested that a hard piece of bread was used because it maintained its shape and did not become soft. It would be improper to say the blessing over an unsightly piece of bread. See, however, A.J. Tawrogi, *Derech Erez Sutta*, p. 33. A.J. Tawrogi suggests economical reasons for using the crusty part of the bread. We consider D.E.R. VI,5 as an admonition to be moderate in eating bread. The hardest and least tasty part of the bread should be eaten first so that the crust, which dries out quickly, is not left over. The explicit reference in D.E.R. to 'ha-Motzi' (the first piece of bread over which the blessing is said), is not the central issue there.

'Ha-Motzi' primarily refers there to the act of breaking bread and the beginning of the meal as such. The text directly following this part of D. E. Z. D. E. Z. VI,5 confirms this explanation: 'When one is about to eat a radish or an onion...'

Cf. also the text following D. E. R. VI,5, where it is stated that it is forbidden to break off a piece of bread that is too large and to put it in one's mouth, lest one gives the impression of being a glutton! A sage, who is required to be modest begins eating the bread from the hard exterior.

**5. When one is about to eat a radish or an onion, he should start eating from the place where the leaves sprout.**

Cf. an analogous statement in D. E. R. VI,8. One may begin eating garlic or an onion only from where the leaves sprout. One who begins to eat garlic or a radish or an onion must begin eating from the hard lower part, where the leaves cling and sprout, not from the upper part at the top of the leaves, which is still tender and soft. If one begins eating from the upper part, then one gives the impression of being gluttonous (see D. E. R. l.c.), which is improper for a sage. On the basis of a baraita that concurs more with the version in D. E. R. VI than with the text under discussion here, one who begins to eat from the upper part of garlic, a radish or an onion does not take the time to remove the protective outer leaves. Cf. TbBeitza 25b and context: One may not eat meat before it has been filled and cut into pieces. By the same reasoning, one must not eat fruit before removing the protective outer leaves.

It is remarked in some commentaries on the basis of *Shul. Ar.*, Or. Haj. 170,15 and 16 that the rule of modesty here in D. E. did not apply on the Sabbath, when one was supposed to enjoy more food than usual in honour of the Sabbath. In the Talmud, one finds an exception made only for the size for the Sabbath in connection with the size of the piece of bread that was broken off at the beginning of the meal for the uttering of 'ha-Motzi'. See TbShab. 117b.

**6. And one should not take a loaf of bread and bite a piece off with his teeth and place it back on the table.**

One may not bite a piece of bread with his teeth and put the rest of the bread back on the table. Cf. the rule in D. E. R. IX,2. One may also not bite off a piece of bread and put the rest back on the dish or offer the rest to another person at the table. Cf. especially TosBer. II,8 , where 'because of danger to life' is given as reason behind this rule. One may feel obliged out of modesty to accept the bitten piece of bread, although being averse to it, and thereby endanger his health. One may may also be repulsed by a bitten piece of bread and not eat, although his body requires nourishment, thereby injuring his health. If one does eat a piece of bread from which another has bitten off a piece, he may take in saliva from that person and contract disease. Intestinal diseases were prevalent in the Tannaitic period; the rabbis were aware of the possibility of transmitting illnesses through unhygienic behaviour. The reason given in D. E. R. IX,2 for forbidden biting off a piece of bread is consideration for the feelings of others at the table who may find such a practice thoroughly distasteful. A sage must take the feelings of others into account whenever possible. For the same reason, one must not take a drink from a goblet and then offer it to someone with whom one is sharing the dish. Cf. D. E. R. IX,3.

### 7. **When one is about to drink in public, one should turn (his face) aside and drink.**

According to a tradition in TbBek. 44b in the name of Rabbi Johanan, it is improper to drink water in public while others look on. It is permitted, however, to urinate in public, because it is harmful to one's health to hold one's urine. There is an unmistakeable correspondence between the content of this statement and the tradition here in D. E. Z. Cf. D. E. Z. VII,3: A scholar must be moderate in eating and drinking, for eating and drinking are private activities and must be free of all exhibitionism. See also D. E. R. X,3: 'He who eats at the market is the companion of a dog.'

It is told in the gemara of TbPes. 86b that Rab Huna astonished his host by emptying a goblet offered to him without turning his face away from his companions. It is thus clear that the custom of turning away one's face while drinking was customary at a meal. According to Rab Huna, the custom at issue applied only to the bride. Cf. especially MPes. VII,13 and TbPes. 86b. The custom of turning away one's face from others while drinking is presented here in D. E. Z. as a rule that applies to all people, which indicates that like the hosts of Rab Huna, those associated with 'derekh 'eretz' were more stringent than Rab Huna. Cf. further, e.g., the *Tosaphists* on TbBek. 44b and the commentaries on *Shul. Ar.*, Or. Haj. 170.4 and *Qitzur Shul. Ar.* 42.12, according to which the rule of turning away from others applied only to the drinking of water. On the basis of D. E. and TbPes. 86b, however, this distinction is not justified.

### 8. **One should not be a trickster (a faultfinder) and not an overpunctilious person and not a glutton.**

No early parallels to this statement are available. Some commentators try to explain this statement in concurrence with the immediately preceding statement. The basis manuscript reads "asqan' (experimenter). A number of manuscripts read "umqan' (trickster); yet other manuscripts (and *Halakhot Gedolot*, ed. I. Hildesheimer, p. 645) read "uqman'. S. Krauss (in: *R. E. J.*, XXXVII (1898), p. 51) associates the terms "umqan' and "uqman' and the immediately following terms 'naqdan' and 'gargeran' with the drinking of a goblet of wine. Cf. also A. J. Tawrogi. *Derech Erez Sutta*, p. 33. S. Krauss derives "uqman' from "aqam' in this explanation, in the meaning of turning and curving as a description of the movements one makes in emptying a goblet to the bottom. "Amqan' may have been derived from this reading, also implying the action of drinking a goblet empty to the bottom. According to S. Krauss, l.c., the reading 'naqdan' ('naqran') was derived from 'naqar'. (Cf. M. Jastrow, *Dictionary*, II, p. 935: 'to keep clean' and interchangeable with 'naqad'. If so the reading 'naqdan' or 'naqran' must be regarded as a variant of "umqan' and hence must be interpreted as 'to drink empty to the last draught.'

'Naqdan' can also be interpreted as 'to drink in small drafts' (derived from 'naqad' = to make points), with the result of increasing the intoxicating effect of alcohol. Cf. A. J. Tawrogi, l.c.. Cf. also J. Harburger, *Massekhet Derech Erez Sutta*, p. 37. According to these interpretations, the concepts "umqan' ('uqman') 'naqdan' and 'gargeran' represent three aspects of the same thing: to till the goblet and drink it to the bottom, to take small sips and drink great quantities.

Entirely different explanations, however, are possible. The word "uqman' can be interpreted as 'trickster'. Cf. M. Jastrow, o.c., p. 1056) and "umqan' can be interpreted as an underhanded and deceitful person. See E. Ben Jehudah, *Millon ha-Lashon ha-'Ibrit*, sub "umqan' and cf. the use of "umqan' in Targum on Prov. 28:6; Ps. 101:4; and Hos. 7:16. "Umqan' may also mean a faultfinder, one who searches deep to find faults in others. Cf. M. Higger, *Massekhtot Derekh 'Eretz*, p. 48 and D. Sperber, *Massekhet Derekh 'Eretz Zuta*, p. 47.

'Naqdan' may be interpreted to mean an over-punctilious person. Cf. the use of the term 'nuqdanin' in TosBer., V,18 (in the sense of overpunctilious persons who reprove children when making a fault in the formula of appealing to partakers to say grace after the meal)! Cf. TjBer. VII [11c]. A number of statements in D. E. Z. VI, are closely related to the context in TosBer. l.c. (rules concerning eating, drinking, the saying of blessings and the order of importance of the great and the small). This may be reason to an analogous interpretation of the term 'naqdan'in the sense of a over- punctilious person and faultfinder. See *'Arukh. ha-Shalem*, ed. A. Kohut, sub 'naqran' and 'nuqdan' as reference to an over-punctilious person and faultfinder. Cf. A. E. Harkavy, *Teshubot ha-Ge'onim* (*Zikkaron la-Rishonim we-gam la-'Aharonim*), I, Berlin 1887, p. 145, sim. 308. On the basis of the manuscripts, we choose the reading "umqan', 'naqdan' and 'gargeran' and interpret: 'Be not a trickster, be not over-punctilious and be not a glutton.'

**9.  And one should overlook an insult and one should not let himself to be honoured by the humilation of his neighbour.**

In this regard, the unequal relationship to one's fellow man is characteristic of 'hasidut'. The hasid shows more consideration for others than for himself. He disregards his own humilation and avoids satisfaction and does not advance himself at the cost of others but overemphasizes the disgrace of another person. Similar behaviour is described in TbMeg. 28a as a characteristic of the pious. In Midr. Teh. 16,11 (ed. S. Buber, 62a), such behaviour is explicitly mentioned in connection with the word 'hasid'. It is already said of Nehunjah ben Haqana (a Tanna of the second generation) in TbMeg. 28a that he never exalted himself by the disgrace of another person. See also the commentary to D.E.Z. II,9.

**10. The beginning of transgression is impure thought, the second stage is scoffing, the third stage is haughtiness, the fourth stage is roughness, the fifth stage is idleness, the sixth stage is causeless hatred and the seventh stage an evil (envious) eye. That is what Solomon said: 'When he speaks fair, believe him not; for there are seven abominations in his heart' (Prov. 26:25).**

The statement is found in its entirely only in later sources. In a lot of statements, however, the notion is found that the commission of transgressions originates in wrong intentions and leads to increasingly worse transgressions. Cf., e.g., Did. III,1ff.. See G. Allon, in: *Tarbitz*, XI (1940), pp. 135–136. Cf. the commentary to D.E.Z. II,17. Cf. Siphrei, Shophetim, Pisqa 187 and A.R.N. [a], XXVI (42a) in a statement by Rabbi 'Aqiba; cf. also TosSot. V,11 in a statement attributed to Rabbi Me'ir. It was typical of the radical inclination of the pious to equate a thought with the deed which it may lead to and to evaluate a minor transgression in light of the worst consequences it may produce. Cf. also A.J. Heschel, *Torah min ha-Shamajim*, I, London 1962, p. XIV. Cf., e.g., the opinion of Resh Laqish in TbSanh. 58b: the very act of raising one's hand to strike someone already makes one a 'bad person'. Hate leads to manslaughter and murder. Cf., e.g., TbJoma 9b; Siphrei, Shophetim, l.c.; and Mat. 5:2. Cf. also other sources. Lust leads to adulterous behaviour. Cf. D.E.Z. III,12 and cf., e.g., TbNed. 20b in connection with the precautions taken by Rabbi 'El'ezer to prevent himself from even thinking of another woman. Cf. Tanh., Naso, § 13 and cf. TbB.M. 107b. Cf. A. Büchler, *Types of Jewish Palestinian Piety*, p. 53ff. and p. 44ff.; cf. also Mat. 5:28. To covet another man's wife or property was already considered a sin among the 'hasidim'. Cf. D.E.Z. I,7 · Cf. TbBer. 55b: 'After your eyes – such is thinking regarding transgression.' Along with the normal halakhah intended for people in general, there was – as it were – also a separate halakhah concerning the thoughts and intentions for the pious. The avoidance of only halakhic transgressions in their actions was not sufficient for them. The pious strove to be free of impure thoughts, to avoid being derisive of others and minimizing transgressions, to be free of haughtiness and cruelty and to avoid idleness, senseless hate and a jealous eye. A jealous eye is regarded here as the ultimate result of impure thoughts. Cf. the answer of Rabbi 'Eli'ezer ben Hyrcanos in M'Abot II,9.

## Derekh Eretz Zuta, chapter VII

**1. There are seven characteristics in an uncultured man: He speaks before him who is greater than he [in wisdom] and enters into the words of his fellow; he is hasty to answer and he does not question according to the halakhah [subjectmatter] and he does not answer according to the subject-matter [halakhah]; he speaks on the last (subjectmatter) first and on the first (subjectmatter) last; and concerning what he has not heart he says: 'I have heart it', and he does not acknowledge the truth.**

For parallels and commentary, see D. E. Z. II,5−7 and D. E. Z. XI, 25 ff.

**2. Fifteen characteristics are mentioned in connection with a sage (scholar): (He is) decorous (pleasant) in his entering, pious (modest) in his sitting, deliberate in knowledge, alert in his deeds, knowing his place, rejoicing at his portion, not claiming merits for himself, (his mind is) absorptive and retentive, he is answering many times (or: fully), putting questions and answering, listening and making additions at each chapter, going to the wise (to seek instruction from them) and he learns in order to teach and he learns in order to practise.**

For parallels and commentary see D. E. Z. III,16.
In a lot of manuscripts this statement is missing in D. E. Z. VII.

**3. A sage (scholar) must be discreet in eating and drinking, [washing], and in anointing, [putting his shoes on and in copulating], in his dressing, in his walking, in his speaking and his spitting, and in (the performing of) his good deeds.**

See the other manuscripts in which the following things are added to the things that are mentioned in the basis manuscript: washing, putting on shoes and copulating. The entire listing clearly corresponds with concepts mentioned in D. E. R. X., pertaining to the behaviour of a sage in a bathhouse. Cf. TbShab. 61a and other sources. At issue here is the order in which one removes his shoes, washes, anoints, and dresses himself, and puts on his 'tallit' ("atiphah'). For the terms contained in the listing, see especially TbBer. 43b, which contains a list of practices that were regarded as unbecoming for a sage, and that could discredit a sage. Cf. D. E. Z. VI,1.

*Discreet in eating and drinking* – this refers not only to moderation in eating and drinking but also to the consideration of eating and drinking as intimate behaviour. Cf. all rules of etiquette pertaining to eating and drinking in *Massekhet Derekh 'Eretz*. Cf. especially statements in D. E. R. VI and see D. E. Z. VI,5–7. In connection with the context of TbBer. 43b, see the forbiddance for a sage to eat frequently with ignorant people.

*Discreet in washing* – See the addition of these words in the manuscripts of D. E. Z. Cf. the rules of etiquette for bathing in D. E. R. X and see TbShab. 61a, where it is stated that a scholar washes himself before anointing himself in a bathhouse. The series of actions listed here in D. E. Z. are not exclusively associated with the behaviour of a sage in a bathhouse. The listing of actions here possibly comprises later additions. Among other things the order in which one dries the parts of the body is also part of the routine of washing oneself. Cf. D. E. R. X,1.

*Discreet in anointing* – this brings to mind the practice of anointing the parts of the body in a specific order. Given the unmistakeable connection with the context of TbBer. 43b (cf. D. E. Z. VI, l.), this statement refers to the habit of the sages not to go out into public wearing perfumed oil on their heads or on their clothing in order to avoid giving incorrect impression that they have homosexual contacts. It could also be misunderstood as a sign of haughtiness or lack of modesty.

*Discreet in his attire* – this calls to mind the sequence in which a sage was supposed to remove his clothes. Cf. TbShab. l.c. It calls especially to mind, however, the fact that sages were to wear clean and simple clothing. Cf. D. E. Z. V,4: A sage must be recognizable from his clothing. Cf. also Siphrei, We-Zot: '. . . and from his clothing at the market.' Cf. also TbShab. 113a: To let one's clothing hang low on any day other than Sabbath was interpreted as a sign of immodesty. Only the richer people who did not have to work in the fields wore long clothing. One was to be especially careful in taking off clothing and in washing it, and one was to make sure that the seam was on the inside. Cf. TbShab. 114a and other sources. In connection with the interpretation of "atiphah' to mean keeping the head covered as a sign of respect for the presence of the Shekhinah, see the commentary to D. E. Z. I,2. Cf. also S. Krauss in: *H. U. C. A.*, XIX (1945–1946), p. 138ff. and in: *Sepher ha-Jobel, . . . Mosheh 'Arjeh Bloch*, 1905, pp. 83–96.

*Discreet in putting his shoes on* – the phrase 'modest in putting his shoes on' has been inserted before 'discreet in his attire' in a number of manuscripts. The phrase may apply to the order in which a sage puts on his shoes. Cf., e.g., D. E. R. X,1· Given the context in Tb Ber.43b (cf. D. E. Z. VI,1) it is possible that the phrase means that scholars should not walk about in public in patched shoes. This would have applied only in summer and in public; however, there would have been no objection to walking around in such shoes in the rainy season because the mud would hide them. Cf. also D. E. R. XI,19: A scholar is not permitted to walk about the market with loosened sandals, for it could be interpreted by others as sign of a arrogant nonchalance.

*Discreet in his going* – see the parallels to D. E. Z. V,4 and the reference there to *Seph. Ben Sira* 19:30. A scholar could be recognized from his way of walking. From the context in TbBer. 43b and TbShab. 113a (cf. TbTa'an. 10b and TbPes. 42a), one can assume that scholars were not to take large steps when walking. Taking large steps was supposed to be harmful to one's eyesight. Here in D. E., however, taking large steps is a sign of immodesty. Scholars were also not supposed to walk erect, out of respect for the omnipresent Shekhinah. Cf. TbQid. 31a. See Tb Ber. l.c., and other parallels.

*Discreet in his speaking* (the use of his voice) – cf. among others, D. E. Z. V,4. Sages speak thoughtfully and softy and in a friendly manner. Cf. also D. E. Z. II,13 'lashon rakkah'.

*Discreet in his spitting* – i. e., when clearing the throat. On the basis of the parallels, the rule to be discreet in spitting may be interpreted as an indication that one is aware of the presence of the Shekhinah. It was forbidden to spit on the Temple Mount and in the 'beit ha-kenesset'. Scholars should not spit just anywhere, and if they must spit, they must do so in an inconspicuous manner. Scholars may not 'make their spit long', i. e., they may not spit in an arrogant conspicuous manner. Cf. TbSot. 47b and parallels. And they may not spit when in the direct presence of others. Cf. TbHag. 5a. They may especially not spit when in the presence of their teacher. Cf. Tb'Er. 99a and D. E. R. X,3 in the manuscripts: 'one who enters a privy makes place to one who leaves, and one should not bring oil in a bottle of glass into a bathhouse because of the danger and one should not spit in a bathhouse because of the danger and one should in no circumstances spit in the presence of others.' The reference in D. E. R. concerns a forbiddance to spit in the bathhouse because of the danger that others may slip and fall.

*Discreet in good works* – Scholars may not make themselves obvious as proud benefactors and donors. The meaning of the term 'tzanua' comes clear here. One must give in secret. S. Krauss (*Talmudische Archäologie*, III, p. 241, note 12) suggests reading 'ma'asim' instead of 'ma'asim tobim', considering that the doing of good deeds may not be subject to limitations. This suggestion, however, rests on the misconception that 'tzanua' (discreet) here means moderation instead of acting quietly and avoiding doing acts of charity in an showy manner. The manuscripts also do not support the suggestion of S. Krauss. The subsequent text in D. E. Z. confirms our explanation here.

**4. As the bride keeps herself in retirement all the time she is in her father's house [and when she makes herself known when she is leaving (her father's house for the wedding-ceremony)] and says: 'Whoever knows anything to bear testimony against me, let him come and testify against me', so a sage**

**has to be modest in his (good) deeds and (yet) be well known by his good works.**

Like the previous statement, this statement means that a sage must be discreet when doing good deeds. As a virtuous bride conceals herself in her father's house from the looks of strange men, the sage must do his deeds in secret. If he is called to account, however, he may attest to his good deeds, just as the bride attests to her innocence upon leaving her father's house. The sage must do his good deeds quietly, but on the other hand, his modesty must not lead others to think that he does no good deeds at all. If necessary, he may attest outright to his deeds. See the explanations of *Maharzav* on Shem. Rab. XLI,5. In the tradition one finds a number of parallels that are closely related to the tradition here in D. E. Z.: Shem. Rab. XLI,5; Shir ha-Shir. Rab. IV,11 and Tanh., Ki-Tissa, ed. S. Buber, § 11 on Ex. 31:18.

The statement here dates back to the to statements attributed to Resh Laqish, found in Shir ha-Shir. Rab. l.c., in the oldest of the parallels. In connection with the originality of the parallel in Shir ha-Shir. Rab., see W. Bacher, *'Aggadot Amora'ei 'Eretz Jisra'el*, I, 1925, p. 150. In one statement, Resh Laqish likens the modesty of a sage to the modesty of a bride. In another statement, the innocence of a sage is compared to the chastity and innocence of a bride, who bears witness to her own chastity and innocence upon leaving her father's house to marry. According to W. Bacher, l.c., the reading in Shir ha Shir. Rab. according to which the bride affirms her own innocence is the oldest. In the other sources mentioned and in D. E. Z. h.l. the two statements of Resh Laqish are combined into one statement and it is the bride herself who challenges *others* to bear witness against her should someone have something with which to impugn her innocence. As a result of a misinterpreted abbreviation, Resh Laqish is replaced in Tanh. l.c. and in Jalq., Cant., r. 391 by Rabbi Levi.

The text in Shem. Rab. l.c. and in Tanh. l.c. reads: '... when she is at the point of entering into the 'huppah' (the bride chamber), she reveals her face...' The text in most manuscripts of D. E. Z. reads: '... and when she goes out (i. e., leaves her father's house for the wedding ceremony), she makes herself known...' ('mepharsemet "atzmah'). The difference in readings here is possibly important. According to L. M. Epstein *(Sex laws and Customs in Judaism*, New York 1967, pp. 36−50 and especially pp. 45−49) the expression 'megalleh panim' (the revealing of the face) refers to the moment at which a bride in Israel removes the veil for the first time. L. M. Epstein suggests that the expression was replaced by the alternative reading 'making herself known in public ('mepharsemet 'atzmah') and that this alternative attests to Babylonian influence and could be explained by the fact that it was far less common for young girls in Babylonia to wear a veil. To assess how common it was for girls and women in Israel to wear a veil is difficult. Opinions concerning this vary very greatly. The covering of the face, head and hair of girls and women surely was not uncommon, however. Cf., e.g., S. Schechter, in: *Ginzei Schechter* I (1928), p. 4; ;Tb'Er. 100b (in which the explanation of R. Dimi also suggests a possible distinction between customs in Israel and Babylonia. Cf. A. R. N. [a] I (2b); P. R. E. XIV and MNed. III,8 (TbNed.30b); Ber. Rab. XVII,8; Jalq., Be-Reshit, r. 23; A. R. N. [b], XLII (49a) and TjSot. [16b]. Although not all questions, concerning the assertion that young girls in Israel who had been given in marriage wore a veil up to the time of their marriage, has been handled here, one may say, that it is not improbable that the reading in the manuscripts of D. E. Z. h. l. has been influenced by Babylonian tradition!

**5. (A sage) should follow the truth but not falsehood, honesty but not robbery, meekness but not haughtiness, peace but not dissension, the council of the old but not the council of the young, a lion but not a woman.**

The statement clearly represents a combination of other elements. A statement in TbBer. 61a (cf. Tb'Er. 18) ascribed to Rabbi Johanan, according to which it is less dangerous to follow a lion than it is to follow a woman, is clearly recognizable. Rabbi Johanan's statement seems to have been derived from *Seph. Ben Sira* 25:16: 'It is better to dwell with a lion and a dragon, than to dwell with a wicked woman.' See ed. M. Z. Segal, p. 155; cf. B. M. Lewin in *Ginzei Qedem, I*, (Derash Rabbenu Hanan'el on TbBer.), Jerusalem 1922, p. 37. Rabbi Hanan'el asserts that a person must fear more for his moral integrity than for his physical well-being. Cf. also the statement of Rabbi 'Aha ben Rabbi Joshijah in TbNed. 20a, according to which it is not permitted to look at the heels of a woman. Cf. also TjHal. II,4 [58c]. Cf. TbShab. 64b; TbBer. 24a; Jalq., Ki-Tetze, r. 931. It is evident from parallels and commentaries that one was afraid to follow a woman, lest she would lift up her clothes while passing a river or stepping over something and thereby make her legs visible. The sight of a woman's legs could arouse undesirable lust in a 'talmid hakham'.

The statement that one should regard the words of elders more important than the advice of youth is closely related to a statement attributed to Rabbi Shim'on ben 'El'azar (another reading Rabbi Shim'on ben 'Ila; see Tos'Ab. Zar. I,19 and parallels).

In connection with avoiding disharmony and dispute, see especially Statements in D. E. Z. XI and the accompanying commentary.

**6. What is meant by showing reverence (to the sages and to his father)? (It is:) He may not sit at his place, he does not contradict his words and he does not cut off his words.**

**What is meant by honouring? (It is:) He gives to eat and to drink, he clothes and puts on (their) shoes, he leads (them) in and out.**

The definition given here for 'showing reverence' and 'honouring' applies to both the relationship to one's parents and to one's teacher. In connection with honouring, cf. Ex. 20:12 and Dt. 5:16. The accusative particle used in these texts has been interpreted in the midrash as an indication that honouring elders and teachers is implied. In connection with 'revering' ('fearing') cf. Lev. 19:3. Cf. also Lev. 19:32: 'You shall stand up before the grey head and honour the old...' See also the explanation of the accusative particle in Dt. 10:20 as a reference to students and scholars. The text here in D. E. Z., however, is principally concerned with reverence and honour for scholars, teachers and elders. Note the additions in the manuscripts of D. E. Z., and the reading of the Gaon of Vilna on D. E. Z. a.l.: ['He honours the wise,] what is meant by one who is honouring the wise... and what is meant by one who does not show reverence...' Reverence is explained as not infringing on the privileges of the old and the wise. This may refer to the situation in the house of study. The sages sit in front and take the first seat and the young students make not take their place. Cf. TosMeg. III,24: 'He does not stay at his place.' Cf. ed. S. Lieberman, pp. 360−361 and see S. Lieberman *Tosephta Ki-Pheshutah*, V, p. 1202. Cf. TbQid. 31b and Bam. Rab. XV, 17. See in a number of manuscripts of D. E. Z. the addition; 'And he does not speak in his place', i. e., the younger person lets the older person or the teacher first and does not, so to say, mow the grass before his feet by saying what the older person or teacher perhaps wishes to say himself. As a student, one may not brutally disprove the words of the teacher and contradict ('satar)' them, i. e., bring to light such a mistake that his teacher becomes ashamed of his own words. One may, however, have a differing opinion and present other arguments concerning a particular matter.

*And he may not cut of his words* – these words do not appear in all manuscripts. The parallels also do not have these words. Therefore, the sources that do not contain these words concur more with the original reading. See in some manuscripts the addition; 'And he may not tip the scale against him', i. e. he may not take the side of the opponent of his father in a dispute. This addition seems to have been borrowed from TbQid. 31b, in which reverence for one's father is discussed. Cf. the explanation of Rashi in TbQid. 31b.

Unlike revering, honouring is interpreted positively, to mean providing food and drink, dressing, and escorting someone inside or outside. Exegetically, this interpretation is connected in the sources with Prov. 3:9: 'Honour the Lord with your wealth.' By way of analogy, one may conclude that one should honour his parents, just as he should honour God, with material goods. Cf., e.g., Mekh. de-R. Jishm., Jitro, par. 8 (ed. M. Friedmann, 69a-b); cf. TbQid. 30b and TbB. M. 32b.

*Dresses him* − (in parallels also 'mekasseh'. Cf. the reading in Mekh. de-R. Jishm. l.c.: 'and with clean clothes'. This primarily brings to mind caring for one's parents in providing them with clean clothing (and food). As remarked earlier, the manuscripts in D. E. Z. suggest a shift in emphasis to honouring the sages. Providing for clothing, then, not only means the concern with clothing of the teacher, it also means the practice of appearing before one's teacher only in clean, tidy clothes and especially not serving dinner while wearing dirty clothes. Cf. TbShab. 119a.

Putting sandals on the feet of one's teacher is also mentioned in the sources as an expression of honour. The words 'leads him in and out' refers to the custom of allowing parents, elders and sages to proceed first upon entering or leaving a place. (customs differed, however, see the commentary to D.E.Z. VI,2). Cf. the reading in TjQid. [61a]: 'u-manhig' (and is leading). The word implies receiving someone and escorting someone inside and escorting him outside, when he is leaving. See A.J. Tawrogi, *Derech Erez Sutta*, p. 37. It is striking that, according to the statement here in D.E.Z. the duties that a person originally was to perform for his parents, such as providing them with clothing and food, are also to be performed for the sages. In the sources, it is considered a sign of reverence for sages to escort them and perform the other duties for them mentioned above. This extension, then, of one's duties to his parents to sages was obviously not self-evident, as is proved by the addition in some manuscripts of D.E.Z.: '(This applies) equally for one's father, one's teacher and the sage.'

### 7. Rabbi Hijja taught: 'Silence is appropriate for the wise, so the more for the fools; and so did Solomon say: 'Even a fool who holds his tongue is counted wise.'(Prov. 17:28)'

This statement is quoted as a baraita in various sources. In TjPes. IX,3 [37a], the statement is ascribed to Bar Kappara (from the period of transition between the Tanna'im and 'Amora'im). In *'Ein Ja'aqob* on Tj. l.c. one finds a reading as in D.E.Z. with Rabbi Hijja. See Bacher in: *R.E.J.*, XXXVII (18989), p. 300. W. Bacher asserts that there are not two versions but one, which has been passed on in the collections of misnajot of Rabbi Hijja as well as Bar Kappara. In connection with these collections, see J.N. Epstein, *Mebo'ot le-Siphrut ha-Tanna'im*, Jerusalem 1957, p. 242; cf. also W. Bacher, *Die Agada der Tannaiten*, II, p. 503, note 7. In A.R.N. [a] XXII (38a), the statement is attributed to Rabbi Shim'on ben Gamli'el (cf.M'Abot. I,17). On the basis of Prov. 17:28, it is concluded that it is better for a fool to keep silent then for a sage. Cf. also the explanation of *Seph. Ben Sira* on Prov. 17:28 (*Sepher Ben Sira* 20:5; ed. M.Z. Segal, p. 119): 'Someone (a fool) who keeps silent is not uncommonly considered wise, but someone who talks much (even he is wise) is often despised.'

Some parallels (cf. TosPes. IX,2 and TjPes. l.c.) and a number of manuscripts of D.E. contain the addition: '... and needless to say a wise man who keeps silent.' These words are superfluous and actually do not concur with the statement to which they have been added, according to which it is particularly appropriate for a fool to keep silent. We therefore consider these words to be a secondary addition and give preference to the version in the basis manuscript in which these words are lacking. The paradox of this addition is pointed up in later sources. See, among others, the remarks of S. Lieberman, *Tosephta Ki-Pheshutah*, IV, p. 532 and A. Steinsalz, *'Ijjunim*, in connection with his edition of the Babylonian Talmud, TbPes. 99a, p. 426.

## Derekh 'Eretz Zuta, chapter VIII

**1. Be pliant like the reed upon which the wind blows from every direction it chooses; for the Torah can only endure in him who is humble in spirit.**

This is a famous comparison that was also known outside Israel. Cf. the commentary to D. E. R. IV,2. This statement is ascribed to Rabbi Shim'on ben 'El'azar in the parallels. Cf., among others, TbTa'an. 20b; A. R. N. [a] XLI (66a) and D. E. R., l.c. In Ms. Epstein (see M. Higger, *Massekhtot Derekh 'Eretz*, introduction, pp. 45—46 and text (p. 120), this statement is attributed to Rabbi Jishma'el. In connection with the political views of Rabbi Jishma'el, see, among others, Siphra, 'Aharei Mot, XIII,14 and cf.TbSanh. 74a and Tb'Ab. Zar. 27b

According to TbTa'an 20a, this statement fits within the opposition of the curse of 'Ahijah the Shilonite, who compared Israel with a reed (see I Kings 14:15) and the blessing of Bileam, who compared Israel with a cedar (see Num. 24:6). In the name of Rabbi Johanan, it is said that preference in this case must be given to the curse, for a reed remains standing while a cedar is eventually blown down by the south wind. In this context the comparison has political overtones, for it is meant that Israel's strength lies in its ability to bend under difficult political circumstances, situations in which proud resistance could lead to uprooting or destroying the people. Cf. Mat. 2:7ff. and Luke 7:24ff., where it is clearly stated in a remark attributed to Jesus that John the Baptist was neither a reed that bends with the wind nor a courtier who adopts to the status quo, but like an unyielding prophet whose refusal to bend ultimately resulted in his imprisonment and death. Regardless of a more detailed explanation of this difficult passage, it is clear that the image of the reed bending with the wind is used here in a political context. It is possible that the comparison of the reed and the cedar was originally used principally to refer to political attitudes. Here in D. E. Z., as well as in D. E. R., l.c., and parallels, however, the statement made by Rabbi Shim'on ben 'El'azar is a general one without political overtones. In D. E. Z. h.l. the statement serves as a general admonition to 'talmidei hakhamim' to be compliant and humble in order to be successful in their studies.

**2. Why is the Torah is likened to water? As water does not flow to a high place but (only) to a low place, so the Torah only dwells with him who is humble in spirit.**

In connection with this self explanatory image, cf. especially D. E. Z. I,4 and D. E. Z. II,3: 'And (be) like a deep (garden)bed, which retains its water.' A rather similar statement passed on in the name of Rabbi Hanina bar 'Idi appears in TbTa'an. 7a.

3. **Keep aloof from anything hideous and (even) from whatever seems hideous.**

4. **And beware of some one who advises you in his own interest.**

3. *Keep aloof from anything hideous...* See the commentary to D. E. Z. I,13 and compare the commentary to D. E. Z. II,16.

    4. *And beware of some one who advises ...* In the parallels, this statement is attributed to Rabbi 'Aqiba. Cf. TbSanh. 76b. The term :'ke-phi darkho' can be interpreted with various nuances of meaning. W. Bacher (see *Die Agada der Tannaiten*, I, p. 274 and see in: *R. E. J.*, XXXVII [1898], p. 302) interprets the term as 'nebenhin' and 'unaufgefordert', thus referring to advice given incidentally without having been requested. He adds that such advice is not given without ulterior motives. One can thus understand the term 'ke-phi darkho' as a reference to the ulterior motives behind the advice. Cf. Rashi on TbSanh. l.c.

    The term may also mean: in his own way, according to his own insight, and not based on the guidelines of the Torah and the tradition. Cf. especially the reading in *Seph. Hasidim*, ed. R. Margaliot (Ms. Bologna), § 137, p. 145. Cf. also *Seph. ha-Jir'ah* of Rabbenu Jonah. Advice must be a reflection of God's will and not the interest of the person giving the advice.

    A statement in *Seph. Ben Sira* serves as a basis to this statement by Rabbi 'Aqiba. See *Seph. Ben Sira* 37:8 (ed. M. Z. Segal, p. 230 and cf. the explanation to this on p. 236): 'Every counsellor points with the hand (i. e. to show the way to go). There is one who counsels a way to himself ("'elaw" is read!). Beware of the counsellor and inform yourself beforehand what is his interest.' On the basis of this interpretation of Ben Sira, we interpret the term 'ke-phi darkho' in D. E. Z. h.l. as 'according to his own interests'.

5. **He who forgoes his rights (to retribution) is pardoned for all his transgressions, for it is said: 'Who is a God like You, That pardons iniquity and passes by transgression' (Mi. 7:18).**

    **Who is forgiven iniquity? He who passes by transgressions.**

The expression 'ma'abir 'al middot' is interpreted in various ways. 'Middot' (from 'madah' = to measure) are those things that are measured out to a person. This may refer to his characteristics and hence to his natural reactions. The expression 'ma'abir 'al middot' thus means that one should surpass his natural reactions and be victorious over his own nature by suppressing his anger and avoiding retribution. 'Middah' can also be interpreted as the share allotted to someone in the sense of his right to retribution. The issue here concerns refusing to punish another person. It is a typical feature of 'hasidut' to remain within the bounds of one's rights ("le-phanim mi-shurat ha-din') and, for the sake of peace and of love, to not completely exercise his rights against another person. An important notion behind this practice is that one is dealt what he deals to others. In TbTa'an. 25b, there appears a tradition according to which the prayer of Rabbi 'Aqiba was heard because he forwent his right to retribution, and the prayer of Rabbi 'Eli'ezer ben Hyrcanos was nor heard because he exercised his right to retribution. The notion of forgiveness appears explicitly in *Seph. Ben Sira* 27:30-28:7; and in the New Testament, cf. Luke 6:37−38; cf. also the prayer in Mat. 6:12 and Luke 11:4; cf. also Mat. 7:2 and Luke 6:37; and see in a statement by Rabbi Hanina, the overseer of priests, see A. R. N. [b] XXVI (27a); cf. the statement of Rabbi Shim'on ben 'El'azar in A. R. N. [a] XVI (32b). Closer examination of the texts mentioned reveals that the notion of forgiving and being forgiven is connected with the realization of the essential equality of people. One's own faults and shortcomings with regard to fulfilling the precepts and to one's relationship with others must serve as the standard by which one judges others. In connection with the special background of this concept and the connection with specific Tannaitic milieu in which such concepts were emphasized, see D. Flusser in: *H. T. R.*, LXI (1968), pp. 107−127. Cf. Mi. 7:18 (Shem. Rab. XVI,2) and TbPes. 113b TbR. ha-Sh. 17a; TbMeg. 28a; TbJoma 23a and TbJoma 87b.

**6. Whoever abases himself for the sake of the words of the Torah, will in the end be exalted by them, for it is said: 'If you have done foolishly in lifting up yourself' (Prov. 30:32). (This has to be read as:) If you abase yourself for the sake of her, you will be exalted by her (i. e. by the Torah).**
**7. Whoever seeks to inquire wisdom by the words of the Torah, one (i. e. Heaven) is adding wisdom to his wisdom, for it is said: 'Give to a wise man and he will be yet wiser' (Prov. 9:9).**

6. The reading 'ha-mitnabbel 'atzmo' in Ms. New York, *J. T.S.*, (cat. E. N. A-dler) no. 4465a is connected with the reading 'ha-menabbel' in the parallels (see TbBer. 63b. Of central importance to this statement is an explanation of Prov. 30:32: 'If you have behaved foolishly by exalting yourself or have devised evil, put your hand on your mouth!' The midrash, however, makes a different caesura: 'If you have made a fool of yourself (by exposing your ignorance) for its sake (i. e., the sake of the Torah), then you will be exalted.' The word 'be-hitnassé' (by exalting yourself) is divided into 'bah' (for its sake) and 'tinnasé' (you will be exalted). In most sources this statement is attributed to Ben 'Azzai. Cf. Ber. Rab. LXXXI, 2 (ed. J. Theodor / Ch. Albeck, p. 969); Midr. ha-Gad. on Gen. 35:1 (ed. M. Margulies, p. 592; cf. the later elaborations in A. R. N. [a] XI (23b) and A. R. N. [b] XXII (23b), where the statement is incorrectly

ascribed to Rabbi 'Aqiba. According to other sources, the statement was made in the name of Rabbi Samuel bar Nahmani. Cf. TbBer. 63b; Jalq. ha-Makh. on Prov. 30:32; Midr. Mishl. on Prov. 30:33; cf. also the deviating tradition in Jalq., Prov., r. 946. On the basis of the parallels mentioned, Prov. 30:32 can be explained as follows: If one makes a fool of himself by asking questions and is laughed by others, he will ultimately become wise and will be exalted by his knowledge of Torah. If one, however, devises plans in order to avoid being laughed at, then one should put his hand on his mouth. In other words, if one does not want to expose his ignorance, he will not learn anything, and when a question is directed at him, he will not be able to give a correct answer.

In connection with this explanation, see especially S.E.R. XIV, ed. M. Friedmann, p. 64. Cf. Jalq., Ki-Tissa, r. 391 and *Tzewat Rabbi 'Eli'zer ha-Gadol*, § 54, ed. Jerusalem 1960, 57a.

See the readings in A.R.N. l.c., where degrading oneself ('mitnabbel') is explained to mean the endurance of privation for the sake of studying the Torah. This, rather than the subjecting oneself to laughter by asking questions, may have been the original meaning behind the statement. See W. Bacher, *Die Agada der Tannaiten*, I, p. 298.

### 8. So long as a man is not a transgressor his fellow-creatures have fear of him, but so long as he is a transgressor he has fear of his fellow-creatures.

As long as one commits no transgressions, he commands the respect of others and does not have to fear that they will discover things that can put him to shame. If one does commit transgressions, he is always afraid of other people lest they discover his transgressions and he be put to shame. This statement is ascribed to both Rabbi Shim'on bar Johai and Rabbi Jishma'el in the parallels. According to D.D. Sperber (*Massekhet Derekh 'Eretz Zuta*, p. 140, the reading 'Rabbi Shim'on bar Johai' arose from the incorrect interpretation of an abbreviation, and the reading ''Rabbi Jishma'el' is correct. M. Friedmann (see Pes. Rab., ed. M. Friedmann, Pisqa 15, 68b), on the other hand, asserts that there were probably two separate versions of the statement, one from the school of Rabbi Jishma'el and one from the school of Rabbi Shim'on bar Johai.

### 9. Whoever makes light of a single word of the words of the Torah deserves to be cut off, for it is said: ' Because he has despised the word of the Lord and he has broken His commandment, that soul shall be utterly cut off, its iniquity rests on it' (Num. 15:31).

This statement does not appear in this place in a number of important genizah fragments. The fact that this statement is also mentioned in the basis manuscript in D.E.Z. VIII,11, supports the assumption that the statement originally belonged there rather than here in D. E. Z. VIII,9. The text in D. E. Z. VIII,12 coheres better with the statement, while the context of D. E. Z. VIII,8 coheres better with the context of VIII,10. The omission of the statement in D. E. Z. VIII,11 (to '... rests on it') in a number of manuscripts was probably a secondary result from shifting the statement to D. E. Z. VIII,9. See, however, A. J. Tawrogi, *Derech Erez Sutta*, pp. 40–41. A. J. Tawrogi states that the statement belonged originally in D. E. Z. VIII,9, and so A. J. Tawrogi was forced to remove D. E. Z. VIII,12 from its original place to shift it to the context of D. E. Z. VIII,9 in order to maintain a logical sequence in that text. In imitation of the Gaon of Vilna on D. E. Z. h.l. A. J. Tawrogi gave the statement of D. E. Z. VIII,12 a new independent form on the basis of TbSot. 4b. These corrections, however, are not supported by the readings in the manuscripts. The statement in D. E. Z. seems to be a shortened, simplified version of an explanation ascribed to Rabbi 'El'azar ha-Mode'i. See Siphrei, Shelah, pisqa 112 (ed. H. S. Horovitz, p. 121); cf. M'Abot III,11 and cf. TbSanh. 99a and other parallels where it is sometimes recorded as a separate baraita.

Whoever does not accept even one word of the Torah or whoever ascribes even one word to Moses himself shows that he rejects the authority of the Torah as a whole and thus is considered to be a despiser of God's words. In the more extensive tradition in TbSanh. 99a (cf. TjSanh. X,1 [27c], the same is said of someone who denies the authority of even one hermeneutic explanation of Scripture in the oral tradition. Elsewhere in the tradition one finds remarks of the opinion that Moses himself made additions to the revealed Torah. Cf., e.g., TbMeg. 31b; Shem. Rab. XLVII (ed. M. Mirkin, p. 188); and A. R. N. [a] II, (5a). See A. J. Heschel, *Torah min-ha-Shamajim*, I, p. 16, and II, chap. VII and chap. IX. According to A. J. Heschel, texts such as those mentioned above represent the points of view of the school of Rabbi Jishma'el, according to which certain parts of the Torah were not literally inspired but bear the influence of people. The Torah was supposed to 'speak the language of people'. Cf. Siphrei l.c. and TbKer. 11a. In statements from the school of Rabbi 'Aqiba (such as Siphrei l.c. and TbSanh. l.c.) were raised objections to the opinion of the school of Rabbi Jishma'el (see also M. Kasher, *Torah Shelemah*, XIX, pp. 333–342). Polemics against such traditions of the school of Rabbi Jishma'el and more likely against Jewish sectarian and Jewish-Christian groups, which did not consider all parts of the Torah and the tradition to be equal of authority, appear in statements such as in TbSanh. l.c. and Siphrei l.c. Cf., e.g., also the polemic in TbBer. 12b; TjBer. I,8 [3c]; and Siphrei, Wa-'Ethannan, pisqa 34 and pisqa 35, where one finds a polemic directed against assertions of difference in the authoritative value between 'The Ten Words' and the rest of the commandments of the Torah. Cf. Did. 21; Gal. 3:19; Hebr. 1:4. See E. E. Urbach, *Hazal*, p. 317, note 70; L. Ginzberg, *Eine unbekannte Jüdische Sekte*, New York 1922, p. 246, note 2; B. J. Bamberger in: *HUCA*, XVI (1941), p. 97ff.

For commentary on the text directly following , see in D. E. Z. VIII,11: 'And what does it mean to say: And her transgressions will be upon her...'

**10. Whoever is shamefaced will not readily sin, for it is said: 'And that fear of Him may be on your faces, that you sin not' (Ex. 20:17). And whoever is not shamefaced will readily sin, for it is said: 'The expression of their face do witness against them' (Is. 3:9).**


Cf. the commentary to D. E. R. I,34b. This statement is cited in most sources as an anonymous baraita and as an interpretation of Ex. 20:20: '... and the fear of Him is upon your face, so that you will not sin.' The phrase 'fear upon your face' is interpreted to mean an expression of shame, the fear of being shamed through transgressions. Shame leads to the fear of committing transgressions. In Mas. Kal. Rab. (ed. M. Higger, p. 134) the statement is treated as if it were uttered by Rabbi Nehorai. In a number of parallels, the text continues with the remark that the fathers of one who shows no shame on his face did not stay at the foot of Mount Sinai. This strongly worded remark implies that such a person places himself outside of the community because he does not allow himself to be corrected by others. Without shame one is not able to repent and therefore has no right to reconciliation with the community. Cf. TjQid. IV [65c] and TbNed. 20a. Cf. also Bam. Rab. VIII,4 and other sources. This continuation, which does not appear in the oldest sources, takes on another form here in D. E. Z. (cf. Mekh. de-R. Jishm., Ba-Hodesh, par. 9 (ed. M. Friedmann, p. 72) and Mekh. de-R. Shim. bar Johai. on Ex. 20:20 (ed. J. N. Epstein / E. Z. Melamed, p. 155). The reading here in D. E. Z., which cites Jer. 3:9 as a Scripture reference, is much more mildly worded.

**11. And whoever makes light of a single word of the Torah deserves to be cut off, for it is said: 'Because he has despised the word of the Lord and he has broken His commandment, that soul shall be utterly cut off, its iniquity rests on it' (Num. 15:31). And what is the meaning of 'its iniquity rests on it'? This teaches that the soul is cut off and that the iniquity rests on it.**

For commentary, see D. E. Z. VIII,9. This statement is probably in the correct place.

*And what is the meaning of...* The verse Num. 15:31 is interpreted as follows: Her transgression will stay with her and will not be atoned by her death. Reconciliation is no longer possible for such a person, who shall not have a share in the World to Come. The double term 'hikkaret tikkaret' is explained by Rabbi 'Aqiba as: cut off from This World and from the World to Come by Heaven. See Siphrei, Shelah, pisqa 112 (ed. H. S. Horovitz, p. 121; cf. TbSanh. 99a and TbSanh. 90b; TbSanh. 13a and other sources. Cf. also the statement in

Mat. 12:31 and Mark 3:29 where it is said that forgiveness is not possible for slander against the Holy Spirit. This probably also refers to entire or partial denial of the authority of revelation and the authority of the tradition.

It is clear that this part of Derekh 'Eretz comprises an anonymous summary of a much larger body of traditions containing statements by various Tannaitic spokesmen on Num.15:31.

**12. Every sage who makes light of washing the hands is reprehensible [more reprehensible is one who eats in the presence of a guest], still more reprehensible is a guest who invites (another guest), still more reprehensible than these three is a guest who causes trouble [to (another) guest].**

**Rabbi Me'ir said: 'Also somebody who takes what is set before him and gives it to the host's child. For it happened that (through such behaviour) a host killed his child.'**

This statement connects with the one directly preceding it. A closely related statement was recorded in the name of Rabbi 'El'azar (ben Pedat): 'Anyone who neglects the washing of the hands will be snatched from This World.' Cf. TbSot. 4b and see A.J. Tawrogi, l.c., mentioned in connection with the commentary on D.E.Z. VIII,9 and remarks there regarding the sequence of statement in D.E.Z. It is striking that the habit of washing the hands is mentioned here in D.E.Z. especially in connection with the 'talmidei hakhamim', who were undoubtedly more conscientious in washing their hands than less learned people. Here in D.E.Z., one who does not wash his hands is simply called contemptible. This statement serves as an introduction to other statements concerning increasingly contemptible forms of behaviour. The statement here pertains to washing hands before a meal.

The manuscripts, contain the addition: 'It is less becoming when one eats in the presence of a guest', i.e., without offering him a portion of one's food. The basis manuscript and a number of important genizah fragments, however, do not contain these words; see especially Ms. New York, J.Th.S. (cat. E.N. Adler) no. 2840) 'megunneh she-sheloshtan' [the most contemptible of the three]). The reading 'megunneh mi-sheloshtan'(more contemptible than these three) implies the mention of four contemptible things, including the addition: 'it is less becoming when one eats in the presence of a guest.' See the interpretation of the addition given by A.J. Tawrogi in *Derech Erez Sutta*, according to which it is contemptible for a host to begin eating before his guest. Cf., however, TbBer. 45b and TbBer. 47a. The host is the first one to break the bread and the first to reach for food. In light of this statement a reverse interpretation, given in the reading in *Menorat ha-Ma'or* of Al-Nakawa (ed. H.G. Enelow, IV, p. 419), is much more understandable: 'It is contemptible for the guest to begin eating before the host.' See, however, the reading 'mi-liphnei' in the manuscripts of D.E.Z. and cf. *Hilkhot Derekh 'Eretz* by Rabbi Jitzhaq ben Hajjim:

'biphnei'. This indicated that it is forbidden for the host to eat in the presence of his guest without offering him something. See also the peculiar explanation in *Nahalat Ja'aqob* on D. E. Z. h.l.: 'The host may take nothing from the food that has already been set before the guest.'

*It is more unbecoming when one guest brings in* ... According to a tradition in TbB. B. 98b, this fragment was part of a statement in *Seph. Ben Sira*, which (according to the reading in TbB. B. 98b) correspondents greatly to the entire context of the listing here in D. E. Z. This is not traceable, however, in the known versions of *Seph. Ben Sira*. A guest must behave in a restrained fashion and not demand rights that actually belong to the host. See the context in TosJom. Tob. IV,10, where it is stated in a remark by Rabbi Shim'on ben Gamli'el that a guest may bring his children along to certain gatherings if it is the custom to do so. See S. Lieberman, *Tosephta Ki-Pheshutah*, V, p. 1014. See also the immediate context in Tos. a.l., which clearly correspondents to the context here in D. E. Z.: It is forbidden for the guest to give food to the children of the host. It is important to note those manuscripts in D. E. that add the following statement after 'When one guest brings in another guest...': 'It is more unbecoming for one to eat before ('liphnei' or 'mi-liphnei') a "talmid hakham".' This means that it is yet more contemptible to begin eating a meal in the presence of a 'talmid hakham' who himself has not begun to eat. Given the reading in all manuscripts according to which the remark concerning washing the hands, and concerning a guest bringing in a guest and eating in the presence of a guest also belongs to this series of (four) increasingly contemptible actions, this can be a later addition.

*Still more reprehensible than these three is* ... In the basis manuscript, only three things are mentioned, while the words 'mi-sheloshtan' suggest four things. Perhaps one has to read 'megunneh she-sheloshtan' (the least unbecoming of the three things) as mentioned. See the supplement in the manuscripts '... (causes trouble) to another guest.' It is most inappropriate of all when one guest troubles another guest.

*Rabbi Me'ir said: 'Also when someone takes (food)...* According to Rabbi Me'ir, it is equally inappropriate for a guest to offer food that has been set before him to members of the host's household. One finds here an abbreviated reading of a baraita, known from TbHul. 94a and D. E. R. IX,7. The accompanying story is only briefly noted here in D. E. Z. See the commentary and parallels to D. E. R., l.c. The earliest reading of the baraita, without the exemplifying story, may be the reading in TosJom Tob IV,10. Note the cohesion of the text there with D. E. Z. h.l. It is striking that the statement and the story are attributed to someone only in *Derekh 'Eretz Zuta*. See TosB. Q. XI,4. It was permitted according to custom for members of the household to give food to each other. The text contains a remarkable reason for guests not being permitted to give their food away. People who are not members of the household (i. e. guests), are guilty of a form of robbery when they give food away. In doing so, they put the food supply of the host at their own disposal and thereby force the host to offer them something else. If the host has nothing more to offer, he is thereby embarrassed in a terrible way.

**13. Whoever lowers himself will be elevated [reflects exactly the tradition he heard], and so Scripture says: 'This shall be no more the same; that which is low upward with it, that which is high downward with it!' (Ez. 21:31)**

A number of manuscripts have a completely different reading: 'Whoever lowers himself determines exactly the traditions he heard', i.e., he will understand the traditions and teachings and be able to repeat them exactly. Cf. the reading of the Gaon of Vilna a.l.: 'Everyone who serves the sages determines exactly the traditions he heard, and everybody who does not exactly determine the tradition he heard deserves death.' Cf. A.J. Tawrogi, *Derech Erez Sutta*, p. 42. This reading, however, must be regarded as an adaption to the tradition that follows in D.E.Z. VIII,14 in connection with Rabbi 'Aqiba, who made incorrect decisions because he did not initially have the humility to learn from the sages. A number of genizah fragments, however, appear to confirm the reading of the basis manuscript; Ez. 21:31, which is quoted in this statement as a Scripture passage, supports on first sight the reading of the basis manuscript more strongly: 'Rase what is low and lower what is high ....' This quotation ,however, is missing in a large number of manuscripts.

Only where content is concerned, preference must be given to the reading of the other manuscripts. One who humbles himself by serving scholars and who studies with them will ultimately be able to make correct decisions. One who does not do so and thereby violates the words of the scholars and the Torah, deserves death. In this sense, the story about 'Aqiba coheres well with the context. See below.

**14a. Whoever transgresses the words of the sages deserves death and whoever declares (always) unfit is himself unfit.**
**14b. Rabbi 'Aqiba said: ' This was the beginning of my attendance upon the sages. Once, I was walking along the road, when I found a corpse which had to be buried according to the Law. I attended it [carrying it four miles] until I brought it to a cemetery [and buried it]. When I came and reported these events before Rabbi 'Eli'ezer and Rabbi Jehoshua, they said to me: 'Every step you have taken is accounted to you as if you have shed blood.' I spoke: 'If I have committed a transgression when I was intended to deserve well, how much more (I committed transgression) when I did not intend to deserve well!' From that moment I did not stop serving the sages.' He (i.e.**

**'Aqiba) used to say: 'Everyone who does not serve the sages deserves death.'**

14a. *Whoever transgresses the words of the sages...* Strong emphasis is placed here on obedience and on the teachings of the sages. The phrase 'words of the sages' are also read in the parallels as 'words of the Scribes' ('dibrei sopherim'). A distinction is already made in Tannaitic sources between 'words of Torah' and 'words of the Scribes.' Cf., e.g., MJeb. II,4; MJad. III,2; TbZeb. 99b; TbSanh. 87a; and MSanh. XI,3. In Tannaitic sources, the phrase 'the words of the Scribes' can mean the words of the sages in general. After the first century, however, the phrase was replaced by 'words of the sages' ('dibrei hakhamim'), and the term 'Scribes' ('sopherim') from know on usually refers specifically to the scribes from the time of Ezra. See W. Bacher, *Die exegetische Terminologie der jüdischen Traditionsliteratur*. Not until the Amoraic period is the phrase 'words of the sages' defined more clearly and distinguished from 'words of the Torah'. See B. de Vries, *Hooflijnen en Motieven in de Ontwikkeling der Halacha*, Haarlem 1959, p. 21. Here in D. E. Z., the phrase 'words of the sages' has a general meaning, but originally it had a somewhat more polemic character. See TbBer. 4b and especially Tb'Er. 21b, where it is stated that one should be more careful with the words of the sages than with 'words of Torah', because every transgression of the words of the sages makes one punishable by death. The hyperbolic wording ('deserves death') are probably attributable to the vehement resistance against the tendency to regard the words of the sages as less important than commandments and forbiddances directly from Scripture. Cf. also the remarks on D. E. Z. VIII,9 and parallels mentioned there such as Siphrei l.c. and TbSanh. l.c., the context of which contain declamations against incomplete acceptance of all oral hermeneutic traditions. It is not necessary to interpret the tradition here in D. E. as an polemic against the Karaites!

See S. Krauss in: *R. E. J.*, XXXVI(1898) p. 206. S. Krauss suggests that the statement here in D. E. is an alternative of the statement: 'And anyone who does not serve the sages deserves to die.' Cf. further A. R. N. [a] XXXVI (end). Like the story about Rabbi 'Aqiba , the statement here in D. E. did , according to S. Krauss, not belong to the original text but was added later on. S. Krauss states that the earlier source is found in Mas. Sem. IV. Such an extensively narrative passage indeed does not fit entirely into the context of this chapter of D. E. Z.

*Whoever declares (another) unfit is himself unfit...* Cf. D. E. R. I,31. Whoever continually declares others unfit is himself unfit. The connection between this statement and the context is unclear. A meaning given in TbQid. 70a is not bearing upon the context here in D. E. Z. The expression originally applied to disqualifying someone from a family of priests for the priesthood, or to disqualifying a woman to mary a priest etc. If someone continually expresses the the suspicion of irregularities in the marriages of other families to disqualify members of those families from the priesthood. Then there exists reason to suppose that he himself must be disqualified from the priesthood. The tradition gives here an example of the psychological insight in what is called presently projection. One who can never speak positively about others is to be suspected of deflecting negative thoughts from himself.

14b. *Rabbi 'Aqiba said: 'This was the beginning* ... See S. Krauss in: *R. E. J.*, XXXVI (1898) p. 306, where he suggests that the story of 'Aqiba is a later addition in this chapter of D. E. Z. According to S. Krauss, the reading 'tehillat zekhuti' in Mas. Sem. must be preferred to the reading 'tehillat shimmushi' here in D. E. Z. He also states that the version in Mas. Sem. predates the reading in D. E. Z. The words 'danti qal we-homer' ('I made an a fortiori reasoning') in Mas. Sem. are also according to his opinion to be preferred to ''amarti' ('I spoke') in D. E. Z. as the earlier reading. The concluding words in Mas. Sem. are partially set in the third person: 'And when someone said this to Rabbi 'Aqiba, he said: 'This was the beginning of my service...''' Cf. further a parallel in TjNaz. VII,1 [56a]. Because Rabbi 'Aqiba lacked daily contact with the sages and practical knowledge of the oral tradition, he broke the halakhic rule 'Met mitzwah qoneh meqomo'. Cf. Tb'Er. 17a; TbB. Q. 81a; TbSot. 45b and TbSanh. 47b. Cf. especially Tos'Er. II,6. See ed. S. Lieberman, pp. 93−94, and see S. Lieberman, *Tosephta Ki-Pheshutah*, III, p. 325, note 31, regarding a statement by Rabbi Jehudah ben Batira. A 'met mitzwah', i. e., a person killed outside of a city district ('tehum') in an open field or alongside the road in time of war, must be buried at the place in which he is found. Such a person acquires, as it were, the ground upon which he lies. His body may be removed only to the side of the road, if it is lying on the road itself. The prohibition against moving a corpse was put into effect because of the danger of removing the body of someone who had been killed by the occupying authorities. Rabbi 'Aqiba violated the words of the sages with every step he took when he was removing the dead body. Whoever transgresses against the words of the sages deserves to die. This led to the remark here in D. E.Z.: '... as if you shed innocent blood...' Cf. the introductory words in D. E. Z. VIII,14a: 'He who transgresses against the words of the sages deserves death.' This introductory sentence cannot be considered an less appropriate alternative to: 'Anyone who does not serve the sages...', but it can be regarded as an appropriate introduction to the story of Rabbi 'Aqiba.

### 15. He who enters a bathhouse should first remove his headcovering and after that he removes his shoes, after that he removes the undergarments, after that he takes off his shirt.

Cf. D. E. R. X,1 and the commentary there. D. E. R. mentions a different sequence for removing clothing: first the shoes are removed, then the headcovering, the coat, the belt, the shirt, and finally the underclothes, which cover the lower body. This sequence seems more plausible than the one mentioned here in D.E.Z., considering that the shirt was probably removed before the 'mikhnasajim', which probably covered the legs and lower body.

The word 'masweh' supposedly means a type of headcovering which, according to D. Sperber (*Massekhet Derekh 'Eretz Zuta*, p. 557), can be compared with the modern Arab 'kephia'. The Gaon of Vilna and A. J. Tawrogi (*Derech Erez Sutta*, p. 45) suggest the reading 'sarbal' (cloak) instead of 'masweh'. There is no reason, however, to deviate from the reading in the manuscripts. The fact that there is no explicit mention of a coat need not cause a problem, as the word 'masweh' can refer to a large cloak that covers the head and the body.

### 16. He who enters a bathhouse should give the honour to some one who is about to leave, and he who is about to leave the privy should give the honour to him who is entering.

[*The end of Derekh 'Eretz Ze'ira, with the help of God, the Almighty*]

It was considered good manners for one entering a bathhouse to show respect to one leaving it by stepping aside and letting the other pass first so that he may go outside (the person leaving could be tired). Once the other person has passed, one may enter the bathhouse. Cf. the commentary to D.E.R. X,2a (see the additions the manuscripts there). When using the toilet, however, the one who has already relieved himself must step aside and let pass the other person who has yet to relieve himself. It would be indecent to let someone who must relieve himself wait longer than is necessary. See the correct reading in M. Higger, *Massekhtot Derekh 'Eretz*. p. 301. Regarding D.E.Z. h.l., cf. the translation of M. Ginsberg in *The Minor Tractates of the Talmud*, ed. A. Cohen, II, p. 588.

A number of commentators interpret 'noten kabod' (should respect) not to mean to make room for another ('noten maqom' in most of the manuscripts in D.E.R. l.c.), but as 'to greet' ('doresh shalom'). One who enters a bathhouse must be the first one to utter a greeting, and one who leaves a toilet must be the first to utter a greeting. In accordance with most of the manuscripts of D.E.R. l.c., preference must be given to the meaning 'to respect' in the sense of making way for someone who is leaving while one is entering.

# Pereq De-Rabbi 'El'azar Ha-kappar

(in some manuscripts the last chapter of 'Jir'at Het' = D.E.Z. I–IV, IX)

## *Derekh 'Eretz Zuta, chapter IX*

1. **Rabbi 'El'azar ha-Kappar said: 'Keep aloof from grumbling, lest you grumble to others and lest you are adding to transgression.**

See all parallels and see the commentary to D.E.Z. I,17.

2. **Love the one who rebukes you [so that you may add to your wisdom] and hate the one who praises you, so that your wisdom does not decrease.**
3. **Love the synagogue so that you will receive your reward every day.**
4. **Love the house of study, so that your children may come to the study of the Torah.**
5. **Love the poor, so that your children will not come to the same (bad) condition.**
6. **Love meekness, so that you may complete your days.**
7. **Love acts of lovingkindness, so that you may be saved from the Angel of darkness.**

2. *Love the one who rebukes...* This statement is closely related to a statement, recorded in A.R.N. [a] XXIX (44a) in the name of Rabbi Shim'on ben 'El'azar. The admonition here in D.E.Z. to embrace rebuke fits completely into the context of practical rules of the sages, who had to guarantee a fruitful learning process. Criticism from others stimulates one's introspection and brings one to improve his behaviour and sharpen his insight. Praise from others, limits one's ability to be critical and thereby one's ability to learn. Cf. also D.E.Z. III,4 and D.E.Z. II,11 and the reference there to M'Abot VI,6 and parallels.

The statements in D.E.Z. IX,2–13, are uniform and stylized. Older traditions have been adapted to the form of these statements.

3. *Love the synagogue ...* One is rewarded for every step made in going to the House of Prayer. Cf. Deb. Rab. VII,2 and parallels. According to some traditions, the rewards are made in This World. In TbBer. 8a, the attainment of

great age is attributed to daily attendance at the synagogue. Cf. Jalq., 'Eqeb, r. 871. Cf. also TbShab. 127a; One already reaps the fruit of attending synagogue in This World. Other traditions mention reward in the World to Come. Cf, e.g., TjBer. V,1; Jalq., Ps., r. 659 and other sources. Women are rewarded for their efforts in stimulating their sons to go to the House of Prayer. Cf. TbBer. 17a.

4. *Love the house of study* ... Children were acquainted early with the House of Study. The good example of the parents could be stimulating for the children.

5. *Love the poor* ... One should love the poor so that his hildren or grand-children do not become poor. Cf. the notions contained in D.E.Z. II,12. Wealth represents a duty, and anyone can lose his possessions at any time through the intervention of Heaven if he is not generous and does not respect the rights of others. Cf. especially a closely related statement by Rabbi 'El'azar ha-Kappar in TbShab. 151b. The statement is ascribed to Bar Kappara, the son of Rabbi 'El'azar ha-Kappar, in the parallel in TjGit. III,7. If one does not become poor himself through being ungenerous and disrespectful, his children or grandchildren will certainly be impoverished. The command to help the poor is based on the concept of identification and solidarity. Cf. in the same strain of thought a statement by Rabbi Gamli'el ben Rabbi (ascribed to Rabban Gam-li'el in TosB.Q. IX,30, by way of Rabbi Jehudah). According to the statement God shows no mercy to those who show no mercy to the poor. See the tradition in TbGit. 7b, based on Nah. 1:12.

6. *Love meekness...* In the oldest traditions, meekness is associated with one's share in the World to Come on the basis of Ps. 37:11 and Is. 61:1. Cf. Mat. 5:4; Did. 3:7−8. For sources in Qumran literature, see D. Flusser in *I.E.J.*, X (1960), p. 20. There is no special reason here in D.E.Z., however, for inter-preting 'that you may complete your days' eschatologically.

7. *Love acts of lovingkindness...* Various traditions reflect the notion that one could prevent an early death or acquire a share in the World to Come by giving alms and doing charitable deeds. The notion is based, among others, on a particular interpretation of Prov. 11:4 (cf. Prov. 10:2): 'Riches do not profit in the day of wrath, but righteousness delivers from death.' I.e., by almsgiving and being charitable, one earns a place in the World to Come. Cf. Prov. 21:21: 'He who pursues righteousness (alsmsgiving) and mercy (act of loving kindness) will find life, righteousness and honour.' The word 'life' in Prov. 21:21 is interpreted in the parallels to refer to being spared an early, unnatural death as well as to the promise of a share in the World to Come.

The expression 'mal'akh ha-tishhoret' is interpreted in different ways. (One parallel in Shir ha-Shir. Rab. I,15 mentions the sparing of one from 'the angel of punishment'. In S.E.R. XI (ed. M. Friedmann, pp. 51−52) there is mention of almsgiving, which keeps one from the reach of the Angel of Death. The expression 'mal'akh ha-tishhoret' can be interpreted as the Angel of Darkness or (according to an interpretation in *Reshit Hokhmah*, Derekh 'Eretz, sha'ar 3) as the Angel of Death, who turns the faces of his victims black. The term is also explained as the angel who takes the lives of those whose hair is still black, i. e., the lives of young people. The reading 'she-temallet me-ha-tishhoret' in *Reshit Hokhmah* l.c. may be interpreted as 'so that you may escape from forced labour.' See the commentary and parallels to D. E. Z. II,15 in connection with the meaning of 'tishhoret' as forced labour. With this meaning, there is a strong connection between the statement here in D. E. Z. and the tradition in TjPe'ah I (see ed. A. M. Luncz, Jerusalem 1908, 4b):'Rabbi 'Aqiba said: "If you give alms from your wealth, then the Holy Praised be He will see to your debts for tributes, fines, capitation tax, and tax on agricultural produce."'" It is entirely possible that the statement here in D. E. Z. originally read: '. . . so that you will be spared conscription into public service (i. e. forced labour).' The word 'mal'akh' may have been added to the text because of the context and because of misunderstanding. See S. Krauss in: *R. E. J.*, XXXVII (1899), pp. 53—54. S. Krauss defends the interpretation of 'tishhoret' as forced labour (as a form of taxation). Whoever gives alms will be spared from forced labour, which was instituted by the Romans. S. Krauss interprets the word 'mal'akh', however, to mean 'messenger', 'deputy' or 'missionary'. The problematic interpretations such as 'Angel of Death' arose later. (The reading 'mal'akh ha-tishhoret' as 'angel of premature death', however, cannot be excluded totally. Cf. M'Abot III,5.

**8. And be heedful to read the 'Shema' and (to pray) the "Amidah', so that you may be saved from the judgement of Gehinnom.**

The basis of this statement is contained in M'Abot II,13: 'Rabbi Shim'on said: "Be careful to read the Shema and the 'Amidah, and when you pray make not your prayer fixed, but as an appeal of mercy and grace before the All Present . . ."' One should be certain to say his prayers on time and with the proper devotion and not to make prayer a routine action. The words 'make not your prayer fixed' can also be interpreted to mean that one should not always say his prayers with the same words or with the same intonation. Cf., e.g. TjBer. IV,4 and TbBer. 29b. In connection with the term 'fixed prayer' and the various interpretations of this term, see I. Jacobson, *Netib Binah*, I, Tel-Aviv 1978, pp. 34 and 37. Among the pious, it is important that one be aware of Him in Whose presence he is saying a prayer. Cf. the custom recorded in the Mishnah (MBer. IV,1) among the early Hasidim of waiting an hour before praying in order to concentrate on the Father in Heaven. The last segment of the statement here in D. E. Z. is related to a statement by Rabbi Hama bar Haninah recorded in TbBer. 15b: 'If one in reciting the Shema pronounces the letters distinctly, hell is cooled for him . . .'

**9. Let your house be open wide, so that you may have no lack of food. Be heedful not to have the doors of your house closed when you sit down to eat and to drink, because the doors of your house may bring you to poverty. 10. Be heedful to honour your wife, so that she does not become barren.**

9. *Let your house be open wide...* This statement seems to be based on M'Abot I,5: 'José the son of Johanan of Jerusalem said: "Let your house be open wide and let the poor be members of your household..."' Hiob, Abraham and Isaac are cited in the parallels as examples to follow, because they opened the doors on all sides of their homes to the poor from all directions. See also D. E. Z. IX,5: 'Love the poor...'

*Be heedful not to have the doors of your house closed...*
The plural form 'doors' may refer to gates that had double doors, such as were found in more distinguished houses. Cf. in Ber. Rab. XLVIII,9 the story of Abraham whose tent was open at all sides. Cf. the explanation of Rabbi Judan pertaining to that context and his discussion of 'diopilos' (= Greek 'diopulos', a gate with two doors); cf. M. Jastrow, *Dictionary*, I, p. 322. Cf. further S. Krauss, *Talmudische Archäologie*, I, p. 36 and p. 38, note 492; see D. Sperber, *Massekhet Derekh 'Eretz Zuta*, p. 148.

10. *Be heedful in honouring your wife ...* Cf. A. J. Tawrogi (*Derech Erez Sutta*, p. 46) suggests the following reading: '... so that she will not be like a barren woman.' Cf. some readings mentioned by M. Higger, *Massekhtot Derekh 'Eretz* , p. 139. The meaning intended is that one should honour his wife so that she does not become an object of scorn like a childless woman. This meaning, however, is not supported by the manuscripts used here in D. E. This interpretation unnecessarily detracts from the context of the statement. A number of commentators suggest that a reading as in the basis manuscript refers to psychic factors that can lead to barrenness in a woman. The statement is also explained to mean that one should show respect to his wife during sexual intercourse. Disrespectful sexual approaches by the man could result in childlessness. Refusal to have intercourse with one's wife is also explained as a form of not honouring one's wife.

The statement here in D. E. Z. is closely related to a statement by Rabbi Helbo (in TbB. M. 59a and other sources): 'Rabbi Helbo said: "A man should always be heedful in honouring his wife, for only because of his wife do blessings rest on a man's home, for it is written: And he treated Abraham well for her sake (Gen. 12:16)"'. The definition of 'blessing' especially includes fertility of the woman, as well as progeny. In TbB. M. l.c., however, 'blessings' are explained by Raba in terms of wealth. In the context here in D. E. Z., attention is focused on the emotional sensitivity of the woman and the duty to approach her with tenderness. Cf. also TbB. B. 10b: 'What is a man to do in order that he may have male offspring?... Rabbi Jehoshua says that he should make his wife glad to perform the marital office.'

**11. Rejoice in sufferings, which come upon you, because sufferings which come upon you will deliver you from diseases of the bed.**

**12. Rejoice at your table, when the hungry benefit from it, so that your days may be prolonged in This World and in he World to Come.**

**13. Rejoice in donating gifts (of charity) within (i. e. in the privacy of) your house, so that the Angel of death may be diverted from you, for it is said: 'A gift in secret averts anger'(Prov. 21:14).**

11. **Rejoice in sufferings...** The statement 'One should rejoice about sufferings more than about his prosperity', made by Rabbi 'Aqiba, is well known. Cf. Mekh. de-R. Jishm., Ba-Hodesh, par. 10 (ed. H. S. Horovitz, pp. 239—240), Siphrei, Wa-'Ethannan pisqa 32, among other sources. Cf. also the statements by Rabbi 'El'ezer ben Ja'aqob and many others mentioned in the same context in that source. There are numerous conceptually related traditions. Suffering makes one to become introspective and to study, it also leads to repentance and reconciliation with Heaven. Confidence in speedy recompense for sufferings in This World for the World to Come was especially strong in the time of Rabbi 'Aqiba and his students, when difficult political circumstances strengthened expectations of the coming of the Messiah.

The basis manuscript reads: 'Rejoice in sufferings... because sufferings which come upon you deliver you from disease of the bed.' One manuscript (Ms. New York, J. T. S., [cat. E. N. Adler] no. 4465a) reads 'diseases from above' (as the counterpart to 'shel mattah' (from below), which clearly indicates that 'shel mittah' (of the bed) was incorrectly interpreted as 'shel mattah' (from below). The Gaon of Vilna suggests in D. E. Z. a.l., the reading 'medinah shel gaihinnom' (from the judgement of gehinnom). Cf. A. J. Tawrogi, *Derech Erez Sutta,* p. 47; and M. Ginsberg in *The Minor Tractates of the Talmud,* ed. A. Cohen, p. 589. This reading, however, is not confirmed by the manuscripts, hence there is no reason to deviate from the reading of the basis manuscript. According to a statement found in TbBer. 5b (cf. Jalq., Is. r. 276) dating back to Rab Huna those who accept their suffering are promised a long life and promised that they will have the good fortune of seeing their offspring. Cf. especially a statement by Rabbi Alexandari in TbNed. 41a, according to which one is only cured of disease if he is forgiven his transgressions (i. e. if he accepts sickness as a form of penance). Rab Hamnuna added further that he gains new vitality in turning to the days of his youth.

12. *Rejoice at your table...* Cf. especially the commentary to D. E. Z. IV,4 and D. E. Z. IX,7: 'Love acts of lovingkindness...' Giving alms and helping the poor gives a long life in This World and through this one earns a share in the World to Come. The background is the concept of 'middah ke-neged middah'. By saving life one earns life.

13. *Rejoice in donating gifts...* This statement is found in clearly comparable form only in later sources. The parallels are based on Prov. 21:14: 'A gift in

secret pacifies anger.' Anger is equated in the parallels with the Angel of
Death. Cf, Midr. Le-'Olam in Jellinek, *Beit ha-Midrash*, III, p. 109; and cf.
*Me'il Tzedaqah* 27c (cf. 74a) with reference to Dt. 9:19 as support for the
identification between 'anger' in Prov. 21:14 and the Angel of Death. Charitable acts must be done within the home, out of view from the public eye.

**14. If one has restrained himself from (performing) a commandment and
occupied himself with some transgression, the Angel of death will get the
start of him.**

This saying should be corrected to read: 'If you have restrained yourself...' Cf.
the commentary to D. E. Z. IV,13–14; and D. E. Z. IV,23. In the manuscripts
concerning this passage in D. E. Z. use is made of both the second and the third
person. The third person may have been used because of the highly negative
nature of the statement. The third person softens the impact of the statement so
that one is not prone to interpret the statement personally. See however the
many manuscripts, that use the second person.

**15. When your feet have brought you if not this way than that way for the
sake of the poor and for the sake of (performing) a commandment, then will
come true about you (what is written:) 'Blessed you shall be when you come
in and blessed you shall be when you go out' (Dt. 28:6).**
**16. If you have guarded your mouth from slander, all your days will be in
peace.**

15. *When your feet...* The blessing 'Blessed shall you be when you come in,
and blessed shall you be when you go out' applies to those people who will spare
no distance or effort to help the poor. This passage is explained as follows in a
statement ascribed to Rabbi Berekhjah (see Deb. Rab. VII,5; cf. TbB. M. 107a
and Rashi in that source): the righteous person is blessed when he is born into
This World guiltless and free of sin, and when he dies he leaves This World just
as guiltless and free of sin. The background belief here is that the fulfilment of
social obligations to others has a conciliatory effect. Anyone who gives alms
and performs charitable deeds earns a place in the World to Come. See also the
commentary to D.E.Z. IV,4; and D.E.Z. IX,7. Cf. also D.E.Z. IV,16 in
connection with the greeting of the righteous after death by God and the angels.

**17. If one has been insolent in the face of some one who is greater than
oneself, one will ultimately be stricken by a skin disease.**
**18. If one has restrained oneself from (performing) some commandment
and has been engaged in some transgression, one's wife will ultimately die
of a stroke (i. e. by a sudden disease). And so Scripture says: 'Son of man,**

**behold, I take away from you the desire of your eyes with a stroke' (Ez. 24:16).**

17. *If one has been insolent...* This statement is found in this form only in later sources. A person, who shows a rude and shameless attitude toward those who deserve to be respected for their knowledge or social status could be punished by contracting a form of leprosy characterized by white spots on the skin. A statement in which haughtiness is mentioned as a cause of leprosy is attributed to Rabbi Johanan in Tb'Ar. 16a. It would be more accurate to correct the statement here in D.E.Z. to read: '...If you are insolent...' In connection with the use of the second rather than the third person in the manuscripts, see the commentary to D.E.Z. IX,14.

18. *If one has restrained oneself ...* The following reading is more accurate: 'If you have restrained yourself...' See commentary to D.E.Z. IX,14. This statement too is found only in later sources. If one does not perform a certain precept when he has the chance to do so, then his wife will die from a plague, i.e., a sudden and abominable disease. Cf. TbM. Q. 28a; Mas. Sem. III and other sources; cf. especially Ez. 24:16.

**19. If you hurry to honour a sage, you will have sons and daughters of the highest degree.**
**20. If you hurry to honour the poor, you will have sons and daughters who occupy themselves with the (study of the) Torah and who will fulfil the commandments in Israel.**

19. *If you hurry to honour a sage ...* This statement does not appear in a number of manuscripts. It is, however, mentioned in various genizah fragments. The context of the statement correspondents strongly to that of D.E.Z. IX,4: 'Love the house of study, so that your children may come to the study of the Torah.' He who honours the sages by having daily contact with them and serving them and thereby learning from them, will have sons and daughters of the highest order. Some of the manuscripts have the reading 'capable of highest order' ('metuqqanim ...').

20. *If you hurry to honour the poor ...* This statement too does not appear in certain manuscripts. Only similar wordings are found in older sources. See a statement by Rabbi 'Eli'ezer in TbB.B. 10b: 'What is a man to do in order that he may have male offspring? Rabbi 'Eli'ezer says that he should give generously to the poor.' Cf. also a statement by Rabbi Jehoshua ben Levi in TbB.B. 9b: 'Rabbi Jehoshua ben Levi said: "He who does charity habitually will have sons which are wise, rich and versed in the aggada..."' Emphasis on the connection between 'talmud Torah' and the concept 'tzedaqah' and 'gemilut hasadim', and between 'talmud Torah', relations with others and social behaviour, is particularly characteristic of the world of 'derekh 'eretz'. Cf., e.g., D.E.Z. I,10b in the manuscripts; D.E.Z. II,9 and II,11; and D.E.Z. V,5.

**21. If you have witnessed the death of a sage, surround him until he departed from you (i. e. until his body is escorted to the burying place).**
**22. If you have witnessed the death of a poor man, stay with him until you have taken him to the grave, so that they will speak about your peace like about the peace of Pinhas ben Eleazar, when you return (from the grave).**

21. *If you have witnessed the death of a sage ...* A number of manuscripts of D. E. Z., which have been influenced by different traditions, read: 'If you have witnessed the death of a sage, go and rent your garments until he is escorted to the burial grounds.' Cf. TosM. Q. II,7 and TbM. Q. 25a and TjM. Q. III,7 and TbShab. 105b. According to these traditions, one who has witnessed the death of a sage counts as a relative and must, among other things, make the customary tear in his garments as a sign of morning. Cf. especially TbSanh. l.c.; TbM. Q. 22b and 25a; TosM. Q.. l.c.; and Mas. Sem. IX (ed. M. Higger, p. 80). If one is not truly a relative of the dead sage, the rent in his clothing may be stitched together as soon as he turned his face away from the bier. See TbM. Q. 25a. The death of a sage means a loss for the entire community; therefore, anyone who witnessed the death of a sage must observe the customs of mourning. This rule certainly applied if one had studied with the dead sage.

22. *If you have witnessed the death of a poor man...* This statement supplements the preceding one. The background here is the concept 'measure for measure'. If one buries another in peace, then he too will return to his place of rest on peace. Cf. a closely related notion contained in a statement by Rabbi Me'ir (made in the name of Rabbi 'Aqiba) in TosMeg. IV,16 and other sources in regard to Qoh. 7:2. One should escort a person to his grave so that he may be escorted to his own grave, lament another so that he himself may be lamented, and bury another so that he himself will be buried. Cf. also in TbM. Q. 25a (cf. TosM. Q. II,17; TjM. Q.. III,7; and Mas. Sem. IX) and a statement by Rabbi Shim'on ben 'El'azar according to which one must observe the customs of mourning for anyone whose death he has witnessed, even if the person was insignificant.

For they will speak about your peace like about the peace of Pinhas ben Eleazar, so that when you return (from the grave....)' Cf. the explanation of M. Higger, *Massekhtot Ze'irot*, p. 135. Cf. also the reading suggested by the Gaon of Vilna: 'If you witnessed the death of a sage, go not away from him, until you brought him to the grave, so that when you die you may enter and rest in the grave on your bed.' (i. e. peacefully). Two statements are combined here into one. Cf. the reading by A. J. Tawrogi influenced by the reading of the Gaon of Vilna, in *Derech Erez Sutta*, p. 49; and cf. M. Ginsberg in *The Minor Tractates of the Talmud*, ed. A. Cohen, II, p. 590. The reading by the Gaon of Vilna and other readings influenced by his reading omit the remark about Pinhas ben Eleazar (from 'when you return' to Eleazar). The remark about Pinhas ben Eleazar contains an implicit reference to Num. 25:10−13. The meaning behind the reference to Pinhas ben Eleazar is not entirely clear. According to one opinion, it means that one who has willingly accompanied a pauper (whose funeral was attended by few) to the grave will be welcomed after his own death by the angels with words of peace. Cf. D.E.Z. IX,15; and D.E.Z. IV,16. Cf. also M. Higger, *Massekhtot Ze'irot* l.c.

Other commentators, though, explain the closing of the statement here in D.E.Z. differently: ... so that people will speak about your peace (i.e., about your prosperity) as about the peace of Pinhas ben Eleazar, when you come back (from the grave). Cf., among others, J. Harburger, *Massekhet Derech Erez Sutta*, pp. 47 and 49 and cf. M. Higger, *Massekhtot Derekh 'Eretz*, p. 55. To judge from the wording here in D.E.Z. (such as 'be-haziratkha'; 'when you return'), the last reading must be considered the most plausible one and the most appropriate one in connection to the implicit reference to Num. 25:10–13. Some manuscripts of D.E.Z. read: '...so that they will greet you...'

**23. If you have noticed that your fellowman is poor and that his economical situation deteriorates and when he stretches out his hand to you for help, do not send him back empty-handed, for it is said: 'He who keeps a command- ment shall know no evil thing, and the heart of the wise knows time and rule.' (Qoh. 8:5).**

**24. If you lend a poor man a 'Sela' or something else in the time of his emergency, it will come true about you (what is written:) 'Then shall you call, and the Lord will answer' (Is. 58:9).**

23. *If you have noticed that your fellowman is poor....* If one's neighbour stretches out his hand for help, one may not send him away empty-handed. The basis manuscript refers to Qoh. 8:5. Other manuscripts cite Prov. 19:16 (which like Qoh. 8:5 also begins with 'shomer') Both passages contain a promise of reward to those who help the poor. Note especially the reference to Lev. 25:25 in some manuscripts. In terms of wording, Lev. 25:25 most closely approxima- tes the statement itself.

Parallels are found in later sources only.

24. *If you lend a poor man a 'Sela' or something ...* This statement is from a much more extensive baraita, mentioned in TbJeb. 62b-63a. Cf. TbSanh. 76b; cf. also D.E.R. II and S.E.R. XVI (ed. M. Friedmann, p. 78).

**25. [If you have lowered yourself, the Holy One blessed be He will lift you up.] If you have made yourself great before your neighbour, the Holy One blessed be He will degrade him [you].**

**26. If others have praised (i.e. cursed or insulted) you, whether at a meeting of the sages or at a meal, make peace with them, so that he [you]**

**may enter in peace and he [you] may rest on your bed (i. e. in your grave, cf. Is. 57:2).**

25. *If you have made yourself great before your neighbour*... Cf. D.E.Z. VIII,6 and D.E.Z. VIII,13 and the commentary. The transition from the use of second to third person ('degrade *him*') in the basis manuscript is striking. The use of the second person is more authentic. The transition to the third person can be explained by the fact that negative statements were set in the third person so that one would not so readily interpret the statement personally and invite misfortune. Cf. also observations in the commentary to D.E.Z. IX,14.

26. *If others have praised you*... No early parallels to this statement have been found. At first sight the reading ('giddelukha' (praised you) is problematic, but it may be regarded as a euphemism for the intended meaning: 'If others have cursed you...' Cf. the reading in *Menorat ha-Ma'or* of Al-Nakawa (ed. H.G. Enelow, IV, p. 433) and 'we-'im heqallu 'otekha 'aherim' (and if others cursed you) and idem *Reshit Hokhmah*, Derekh 'Eretz, sha'ar 3. M. Higger, however, suggests reading ''im gazelukha' (if others have robbed you). See M. Higger, *Massekhtot Ze'irot*, p. 135. The manuscripts, however, do not support this reading, and the content of that reading does not correspondent well to that of the statement here in D.E.Z. D. Sperber suggest the same reading, but in the sense of: 'If others rob you of your honour...', i.e. if one is taunted and hurt by others. See D. Sperber, *Massekhet Derekh 'Eretz Zuta*, p. 65. D. Sperber refers to TbBer. 6b, where it is said that one who does not return a greeting is a robber. D. Sperber's reading is plausible, but the manuscripts do not conform it. If one accepts the readings 'gadelu' or 'kabedu' as euphemisms, however, the manuscript readings do not need to be revised. Cf. the reading of the Gaon of Vilna a.l.:'we-'im jaribu 'immekha' (and if they strive with you; when they accuse you).

With regard to the conclusion of the statement here in D.E.Z., cf. especially Is. 57:2 and parallels in D.E.Z. IV,16.


27. **And so Rabbi 'Eli 'ezer [better reading: Rabbi 'El'azar ha-Kappar] used to say: 'Great is peace and hated is dissension. Great is peace for even when Israel would worship idols but peace is (maintained) among them, the All Present blessed be He says: "I am not able to injure them", for it is said: "Ephraim is joined to idols, let him alone" (Hos. 4:17). But when they became divided, what is said about them? "Their heart is divided, now they shall bear their guilt" (Hos. 10:2).'**
28. **How? A house in which there is dissension will ultimately be destroyed, and the sages say: 'Dissension in a house (leads to) cunning evil'.**
29. **A Town in which there is dissension will ultimately be destroyed, and the sages say: 'Dissension in a town (leads to) shedding of blood.'**

30. **A synagogue in which there is dissension will ultimately be cut into pieces. [Other reading: will ultimately destroyed and the sages say 'will ultimately be cut into pieces.']**
31. **Two sages in one city and so two courts of law between which there is dissension will ultimately lead to death.**

27. *Rabbi 'Eli'ezer the Great [better reading; Rabbi 'El'azar ha-Kappar] used to say...* In Siphrei, Naso, pisqa 42 (ed. H. S. Horovitz, p. 46), this statement is ascribed to Rabbi 'El'azar, the son of Rabbi 'El'azar ha-Kappar, as the conclusion to a midrash. In D. E. Z., the statement serves as an independent introduction to a series of statements.

*Great is peace for even if Israel...* Peace is great, for even if Israel is guilty of idolatry, it is preserved by its internal unity. On the basis of Siphrei l.c., this statement (along with the preceding one) must be attributed to Rabbi 'El'azar, the son of Rabbi 'El'azar ha-Kappar. Cf. Bam. Rab. XI,7 and Jalq., Ps., r. 711 and other sources. Cf. Tanh. (Jash.), Tsav, § 7 and Pes. Rab. (ed. M. Friedmann, 199b) and other sources that read: Rabbi 'El'azar ha-Kappar. The wording here in D. E. Z. IX,2 (*... says, as it were, the Holy praised be He: 'I am unable to harm them'*) is found in nearly identical form in Ber. Rab. XXXVIII,6 (see ed. J. Theodor / Ch. Albeck, pp. 355–356): 'I am unable to have dominion over them.' This reading seems authentic. Siphrei l.c. and other parallels contain a less forceful reading: '... The Omnipresent, as it were, says: "Satan is unable to harm them..."' It is said in the context of Ber. Rab. l.c., that the generation from the time when the Tower of Babel was built, was spared even though they were guilty of idolatry, because they were at one with each other. The generation from the flood was divided, and thus was not saved. It is explained in *Mishnat Rabbi 'Eli'ezer* (ed. H. G. Enelow, I, p. 78) that God was willing to forgive Israel after the episode of the Golden Calf because they were at one with each other. This was not so, however, with Korah and his followers, and his punishment was explained as the consequence of the dissension he caused in Israel. Cf., e.g., Deb. Rab. XVIII,4. Cf. the tradition in D. E. Z. XI,5 and parallels, where it is stated that the harmony of Israel (i. e. the lack of dissension in Israel) made Israel eligible to receive the Torah.

28. *How? A house in which there is dissension ...* Although this statement is recorded only in later sources, it is recorded as a baraita. According to the rabbis, the residents of a house in which dissension reigns will devise evil plans against each other. Cf. M. Higger's translation (*Massekhtot Derekh 'Eretz*, p. 560: '... leads to unchastity...'

30. *A synagogue in which there is dissension ...* Some manuscripts read: 'A synagogue in which there is dissension will ultimately be destroyed and the wise say: "(A synagogue in which there is dissension) will in the end be cut in pieces."' The Gaon of Vilna reads: '... will ultimately become a house of

sectarians' but this reading is not supported by the manuscripts. The Gaon of Vilna's reading seems to have been influenced by TbJeb. 96b.

31. *Two sages in one city...* See the manuscripts. The earliest reading probably only mentioned two sages in one city, based on Talmudic traditions. Cf. TbSot. 49a and TbTa'an. 8a. The element about the two courts of law was probably added later on. In accordance with the parallels (see *Menorat ha-Ma'or* of Al-Nakawa; ed. H. G. Enelow, IV, p. 298; *Ma'alot ha-Middot*, ed. Eshkol, p. 329 and Midr. ha-Gad. on Num. 32:5), preference must be given to the reading 'we-ken' (*and so*) rather than 'we-hen', the reading in the basis manuscript.

## 32. 'Abba Sha'ul said: 'Dissension between courts of law is the destruction of the world.'

In connection with the concept of a world that cannot survive without peace, see the mentioned parallels in connection with D. E. Z. XI,1. A fixed system of justice is one of the pillars of human society. The commandment to institute courts is one of the Noachitic commandments. Cf. TbSanh. 56a ff. Cf, also M'Abot I,18!

## 33. 'Abba José ben Johanan (read: Hanin) said in the name of Shemu'el ha-Qatan (Samuel the Small): 'This world, what is it like? (It is like) the eyeball of flesh and blood. The white which is in it is the ocean, which surrounds the whole world. The dark colour (i. e. the iris) is the inhabited world. The pupil in the dark colour (i. e. the iris) is Jerusalem. The reflected face in the pupil is the Temple. May it be Your wish that it will be rebuilt speedily in our days.' End.

The word ''Abba' (see also D. E. Z. IX,32) was added to personal names as a sign of respect. It is difficult to ascertain the identity of the 'Abba José ben Johanan mentioned here. W. Bacher, *Die Agada der Tannaiten*, p. 46, note 2 suggests the reading: 'Abba José ben Hanin (cf. the manuscripts here in D. E. Z. that read 'Hanan' or 'Hanin'). W. Bacher suggests that confusion has occurred with José ben Johanan mentioned in M'Abot I,4. Similar confusion is evident from the comparison between the reading of TosMen. XIII,21 (ed. M. S. Zuckermandel, p. 533 with the name: 'Abba José ben Johanan) and a parallel in TbPes. 57a (which reads: Abba Joseph ben Hanin [Hanan]). Cf. also TjSheq. VI,2 and TbSheq. 17a. 'Abba José ben Hanin is also mentioned in MMid. II,6. He probably lived in the first generation of the Tanna'im. See R. Halperin, *'Atlas 'Etz Hajjim*, IV, p. 121 and A. B. Hyman, *Toledot Tanna'im we-'Amora'im.*, p. 726 and W. Bacher, l.c.; cf. TbPes. 57a; TbSot. 20b; and Siphrei, Ba-Midbar, pisqa 8.

Such an early dating of the transmitter, here in D. E. Z., however, makes implausible the suggestion that this spokesman was transmitting the statement in the name of Shemu'el ha-Qatan. It is more likely that the transmitter was (in accordance with a tradition in TjKil. II,4) a contemporary of Rabbi 'El'azar ben Rabbi Shim'on. Tj. l.c., reads 'Abba José ben Johanan: with the addition of 'ish j-n-w-h' (= ''ish jewani', i. e. the Greek). The same person is mentioned in TosKil. II,1 as 'Abba José Hanan [Hanin] [Hanun] the Greek. It is possible that this person was the 'Abba José ben Johanan of Jerusalem, speaking in the name of Rabbi Me'ir in TbJeb. 53b. The abbreviation of the addition 'the Greek' was possibly incorrectly interpreted in TbJeb. 53b as 'isj Jerushalajim' (the man of Jerusalem). Cf. the reading mentioned in TosMen. XIII,21. See A. B. Hyman, l.c., and R. Halperin l.c.

The central place and meaning of the Temple in the world is illustrated by comparison here in D. E. Z. It would be incorrect to interpret the statement merely as an astrological observation. According to D. Sperber (*Massekhet Derekh 'Eretz Zuta*), the words 'the face in the pupil [is referring] to the Temple' here in D. E. Z., refer to the heavenly Temple, which is a reflection of the Temple on earth. Jerusalem is regarded as the navel of the world. The prayer for the restoration of the Temple was added later to the statement of Shemu'el ha-Qatan and thus does not appear in some manuscripts. After the fall of the Temple, the prayer for the restoration of the Temple became part of the Eighteen Benedictions and involved an adaption of existing formulas for blessing the Temple and for sacrificial rites. Cf., e.g. *Seph. Ben Sira* 51,12; TjBer. IV,5 [8c]; TjR. ha-Sh. IV,5 [59c]; Waj. Rab. VII,2; and Pes. Rab. pisqa 25 (ed. M. Friedmann, 158b).

It is difficult to date the addition precisely. The wording of the addition is related to that of a prayer recorded in a baraita in TbB. M. 28b. The statement as a whole was probably intended as the closing to D. E. Z. IX.

# Pereq Rabbi Shim'on

## *Derekh 'Eretz Zuta, chapter X*

**1. Shim'on ben Johai said: 'The week (of seven years) on the end of which the son of David will come, the first year becomes true: "And I caused it to rain upon one city and I caused it not to rain on another city" (Am. 4:7). The second year arrows of famine will be sent forth. (During) the third year there will be a great famine and in the course of that men, women and children will die; and pious men and men of deed [will be reduced in number]; and the Torah will be forgotten by its students. (During) the fourth year there will be plenty and there will be not plenty. (During) the fifth year there will be a great plenty, one will eat, drink and rejoice. (During) the sixth year there will be sounds (or voices, or rumours). (During) the seventh year wars (will be waged), at the conclusion of the seventh year the son of David will come.'**

This and the following statements describe the so-called 'birth pangs of (i.e. preceding the advent) the messiah', the stages of suffering and oppression preceding the coming of the messiah. The apocalypse of Baruch (chap. 27) already mentions twelve such stages preceding the Messianic Era. The fifth stage brings with it drought and famine. The Apocalypse of Abraham (ed. G. H. Box, London 1918, chap. 30, pp. 82–84) mentions ten plagues. With respect to the concept 'birth pangs of the messiah', see, among others, TbSanh. 98b; Mat. 24:8 and Mark 13:8. Examples of the birth pangs of the messiah are also found in the New Testament. Cf. Mat. 24:4–31; Mark 13:5–27; and Luke 21:8–28.

One may assume that the illustrations in the above-mentioned texts were greatly influenced by the social and political circumstances at the end of the Second Temple Period, i.e., in the time of the uprising and of the fall of the Temple and later of the Bar Kokhba period. Cf. J. Klausner, *Die Messianische Vorstellungen des jüdischen Volkes*, p. 49; cf. also P. Bogaert, *L'Apocalypse de Baruch*, Paris 1969, p. 60.

The statement here in D. E. Z., concerning the week of seven years preceding the Messianic Era dates back to a tradition recorded in TbSanh. 97a as a baraita. This statement is ascribed in Shir ha-Shir. Rab. II,13 to Rabbi Johanan. Cf. also Midr. Seder 'Olam Zuta, 91 and *Pugio Fidei* (of R. Martini) pp. 783, 846 and 884.

The statement at issue here is attributed in D.E.Z. to Shim'on bar Johai. This is probably correct, considering the circumstances under which Rabbi Shim'on lived. The erroneous attribution of the statement to Rabbi Johanan in Shir ha-Shir. Rab. l.c., was probably made on the basis of a statement in the immediate context of the statement under discussions that appears in TbSanh. l.c. See also J. Klausner, o.c., p. 52.

The concept 'week' as a week of years, as used in D.E.Z., can be compared with that used in Dan. 9:27. Also elsewhere in the tradition appears this concept of a cycle of seven years, preceding the advent of the messiah. Cf. the tradition of Rabbi 'Aba or Rabbi 'Aha in TjBer. II,4 (4c-5a) and cf. TbMeg 17b(Raba). It is concluded here in D.E.Z. on the basis of Amos 4:7 that God will manipulate nature before the final redemption so that one place will be blessed with rain and abundance, while another will be ravaged by drought and famine.

*During the second year 2...* During the second year arrows of famine will be sent forth. According to Rashi on TbSanh. 97a 'arrows of famine' is an image of moderate famine and the lack of abundance for everyone. These places that enjoyed abundance in the first year will also be confronted with an increasing scarcity of food.

*(During) the third year ...* The third year will bring complete and devastating famine that will claim the lives of many men, women and children. Cf. especially II Bar. 27:7[5] ff.: 'In the third stage many will die.' Cf. also the Apoc. of Abraham, chap. 30, regarding the fourth and eighth plagues; cf. also Mat. 24:7; Mark. 13:8 and Luke 21:11. The number of 'hasidim' and ''anshei ma'aseh' (men of the deed) will decrease. This interpretation is based on a reading such as is found in Shir ha-Shir. Rab. II,13 and a number of manuscripts of D.E.Z. Reference to 'hasidim' and ''anshei ma'aseh' is typical of the early Tannaitic period. Cf. especially, A. Büchler, *Types of Jewish Palestinian Piety*, p. 1 ff. The word 'hasid' refers to someone who behaves in a correct and loving manner toward others. The word ''anshei ha-ma'aseh' refers to those who not only try to avoid transgression but try to fulfil the positive precepts with as much love and devotion as possible. For such people, the performance of deeds motivated by loving kindness was more important than study. See A. Büchler, o.c., p. 48. Cf. statements in MSot. IX,15 and TosSot. XV,5 about the disappearance of the 'hasidim' after the death of Rabbi José Qatnuta (Qetonit) and the disappearance of the 'Men of the deed' after the death of Rabbi Haninah ben Dosa. It is clear from the general context of the passages mentioned that the experience of the disappearance of the 'hasidim' and the 'men of the deed' was a hall mark of the period after the fall of the Temple. The difficulties experienced especially in that period were perceived as the birth pangs of immanent deliverance. See especially the statement of Rabbi Pinhas ben Ja'ir in the tradition in MSot. l.c., where the decline of the ''anshei ma'aseh' is mentioned as a characteristic of the 'birth pangs of the messiah.' In the same context see also the statement of Rabbi 'Eli'ezer ha-Gadol in connection with

the decline of the study of the Torah and the quality of the scholars after the fall of the Temple. Cf, Rashi on the parallel in TbSanh. 79a. Rashi declares that knowledge of the Torah will decline in the third year as a result of the famine of the students, who will not be able to concentrate because of hunger. Cf. also *Nahalat Ja'aqob* on D.E.Z. a.l. See also J. Klausner, o.c., p. 48, where he states that the decrease in the number of the scholars and the decline of the knowledge of the Torah were especially characteristic of the Hadrianic period (and after 117 C.E.) and the time of Rabbi 'Aqiba and his students. Cf, especially TbShab. 138b (and Mekh de-R. Jishm., Bo, par. 12 and Leq. Tob, Bo, on Ex. 12:26) and compare this with Tos'Ed. I,1ff., which contains the original form of the tradition in TbShab. 138a, which is used in the Tosephta to point up the differences of opinion between the various schools. The notion of forgetting the Torah is of central importance in TbShab. and, as in Tos. l.c., and is based on Am. 8:11ff.: 'Behold, the days come, says the Lord, that I will send a famine in the land, not a famine of bread... but of hearing the words of the Lord... They shall wander from sea to sea... They shall run to and fro to seek the word of the Lord, and shall not find it.'

*(During) the fourth year*... Neither famine nor plenty will dominate in the fourth year. The harvest will be too great to speak of famine but too small to speak of plenty. This is clearly a reference to recovery from the devastating hunger of the third year.

*(During) the fifth year there will be plenty* ... In the fifth year, there will be abundance and the knowledge of the Torah will return to the students. Because there will be sufficient food, students will again be able to study properly. Cf. Rashi on TbShab. 97a, where he attributes the loss of knowledge of the Torah in the third year to the starvation of the students. The remark about the return of the knowledge does not appear in the manuscripts of D.E.Z., but it appears in the parallels. Cf. TbSanh. 97a; Shir ha-Shir.Rab. II,13 and other sources. Cf. the reading of D.E.Z., a.l. by the Gaon of Vilna. The addition about the return of the knowledge of the Torah has taken various forms in the parallels.

In TbSanh. 97a, one finds the words 'the Torah returns to those who study it'. These words also appear in S.E.Z. XI (ed. M. Friedmann, p. 11); in Midr. ha-Gad., Mi-Qetz, on Gen. 41:1 (ed. M. Margulies, p. 683); and in Jalq., Am., r. 549. Pes. de R.K., pisqa 5 (ed. B. Mandelbaum, p. 97) reads: 'we-Torah hozeret le-hiddushah' (and the Torah [study] becomes new again). Shir ha-Shir. Rab. reads: 'we-ha-Torah hozeret le-Jisra'el u-mithaddeshet le-Jisra'el' (and the Torah becomes new again and is renewed for Israel).

The reading in TbSanh. 97a is probably the original one. The readings in Pes. de-R. K. and Shir ha-Shir. Rab. must be considered as much later changes. Cf. J. Klausner, *Die messianische Vorstellungen des jüdischen Volkes*, p. 53. Cf. also W.D. Davies, *Torah in the Messianic Age*, Cambridge 1952, p. 75. Cf., however, I.H. Weiss, *Dor Dor we-Doreshaw*, I, repr. Jerusalem, p. 215, note 4, who asserted that both readings stem from the original stage of development of the text. The readings in Pes. de-R. K. and in Shir ha-Shir. Rab. refer not to a replacement of the Torah, but to the restoration of the knowledge of the Torah. The word 'renewal' means that the Torah will have again its authority, and to previous unknown proportions. The literal translation of the words 'we-ha-Torah hozeret le-hiddushah' is: The Torah will return to its newness. Cf. J. Klausner, o.c., p. 54; A. Aptowitzer, *Parteipolitik der Hasmonäerzeit im rabbinischen und Pseudepigraphischen Schrifttum*, Vienna 1927 and W.d. Davies, o.c., p 76. The reading in Pes. de-R. K. and in Shir ha-Shir. Rab. must therefore be regarded as a variant of the reading 'we-ha-Torah hozeret le-hiddushah'.

*In the sixth year, sounds...* According to Rashi (TbSanh. l.c.) this is a reference to Is. 27:13: 'And in that day the great Shophar will be blown ...' The sounding of the great Shophar refers to an announcement of the messianic Era (cf. IV Ezra 6:22). A comparison with related texts in apocalyptic literature leads one to assume that 'qolot' (voices) here in D.E.Z. actually refers to sounds of natural violence, such as the crashing of the waves of the sea, thunder, the sounds produced by earthquakes etc. Cf., e.g., IV Ezra 5:7 (in ed. A. Kahane [*Ha-Sepharim ha-Hitzonim la-Tora, la-Nebi'im, la-ketubim u-she'ar Sepharim Hitzonim*], repr. Jerusalem 1978, p. 569. See M. Stone, *The Armenian Version of IV Ezra*, Missoula 1979, p. 65.

Other explanations are possible, however. The word 'qolot' (voices) may be explained as rumours about immanent events and about the coming of the messiah. Cf. M. Stone, o.c., p. 65 (l. 6a): '...and tellers of tales shall be mighty.' Cf. *Midr. 'Aggadot ha-Mashiah*, in A. Jellinek, *Beit ha-Midrash*, III, p. 141. Cf. also Mat. 24:6; Mark. 13:7 and Luke 21:9, all of which mention hearing rumours about war.

The messiah is supposed to come at the end of the so-called 'year week'. Cf. various statements in TjBer. II,4, according to which the deliverance of Israel will take place in the seventh year. Cf. also TbMeg. 17b, where it is said that the deliverance in the seventh year is the reason for mentioning deliverance in the seventh blessing of the Eighteen Benedictions.

**2. Rabban Gamli'el said: 'In the generation when the son of David comes the house of assembly will be (used as a place of) unchastity; Galilee will be destroyed and the people of Galilee will go around from city to city and will be shown no compassion and the wisdom of Scribes will become vapid, sin-fearing people will be despised, the face of the generation will be like the face of a dog, truth will be lacking and he who departs from evil will make himself a pray.'**

Unlike D.E.Z., the parallels do not attribute this statement to Rabban Gam-li'el, but to Rabbi Jehudah. Cf. TbSanh. 97a; S.E.Z XVI (ed. M. Friedmann, p. 11); and Midr. ha-Gad., Mi-Qetz, ed. M. Margulies, p. 685. On the basis of a misinterpreted abbreviation Rabbi José is cited in Ms. Florence of TbSanh. l.c., as the spokesman. In Pes. de-R. K. o.c., p. 98 and in Pes. Rab. XV (ed. M. Friedmann, p. 75), Rabbi 'Abin ('Abun) is mentioned as spokesman. According to Shir ha-Shir. Rab. II,13, Resh Laqish is the spokesman. According to J. Klausner, *Die messianische Vorstellungen des jüdischen volkes*, p. 51, however, this last reading is incorrect. In TbSot. 49b (cf. MSot. IX,15), the statement is attributed to no one. In connection with the later additions to the Mishnah, see Ch. Albeck, *Seder Mo'ed*, (Mishnah Sotah), p. 394. According to J. Klausner, the statement should be attributed to Rabbi Jehudah. He claims that the attribution in D. E. Z. of the statement to Rabban Gamli'el is incorrect. There is no urgent reason, however, for excluding the possibility that Rabban Gamli'el the Second of Jabneh was the spokesman.

It is clear from the words used in this statement that it is quite old. The term 'beit ha-wa'ad' (gathering house) refers to a place where a group of scholars studied together. Houses of study will deteriorate into brothels. Galilee will be destroyed in the period directly preceding the coming of the messiah. This notion was most likely directly influenced by the situation in Galilee after the fall of the Temple in the year 70 C. E. This indicates that the statement here dates from shortly after 70 C. E., given that Galilee, unlike Judea, was mainly spared of the destruction caused by the Bar Kokhba uprising. The words 'and Gablan will be destroyed' do not appear in D. E. Z., but they appear in the parallels. The wording does not give the impression of being a later addition. According to W. Bacher, *Die Agada der Tannaiten*, II, p. 222, Gablan refers to Gaulanitis, the region of Basan lying to the east of the sea of Kinneret. Gaulanitis belonged to the land ruled by Herodus Philippus, Agrippa I and Agrippa II. After 106 C. E., Basan came under the rule of the Roman province Arabia. See B. Z. Segal, *Ha-Geographia ba-Mishnah*, pp. 54, 59 and 60. Gablan is the Aramaic form of Golan (Gaulanitis), it refers to a fairly large city after which the district of Gaulanitis was named. Cf. also I. S. Horovitz, *'Eretz Jisra'el u-Shekhunoteiha*, Vienna 1923, p. 194. See also, however, A. Neubauer, *Geographie du talmud*, repr. Hildesheim 1967, p. 66. A. Neubauer identifies Gablan with Gabalena, a region in the the south of Israel.

Galilee and Gaulanitis together formed the region of Israel where the most important Jewish settlements were established after the Bar Kokhba uprising in 135 C. E. See M. Avi Yona, *Geschichte der Juden im Zeitalter des Talmud*, Berlin 1962, p. 16ff. It is therefore plausible that expectations of the birthpangs of the messianic Era apply to those regions, if one agrees that Rabbi Jehudah made this statement here in D. E. Z.

*And the people of Galilee will go from city to city*... Cf. Pes. de- R. K. l.c.; Pes. Rab. l.c.; and Shir ha-Shir. Rab. l.c. TbSanh. reads: '... and the people who live along the borders (or the people of Gebul?) ...' See D. Castelli, *Il Messia secondo Gli Ebrei*, Firenze 1874 , p. 298. D. Castelli suggests that

'Gebul' is the name of a place in Idumea. Cf. also M. Jastrow, *Dictionary*, I, p. 205, sub 'gebul' and idem, p. 207 sub 'Gabla'. M. Jastrow identifies 'Gebul' with Gabalena in Idumea, southwest of Jerusalem. The reading ''anshei ha-gebul' also appears in MSot. IX,15. Rashi on TbSanh. l.c. reads 'people from the border of the land Israel.' W. Bacher o.c., p. 222, considers 'people of Galilee' to be the original reading. J. Klausner, o.c., p. 50, on the other hand, suggests that ''anshei gebul' (people who live along the borders) is the original reading, and that is was later replaced by 'people of Galilee'. In agreement with J. Klausner it must be regarded plausible that 'people of Galilee' is a replacement of the original reading ''anshei ha-gebul'. See the reading in S. E. R. l.c., of 'people of Golan'. According to I. S. Horovitz. o.c., pp. 180 and 194 'gebul' is a name of a place that also stands for 'Gablan' (= Golan), the entire region of the high plateau of Golan.

In light of the entire context, one may assume that the people of the highlands of Golan (Gaulanitis) will go from city to city in search of shelter and food. The background notion is that the Jewish population in Galilee will be reduced to such a small group that the border regions (such as the highlands of Golan) will no longer be inhabited by Jews.

*The wisdom of the scribes shall become vapid . . .* This statement is associated in Pes .Rab. l.c. and Pes. de-R. K. l.c., with a statement by Rabbi Nehorai. Cf. Jer. 49:7.

The wisdom of the Scribes (sopherim) will be spoiled, i.e., the wisdom of teachers will deteriorate greatly. The word 'sopherim' was used especially in the Tannaitic period (of the second century) to refer to teachers who instructed children in Scripture and scribes of Torah scrolls. Cf. W. Bacher, 'E*rkhei Midrash Tanna'im*, Tel-Aviv 1923, sub 'sopherim'; see J. N. Epstein, *Mebo'ot le-Siphrut ha-Tanna'im*, p. 503. The term 'hokhmat sopherim' already appears in *Seph. Ben Sira* 38:24. In the generation before the coming of the messiah, one will no longer be able to receive Torah instruction of good quality, and scribes will no longer write Torah scrolls according to the prescribed rules. The generation will be deprived of instruction in the Torah. In agreement with J. Klausner, o.c., p. 48, the images used here can be associated with the experiences of the Hadrianic persecutions · Cf., e.g., a statement by Rabbi Natan in Mekh. de-R. Jishm., Jitro, par. 6 (ed. M. Friedmann, 68b). Cf. especially in MSot. IX,15 the statement ascribed to Rabbi 'Eli'ezer ha-Gadol with the following content: after the fall of the Temple, the scholars (who gave instruction in the entire oral tradition) became 'sopherim' and the 'sopherim' became schoolgovernors. See also D. E. Z. X,1, concerning the loss of knowledge of the Torah and the sharp decline in the number of scholars.

The words *Truth will be lacking and he who departs (keeps himself away) from evil will make himself a pray (will be bereft)* were borrowed from Is. 59:15 (read: 'mishtolel'). The words 'will be bereft' can be explained figuratively to mean:: will be bereft of reason and will be considered as senseless. Cf. espe-

cially a statement ascribed to Rabbi Jannai in Midr. ha-Gad., Mi-Qetz, ed.
M. Margulies, p. 685: 'What means "who keeps himself away from evil will be
bereft?"... (It means that) anyone who fears Heaven will be considered crazy.'
Cf. also Rashi on TbSanh. 97a. Rashi refers to Hiob 12:18 (cf. Mi. 1:8): 'He
leads counsellors away spoiled ("sholal") and makes the judges fools'. The
word 'sholal' is parallel here to 'fools'. This also appears to have been the
explanation given by the school of R. Shila (see the context in TbSanh. l.c.).
Midr. ha-Gad. l.c. contains another explanation ('mizdolal 'al ha-beriot'): 'will
be despised by his fellowmen'. As in Is. l.c., however, the original meaning was:
'He who keeps himself from evil makes himself prey...' Cf. also Targum on Is.
l.c.

*And the face of the generation will be like the face of a dog...*

Like the face of a dog, the face of the generation will be expressionless and
unable to indicate shame. In some parallels, this statement is recorded separately and ascribed to Rabbi Jannai. Cf. Pes. de-R. K. o.c., p. 98. In Shir ha-
Shir. Rab. l.c., the statement is attributed to Rabbi 'Aba bar Kahana. Shir ha-
Shir. Rab. l.c. contains the addition of an interpretative statement by Rabbi
Levi: 'The son of David will only come in the generation of which the face is
impudent and who deserves extinction.' Cf. Shem. Rab. XLII,9 and TbBeitza
25a.

3. **Rabbi Nehorai said: 'In the generation when the son of David comes the
young will put the old to shame and the old will stand up before the young, a
daughter will rise up against her mother, a daughter-in-law against her
mother-in-law, and a son will not be ashamed in the presence of his father.'**

The wording in TbSanh. 97a indicates that this statement applies to a Tannaitic
tradition. Rabbi Nehorai here is probably Rabbi Nehorai, a Tanna of the fourth
generation. See, however, J. Klausner, o.c., p. 51, who suggests on the basis of
Tb'Er. 13b that Rabbi Me'ir made the statement. The image of enmity between
different generations and between close relatives was typical of the representa-
tions of the 'birthpangs of the messiah', i.e., the suffering that would occur
before the coming of the messiah. In I Hen. 99:5 (regarding the merciless
abandonment of young children who are still suckling); in IV Ezra V. Cf. ed.
M. Stone (*The Armenian Version of IV Ezra*, pp. 65–66): ' And men shall fight
with one another, sons with fathers and fathers with sons, daughters opposed to
one another, brothers with brothers, friends with acquaintances, nations with
nations, peoples with peoples, priests with priests and ministrants with ministrants... and wisdom shall depart from the saints.' In II Bar. 48:32 and in Mark.
13:12 (cf. Mat. 10:21 and Luke 21:16), one finds similar illustrations of children
fighting their parents and parents merciless fighting their children. Cf. especially Mi. 7:6, which contains a statement upon which the statement here in
D. E. Z. is based: 'For the son despises his father, the daughter rises up against

her mother, the daughter-in-law against her mother-in-law; the members of one's household will rise up against him.'

Boys will make the faces of their parents white – i. e., they will shame them. There will be no longer respect for parents. Shir. ha-Shir. Rab. l.c. and S. E. R. l.c. contain a short reading that concurs with the reading here in D. E. Z. Other parallels (TbSanh. l.c.; MSot. l.c.; Pes. Rab. l.c. and Pes. de-R. K. l.c.) contain a number of elements that probably did not belong to rabbi Nehorai's statement. The phrase 'the face of the generation will be the face of a dog' is one such an element. The tradition in D. E. Z. is clearly not dependent here on the Talmud tradition!

**4. Rabbi Nehemjah said: 'So [other reading: the generation when the son of David will come] impudence will increase, high prices will be corrupt, the vine will yield its fruit yet wine will be (sold) for a high price; and the Kingdom will be converted to heresy and there will be no reproof.'**

There are sharply different explanations of this statement by Rabbi Nehemjah, a student of Rabbi 'Aqiba and a survivor of the Bar Kokhba revolt. In MSot. l.c., the first words of the statement are recorded anonymously and in Aramaic, with the introductory word: 'In the footsteps of the messiah ...', i.e., just before the coming of the messiah, the brutality will be great... In S. E. R. l.c., the statement begins: 'Rabbi Nehemjah said: "In the generation when the son of David comes..."' In Shir ha-Shir. Rab. l.c., it begins: 'Rabbi Nehemjah said: "Before the days of the messiah..."' The wording in S. E. R. was probably the original wording of the reading in D. E. Z. and was replaced by 'And so' in D. E. Z. for the sake of convenience. Both Shir ha-Shir. Rab. l.c. and S. E. R. l.c. read: "we-'oniut tirbeh' (the poverty will increase) instead of 'we-'azut tirbeh' (the brutality will increase).

The words 'we-ha-joqer je'awwet' are explained in very different ways: 1) High prices will pervert people, i. e. scarcity and high prices will cause people to lose their honesty; 2) as in D. E. Z. 'we-ha-joqer je'uwwat' can be explained to mean that the expensiveness of things will itself be perverted. While there will be no real scarcity, prices will be driven up by speculators. This explanation connects with the text directly following the statement, in which it is said that the wine will be expensive despite a plentiful grape harvest.

MSot. l.c. reads 'we-ha-joqer ja'amir'. This is also explained in different ways. J. Klausner o.c. (p. 49) derives 'ja'amir' from "'amir' which means 'Wipfel' (cf. Is. 17:6,9). He translates the statement as follows: 'Die Theuerung wird ihren Wipfel erreichen.' It would be more correct, however, to read: 'And the prices will be inflated (fat)', i. e., prices will be deliberately kept high by speculators. Cf. Ch. Albeck, Mishnah, *Seder Mo'ed*, p. 262 and W. Bacher, *Die Agada der Tannaiten*, II, p. 236, note 3. Such an explanation fits superbly with the explanation given in point 2 above and with the immediate context.

Shir ha-Shir. Rab. reads 'we-joqer howeh' (and the prices will remain high). Cf. the use of the expression in TbShab. 32b. This can also be explained to mean that prices will not depend on the availability of products because consumers will be exploited by artificial inflation. Poverty will result not from scarcity but from exploitation. See J. Klausner, l.c. He derives j-'-w-t' from "et" (time) and explains: 'the prices will remain high'. W. Bacher, l.c., suggests that 'ja'wot' ('je'awwet') is a corruption of 'ja'iq', and he translates and explains: 'The prices will oppress the people'.

In entirely different explanations 'joqer' is read as 'the nobility'. Respectable people will become corrupt and become deceitful. Cf. Rashi on TbSanh. 97a. The reading in MSot. l.c.

('we-ha-joqer ja'amir') similarly explains: 'and the nobility will be oppressive'. Cf. M. Jastrow, *Dictionary*, I, l.c. Cf. J. Harburger, *Derech Erez Sutta*, p. 53 and D. Sperber, *Massekhet Derekh 'Eretz Zuta*, p. 68. According to yet another explanation, honour ('joqer' interpreted as 'kabod' = honour) will be perverted, i.e., people will no longer respect each other. Cf., among others, Rashi on TbSanh. 97a.

On the basis of the context of the statement, preference must be given to the explanation according to which prices are artificially kept high and will remain high, despite the abundance of products. The grape harvest will be large, but wine will still remain expensive. Cf., however, the interpretative reading in Shir ha-Shir. Rab. l.c. which says that the grape harvest will indeed be large, but that the wine will spoil. Rashi on TbSanh. l.c. explains differently: 'The grape vine will be blessed but the grape as product will not be blessed' (cf. Shir ha-Shir. Rab. l.c.). Because of the terrible circumstances, the tendency to consume too much alcohol will be great, which will cause a shortage of wine despite a large grape harvest and keep the price of wine high. Some manuscripts of D. E. Z. read: 'And the grapevine will *not* produce much fruit.' This reading, however, represents an later attempt at removing the intended contradiction in the statement.

*And the Kingdom will be converted to heresy* ... 'Malkut' here most likely refers to the Roman Empire. 'Minim' refers to Jewish Gnostic and Jewish antinomistic or Jewish-Christian groups that may have been influenced by gnosticism.

The statement at first sight refers to the conversion of the Romans to Christianity under Constantine the Great in 313 C. E. See, however, R. T. Herford, *Christianity in Talmud and Midrash*, repr. New York 1966, p. 207ff. It is possible that the statement here is an interpolation from the time of Constantine in the scope of the statement by Rabbi Nehemjah. This possibility must not be excluded simply because the statement appears in MSot. IX. 15, considering that it was not part of the original Mishnah context. Herford's argument that such a late tradition could not have appeared in the Mishnah is thus refuted. In connection with the opinion that MSot. IX,15 was not incorporated into the

Mishnah texts until later, see Ch. Albeck, Mishnah, *Seder Nashim*, MSot., notes on p. 394, and see J. N. Epstein, *Mebo'ot le-Siphrut ha-Tanna'im*, p. 406. Cf. also J. N. Epstein, *Mabo le-Nusah ha-Mishnah*, II, Jerusalem 1948, p. 976. The words 'we-ha-malkut tehaphekh le-minut' do not appear in Ms. Leningrad (published by A. I. Katsch in *Ginzei Mishnah*, Jerusalem 1970, p. 77. They also do not appear in the Pisarro or Constantinople Edition of the Mishnah (ed. Jerusalem 1970, p. 200) or in the Ms. Parma (ed. Jerusalem 1970). The wording appears only in Ms. Kaufmann. See R. Kimelman in *Jewish and Cristian Self-definition*, ed. E. P. Sanders e.a., p. 228, note 18. Cf. also TjSot. [24c], which also does not contain the words here in D. E. Z. about the conversion of the Kingdom to Christianity. It is, however, probable, as stated by R. T. Herford, that there is no direct reference in this statement to the conversion of Constantine; rather, the statement gives a general impression of the degeneration of civilization (including Rome) to heresy. According to the statement under discussion the abandonment of of values and the degeneration to heresy take similar form everywhere. Although 'malkut' refers to Rome, it also refers to the heathen world in general. The tradition in TbSanh. 97a (cf. Midr. ha-Gad. l.c.) supports this assumption: 'This supports the words of Rabbi Jitzhaq. Rabbi Jitzhaq said: "The messiah will not come until the entire world has degenerated into heresy."' Cf. also the parallels in S. E. Z. l.c. The subsequent text in TbSanh. 97a must be explained along similar lines: 'Raba said: "What verse proves it? (It is proved by the words:) If it is all turned white he is clean (Lev. 13:13)."' Only when the whole world is contaminated (like a leper who has become totally white from his illness) will it be ready for the coming of the messiah.

The term 'heresy' in this statement does not imply that heathens remain simply heathens who are neutral toward Israel and the Torah. Rather, it refers to their attitude toward Israel, typical of heretics in the second century, i. e., an attitude of hostility and antinomism. It also refers to Jewish antinomism, see among others, R. Kimelman in o.c., pp. 226 and 228 ff. J. Klausner, o.c., p. 51; Cf. M. Goldstein, *Jesus in the Jewish Tradition*, 1950, p. 46 ff.; A. Büchler, *Studies in Jewish History*, Oxford 1956, p. 271 and idem, p. 272; S. Lieberman, in: *A. I. Ph. H. O. S.*, VII (1944), p. 398; M. Simon, *Verus Israel*, Paris 1964, p. 238; H. Hirschberg in *J. B. L.*, LXII (1943), pp. 73–87; K. G. Kuhn in: *Judentum-Urchristentum-Kirche*, ed. W. Eltester, 1960, p. 39 ff.; and G. Alon, *Mehqarim be-Toledot Jisra'el*, ed. S. Safrai, I, Israel 1957, p. 129 e.a.

**5. Rabbi José said: 'Two are better than three, alas for the one thing which goes and does not return.'**
**6. He used to say: 'One does not appoint as leader of the community one who belongs to the bloodletters, tanners or bath-attenders, and one does not appoint any of them as an administrator.'**

7. **He used to say: 'Those who dwell in villages and those who travel in the deserts their life is (actually) no (real) life, and their money is not theirs.'**

5. *Rabbi José said Two are better...* It is clear from the parallels that this statement must be ascribed to Rabbi José ben Qisma. See TbShab. 152a and S. E. Z. XVI. This statement does not belong to the eschatological texts of the first section of this chapter. See, however, *Nahalat Ja‘aqob* on D. E. Z. a.l., which contains an attempt to reconcile this statement with the preceding one.

The statement is in the form of a riddle. *Two are better than three* means that it is better to walk on two healthy legs when one is young than it is to walk with the help of a cane in old age.

*And also for the one thing that goes and does not return...* – this is explained as the youth. Cf. the reading in S. E. Z. XVI (ed. M. Friedmann, p. 12): 'Alas for the youth, which does not return.' Compare this with the explanation of Rab Hisda in TbSanh. l.c.. Cf. the sources mentioned in D. Sperber, *Massekhet Derekh 'Eretz Zuta*, p. 155, which indicate a correspondence between the statement here in D. E. Z. and Greek proverbs. D. Sperber refers to the famous riddle of the Sphinx: 'What has a voice, sometimes two legs, sometimes three, and sometimes four...' Some manuscripts in D. E. Z. read: 'Three are good, but alas to the one thing ...' This is imprecise. Cf., however, J. Harburger, *Massechet Derech Erez Sutta*, p. 53, note 1. J. Harburger considers this reading as an alternative saying, expressing the idea that the walking with the help of a cane in old age is always better than loosing life. As long as one lives, he can always strive toward perfection. Once he is dead, that is no longer possible.

6. *He used to say: 'One does not appoint as leader...* Rabbi José ben Qisma probably made this statement as well as the preceding one. The parallels contain only anonymous statements. TbQid. 82a contains a list of categories of workers who have frequent contact with women in their professions and whose character is thus considered spoiled. Such professionals include goldsmiths (who make jewels for women), carders (who card the wool with a comb for women's garments), bloodletters (law-class surgeons), bathing attendants, tanners etc. The last three categories mentioned here also appear in D. E. Z. In TbQid 82a it is said that of these persons neither a king nor a High Priest may be appointed. While the word 'gara'' can mean 'barber', it specifically means 'bloodletter' in TbQid. l.c. The professions of barber and bloodletter often went together. Cf. however, *Sepher ha-Hinnukh* (509) 'lo sappar' (no barber).

The word 'bannai' literally means a builder, but it does not have this meaning in D. E. Z. See, however, M. Higger, *Massekhtot Derekh 'Eretz*, p. 82. M. Higger translates 'bannai' as: 'builders', as does M. Ginsberg in *The Minor Tractates of the Talmud*, ed. A. Cohen, II, 1965, p. 594. J. Harburger., *Massechet Derech Erez Sutta*, p. 52, gives the peculiar reason for not appointing a builder as an administrator that builders are exposed to too many dangers and that the continuity of their function as leaders of the community is not guaranteed. See, however TbQid. 82a, where 'ballan' (bathing attendant) appears instead of 'bannai'. The word 'bannai' must be regarded as derivative of 'balnai' (bathing attendant). See M. Friedmann, notes to S. E. Z. XVI (p. 9) and MMiqw. IX,6 of which text the commentaries also interpret 'banna'im' as 'ballanim' (bathing attendants). Regarding MMiqw. l.c., cf. Ch. Albeck, ed. of the Mishnah, *Seder Tohorot*, p. 367; cf. Targ. Est. 6:12 'bannai de 'as*h*ei jateh' (a bathing attendant who washed him). Cf. *Derekh Hajjim* (in D. E. Z., ed. J. E. Landa, repr. Tel-Aviv 1971) on D. E. Z. h.l. with the explanation: 'we-ha-bannai hajnu ha-mehammem ha-merhatz' (the bathing attendant, who is the one who heats the bathhouse) and cf. Rashi on TbShab. 114a, sub ''-l-j-j-r-n': 'u-banna'im – lashon bei b-n-i' (... term of bathhouse). Cf. TjTer. VIII (end) 'bei b-n-i' = 'beit balnai', 'beit ha-merhatz'. Cf. TjShab. VIII (end) and cf. Ber. Rab. XXXIII,3 (ed. J. Theodor / Ch. Albeck, p. 307 'bei b-n-i' = 'beit balnai' = 'beit ha-merhatz'; And cf. D. Sperber, o.c., p. 156. Cf. further S. Krauss, *Griechische und Lateinische Lehnwörter im Talmud, Midrasch und Targum*, II (repr. 1964), pp. 158b and 159b. S. Krauss also derives 'bannai' from 'balnai' (bathing attendant). Cf. S. Lieberman, *Tosephta Ki-Pheshutah*, VIII, p. 983, note 73. S. E. Z. probably contains the earliest known reading of the statement under discussion. See the note of M. Friedmann l.c. According to the reading in S. E. Z., persons in the categories mentioned could not be appointed to King, Nasi or High Priest (cf. TbQid 82a: 'neither a king nor a High Priest'). They were not even allowed to be guardians to orphans. Only the term 'parnas' (leader, director) is used here in D. E. Z. 'Parnasim' were community leaders who attended to arranging religious matters, social provisions and education. They were appointed by the Nasi. Cf., Avi Yonah, *Geschichte der Juden im Zeitalter des Talmud*, p. 59. The term 'parnasim' as used here in D. E. Z. represents a later, simplified reading.

7. *He used to say: 'Those who dwell in villages* ... This statement was according to the redactor of D. E. Z. also made by Rabbi José ben Qisma. A closely related statement recorded in Tb'Er. 55b in the name of Rab contains the expression 'joshebei tzeriphin' (dwellers of huts) instead of 'joshebei kepharim' (dwellers of villages). Cf. Rashi on Tb'Er. 55b: 'tzariph': a temporary shelter for wandering shepherds. Preference must be given to the reading in Tb'Er. Cf. also W. Bacher, *Die Agada der Tannaiten*, I, p. 399, note 4. In Tb'Er. one finds a related statement in the name of Rabbi 'Eli'ezer, the citizen of Biria. See R. Rabbinovicz, *Seph. Diqduqei Sopherim* on Tb'Er. l.c.

Biria is a place name. It could be Bira, southwest of Gush Halab, or Kephar Birim, northwest of Gush Halab. Cf. R. Halperin, *'Atlas 'Etz Hajjim*, IV, p. 141. The statement reads: 'Dwellers of huts are like dwellers of graves.' This statement as well as the statement here in D. E. Z. are attributed in S. E. Z. XVI (ed. M. Friedmann p. 12) to Rabbi 'Eli'ezer ben Ja'aqob. M. Friedmann suggests that Rabbi 'Eli'ezer, the man of Biria, is Rabbi 'Eli'ezer ben Ja'aqob. The original reading may have read 'Abba Biria (Bira'a) of the school of Rabbi

'Eliʿezer ben Jaʿaqob or 'Abba Biria in the name of Rabbi 'Eliʿezer ben Jaʿaqob. Cf. TbʿEr. 19a; TbMen. 13b and R. Halperin o.c., p. 116. It is likely that this combination of names has been corrupted in various sources, including in S. E. Z. l.c. and TbʿEr. l.c. In various readings of TbʿEr. l.c. one still finds the reading: "Ula the man of Biria.' Cf. TbMeg. 4a.

In any case, two originally separate statements have been combined in S. E. Z. l.c. It is stated in the parallel in TbʿEr. l.c., that the daughters of people who live in huts are really not the daughters of those people (because they are constantly at risk of being robbed or raped). Cf. the manuscripts in D. E. Z., that add accordingly: '. . . and their children are not of their own.'

**8. Four kinds of 'perutot' (i. e. income) are without a sign of blessing, and they are: the income of scribes, the income of interpreters, and the income that has to come from overseas and (the income of) someone who marries a woman for the sake of a (profitable) marriage-contract. For they will not be able to leave (the money) to their children or their grandchildren.**

This statement is, among other things, dated back to a baraita recorded in TbPes. 50b. In the phrase 'the payment of scribes', 'scribes' are writers of Torah scrolls, 'tephillin' and 'mezuzot'. The copying of sacred texts is a self-understood duty and must not be source of income. Sacred texts should be written out of love for Heaven and not for the sake of monetary gain. According to, among others, Mas. Kal. Rab. X (ed. M. Higger, p. 340) is stated as an explanation that one mistake in copying sacred texts can bare consequences for the world. This probably explains extreme statements such as in A. R. N. [a] XXXVI (54b), according to which scribes will have no share in the World to Come. Cf. S. Lieberman, *Tosephta Ki-Pheshutah*, II, p. 854. Cf. commentary and references to D. E. R. XI,7.

The 'meturgeman', who repeated the words of the sage on Sabbath, during the sage's sermon, in a loud voice to listeners, should also not accept money for anything that amounts to the fulfilment of a commandment (learning and teaching). Besides one should not accept payment for deeds performed on the Sabbath. Although there is no mention of outright transgression, money for such a deed performed on the Sabbath will not be blessed.

Someone who earns money that comes from overseas is at a great risk of losing that money in case of shipwreck or robbery. Cf. also D. E. R. II,6.

*And someone who marries a woman . . .* This statement occurs in D. E. Z., in place of 'payment of orphans' in TbPes. l.c. (this refers to income gained from supervising the finances of an orphan; no one can check whether the supervisor of these finances is taking too much for himself; such income always brings with it the suspicion of dishonesty).

One who marries a woman in order to enjoy the profit of assets she brings with her into the marriage, will not enjoy these profits. A marriage must be concluded for the sake of Heaven, not for monetary gain. Cf. D. E. R., I,29. The words *for they will not be able to leave (the money) to their children or grandchildren* here in D. E. Z. also appears as an addition to the baraita in TbPes. l.c.

**9. There are some who marry a woman for sexual voluptuousness, there are some who marry a woman for money, there are some who marry a woman for a high (social) position and there are some who marry for the sake of Heaven.**

**About those who marry for sexual voluptuousness Scripture declares: 'They have dealt treacherously against the Lord, for they have begotten strange children' (Hos. 5:7) [other readings continue with: About those who marry a woman for money Scripture declares:] 'Now shall the New Moon devour them with their portions' (ibid).] (This means:) a month comes and a month goes and their money is gone. Those who marry a woman for a high position will ultimately be fetched down from their high position. From those who marry for the sake of Heaven will ultimately spring forth children children who will deliver Israel.**

This statement has been composed from a number of traditions. The statement could be made more complete by adding an introduction based on parallels. Cf. S. E. R. III (ed. M. Friedmann, p. 167) and Midr. ha-Gad. on Dt. 21:18 and Jalq., Ki-Tetze, r. 925: 'There are four variants of "derekh 'eretz"' (i. e. concerning the relationship between men and women). TbQid. 70a contains a tradition in the name of Rab, that partially corresponds with D.E.Z. h.l.: 'Whoever marries a woman for the sake of money will have unworthy children, as it is said: "They have dealt treacherously against the Lord, for they have born strange children" (Hos. 5:7). And should you think their money is saved (for them), therefore it is stated: "Now shall the New Moon devour them with their portions" (idem).' The tradition in D.E.Z. is much more differentiated (see the additions in other manuscripts) and the first part of this passage from Hos. 5:7 is applied here in D.E.Z. to those who marry for the sake of sexual indulgence, and not for the sake of money, as remarked in the statement by Rab. This application of Hos. 5:7 here in D.E.Z., in which 'strange children' are explained as 'children of adultery', correspondents more strongly to the original meaning in Hosea! See J. Harburger, *Massekhet Derech Erez Sutta*, p. 52, note 9. J. Harburger adopted the text of D.E.Z. h.l. to the version in TbQid. 70a by reading 'who marries for the sake of money' instead of 'who marries for sexual indulgence'.

The words *A month comes and a month goes* ... in the text directly following the statement here in D.E.Z. is a paraphrased explanation of the second portion of the passage from Hos. 5:7 ('now shall the New Moon devour them

with their portions'), an explanation that is ascribed in TbQid. 70a to Rab
Nahman bar Jitzhaq. In light of the reading in TbQid. 70a, the reading in the
basis manuscript of D.E.Z. must be considered defective. With the aid of Ms.
Oxford Bodleian (cat. A. Neubauer) no. 2339 , one can reconstruct the text as
follows: 'Of him, who marries for sexual indulgence, Scripture declares: "They
have dealt treacherously, for they have born strange children." Of him, who
marries for the sake of money, Scripture declares: "Now shall the New Moon
devour them with their portions." What does this imply? A month comes and a
month goes and their money is lost.' See also commentary and parallels to
D.E.R. I,29.

S.E.Z. II (ed. M. Friedmann, p. 177) and Midr. ha-Gad. on Dt. 21:18
contain a detailed version of this statement in which it is said that one who
marries a woman for financial benefits will be dependent on others for financial
help. It is also said that a man who marries a woman sheerly for sexual reasons
will have a rebellious son. This statement is based on Dt.21:11. Cf. Tanh., Ki-
Tetze, § 1 (ed. S. Buber, 17a) and Jalq., Ki-Tetze, r. 921. See also to the many
Biblical examples cited in those sources. (Abshalom the son of David and
Ma'akha the daughter of Talmi, for example are mentioned as examples of
rebellious children born of lascivious relationships).

Given the wording of the statement, there is clearly a direct connection (as in
the context of TbQid. 70a) between the words 'a woman who is not suited for
him ("ishah she-'einah hogenet lo') and the statements about marrying a
woman for the sake of sex or for the sake of money. One may thus accordingly
refer to pronouncements about the severity of consequences of marrying an
unsuitable wife ('she 'einah hogenet'). Cf. e.g. the statement of Rabbi 'Aqiba in
A.R.N. [a] XXVI (42a) and cf. Siphrei, Ki-Tetze, pisqa 235 (the statement of
Rabbi Jehudah and the subsequent text; cf. TbKet. 25b) and cf. the statement
in TosSot. V,11 ascribed to Rabbi Me'ir. See also S. Lieberman, *Tosephta Ki-
Pheshutah*, VIII, p. 662.

*Those who marry a woman for a high position ...* Anyone who marries a
woman for status and social position will ultimately be humiliated. See also
parallels with other wording according to which such a person will have a
descendant who will decimate his progeny. This wording is based on the
example of King Jehoshaphat, King of Judah, who mated with the house of
Ahab (the king of Northern Israel) by marrying his son Joram to Ataljah, who
murdered almost the entire royal family of Jehoshaphat after the death of her
son Ahazjah. (See II Kings 11:1ff.); see Midr. ha-Gad. on Dt. 21:18; S.E.Z. II
(ed. M. Friedmann, p. 177), and Jalq., Ki-Tetze, r. 925. Cf. in the same sources
the example of Amram who married for the sake of Heaven and who produced
Moses and Aaron; and the example of Boaz, whose descendants included King
David. Cf. further D.E.R. I,29.

10. **The adornment of God is mankind, the adornment of mankind is his clothes, the adornment of the Torah is wisdom and the adornment of wisdom is grey hair; the adornment of youth is fear of sin, the adornment of an ignoramus (an "am ha-'aretz') is poverty.**

Man is considered the adornment of God. In some rabbinical texts 'image and likeness' (cf. Gen. 1:27) are explained as the 'honour' (kabod) of the Creator, represented by the existence of man. Cf., e.g., Deb. Rab. XI,3 and Tanh., Pequdei, § 2. In other texts, man is simply termed as ''iqonia'(image). Cf., e.g., Tanh., Mishpatim, § 19 and Bam. Rab. IV,4. This reflects the notion that the defilement of human dignity implies a defilement of God Himself. Cf., e.g., MSanh. VI,4 and TbSanh. 46b in relation to Dt. 21:22−23. It also makes up part of the well-known concept of 'la'ag boré', i. e. behaviour that is offensive to the Creator and actions in which one shows no regard for human dignity. Taking care of the body and showing respect for the human person have to be considered a homage to God. Cf., e.g., Hillel's statement in Waj. Rab. XXXIV,7 and cf. TbShab. 50b in connection with taking care of the body. Cf. also TbTa'an. 11a, which contains a statement, expressing disapproval of neglect of the body. Paying tribute to the Creator, then, is the reason behind the emphasis placed by the sages on rules for maintaining health, and taking care of one's appearance and clothes. These rules were especially important to scholars, for scholars were especially associated with the presence of God. It is said of Israel that it became the adornment of God, when it accepted the Torah. Cf., e.g., Shem. Rab. LI,8 and TjMa'as.Shen. (end).

The scholar must have a pleasant appearance and wear clothes that are well taken care of, for contempt of them would mean contempt for the Torah and for God. But that which applies especially to the scholar applies ultimately to everyone. In some later sources, the opening of the statement here in D. E. Z. is attributed to Ben Sira. Cf. *Shiblei ha-Leqet ha-Shalem* (ed. S. Buber sim. 58, 23a), which cites the Tanh. (Cf. *Tanja Rabbati*, sim. 10; see Tanh., Tzav, ed. S. Buber § 3, 7b and notes. Cf. Introduction Tanh. ed. S. Buber, 50a and cf. Midr. Jelammedenu in A. Jellinek, *Beit he-Midrash*, VI, p. 85. Cf. S. Schechter in: *J. Q. R.*, III, (1891), p. 307, notes 85−87. The statement does not appear in the known readings of Seph. Ben Sira. Seph. Ben Sira does, however, contain a related statement according to which someone is noticed for his manner, facial expressions and clothing. See Seph. Ben Sira 19:25[26] (see ed. M. Z. Segal, p. 39 note 9). Cf. also D. E. Z. V,4 concerning the clothing of scholars.

*The adornment of an "am ha-'aretz' ...* Poverty adorns the "am ha-'aretz', who occupies himself more with worldly things than with the study of the Torah. In connection with the interpretation of the word 'me'era' as poverty, see M. Jastrow, *Dictionary*, II., p. 724. The "am ha-'aretz' only misuses his wealth. Wealth and succes only keep him even more from studying the Torah.

Only poverty can bring a person to study the Torah. Cf. the commentary of
J. Harburger, *Massekhet Derech 'Erez*, p. 55, note 10.

Less plausible interpretations include: 'The adornment of the "'am ha-
'aretz" is destruction' and 'The adornment of the "'am ha-'aretz" is curse'. Cf.,
however, especially the commentary in *Derekh Hajjim* on D. E. Z. in *Massekhet
Derekh 'Eretz Zuta*, ed. J. E. Landa (repr. Tel-Aviv 1971): a curse upon the
income of the "'am ha-'aretz"', gained from robbery and exploitation is a just
reward for him. Thus he learns that this method of earning an income is
improper. There is no essential difference between this interpretation and the
one given above ('me'erah = poverty). An interpretation according to which it
is sanctioned to curse or destroy an "'am ha-'aretz' himself is not plausible in this
context of good will towards others and other characteristics of 'derekh 'eretz'.

**11. He who has learned Scripture but not 'mishnah', behold that one is
empty headed. He who has learned 'mishnah' but did not study Scripture is
an ignoramus. He who has studied Scripture and 'mishnah' but did not
explain is wise. He who has studied Scripture and 'mishnah' and (also) has
explained is a man of insight (i. e. of deeper understanding). For the one
who has studied neither Scripture nor 'mishnah' it would have been better
to have never been born.**

This statement is related to a tradition in TbSot. 22a. One who has studied
Scripture but not oral tradition is considered empty-headed. Such a person
clearly is at most interested in theoretical knowledge of Scripture, not in putting
the Torah into practice. One who does have knowledge of oral tradition (i. e.,
of halakhot) but not of Scripture is an "'am ha-'aretz'. In other words, someone
who does want to put the Torah into practice and acquires some knowledge of
oral tradition but who at the same time does not study Scripture and who has no
interest in the intricate relationship between oral tradition and Scripture is and
remains an "'am ha-'aretz'. According to a statement by Rabbi 'El'azar in
TbSot. 22a, however, an 'am ha-'aretz' has knowledge of both oral tradition
and Scripture but lacks the daily contact with scholars made by serving them.
The knowledge of an "'am ha-'aretz' is unrefined and incomplete, and therefore
(according to the statement of Hillel in M'Abot II,5), he will never attain the
religious refinement necessary for one to become a 'hasid' (whose behaviour
toward others and whose relationship to God cannot be criticized). Cf. commentary and parallels to D. E. Z. III,15.

Someone who does study Scripture and oral tradition in the form of halakhic
rules but who offers no explanation of the relationship between the two is called
a sage here in D. E. Z. Someone who not only studies Scripture and halakhic
rules, but also midrash-halakhah and midrash-aggadah is called a man of
insight. By implication, then, 'peirush' (knowledge of midrash-halakhah and of
midrash-aggada) is valued more highly in this statement then 'mishnah' alone,

i. e. the activity of learning halakhic rules, and the learning of halakhic rules is valued more highly than 'Miqra' (the study of Scripture only). Cf. D. E. Z. IV,2 and the commentary and parallels mentioned there. See, finally, TbSot. l.c., where Jer. 31:27 is quoted in connection with someone who studies neither Scripture nor oral tradition: 'I will sow the house of Israel... with the seed of man and with the seed of beast.'

The statement in D. E. Z. clearly deals with the milieu of scholars. There are also other traditions in which persons who lack knowledge of Scripture and oral tradition are judged much more mildly. Cf., e.g., S. E. R. II (ed. M. Friedmann, p. 13): 'Even if he only has knowledge of "derekh 'eretz" (good habits) and of Scripture, his reward is before Me, as long as he refrains from transgression. Even if he has no knowledge of Scripture or of 'mishnah' but does arise early to go to the synagogue and to the house of study and returns late from the house of study... then his reward is before Me.' Cf. also S. E. Z., ed. M. Friedmann, pp. 69 and 82, which contain somewhat positive statements about the ''am ha-'aretz'. The reverse applied to someone who was guilty of committing transgressions and doing unseemly things, even if he had knowledge of Scripture and 'mishnah'. Cf. S. E. R., ed. M. Friedmann, p. 69.

## 12. Wisdom without fear (of transgression) is despicable. One who possesses neither wisdom nor fear is a fully wicked person.

The thoughts implied in the previous statement are further developed here. The explanation of Scripture of the oral tradition and the discussions pertaining to it are definitely more important than 'mishnah' (the collecting and studying of halakhic rules) and 'Miqra' (study of Scripture) alone, considering that the learning process is geared toward seeking applications of the Torah to daily life. This cannot happen without 'peirush' and 'talmud', which is used as the basis for making halakhic rules and decisions. In this statement, 'wisdom' ('hokhmah') means knowledge of the tradition in general, and 'fear of transgression' refers to the intention of putting what one has learned into practice and avoiding transgression. It is declared in various statements that knowledge that is not put into practice will not be perpetuated. Cf. e.g., M'Abot 11,9; M'Abot III,17; Shem. Rab. XXX,1; Midr. Zuta, Cant., ed. S. Buber, p. 2: Ag. Ber. XXXIII on Qoh. 12:13 (ed. S. Buber, pp. 65–66; and A. R. N. [a] XXII (37b/38a).

Studying without the intention of applying the knowledge acquired is strongly condemned. In TjBer. I,5 , it is even said that it would have been better had one, who studies without intending to put his knowledge into practice, not been born. According to a statement ascribed to Rabbi Johanan: 'It would have been better had he got the placenta in his face and not come into the world.' The rabbis were acutely aware of the dangers of theoretical and speculative study not put to practical use.

Someone who has both the wisdom and the fear of transgression is termed
here in D. E. Z. 'fully righteous'. The concept of 'fear of transgression' not only
refers to avoiding infractions of the halakhic rules, it also refers to the development of the sensitivity to what is good and what is evil. Such sensitivity puts one
at a higher moral and religious level than does just strictly observing the
halakhah. Cf. A. Büchler, *Types of Jewish Palestinian Piety*, p. 28: 'It would be
a mistake to think a sin-fearing man to be one of a negative virtue, one who
merely avoids sin.' Cf. also idem, p. 29: "The sin-fearing quality would then
refer to the deliberate avoidance of an action that constituted an offence only
for the very sensitive donor, but was for the average and observant Jew not
approaching sin.'

A. R. N. [a] XXIX contains a statement by Rabbi Jitzhaq bar Pinhas: 'Someone who has knowledge of midrash but no knowledge of halakhic rules has not
tasted wisdom. Someone who has knowledge of halakhic rules but not of
midrash has not tasted fear of transgression.' By implication, then, wisdom is
associated with knowledge of halakhic rules and fear of transgression is associated with knowledge of midrash! By learning midrash ('peirush') one elevates
not only his deeds but his middot, i. e., his characteristics and intentions. Just by
studying midrash and halakhah, one acquires the greater sensitivity implied in
the term 'fear of transgression', and only when he has acquired that sensitivity is
he considered 'fully righteous'!! With regard to the interpretation of 'hokhmah'
as knowledge of halakhah, cf., e.g., TbNid. 69b and the commentary of
Maharasha contained there. Cf. also A. J. Heschel, *Torah min ha-Shamajim*, I,
1962, p. II.

# Pereq Ha-shalom

## *Derekh 'Eretz Zuta, chapter XI*

1. **Rabbi Jehoshua [ben Levi] said: 'Great is peace, for peace in the land (the world) is like leaven to the dough. Had not the Holy One blessed be He created and given peace to the land, the sword and the wild beasts would have devastated the land. What is the argument? (Because there is written:) "And I will give peace to the land ( ... and I will cause evil beasts to cease out of the land, neither shall the sword go through your land") (Lev. 26:6). And 'land' means nothing else than Israel, for it is said: 'And (all the nations) shall call you happy, for you shall be a delightsome land' (Mal. 3:12), and it says: "Behold the whole land (earth) sits at rest and is silent" (Za. 1:11). That is Israel. It is written: "A generation goes and (another) generation comes, and the earth (read: the land) abides for ever" (Qoh. I:4). One kingdom comes and (another) kingdom goes, but Israel abides for ever.'**

**Solomon said: Although one generation goes and another generation comes, one kingdom goes and another kingdom comes one decree goes and another decree comes upon the enemies of Israel (it is to say: on Israel) 'And the earth (read: the land) abides for ever', Israel abides for ever. They are not destroyed and they will not be destroyed, for it is said: 'For I the Lord of Hosts have not changed, and so, you sons of Jacob are not destroyed' (Mal.3:6). Just as I have not changed [and as I will not change in the future] so you sons of Jacob are not destroyed and will not be destroyed in the future. But (as Scripture says it:) 'You that cleave unto the Lord your God are alive, everyone of you this day' (Dt. 4:4).**

Peace in the land is like leaven in the dough. Cf. the figurative use of the expression 'leaven in the dough' in, e.g., TbKet. 10b; TbNid. 8b and TbNid. 64b.

The reading 'Rabbi Jehoshua ben Levi' is supported by the manuscripts. Cf. also the parallels in Jalq. Re'ub. on Lev. 26:6, p. 84. If God had not brought peace to the land (to earth), then the sword and wild animals would have ruined the land. Lev.26:6 is cited as reference: 'And I will give peace in the land ... and I will rid evil beasts out of the land, neither shall the sword go through your land.' The word ''aretz' in this passage applies to Israel, on the basis of analogous reasoning and comparison with Mal. 3:12, where "aretz' applies specifically to Israel. Similar reasoning is attributed to Rabbi Jitzhaq in Qoh. Rab. I,4. Cf. also Midr. Teh. 36,8 and Midr. le-Hanukkah in A. Jellinek, *Beit ha-Midrash*, I, p. 134. According to W. Bacher (*Aggadot ha-'Amora'im*, II, p. 206, note 2) that statement should be ascribed to Rabbi Jitzhaq Nappaha. He also notes that Rabbi Jitzhaq Nappaha made a statement in Qoh. Rab. I,4 that correspondents to the conclusion of the statement contained in D. E. Z. h.l.: 'A generation comes and a generation goes ...' Cf. Midr. Teh.. l.c. and Midr. le-Hanukkah l.c.

In Midr. ha-Gad. on Lev. 26:2 (ed. A. Steinsalz, p. 732) it is concluded on the basis of Lev. 26:4 that nothing is greater than peace. The same is concluded on the basis of Is. 45:7 (as it appears in the prayer-formulation ('He who makes peace and creates all things') in 'Jotzer 'Or' (The berakhah preceding the morning-'Shema'; Cf. the parallel in Bam. Rab. XI,7, where this 'Scripture passage' is introduced with 'we say ... '). The subsequent statement in Midr. ha-Gad. l.c. is related to the opening of the statement here in D. E. Z. ('Great is peace for it is like leaven in the dough. For if there were no peace, the wild beasts would ruin (the land) and the roads would run in all directions and the commerce would decline. But since peace has been given in the world, such disasters have ended.')

The described opening of the traditions in Midr. ha-Gad. is based on an explanation of Is. 45:7 ascribed to Rabbi Hananjah, the overseer of the priests. See Siphrei, Naso, pisqa 42 (ed. H. S. Horovitz, p. 47). Cf. Midr. Leq. Tob on Num. 6:26. This opening appears anonymously in a large number of other parallels, Cf. especially Siphra, Be-Huqqotai, pereq I (end): '... Scripture says: "And I will give peace in the land..." (Lev.26:6). This shows that peace weights against all things. Thus is also said: "He who makes peace and creates evil" (Is. 45:,7). This also shows that peace weights against all things.' Cf. Midr. ha-Gad. l.c. According to M. Higger *Massekhtot Ze'irot*, pp. 19−20, the Siphra text is the source of the statement here in D. E. Z. It must be assumed, that the two statements made by Rabbi Jitzhaq Nappaha mentioned above were added to that text. D. E. Z. h.l. (1b) contains a far more extensive reading of the explanation of Rabbi Jitzhaq Nappaha than the source Qoh. Rab. I,4. The term 'haters of Israel' must be considered as an euphemism. It refers actually to Israel itself as a whole, but given the negative content of the statement, the euphemistic term was used. Cf., e.g., the use of the expression in *Mishnat Rabbi 'Eli'ezer*, ed. H. G. Enelow, p. 310.

A tradition closely related to the explanation of Is. 45:7 is contained in A. R. N. [b] XXIV (25a), where it is stated that peace was the first thing to be created and that it was essential for all things that followed in creation. The wording in 'Jotzer 'Or' ('Who creates light ... makes peace and creates all things...') is interpreted in A. R. N. l.c., as an indication of the sequence of the creation of things. Peace was created first and then all things. The statement in

A. R. N. l.c. dates back to the time of Rabban Gamli'el II. See also *Midr. Gadol u-Gedolah* in A. Jellinek, *Beit ha-Midrash*, III, p. 127. See also *Mishnat Rabbi 'Eli'ezer*, ed. H. G. Enelow, p. 68.

2a. **There (i. e. in Mishnah 'Abot) we learn: Rabban [Shim'on ben] Gamli'el said: 'On three things the world is based: on justice, truth and on peace.'**
2b. **Rabbi [Muna] said: 'And the three are one thing, (because) when justice is done truth and peace have been realised. And the three are mentioned in one verse: 'Pronounce a judgement of truth, justice and peace in your gates' (Za. 8:16). Wherever there is (pronounced a judgement of) justice, there is peace; and wherever there is (realised) peace there is justice.'**

The basis manuscript incorrectly reads 'Rabban Gamli'el instead of 'Rabban Shim'on ben Gamli'el II'. Cf. M'Abot I,18. This statement from M'Abot is a variant of the statement of Shim'on the Righteous in M'Abot I,2. The statement was probably inspired by the image of the three-legged table, which was in common use at the time when the statement was first made. Three-legged tables were used because the floors of that time were rarely even and it was difficult to construct a table with four straight legs with the tools available at that time. Cf. S. Safrai in *The Jewish People in the First Century*, ed. S. Safrai e.a., chap. XIV, p. 738; and cf. S. Krauss, *Talmudische Archäologie*, I, pp. 59 and 378, note 16, where the so-called 'Mensa Tripes' is described. Cf. the parallel in Deb. Rab. V,1: 'Rabbi Shim'on ben Gamli'el said: "Do not despise the administration of justice, for that is one of the three legs of the world..."'.

While the term 'teninan' sometimes refers to a baraita, it refers here in D. E. Z. to a place in the Mishnah. See W. Bacher, *Die exegetische Terminologie*, II, p. 238.
'Taman' refers to common assumed parts of the tradition. See W. Bacher, o.c., p. 237. Cf. also the tradition in TjTa'an. IV,2 [68a] and TjMeg. III,6 and Pes. de-R. K. (ed. B. Mandelbaum, I, p. 309). Cf. M. Ginsberg in *The Minor Tractates of the Talmud*, ed. A. Cohen, II, p. 597, note 11. M. Ginsberg suggests that 'taman' refers to Babylonia. This suggestion, however, is implausible.

This statement in D. E. Z. preserves a very early form of the tradition of Rabbi Shim'on ben Gamli'el. According to W. Bacher the deduction in M'Abot (in editions) based on Za. 8:16 did not belong to the statement of Rabbi Shim'on ben Gamli'el. See W. Bacher, *Die Agada der Tannaiten*, II, p. 328. Za. 8:16 was added to the statement of Rabbi Shim'on ben Gamli'el on the basis of a statement of Rabbi Muna. So some manuscripts of D. E. Z. h.l. with the reading: ' And Rabbi Muna says...' Cf. Z. Frankel in: *M. G. W. J.*, X (1861),

p. 413 and see notes to Ch. Taylor, *Sayings of the Jewish Fathers*, p. 5 of the text. Cf. TjTa'an. IV,2 [68a], in which the following statement was added after the famous statement by Shim'on the Righteous of M'Abot: 'And (one finds) these three in one verse . . .' Cf. Jalq.,Is., r. 475.

In TjTa'an. l.c. (cf. TjMeg. l.c.) the following words were added to the words of Rabban Shim'on ben Gamli'el: 'The three are one thing, if justice has been realised, truth has been realised, and peace has been realised.' The same words are attributed here in D. E. Z. to Rabbi Muna (cf. the reading in Pes. de-R. K. l.c., where all statements concerned are attributed to Rabbi Shim'on ben Gamli'el). The reading in D. E. Z. dates back to a very early time, according to our opinion. The words from 'Where ever there is justice there is peace . . .' are probably a later addition to the words of R. Muna.

The central concept in the statement is 'din', justice. This is confirmed by the context in the parallel in Deb. Rab. V,1, where Rabbi Shim'on ben Gamli'el opens with the words: 'Do not despise justice, for it is one of the three legs of the world.'Cf. also Jalq., Shophetim, r.907 and Tanh., Shophetim, § 15 and the commentary attributed there to Rabbi Jehoshua ben Levi on the statement of Rabbi Shim'on ben Gamli'el. ('. . . and all depends on justice . . .'). Human society cannot exist without an organized system of justice. Justice is one of the Noachitic commands. Cf. TbSanh. 56a and parallels. 'Truth' and 'peace' can be considered as further definitions of the concept of 'justice'. A society cannot survive if it complies only with formally organized justice. Justice must be based on truth, equal consideration of all factors and on the will for peace, i. e., the will to restore damaged relationships and to bring the parties involved to reconcile. Justice must involve more than the application of existing rules. The concept ('din 'emet' (justice of truth) was common. Cf., e.g., a statement by Rabbi Jonatan in TbSanh. 7a; TbSanh. 10a and TbMeg. 15b; cf. also Tanh., Shophetim, § 8, and idem ed. S. Buber, § 7.

In some traditions, emphasis is placed on the combination of law and peace. Cf. ,e.g., TbSanh. 6b in a statement of Rabbi Jehoshua ben Qorha, where Za. 8:16 is of central importance. Cf. Siphrei Deb., pisqa 17; TosSanh. I,3. The explanations in such parallels are in agreement with the saying of Rabbi Muna in D. E. Z. If justice is truly pronounced, then the demands for truth and peace are already met. There can be no contradiction among the three. Cf. The commentary of *Nahalat Ja'aqob* on D. E. Z., h.l. Cf. the statement of Rabbi Simai in Mekh. de-R. Shim. bar Johai on Ex.18:23 (ed. J. N. Epstein / E. Z. Melamed) pp. 133–134 and cf. parallels, according to which one who bends the laws for the sake of peace does nothing to promote peace.


3. **Rabbi Jehoshua [ben Levi] said: 'Great is peace, for when Israel stood at the mount Sinai and said: "All that the Lord has spoken we will do and obey" (Ex. 24:7) [The Holy One, blessed be He, rejoiced in them and] He**

**gave them His Torah and blessed them with peace [for it is said: "The Lord will give strength unto his people. The Lord will bless His people with peace" (Ps. 29:11)].**
**And it is said: "The Torah of the Lord is perfect."(Ps. 19:8)'**

This statement is ascribed to Rabbi Jehoshua ben Levi in certain manuscripts and in Jalq. Re'ub. on Ex. 24:7 (65a). Cf. also the opening of this chapter in D. E. Z. Peace is great because Israel was blessed with peace after receiving the Torah. It is here that Israel was blessed with peace after it stated its intention to put the Torah into practice in Ex. 24:7. The relationship between the content of the statement and Ps. 19:8, which is cited in the basis manuscript, is not clear. The relationship between the content of the statement and Ps. 29:11 found in other manuscripts is far more logical. Cf. also the parallel in Jalq. Re'ub., l.c.

The reading with Ps. 29:11 thus deserves preference. The word "oz', power, in Ps. 29:11 is interpreted as a reference to the Torah. The statement here in D. E. Z. is especially related to traditions in which Ex. 24:7 and the words spoken by Israel are cited as the reason why the Torah was given to Israel and not to the other peoples. Cf. Mekh. de-R. Jishm., Jitro, par. 5 (ed. M. Fried-mann, 66b); Siphrei, We-Zot, pisqa 343; Midr. Tan. (ed. D. Hoffmann, p. 210: Midr. Leq. Tob on Dt. 33:2; Jalq. ha-Makh. on Hab., p. 39; Midr. 'Eikh. Rab. on Lam. 3:1; Midr. Shem. Rab., XXX,9; Bam. Rab. XIV,22. Cf. M. Kasher, *Torah Shelemah*, on Ex. 24:7. Cf. especially those traditions in which peace is called great and in which it is stated that peace is given to those who learn Torah. Cf. Siphrei, Naso, pisqa 42 (ed. H. S. Horovitz p. 47); cf. Waj. Rab. IX,9; Bam. Rab. XI,7; TbBer. 64a (Rabbi Hanina); and TbTam. 32b (end; Rabbi 'El'azar ben 'Azarjah: 'The disciples of the wise increase peace in the world . . .'). Cf. also Rabbi's statement on Ps. 29:11 in Siphrei, Naso, pisqa 42; Bam. Rab. XI,7; Midr. Leq. Tob on Num. 6:26: The word 'peace' in the blessing of the priest in Num. 6:26 refers to the peace of the Torah. Peace and Torah are more or less equated here on the basis of Ps.29:11.

Cf, also Tanh. Tzav, § 3 (ed. S. Buber § 5, 8b) in which peace and the content of the Torah are clearly identified with each other. Cf, also Bam. Rab. XI,7; Bam. Rab. XXI, (beginning); Jalq., Naso, r. 711; Jalq. ha-Makh. on Ps. 29, § 37 (end); Pes. de-R. K. (10b) and Tanh., Jitro, § 9. See also the statement of Hizkia in D. E. Z. chap.XI,5, where the peace of Israel is cited (on the basis of Prov. 3:17) as a condition necessary for the revelation of the Torah.

A later parallel in P. R. E. XLI assumes an explicit connection between the content of the statement of Rabbi Jehoshua ben Levi and the subsequent statement by Hizkia (see D. E. Z. XI,5). The parallel cites Ex. 24:7 as an indication of Israel's unity, which unity (peace) made Israel eligible to receive the Torah. Cf, also the wording in Shir ha-Shir. Rab. III,7. Cf. especially the later tradition in *Mishnat Rabbi 'Eli'ezer* (ed. H. G. Enelow, p. 67), where peace is termed the reward for devotion to the Torah and where it is stated that peace is a necessary condition for receiving the Torah.

**4. Hizkiah said: 'Great is peace for in connection to all the commandments of the Torah it is written: 'If you see (the ass of your enemy...)' (Ex. 23:5), 'If you meet (your enemy's ox...)' (Ex. 23:4), 'If (a bird's nest would chance to be before you...)' (Dt. 22:6), 'If you built (a new house...)' (Dt. 22:8), if you chance upon (the occasion to fulfil) a commandment you are bound to perform it, but in connection with peace it is written: 'Seek peace and pursue it' (ps. 34:15). (That means:) seek it in your place and follow it (when it flies from you) to another place.'**

Hizkiah here was the son of Rabbi Hijja and an Amora of the first generation. He was also the mentor of Rabbi Johanan and a contemporary of Bar Kappara. A direct parallel to this statement appears in Waj. Rab. IX,9 along with the following statement (in D.E.Z. XI,5) by Hizkiah, introduced with the words 'Hizkiah said two things' and followed by 'Hizkiah said yet something else.' Dt. 22:8 mentioned here in D.E.Z., is not mentioned in the reading in Waj. Rab. l.c. Cf. *Midr. Seph. We-Hizhir* (ed. A. Scheiber, 34b); Bam. Rab. XIX,27; Tanh., Huqqat, § 22; Jalq., Naso, r. 711; idem. Ps., r. 711; Jalq. ha-Makh. on Ps. 29, § 42; Midr. ha-Gad., Tzav (ed. N.E. Rabinowitz, p. 141), and *Mishnat Rabbi 'Elie'zer* (ed. H.G. Enelow, p. 71).

The fulfilment of a precept of the Torah depends in general on a situation favourable to the fulfilment of such a precept. When it is not possible to fulfil the precept, it is not required to do so. One important exception to this rule, however, is the command to strive for peace. One must strive for peace even in unfavourable situations. One must bring peace to all places where there is no peace, not only when others ask for peace. One is required to take the first steps in realizing peace. One must pursue peace even if it does not meet him and even, as it were, flees from him. M'Abot I,12 contains a well-known statement by Hillel that is closely related to the statement here in D.E.Z.: 'Be of the disciples of Aaron... love peace and pursue it ...' Note the explicit connection made in A.R.N.[b], XXIV (25a) between the statement ascribed here in D.E.Z. to Hizkiah and the statement of Hillel. A statement closely connected to the last part of the statement of Hizkiah here in D.E.Z. is found in A.R.N.[a], XII (26a) and ascribed to Rabbi Shim'on ben 'El'azar. Cf. the formal correspondence with an anonymous tradition in TjPe'ah I,1: 'Avoid evil, do good, seek peace and pursue it' (Ps. 34:15).

Seek peace (when she is) on your place and follow her to another place. The origin of the statement must be sought in an explanation of Ps. 34:15 as given in, for example, TjPe'ah, l.c. and A.R.N.[a] l.c., according to which one must leave his place and pursue peace from one place to the other. See *Mas. Kal. Rab.* ed. M. Higger, introduction, p. 74.

5. **Hizkiah said: 'Great is peace, for in connection with all journeys of Israel it is written: "And they journeyed and they encamped" (Num. 33:5; the plural number, implying the following) they were journeying in dissension and encamping in dissension. When they, however, came to mount Sinai, they (all) encamped (forming) one camp (i. e. as one man, based on the singular form, for it is written:) "And there Israel encamped (singular form)" (Ex. 19:2). The Holy One blessed be He said: "Since they (Israel) hated dissension and loved peace and became one encampment, behold this is the moment to give them My Torah."'**

The harmony of Israel qualified it to receive the Torah. The source of this statement is recorded in traditions such as those found in Mekh. de-R. Jishm., Jitro (Ba-Hodesh), par. I (ed. H. S. Horovitz, p. 206 and ed. M. Friedmann, p. 62). Cf. also Targ. Pseudo Jon. on Ex. 19:2, where reference is made to Israel's harmony at the foot of Mt. Sinai. These traditions discuss the singular form used in Ex. 19:2: 'wa-jihan (sham)' in place of 'wa-jahanu' as found in other places in the Torah. The singular form is explained as a reference to Israel as one person, which was not divided by dissension when it stood at the foot of Mt. Sinai. This explanation is cited in the statement by Hizkiah as an indication that the lack of dissension was considered sufficient reason to hand the Torah to Israel. This exegesis implicitly answers the question as to why the Torah was not given to Israel immediately after the Exodus out of Egypt. Only when Israel had achieved complete harmony could the Torah be revealed to it. Cf. the expression 'hamonia 'ahat' in 'Eikh. Rab. Petihta, § 20; cf. the expression ''aggudah 'ahat' in other parallels. P. R. E. contains a combined statement that is related to Hizkiah's statement and recorded in the name of Rabbi 'Eli'ezer. Waj. Rab. XIX, 4 (ed. M. Margulies, p. 424) contains in the name of Rabbi Kohen a statement very closely related to that of Hizkiah according to which the Shekhinah was able to descend from Mt. Sinai when the dissension, that until then had command over the people, had been brought to an end. Cf. Midr. Qoh. Rab. X,18; Pes. de-R. K. (ed. S. Buber, 106a) and Tanh., Jitro, § 10.

6. **Adonia was slain for no other reason than that he was a creator of dissension and not because of Abishag ... [other reading: and it is permitted to slander about a person who creates dissension]. For so spoke Natan to Batsheba: 'I shall also come in after you and complete your words' (I. Kings 1:14).**

Two traditions recorded in TjPe'ah I,1 provide the background to this statement. In that source, I. Kings. 1:14 is cited in a statement made by Rabbi Samuel bar Nahman in the name of Rabbi Jonatan as proof that one may speak ill of quarrelsome persons and persons who sow unrest. According to this statement, the prophet Natan declared himself ready to affirm the words

spoken by Batsheba to the unsuspecting King David (I Kings 1:11) about the
bad intentions of Adonia (who wanted to gain power). It is clear from this
explanation that the the manuscripts that read not 'and not because of Abishag'
but 'and it is permitted to speak ill about a quarrelsome person' must be
preferred to the basis manuscript of D.E.Z. The statement quoted from I
Kings 1:14 becomes clear only in light of the last reading.

The opening of the statement here in D.E.Z., according to which the death
of Adonia occurred because he caused dissension, concurs with a statement
made by Rabbi José in a conversation with Rabbi Zeira, recorded in TjPe'ah,
l.c. The background of this tradition is contained in the story of I Kings 2:13ff.
There it is recorded that Adonia wanted to marry the concubine of his father,
King David. Solomon (who had already been declared as the successor to the
throne) construed this as an illegitimate claim by his brother to the throne, and
therefore had him killed. The intended marriage of Adonia and Abishag was
nothing more than an alibi for Solomon to kill his brother, who had already
caused much dissension in his efforts to invalidate Solomon's claim to the
throne. The midrash emphasizes that the dissension caused by Adonia was the
true reason for his death. The context of the parallels also mention examples of
kings who died because they caused dissension, such as Joram in whose place
Jehu was anointed, and Ataljah, in whose place Joash was anointed. Cf.
TosSanh. IV,11; TjSheq. VI, 1 [49c]; TjSot. VIII (22c); TbHor. 11b andTbKer.
5b.

7. **Rabbi said: 'All falsehoods are forbidden, but it is permitted to utter a
falsehood to maintain peace, as we find it in connection with Sarah who
said: [other reading: Bar Kappara said: 'Great is peace for so we find the
Torah speaking falsehood to maintain peace between Abraham and Sarah,
for it is said:] "And Sarah laughed within herself (saying:) My Lord being
old . . ." And the angel alternated (the words of Sarah) saying for the sake of
peace (her words in this form:) "(Shall I of a surety bear a child) I who am
old?" (Gen. 18:13).'**

This statement is found recorded in the sources not in the name of Rabbi. A
related tradition, recorded in the name of, among others, Bar Kappara (a
student of Rabbi) is found only for the section of the statement from 'So we find
in connection with Sarah' onward. See other manuscripts here in D.E.Z. that
read: 'Bar Kappara said: "Great is peace, for we find untrue words in the Torah
spoken in order to keep peace between Abraham and Sarah..."' Cf. e.g., Ber.
Rab. LXVIII,18; Waj. Rab. IX,9; Midr. Leq. Tob on Gen. 18:12−13; Jalq.,
Wa-Jera, r. 82; and Midr. ha-Gad., Tzav (ed. N.E. Rabinowitz, p. 141)

There exists also another tradition nearly identical to that of Bar Kappara,
recorded in the name of Rabbi Jishma'el or a representative of his school. Cf.
TbJeb. 65b; TbB.M. 87a; Siphrei, Naso, pisqa 42 (ed. H.S. Horovitz, p. 46);

Bam. Rab. XI,7; Pes. Rab. (ed. M. Friedmann, 197b); cf. Midr. Leq. Tob on
Num. 6:26: Jalq., Naso, r. 711 .

In TjPe'ah I,1 [16a] Rabbi Hanina is cited as the spokesman of a statement
that is nearly identical to the above-mentioned statement made by Bar kappara. Some traditions show a closely related tradition in the name of Rabbi
Shim'on ben Gamli'el: 'Know how much ink has been spilled and how many
writing-pens have been broken... to write something that is not (true) in the
Torah for the sake of peace. See how great is the power of peace, and so you
find in connection with Sarah...' See Tanh., Tzav (ed. S. Buber, § 10 (9b);
Tanh., Shophetim. § 18 and Midr. Jelammedenu (in L. Grünhut, *Sepher ha-
Liqqutim*, 55b). With regard to Rabbi Shim'on ben Gamli'el, cf. also Waj. Rab.
IX,9 (ed. M. Margulies, pp. 189–190) and parallels mentioned there.

The difference between the words of Sarah in Gen. 18:12 and the version of
these words spoken by the Angel in the presence of Abraham (Gen. 18:13) is
explained as an attempt by the Angel to distort Sarah's insulting words in a
positive manner in order to keep peace between Abraham and Sarah.

**8.  And so [other reading: Bar Kappara said: Great is peace, for so] we find
that the prophets uttered falsehoods to maintain peace between Manoah
and his wife, because Scripture says '(Behold now) you are barren (and
have not borne, but you shall conceive and bear a son)' (Judg. 13:3); but in
the end there is no mention at all of her being barren.**

Waj. Rab. IX,9 contains three statements by Bar Kappara about peace, the
second of which concurs with the statement here in D. E. Z. See other manuscripts in D. E. Z. that read: 'Bar Kappara said: "Great is peace, for we find in
connection with the prophets..."' Cf. also Jalq., Shophetim, r. 68; Jalq., Ps., r.
712; and *Midr. Seph. We-Hizhir*, Tzav, 35a.

The statement can be explained as follows: The wife of Manoah did not tell
everything to her husband (see Judg. 13:6) the angel had said to her (see Judg.
13:3), i. e., she neglected to tell him that the angel talked about her infertility.
According to the midrash, the prophet (the book of Judges belongs to the 'early
prophets') is giving an example that clearly illustrates that it is sometimes
permitted not to tell the whole truth, if it preserves peace between man and
wife. Cf. especially the reading in Midr. ha-Gad. on Gen. 18,12–13 and
*Mishnat Rabbi 'Eli'ezer*, where it is said that the Scripture *covers words*. The
explanation is based on the fact that the angel himself (see Judg. 13:3ff.) did not
tell Manoah, what he told his wife about her infertility. Cf. the readings that
have the wording: 'Great is peace, for the angel changed his words [for Mano-
ah]...' Cf. Siphrei, Naso, pisqa 42 (ed. H. S. Horovitz, p. 46); Bam. Rab. XI,7;
Midr. Leq. Tob on Num. 6:26; Jalq. ha-Makh. on Ps. 29 (§ 37). See also the
extensive explanation given in Waj. Rab. IX,9 and in a number of above
mentioned and other parallels, where it is said that the angel only told a half-

truth to Manoah. The reading in D. E. Z. h.l., is clearly an abridged reading of
the midrash ascribed to Bar Kappara.

9.  **And so [other reading: Bar Kappara said: Great is peace, for among the
angels there is no enmity, no jealousy, no hatred, no sectarism, no rivalry
and no dissension (and yet it is needed) that] the Holy One blessed be He
makes peace [among them], for it is said: 'Dominion and fright are with
Him, He makes peace in his high places' (Hiob 25:2). 'Dominion', that is
Michael. And 'fright', that is Gabriel. They (i. e. the heavenly creatures) do
not injure one another, some being of fire and others of water. How much
more (it is needed to make peace between) men, among whom all these
(evil) dispositions exist.!**

The basis manuscript in D. E. Z. clearly contains a defective reading here: 'And
so the Holy One blessed be He made peace among them...' These words can
only refer to that which is stated explicitly at the beginning of this statement in
other manuscripts The words *among whom all these dispositions exist* applies to
the characteristics of the angels mentioned at the beginning of this statement in
other manuscripts The statement here in D. E. Z., up to 'Rabbi Shim'on
said...') can be dated back to different traditions. The opening of the statement is based on a tradition of Bar Kappara (as stated in other manuscripts), in
which Hiob 25:2 is of central importance. Cf. Waj. Rab. IX,9; Deb. Rab. V,12;
*Midr. Seph. We-Hizhir* on Lev. 7:11 (35a); Midr. ha-Gad., Tzav (ed. N. E.
Rabinowitz, p. 141; cf. also other sources.

The statement of Bar Kappara is interwoven here in D. E. Z. with a statement
that is ascribed elsewhere to Resh Laqish and that also comprises an explanation on Hiob 25:2. The phrase 'dominion and fear are with Him' is interpreted
here to mean that Michael and Gabriel are with Him. In this interpretation,
Michael represents the element snow (water) and Gabriel represents fire. The
continuation of the text in Hiob 25:2 ('He makes peace in His high Places') is
explained to mean that God reconciled water and fire by creating peace
between Michael and Gabriel. Cf. Deb. Rab. V,12 (directly preceding the
statement of Bar Kappara); Ber. Rab.XII,8; *Ma'alot ha-Middot*, Ma'alat Shalom (ed. Eshkol, p. 323; and Targ. on Hiob 25:2 (different).

In some traditions, a nearly identical statement is ascribed to Rabbi Ja'aqob
de Kephar Hanin (an Amora of the third generation) and not Resh Laqish. See
Pes. de-R. K. and Jalq.,Wa-Era, r. 186. The correspondence of the words in
those sources with these here D. E. Z. is unmistakable. The statement of Rabbi
Ja'aqob of Kephar Hanin was probably attributed by mistake to Rabbi Johanan
in Bam. Rab. XII,88. In connection with Hiob 25:2, however, another statement is indeed attributed to Rabbi Johanan. Cf. TjR. ha-Sh. II,5 [68a]; Deb.
Rab. V,12; and Midr. ha-Gad. on Lev. 9:1.

Rabbi Shim'on bar Johai made a very similar statement in connection with Hiob 25:2 in which it is said that the firmament represents the element water and the stars (or angels) the element fire, and that God preserves peace between the two. Cf. Ps. 104:3−4: 'He makes His upperrooms in the waters... He makes the winds His messengers and He makes raging fire His servants.' Cf. Bam. Rab. XII,8; Shir ha-Shir.Rab.III,2; Midr. Hazit on Cant. 3,2 and Ag. Shir ha-Shir. (ed. S. Schechter, p. 4); Tanh., Wa-Jiggash, § 6; Pes. de R. K., ed. S. Buber, 3a; Jalq., Wa-Era, r.186; Jalq., Hiob, r. 912; and Midr. ha-Gad. on Lev. 9:1 (ed. A. Steinsalz, p. 211).

The statement here in D. E. Z. represents a combined, abridged reading of the content of the statements of Bar Kappara and Resh Laqish. The explanation of 'Shamajim' as a combination of ''esh' (fire) and 'majim' (water) is related to those explanations according to which God reconciles water and fire, elements represented by the angels Michael and Gabriel or by the firmament and the stars or heavenly bodies. Cf. *Seph. ha-Bahir*, § 59 (ed. R. Margaliot, 27a). Fire and water here probably represent the concepts of 'middat ha-din' (God's quality of righteousness and 'middat ha-Rahamim' (God's quality of mercifulness). The earthy and heavenly reality are determined by God's righteousness and mercifulness, qualities which contradict each other according to human standards but which are kept in harmonious balance by God. Peace created by God is essential to the preservation of the harmony between these qualities in Heaven as well on earth. See M. Karib, *Me-Sod Hakhamim*, Jerusalem 1976, p. 26 regarding a statement by Rabbi Johanan in Ber. Rab. X,3; cf. also the commentary to Bahja ben Asher on M'Abot I,12, mentioned in *Menorat ha-Ma'or*, ed. H. G. Enelow, p. 522.

## 10.  Rabbi Shim'on [better reading: Rabbi Jishma'el] said: 'Great is peace for the Holy One blessed be He permitted His Name, although written in holiness, to be blotted out in water (by the priest), in order to maintain peace between a husband and his wife.'

The reading of 'Rabbi Shim'on' in the basis manuscript is not confirmed by the parallels. The reading 'Rabbi Jishma'el ' is more plausible on the basis of the context in the parallels and other manuscripts here in D. E. Z. The parallel in TosShab. XIII,5 also reads 'Rabbi Jishma'el'. Cf. among others TbShab. 116a and Waj. Rab. IX,9. Cf., however, the reading 'De-Bei Rabbi Jishma'el' (the school of Rabbi Jishma'el) in Midr. ha-Gad. on Gen. 18:12 (ed. A. Steinsalz, pp. 301−302) and cf. the reading 'wa-jomer Mar' in TbHul. 141a. Deb. Rab. V,12 contains a statement analogous to the one here in D. E. Z., recorded in the name of Rabbi 'Aqiba. In TbNed. 66b, Rabbi makes a remark to Rabbi Shim'on from which it is evident that he knew of the tradition attributed in the parallels to Rabbi Jishma'el. The statement of Rabbi Jishma'el was probably used originally in discussions about the relationship one should have to the

Scriptures of the Minim in the form of a reasoning from light to heavy (a fortiori). If Gods name may be effaced for the sake of preserving peace between a man and a woman (this is an reference to the ritual that a wife suspected of having committed adultery had to undergo [see Num. 5:12ff. and see especially verse 23]), then scriptures that cause dissension and conflict may be effaced all the more. Cf. the traditions in TossShab. XIII,5 and TbShab. 116a; TjShab. XVI,1 [16c]; TjSot.I,4; TbNed. 66b; TbNed. 141a; Siphrei, Naso, pisqa 16 (ed. H.S. Horovitz, p. 21); and Midr. ha-Gad., Tzav (ed. N.E. Rabinowitz, p. 141). In other probably later forms of the statement (such as here in D.E.Z.), the statement is divorced from the a fortiori reasoning.

**11.   And [ other reading: Rabbi Jehoshua ben Levi said:] great is peace, for the covenant of priesthood was made with peace, for it is said: 'Behold, I give him My covenant of peace' (Num. 25:12).**

See M. Higger, *Massekhtot Ze'irot*, p. 149, and W. Bacher, *Die Agada der Tannaiten*, I, p. 186. The question arises here whether 'Rabbi Jehoshua' is actually Rabbi Jehoshua ben Levi. Cf. the opening of *Pereq ha-Shalom*. The fact that so many statements that appear anonymously in the basis manuscript and parallels are ascribed to Rabbi Jehoshua in other manuscripts raises doubts about the originality of the readings in those manuscripts Cf. especially W. Bacher, *Die Agada der Tannaiten*, I, p. 186;

   No direct source or parallel to this statement has been found. The passage from Num. 25:12 cited in this statement does appear in one tradition in connection with Pinhas, who recorded a 'bond of peace' as a reward for his behaviour at Ba'al Pe'or, where he slew Zimri (see Num. 25:1ff.). The statement here in D.E.Z. may refer to that same tradition. Cf., e.g., Ibn Ezra on Num. 25:12. Receiving a 'bond of peace' meant that Pinhas and his descendants did not had to fear revenge from Zimri and his descendants. Cf. also TbZeb. 101b. Cf. also Rashi on TbSanh. 82b.

**12.   And [other reading: Rabbi Jehoshua ben Levi said:] great is peace for so the Name of the Holy One blessed be He is called 'Peace', for it is said: 'And he called it (i.e. the altar) Adonai Shalom' (Judg. 6:24).**

Like the previous statement, this statement is recorded anonymously in the basis manuscript and attributed to Rabbi Jehoshua in other manuscripts. The parallels do not mention Rabbi Jehoshua as spokesman, but the statement is recorded there in the name of an otherwise unknown individual, Rabbi Judan bar Joseph. (see Waj. Rab. IX,9; ed. M. Margulies, p. 190) or Rabbi Judan bar José. Cf. the reading 'Rabbi Judan' in *Midr. Seph. We-Hizhir* on Lev. 7:11, 35a. The different readings probably resulted from various interpretations of one abbreviation. The interpretation of 'Rabbi J.' as Rabbi Jehoshua (in D.E.Z.) is plausible. In Judges 6:24, it is told how Gideon built an altar and called it 'The Lord is Peace'. The midrash concludes accordingly that one of God's names is 'Peace'.

**13a. Rabbi Hijja [bar 'Abba] said: 'Therefore it is forbidden to a man to extend a greeting to his fellowman (lit. to inquire after the peace of his fellowman) on a filthy place. What is the argument? (For it is written:) "And Gideon built an altar there unto the Lord and called it Adonai Shalom" (Judg. 6:24).'**
**13b. Now if an altar, which does not eat and does not drink and does not smell and does not speak and which was erected only for the atonement of Israel, is called peace, how much more so One Who loves peace and pursues peace and Who establishes peace and Who maintains peace between a husband and his wife.**

13a. *Rabbi Hijja...* Rabbi Hijja bar 'Abba is mentioned as the spokesman of this statement in the manuscripts of D. E. Z. Rabbi Tanhum bar Judan is mentioned as the spokesman in the parallel in Waj. Rab. IX,9 (ed. M. Margulies, p. 190) and in *Midr. Seph. We-Hizhir* on Lev. 7:11 (35a). Rabbi Tanhum the son of Rabbi Hijja (a man of Kephar Akko) is mentioned as the spokesman in Midr. ha-Gad. on Lev. 7:11. The question remains as to whether this is the original reading or a later harmonization of two different readings. Cf. a closely related tradition in D. E. R. X,4−6 and see there the commentary and parallels. Cf. especially TbShab. 10a and TjShab. II,3 [4c] Cf. especially S. Lieberman, *Tosephta Ki-Pheshutah*, I, p. 26 on TosBer. II,2.

One may not greet in an inappropriate place (where people are undressed, for example, or in close proximity to excrements etc.), i. e., one may not ask for the 'shalom' of someone, because 'Shalom' is another name for God and thus may not be spoken in an impure or degrading place. Cf. TbShab. 11a, where for the same reason, it is said, in connection with a discussion about whether one may extend a greeting in a bathhouse: 'One may not extend a greeting there.' This supports the opinion of Rab Hamnuna in the name of 'Ulla, who said: 'It is forbidden for one to greet another in the bathhouse for it is said: ... "and called it The Lord is Peace "(Judg. 6:24).' The content of the statement connects directly to the explanation of Judg. 6:24 given above.

13b. *Now if an altar...* This incomplete statement which has been adapted to the context here in D. E. Z., is based on a tradition recorded in the sources in the name of Rabbi Johanan ben Zakkai. The sources contain two versions of the statement by Rabbi Johanan ben Zakkai. The statement departs from an explanation of Dt.27:6, where it is said that unhewn stones, must be used to built the altar at Mt. Ebal. The reasoning behind this is as follows: If those stones, which (unlike) people cannot see, hear, speak, etc, may not be touched by the iron of the sword because they bring peace to Israel and reconcile Israel and its father in Heaven, people, of flesh and blood, who can see, hear, speak, etc., will all the more so be spared from the sword of their enemies, when they will create peace between men and women, between cities and between peoples. Cf. W. Bacher, *Die Agada der Tannaiten*, I, p. 29 ff. in connection with the term 'ke-min homer'. Cf. the sources in Mekh. de-R. Jishm., Jitro, Ba-Hodesh, par. 11 (ed. M. Friedmann, 74a and ed. H. S. Horovitz, p. 244); Tanh., Jitro, (end); Jalq., Qedoshim, r. 624 and *Mishnat Rabbi 'Eli'ezer* (ed. H. G. Enelow, p. 86). In the TosB. Q. VII,7; Mekh. de-R. Shim. bar Johai, Jitro, on Ex. 20:22 (ed. J. N. Epstein / E. Z. Melamed, p. 157) and in TbSem. VIII (cf. Jalq., Mishpatim, r. 318), the statement appears in a more extensive context and is introduced by an explanation according to which 'iron' in Dt. 27:5 alludes to the sword as a symbol of punishment, given that the sword was made of iron. According to the tradition, the 'sons of the Torah' will be spared of destruction by the sword, because, like the altar, they bring about reconciliation in the world. Cf. W. Bacher, *Die Agada der Tannaiten*, I, p. 28. One notion behind this statement is that from the destruction of the Temple and the disappearance of the altar and of the possibility of bringing about reconciliation by offerings onward, study and deeds of charity had to create peace in the world. Cf. the well known statement by Rabbi Johanan ben Zakkai in A. R. N. [a], IV (11a) and parallels.

The reading 'u-mesim shalom' (*Who establishes peace*) in the basis manuscript is to be preferred to the reading 'u-maqdim shalom...' in the manuscripts. See the parallels, most of which read 'u-metil shalom'. Cf. especially the reading 'u-mesimot shalom' in Pes. Rab. (ed. M. Friedmann, 199b). The reading 'between a husband and his wife' in the basis manuscript must also be preferred to the reading 'between Israel and their father in heaven' in the other manuscripts.

### 14. And [other reading: Rabbi José the Galilean said:] also the name of the messiah is called 'Peace', for it is said: '(And his name shall be called...) Father of Eternity, Prince of Peace' (Is. 9:5).

This statement is recorded anonymously in the basis manuscript and in the name of Rabbi José the Galilean in the other manuscripts. There are no direct parallels to this statement. See J. Klausner, 'The Name and Personality of the Messiah' in: *Messianism in the Talmudic Era*, ed. L. Landman, New York 1979, p. 219, with respect to the name 'Shalom' for the Messiah: 'This name did not take root in Jewish literature or became current among common people or scholars.; it remained the individual creation of José the Galilean.' See the commentaries on Is. 9:5.

According to the commentaries, the name 'Prince of Peace' in Is. 9:5 is the name of the child whose birth was announced by the prophets. As in a tradition in TbSanh. 94a, eight names are attributed to Hezekiah on the basis of Is. 9:5. These names included 'prince' and 'peace' (which here are considered two separate names). In a statement of Bar Kappara in the context of that tradition Hezekiah was considered a potential messiah of his time. In traditions such as this one, there was an implicit connection between the name 'peace' and the names of a messianic person. Cf. a tradition in Midr. Mishl. (ed. S. Buber, p. 87) that lists eight names for the messiah, including 'Eternal Father of Peace' (cf. Is. 9:5). See R. Patai, *The Messiah Texts*, chap. II, pp. 16–22.

**15. And [other reading: Rabbi Jehoshua said] great is peace for Israel is called 'Peace', for it is said: 'For (as) the seed of peace (the vine shall give her fruit)' (Za. 8:12). To whom belongs peace? To 'the seed (the children) of peace'.**

The basis manuscript records this statement anonymously, while other manuscripts attribute this statement to Rabbi Jehoshua. See the remarks on D. E. Z. XI,11. The statement is based on Za. 8:12: 'For as the seed of peace, the wine shall give her fruit . . . ' The midrash interprets 'the seed of peace' figuratively as Israel. The continuation of the statement 'To whom belongs peace . . .' was probably added later.

**16. And [other reading: Rabbi José the Galilean said:] great is peace for (even) in time of war one should only begin by (offering) peace, for it is said: 'When you draw night unto a city to fight against it, then you have to proclaim peace unto it' (Dt. 20:10).**

This statement is also recorded anonymously in the basis manuscript, while it is attributed to Rabbi José the Galilean in others. The attribution is in this case supported by a number of parallel-texts. Cf. Waj. Rab. IX,9 (ed. M. Margulies, p. 190) and *Midr. Seph. We-Hizhir*, Tzav, on Lev. 7:11. One must try to promote peace even in times of strive and warfare. See Dt. 20:10.

**17. And so regarding the king messiah, he comes only with (words of) peace [other reading: Rabbi José the Galilean said: Great is peace, for when the messiah will be revealed to Israel he begins (his message) only with (words of) peace], for it is said: 'How beautiful upon the mountains are the feet of the messenger (of good tidings that announces peace)' (Is. 52:7).**

The sequence of statements is different in the manuscripts of D. E. Z. The words *and so* can be better connected to the statement in D. E. Z.XI,14, where peace is also discussed in connection with the messiah. On the other hand, however, one may assume in favour of the sequence in the basis manuscript that two statements attributed to Rabbi José the Galilean appear here together. The statement here in D.E.Z.XI, 17 is recorded anonymously in the parallels. The background of the statement is Is. 52:7: 'How beautiful upon the mountains are the feet of him who brings good tidings, who announces peace... who says to Zion "Your God is King."' The redemption of Zion and Jerusalem and peace are both mentioned in this statement and its eschatological context. As for a number of other statements in this chapter, no parallels have been found in the sources for this statement.

**18. Rabbi said [other reading: Rabbi Jehoshua said: Great is peace for in the future (i.e. in the hereafter) the Holy One blessed be He will support the righteous with peace, for it is said: 'You steadfast mind, you keep in (perfect) peace' (Is. 26:3); Rabbi Jehoshua said:] 'Great is peace, for it is assigned to the living and it is assigned to the dead. To the living, for it is said: "And Jitro said to Moses: Go in peace" (Ex. 4:18). Whence to the dead? (To the dead, for it is written:) "But you shall go to your fathers in peace" (Gen. 15:15).'**

The basis manuscript reads: 'Great is peace, for it is assigned to the living and it is assigned to the dead...'. Other manuscripts read: 'Rabbi Jehoshua said: "Great is peace, for in the future (in the hereafter) the Holy One blessed be He will support the righteous with peace, for it is said: Your mind stayed in you, you keepest in perfect peace" (Is. 26:3).' In connection with the reading 'Rabbi Jehoshua' in the manuscripts, see D.E.Z. XI,11. In the parallels, peace is called great because (based on Jer. 34:5: 'And you will die in peace.' and Gen. 15:15 ('But you shall go to your fathers in peace.') even the dead need peace. The statement here in D.E.Z. appears to be an elaboration on that tradition. This statement is most closely related to the parallel in Ag. Esther, par. 9 (ed. S. Buber, 41b), where peace is also mentioned in connection with both the living and the dead.

**19. Rabbi Jehoshua said: 'Great is peace for when the world was created the Holy One blessed be He made peace between the upper-world and the lower-world. The first day (He created) heaven and earth; the second day "Let there be a firmament between the waters" (Gen. 1:6); the third day: "Let the waters beneath the heaven flow together" (Gen. 1:9); the fourth day (He created) the lights in the firmament of the heaven; the fifth day: "Let the waters swarm (with living creatures)" (Gen. 1:20); the sixth day He created man. He created the body of the lower-world, for it is said: "Then the Lord, God, formed man from the dust of the earth" (Gen. 2:7) · And He created his soul from the upper-world, for it is said: "And He blew a breath of life in his nostrils" (ibid.).'**

**20. [other reading: Rabbi Shim'on ben Gamli'el said: 'Great is peace for we find that the tribes reported an untrue statement to maintain peace between Joseph and his brothers, for it is said: "And they sent a message unto Joseph, saying: Your father did command (before he died saying: So shall you say unto Joseph: Forgive, I pray you now, the transgression of your brothers and their sin)" (Gen. 50:16). But we do not find that he (i. e. Jacob) had given them any command (like that).']**

Other manuscripts read (XI,20): 'Rabban Shim'on ben Gamli'el said: "Great is peace, for we find that the tribes spoke untrue words in order to maintain peace between Joseph and his brethren, as it is stated . . .'

In the parallels to the reading of this statement in the basis manuscript, the statement is not ascribed to Rabbi Jehoshua but to Rabbi Shim'on ben Halaphta or (in a similar form) to Rabbi Shim'on ben Laqish. Cf., e.g., Waj. Rab. IX,9 (ed. M. Margulies, p. 193); *Midr. Seph. we-Hizhir* on Lev. 7:11 (35b); Jalq., Ps., r. 712; and Jalq., Naso, r. 711, all of which read 'Rabbi Shim'on ben Halaphta'. Cf. also Ber. Rab. XII,8, which reads 'Rabbi 'Azarjah in the name of Rabbi Shim'on ben Laqish' (see ed. J. Theodor / Ch. Albeck, p. 106, notes); see W. Bacher, *Amora'ei 'Eretz Jisra'el*, I, p. 190, note 4. Cf. the notes of S. Buber in Tanh., ed. S. Buber, Be-Reshit, § 15.; Jalq., Prov., r. 935; Midr. ha-Gad. on Lev. 7:11; and Midr. Leq. Tob on Gen. 2:3 (9b), all of which have a reading in the name of Shim'on ben Laqish. The reading 'Rabbi Jehoshua' in D.E.Z. (basis manuscript) is thus in no way confirmed by the parallels. The parallels all contain greatly different readings. In order to nullify every antagonistic argument of the upper world against the lower world, the works of the creation of God are, according to the midrash, evenly distributed throughout the upper and lower world in four pairs. The first day and first pair are a reference to Gen. 1:1 ('the heaven and the earth'). The second and third days and the second pair refer to Gen. 1:6 (". . . on the second day the firmament', referring to the upper world) and to Gen. 1:9 (the seas were created on the third day and belong to the lower world). The third pair of creations took place on the fourth and fifth day, the heavenly bodies (belonging to the upper world) on the forth day (Gen. 1:14) and creatures that live in the water (belonging to the lower world) on the fifth day (Gen. 1:20). With respect to the sixth day, the parallels are more extensive and contain God's opinion that creating something only for the upper world or only for the lower world disturbs the harmony and balance between the two worlds. Therefore man was created on the sixth day, belonging to the upper world (his soul) and to the lower world (his body), to keep the balance in creation. The reading here in D.E.Z. is incomplete. 'Shalom' is presented here as a harmony effected by God between the spirit and material, on which all of creation depends. With respect to other readings in the manuscripts, cf. Waj. Rab. IX,9 (ed. M. Margulies, pp. 189–190; Ber. Rab.

C,8 (ed. J. Theodor / Ch. Albeck, p. 1293, and references there) and Midr. ha-
Gad. on Gen. 3:16 (ed. A. Steinsalz, p. 877 and notes to line 14).

**21. Rabbi Shim'on ben Gamli'el said: 'Great is peace, for Aaron the
(High-)Priest is praised only for peace, for [he loved peace and] he pursued
peace and he was first in greeting with (a salutation of) peace and he
established peace [other reading: and he answered with (a salutation of)
peace], for it is said: "He walked with Me in peace" (Mal. 2:6).**

**This teaches us that when he saw (two) men hating one another, he would
go to one of them and say to him: "Why do you hate So-and-So? He has
already come to my house and prostrated himself before me saying: I have
sinned against So-and-So, go and pacify him." And then he left this man
and went to the second and spoke to him like to the first. And so he
established peace [,love] and fellowship between a man and his fellow. And
with reference to this it is said: "And he did turn many away from iniquity"
(ibid.).'**

This statement is based on Mal. 2:6, which, according to the midrash, applies to
Aaron, the forefather of the priests: 'Torah of truth was in his mouth and
unrighteousness was not to be found on his lips. He walked with Me in peace
and sincerity, and he brought many back from unrighteousness.' Cf. also the
explanations of this verse in relation to Aaron in the commentaries. Cf. also,
e.g., Ber. Rab. XCIX,5; Shem. Rab. V,10; Shem. Rab. XXXVIII,5; Waj.
Rab. III,6; Pes.de-R. K. (ed. S. Buber, 46a and 168b;), idem ed. B. Mandelbaum, p. 385 and idem ed. B. Mandelbaum p. 85.

The first part of the statement here in D. E. Z. XI,21a, occurs anonymously
and separately in the sources. Cf. Bam. Rab. XI,7; Jalq., Naso, r. 711; Jalq. ha-
Makh. on Ps. 29, § 37; and *Midr. Gadol u-Gedolah*, in A. Jellinek. *Beit ha-
Midrash*, III, p. 129. In these sources, this portion of the statement is supported
by Mal. 2:5. Here in D. E. Z., however, only Mal. 2:6 is cited. One may assume
like M. Higger, that the source of the rest of the statement (XI,21b) must be
sought in Siphra (Shemini, end of Petihta). See *Mas. Kal. Rab.* ed. M. Higger,
introduction, p. 74.

The statement of Rabbi 'El'azar ben Rabbi José the Galilean in the sources
must be regarded as a further elaboration of the tradition in Siphra. Cf.
TosSanh. I,2; TjSanh. I,1 [18b]; TbSanh. 6b; cf. Midr. ha-Gad. on Dt. 1:17.
The traditions in A. R. N. are even more detailed and extensive (see A. R. N.
[a], XII [24b-25a]; A. R. N. [b] XXIV [25a-b]; cf. Jalq., Mal., r. 588). The
tradition in A. R. N. [a] is recorded in the name of Rabbi Me'ir. Cf. the
manuscripts in D. E. Z. that supplement the passage from Mal. 2:6 as follows:
'And he brought back many from unrighteousness.' Only in Midr. ha-Gad. as in
D. E. Z. is everything attributed to RabbiShim'on ben Gamli'el. The reading

here in D.E.Z. should be corrected and read: 'for he loved and pursued piece and established piece'.

Hillel had already made a statement in which Aaron was set forth as an example of one who loved and pursued peace. Cf. M'Abot I,12.

**22. Rabbi Jehoshua said: 'A prophet is called "angel" (messenger) and the sage is called "angel", [the prophet is called "angel" for it is said: "Then spoke Haggai the messenger (lit.: angel) of the Lord" (Haggai 1:13). And the sage is called "angel"], for it is said: "For he is the messenger (lit.: angel) of the Lord of Hosts" (Mal. 2:7). Is it possible (to argue) that this applies to a priest who is an ignoramus ("am ha-'aretz')? (No, and therefore) Scripture says: "And they should seek the Law at his mouth" (Mal. 2:7).'**

This statement is attributed to Rabbi Jehoshua only here in D.E.Z. See the commentary on D.E.Z. XI,11. It is clair from the parallels that this statement represents a combination of various statements. Prophets and sages are compared with angels here in D.E.Z. In light of the context of D.E.Z. XI,22, however, it is probable that the original reading of the statement mentioned 'the priest' instead of the 'the sage'. Cf. the reading of the Gaon of Vilna a.l. The comparison of priests with angels is based on Mal. 2:7. Cf. the explanation of Mal. 2:6 in connection with the preceding statement. The statement here is an associative explanation of the context of Mal. 2:6, where Scripture continues with: 'For the priests lips should keep knowledge, and they should seek the law at his mouth, for he is *the angel* of the Lord of Hosts.' One also finds sources in which prophets are identified with angels on the basis of various passages from Scripture, such as Num. 20:16: '...sent an angel and led us out of Egypt.' The angel in this passage is identified with the prophet Moses. Pinhas was similarly associated with an angel, see commentary to Judg. 2:1. In some traditions reference is also made to Ps. 103:20 (see Waj. Rab. I,1 [ed. M. Margulies, p. 2]) and II Chron. 36:,16. Waj. Rab. I,1 contains a tradition in the name of Rabbi Johanan according to which, on the basis of Hag. 1,13 prophets are compared to angels (see ed. M. Margulies, p. 2 notes). Cf. the manuscripts in D.E.Z. in which Hag. 1:13 had been added as reference. In a related statement by Rabbi Johanan, the Rab (teacher) is compared with an angel on the basis of Mal. 2:7. These parallels explain why the prophet and the scholar are compared to angels in this statement in D.E.Z., and not the prophet and the priest as would be in accordance with the following text in D.E.Z. The reading 'Rabbi Jehoshua' here in D.E.Z. might be an erroneous interpretation of the abbreviated name of Rabbi Johanan (see the sources mentioned).

In Jalq. Re'ub., the statement appears in an even more general form. In that statement, each person who has 'hasidut' within him is compared with an angel.

See Jalq. Re'ub., Naso.; Cf. Jalq. ha-Makh. on Ps. 119., § 9 and Tanh., Wa-
Jiqra, § 1 in regard to II Chron. 36:16.

**23a.  And also [other reading: Rabbi Jehoshua of Sikhnin said in name of
Rabbi Levi:] great is peace, for all prayers and benedictions conclude with
(words of) peace.**
**23b.  [(Later addition): This is so in connection with benedictions, but how
is it in connection with offerings? Scripture says: 'This is the Torah of the
burnt-offerings, the meal-offerings, the sin-offerings, the guilt-offerings
and the peace-offerings' (Lev. 7:37). Now (in Lev. l.c.) I only have evidence (in connection with offerings) in general, in (connection with offering in)
detail, whence is it proven? (It is proven by:) 'And this is the Torah of the
meal-offering' (Lev. 6:7,14), 'And this is the Torah of the peace-offering'
(Lev. 7:11). I only have (evidence in connection with peace in) This World,
in connection with the World to Come, whence it is proved? For it is said:
'For so says the Lord, behold I do run to her peace like a river' (Is. 66:12).]**
**23c.  The reading of the 'Shema' concludes with peace: 'And spread over us
the tabernacle of Your peace'. The Benediction of the Priests concludes
with peace: 'And the Lord give you peace' (Num 6:26). The "Amidah'
concludes with peace [other reading: All benedictions (i. e. of the 'Amidah') conclude with peace] '(Blessed are You ...) Who makest peace in His
High Places' (see Hiob 25:2).**

23a. *And also [Rabbi Jehoshua of Sikhnin said in the name of Rabbi Levi]...*
The basis manuscript mentions no spokesman for this statement, only an
anonymous connection with the preceding statement. Other manuscripts and a
number of parallels attribute the following statement here in D. E. Z. to Rabbi
Jehoshua of Sikhnin in the name of Rabbi Levi, or simply to Rabbi Levi. Cf.,
e.g., Midr. Jelammedenu, Wa-Jera, 9 in L. Grünhut, *Sepher ha-Liqqutim*, III,
55b; Deb. Rab. V,12 and Tanh., Tzav, ed. S. Buber § 10.
   The statement appears anonymously in a number of other parallels. The
names of the person who originally transmitted the tradition appear in Waj.
Rab. IX,9: 'Rabbi Mani [Rabbi Mana] of Sha'ab (a place in Galilee) and Rabbi
Jehoshua of Sikhnin in the name of Rabbi Levi.' Cf. Jalq. Ha-Makh. on Nah.
2:1 (p. 13); *Midr. Seph. We-Hizhir*, Tzav (35b); and Midr. ha-Gad., Naso, on
Num. 6:12. The detailed statement, which ultimately must be ascribed to Rabbi
Levi, is based on a much shorter statement by Rabbi 'El'azar ha-Kappar.
According to that statement, the Eighteen Benedictions end with the words
'we-jasem lekha shalom'. In some parallels of the statement of Rabbi 'El'azar
ha-Kappar, the Eighteen Benedictions are called 'All Blessings'!! Cf. Siphrei,
Naso, pisqa 42: 'Rabbi 'El'azar said: 'Great is peace, for one ends All Blessings
(i. e. the Eighteen Benedictions) with 'peace', for it is said: 'The Lord bless you

and the Lord keep you and the Lord shine upon you and be graceful to you...
*and give you peace.*' Cf. Jalq., Ps. 29, r. 711; Jalq. ha-Makh. on Ps. 29, § 37;
Midr. Leq. Tob on Num. 6:26; and *Menorat ha-Ma'or* of Al-Nakawa, ed.
H. G. Enelow, p. 546. Another parallel reads: 'The entire Tephillah.' Cf. Bam.
Rab. XI,7: 'Rabbi 'El'azar ha-Kappar said: 'Great is peace, for one ends the
entire Tephillah ...' Yet another reading mentions: 'the blessing of the priests.'
Cf. the reading in Tanh., Tzav, ed. S. Buber, § 10. Because of the strong
connection with the statement here in D. E. Z., the statement of Rabbi 'El'azar
ha-Kappar is there incorrectly attributed to Rabbi Levi. Cf. Siphrei, Shophetim, pisqa 199 (ed. L. Finkelstein, p. 237): 'Great is peace, for one concludes
the blessing of the priests ...'. The remark of Rabbi El'azar ha-Kappar about
the end of the Eighteen Benedictions is expanded in the statement by Rabbi
Levi here in D. E. Z., according to which all blessings and prayers end with
'peace.' The statement is followed by a series of examples.

The above-mentioned statement by Rabbi 'El'azar ha-Kappar raises a number of questions. In the repetition of the Eighteen Benedictions the 'blessing of
the priests' is added in before the last blessing ('Sim Shalom'). Cf., e.g. TbMeg.
17b-18a and I. Elbogen, *Ha-Tephillah be-Jisra'el*, Jerusalem 1972, p. 46. It is
implied in the statement of Rabbi 'El'azar ha-Kappar that the entire prayer of
the Eighteen Benedictions is concluded at the end of the blessing of the priests
with the words '...and He give you peace' (Num. 6:26). Cf. especially the
reading in Bam. Rab. XI,7 ('... for one concludes the entire Tephillah...') and
the reading in a statement by Rabbi Shim'on ben Halaphta in Bam. Rab. XI,7
'... the blessing of the priests after the blessings (of the Eighteen Benedictions)
also ends with the word 'peace'.'

The Eighteen Benedictions ending with the blessing 'Sim Shalom' ended in
Israel with ''oseh shalom' (see further in the commentary), not with 'we-jasem
lekha shalom' (and may He give you peace), as suggested in the statement of
Rabbi 'El'azar ha-Kappar. One solution to this problem would be to assume
that the Eighteen Benedictions originally ended with the blessing of the priests
and with the words '... and give you peace' ('we-jasem le-kha shalom'). It is
highly probable that the blessing 'Sim Shalom' arose from the blessing of the
priests preceding it! The question put in TbMeg.17a-18b as to why one says 'Sim
Shalom' after the blessing of the priests supports this assumption.

Old sources mention the blessing of the priests instead of 'Sim Shalom' (see
MTam. V,1 and TjR. ha-Sh. IV,5) as the conclusion to the prayer from which
the present-day Eighteen Benedictions evolved. See I. Elbogen, *Ha-Tephillah
be-Jisra'el*, p. 46. (Cf. I. Elbogen, *Die jüdische Gottesdienst in seiner geschichtlichen Entwicklung*, p. 31 and p. 59, where I. Elbogen, however, suggests on the
basis of the sources mentioned that the term 'blessing of the priests' ('Birkat
Kohanim') refers to 'Sim Shalom'. Cf. especially G. Allon in: *Tarbiz*, XIV, vol.
II, pp. 70–72. G. Allon tries to prove that the Eighteen Benedictions in Israel
ended with the words 'ma'jan berakhot 'oseh shalom'. This conclusion of 'Sim

Shalom' is supposed to have functioned as a reference to God (see idem p. 73) and as a counterbalance to the notion suggested by the blessing of the priests preceding it, that the priest, not God, was the source of the blessing. This view, then, implies that the blessing 'Sim Shalom' evolved from the blessing of the priests preceding it (as the original conclusion). This explains why one reading of the statement of Rabbi 'El'azar ha-Kappar mentions the conclusion to 'the blessing of the priests' and the other reading of his statement mentions 'all blessings', with both referring to the conclusion to the Eighteen Benedictions.

Both readings are combined in Bam. Rab. XI,7 and in Jalq. ha-Makh. on Ps. 29, § 37 because it was no longer realized that there are two different readings of one statement. As stated above, the statement of Rabbi 'El'azar ha-Kappar, in which the term 'all blessings' applied only to the old version of the Eighteen Benedictions, was explained in the statement of Rabbi Levi to apply to all blessings (in general), which resulted in the peculiar assertion that all blessings end with 'peace'. The sequence in the statement in D. E. Z. h.l. is incorrect. The words 'the reciting of the Shema' (23c) onward to the end of the statement should be placed in after the words 'one concludes with 'peace' (23a), in accordance with the order in the parallel Waj. Rab. IX,9 and other parallels. See also M. Higger, *Massekhtot Ze'irot*, p. 150. Cf. also the reading of the Gaon of Vilna a.l. The section from This is so in connection with benedictions... ' (23b) to ' ... the reciting of the Shema') is clearly a later addition. The fact, however, that the addition already appears in Waj. Rab. l.c. may attest to the great age of this addition. Cf. also Deb. Rab. V,15.

23c. *And spread over us the tabernacle of Your peace...* These words were spoken at the end of the second blessing ('Hashkibenu') after the Shema on the eve of the Sabbath and holidays.

*Who makest peace in His high places.* An other reading : 'Who makest peace.' This refers to the conclusion of the Eighteen Benedictions, which (according to Babylonian tradition) ended on the Ten Days between Rosh ha-Shannah and Jom Kippur with the words 'Blessed are You, O Lord, *Who makest peace.*' There are indications that the Eighteen Benedictions were concluded in Israel also on other days with the same or nearly identical words. See G. Allon, l.c. and S. Schechter in *J. Q. R.*, X, (1898) p. 659, which contains a fragment of 'Sim Shalom' ending with 'sim shalom 'al Jisra'el, kakh tebarrekhenu kulanu be-shalom ma'jan ha-berakhot we-'oseh shalom'.

See also S. Schechter's remarks on this fragment. Cf. also the reading of a geniza fragment by J. Mann, in *HUCA* II (1925), p. 307 with the following wording: 'sim shalom 'al Jisra'el... ki tob be-'eineikha le-barrekh 'e[t 'ammekha] Jisra'el be-shalom, barukh 'atta ha-Shem 'oseh ha-[shalom].'

Cf. also a fragment recorded by A. Marmorstein, in: *Ha-Tzopheh*, VI, p. 56: 'barukh 'atta ha-Shem m-w-'-n ha-berakhot 'oseh ha-shalom.'. See also I. Jacobson, *Netib Binah*, I, p. 296 with a geniza fragment: 'barukh 'atta ha-Shem 'oseh ha-shalom.'

And see I. Elbogen in: *HUCA*. III (1926), p. 224 in a piut of Kalir (Kilir): 'barukh 'atta ha-Shem ha-metzawweh kol ha-berakhot we-'oseh ha-shalom.'

Cf. also Num.Rab. V,15, ed. by M. Weiss in Ha-Tzopheh vol. XIII p. 14. See further in *Seder Rab 'Amram Gaon* (ed. N.N. Coronel,18a) in ed. E.D. Goldschmidt p. 50, concerning the daily Minhah prayer:

'u-mesajjem 'ad 'oseh shalom ke-derekh she-mitpallelin ba-shaharit.' Cf. further Jalq., Sam., r. 80 and comments in relation to this source in I. Jacobson, o.c., p. 264 and *Shiblei ha-Leqet,* 18. Cf. also remarks in I. Jacobson, o.c., p. 265; Midr. Ps. 29, §2 (ed. S. Buber, 116b); and I. Elbogen, D*er Jüdische Gottesdienst in seiner geschichtlichen Entwicklung*, p. 59. See especially G. Allon l.c., according to whom the conclusion to the Magen 'Abot (... 'me'ein ha-berakhot. 'El ha-hoda'ot, le-hoda'ot la-'Adon ha-shalom') spoken on the eve of the Sabbath actually belongs to the concluding blessing of the Eighteen Benedictions in Israel (in the old sources we read, however, 'ma'jan ha-berakhot' [cf. 'ha-metzawweh berakhot'] in stead of 'me'ein he-berakhot' [fitting forms of blessings] in Magen 'Abot!). Magen 'Abot is actually a summary of the Eighteen Benedictions. See G. Allon. l.c., note 4. According to G. Allon, the Eighteen benedictions in Israel ended with the words 'me'ein ['ma'jan'?] ha-berakhot 'oseh shalom'. They also end with the same words in the reading of the statement here in D.E.Z. in Waj. Rab. IX, 9 (ed. M. Margulies, p. 194: 'ba-tephillah: m-'-j-n ha-berakhot'.

Cf. *Midr. Seph. We-Hizhir*, Tzav, on Lev. 7:11 (35b), and cf. there the later reading adapted to Magen 'Abot:... 'me'ein ha-berakhot le-hoda'ot la-'Adon ha-shalom.' Cf. also *Menorat ha-Ma'or* of Al-Nakawa, ed. H.G. Enelow, p. 546 with additions concerning the adoption of the later custom of reciting Magen 'Abot on the eve of the Sabbath.

The reading in the basis manuscript, according to which the Eighteen Benedictions ended with ''Oseh shalom bi-meromaw' is not confirmed by the sources. On the basis of other manuscripts on this section of *Pereq ha-Shalom* the word 'be-meromaw' must be deleted. Only ''Elohai Netzor' prayer added after the Eighteen Benedictions, ended with that wording (cf. TbBer. 17a).

**24. [Most manuscripts are ending Pereq ha-Shalom as follows: Rabbi Jehoshua ben Levi said: ' The Holy One blessed be He said to Israel: "You have brought about that My Temple is destructed and My children were exiled. Ask for her peace (i.e.the peace of Jerusalem) and I will forgive you." Therefore it is written: "Pray for the peace of Jerusalem" (Ps. 122:6); and it says: "And seek the peace of the city" (Jer. 27:7) and it says: "Peace be within your walls, rest within your palaces" (Ps. 122:7); and it says: "For my brothers and companions sake, I will now say: Peace be within you" (Ps. 122:8). The Holy One blessed be He will cause him who loves peace, pursues peace and offers a salutation of peace and returns a**

salutation of peace, to inherit This World and the World to Come, for it is said: "But the meek shall inherit the land and delight themselves in the abundance of peace." (Ps. 37:11).]

25.  There are seven characteristics in an uncultured man and seven characteristics in a wise man. In an uncultured man: He interrupts the words of his fellow, he is hasty to answer and he speaks before him who is greater (in wisdom and years) than he is, and he answers at the first (question) last and at the last (question) first, and he does not acknowledge the truth and he feels ashamed to learn (of others) and to say: 'I have not heard (of it)'. But the sage is not like this, he does not interrupt the words of any man.

See the conclusion of *Pereq ha-Shalom* in other manuscripts. In the basis manuscript this statement is followed by an exceedingly long text containing exegetical remarks based on the tradition from M'Abot V,7. See the general remarks in connection with D.E.Z. VII, 1.

The context of this explanation does not belong to *Pereq ha-Shalom*. In accordance with other manuscripts, one must conclude that *Pereq ha-Shalom* ended with a far shorter statement, which other manuscripts contain instead of this long exegetical addition.

(26).  This is Aaron. Moses was angry with him and commanded him to eat of what was sanctified and disqualified (from being eaten), but he (i.e. Aaron) did not became angry with him and he did not say: 'They (i.e. my sons Eleazar and Ithamar) are mourning (so they may not eat of any offering), make your words short', but he waited until he (i.e. Moses) concluded (his words) and (only) after that he answered him, for it is said: 'And Aaron said unto Moses: This day ...' (Lev. 10:19). 'This day my sons died and then I shall bring an offering?! This day my sons died and then we shall eat of the offerings?! If then the tithe is forbidden to a mourner how much more should the sin-offering, which is a more serious case, be forbidden to a mourner!' Therefore, Aaron followed a reasoning from light to heavy (i.e. an a fortiori reasoning).

(*He does not interrupt the words of any man*,) *This is Aaron* ... See Ms. Epstein, mentioned in A.R.N., ed. S. Schechter, 56b-57a. Cf. the wording in the source in M'Abot: 'We-'eino nikhnas be-dibrei habbero' See further the parallels mentioned in connection with D.E.Z. VII,1 and cf. especially the wording in TosSanh. VII,10: 'lo jehe qophets le-tokh dibreihen'.

In its original context, the statement applied to the sage's behaviour toward colleagues, students and teachers. The wording here in *Pereq ha-Shalom*, however, has a far more general application. In connection with D.E.Z. XI,

26a, see the parallels in A. R. N. [a], XXXVII (56a) and in A. R. N. [b], XL (66a). The source of this statement must be sought in an explanation of Rabbi Nehemiah in TbZeb. 101a. Cf. the reading in Waj. Rab. XIII,1. Cf. also TbZeb. 16b (in the explanation of Rabbi 'El'azar); TbPes. 82b; and TjPes. VII,8 and cf. other sources.

In Waj. Rab., emphasis is placed on the fact that Moses forgot a tradition in his rage and indignation toward Aaron, Eleazar and Itamar for not eating the specified parts of an offering (a goat) in a sacred place, as he had commanded (see Lev. 10:16). He forgot the fact that Aaron and his surviving sons were in a mourning after the deaths of Nadab and Abihu and thus were not at all supposed to partake of the offering.

The background of the statement here in D. E. Z. (and in A. R. N.) is an explanation of Lev. 10:12−20. After two of Aaron's sons had died, Moses asked himself why Aaron and his two surviving sons completely burned the offering instead of eating parts of the offering specified for them in a clean place (Lev:10,12). Moses bursted out in anger not at Aaron himself, but at Eleazar and Itamar. Because they were in mourning, however, they were not supposed to heed the command of Moses. Cf. the explanation of Rabbi Nehemiah, Rabbi Shim'on and Rabbi Jehudah in TbZeb. 101a-101b. Cf. especially parallels and commentary to D. E. Z. II,5. Because Eleazar and Itamar were in mourning, the sin-offering was not valid and should not have been eaten in a sacred place. Cf. the statement here in *Pereq ha-Shalom*: 'and he commanded him to eat from the sanctified offering that was disqualified.' In the statement of Rabbi Nehemiah in TbZeb., emphasis is placed on the fact that Moses is prepared to openly admit his ignorance and his mistake. Moses had in his anger overlooked the fact that Aaron and his sons were in mourning and they were right in burning the offering.

In Waj. Rab., emphasis is placed on the fact that Moses forgot the halakhah in his rage. Here in *Pereq ha-Shalom* (and in A. R. N.) emphasis is placed on the fact that Aaron and his sons did not interrupt Moses but let him have his say, even though they knew that the anger of Moses was unjustified. Only after finishing his words Aaron made Moses realize that his anger was unjust by using reasoning from light to heavy (a fortiori). Details of his response are not given here in *Pereq ha-Shalom*, but the details are contained in the explanation given by Rabbi Nehemiah in TbZeb. 101a. Cf. Waj. Rab. XIII,1 and TbZeb. 16b. See especially the readings in A. R. N. l.c. It is apparent from these readings that the text in *Pereq ha-Shalom* is an incomplete paraphrase. The quotation from Lev. 10:19 is recorded incorrectly, which strengthens the conviction that the text in *Pereq ha-Shalom* is a late and inaccurate addition. Aaron reasoned with Moses and convinced him that he was right. Moses acknowledged this. See especially the discussion in Siphra, Shemini, per. II. Cf. also Targ. Ps. Jon. on Lev. 10:19; M. Higger, *'Otzar ha-Baraitot*, no. 1175, p. 339; idem VII, no. 695, p. 201; and Midr. ha-Gad. on Lev. 10:19. Moses incorrectly assumed that since an exception was made that mourning did not make one ineligible to eat the meal offering in a sacred place (see Lev. 10:13), an exception should also have been made where eating the sin-offering was concerned. See Siphra, Shemini, per. II. The words 'such as these' in Aaron's answer to Moses in Lev. 10:19 ('As things such as these have befallen me, would it have been good in the eyes of the Lord had I eaten the sin offering to day?) are explained by Rabbi Nehemiah as an indirect reference to the deaths that same day of Nadab and 'Abihu (see Lev. 10:1−2). Moses openly acknowledged his mistake. The reading in *Pereq ha-Shalom* corresponds most closely to the reading in A. R. N. [a], l.c.

(27). **And so acted the Holy One blessed be He in connection with Abraham, when he begged for (the salvation of) Sodom and when he said to Him: 'Behold now I have taken heart to speak' (Gen. 18:31). And He waited until he (i. e. Abraham) concluded his words and (only) after that He answered, for it is said: 'And the Lord left after He finished to speak with Abraham' (Gen. 18:33). If then the Holy One blessed be He did not want to interrupt the words of a man of flesh and blood, how much more should not a man of flesh and blood, who is dust, worm and maggot, interrupt the words of his fellowman.**

See the readings in A. R. N. [a] and A. R. N. [b] l.c. A. R. N. contains a more extensive connection with the preceding example of Aaron and Moses. A. R. N. [a] places emphasis on the fact that Moses first directed his anger at Aaron's sons Eleazar and Itamar, and not at Aaron himself. See Lev. 10:16. This statement is explained by the notion that it is natural to direct one's anger at someone smaller rather than someone older or more important than oneself. Thus it is said: 'Aaron was greater than Moses, but still greater is the Holy One blessed be He.' This is used as an introduction of the example of God, who did not interrupt Abraham. (See especially A. R. N. [b], with which the reading here in *Pereq ha-Shalom* most closely correspondents). This introduction strengthens the final conclusion that the fact that God Who is greatest, does not interrupt the mortal Abraham, there is all the more reason for an ordinary mortal not to interrupt another while he is speaking. See the more extensive explanation in A. R. N.

[See in A. R. N. [a] and [b] the end of the statement ('For it is said: "He finished speaking to Abraham..." [Gen 18:33). God said to Abraham, as it were, "See, I am leaving you" upon which Abraham returned to his place (Gen 18:33).') After finishing speaking to Abraham God, as it were, asked permission to Abraham to take leave of him before Abraham returned to his place. This additional explanation is connected with a a fortiori reasoning, according to which it is not permitted for one to leave someone without announcing that he is leaving and without asking permission to do so. One should behave toward another person as God behaved toward Abraham. See commentary and parallels in D. E. R., V,1−2.]

Cf. also Tanh., Wa-Jera, § 8. Cf. a related explanation by Rabbi Shim'on bar Johai in Siphrei Be-Ha'alotkha, pisqa 103, on Num. 12:6. Cf. also Mas. Kal. Rab. IV, ed. M. Higger, p. 253, where the admonition not to interrupt another who is speaking is traced back to Jer. 43:1−2.

**28a. And he is not hasty to answer. Like Elisha, son of Barakh'el of Buz, for it is said: 'Wait a little for me, and I will inform you' (Hiob. 36:2).**
**28b. And Moses spoke to Eleazar and Itamar: 'Why do you not eat the sin-offerings?' (Lev. 10:17); and they did not answer him until the great (i. e. their father Aaron) came and answered, for it is said: 'And Aaron spoke unto Moses' (Lev. 10:19).**

28b. *And Moses said to Eleazar and Itamar ...*

This statement contains an explanation that illustrates the words *And he* (does not) *speaks before him who is greater* and the words borrowed from M'Abot V,7: 'The wise man does not speak before him who is greater than he in wisdom.' Eleazar and Itamar did not themselves answer the question of Moses (Lev. 10:16−17) but instead let their father Aaron, who was greater than they, answer the question (Lev. 10:19). Although Eleazar and Itamar also knew the halakhah and could have responded to the question of Moses, they let their father answer for them. See especially Siphrei Zuta on Num. 31:21 and Waj. Rab. l.c. A. R. N. contains not this example but an example based on Ex. 4. See D. E. Z. XI, 30.

**29a. You can compare it with a woman, who was angry with her son and she made her daughter in law to hear it. So Moses, when he was angry with the sons of Aaron, he made Aaron to hear it and to tell it to them. It belongs to the general behaviour of man that he puts his eye on the younger of the members of his house, when he is angry with them.**
**29b. And so the Rab (teacher) puts his eyes on the great of them (i. e. of his pupils) for it is said: 'And Moses said unto God; I Pray, take another messenger, whoever You want to take' (Ex. 4:13). And He put His eyes on Michael.**

29a. *You can compare it with a woman ...* This refers to a woman who direct her rage at her daughter in law because she is enraged at her son. This example is raised to illustrate the fact that Moses did not express his anger at Aaron for burning the entire offering, but expressed it at his sons Eleazar and Itamar. See Lev. 10:16−17.

The comparison with the woman who is angry at her daughter -in-law is missing in the parallels and this must be regarded as a later addition. The point of the explanation of Lev. 10:16–17 is that Moses directed his anger toward the sons of Aaron while he is actually angry at Aaron himself. The reaction of Moses is natural, for it is natural to strike out at the youngest.

The statement should be corrected to read: 'So did Moses express his anger at the sons of Aaron so that Aaron would hear him. It is a principle of 'derekh 'eretz' that one turn his eyes (i.e. direct his anger) toward the youngest when angry at his son or a member of his household.' The reading in *Pereq ha-Shalom* is vague and incomplete. The term 'derekh 'eretz' here means 'a natural human reaction.' See Mekh. de-R. Jishm., Wa-Jehi Be -Shallah, par. 6 (ed. M. Fried-mann, 52a); Mekh. de-R. Shim. bar Johai on Ex. 17:2 (ed. J.N. Epstein / E.Z. Melamed p. 117) and Jalq., II Sam., r. 139.

29b. *And so the teacher puts his eyes...* The text here in *Pereq ha-Shalom* is different from the parallels in A.R.N. The reading and sequence in A.R.N. [a], XXXVII (56a) is more comprehensible: 'It is said that when one holds a feast for his students, he turns his eyes to the greatest student, but when he is angry, he expresses his anger to the smallest because it is written: "And he was angry at Eleazar..."' (See ed. S. Schechter, 56a [it is more correct to read: 'When one instructs his students, he directs his eyes only at the greatest...']).

*For it is said: And Moses said to the Lord 'Send take another messenger whoever You want to take...'* The explanation that follows these words illus-trates the words 'The wise man does not speak before him who is greater...' in M'Abot. V,7. This request by Moses is explained in the midrash as a request by Moses not to send himself but to send his brother Aaron. According to the rabbinical explanation in the midrash, the request is made out of respect on the part of Moses for the older brother Aaron. Cf. Shem. Rab. III,16; cf. Midr. ha-Gad. on Ex. 4:13; and see *Mishnat Rabbi 'Eli'ezer*, ed. H.G. Enelow, I, p. 17. See Midr. ha-Gad. on Gen. (ed. M. Margulies, introduction, p. 26); Midr. ha-Gad. on Dt. 33:9; Midr. Tan., ed. D. Hoffmann, p. 215; Midr. Ag. on Ex. 4:13; Tanh., Shemot, § 21 and § 27; and Tanh., Shemot, ed. S. Buber, § 21 and § 24). Moses emphasized in his plea for Aaron, that Aaron had been a messenger and prophet for God for a long time. The quotation from Ex. 4:13 is explained in that midrash to mean: 'Send as messenger one You usually send as messenger.' A tradition appears in the same context according to which Moses asks God to send His angels as messengers. These two explanations are combined here in *Pereq ha-Shalom* and in A.R.N.[b] l.c. and Michael has come to replace 'angels' in most texts. In A.R.N. [b] it is stated additionally that Michael is the greatest of all (because in making a respectful request, one lets the greatest go first.)

The quotation from Ex. 4:13 is used more clearly in *Pereq Ha-Shalom* as evidence for the statement that a teacher puts his eye on the greatest student first (see A.R.N. [a] l.c.); meant is the situation of a respectful request.

**30.  And he does not speak before some one who is greater than he. (This is said) of Moses, who was worthy to speak but said to Aaron his brother to speak (in his place). And he (i.e. Moses) heard the message out of the mouth of the Holy One blessed be He, and Aaron (heard it) out of the mouth of Moses, for it is said: ' (Aaron spoke all the words which the Lord spoke unto Moses)... And the people trusted' (Ex. 4:30−31).**

*(This, is said) of Moses...* It is concluded on the basis of Ex. 4:30 that Aaron ultimately spoke because Moses had him to do so, out of respect for his wisdom and age. According to the midrash, Moses heard the commandments from the mouth of God himself and then whispered them to Aaron in order to impel him to speak before the public. He thus let Aaron speak not because he himself was afraid or unable to do so, but because he wished to show respect for his older brother. According to this midrash the excuses of Moses for not speaking publicly do not signify an attempt to escape his duty, but rather signify an attempt to do honour to his brother in an inconspicuous manner. Cf. especially the reading in A. R. N. [a] l.c. and see A. R. N. [b] l.c., where this explanation has been combined with the above given explanation of Ex. 4:13. Cf. also the explanation of Lev. 10:19 in D. E. Z. XI,28.

**31a.  (And he answers) according to the question. This is Judah (who said:) 'I will be a surety for him' (Gen. 43:9).**

   **Beside the question. This is Ruben, for it is said: 'I will kill my two sons'(Gen. 42,37). Was Jacob his father then a murderer? Therefore they (i.e. the sages) say: '[One does not answer] on senseless words.'**
**31b.  And Rabbi 'Ele'azar said regarding our Rabbi (Tarphon): 'When a man said something full of sense, he would say: 'Pomegranate and blossom'; when a man said something senseless, he would say: 'My son will not go with you' (Gen. 42:38).**

31a−b.  *(And he answers)...* This statement explains the words borrowed from M'Abot V,7: 'He asks questions according to the subjectmatter...' This statement originally occurred in the scope of rules of good practices in the house of study during asking and answering questions. Such practices encouraged the learning process. Cf. parallels and commentary to D. E. Z. I,3, and II,5. Cf. the various readings contained in the sources mentioned there, such as 'Ask according to the halakhah and answer according to the subject matter.' This reading applies better to the example of Judah given here, considering that it concerns an answer. See, however, the parallels in A. R. N. l.c.: 'Ask according to the subject matter, that is Judah.'

   *Not in accordance with the subject matter (beside the question). That is Ruben...* See Gen. 42:37. The duty to ask and answer questions in accordance with the subject at hand, which originally was one of the rules governing the behaviour in the house of study, is generalized in this example to mean that one should avoid making irrelevant statements altogether.

This example can be traced back to a statement that probably must be ascribed to Rabbi 'Abba. See Midr. ha-Gad. on Gen. 42:37, ed. M. Margulies, p. 729; and cf. Ber. Rab. XCI,9. According to the sources mentioned, Jacob addressed Ruben as a 'fool' after he made an irrelevant statement, and he said to him: 'This first born is a fool'. Ruben's words are characterized in the sources and commentaries mentioned as the epitome of foolishness for three reasons: 1) Ruben's sons were the sons (grandsons) of Jacob himself. Jacob loved his grandsons. See Ber. Rab. l.c. 2) Jacob was of course no murderer, which means he would have not killed children, let alone his own grandchildren. 3) Even if Jacob would have killed his own grandchildren, he would still not have been able to assure Benjamin's safety. (Judah, however, was prepared to actively assure the safety of Benjamin's life).

The tradition contained in D.E.Z. XI,31b is highly corrupt and must be corrected on the basis of the sources. See especially Ber. Rab. XCI,9: Rabbi Hanina and Rabbi Marinus in the name of Rabbi Nehorai ('Abba Nehorai): 'Whenever someone made a sensible remark to Rabbi Tarphon, he was to say: 'Pomegranate and blossom'. Whenever someone made a senseless remark to him, he was to say 'My son does not go with you.' Cf. in A.R.N. [b], XL (56b): 'Rabbi Nehemiah and Rabbi Marinus in the name of Rabbi Nehorai ...' This represents a wordplay on Jacob's reaction to Ruben's senseless suggestion. In D.E.Z. "al haphlagah' must be corrected to read: 'al ha-battalah' (on senseless words) (Cf. especially the version in A.R.N. [b], XL [56b]: 'we-halo 'ein meshibin 'al dibrei ha-battalah [and is it not true that one should not answer on senseless words?]). The reading 'Rabbi 'El'azar in the name of our Rabbi' in D.E.Z. is clearly corrupt.

**32. He answers at the first (question) first and at the last (question) last. This is Rebecca, for it is said: 'And he spoke, whose daughter are you ...?'; 'And she spoke: I am the daughter of Betuel'; 'And she said unto him: We have straw as well as food in abundance' (Gen. 24:23−25).**

**Another interpretation: They are the men of Haran, for Jacob said unto them: 'My brothers, where do you come from? And they said: We come from Haran. And he said: Do You know Laban, is he doing well? And they said: We know him.' (cf. Gen. 29:4−5)**

32. *He answers the first question first ...* A scholar must answer questions in the order in which they are asked. This rule applied to the scholars in the house of study. Cf. parallels to D.E.Z. II,5. The version here in D.E.Z. corresponds both to A.R.N. [a] l.c. and to A.R.N. [b] l.c. According to an explanation of Gen. 24:23−25, Rebecca answers Eliezer's questions to her precisely in the order in which they have been asked. She first answered the question as to

whose daughter she was and then the question as to whether there was a place to spend the night. The second example of the men of Haran who answer questions put to them by Jacob (see Gen. 29:4 ff.) is less striking because Jacob asks his questions one by one and they have no choice but to answer them one by one.

In A. R. N. [b], the example of the men of Haran is used in support of completely different admonition based on M'Abot V,7. It applies there to the maxim: '(The sage says) of things that he knows, that he knows them; of things he does not know, he says he does not know them.' According to Gen. 29:6 e.g., the men of Haran refer to Rachel in answering the question how Laban is, for Rachel is his daughter and is able to tell more. Cf. also M. Kasher, *Torah Shelemah*, on Gen. 29:4 ff., p. 958, § 16.

Yet more examples, of Sarah and Jacob, appear in A. R. N. [a] but without Scripture references. In connection with the example of Jacob, cf. Rashi on Gen. 32:19 ('When Jacob instructed his servant who was to meet Esau, Jacob anticipated possible questions and provided the answers in proper order.') Cf. also Gen. 31:27 ff. Laban puts the questions to Jacob. Laban first asks him why he has fled in secret (vs. 27) and then why he has stolen the house-gods. According to vs. 31, Jacob does not answer the last question first, but answers the first question first and the last question last (vs. 32). See Rashi a.l. Cf. Midr. Ag. on Gen. 31:31 and Midr. Leq. Tob. on Gen. 31:31.

The example of Sarah is possibly a mistake. One may assume that 'Rebecca' must be read instead of 'Sarah'. See J. Goldin, *The Fathers according to Rabbi Nathan*, p. 215, note 62.

**33. And he acknowledges the truth. This is Moses, our teacher, for it is said: 'When Moses heard this, it was good in his eyes' (Lev. 10:20). And also the All Present acknowledged the truth to the daughters of Zelaphead, for it is said: 'So the daughters of Zelaphead spoke (right)' (Num. 27:7). And it says: 'The tribe of the sons of Joseph spoke (right)' (Num. 36:5). They spoke beautifully and in a just order. Happy is the man whose words are acknowledged by the Lord.**

*And he acknowledges the truth* This is connected with the example of Moses, based on Lev. 10:20. Cf. commentary and parallels to D. E. Z. XI,26. Cf. especially TbZeb. 101a. Cf. also A. R. N. [a] and [b] l.c. Moses frankly admitted that his anger at Eleazar, Itamar and Aaron was unjustified, because they were not at all allowed to partake of the sin-offering while he had instructed them to do so. See especially Siphra, Shemini, per. 2. Moses is not ashamed to admit that he has not heard of the tradition of the a fortiori reasoning, which Aaron had used to defend his decision. See especially D. E. Z. II,7.

A second example is based on God's own behaviour in accordance with Num. 27:7. God speaks here to Moses and recognizes the claims of the daughters of

Zelaphead to their inheritance. See Num. 27:1ff. and Num. 36:5, where God informs Joseph of a measure to prevent the legacy of his tribe from falling into the hands of others through the conclusion of marriages by Zelaphead's daughters. In both cases, God's decision is based on a convincing human plea. See A. R. N. [b], where Num. 36:5 is also cited as an example. Cf. especially the parallel in Mekh. de-R. Jishm., Ba-Hodesh, par. 9 (ed. M. Friedmann, 72a); and cf. Siphrei, Pinhas, pisqa 143.

**34. And he does not feel ashamed to learn. This is Moses our teacher, for it is said: 'And Moses brought their case for judgement before the face of the Lord' (Num. 27:5).**

Cf. the commentary and parallels in connection with D. E. Z. II,7 and cf. M'Abot V,7ff.

# Bibliography

## a. Works referred to in the book

Aberbach, M.,('Educational Institutions and Problems during the Talmudic Age' (Seating Arrangements in the Palestinian and Babylonian Academies during the Talmudic Age), in: *Hebrew Union College Annual*, XXXVII (1966), p. 107 ff.

—, 'Elijah', in: *Encyclopedia Judaica*, VI, col. 632 ff.

Abrahams, I., 'The "Fear of Sin"' in: *Jewish Quarterly Review*, X (1898), pp. 660–661.

—, "The Bodleian MSS. entitled 'The Fear of Sin'", in: *Festschrift zum 80. Geburtstage M. Steinschneider*, II, Leipzig 1896; repr. Hildesheim 1975, p. 72 ff.

Abram, I. B. H., *Joodse Traditie als Permanent Leren*, Waddinxveen 1980.

Albeck, Ch., *Mabo la-Talmudim*, Introduction to the Talmud, Babli and Yerushalmi, Tel-Aviv 1969; repr. 1975.

Allon, G.,'Halakhah she be-Torat J"b" ha-Shelihim' in: *Tarbitz*, XI (1940), p. 127 ff. (Ma'amar she-nishtaqqa 'Injano?, pp. 135–136)

—, *Toledot ha-Jehudim be-'Eretz Jisra'el bi–Tequphat ha-Mishnah we-ha-Talmud* (History of the Jews in Palestine in the period of the Mishnah and the Talmud), ed. S. Safrai, Ha-Qibbutz ha-Me'uhad 1953 (-1955); repr. 1975.

—, *Mehqarim be-Toledot Jisra'el*, (ed. S. Safrai) Ha-Qibbutz ha-Me'uhad 1957–1958.

Aptowitzer, A., 'Le traité de Kalla', in: *Revue des études juives*, LVII (1909), p. 248.

Aptowitzer, V., *Parteipolitik der Hasmonäerzeit im rabbinischen und Pseudepigraphischen Schrifttum*, Vienna 1927.

Avi-Yona, M., *Geschichte der Juden im Zeitalter des Talmud*, Berlin 1962.

Bacher, W., 'Das Targum zu Hiob', in: *Monatschrift für Geschichte und Wissenschaft des Judentums*, XX (1871), p. 208 ff.

—, *Die Agada der Tannaiten*, I + II, Strassburg 1884–1890 (second rev. ed. vol. I, 1903); repr. Berlin 1965.

—, 'Observations sur la liste des rabbins mentionnés dans le Traité Derech Ereç', in: *Revue des études juives,* XXXVII (1898), pp. 299–303.

—, 'Qirqisani, the Karaite and his work on Jewish Sects', in: *Jewish Quarterly Review*, VII (1895), p. 687 ff.

—, 'Ausdrücke in der Tradition', in: *Jewish Quarterly Review*, XX (1908), p. 581 ff.

—, *Die Agada der Palästinensischen Amoräer*, I–III, Strassburg 1892–1899; repr. Hildesheim 1965; transl. in Hebrew by A. S. Rabinovitz: *'Amora'ei 'Eretz Jisra'el*, 1925–1927;

—, *Die exegetische Terminologie der jüdischen Traditionsliteratur*, Leipzig (1899-)1905; repr. Darmstadt 1965. Idem, transl. in Hebrew by A. S. Rabinovitz: *'Erkhei Midrash Tanna'im*, Tel-Aviv 1923.

Baer, Y., *Jisra'el ba-'Ammim*,(Israel among the nations); an essay on the history of the period of the Second Temple and the Mishnah and on the foundations of the Halacha and Jewish religion, Jerusalem 1955.

Bamberger, B. J., 'Revelation of Torah after Sinai, an aggadic Study', in: *Hebrew Union College Annual* , XVI (1941), p. 97 ff.

Ben Yehudah, E., *Millon ha-Lashon ha-'Ibrit*, A Complete dictionary of ancient and Modern Hebrew, Jerusalem 1910–1959.

Bergmann, J.,'Zur Geschichte religiöser Bräuche' in: *Monatschrift für Geschichte und Wissenschaft des Judentums*, LXXI (1927), p. 161 ff. (II Kerze und Fackel, pp. 162–165)

Bickermann, E. J., 'The Civic Prayer for Jerusalem', in: *Harvard Theological Review*, LV³ (1962), p. 163 ff.

Blau, L., 'Aus den talmudischen Randnoten des Herrns Rabbinatpräses S. L. Brill in Budapest,' in: *Monatschrift für Geschichte und Wissenschaft des Judentums*, XLI (1897), p. 105 ff. (Aussertalmudische Tractate, pp. 111–112)

Bogaert, P., *L'Apocalypse de Baruch*, Introduction, traduction du Siriaque et commentaire, Paris 1969.

Böhl, F., *Gebotserschwerung und Rechtsverzicht als ethisch-religiöse Normen in der rabbinischen Literatur*, Frankfurter Judaistische Studien, ed. A. Goldberg, I, Frankfurt am Main 1971.

Bonsirven, J., *Le Judaisme Palestinien au temps de Jésus Christ, sa théologie*, Paris 1935.

Bousset, W., (and Gressman H.), *Die religion des Judentums in Späthellenistischen Zeitalter*, Tübingen 1926; repr. 1966.

Brill, J., see L. Blau: 'Aus den Talmudischen Randnoten de Herrns Rabbinatpräses S. L. Brill in Budapest' in: *Monatschrift für Geschichte und Wissenschaft des Judentums*, XLI (1897), p. 105 ff.

Brüll, N., *Jahrbücher für jüdische Geschichte und Literatur*, (1874–1890), II, pp. 128–129, IV p. 401 ff., VII p. 48.

Buber, M., see H. Kosmala.

Büchler, A., *Der galiläische Am ha-Arets des zweiten Jahrhunderts*, Beiträge zur innern Geschichte des Palestinänsischen Judentums in den ersten zwei Jahrhunderten, Wien 1906; repr. Hildesheim 1968.

—, 'Familienreinheit und Familienmakel in Jerusalem vor dem Jahre 70', in: *Festschrift Adolph Schwartz zum 70 Geburtstag*, ed. S. Krauss, Berlin 1917, p. 133 ff.

—, *Types of Jewish-Palestinian Piety*, from 70 B. C. E. to 70 C. E., The Ancient Pious Men, London 1922; repr. 1969.

—, *Studies in Sin and Atonement*, London 1928.

—, *Studies in Jewish History*, Oxford 1956.

Castelli, D., *Il Messia secondo Gli Ebrei*, Firenze (Florenz) 1874.

Charles, R. H., *The Apocrypha and Pseudepigrapha of the Old Testament in English*, II, Oxford 1913; repr. 1976.

Cohn, L., 'Beiträge zur Sacherklärung der Mischnah', in: *Monatschrift für Geschichte und Wissenschaft des Judentums*, XX (1871), p. 494 ff.

Dalman, G., *Arbeit und Sitte in Palestina*, Gütersloh 1928–1942; repr. Hildesheim 1964.

Davies, W. D., *Torah in the Messianic Age*, Cambridge 1952.

Derenbourg, J., *Essai sur l'histoire et la geographie de la Palestine d'apres les Talmuds et les autres sources rabbiniques*, Premiere partie: histoire de la Palestine depuis Cyrus jusqu'a Adrien, Paris 1867; repr. Westmead, Farnborough, Hants 1971.

Edelmann, Z. H., ed. of Kaphtor u-Pherah (of Estori ha-Parhi), Berlin 1851; repr. 1959.

Ehrman, A., edition of: *Qiddushin*, Jerusalem / Tel-Aviv 1967.

Eisenstein, J. D., *'Otzar Dinim we-Minhagim*, repr. Tel-Aviv 1975.

Elbogen, I., *Der jüdische Gottesdienst in seiner geschichtlichen Entwicklung*, , Hildesheim 1967 ;repr. of ed. Frankfurt a. Main 1931.

—, *Ha-Tephillah be-Jisra'el*, Jerusalem 1972.

*Encyclopedia Talmudit*, ed. M. Berlin and S. J. Zevin, Jerusalem 1946–1980.

Epstein, A., *Beiträge zur jüdische Altertumskunde*, I, 1887, pp. 113 ff. – -, *Mi-Qadmonijjot ha-Jehudim*, II, 1887. See ed. A. M. Habermann, Jerusalem 1957, (1950-)1957, II, pp. 104–106.

—, 'Die Pardes als Quelle für die Literaturgeschichte der Juden in Deutschland' in: *Monatschrift für Geschichte und Wissenschaft des Judentums*, LII (1908) p. 710 ff.

Epstein, J. N., *Mabo le-Nosah ha-Mishnah*, Jerusalem 1948.

—, *Mebo'ot le-Siphrut ha-Tanna'im*, Mishnah, Tosephta u-Midreshei Halakhah, Jerusalem 1957.

Epstein, L. M., *Sex laws and customs in Judaism*, repr. New york 1967.

Finkelstein, L., *Akiba, Scholar, Saint and Martyr*, Philadelpia 1936; repr. 1962.

Flusser, D., 'Ha-Dualizem "Basar Ruah" bi-Megillot Midbar Jehudah u-bi-"Berit Hadashah' in: *Tarbitz*, XXVII (1958), p. 158 ff.

—, 'Blessed are the Poor in Spirit', in: *Israel Exploration Journal*, X (1960), p. 1 ff.

—, *Jahadut u-Meqorot ha-Notzrut*,(Hotz. ha-Qibbutz ha-'artzi, ha-Shomer ha-Tza'ir), Israël 1979.

—, 'A New Sensitivity in Judaism and the Christian Message', in: *Harvard Theological Review*, LXI (1968), p. 107 ff.

—, 'Hillels Selfawareness and Jesus', in: *Immanuel*, IV (1974), p. 31 ff.

Friedmann, M., *Seder 'Eliahu Rabba and Seder 'Eliahu Zuta (Tanna d'be Eliahu)*, *Pseudo-Seder 'Eliahu Zuta*, Jerusalem 1969 (repr. of ed. Wien 1902–1904). (Introduction to Pseudo-Eliahu Zuta)

Gaster, M., *Sepher ha-Ma'asiot, The Exempla of the Rabbis*, New York 1968.

Geiger, A., *Zeitschrift der deutschen Morgenländischen Gesellschaft*, VI.

Ginsberg, M., Transl. of Derekh 'Eretz Rabba and Derekh 'Eretz Zuta in: *Massekhtot Qetannot, The Minor Tractates of the Talmud* , ed. A. Cohen, II, London 1971.

Ginsburger, M., edition of: *Targum Pseudo-Jonathan*, Berlin 1903.

Ginzberg, L., *Geonica*, II (Geniza Studies), 1909; repr. New York 1968.

—, *Eine unbekannte jüdische Sekte*, New York 1922; repr. Hildesheim 1972.

—, *Genizah Studies in Memory of Solomon Schechter*, I, New York 1928.

—, *Seridei Jerushalmi*, (Yerushalmi Fragments), The Jewish Theological Seminary of America 1909; repr. Jerusalem 1969).

—, *The Legends of the Jews*, I-VII, Philadelphia 1909–1938; repr. 1968.

—, *Perushim we-Hiddushim bi-Jerushalmi*, , A commentary on the Palestinian Talmud, I–IV, New York 1941–1961.

—, 'Derek Erez Rabbah' in: *J. E.*, IV, pp. 526–52; 'Derek Erez Zuta' in: *J. E.*, IV, pp. 528–529.

Goldberg, A., *Frankfurter Judaistische Studien*, Erlösung durch Leiden, Drei Rabbinische Homilien über die Trauernden Zions und den leidenden Messias Efraim (PesR 34.36.37), IV, Frankfurt am Main 1978.

—, *Untersuchungen über die Vorstellung von der Schekhinah in der frühen Rabbinischen Literatur, Talmud und Midrasch*, Berlin 1969.

Goldberg, M., *Derech Erez Rabba*, nach Handschriften neu edirt und übersetzt, Breslau 1888.

Goldin, J. , *The Fathers according to Rabbi Nathan*, New Haven 1955; repr. 1967.

Graetz, H., 'Zur Geschichte und Chronologie Agrippa's II der Procuratoren und der Hohenpriester seiner Zeit', in: *Monatschrift für Geschichte und Wissenschaft des Judentums*, XXVI (1877), p. 337 ff.

Greefield, J. C., 'Prolegomena', in: G. Odeberg, *Third Enoch or the Hebrew Book of Enoch*, Cambridge 1928; repr. New York 1973, (pp. XXXI–XXXII).

Guttmann, J., 'Ueber zwei Dogmengeschichtlichen Mischnastellen', in: *Monatschrift für Geschichte und Wissenschaft des Judentums*, XLII(1998), p. 289 ff.

Hakohen, M., 'Pereq Massekhet Jir'at Het', in: *Sinai Jub. Volume*, ed. J. L. Maimon, Jerusalem 1985.

Halivni, D., 'On the supposed anti-ascetism or anti-Nazritism of Simon the Just', in *Jewish Quarterly Review*, LVIII, 1968, p. 243 ff.

Halperin, R, '*Atlas 'Etz Hajjim*, IV, Tel-Aviv 1980.

Harburger, J., *Massechet Derech Erez Sutta*, Eine Sammlung der reinsten und kernhaftesten Sitten- und Anstandslehren der ältesten Rabbinen, Bayreuth 1939.

Harkavy, *Ziqqaron la-Rishonim we-gam la-'Aharonim*, IV, Ziqqaron ka-mah Ge'onim u-be-jihud Rab Sherira Gaon we-Rab Hai beno we-ha-Rab Jitzhaq 'Alphasi, Berlin 1887. Quoted as *Teshubot ha-Ge'onim*.

Heinemann, J., 'Birkat ha-Zimmun and the Haburin-means', in: *Journal of Jewish Studies*, XIII, $^{1-4}4$ (1962), p. 23 ff.

—, *Ha-Tephillah bi-Tequphat ha-Tanna'im we-ha-'Amora'im*, Jerusalem 1966.

Herford, R. T., *Christianity in Talmud and Midrash*, New York 1966.

Herr, D., 'The Historical Significance of the Dialogues between Jewish Sages and Roman Dignitaries' in: *Scripta Hierosolymitana*, XXII, Studies in Aggadah and Folk-Literature, Jerusalem 1971, p. 123 ff.

Heschel, A. J., *Torah min ha-Shamajim be-'Aspaqlaria ha-Dorot*, (Theology of Ancient Judaism), I–II, London 1962–1965.

Higger, M., *Massekhtot Ze'irot*, (1929) repr. Jerusalem 1970.

—, *Massekhtot Derekh 'Eretz*, New York 1935.

—, 'Pereq Qinjan Torah', in: *Horeb*, II(1935), p. 284 ff.; and 'Massekhet 'Abot we-Qinjan Torah', in: *Horeb*, VII, (1943), p. 110 ff.

—, *'Otzar ha-Baraitot*, I–X, New York 1938–1948.

Hildesheimer, I., edition of: *Halakhot Gedolot*, repr. Jerusalem 1971–1980.

Hirschberg, H., 'Allusion to the Apostle Paul in the Talmud', in: *Journal of Biblical Literature*, LXII (1943), p. 73 ff.

Horovitz, I. S., '*Eretz Jisra'el u-Shekhunoteiha*, Palestine and the adjacent countries. A geographical and historical encyclopaedia of Palestine, Syria and the Sinai Peninsula, Vienna 1923.

Horovitz, J., *Die Josepherzählung*, Frankfurt am Main 1921.

Horst, P. W. van der, *The Sentences of Pseudo-Phocylides*, with introduction and commentary, Leiden 1978.

Hyman, A. B., *Toledot Tanna'im we-'Amora'im*, repr. Jerusalem 1964.

Jacobson, J., *Netib Binah*, I, Tel-Aviv 1978.

Jastrow, M., *A Dictionary*, of the Targumim, The Talmud Babli and Yerushalmi, and the Midrashic Literature, I–II, New York 1950.

Jellinek, A., *Beit ha-Midrash*, Sammlung kleiner Midraschim, Leipzig 1853–1877; repr. Jerusalem 1967.

Kadushin, M., *Organic Thinking*, A study in Rabbinic thought, New York 1938.

—, *Worship and Ethics*, Northwestern University Press 1964, (chap. III).

Kahana, A., *Ha-Sepharim ha-Hitzonim la-Torah, la-Nebi'im, la-Ketubim u-She'ar Sepharim Hitzonim*, Tel-Aviv 1941.

Kahle. P., *Palästina Jahrbuch des deutschen evangelischen Instituts für Altertumswissenschaft*, Jerusalem 1910.

Kanovitz, J., *Me'arekhot Tanna'im*, I–IV, 1967–1969.

Karib, M., *Me-Sod ha-Hakhamim*, Jerusalem 1976.

Kasher, M., *Torah Shelemah*, Talmudic-Midrashic Encyclopedia of the Pentateuch, Jerusalem 1961–1975.

Katsch, A. I., *Ginzei Mishnah*, Fragments from the cairo Geniza in the Saltykov-Schedrin Library in Leningrad, Jerusalem 1970.

Kimelman, R., 'Birkat Ha-Minim and the Lack of Evidence for Anti-Christian Jewish Prayer in Late Antiquity', in: *Jewish and Christian Self-definition*, ed. E. P. Sanders, A. I. Baumgarten a. o., II, London 1981, p. 226 ff.

Klausner, J., *Die Messianischen Vorstelllungen des jüdischen Volkes im Zeitalter der Tannaiten*, Krakau 1903; repr. Berlin 1904.
Cf. –; *The Messianic Idea in Israel*, New York 1955.

—, *Jesus von Nazareth*, Seine Zeit, sein Leben, seine Lehre, (Berlin 1930) erw. Auflage, Jerusalem 1952³ (original title: *Jeshu ha-Notzri, Zemanno, Hajjaw we-Torato*, 1922; tranl. by H. Danby, London 1925).

Klein, S., *Beiträge zur Geographie und Geschichte Galileas*, Leipzig 1909, 47. [Cf.- – , '*Eretz ha-Galil*, Galilee, Geography and History of Galilee from the return from Babylonia to the conclusion of the Talmud, ed. Y. Elizur, Jerusalem 1967.]

Kohler, K., 'The Pre-Talmudic Haggada', in: *Jewish Quarterly Review*, V (1893) , p. 399 ff.

Kosmala, H., 'Martin Buber', in: *Annual of the Swedish Theological Institute*, IV (1965), p. 13 ff.

Krauss, S., *Griechische und Lateinische Lehnwörter im Talmud, Midrasch und Targum*, II, Berlin 1899 (repr. Hildesheim 1964). Also quoted as *Lehnwörter*.

—, 'The Jews in the Works of the Church Fathers' in: *Jewish Quarterly Review*, V (1893), p. 122 ff.

—, 'Le Traité Talmudique "Derech Ereç"', in: *Revue des études juives*, XXXVI (1898), pp. 27–46. And continued in: *Revue des études juives*, XXXVII (1898), pp. 299–303.

—, 'Die Ehe zwischen Onkel und Nichte', in: *Studies in Jewish Literature in Honour of K. Köhler on the occasion of his 70th birthday*, Berlin 1913, p. 165 ff.

—, *Talmudische Archäologie*, I – III, Leipzig 1910 – 1912 (repr. 1966).

—, 'Die religionsgeschichtlich erklärte Baraita' in: *Monatschrift für Geschichte und Wissenschaft des Judentums*, LXXII (1928), p. 477 ff.

—, 'The Jewish Rite of Covering the Head', in: *Hebrew Union College Annual*, XIX (1945–1946), p. 121 ff.

Kuhn, K. G., 'Giljonim und Sifre Minim', in: *Judentum-Urchristentum-Kirche*, Festschrift Joachim Jeremias, ed. W. Eltester, Berlin 1964, p. 39 ff.

Kuhn, P., *Gottes Selbserniedrigung in der Theologie der Rabbinen*, München 1968.

Lachs, S. T., 'Rabbi Abbahu and the Minim', in: *Jewish Quarterly Review*, LX, 1970, p. 202 ff.

370 Bibliography

Landa, J.E., *Massekhet Derekh Eretz Zuta*, im Bi'ur Derekh Hajjim we-'Orhot Hajjim . . . 'im haggahot ha-Gaon Rabbenu Eliahu me-Vilna, Vilna 1872; repr. Tel-Aviv 1971.

Lazarus, M., *Die Ethik des Judentums*, I–II, Frankfurt am Main 1898–1911.

Lerner, M. B., in: *The Literature of the Sages I,* Compendia Rerum Iudaicarum ad Novum Testamentum, ed. S. Safrai, Assen / Maastricht 1987, p. 379 ff.

Levy J., *Neuhebräisches und Chaldäisches Wörterbuch*, über die Talmudim und Midraschim, ed. L. Goldschmidt, Berlin 1924; repr. Darmstadt 1963.

Lewin, B. M., *'Otzar ha-Ge'onim*, Haifa-Jerusalem 1928–1962.

—, *Ginzei Qedem*, A Geonitic Scientific Periodical,I + II (I-VI) Haifa-Jerusalem 1922–1944.

Lieberman[n], S., *Greek in Jewish Palestine*, Studies in the literary transmission, beliefs and manners of Palestine in the First Cent. B. C. E. – Fourth Cent., New York 1942; repr. New York 1963.

—, *Tosephta Ki-Pheshutah*, New York, 1955–1973.

—, 'The Martyrs of Caesarea', in: *Annuaire de L'Institute de Philologie et d'Histoire Orientales et Slaves*, VII, (1944), p. 398.

Löw, I., 'Die Finger', in: *Gedenkbuch zur Erinnerung an David Kaufmann,* ed. M. Brann and F. Rosenthal, Breslau 1900; repr. Jerusalem 1970.

Lowe, W. H., *The Mishnah on which the Palestinian Talmud rests*, edited from the unique MS presented in the University Library of Cambridge, Cambridge 1883.

Maier, J., *Jesus von Nazareth in der talmudischen Ueberlieferung*, Darmstadt 1978.

Mann, J., 'Genizah Fragments of the Palestinian Order of Service' in: *Hebrew Union College Annual*, II, (1925), pp. 306–307.

—, *The Bible as read and preached in the old synagogue*, A study in the cycles of the readings from Torah and Prophets . . . , New York 1940–1966; repr. vol. I, 1971.

Margoliouth, G., 'Gleanings from the Yemenite Liturgy', in: *The Jewish Quarterly Review*, XVII, (1905), p. 690 ff.

Marmorstein, A., 'The Unity of God in Rabbinic Literature' in: *Hebrew Union College Annual*, I (1924), p. 467 ff.

—, *The Old Rabbinic Doctrine of God*, I, The names and atributes of God, London 1927; repr. Farnborough 1969.

—, 'Eine angeblich Korrupte Borajta', in: *Monatschrift für Geschichte und Wissenschaft des Judentums*, LXXII, (1928), p. 391 ff.

—, 'Judaism and Christianity in the Middle of the Third Century', in: *Hebrew Union College Annual*, X, (1935), p. 223 ff.

Melamed, E. Z., *Pirqei Minhag we-Halakhah*, Jerusalem 1970.

Montgomery, J. A., 'Ascetic Strains in early Judaism', in: *Journal of Biblical Literature*, (1932), p. 184 ff.

Moore, G. F., *Judaism*, I–III, Cambridge 1927- 1930; repr. 1970–1971 (two vol.).

Neubauer, A., *La Géographie du Talmud*, Paris 1868; repr. Hildesheim 1967.

Ostrinsky, M., *The Ethics of Derek Eretz Raba and Zuta*, Chigago 1928.

Patai, R., *The Messiah Texts*, A major New Book of Revelation Expressing the Age-old Dream of a Great People, New York 1979.

Poznanski, S., 'Besprechungen' in: *Monatschrift für Geschichte und Wissenschaft des Judentums*, LXI, (1917), p. 229 ff. (Epstein Dr. J. N. Der Gaonäische Kommentar zur Ordnung Tohoroth)

Rabbiniowicz, I. M., *Legislation Civile du Talmud*, V, 1880.

Rabbinovicz, R., *Sepher Diqdukei Sopherim*, I—XII, 1867 –; repr. New York 1960.

Rabin C., *Qumran Studies*, (Scripta Judaica 2), Oxford 1957.

Reifmann, J., 'Qunteres Ruah Hadashah', in: *Beit Talmud*, IV (1885), p. 84.

Renan, E., *Les Evangiles et la Seconde Generation Chretienne*, Paris 1881.

Rosenzweig, R., *Solidarität mit den Leidenden im Judentum*, Berlin 1978.

Rubanov, P., 'Ha-Massekhtot Derekh 'Eretz we-Kallah', in: *Horeb*, IV, (1937), p. 207 ff.

Safrai, S., in: *The Jewish People in The First Century*, II, ed. S. Safrai, M. Stern, e.a., Assen / Amsterdam 1976.

—, 'Mishnat Hasidim be-Siphrut ha-Tanna'im', in: *We-Hinnei 'Ein Joseph. Qobetz le-Zikhro shel Y. Amorai*, Tel-Aviv 1973, p. 136 ff. See the English transl. 'Teachings of Pietists in Mishnaic Literature' in: *Journal of Jewish Studies*, XVI (1965), p. 15 ff.

Schäfer, P., *Rivalität zwischen Engeln und Menschen*, Untersuchungen zur rabbinischen Engelvorstellung, Berlin / New York 1975.

Schechter, S., in: *Ginzei Schechter*, I, (1928).

—, 'Baraita de-Masekhet Nidda' in: *Jewish Quarterly Review*, III (1891), p. 340 ff.

—, 'The Quotations from Ecclesiasticus in Rabbinic Literature' in: *The Jewish Quarterly Review*, III (1891), p. 683 ff.

—, 'Genizah Specimens', in: *Jewish Quarterly Review*, X (1898), repr. pp. 657 and 659.

Schechter, J(oseph)., *'Otzar Ha-Talmud*, Tel-Aviv 1963.

Scheftelowitz, J., 'Ein Beitrag zur Methode der vergleichenden Religionsforschung' in: *Monatschrift für Geschichte und Wissenschaft des Judentums*, LXV (1921), p. 107 ff.


Schiffman, I.H., 'At the Crossroads: Tannaitic Perspectives on the Jewish-Christian Schism', in: *Jewish and Christian Self-definition*, ed. E. P. Sanders, A. I. Baumgarten a.o., II, London 1981, p. 115 ff.

Scholem, *Major Trends in Jewish Misticism*, New York 1941; repr. London 1954.

—, *Jewish Gnosticism, Merkabah Mysticism and Talmudic Tradition*, New York 1965.

Schwab, M., *Le Talmud de Jerusalem traduit pour la premiere fois*, Paris 1871; repr. Paris 1972; Eng. ed.: *The Talmud Jerusalem*, I, Berakhot, New York 1969; repr. of ed. London 1886.

Segal, B. Z., *Ha-Geographiah ba-Mishnah*, Jerusalem 1979.

Sharbit, S.,'Qeri'at 'Abot ba-Shabbat we-ha-baraitot she-nispahu lah', in: *Bar Ilan*, XVII (1976), p. 184.

Silver, A.H., in: *Messianism in the Talmud Era*, Selected essays with an introduction, ed. L. Landman, New York 1979.

Simon, M. , *Verus Israël*, Les relations entre Juifs et Chrétiens sous l'Empire Romain, Paris 1964.

Sperber, D., *Massekhet Derekh Eretz Zuta*, Jerusalem 1982.

Steinschneider, M., *Catalogus Librorum Hebraeorum*, Berolini 1852; repr. Hildesheim 1964.

Stern, M., *The Jewish People in the First Century*, Compendia Rerum Iudaicarum ad Novum Testamentum, ed. S. Safrai, M. Stern a.o., vol. II.

Stone, M., *Religion in Antiquity, Essays in Memory of E. R. Goudenough*, Leiden 1968.

—, *The Armenian Version of IV Ezra*, Missoula 1979.

Strack, H. (and Billerbeck, P.), *Kommentar zum Neuen Testament aus Talmud und Midrasch*, München 1922 – 1928.

Straschun, D. O., in: *Ha-Maggid*, IX (1865), p. 333.

Taubes, Ch. Z., *'Otzar ha–Ge'onim le-Massekhet Sanhedrin*, Teshubot u-Pherushim, Jerusalem 1966.

Tawrogi, A. J., *Der Talmudische Tractat Derech Erez Sutta*, nach Handschriften und seltenen Ausgaben mit Parallelstellen und varianten kritisch bearbeitet, übersetzt und erläutert, Königsberg, 1885.

Taylor, Ch., *Saying of the Jewish fathers*, Cambridge 1897–1900; repr. Jerusalem 1970.

Urbach, E. E.., in: *Baer, Yitzhak, Sepher Jobel*, Jubilee volume on the occasion of his 70th birthday, ed. S. W. Baron, B. Dinur and others, Jerusalem 1961, p. 48 ff.

—, *Hazal*,(The Sages, their concepts and beliefs), Jerusalem 1978.

—, *Sepher Pitron Torah*, Jerusalem 1978.

Vogelstein H. and Rieger P., *Geschichte der Juden in Rom,*, I, 1895, (see the ed. by M. Hadas, Jewish Publication Society of America 1940).

Vries, B. de, *Hoofdlijnen en Motieven in de Ontwikkeling der Halachah*, Haarlem 1959.

Weiss, I. H., *Dor Dor we-Doreshaw*, I–IV 1871–1891; repr. Jerusalem / Tel-Aviv.

Wertheimer, A., *Batei Midrashot*, Jerusalem 1952–1955; repr. 1980.

Winter, P. and Wünsche A., *Die jüdische Literatur seit Abschluss des Kanons*,I, Berlin 1897, (pp. 630–650).

Wolff, C., *Bibliotheca Hebraea*, II, ed. Hamburg 1721; repr. Bologna 1967.

Zucker, M., *'Al Targum Rasag 'al ha-Torah*, New York 1959.

Zunz, L., *Die Gottesdienstliche Vorträge der Juden*, Frankfurt am Main 1892; repr. Hildesheim 1966, chap. VII (Etische Hagada). See Hebr. transl. and notes in ed. CH. Albeck, Jerusalem 1954; repr. 1974.

## b. Editions, description and commentary

Talmud Babli, ed. Venice 1550 (first ed. 1547), contains D. E. R. chap. I–IX and D. E. Z. chap. I–IV and chap. IX–XI.

Cf. Higger, *Massekhtot Derekh 'Eretz*, New York 1935, Mabo, pp. 43–44. Cf. M. Steinschneider, *Catalogus Librorum Hebraeorum*, Berolini 1852, Copy Hildesheim 1964, no. 1405, no. 1410, no. 1636, no. 1637. Cf. C. Wolff *Bibliotheca Hebraea, II,* Hamburg 1715–1733; repr. 1969, p. 1283, n. 139. Cf. introduction to Pseudo 'Eliahu Zuta, ed. M. Friedmann, Jerusalem 1969, pp. 1–2.

*Derekh 'Eretz*, ed. Riva di Tarento, 1561 (ed. D. Hedegärd, Lund 1951). It contains D. E. Z. chap. I–IX and D. E. R. chap. III–IX.

Cf. introduction to Pseudo 'Eliahu Zuta, ed. M. Friedmann, 12. Cf. D. Sperber, *Massekhet Derekh 'Eretz Zuta*, Jerusalem 1982, p. 167.

*Hilkhot Derekh 'Eretz*, of Rabbi Jitzhaq ben Hajjim, Cracow 1595. It contains parts of D. E. Z. chap. I, chap. III–IV, chap. V-VI and chap. VIII; and parts of D. E. R. chap. III-VII. Cf. M. Higger, *Massekhtot Derekh 'Eretz*, pp. 29–30.

*Opus Itinerarium Tripertitum*, Shabbetai Bass, Amsterdam 1680. Zie M. Steinschneider, *Catalogus Librorum Hebraeorum*, Berolini 1852. 2230.

*Hilkhot Derekh 'Eretz, Belehrung der jüdisch-Teutschen Red- und Schreibart*, J. Wagenseil, Königsberg 1699. Cf. C. Wolff, *Bibliotheca Hebraea*, II, p. 1283, n. 139.

*'Or lo be-Tzion*, Hiddushei Massekhet Berakhot we-Hiddushim 'al Massekhtot Qetannot, added to *'Or Ne'elam* of Rabbi Jitzhaq Saeckel Ethausen, Karlsruhe 1765.

*Regel Jesharah*, Rabbi Gedaljah ben Jisra'el Lipschütz, Dyhernfurt 1776. (Notations on the Talmud).

*Catalogus Oppenheim*, 1782, no. 556.

*Binjan Jehoshua*, Rabbi Jehoshua Falk, Dyhernfurt 1788. Commentary on 'Abot de Rabbi Natan, Massekhet Semahot, Derekh 'Eretz Rabbah, Derekh 'Eretz Zuta and Pereq ha-Shalom.

*Nahalat Ja'acob*, Rabbi Ja'acob Naumburg, Fürth 1793. Printed in Talmud Babli from ed. Vilna 1883. Commentary on D. E.

*Mar'eh Meqomot we–haggadot Hagrab*, Rabbi Jeshajah Berlin, Dyhernfurt 1800–1804. Printed in Talmud Babli from ed. Vilna 1883.

*Kikkar l-'Adon*, Rabbi Hajjim Joseph David Azulai. Printed together with *Debash le-Pi*, Livorno 1801 (ed. I 115b-120b, ed. II 278b-292a).

*Haggahot le-ha-Gaon Rabbi 'Eliahu Vilna*, Salkowo 1803. Printed in Talmud Babli from ed. Vilna 1883.

*Massekhtot we-Halakhot Qetannot*, (Massekhet Kallah, Massekhet Derekh 'Eretz, Massekhet Semahot, Massekhet Sopherim), Polna 1803.

*Massekhet 'Abot u-Massekhtot Qetannot*, ed. Salkowo 1804. [With commentary of Rashi and of Hagra and with the Massekhtot Qetannot (also D. E. R. and D. E. Z.).]

*Hamesh Sepharim*, Rabbi Abraham Frieseck, Luneville 1807 (ed. of Derekh 'Eretz).

*Simhat Jehudah*, Hiddushim al Massekhet Keritot we-'al Massekhtot Qetannot, Rabbi Jehudah Nager, Pisa 1816.

*Me'orei 'Or*, Rabbi Aaron ben Rabbi Aberle Joseph Worms, Dajjan of Metz, seven volumes, Metz 1790–1831, vol. VII Q*en Tahor* (1831), pp. 65–66. Commentary.

*Massechet Derech Erez Sutta*, Eine Sammlung der reinsten und kernhaftesten Sitten- und Anstandslehren der ältesten Rabbinen, J. Harburger, Bayreuth 1839 · [textedition]

*We-lo 'od 'ella*, Rabbi Jehoshua Mosheh Krispin, Izmir 1853.

*Massekhet Derekh Eretz Zuta,* im Bi'ur Derekh Hajjim we-'Orhot Hajjim... im Haggahot ha-Gaon Rabbenu 'Eliahu me-Vilna, ed. Rabbi Jitzhak 'Eliahu Landa, Vilna 1872; repr. Tel-Aviv 1971.

*Minhat Jehudah*, Rabbi Jehudah Epstein, Warschau 1977.

*'Einei kol Haj*, Rabbi Hajjim Palache (Palaggi), Izmir 1878.

*Massekhet Derekh 'Eretz*. [Short commentary and translation Hebrew-German, Vilna 1878. See D. Sperber, *Massekhet Derekh 'Eretz Zuta*, Jerusalem 1982, 168.]

*Derekh 'Eretz*, Il falso progresso volgariz, di E. Pontrimoli, con introdduzioni, Padua 1879.

*Haggahot Rabbi Ja'acob Emden*, printed in Talmud Babli, from ed. Vilna 1883.

*Massekhet Derekh 'Eretz Zuta*, ed. Vilna 1884.

*Der talmudische Tractat Derech Erez Sutta*, nach Handschriften und seltenen Ausgaben mit Parallelstellen und Varianten kritische bearbeitet, übersetzt und erläutert, A. J. Tawrogi, Königsberg 1885. [Ed. of the Talmud Babli worked up: ed. Vilna 1843, ed. Wien 1847, ed. Berlin 1865 and ed. Vilna 1878].

*Mi-Qadmonijjot ha-Jehudim*, A. Epstein, 1887 See A. M. Haberman, *Kitbei Rabbi Abraham Epstein*, (1950-)1957, pp. 104–106.

Cf. M. Higger, *Massekhtot Derekh 'Eretz*, Mabo, pp. 45–46.

*Massechet Derech Erez Rabba,* Der talmudische Tractat Derech Erez Rabba, nach Handschriften neu edirt und übersetzt, M. Goldberg, Breslau 1888.

Winter, p., und Wünsche A., *Die jüdische Literatur seit Abschluss des Kanons*, I, Berlin 1897, pp. 630−650. German translation of D. E. R., D. E. Z. and Pereq ha-Shalom.

*Massekhet Derekh 'Eretz Zuta*, (with haggahot Hagra), ed. Rabbi David Weissman, Warschau 1903. See D. Sperber, *Massekhet Derekh 'Eretz Zuta*, Jerusalem 1982, p. 169.

*Massekhet Derekh 'Eretz Zuta, Prozdor le-Talmud*, ed. Warschau 1912. See D. Sperber, o.c. p. 169.

*Massekhet Derekh 'Eretz*, ed. J. N. Brandspiegel, Piotrkow (Petrograd) 1914. See D. Sperber, o.c., p. 169.

*Massekhet Derekh 'Eretz Zuta*, Rabbi Ezekhiel Pisechavitz (with transl. Hebrew-German), Vilna 1915. See D. Sperber, o.c., p. 169.

*Massekhtot Ze'irot*, ed. M. Higger, 1929. Edition with additions (= Hosaphot le-Massekhtot Ze'irot, Jersusalem 1935) Jerusalem 1970. [The work contains text and commentary to D. E. Z. and Pereq ha-Shalom.]

*Massekhtot Derekh 'Eretz*, the Treatises Derek Erez, Pirke ben Azzai, Tosefta Derek Erez, edited from Mss. with an introduction, notes, variants and translation, ed. M. Higger, New York 1935.

*'Or ha-Jashar*, Rabbi Samuel Isaac Hillman (commentary on the tractates of the babylonian Talmud, including the Minor Tractates, Jerusalem 1921−1945.

*Massekhtot Derekh 'Eretz*, ed. A. Fritzker, Tel-Aviv 1950.

*Zaphenat Pa'neah*, Rabbi Joseph Rozin, the genius of Rogachov, ed. M. Kasher, Jerusalem 1962.

*The Minor Tractates of the Babylonian Talmud*, ed. A. Cohen, London 1965 (repr. 1971): translation of D. E. Z. by M. Ginsberg in vol. II, p. 567 ff.; translation of D. E. R. by M. Ginsberg, vol. II, p. 529 ff.

*Massekhtot Ze'irot*, ed. M. Higger, Jerusalem 1970 (= Massekhtot Ze'irot ed. New York 1929 combined with Hosaphot le-Massekhtot Ze'irot [Jerusalem 1935]).

*Massekhet Derekh Eretz Zuta*, ed. D. Sperber, Jerusalem 1982.

## c. Parts of Derekh 'Eretz in the sources

*'Arba'ah Turim*, Or. Haj., sim. 170. Sayings from D. E. R. chap. VI−IX. See the description by M. Higger, *Massekhtot Derekh 'Eretz*, Mabo, p. 30.

*Halakhot Gedolot*, ed. E. Hildesheimer, Berlin 1888; pp. 644−647: D. E. Z. chap. V-VIII; pp. 647−652: D. E. Z. chap. I−IV, chap. IX. See ed. Jerusalem 1971 (1980) I, 3b−4b: D. E. R. chap. I.

*'Ibbur Shanim*, see Tiqqun Jissahar.

*Ma'alot ha-Middot*, of Rabbi Jehiel ben Jequtiel ben Benjamin ha-Rophe of Rome (13th century) ed. Cremona 1556, repr. Jerusalem 1978 (Eshkol). See Pereq Derekh 'Eretz: sayings from D. E. Z. chap. I−IX and from chap. XI; and from D. E. R. chap. III−XI.

*Mahzor Vitry*, ed. S. Hurwitz, repr. Jerusalem 1963. Sim. 531, pp. 724 -735: D. E. R. . Sim. 530, pp. 721−723: D. E. Z. D. E. Z.: parts of chap. I, chap. VIII, and chap. IX. D. E. R.: parts of chap. I and chap. II−XI. See also the description by M. Higger, *Massekhtot Derekh 'Eretz*, New York 1935, Mabo p. 47.

*Massekhet Kallah Rabbati*: see the edition in *Hamishah Qunteresim*, N. Coronel, Vienna 1864. This work contains Massekhet Kallah and Massekhet Kallah Rabbati. Massekhet Kallah Rabbati contains baraitot and sayings of D.E.Z., chap. I – chap.III and of D.E.R. chap. III–XI. See also the introduction to Nispahim le-Seder 'Eliahu Zuta, ed. M.Friedmann, pp. 14–15. See the critical edition of Massekhet Kalla Rabbati of M. Higger, New York 1936, pp. 212–273.

*Menorat ha-Ma'or*, of Rabbi Jisra'el Al-Nakawa, ed. H.G. Enelow, IV, New York 1932. See Pereq Derekh 'Eretz, pp. 399–451. Sayings from D.E.Z. chap. I-VI and from chap. VIII–XI; and sayings from D.E.R. chap. I-VII and from chap. IX–XI. See also the description by M. Higger, *Massekhtot Derekh 'Eretz*, Mabo, pp. 35–36.

*'Orhot Hajjim*, of Rabbi Aaron den Jacob ha-Kohen of Lunel, Florence 1750. See Hilkhot Se'udah.

*Pirqei Rabbenu ha-Qadosh*, ook genoemd: Midrash Ma'aseh Torah or Huppat 'Eliahu. See in Menorat ha-Ma'or of R. Jisra'el Al-Nakawah, ed. H.G. Enelow vol. IV. See Kol Bo, sim. 118. See S. Schönblum, *Shelosha Sepharim Niphtahim*, Lemberg 1877. See H.M. Horovitz, *Kebod Huppah*, Frankfurt am main 1888. See L. Grünhut, *Sepher ha-Liqqutim*, III, Jerusalem 1899 (repr. 1967), pp. 33–90. See M.Higger in *Horeb* VI, 1942, p. 146 ff. See S.A. Wertheimer, *Battei Midrashot*, II, pp. 45–73.

*Pirkei Abot con su Ladino*,, Isaac b. Moses di Phas, Florence 1749. See the description by M. Higger, *Massekhtot Derekh 'Eretz*, Mabo, p. 21.

*Reshit Hokhmah*, Of Rabbi 'Eliahu Di Vidas, Venice 1579 (also ed. of Amsterdam and Constantinopel). See Pereq Derekh 'Eretz. The work is based on Menorat ha-Ma'or of Rabbi Jisra'el Al-Nakawa.

*Seder 'Olam Zuta*, per. XCIX; contains parts of D.E.Z. chap. X.

*Seder Rab 'Amram Gaon* (d. 875), ed. N. Coronel, Warschau 1865, repr. 1965, p. 30 ff.(Seder Minhah le-Shabbat). It contains D.E.Z. chap. I and a part of D.E.Z. IV. The text of ed. N.N. Coronel is based on Ms. British Library Or. 1067 (Marg. 206) with additions not belonging to the original Siddur of Rab 'Amram. This [parts of Derekh 'Eretz are not found in ed. A.L. Frumkin, Jerusalem 1912 and also not found in ed. D. Goldschmidt, Jerusalem 1972. See also D. Sperber, *Massekhet Derekh 'Eretz Zuta*, Jerusalem 1982, p. 172. See ed. D. Hedegärd (Riva di Tarento 1561), Lund 1951.

*Sepher ha-Roqeah ha-Gadol*, of Rabbi 'Eli'ezer ben Jehudah, ed. Jerusalem 1967, p. 5 ff. (Hilkhot Hasidut). See also sim. 29.

*Sepher ha-Musar*, of Rabbi Jehudah Kl"tz (Constantinopel 1546), ed. S.Ch. Lieberman, Jerusalem 1973. See chap. XX: sayings from D.E.Z. chap. I–II, from chap. III-VI, and from chap. IX. Sayings from D.E.R. chap. I-VII.

*Sepher Musar*, of Rabbi Joseph ben Jehudah Ibn Aknin (1150–1220), ed. W.Bacher, Berlin 1910; repr. Jerusalem 1967, p. 139–144. Sayings from D.E.Z.: chap. I–IX. See also the description of M. Higger, *Massekhtot Derekh Eretz*, Mabo , p. 18.

*Sepher ha-'Aggudah*, of Rabbi Alexander Süslin ha-Cohen of Frankfurt (d. 1349) ed. Cracow 1571 (critic. ed. Jerusalem 1966). Sayings from D.E.R. chap. III–XI. See the description by M.Friedmann in his ed. of S.E. (Jerusalem 1979), Mabo on S.E.Z., p. 2.

*Shulhan shel 'Arba*, of Rabbi Bahja ben Asher (13th century). See Kitbei Rabbenu Bahja, ed. Ch. Chavel, Jerusalem 1970. Sayings from D.E.Z. chap. I, from chap. V-VII and from chap. IX; and sayings from D.E.R. chap. III, and from chap. VII–IX.

*Tiqqun Jissahar*, of Rabbi Issahar Susan, Constantinopel 1564 (=*'Ibbur Shanim*, Venice 1579). D. E. Z. chap. I.

# Index of Rabbis

---

* See R. Halperin, *'Atlas 'Etz Chajjim*, IV, Tel-Aviv 1980, p. 228.

# Index Subjects

# Index of references

## Scripture (including Targums)

## Apocrypha

## Pseudepigrapha

## New Testament

## Wisdom